Lecture Notes in Computer Science

Founding Editors

Gerhard Goos
Juris Hartmanis

Editorial Board Members

Elisa Bertino, *Purdue University, West Lafayette, IN, USA*
Wen Gao, *Peking University, Beijing, China*
Bernhard Steffen, *TU Dortmund University, Dortmund, Germany*
Moti Yung, *Columbia University, New York, NY, USA*

The series Lecture Notes in Computer Science (LNCS), including its subseries Lecture Notes in Artificial Intelligence (LNAI) and Lecture Notes in Bioinformatics (LNBI), has established itself as a medium for the publication of new developments in computer science and information technology research, teaching, and education.

LNCS enjoys close cooperation with the computer science R & D community, the series counts many renowned academics among its volume editors and paper authors, and collaborates with prestigious societies. Its mission is to serve this international community by providing an invaluable service, mainly focused on the publication of conference and workshop proceedings and postproceedings. LNCS commenced publication in 1973.

Mike Hinchey · Bernhard Steffen
Editors

The Combined Power of Research, Education, and Dissemination

Essays Dedicated to Tiziana Margaria on the Occasion of Her 60th Birthday

Springer

Editors
Mike Hinchey
University of Limerick
Limerick, Ireland

Bernhard Steffen
TU Dortmund
Dortmund, Germany

ISSN 0302-9743   ISSN 1611-3349 (electronic)
Lecture Notes in Computer Science
ISBN 978-3-031-73886-9   ISBN 978-3-031-73887-6 (eBook)
https://doi.org/10.1007/978-3-031-73887-6

© The Editor(s) (if applicable) and The Author(s), under exclusive license
to Springer Nature Switzerland AG 2025

This work is subject to copyright. All rights are solely and exclusively licensed by the Publisher, whether the whole or part of the material is concerned, specifically the rights of translation, reprinting, reuse of illustrations, recitation, broadcasting, reproduction on microfilms or in any other physical way, and transmission or information storage and retrieval, electronic adaptation, computer software, or by similar or dissimilar methodology now known or hereafter developed.
The use of general descriptive names, registered names, trademarks, service marks, etc. in this publication does not imply, even in the absence of a specific statement, that such names are exempt from the relevant protective laws and regulations and therefore free for general use.
The publisher, the authors and the editors are safe to assume that the advice and information in this book are believed to be true and accurate at the date of publication. Neither the publisher nor the authors or the editors give a warranty, expressed or implied, with respect to the material contained herein or for any errors or omissions that may have been made. The publisher remains neutral with regard to jurisdictional claims in published maps and institutional affiliations.

Cover illustration: A graphical, formal methods-driven service-oriented system design, proposed by the honoree and collaborators in 1994.

This Springer imprint is published by the registered company Springer Nature Switzerland AG
The registered company address is: Gewerbestrasse 11, 6330 Cham, Switzerland

If disposing of this product, please recycle the paper.

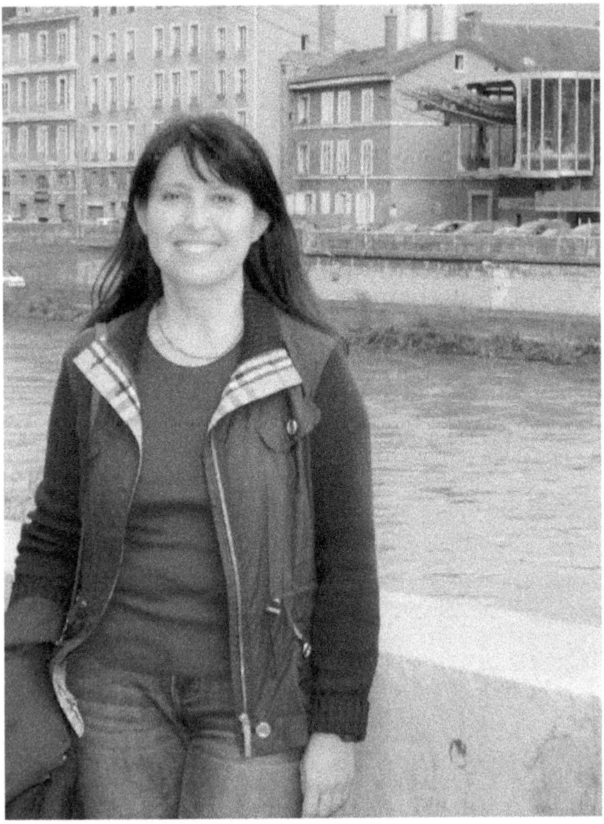

Preface

This Festschrift is dedicated to Tiziana Margaria on the occasion of her 60th birthday.

Comments B. Steffen

Tiziana is Catholic, yet when it comes to software engineering she adopts Luther's approach, translating the Latin (code) to the vernacular (service-oriented models). This is her passion, bringing programming to the people, not by educating everybody in computing, as many propose, but by bringing programming to the people in a low-code/no-code fashion. Tiziana has used the Luther metaphor many times in projects, talks, and lectures.

We've worked together on this mission for decades, developing graphical modeling environments, introducing automatic mediation to make services compatible, and always striving for simplicity: systems should simply work.

Other historical references are helpful here, like when Gottlieb Daimler was asked about the potential market for cars and replied that it will be small because it's limited by the number of chauffeurs that would be required. And back then the average distance between wheel changes was 10 miles, which explains why cars carried so many spares even for short trips.

The success of cars strongly depended on the development of a complex street infrastructure, wheels lasting much longer is due not just to better wheels but to improved streets! And we are still waiting for a corresponding development in software engineering.

Tiziana always foresaw a similar requirement for software engineering, and she has started numerous projects and initiatives in this direction. The most recent is R@ISE, a research project for PhD students, addressing immersive software engineering.

There's a reason the reality is still behind, changing to true service orientation is invasive and requires upfront investment. Thus many stick to the traditional development style despite its much worse total cost of ownership.

We know Tiziana will not give up, and we are happy to join her 'fight' on all fronts: research, education, and dissemination.

Comments M. Hinchey

I first encountered Tiziana and Bernhard almost exactly 30 years ago. I was co-organizing a minitrack at HICSS (Hawaii International Conference on Systems Sciences) with Jonathan Bowen (then at the University of Oxford). Tiziana and Bernhard submitted two excellent papers which were easily accepted, but the other submissions were quite poor. The minitrack didn't take place but Tiziana and Bernhard's papers were moved to the main conference.

We really got to know each other through FMICS, and the ISoLA conferences, in Cyprus, Crete, Corfu, and even at Loyola University, Maryland, USA, where I was based at the time. Both became great friends, as we collaborated on formal methods, automata learning, and other areas applied to NASA space exploration missions, resulting in several patents related to automated code generation.

I eventually managed to convince Tiziana to take a position at the University of Limerick, Ireland, rather than at another institution she was considering. She became Head of Department and used this to engage with many other people throughout the university, making connections and collaborations that benefited from her interests not just in computing formal methods, and no-code/low-code, but also the use of technology in all sorts of areas – healthcare, history and genealogy, and community engagement.

The range of her interests and expertise is truly impressive. She is a great researcher, a wonderful person, and a fantastic friend.

Throughout her career Tiziana's successes have been motivated by how best to advance science and engineering through the implementation of techniques in challenging applications. The chapters in this volume by leading researchers are representative of a community that shares this drive, and we hope the readers will benefit from these efforts and make their own contributions.

August 2024

Mike Hinchey
Bernhard Steffen

My Mom – My Role Model

Barbara Steffen

Daughter
mail@barbara-steffen.de

Abstract. Growing up, I never questioned the notion of equal opportunity, as my mother always encouraged me to take on challenges, from sports to international education. These experiences instilled in me a mindset of resilience and confidence, despite societal biases that often hold women back. I discuss the challenges women face in navigating a male-dominated world, emphasizing the importance of perseverance, optimism, and finding your own path. Through my mother's example, I learned to question societal norms and pursue opportunities with confidence. Her journey and unwavering support taught me to see obstacles as opportunities for growth. Ultimately, I am committed to recognizing and nurturing (female) potential, motivation, and willpower and encouraging others to embrace their strengths to create, walk, and adapt their own paths to success.

Keywords: Female Role Model · Strong Women · Personal Growth · Creating over Waiting

Before I left home, I never imagined that being a woman could limit my potential. I never wondered whether it could hold me back. In 2013, I still took equal opportunity for granted. This mindset was not innate but nurtured by the role models in my life. My mother is not the only strong woman in our family, but she was certainly the most influential. She constantly sought new opportunities and encouraged me to embrace them. While there were many times when I was scared, hesitant, unsure, it was she who believed in me, she who pushed me, she who made me do it and eventually taught me how to keep going, pushing, and growing.

It started when I was a kid. My mother suggested I take up swimming and skiing. These activities became influential in my life. I became a proficient swimmer and later transitioned to triathlon, eventually becoming a state champion. A few years later I also earned a first-level skiing instructor certificate, allowing me to teach 3- to 7-year-olds how to go from "pizza slice" to "pommes frites" (actual technical vocabulary – believe me) and from blue to red slopes. Although my mother was not a fan of these sports, she insisted that my brother and I learn them.

Fig. 1. The many facets of Tiziana: Skiing with the family, meeting the Irish president, and enjoying a stroll in Limerick.

She also encouraged me in areas more aligned with her own interests. While some of my peers spent a school year abroad, I attended two university summer programs. The first was a nine-week program in California. My English was pretty poor at the time – a fact my English teacher kept emphasizing. Nevertheless, my mother believed in me and sent me to university. I was 16, and it was the first time I had been away for so long, so far, and so independent – living on my own and taking care of myself.

I came back a more thoughtful, capable, mature, and 'heavier' version of myself. All my grades improved, and I realized that I could do well if I wanted to. It was not others pushing me; now it was me delivering. Two years later, I did something similar in Shanghai, China. Four years after that, I graduated at the top of my class. These experiences instilled a mind-set of seeking and seizing new opportunities on my own.

Meeting other women who were more cautious made me realize that this attitude is not universal. For example, six months into my bachelor's program, the top 5% of students were invited to join an interdisciplinary honors program. Although more female than male students qualified, in the end there were six men and myself from my program. Female students feared the impact of the extra workload on their grades, while some males without the grades asked to join so they could spend more time with their friends who had the grades and participated.

This is not unique. I have heard many stories illustrating how women often worry about potential failure, while men tend to be more optimistic, assuming they will figure it out as they go. Studies support this, showing that women often underestimate their abilities and performance, while men overestimate theirs [2]. Interestingly, while men attribute success to their skills and failure to external factors, women often see it the other way around. Unfortunately, this perception is not limited to women themselves; also, colleagues and the media are quick to attribute women's achievements to external factors [2].

In the workplace, women still face stereotypes and assumptions that require us to prove ourselves again and again. We must find our place, our strengths, and our strategy by reflecting on how we are perceived and what is expected of us to engage and lead effectively. Initially, situations may be more challenging for women. While men may be perceived as natural leaders, it is up to us women to persevere, remain optimistic, find allies, and correct these perceptions over time.

In 2024, I am convinced that equal opportunities are still nothing we can take for granted. While my mother still heard a professor saying that a woman could never get the highest grade in his class or had to deal with her Ph.D. student being mistaken for the boss, my generation benefits from the strong women who came before us. Yet, we still face challenges.

Even today, women in the workplace hear statements like, "We should take you to the client – that will smooth the deal", "Can I ask you a question, or are you just here to look pretty?", "She was probably hired for the quota", "We shouldn't promote her now as she probably gets pregnant soon". Believe me when I say that these statements are still harmless compared to what many women hear on a regular basis. Some hear these statements more often than others, but probably every woman has encountered them in one form or another.

These comments suck. But we still live in a time where they are often written off as little jokes – nothing to take too seriously. This is where we women have to decide whether to stand up for ourselves "making us difficult to work with" or just brush them off. Whether they are jokes or serious, these statements diminish our position, our thoughts, our ideas, our passion, our energy, our influence, and our leverage. Each joke symbolizes a moment in which we do not feel and are not taken seriously. Not understanding why we make such a big deal out of it signals the superficiality of many today. Next time, test the joke: would you laugh if your daughter was the target?

It is often suggested that women are to blame – that we are not clear, firm, or persistent enough. But it is more complicated than that. We are expected to operate and excel in a male-dominated world. We are supposed to play by the same rules, yet they are completely different for us. Consider Flynn and Anderson's study in 2003 [1], which used a Harvard Business case study of Heidi Roizen, a real-life entrepreneur with an extensive network. One group read about Heidi, while another group read about Howard, just a little name swap. Despite identical accomplishments, students preferred to work with Howard. He was perceived as likeable, while Heidi was perceived as selfish. This shows that women are held to different standards. Our achievements and decisiveness are not rewarded in the same way as men's. Thus, "to protect ourselves from being disliked, we question our abilities and downplay our achievements, especially in the presence of others" as put by Sheryl Sandberg in Lean In [2].

So, it is not easy for women. Navigating this world involves impossible trade-offs: being strong, decisive, and ambitious while also being nice, kind, caring, listening, and supportive. This also explains the results of studies showing that women are expected to be more communal and helpful, with their favors taken for granted, while men's favors are more valued and generally reciprocated.

So how should we behave? How do we succeed? There is no one right way. It is up to each of us to find our own way. We may not always fit in, but that should not deter us. It is when we embrace our differences, stay true to our goals, get up at least one more time than we fall, and create our own path that we truly grow. For orientation role models are key.

While others searched for female role models, I never had to. I never assumed that me being a woman could seriously hold me back. My parents, especially my mother, never questioned my abilities. She encouraged me with "do it, try it" and taught me to try, act, reflect, grow, and prove myself over and over again. Thanks to my mother, difficult experiences make me question society and the idiots who make the stupid comments, not myself. This attitude opens me to new opportunities and challenges.

I cannot imagine losing both my parents at the age of 23. For my mom, it meant becoming the independent superhero that she is. She learned to swim by jumping into the cold water. In times of constant change, that ability to adapt and have a vision is critical to survival. It also explains why and how she moved from Italy to Germany and now to Ireland. Why she has started a company. Why she continually initiates new projects. Why she loves interdisciplinary work. Why she wants to put theory into practice. And especially where she takes the courage and energy from. It is about finding and, if necessary, even creating the right way, rather than following the standard steps. Wherever opportunities lurk, it is up to each of us to see, dare, act, and adapt to make them a reality.

These are the skills and mind-set that free and empower you to create your life. When things go wrong, you change your perspective, strategy, and direction until it fits again. I have adopted many aspects of this approach, working not for my bank account or title, but for opportunities to grow and prepare for future challenges. This is the only way that allows you to stay calm and adapt when everything around you is changing.

Though I may not realize it every day, the woman I am – seeking new opportunities and challenges – is a product of my mother's influence: She came to life through my mother literally and figuratively. Seeing a strong woman who always sees the bigger picture and follows her own path has been invaluable.

Some friends lack (s)heroes and wish they had a female role model, but I never lacked one. I always had the strongest woman I know in front of me – a woman who entered a male-dominated world, found her way, and achieved impressive results. Not every idea or project is successful, but this mindset leads to more successes and new realities than playing it safe and being mainstream. To everyone reading this, think of the women in your life. Let's take the meta-view and empower them to learn to empower themselves. Thank you, Mom, for all you have taught me and the lessons yet to come. Happy 60th birthday – I love you!

PS: Of course, the attitude of always getting up – at least one more time than you fall – applies to everyone. It is a message not only for women, but is lived by anyone who dares to take responsibility, dares to take initiative, and dares to grow.

References

1. Flynn, F., Anderson, C.: Heidi vs. Howard: An examination of success and likeability. Columbia Business School and New York University (2003)
2. Sandberg, S.: Lean In. W H Allen, London (2015). https://doi.org/10.3390/app13106008

Omnipresence

Bruno Steffen

Technical University Dortmund, Germany
`bruno.steffen@tu-dortmund.de`

Abstract. The widespread usage of digital technologies has proven to increase mental health issues among the populus, mostly caused by decreased sleep quality [2]. However, especially recent years have shown that many have benefitted from digitalization. The extensive adoption of remote work leads to less stress, more efficiency, and better quality of work for many digital workers [1]. Tiziana adopted this trend early, effectively enabling her to be everywhere she needs to be, while simultaneously striving forward in her prolific professional journey.

Keyword: Remote Work

1 Everywhere at Once

It is easy to inspire and excite a Margaria/Steffen family member. In fact, the de-facto standard topics at family dinners are new ideas to improve processes or circumstances in private or professional life. Referencing the famous Thomas Edison quote "vision without execution is hallucination", it has to be said that one requires a lot of energy and dedication to follow through on great ideas. This is an attribute that I learned from my mother at an early age: To grow and mature a vision into reality, you need to feed it with time and dedication.

Tiziana did just that on many ends, with one of the more recent and well-fed realities being the Research at Immersive Software Engineering program at the University of Limerick[1]. But great execution can take many shapes, such as to follow through on promises and plans. My mother has yet to let me down on a promise she made. She is exceptionally great at sensing when something is important to me and assisting me through guidance or sheer presence. In a sense, Tiziana is omnipresent. Not a birthday missed, nor an important event such as the participation of my formula student team at the Hockenheimring. My mother was the first person to offer me support in my studies or at home when a garment needed stitching. One of my fondest memories when traveling has been a trip between the two of us, when she spontaneously decided to take me with

---

[1] https://www.software-engineering.ie/raise/.

her to Montreal for a conference in 2019. When her duties were done, we managed to incorporate a sightseeing bonanza and great food along the way. I can only thank her, but also, I know she has a little secret, to make these things possible.

She adapted to her ambitions for travel and family by being one of the earliest adopters of remote work practices. The technology to work from anywhere on the globe as a digital worker is prevalent, however, these tools only work well in combination with dedication to be productive no matter where you are. I personally struggle to be productive when I am not in my typical work and studies zone at my university, I need this dedicated space. This is why I deeply admire her ability. When I think of Tiziana in the context of remote work, the first place that comes to my mind is Cantoira.

(a) Tiziana at the peak of our most beloved summit called St. Cristina

(b) Me and my mother right before entering a hiking path in 2015

Fig. 1. Pictures of Tiziana in her favourite place, Cantoira

Tiziana always felt a strong connection to her Italian roots, especially to his adorable alpine village, where she spent all of her summer vacations in her youth. And so did we, for three weeks every year. While it was not obvious to me when I was young, I now feel the same pull toward this scenic, tranquil, and peaceful location. No more than twenty years ago, a stay at this place would have meant a total disconnect from ordinary life, especially from work. One could maintain the ethos towards the location as back in the days, but one could also combine the best of both worlds, due to the widespread adoption of the internet across the globe: Enjoy the Italian sun, the cuisine, and the hospitality while simultaneously getting the work done. My mother is an expert in this lifestyle, a lifestyle I might get into when the time is right. For now, I let my mother enjoy this place and wish her the very best on her sixtieth birthday.

References

1. Hall, C.E., Davidson, L., Brooks, S.K., Greenberg, N., Weston, D.: The relationship between homeworking during covid-19 and both, mental health, and productivity: a systematic review. BMC Psychol. **11**(1), 188 (2023)
2. Makin, S.: Searching for digital technology's effects on well-being. Nature **563**(7733), S138–S140 (2018)

Bridging Theory and Practice: Tiziana Margaria's Strategic Leadership in Bridging Academia and Industry

Salim Saay

Department of Computer Science and Information Systems, University of Limerick, Ireland
`Salim.Saay@ul.ie`

Abstract. This Festschrift honours Tiziana Margaria for her exceptional contributions to bridging academia and industry in computer science and software engineering. Tiziana's leadership at the University of Limerick, particularly in establishing the Immersive Software Engineering (ISE) program, exemplifies her commitment to integrating theoretical knowledge with practical applications. Her strategic initiatives, such as the R@ISE project, have significantly advanced research and education. As a mentor and a leader, Tiziana has inspired many colleagues in computer science at the University of Limerick and the Lero - The Irish Software Research Centre, fostering an environment of innovation and collaboration. Her roles in various prestigious organizations and conferences highlight her influence in shaping software engineering policies and practices. This tribute acknowledges her profound impact on the academic community and her dedication to advancing the field and supporting her colleagues and students.

Introduction

It is with great pleasure and admiration that I contribute to this Festschrift in honour of Tiziana Margaria. Since our first meeting in 2019, when I applied for my postdoctoral studies, I have had the privilege of working closely with Tiziana on my postdoc project for one and a half years and several more research projects after that, gaining a deep appreciation for her as a highly professional and supportive colleague and a remarkable leader in our field.

Throughout working on several projects with Tiziana, she has demonstrated an extraordinary capacity for critical thinking and problem-solving. Her insights and expertise have been invaluable, and her commitment to excellence has set a high standard for all of us. Moreover, her support and encouragement have been instrumental in my professional development. I am deeply grateful for the opportunity to work with Tiziana and to learn from her.

Tiziana's unwavering dedication to advancing research, her contributions to the computer science and information system department at the University of Limerick, especially her initiative on establishing the Immersive Software Engineering (ISE) course and the Research at ISE (R@ISE) project and her exceptional ability to inspire and guide her research team has left an indelible mark on all who have had the opportunity to work with her. ISE and R@ISE are the two main initiatives of Tiziana that focus on industry requirements and bridge the gap between academia and industry. Tiziana's leadership style, characterized by a perfect blend of rigorous academic standards and compassionate mentorship, has fostered an environment where innovation and collaboration thrive.

A Personal Reflection

I clearly remember my first online meeting with Professor Tiziana when I planned to apply for a Marie Skłodowska-Curie's postdoctoral fellowship in 2018. Tiziana's guidance on transformation of the Broker Architecture I designed during my PhD study to low-code/no-code platform was not only insightful but delivered with such passion that it immediately captured my interest in the low-code/no-code platform. Over the years, Tiziana has been more than a project supervisor and a colleague; she has been a mentor and a kind advisor. Her guidance was instrumental in the development of my career path and research, where she generously contributed her expertise and encouragement, highlighting her supportive and inspiring nature.

Academic Contributions

Tiziana's contributions to the field of computer science, and software engineering are extensive and multifaceted. She has been an influential educator at universities for over two decades, imparting knowledge and fostering a generation of software engineers well-versed in both the theoretical and practical aspects of the field. As a professor of Software Systems at the University of Limerick (UL) and Principal Investigator in Lero, her role extends beyond lecturing to shaping the curriculum and the educational approaches in software engineering. Her leadership as the head of the department at the University of Limerick has been pivotal. In this role, she has been instrumental in setting strategic directions for the department, enhancing its research output, and improving the quality of education.

Tiziana established the Immersive Software Engineering (ISE) course that is an industry-oriented course designed based on industry requirements at the University of Limerick. This program is notable for its hands-on, real-world approach to teaching software engineering, integrating industry experience with academic learning to better prepare students for professional challenges. Her initiative on R@ISE has contributed to the academic understanding and pedagogical advancements in immersive learning environments and it is a great contribution to the enhancement and sustainability of the low-code no-code platform.

As the Vice President of the European Association of Software Science and Technology (EASST), Tiziana actively contributes to the shaping of software science policies and the dissemination of knowledge across Europe. She served as President of FMICS, the ERCIM Working Group on Formal Methods for Industrial Critical Systems, highlighting her expertise in formal methods for high-assurance systems that are crucial for safety-critical applications. Her role as a co-founder of the TACAS (Tools and Algorithms for the Construction and Analysis of Systems) and ISoLA (International Symposium On Leveraging Applications of Formal Methods) series of conferences has been influential in setting the agenda for discussions on the development and application of formal methods and tools. Through her various roles and initiatives, Tiziana has been a strong advocate for the application of formal methods, model-driven design and low-code no-code in academia.

As we celebrate Tiziana's contributions to our field and her profound impact on those around her, this Festschrift stands as a testament to her achievements and the respect she commands within the academic community. It is an honour to acknowledge her exceptional work and to express my heartfelt appreciation for her leadership. Professor Tiziana Margaria's contributions are characterized by her dedication to improving both the theoretical foundation and practical applications of software engineering, making significant impacts in academia.

Conclusion

The remarkable contributions of Tiziana Margaria become evident in how she has not only shaped the research and education in computer science and software engineering at the University of Limerick but also significantly influenced the lives and careers of countless individuals within the academic community and beyond. Her pioneering efforts in establishing the Immersive Software Engineering course (ISE), and R@ISE led to bridging the gap between academia and industry, her strategic leadership within the department, and her passionate commitment to rigorous academic inquiry are just a few highlights of a career marked by relentless pursuit of excellence. Tiziana's ability to merge high academic standards with compassionate mentorship has created a dynamic and innovative environment that not only fosters intellectual growth but also nurtures professional development. Her accolades, leadership roles, and continuous engagement in high-level initiatives reflect a career dedicated to advancing not just her field but also the people within it. As we honour her achievements and her enduring impact on the community, this Festschrift celebrates her as a beacon of inspiration and a pillar of support in the ever-evolving landscape of software engineering. The gratitude expressed by colleagues and students alike underscores the profound and positive influence she has had on all who have had the privilege to work alongside her.

Tiziana, thank you for being an exemplary role model and for your unwavering dedication to advancing knowledge and fostering growth within our discipline. Your legacy of excellence and support will continue to inspire us all.

With deepest respect and gratitude,
Salim Saay

How Long Does It Take to Become (Scientific) Friends?

Wolfgang Ahrendt

Department of Computer Science and Engineering, Chalmers University
of Technology, Gothenburg, Sweden

I have a very fresh memory of my first encounter with Tiziana Margaria. Tiziana visited one of the divisions at my department. Her host had beforehand spread an invitation to join an informal meeting with some very interesting visitor called Tiziana Margaria. The meeting was intended as a platform to chat about possible collaborations in research and education. Intrigued by the invitation, so I crossed the city centre, and the river floating through Gothenburg, to attend the meeting. Our department is spread over two campuses, with non-negligible commuting time. I arrived somewhat late. Tiziana and I got introduced, and started telling each other what either of us is interested in and working on. Within a fraction of a minute, we were engaged in an awesome conversation, and kept going like that. It was great to, at a high speed, discover a lot of common interests. The fact that our respective works address complementary aspects of our common interests only made the exchange more exciting. Not to speak of the personal chemistry, which 'clicked' directly. In this way, a meeting which was intended for a group of people quickly turned into a bilateral communication between me and Tiziana. Understandably, the other people started leaving, politely of course. But Tiziana and I went on talking for a long while. To be clear, it is me to blame for hijacking a meeting, and thereby Tiziana herself, from my colleagues. (Tiziana is too kind for that.) But I could not resist taking the opportunity.

Ever since that day, I am glad to call Tiziana a great scientific and personal friend. We visited each other, contributed to each other's events, and took many opportunities to meet and interact in many ways. Among others, she kindly invited me and my colleague Gerardo Schneider to visit her at the University of Potsdam (where Tiziana worked at that time) for giving guest lectures for her students. The lectures were even broadcast to the University of Dortmund. As a curiosity, the picture on my homepage[2] is taken in the context of that visit, during a great evening we had in Berlin.

I have always been amazed by Tiziana's breadth as a scientist, by her unmatched networking and community building skills, organisational competence, her creativity, innovative mind set, effectivity, and, oh my, astonishing productivity. What else do you want! All of that is combined with incredible kindness, care, and the ability to connect to each and everyone. I could elaborate on all of this, but let me just give an example. When I acted as PC chair of the iFM (integrated Formal Methods) conference 2019, we invited Tiziana to give a keynote. Her talk on the subject of *digital twins*, a topic

---

[2] This may change soon. The photo does not anymore reflect my current age, sadly.

with high coverage in the literature today but much less known back then, was not only very well received, but also led to related activities of various people in the room and in the community. Tiziana also contributed a very well cited paper [1] to the conference proceedings, which is not a given for invited papers.

We now celebrate Tiziana's 60th birthday. (Is that possible? Can someone do the Math again?) For me, this is a great opportunity to express my gratitude for all her contributions to the community, and for her great scientific and personal friendship.

As far as Tiziana and myself are concerned, the answer to the question in the title is: less than a minute.

Reference

1. Margaria, T., Schieweck, A.: The digital thread in industry 4.0. In: Ahrendt, W., Tapia Tarifa, S.L. (eds.) Integrated Formal Methods. IFM 2019. LNCS, vol. 11918, pp. 3–24, Springer, Cham (2019). https://doi.org/10.1007/978-3-030-34968-4_1

Contents

The Combined Power of Research, Education and Dissemination 1
   Bernhard Steffen and Mike Hinchey

The Big Game: The Italian Avenue of Attack to Cybersecurity Skill
Shortage 19
   *Gaspare Ferraro, Nicolò Maunero, Sonia Montegiove,
and Paolo Prinetto*

Education and Society 35
   Gino Yu

From Otter to ISoLA 44
   Martin Wirsing

A Quantum-Like Intellect: Celebrating the Profound Impact of Tiziana
Margaria, Professor and Friend 50
   Cristina Seceleanu

The Softer Side of a Formal Methods Researcher 55
   Barry D. Floyd

The Power of Models for Software Engineering 67
   Ina K. Schieferdecker

Unveiling Modeling Patterns in Workflow Sketches: Insights for Designing
an Abstract Workflow Language for Scientific Computing 81
   Anna-Lena Lamprecht

The Isolette System: Illustrating End-to-End Artifacts for Rigorous
Model-Based Engineering 93
   John Hatcliff and Jason Belt

A Case-Study on Structured Modeling with Internal Domain-Specific
Languages 118
   Steven Smyth, Tim Tegeler, Daniel Busch, and Steve Boßelmann

Semantic Reflection and Digital Twins: A Comprehensive Overview 129
   *Eduard Kamburjan, Andrea Pferscher, Rudolf Schlatte,
Riccardo Sieve, Silvia Lizeth Tapia Tarifa, and Einar Broch Johnsen*

Assessing Static and Dynamic Features for Packing Detection 146
  Charles-Henry Bertrand Van Ouytsel, Axel Legay, Serena Lucca,
  and Dimitri Wauters

Towards a Framework for Transitioning from Monolith to Serverless 167
  Giuseppe De Palma, Saverio Giallorenzo, Jacopo Mauro,
  Matteo Trentin, and Gejsi Vjerdha

Computing Inflated Explanations for Boosted Trees: A Compilation-Based
Approach 183
  Alnis Murtovi, Maximilian Schlüter, and Bernhard Steffen

The AI Act and Some Implications for Developing AI-Based Systems 202
  Martin Leucker

Recognizing Hand-Based Micro Activities Using Wrist-Worn Inertial
Sensors: A Zero-Shot Learning Approach 215
  Fadi Al Machot, Habib Ullah, and Florenc Demrozi

A Modal Logic Analysis of the MUTEX Variable Coverage Theorem 235
  Michael Mendler

Timing is All You Need 259
  Susanne Graf, Bengt Jonsson, Behnam Khodabandeloo,
  Chengzi Huang, Nikolaus Huber, Philipp Rümmer, and Wang Yi

Three Ways of Proving Termination of Loops 280
  Krzysztof R. Apt, Frank S. de Boer, and Ernst-Rüdiger Olderog

Formal Verification of BDI Agents 302
  Thomas Wright, Louise A. Dennis, Jim Woodcock, and Simon Foster

Formal Methods for Industrial Critical Systems: 30 Years of Railway
Applications 327
  Maurice H. ter Beek, Alessandro Fantechi, and Stefania Gnesi

A Manifesto 4 Longevity as a Biomedical Paradigm Shift - Challenging
Entrenched Wisdoms in Healthcare Economics 345
  Christoph Rasche, Andrea Braun von Reinersdorff,
  and Andreas Bertram

Death and Burial Data: Ireland 1864–1922 – an Interdisciplinary
Collaboration 365
  Ciara Breathnach and Rachel Murphy

Author Index 377

The Combined Power of Research, Education and Dissemination

Bernhard Steffen[1](✉) and Mike Hinchey[2]

[1] Chair for Programming Systems, TU Dortmund University, Dortmund, Germany
steffen@cs.tu-dortmund.de
[2] Department of Computer Science and Information Systems, University of Limerick, Limerick, Ireland
mike.hinchey@lero.ie

Abstract. Service-orientation should not refer to an architecture, but to a mindset. At least this is how Tiziana views the term, as a very generic approach to modularization tailored to support what she calls user-centric modelling. Tiziana has been 'living' service orientation for three decades now. She applied it in industrial projects, in teaching, and in research, e.g., to establish a well-founded style of low code/no code system development. This paper sketches her corresponding contributions, as well as the content of this Festschrift.

Keywords: Service Orientation · Low-Code/No-Code · MDD · formal Methods · Model Checking · Model Synthesis · Automata Learning

1 Tiziana's Background

Tiziana studied electrical engineering at the Politecnico di Torino. I (Bernhard) got to know her in 1990 during the second workshop on Computer Aided Verification (CAV) at Rutgers (USA). She presented a paper of colleagues who did not want to travel, in contrast to her: Tiziana loves travelling!

Without going into detail: We married two years later in Aachen. The result: More than 200 joint publications and two kids: Barbara's and Bruno's impression of having Tiziana as a mother is sketched in [86]. The remainder of the paper will focus on science, and here, in particular, on Tiziana's mission: programming for everybody, a topic dominating our common research.

However, before we dive into Tiziana's software engineering perspective let me recall my impressions of her work in hardware verification. When I met her first, she was using the theorem prover OTTER to verify hardware designs [15,16,48,49], and also our first joint paper was about hardware verification [46].

From my perspective, the approach with Monadic second order logic to verify sequential circuits was particularly elegant [34,50,98]. It turned out that the same underlying tool, MoSeL, could favourably be used to optimize planning tasks [5] like service compositions [58]. In a sense, this paper witnesses how her early work also influenced her later work on service orientation.

2 Thinking in Services

Our scientific cooperation started intensifying with what one could regard as the first step toward service orientation. The symbolic treatment of software components using taxonomic classifications. The point of this approach is to represent software components, as well as input and output types with self-explanatory names and to model their compatibility with a directed graph, the so-called universe [89,95]. This way, executable components sequences are nothing but paths of the universe. We developed a tableaux-based algorithm to automatically synthesize executable component (service) compositions for increasingly complex scenarios [5,21,40,41,56,95].

A particularly interesting application of this approach was the Electronic Tool Integration (ETI) platform, where we used synthesis to automatically synthesize mediators, i.e., transformations of types that make the output type of a component compatible to the input type of its successor [44,51,59,89]. Our goal was to ease the experimentation with combinations of functionalities of different verification tools [53].

It was within an industrial project with Siemens Nixdorf where we first used our taxonomy-based component modeling paradigm [92] which we later also used in larger scale [10,90,93,94]: It was the foundation of the Service Definition Environment for telecommunication services. In this project we were able to reduce the time to market of these services by a factor of 5. The reason for this improvement, which won us a European IT Award in 1996, was our model checking-based consistency control [11,88] based on an incrementally increasing set of temporal constraints, an approach Tiziana followed over the years [30,32,91].

The same mindset was also the reason for our success in a project with Siemens on testing. We built a service-oriented environment for test case definition [26,72]: Individual test cases were simply sequences of small test services that were designed to provide an intuitive understanding of what is tested. It was this intuitive understanding which triggered us to aggregate the test-based observations in concise models. Combined with an optimization taken from active automata learning [3] this resulted in what is called test-based modeling today [29,45,77]. The results were so promising that we continued with the development of corresponding tool suites [69,76].

As detailed in [67], Tiziana has worked in a service-oriented mindset already a decade before the term was officially coined. Based on her experience with our development environment jABC [96], she viewed service orientation as an angle to continuously [57] reach out to different application domains [52,63], like business [47,64], biology [39,56], and, more technically, also compiler technology [31,87]. Important for the success here is the focus on simplicity [55,62,65].

3 The Time in Limerick

In September 2014 she moved to the University of Limerick in Ireland as a full professor and Chair of Software Systems. At the same time, Margaria joined

Lero[1], the Science Foundation Ireland Research Centre for Software in Limerick, as a principal investigator. Margaria currently co-leads the research strand on Methods and is a member of its Executive Committee. The main projects concerned automatic face recognition [23] and the development of a secure-by-hardware system development environment [100], that led to the infusion of formal methods [18] and the development of a generative platform for holistic security [24]. More recently, the work with Kevin Moerman on SimuLimb concerns an open source development platform for the personalised design of prosthetic sockets [70].

At the same time she engaged herself intensely with initiatives that bring IT closer to girls (Google RAISE award in 2015) [38], to 1st year students in Computer Science [22], and to historians via transcription applications and classifiers [35]. This cooperation led her to the UL 2013 Team Teaching Award for innovative interfaculty interdisciplinary teaching, jointly with Ciara Breathnach and Rachel Murphy [28] (Fig. 1).

Fig. 1. Ciara Breathnach (AHSS), Tiziana Margaria (SEN) and Rachel Murphy (AHSS) Winners of the UL Excellence in Teaching Team Award 22/23

On scholarship in IT education, she co-chairs the IEEE CELT symposium since 2015, editing a special issue of TETC [36] and championing Open Education Resources (OER) initiatives. She led the Eirenteering project in UL, in

---
[1] Lero: https://lero.ie.

collaboration with Marina Marchisio and Matteo Sacchet at the University of Torino [43] and is now leading the UL team in the Blockchain for Sustainability ERASMUS+ project (http://bc4eco.eu) with Aalborg University (DK) and Tallinn Univ. of Technology (EST). Here, she published on the multidisciplinary approach (blockchain, design science and ecology/environmental case studies) using canvas and design thinking tools [75].

From 2015 to 2021, Tiziana headed the University of Limerick's Department of Computer Science and Information Systems (CSIS) in the Faculty of Science and Engineering.

In 2016 she joined Confirm[2], the SFI-funded research centre on Smart Advanced Manufacturing. She co-led the Hub on Cyberphysical systems with Dirk Pesch, and carried out platform projects on the Digital Thread [61], on digital twin data management [60], Edge IoT [54], preventive maintenance [17], and digitalization and risk management in industry 5.0 [79].

Since 2018 she is the co-director and Executive Committee member of the national Centre of Research Training in AI[3] In this context, she has cooperated with Ciara Breathnach on open source tools for the development of web applications that support the transcription of original registers from the Irish civil registration [82], the classification [73] and automatic transcription [14]. This successful cooperation led to the organization of the first Digital Humanities track at AISoLA 2023 [12], her collaboration with the European Society of Historical Demography (ESHD)[4], with several conference tracks and presentations, and her membership in the GreatLeap EU COST action[5]

In healthcare, she is principal investigator of the Limerick Digital Cancer Research Centre (LDCRC) where she leads the Data Management and Workflow platform (D5)[6], and member of the Health Research Institute (HRI)[7] In the context of the UL Cancer Network, she has cooperated with cell biologist of the Bernal Institute on improving imaging analysis with a new generation of AI and LCNC tools [7], with haematologists in the diagnosis of Multiple Myeloma [9] and with the Public and Patient Involvement group (PPI) to produce a health information portal and AI-based classifiers that help combat the misinformation on cancer for patients and the public [8].

Since 2023 she leads the R@ISE project[8], a Science Foundation Ireland Strategic Partnership Program on Low-code/No-code software development for high assurance software, in cooperation with co-funding industrial partners ADI, Stripe, Tines, Johnson & Johnson and the Limerick City and County Council. Its ambition over 5 years is to create a new generation of XMDD-based software and systems development platform [63,66], which will include lightweight

---

[2] Confirm: www.confirm.ie.
[3] CRT-AI: https://www.crt-ai.ie.
[4] ESHD:https://eshd2023.eshd.eu.
[5] GreatLeap EU COST: https://greatleap.eu.
[6] LDCRC D5: https://www.ul.ie/limerick-dcrc/research-in-d5-the-digital-cancer-patient/d5-data-management-and-workflow.
[7] HRI: https://www.ul.ie/hri/person/hri-member/prof-tiziana-margaria.
[8] R@ISE SFI SPP: https://www.software-engineering.ie/raise/.

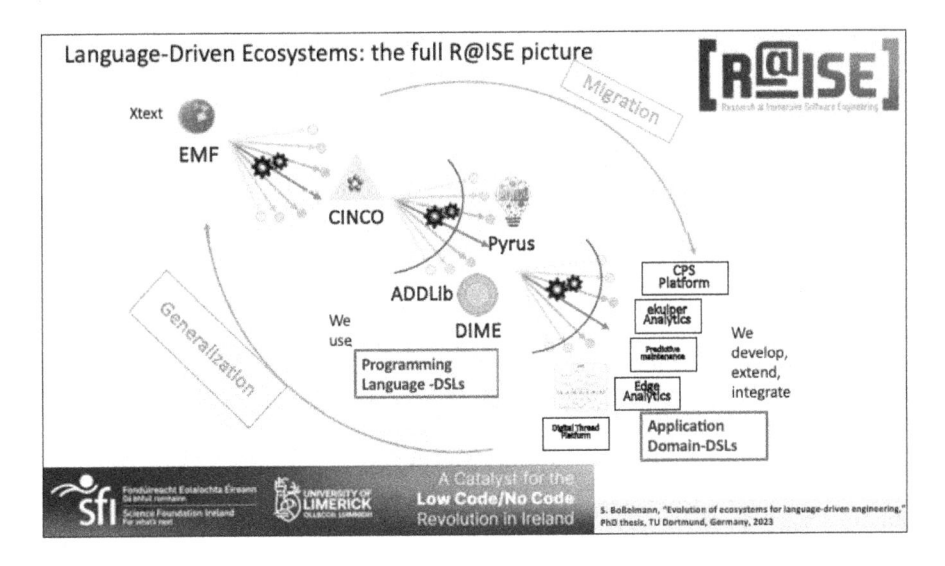

Fig. 2. The R@ISE architecture: a LC/NC platform in the cloud

formal methods and make the development accessible to a much wider range of individuals, including those who cannot code (see Fig. 2). In this context, she has organized twice the R@ISE Spring Conference in Limerick, and with Mike Hinchey the R@ISE tracks at AISoLA 2023 [9] and ISoLA 2024.

Tiziana is a Fellow and the current president of the Irish Computer Society[9] and a fellow of the Society for Design and Process Science[10] specifically for the transdisciplinary character of her work.

She is a member of the Board of the ERCIM Working Group on Formal Methods for Industrial Critical Systems (FMICS), serves as a member of the Steering Committee of the European Joint Conferences on Theory and Practice of Software (ETAPS), and is a vice-chair of the Design and Engineering of Electronic Systems working group of the International Federation for Information Processing (IFIP).

4 The Contributions of the Festschrift

In this volume we have three clusters of contributions, of increasing level of technicality: personal statements, papers that sketch research aspects that go beyond the technical level, and technical papers that, beside their specific contribution to formal methods, AI and other technical subjects, still reconnect with aspects of the research by Tiziana.

---

[9] ICS: https://ics.ie.
[10] https://www.sdpsnet.org [83].

4.1 Personal Statements

Personal statements were provided by **Barbara Steffen** [86], **Bruno Steffen** [97], **Salim Saay** [80] and **Wolfgang Ahrendt** [1]: literally friends and family, whereby family has also published with her or nearby.

4.2 Research and Beyond

In [19] **Paolo Prinetto** et al. present "The Big Game," a significant Italian initiative aimed at: (a) raising cybersecurity awareness, education, and training, (b) addressing the cybersecurity skill shortage, (c) reducing the gender gap and increasing girls' interest in cybersecurity, and (d) creating and growing communities of young cyber defenders and high school teachers involved in cybersecurity. It analyzes the program's key features and activities, highlighting its institutional recognition and alignment with the Italian National Cybersecurity Strategy 2022–2026.

In [103] **Gino Yu** explores how recent advancements in artificial intelligence and digital technologies are transforming culture, education and employment. It emphasizes the need to reassess educational approaches to adapt to these changes. Starting with a historical perspective on knowledge and societal norms, it examines the different roles of traditional mythologies and the impact of technology on our connection to nature and mystical experiences. After the digital and internet revolution, with the dychotomy between digital natives and immigrants identified in the early 2000, AI is now introducing a new divide between the educators and the pupils (both in an extended sense). The paper argues for an updated educational framework that fosters self-knowledge, critical thinking, and prepares students for the complexities of the digital and AI age.

In [101] **Martin Wirsing** recollects the development of Tiziana from a hardware verifier to her current roles in Limerick and several associations and communities. It is a special collection as it reconnects to her early times in Passau, over the German stops and achievements until the present. Although they never directly collaborated, Wirsing highlights her significant contributions to model-driven development tools and methods, many in collaboration with her husband, Bernhard Steffen. It also touches on her work with Mike Hinchey, her innovative applications of digital techniques, and her involvement with the ISoLA conference series, which she co-founded and has co-chaired for 20 years and the STTT journal.

In [84] **Cristina Seceleanu** reflects on many aspects of Tiziana both in research and in her way to approach research, mentorship and life in general. With wit and charme corroborated by hard facts and evidence (papers, conferences, events, joint activities in ressearch but also education and eduation management), she recalls activities, events, successes and attempts that show how Tiziana "functions" in a quantum-like fashion of "cleverness and quick reactions".

In [20] **Barry Floyd** recalls some of the projects and activities he carried out with Tiziana, and it is a collection that touches on work on simplicity in IT, on her proactive engagement for an interdisciplinary (with economists, historians, healthcare experts and more) and interfaculty collaboration (Science and Engineering with the Business school in Potsdam and now with the Humanities in Limerick), as well as her push, in Potsdam and then in Limerick, for a broader understanding of education and professionalism, that led to initiatives for her PhD students (at ISoLA) but also to fundamental reforms of IT courses in Potsdam and Limerick.

4.3 Research Contributions: FM, AI and Beyond

For this larger group, we organize the contributions in five thematic clusters: MDD, Software Systems Engineering, AI and ML, Formal Methods, and Applications. Some contributions overlap across the clusters, and there we have chosen the predominant one. Again, within each section the contributions are ordered along the time the authors "joined" Tiziana's professional life. In case of multiple authors, the most ancient connection counts.

Model Driven Design and Engineering

In [81] **Ina Schieferdecker** outlines the origins of scientific modelling, the use of models in Model-Driven Software Engineering (MDSE) and its evolution over the decades, with different approaches: Tiziana's OTA enforcing coherence by design vs. a ModelBus approach that re-establishes coherence through model transformations. The challenges posed by AI and a new Internet of Collaboration will again require new approaches to the design, development, management and use of models for software engineering as well as for corresponding tools.

In [37] **Anna-Lena Lamprecht** reconnects with her and Tiziana's work on using workflows as a (MDD) means to ease the production of scientific analyses by non-CS students who cannot program. Here, she analyzes modeling patterns from 172 workflow sketches created by students in a beginners' scientific workflow management course. As a step towards LC/NC, the abstraction can help novices intuitively model correct workflows, even when free to choose their own styles. The findings suggest that extending classical control-flow modeling with optional data nodes can effectively form an abstract workflow specification language. These insights are useful to leverage users' natural inclinations in scientific computing, enhancing usability and functionality.

Software Systems Engineering

In [27] **John Hatcliff** and **Jason Belt** reflect on what it takes for a case study to be a good teaching example for formal methods. They connect to Tiziana's One Thing Approach (OTA) to MDD by presenting a safety-critical system, the Isolette (an infant incubator), with a rich set of (FM) artifacts. They use AADL for system models, the HAMR tool, the GUMBO contract language, and the Slang/Logika framework for testing and verification, and demonstrate a rigorous process from concepts and requirements to deployment on the formally verified seL4 microkernel. They then reflect on what is needed in terms of educational resources and tutorials for introducing students and industry teams to formal methods integrated with model-based development.

In [85] **Steven Smyth, Tim Tegeler, Daniel Busch,** and **Steve Boßelmann** present KTML, a Kotlin library for creating well-structured and type-safe HTML documents and apply it to the Tangle project, which is part of a professional conference management system that generates various conference program views during conferences. The key aspect here is to support simplicity of code writing and GUI generation by making use of Kotlin's ability to support internal DSLs. Internal DSLs use the host language's capabilities but are embedded entirely within the existing ecosystem of tools and supports, so that developers can profit of higher abstractions and efficiency without having to learn new notations. Abstract and domain-specific thinking are of great benefit for producing more sophisticated views and scaling to hundreds of users.

In [33] **Eduard Kamburjan, Andrea Pferscher, Rudolf Schlatte, Riccardo Sieve, Silvia Lizeth Tapia Tarifa** and **Einar Broch Johnsen** explore the fundamental concepts of semantic reflection, its applications in digital twins, and its links to formal methods. Semantic reflection combines reflection in programming languages, allows a program to represent and query its own runtime state, with semantic technologies for internal and external knowledge representation in a formal and domain-specific fashion. Applied to digital twins, it helps model the architecture and configurations of digital twins during both development and operation, and enable digital twins to access their own runtime configuration in order to adapt their future behavior.

In [99] **Axel Legay et al.** compare the effectiveness of static and dynamic features in detecting packed malware with machine learning classifiers. Packing is a common technique used by malware to evade detection and complicate reverse engineering. While static features include headers, entropy, and section permissions, dynamic features encompass API calls and runtime behaviors. They evaluate the impact of these features on detection accuracy across different datasets and show that the use of dynamic features within a machine learning framework can yield impressive results, matching or even exceeding those achieved with static features. However, their significant extraction cost should also be considered when designing an efficient malware analysis toolchain.

In [74] **Jacopo Mauro** et al. introduce Fenrir, a programming framework that aims to make the development of serverless applications as seamless as possible by letting developers write serverless architectures as traditional, monolithic programs. It uses annotations to mark which parts of a monolithic code should be deployed in a serverless fashion, followed by transformations. Based on these annotations, Fenrir generates a deployable serverless codebase, facilitating quick development and testing cycles while maintaining consistent execution semantics between monolithic and serverless code.

AI and ML

In [71] **Alnis Murtovi, Maximilian Schlüter** and **Bernhard Steffen** address the problem of explaining classifications in meaningful terms for humans, based on the notion of inflated explanations, that express the "distance" one or more features have to go for a classification outcome made by tree-ensembles to change. They introduce the first algorithm for generating inflated (abductive) explanations for gradient boosted trees, the current de facto standard for tree-based classifiers. The algorithm employs a compilation approach based on algebraic decision diagrams.

In [42], **Martin Leucker** discusses the change of legal and practical situation in the development of safety critical systems as a consequence of the introduction of the EU AI Act. Including AI components in otherwise regulated domains adds layers of risk, and thus more complex requirements to already costly and complicated software engineering processes and certification norms. Using formal methods is beneficial to provide evidence for correctness as well as evidence for errors, thanks to the rich collection of approaches and tools meanwhile available for the analysis of systems as well as for the investigation of AI and ML components. Still, several open research challenges accompany the establishment of a roadmap towards a systematic formal methods-based conformity assessment to the regulatory affairs.

In [2] **Fadi Al Machot, Habib Ullah** and **Florenc Demrozi** try to recognize a set of hand-based Activities of Daily Living using inertial sensor data, introducing a two-level segmentation strategy. They examine the efficacy of Zero-Shot Learning (ZSL) for activity recognition, using Sentence-BERT (S-BERT) for semantic embeddings and Variational Autoencoders (VAE) to connect seen and unseen classes. The accuracy results on small datasets are promising, underscoring ZSL's potential to enhance activity recognition systems, crucial for applications in healthcare, human-computer interaction, and smart environments.

Formal Methods

In [68] **Michael Mendler** investigates how in the theory of shared-memory distributed systems the existence of algorithms depends on subtle assumptions at the level of granularity of interaction, both regarding scheduling and memory models. He revisits the Variable Coverage (VC) Theorem from an axiomatic perspective, and formalizes mostly informal proofs using modal logic. This abstraction helps separate the purely combinatorial parts of the proofs from those aspects that pertain to the read/write interaction architecture and those that relate to the concrete mutex synchronisation problem. This way he can now characterise the key limitation of the read/write memory model, from which the impossibility result ultimately stems, in a single closure axiom: the Variable Cover Axiom, which plays a role akin to the Pumping Lemma for regular or context-free languages.

In [25] **Susanne Graf, Bengt Jonsson, Wang Yi** et al. study the problem of defining deterministic execution semantics of asynchronous data-flow languages in the presence of time. By designing appropriate complete partial orders of timed streams, they define a denotational semantics, this way staying close to the original definitions for Kahn process networks, yet they are able to handle zero-delay feedback loops. This theory underpins the MDD tool-chain for the MIMOS model of computation for embedded systems.

In [4] **Krzysztof Apt**, **Frank de Boer** and **Ernst-Rüdiger Olderog** explore three proof rules for establishing the termination of while programs and demonstrate their proof-theoretic equivalence. They highlight practical differences between these theoretically equivalent rules and discuss applications within the design by contract paradigm.

In [102] **Jim Woodcock** et al. present a formal modeling and verification approach using Hoare Logic, Isabelle/HOL and Z-Machines for intelligent agent systems, grounded in Beliefs, Desires, and Intentions (BDI). Used to represent autonomous robots, virtual characters in simulation environments and more, BDI-based systems are increasingly relevant for real-world applications: the presented case study is a nuclear inspector robot, and the method is able to verify invariants and uncover bugs in its behavior.

Applications

In [6] **Maurice ter Beek**, **Alessandro Fantechi** and **Stefania Gnesi** leverage the long term collaboration in the FMICS working group of ERCIM to reflect on 30 years of FMs in railway applications. They summarize the main case studies, achievements and challenges of applying FMs in the transportation and specifically railway controlling domain, the many collaborative projects, mostly international, that have been carried out in this time span, and the relation this has with many ISoLA tracks organized over the years. They also reflect on the need to educate software designers in Formal Methods for better future safety and mission-critical systems.

In [78] **Christoph Rasche**, **Andrea Braun von Reinersdorff**, and **Andreas Bertram** sketch a paradigm shift in the approach towards longevity: away from sickcare' that repairs when damage is done towards proactive healthcare and lifecare that avoid and preempt conditions and loss of quality of life. In the 360-degree One-Health-Concept (OHC) healthcare and lifecare are seen as strategic assets in which society should invest at the micro, meso, and macro levels. The measures are holistic, apply to everyone and lead to prolonged and increased wellbeing of people in their environment and of the environment itself. This AMLEGA approach depends on a new understanding of value, motivations and rewards, for the good of individuals, communities, society and also institutional and economic actors. The "Manifesto 4 Longevity" is a new decalogue that considers political, ecological, societal, and economic ecosystems as mediating factors of sustainable health and longevity.

In [13] **Ciara Breathnach** and **Rachel Murphy** recount how Historical Big Data has posed challenges for successive national administrations. While digitization has ensured the survival of invaluable social history artifacts, it has also created new problems. Over the past 50 years, digitization has served to remove fragile cultural artifacts from the handling environment' through imaging. However, that's not what historians, demographers and population researchers need to proficiently answer their many and changing questions. The digitization life cycle has evolved into complex workflows enabling interlinkage, migration and a much wider access. The cooperation with Tiziana in several projects and initiatives has led to advances due to MDD and Low-Code/No-Code approaches like DIME to create historian-ready applications, the use of AI and ML for support and automation of data transcription, and to the emergence of a collaboration mindset that stresses the centrality of diverse contributions towards achieving common goals.

References

1. Ahrendt, W.: How long does it take to become (scientific) friends? In: Hinchey, M., Steffen, B. (eds.) The Combined Power of Research, Education, and Dissemination. LNCS, vol. 15240, pp. xxi–xii. Springer, Cham (2024)
2. Al Machot, F., Ullah, H., Demrozi, F.: Recognizing hand-based micro activities using wrist-worn inertial sensors: a zero-shot learning approach. In: Hinchey, M., Steffen, B. (eds.) The Combined Power of Research, Education, and Dissemination. LNCS, vol. 15240, pp. 215–234. Springer, Cham (2024)
3. Angluin, D.: Learning regular sets from queries and counterexamples. Inf. Comput. **75**(2), 87–106 (1987)
4. Apt, K.R., de Boer, F.S., Olderog, E.R.: Three ways of proving termination of loops. In: Hinchey, M., Steffen, B. (eds.) The Combined Power of Research, Education, and Dissemination. LNCS, vol. 15240, pp. 280–301. Springer, Cham (2024)
5. Astesiano, E. (ed.): Fundamental Approaches to Software Engineering. LNCS, Springer, New York (1998). https://doi.org/10.1007/978-3-031-30826-0
6. Maurice H. ter Beek, A.F., Gnesi, S.: Formal methods for industrial critical systems: 30 years of railway applications. In: Hinchey, M., Steffen, B. (eds.) The Combined Power of Research, Education, and Dissemination. LNCS, vol. 15240, pp. 327–344. Springer, Cham (2024)
7. Brandon, C., et al.: Cinco de bio: a low-code platform for domain-specific workflows for biomedical imaging research. BioMedInformatics **4**(3), 1865–1883 (2024). https://doi.org/10.3390/biomedinformatics4030102
8. Brandon, C., Doherty, A.J., Kelly, D., Leddin, D., Margaria, T.: HIPPP: health information portal for patients and public. Appl. Sci. **13**(16) (2023). https://doi.org/10.3390/app13169453. https://www.mdpi.com/2076-3417/13/16/9453
9. Brandon, C., Singh, A., Margaria, T.: Model driven development for AI-based healthcare systems: a review. In: Proceedings of the AISoLA 2023. LNCS, vol. 14129. Springer, Cham (2024)
10. Braun, V., Margaria, T., Steffen, B., Yoo, H.: Rychly: safe service customization. In: Proceedings of the IN 1997, pp. 4–7. IEEE Communications Society Press, Colorado Springs (1997)
11. Braun, V., Margaria, T., Steffen, B., Yoo, H.: Automatic error location for IN service definition. In: Margaria, T., Steffen, B., Rückert, R., Posegga, J. (eds.) Services and Visualization Towards User-Friendly Design. LNCS, vol. 1385, pp. 222–237. Springer, Heidelberg (1998). https://doi.org/10.1007/BFb0053508

12. Breathnach, C., Margaria, T.: Digital humanities and cultural heritage in AI and IT-enabled environments. In: Proceedings of the AISoLA 2023, Special Track Digital Humanities and Cultural Heritage in AI and IT-Enabled Environments. LNCS, vol. 14129. Springer, Cham (2024)
13. Breathnach, C., Murphy, R.: Death and burial data: Ireland 1864–1922 - an interdisciplinary collaboration. In: Hinchey, M., Steffen, B. (eds.) The Combined Power of Research, Education, and Dissemination. LNCS, vol. 15240, pp. 365–376. Springer, Cham (2024)
14. Breathnach, C., Murphy, R., Schieweck, A., O'Shea, E., Clancy, S., Margaria, T.: Curating history datasets and training materials as OER: an experience. In: 2023 IEEE 47th Annual Computers, Software, and Applications Conference (COMPSAC), pp. 1570–1575. IEEE (2023)
15. Camurati, P., Margaria, T., Prinetto, P.: The OTTER environment for resolution-based proof of hardware correctness. Microprocess. Microprogramming **30**(1), 421–428 (1990). Proceedings Euromicro 90: Hardware and Software in System Engineering
16. Camurati, P., Margaria, T., Prinetto, P.: Resolution-based correctness proofs of synchronous circuits. In: Proceedings of the Conference on European Design Automation, EURO-DAC 1991, Washington, DC, USA, pp. 11–15. IEEE Computer Society Press (1991)
17. Chaudhary, H.A.A., Guevara, I., John, J., Singh, A., Margaria, T., Pesch, D.: Low-code Internet of Things application development for edge analytics. In: Camarinha-Matos, L.M., Ribeiro, L., Strous, L. (eds.) IFIPIoT 2022, vol. 665, pp. 293–312. Springer, Cham (2022). https://doi.org/10.1007/978-3-031-18872-5_17
18. Farulla, G.A., Indaco, M., Legay, A., Margaria, T.: Model driven design of secure properties for vision-based applications: a case study. In: Proceedings of the International Conference on Security and Management (SAM), p. 159. The Steering Committee of The World Congress in Computer Science, Computer (2016)
19. Ferraro, G., Maunero, N., Sonia, M., Prinetto, P.: The big game: the Italian avenue of attack to cybersecurity skill shortage. In: Hinchey, M., Steffen, B. (eds.) The Combined Power of Research, Education, and Dissemination. LNCS, vol. 15240, pp. 19–34. Springer, Cham (2024)
20. Floyd, B.D.: The softer side of a formal methods researcher. In: Hinchey, M., Steffen, B. (eds.) The Combined Power of Research, Education, and Dissemination. LNCS, vol. 15240, pp. 55–66. Springer, Cham (2024)
21. Freitag, B., Margaria, T., Steffen, B.: A pragmatic approach to software synthesis. SIGPLAN Not. **29**(8), 46–58 (1994)
22. Gossen, F., Kühn, D., Margaria, T., Lamprecht, A.L.: Computational thinking: learning by doing with the Cinco adventure game tool. In: 2018 IEEE 42nd Annual Computer Software and Applications Conference (COMPSAC), vol. 1, pp. 990–999. IEEE (2018)
23. Gossen, F., Margaria, T.: Comprehensible people recognition using the Kinect's face and skeleton model. In: 2016 IEEE International Conference on Automation, Quality and Testing, Robotics (AQTR), pp. 1–6 (2016). https://doi.org/10.1109/AQTR.2016.7501309
24. Gossen, F., Margaria, T., Neubauer, J., Steffen, B.: A model-driven and generative approach to holistic security. In: Flammini, F. (ed.) Resilience of Cyber-Physical Systems. ASTSA, pp. 123–147. Springer, Cham (2019). https://doi.org/10.1007/978-3-319-95597-1_6

25. Graf, S., et al.: Timing is all you need. In: Hinchey, M., Steffen, B. (eds.) The Combined Power of Research, Education, and Dissemination. LNCS, vol. 15240, pp. 259–279. Springer, Cham (2024)
26. Hagerer, A., Margaria, T., Niese, O., Steffen, B., Brune, G.: Efficient regression testing of CTI-systems: testing a complex call-center solution. Ann. Rev. Commun. (2002)
27. Hatcliff, J., Belt, J.: The isolette system: illustrating end-to-end artifacts for rigorous model-based engineering. In: Hinchey, M., Steffen, B. (eds.) The Combined Power of Research, Education, and Dissemination. LNCS, vol. 15240, pp. 93–117. Springer, Cham (2024)
28. Health Research Institute (HRI): on LinkedIn: Sincere Congratulations to HRI Members, Tiziana Margaria and Dr. Ciara Breathnach on receiving the prestigious UL Teaching Excellence award (team) 2022/23 (2023). https://www.linkedin.com/feed/update/urn:li:activity:7102954744142286848/. Accessed 07 Aug 2024
29. Hungar, H., Margaria, T., Steffen, B.: Test-based model generation for legacy systems. In: Proceedings of the International Test Conference, ITC 2003. IEEE (2004)
30. Jonsson, B., Margaria, T., Naeser, G., Nyström, J., Steffen, B.: Incremental requirement specification for evolving systems. Nord. J. Comput. **8**, 65–87 (2001)
31. Jörges, S., Margaria, T., Steffen, B.: Genesys: service-oriented construction of property conform code generators. Innov. Syst. Softw. Eng. **4**(4), 361–384 (2008)
32. Jörges, S., Lamprecht, A.L., Margaria, T., Schaefer, I., Steffen, B.: A constraint-based variability modeling framework. Int. J. Softw. Tools Technol. Transfer **14** (2012). https://doi.org/10.1007/s10009-012-0254-x
33. Kamburjan, E., Pferscher, A., Schlatte, R., Sieve, R., Tapia Tarifa, S.L., Johnsen, E.B.: Semantic reflection and digital twins. In: Hinchey, M., Steffen, B. (eds.) The Combined Power of Research, Education, and Dissemination. LNCS, vol. 15240, pp. 129–145. Springer, Cham (2024)
34. Kelb, P., Margaria, T., Mendler, M., Gsottberger, C.: Mosel: a flexible toolset for monadic second-order logic. In: Brinksma, E. (ed.) TACAS 1997. LNCS, vol. 1217, pp. 183–202. Springer, Heidelberg (1997). https://doi.org/10.1007/BFb0035388
35. Khan, R., Schieweck, A., Breathnach, C., Margaria, T.: Historical civil registration record transcription using an extreme model driven approach. In: Proceedings of the Institute for System Programming of the RAS, vol. 33, no. 3 (2021)
36. Lamberti, F., Margaria, T., Chan, H.C.B.: Guest editorial: Special section on computing education & learning technologies. IEEE Trans. Emerg. Top. Comput. **6**(1), 5–6 (2018). https://doi.org/10.1109/TETC.2017.2769223
37. Lamprecht, A.L.: Unveiling modeling patterns in workflow sketches: insights for designing an abstract workflow language for scientific computing. In: Hinchey, M., Steffen, B. (eds.) The Combined Power of Research, Education, and Dissemination. LNCS, vol. 15240, pp. 81–92. Springer, Cham (2024)
38. Lamprecht, A., Margaria, T., McInerney, C.: A summer computing camp using ChainReaction and jABC. In: 40th IEEE COMPSAC, Atlanta, GA, USA, 10–14 June 2016, pp. 275–280. IEEE Computer Society (2016)
39. Lamprecht, A.L., Margaria, T., Steffen, B.: From Bio-jETI process models to native code. In: 14th IEEE International Conference on Engineering of Complex Computer Systems, ICECCS 2009, Potsdam, Germany, 2–4 June 2009, pp. 95–101. IEEE Computer Society (2009). http://www2.computer.org/portal/web/csdl/doi/10.1109/ICECCS.2009.50

40. Lamprecht, A.L., Naujokat, S., Margaria, T., Steffen, B.: Synthesis-based loose programming. In: 2010 Seventh International Conference on the Quality of Information and Communications Technology. IEEE (2010)
41. Lamprecht, A.L., Naujokat, S., Margaria, T., Steffen, B.: Semantics-based composition of EMBOSS services. J. Biomed. Semant. **2**(Suppl. 1), S5 (2011)
42. Leucker, M.: The AI Act and some implications for developing AI-based systems. In: Hinchey, M., Steffen, B. (eds.) The Combined Power of Research, Education, and Dissemination. LNCS, vol. 15240, pp. 202–214. Springer, Cham (2024)
43. Marchisio, M., Margaria, T., Sacchet, M.: Automatic formative assessment in computer science: guidance to model-driven design. In: 2020 IEEE 44th (COMPSAC), pp. 201–206 (2020)
44. Margaria, T., Nagel, R., Steffen, B.: Remote integration and coordination of verification tools in JETI. In: 12th IEEE International Conference and Workshops on the Engineering of Computer-Based Systems (ECBS 2005). IEEE (2005)
45. Margaria, T., Niese, O., Raffelt, H., Steffen, B.: Efficient test-based model generation for legacy reactive systems. In: Proceedings. Ninth IEEE International High-Level Design Validation and Test Workshop (IEEE Cat. No.04EX940). IEEE (2004)
46. Margaria, T., Steffen, B.: Distinguishing formulas for free. In: 1993 European Conference on Design Automation with the European Event in ASIC Design. IEEE Computer Society Press (2002)
47. Margaria, T., Steffen, B.: Service engineering: linking business and IT. Computer (Long Beach Calif.) **39**(10), 45–55 (2006)
48. Margaria, T.: Efficient RT-level verification by theorem proving. In: IFIP transactions/A, Computer Science and Technology, vol. 1, pp. 696–702. North-Holland, Amsterdam [u.a.] (1992)
49. Margaria, T.: Hierarchical mixed-mode verification of complex FSMs described at the RT level. In: Proceedings of the IFIP TC10/WG 10.2 International Conference on Theorem Provers in Circuit Design: Theory, Practice and Experience, pp. 59–75. North-Holland Publishing Co., NLD (1992)
50. Margaria, T.: Fully automatic verification and error detection for parameterized iterative sequential circuits. In: Margaria, T., Steffen, B. (eds.) TACAS 1996. LNCS, vol. 1055, pp. 258–277. Springer, Heidelberg (1996). https://doi.org/10.1007/3-540-61042-1_49
51. Margaria, T.: Web services-based tool-integration in the ETI platform. Softw. Syst. Model. **4**(2), 141–156 (2005)
52. Margaria, T.: Service is in the eyes of the beholder. Computer (Long Beach Calif.) **40**(11), 33–37 (2007)
53. Margaria, T., Braun, V., Kreileder, J.: Interacting with ETI: a user session. Int. J. Softw. Tools Technol. Transf. **1**(1–2), 49–63 (1997)
54. Margaria, T., Chaudhary, H.A.A., Guevara, I., Ryan, S., Schieweck, A.: The interoperability challenge: building a model-driven digital thread platform for CPS. In: Margaria, T., Steffen, B. (eds.) ISoLA 2021. LNCS, vol. 13036, pp. 393–413. Springer, Cham (2021). https://doi.org/10.1007/978-3-030-89159-6_25
55. Margaria, T., Hinchey, M.: Simplicity in IT: the power of less. Computer (Long Beach Calif.) **46**(11), 23–25 (2013)
56. Margaria, T., Kubczak, C., Steffen, B.: Bio-jETI: a service integration, design, and provisioning platform for orchestrated bioinformatics processes. BMC Bioinform. **9**(Suppl. 4), S12 (2008). https://doi.org/10.1186/1471-2105-9-S4-S12

57. Margaria, T., Lamprecht, A.L., Steffen, B.: Continuous model-driven engineering. In: Software Technology: 10 Years of Innovation in IEEE Computer, pp. 139–154. Wiley, Hoboken (2018)
58. Margaria, T., Meyer, D., Kubczak, C., Isberner, M., Steffen, B.: Synthesizing semantic web service compositions with jMosel and Golog. In: Bernstein, A., et al. (eds.) ISWC 2009. LNCS, vol. 5823, pp. 392–407. Springer, Heidelberg (2009). https://doi.org/10.1007/978-3-642-04930-9_25
59. Margaria, T., Nagel, R., Steffen, B.: jETI: a tool for remote tool integration. In: Halbwachs, N., Zuck, L.D. (eds.) TACAS 2005. LNCS, vol. 3440, pp. 557–562. Springer, Heidelberg (2005). https://doi.org/10.1007/978-3-540-31980-1_38
60. Margaria, T., Ryan, S.: Data and data management in the context of digital twins. In: Crespi, N., Drobot, A.T., Minerva, R. (eds.) The Digital Twin, pp. 253–278. Springer, Cham (2023). https://doi.org/10.1007/978-3-031-21343-4_10
61. Margaria, T., Schieweck, A.: The digital thread in industry 4.0. In: Ahrendt, W., Tapia Tarifa, S.L. (eds.) IFM 2019. LNCS, vol. 11918, pp. 3–24. Springer, Cham (2019). https://doi.org/10.1007/978-3-030-34968-4_1
62. Margaria, T., Steffen, B.: Lightweight coarse-grained coordination: a scalable system-level approach. Int. J. Softw. Tools Technol. Transfer **5**, 107–123 (2004). https://api.semanticscholar.org/CorpusID:25252712
63. Margaria, T., Steffen, B.: Agile IT: thinking in user-centric models. In: Margaria, T., Steffen, B. (eds.) ISoLA 2008. CCIS, vol. 17, pp. 490–502. Springer, Heidelberg (2008). https://doi.org/10.1007/978-3-540-88479-8_35
64. Margaria, T., Steffen, B.: Business process modelling in the jABC: the one-thing-approach. In: Cardoso, J., van der Aalst, W. (eds.) Handbook of Research on Business Process Modeling. IGI Global (2009)
65. Margaria, T., Steffen, B.: Simplicity as a driver for agile innovation. Computer (Long Beach Calif.) **43**(6), 90–92 (2010)
66. Margaria, T., Steffen, B.: eXtreme model-driven development (XMDD) technologies as a hands-on approach to software development without coding. In: Tatnall, A. (ed.) Encyclopedia of Education and Information Technologies, pp. 732–750. Springer, Cham (2020). https://doi.org/10.1007/978-3-319-60013-0_208-1
67. Margaria, T., Steffen, B., Reitenspieß, M.: Service-oriented design: the roots. In: Benatallah, B., Casati, F., Traverso, P. (eds.) ICSOC 2005. LNCS, vol. 3826, pp. 450–464. Springer, Heidelberg (2005). https://doi.org/10.1007/11596141_34
68. Mendler, M.: A modal logic analysis of the mutex variable coverage theorem. In: Hinchey, M., Steffen, B. (eds.) The Combined Power of Research, Education, and Dissemination. LNCS, vol. 15240, pp. 235–258. Springer, Cham (2024)
69. Merten, M., Steffen, B., Howar, F., Margaria, T.: Next generation LearnLib. In: Abdulla, P.A., Leino, K.R.M. (eds.) TACAS 2011. LNCS, vol. 6605, pp. 220–223. Springer, Heidelberg (2011). https://doi.org/10.1007/978-3-642-19835-9_18
70. Moerman, K.M., Solav, D., Sengeh, D., Herr, H.: Automated and Data-driven Computational Design of Patient-Specific Biomechanical Interfaces (2016). https://engrxiv.org/index.php/engrxiv/preprint/view/17. https://doi.org/10.31224/osf.io/g8h9n. Accessed 07 Aug 2024
71. Murtovi, A., Schlüter, M., Steffen, B.: Computing inflated explanations for boosted trees: a compilation-based approach. In: Hinchey, M., Steffen, B. (eds.) The Combined Power of Research, Education, and Dissemination. LNCS, vol. 15240, pp. 183–201. Springer, Cham (2024)
72. Niese, O., et al.: Library-based design and consistency checking of system-level industrial test cases. In: International Conference on Fundamental Approaches to Software Engineering (2002)

73. O'Shea, E., Khan, R., Breathnach, C., Margaria, T.: Towards automatic data cleansing and classification of valid historical data an incremental approach based on MDD. In: 2020 IEEE International Conference on Big Data (Big Data), pp. 1914–1923 (2020)
74. Palma, G.D., Giallorenzo, S., Mauro, J., Trentin, M., Vjerdha, G.: Towards a framework for transitioning from monolith to serverless. In: Hinchey, M., Steffen, B. (eds.) The Combined Power of Research, Education, and Dissemination. LNCS, vol. 15240, pp. 167–182. Springer, Cham (2024)
75. Peruccon, A., Lyons, R., de Gotzen, A., Margaria, T., Simeone, L.: Bc4eco - using visual tools for a shared understanding and pedagogical approach across an interdisciplinary consortium. In: 2023 IEEE 47th Annual Computers, Software, and Applications Conference (COMPSAC), pp. 1890–1895 (2023). https://doi.org/10.1109/COMPSAC57700.2023.10223442
76. Raffelt, H., Steffen, B., Berg, T., Margaria, T.: LearnLib: a framework for extrapolating behavioral models. Int. J. Softw. Tools Technol. Transf. **11**(5), 393–407 (2009)
77. Raffelt, H., Steffen, B., Margaria, T.: Dynamic testing via automata learning. In: Yorav, K. (ed.) HVC 2007. LNCS, vol. 4899, pp. 136–152. Springer, Heidelberg (2008). https://doi.org/10.1007/978-3-540-77966-7_13
78. Rasche, C., Braun von Reinersdorff, A., Bertram, A.: A manifesto 4 longevity as a biomedical paradigm shift - challenging entrenched wisdoms in healthcare economics. In: Hinchey, M., Steffen, B. (eds.) The Combined Power of Research, Education, and Dissemination. LNCS, vol. 15240, pp. 345–364. Springer, Cham (2024)
79. Ryan, S., Margaria, T.: Digitalisation for organisations in industry 4.0: a working example. In: ITM Web of Conferences. vol. 51. EDP Sciences (2023)
80. Saay, S.: Bridging theory and practice: Tiziana Margaria's strategic leadership in bridging academia and industry. In: Hinchey, M., Steffen, B. (eds.) The Combined Power of Research, Education, and Dissemination. LNCS, vol. 15240, pp. xvii–xix. Springer, Cham (2024)
81. Schieferdecker, I.K.: The power of models for software engineering. In: Hinchey, M., Steffen, B. (eds.) The Combined Power of Research, Education, and Dissemination. LNCS, vol. 15240, pp. 67–80. Springer, Cham (2024)
82. Schieweck, A., Murphy, R., Khan, R., Breathnach, C., Margaria, T.: Evolution of the historian data entry application: supporting transcribathons in the digital humanities through MDD. In: 2022 IEEE 46th Annual Computers, Software, and Applications Conference (COMPSAC), pp. 177–186. IEEE (2022)
83. SDPS: SDPS Fellows. https://www.sdpsnet.org/sdps/index.php/about-sdps/fellows/195-dr-tiziana-margaria. Accessed 1 Aug 2024
84. Seceleanu, C.: A quantum-like intellect: celebrating the profound impact of Tiziana Margaria, professor and friend. In: Hinchey, M., Steffen, B. (eds.) The Combined Power of Research, Education, and Dissemination. LNCS, vol. 15240, pp. 50–54. Springer, Cham (2024)
85. Smyth, S., Tegeler, T., Busch, D., Boßelmann, S.: A case-study on structured modeling with internal domain-specific languages. In: Hinchey, M., Steffen, B. (eds.) The Combined Power of Research, Education, and Dissemination. LNCS, vol. 15240, pp. 118–128. Springer, Cham (2024)
86. Steffen, B.: My mom - my role model. In: Hinchey, M., Steffen, B. (eds.) The Combined Power of Research, Education, and Dissemination. LNCS, vol. 15240, pp. ix–xii. Springer, Cham (2024)

87. Steffen, B., Gossen, F., Naujokat, S., Margaria, T.: Language-driven engineering: from general-purpose to purpose-specific languages. In: Steffen, B., Woeginger, G. (eds.) Computing and Software Science. LNCS, vol. 10000, pp. 311–344. Springer, Cham (2019). https://doi.org/10.1007/978-3-319-91908-9_17
88. Steffen, B., Margaria, T.: METAFrame in practice: design of intelligent network services. In: Olderog, E.-R., Steffen, B. (eds.) Correct System Design. LNCS, vol. 1710, pp. 390–415. Springer, Heidelberg (1999). https://doi.org/10.1007/3-540-48092-7_17
89. Steffen, B., Margaria, T., Braun, V.: The electronic tool integration platform: concepts and design. Int. J. Softw. Tools Technol. Transfer (STTT) **1**(1–2), 9–30 (1997)
90. Steffen, B., Margaria, T., Braun, V., Kalt, N.: Hierarchical service definition. Ann. Rev. Commun. **51** (2003)
91. Steffen, B., Margaria, T., Claßen, A., Braun, V.: Incremental formalization. In: Wirsing, M., Nivat, M. (eds.) AMAST 1996. LNCS, vol. 1101, pp. 608–611. Springer, Heidelberg (1996). https://doi.org/10.1007/BFb0014354
92. Steffen, B., Margaria, T., Claßen, A., Braun, V.: The METAFrame'95 environment. In: Alur, R., Henzinger, T.A. (eds.) CAV 1996. LNCS, vol. 1102, pp. 450–453. Springer, Heidelberg (1996). https://doi.org/10.1007/3-540-61474-5_100
93. Steffen, B., Margaria, T., Claßen, A., Braun, V., Nisius, R., Reitenspieß, M.: A constraint-oriented service creation environment. In: Margaria, T., Steffen, B. (eds.) TACAS 1996. LNCS, vol. 1055, pp. 418–421. Springer, Heidelberg (1996). https://doi.org/10.1007/3-540-61042-1_63
94. Steffen, B., Margaria, T., Claßen, A., Braun, V., Reitenspieß, M.: An environment for the creation of intelligent network services. In: Intelligent Networks: IN/AIN Technologies, Operations, Services and Applications - A Comprehensive Report, pp. 287–300. IEC: International Engineering Consortium (1996)
95. Steffen, B., Margaria, T., Freitag, B.: Module configuration by minimal model construction. Technical report. Fakultät für Mathematik und Informatik, Universität Passau (1993)
96. Steffen, B., Margaria, T., Nagel, R., Jörges, S., Kubczak, C.: Model-driven development with the jABC. In: Bin, E., Ziv, A., Ur, S. (eds.) HVC 2006. LNCS, vol. 4383, pp. 92–108. Springer, Heidelberg (2007). https://doi.org/10.1007/978-3-540-70889-6_7
97. Steffen, B.: Omnipresence. In: Hinchey, M., Steffen, B. (eds.) The Combined Power of Research, Education, and Dissemination. LNCS, vol. 15240, pp. xiii–xv. Springer, Cham (2024)
98. Topnik, C., Wilhelm, E., Margaria, T., Steffen, B.: jMosel: a stand-alone tool and jABC plugin for M2L(Str). In: Valmari, A. (ed.) SPIN 2006. LNCS, vol. 3925, pp. 293–298. Springer, Heidelberg (2006). https://doi.org/10.1007/11691617_18
99. Van Ouytsel, C.H.B., Legay, A., Lucca, S., Wauters, D.: Assessing static and dynamic features for packing detection. In: Hinchey, M., Steffen, B. (eds.) The Combined Power of Research, Education, and Dissemination. LNCS, vol. 15240, pp. 146–166. Springer, Cham (2024)
100. Varriale, A., Vatajelu, E.I., Di Natale, G., Prinetto, P., Trotta, P., Margaria, T.: Secube^{TM}: an open-source security platform in a single SOC. In: 2016 International Conference on Design and Technology of Integrated Systems in Nanoscale Era (DTIS), pp. 1–6 (2016). https://doi.org/10.1109/DTIS.2016.7483810
101. Wirsing, M.: From OTTER to ISolA. In: Hinchey, M., Steffen, B. (eds.) The Combined Power of Research, Education, and Dissemination. LNCS, vol. 15240, pp. 44–49. Springer, Cham (2024)

102. Wright, T., Dennis, L.A., Woodcock, J., Foster, S.: Formal verification of BDI agents. In: Hinchey, M., Steffen, B. (eds.) The Combined Power of Research, Education, and Dissemination. LNCS, vol. 15240, pp. 302–326. Springer, Cham (2024)
103. Yu, G.: Education and society. In: Hinchey, M., Steffen, B. (eds.) The Combined Power of Research, Education, and Dissemination. LNCS, vol. 15240, pp. 35–43. Springer, Cham (2024)

The Big Game: The Italian Avenue of Attack to Cybersecurity Skill Shortage

Gaspare Ferraro[1], Nicolò Maunero[2](✉) [iD], Sonia Montegiove[3], and Paolo Prinetto[4]

[1] CINI Cybersecurity National Lab, Genua, Italy
gaspare.ferraro@cybersecnatlab.it
[2] MT School for Advanced Studies, Lucca, Italy
nicolo.maunero@imtlucca.it
[3] CINI Cybersecurity National Lab, Todi, Italy
sonia.montegiove@cybersecnatlab.it
[4] CINI Cybersecurity National Lab, Turin, Italy
paolo.prinetto@cybersecnatlab.it

Abstract. The paper presents *The Big Game*, one of the most significant and effective Italian set of comprehensive and integrated actions aimed at: (a) raising *cybersecurity awareness, education & training* in the country, (b) tackling the *cybersecurity skill shortage*, (c) reducing the gender gap, increasing girls' interests in the topic, and (d) creating and growing both a community of *cyber defenders* by investing in young talents, and, at the same time, a community of *high school teachers* more and more involved in cybersecurity issues.

Both the key features of the program and its several composing activities are analyzed, pointing out its institutional recognitions and its fulfillment with the Italian National Cybersecurity Strategy 2022–2026.

Keywords: Cybersecurity · educations and training · gamification · gender gap · young talents

Statement of Appreciation

The present paper has been written in appreciation of the interest that Tiziana Margaria has systematically shown, for the whole span of her very prestigious carrier, to the educations and training of young people. More recently, with the increasing role played on our everyday life by cybersecurity related issues, we spent together a lot of time brainstorming and sharing experiences about the best ways to raise, at a same time, young people's awareness on these topics and, more generally, their interests towards STEM carriers.

1 Introduction

According to DESI [5], 46% of EU individuals (age 16–74) lack the digital skills needed in a world that has changed and continues to change rapidly. The situation is certainly no better when one goes to investigate the level of knowledge and awareness of young people, particularly young women, who are often less interested in ICT issues and reluctant to be engaged in awareness-raising activities on these topics.

Concurrently, cybersecurity is becoming more and more important in todayś increasingly digitalized and connected world. Unfortunately, the constant increase of cybersecurity requirements is not properly supported by the availability of the requested workforce. Just to mention, according to the European Union, in 2022, "the shortage of cybersecurity professionals in the EU ranged between 260,000 and 500,000, while the EUś cybersecurity workforce needs were estimated at 883,000 professionals. In addition, women only amounted to 20% of cybersecurity graduates and to 19% of information and communications technology specialists" [1],

Several avenues of attack have been paved both at the central level, mainly via ENISA, and at the single member state level.

At the EU level, the *Cybersecurity strategy of the European Union* [6], engraves, among the others, the aim to foster awareness, skills development, and career opportunities in cybersecurity using a variety of games and cybersecurity challenges. These goals have been then further developed within the frame of the recently proposed *Cybersecurity Skills Academy* [1]. This falls into the scope the European Year of Skills 2023 [3] of the European Union. The Academy is designed to bring together private and public initiatives aimed at promoting cybersecurity skills at European and national levels. The ultimate objective of the Academy is to increase the European cybersecurity workforce and upskill cybersecurity professionals and make them visible on an online platform.

At the member state level, for instance, the Italian National Cybersecurity Strategy 2022–2026 [7] has been set up to address these needs and it aims at planning, coordinating, and implementing security measures to make the country safer and more resilient. The strategy seeks to achieve 82 measures by 2026.

In the sequel of the present paper, *The Big Game*, one of the most significant and effective Italian approach, fully coherent with the National Strategy, is presented.

The paper is organized as follows: the next section introduces the overall structure of *The Big Game* program, presenting its organizers and outlining its key features. The following sessions focus on the characteristics and structure of the main components of the program, and namely *CyberChallenge.IT*, *OliCyber.IT*, *CyberTrials*, *TeamItaly*, and *CyberHighSchools*. The last session (VIII) eventually concludes the paper, outlining the actions already foreseen to increase the overall impact of the program in the Italian cybersecurity landscape.

2 The Big Game

The Big Game is a comprehensive and integrated set of actions aimed at: (a) raising *cybersecurity awareness, education, & training* in the country, (b) tackling the *cybersecurity skill shortage*, (c) reducing the gender gap, increasing girls'

interests in the topic, and (d) creating and growing both a community of *cyber defenders* by investing in young talents, and, at the same time, a community of *high school teachers* more and more involved in cybersecurity issues.

As sketched in Fig. 1, *The Big Game* includes 3 main "lines": *Training*, *CTF's*, and *CyberHighSchools*. Depending of their nature, one or more editions of each program is run annually.

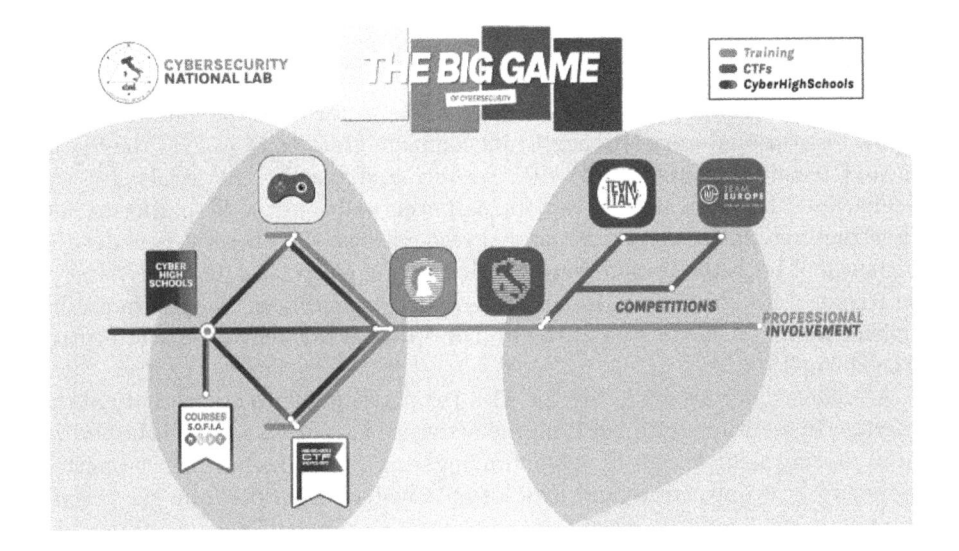

Fig. 1. A global picture of *The Big Game* program.

Before entering the specific implementation details of each composing program, we are going to first introduce the organizer briefly, and then pointing out some key features of the overall program.

2.1 The Organizers

The Big Game program is organized and managed by the CINI *Cybersecurity National Lab*[1].

Established on the 6/12/1989, CINI[2] (National Interuniversity Consortium for Informatics) is a consortium of 52 publicly funded Italian universities and is today the main point of reference for the national academic research in the fields of Computer Engineering, Computer Science, and Information Technologies. The consortium is under the supervision of the competent Italian Ministry for University and Research and is currently equipped with 10 Thematic R&D National Labs, distributed throughout the whole national territory, the preeminent one being the *Cybersecurity National Lab*.

---
[1] https://cybersecnatlab.it.
[2] https://www.consorzio-cini.it.

The Lab is organized as a network of 65 interconnected Nodes, located in major Italian Universities, research Institutions, and military academies. The Lab aims at fostering the Italian national cybersecurity ecosystem, via the promotion of a continuous process of aggregation of R&D structures in a multi- and inter-disciplinary perspective, pushing synergisms and joint activities between the public and the private sector. Among these activities, the flagship one in the field of educational and training is definitely *The Big Game* program.

2.2 Key Features

Among the program's key feature, we would like to focus on the following ones: (a) the institutional recognitions, (b) its complete gratuitousness, (c) the teaching and training approach, (d) the teaching and training materials, (e) the peculiarity of teachers and instructors, and eventually (e) the IT platforms and infrastructures. In terms of institutional recognitions, the program is under the patronage of both the Italian *National Agency for Cybersecurity* (ACN) and of the Italian *Data Protection Authority* (GPDP). In addition, the program fully implements the Measure #65 of the Italian National Strategy on Cybersecurity 2022–2026 [7].

Attendance is *completely free* for ALL the participants to any activity of the program. In addition, until 2021, all the activities have been accomplished without exploiting a single cent of public funding, everything having been supported by the involved universities and by a lot of industrial sponsors from the private sector.

The various activities of *The Big Game* are ALL characterized by peculiar and custom *game-based approaches*. These systematically introduces the various cybersecurity themes exploiting a proper mix of theory and fundamental concepts with *gamification*, that always require attending competitions in virtual arenas that properly simulate and emulate real IT and OT infrastructures, network scenarios, and operational environments. In particular, gamification is used as a tool to increase student engagement and motivation, as well as to promote learning and retention of course material [9,11]. The proposed model is unique in the international scenario; in fact, it not only exploits gaming for attracting people, regardless their age, but also provides significant and solid inter- and multi-disciplinary training paths. These systematically cover, at different level of depth and details, foundations, technical, scientific, legal, and ethical aspects of issues related to various aspects of cybersecurity.

Teachers and instructors of the various activities include not only professors, researchers, and experts in the various fields of cybersecurity provided by the involved universities, but also members of the best Italian Capture-the-Flag teams, composed of participants to elder editions of *CyberChallenge.IT* (see Sect. 3) and of members of the Italian National Cyberdefender *TeamItaly* team (see Sect. 6).

The overall program exploits advances IT infrastructures that have been entirely in-house developed and managed by the *Cybersecurity National Lab*. These currently support the admission tests, the training phases, the various competitions, the portal, and the website. All the developed infrastructures are continuous upgraded and improved and are today characterized by a very high-quality level in terms of security, dependability, scalability, and deployment solutions. It is worth mentioning that the organizers of both the 2022 and 2023 edition of the *International Cybersecurity Challenge* (ICC)[3] that took place in Athens (Greece) and San Diego, CA, (USA), respectively, after an international selection process, selected the *Cybersecurity National Lab* as the official provider of both the Attack/Defense infrastructures and the related challenges.

All the teaching and training materials have been developed in house, partly in English and partly in Italian; they are systematically peer reviewed during the preparation phase and updated and upgraded after each edition. In addition, all the challenges used in the various final competitions are always brand new and developed in-house, as well. After each competition, the proposed challenges are included in the training paths of the next editions. Most of the basic training material is *freely accessible* through the new *Training Portal* of the *Cybersecurity National Lab*[4]. It currently includes 20+ hours of lectures and 300+ exercises (challenges) on the most relevant cybersecurity topics.

In addition, to properly support Network and Hardware security training, a Hybrid CyberRange, named PAIDEUSIS [8], has been implemented. Physically located in Lucca, at the IMT premises, the CyberRange can be remotely accessed to fully exploit its facilities, that today includes: 4 powerful servers, with 200+ USB interfaces for VMs, 40 modems/routers[5], 40 Open security Platforms [14], 40 Platforms for Side Channel attacks[6], 40+ platforms for IoT and IIOT [14], 40+ FPGA-based architectures[7], SCADAs & ICS'[8], CanBus Infrastructures [14].

In conclusion of this section, it is worth pointing out the concurrent in-house availability of the required IT infrastructures and of the recorded training materials, in addition to the possibility of remotely accessing the CyberRange, allowed us to continue the regular delivering of our programs even during the Covid19 pandemic restrictions, simply switching from in-presence activities to their remote delivery.

3 CyberChallenge.IT

CyberChallenge.IT is the first Italian training program in cybersecurity for high-school, undergraduate, and graduate students (aged 16–24) that aims at significantly reducing today's cyber workforce shortage in Italy, by identifying, attracting, recruiting, and placing the next generation of cybersecurity professionals, thus making their skills available to the Country.

---

[3] https://www.ic3.games.
[4] https://training.olicyber.it.
[5] https://www.tiesse.com/prodotti/switch-e-gateway/.
[6] https://www.newae.com/products/NAE-CW1101.
[7] http://www.pynq.io.
[8] https://www.tridium.com/us/en.

In particular, the program aims to create and grow the cyberdefender community by (a) stimulating interest in STEM areas and mainly in computer science/engineering; (b) identifying and properly tutoring young cyber talents, thus contributing to their professional grow; (c) facing real-world multi-disciplinary challenges in different fields of cybersecurity, including both Red-Teaming and Blue-Teaming, ethical and legal aspects; (d) sharing professional employment opportunities offered by program's private and public sponsors and stakeholders.

Each edition is run annually from January to July in 40+ locations, aka Training Nodes, (Universities, Regional Centers, Military Academies) spread over the whole nation. The 8 editions of the program recorded so far 29,270 students enrolled, and 4,550 participants. An overview of the various editions is in Table 1, whereas detailed statistics for the various editions are available via the program website[9]. It is worth pointing out that the implementation of the program has been made possible just by the peculiar "national" feature of the Cybersecurity National Lab: none Italian university, even the biggest ones, would have had the capability to realize it by their own, reaching today levels.

Table 1. CyberChallenge.IT Attendance.

Year	Venues	Schools	Total #	Gender M	F	O	Origin Schools #	%	Universities #	%	Admitted #	%
2017	1	-	683	603	80	-	57	8.35	626	91.65	26	3.81
2018	8	-	1866	1698	168	-	583	31.24	1283	68.76	160	8.57
2019	18	19	3203	2830	373	-	1341	41.87	1862	58.13	360	11.24
2020	28	114	4452	3848	604	-	1960	44.03	2492	55.97	560	12.58
2021	33	184	4902	4258	644	-	2255	46.00	2647	54.00	671	13.69
2022	34	316	5344	4642	661	48	2461	46.05	2883	53.95	754	14.11
2023	43	503	4720	4101	567	52	2066	43.77	2654	56.23	944	20
2024	43	600	4114	3576	496	40	1735	42.17	2379	57.83	942	22.90

Since 2021, *CyberChallenge.IT* has been recognized by the Italian Ministry of Education as a "Project for the Enhancement of Excellences" [12]. As a consequence, the Ministry grants yearly top ranked high school students several awards and prizes. In addition, many Italian universities recognize credits according to the European Credit Transfer and Accumulation System (ECTS) [2] to CyberChallenge.IT participants.

3.1 Workflow

Each program edition includes 4 main phases: Admission Tests, Training team clustering, Training path, and Final competitions. Participants are selected

---
[9] https://cyberchallenge.it/stats.

through a sequence of on-line tests, aimed at an initial selection and at the composition of the Training Teams, respectively. Once admitted, attendees are clustered in Training Teams of 20 people each (plus 5 alternates), and each team is trained in one of the program's Training Nodes.

In particular, the selection process consists of multiple stages, including a web-based on-line pretest and two in-presence admission tests organized simultaneously in all the Training Nodes.

Registered students can train themselves in preparation for the admission test exploiting a custom in-house developed software platform. On this platform, students can face the proposed quizzes and submit their solutions of the programming problems to get an automatic evaluation. Both correctness and performances are considered during the scoring.

At the end of the registration period, admitted students must attend an in-presence test, which consists of two different activities, carried out concurrently through all the Country in all the Training Nodes. In the morning, students are asked to answer some quizzes, similar albeit more complex than the on-line pretest. The best ranked students are then admitted to the afternoon programming phase, in which they are asked to solve three programming problems, freely exploiting the preferred programming language among C/C++, Java, or Python.

The training program aims at providing the methodological and practical foundations required to analyze weaknesses, vulnerabilities, and possible attacks, identifying the most suitable solutions to prevent them, in different fields of cybersecurity. Specifically, the covered topics are clustered into 8 *Topic Areas* (Introduction to Cybersecurity, Cryptography, Hardware Security, Software Security, Network Security, Web Security, Attack/Defense, Ethics & Soft Skills), in turn composed of 24 *Modules*. Typically, each module spans a week timeframe and includes 6 h of proctored activities (2 of lectures and 4 of hands-on activities). These are organized to guide students, step-by-step, in solving Capture the Flag (CTF) challenges of increasing complexity. No previous knowledge in cybersecurity is assumed. Teaching and training activities are scheduled locally in time slots compatible with the school and university activities of the participants, including, in some cases, Friday afternoon or Saturday morning. The training path targets both *BlueTeaming* and *RedTeaming*. The complete training program spans 12 weeks and the set of modules to be covered at each Training Node is freely selected locally.

The training process ends with *two final competitions*, organized at the Training Node level and at the National level, respectively. The former one is a Jeopardy style CTF run concurrently by all the attendees of all the Training Nodes. The latter i.e., the *Italian CTF championship in Cybersecurity*, is an Attack-Defense style CTF, attended by teams of 6 members each, one per Training Node, and organized each year in a specific location. Where all the teams physically convey.

4 OliCyber.IT

In 2020, we realized that out of 2,035 high-school students initially enrolled to the CyberChallenge.IT program, just 156 were admitted, having passed all the admission phase. The high failure rate was in primis devoted to the fact that they had to compete with undergraduate and graduate university students, who obviously have different background and skills. Thus, we decide to start a brand-new program targeting just high-school students and we called it **OliCyber.IT**, *the Italian Cybersecurity Olympiads*.

4.1 Mission

OliCyber.IT, the Italian Cybersecurity Olympiads[10], is a training and competition program that targets the students of all years of all Italian high schools, aiming at encouraging and incentivizing their approach to the challenges of cybersecurity. In particular, OliCyber.IT aims to create and grow a community of cyberdefenders by investing in young people stimulating their interest in technical and scientific aspects of computer engineering, computer science, and cybersecurity. In addition, the program aims to identify young talents and contribute to their career guidance and training, including by sharing the opportunities offered by various training paths on cybersecurity topics.

The program draws on the experience and tools developed as part of the *CyberChallenge.IT* program, which, as we have seen, can be accessed upon reaching the age of 16. From this point of view, the *Italian Cybersecurity Olympiads* stands as a "propaedeutic" program to *CyberChallenge.IT*, which is seen as its natural downstream complement. The 4 editions of the program recorded very significant numbers: a total of 11,430 enrolled.

In terms of institutional recognition, the *OliCyber.IT* program is recognized by the Ministry of Education as a *Pathway for Transversal Skills and Orientation* (PCTO) [4]. In addition, since 2021, in a way similar to CyberChallenge.IT, the same Ministry also recognizes *OliCyber.IT* as a *Project for the Enhancement of Excellences*.

4.2 Workflow

The various phases of each program edition can be summarized as follows:

1. Participation (free of charge) in the *CyberHighSchools* program by high schools;
2. The enrollment (free of charge) in the program by interested students;
3. A high school-level selection phase for all enrollees, held simultaneously online, and aimed at selecting the best students from each federated institution;

---

[10] https://olicyber.it.

4. A second territorial selection phase, in which those admitted from the first selection take part, aimed at selecting the best 100 students who will participate in the national competition;
5. An in-person training phase that, in the 2023 edition, involved more than 360 students among those admitted to the territorial selection, divided geographically (North, Central, South Italy) in 3 one-week "Training camps", each with about 120 participants. An in-depth discussion of the camps is provided in the next section;
6. The final national in-person competition: the Italian Cybersecurity Olympiads, followed the next day by a national awards ceremony, attended by VIPs and representatives of Italian institutions.

4.3 Training Camps

One of the main problems encountered in the first editions of the Italian Cybersecurity Olympiads was the "gap" in theoretical knowledge required between the different phases of the program. If, in fact, passing the school selection requires only good logical ability and some basic scholastic knowledge, the territorial phase, in CTF format, requires technical and practical knowledge in cybersecurity that can only be acquired through education and training specific to this type of event. This phenomenon, while in some cases it was seen by the more competitive students as a challenge to overcome and a new opportunity to prove themselves, unfortunately represented a reason for "abandonment" for most of the students who, having passed the previous phase, found great difficulty in solving the exercises proposed in this phase. Starting with the 2023 edition, the problem has been addressed and solved by creating more activities and growth opportunities for the students in the initial stages of the project. A first significant step in this direction was the creation of the *training.olicyber.it* portal, which, through video lectures and exercises, makes available to the boys the tools to continue in the later stages. A further step was the creation of a series of events, called "Training camps", to allow students to learn about this world thanks to mentoring from more experienced participants who have had a similar experience in the past. The main objective is to bring participants, at the end of the camp, to have the necessary tools and knowledge to face the territorial selection phase. These activities have taken strong inspiration from the local and national internships of the Math and Computer Science Olympiads, which, over the years, have shown how intensive training activities by former participants and organizers, carried out in presence even at the local or regional level, are essential to grow the project. Those who have successfully passed the school selection are informed of the opportunity to participate in the camps on a first-come first-served basis and consent from the school's lead teacher, who will also, accordingly, justify their absence from school classes. Each edition of the camp includes 40 h of training recognizable as PCTO and divided between:

- 4 introductory hours aimed at the setup of working tools and methodology;

- 32 h of training divided into 4 days of 8 h each, specifically dedicated to scripting in python, network security, web security, software security and cryptography, alternating between theoretical and laboratory meetings;
- 4 h of simulation of a competition.

The training of each camp was taken care of by 8 different tutors, 2 per class (web, crypto, software) and 2 additional ones, who followed the participants' training during the whole week. All training materials used in the camps are made available via the official project communication channels.

5 CyberTrials

In 2022 we realized that the issue of gender gap in *OliCyber.IT* was getting worst and worst. In order to try to tackle it effectively, we started **CyberTrials**, a custom entry-level, game-based training program for high-school girls. The purpose of the initiative is to promote the topics of cybersecurity and online civic-mindedness, providing tools for understanding and deepening that make it concretely possible to master technological topics. Through face-to-face meetings, in-person initiatives, and organized competitions among participants, *CyberTrials* provides an opportunity for anyone - even those without prior technical knowledge - to master the theoretical tools of online safety. In addition, the program aims at (a) Breaking down gender barriers in STEM subjects by setting up a cybersecurity accelerator pathway aimed at anyone and suitable for anyone regardless her scientific or humanities oriented background; (b) Providing girls with the basic knowledge needed to operate safely in the digital realm, both in defensive and offensive conditions, with responsible attention to hacker ethics; (c) Strengthening understanding of phenomena such as social networks, stalking, data processing and online scams, to provide useful and concrete tools for reading the digital world and protecting against its distortions.

5.1 Program Structure

The training program aims at enabling the participants to acquire basic technical skills and a general understanding of some aspects of cybersecurity, including Networks, Web, OSInt, Threat modeling, Social Engineering, Computer forensics, Cryptography and Steganography. These competencies are complemented with soft skills, including Self-management skills, Legal and ethical aspects, Team building, and Communication skills. All of these topics are presented weekly, in 2-hours modules.

Alongside traditional lectures, the program offers CTF-based, hands-on sessions, carried out during the entire training process in order to consolidate the concepts learned. Once again, we resort to gamification, i.e., the use of game elements, such as points, badges, and leaderboards, in non-game contexts to engage and motivate the participants [13]. In particular, each week 3 new challenges are released just at the end of the presented module. A peculiarity of CyberTrials is to be based on a continuous storytelling, where all the presented challenges are integrated with the main story through references, descriptions, hints, and additional materials (implementation details can be found in [10]).

To increase their involvement in the game, the girls are forced to play in teams of up to five people, chosen randomly, in order to foster relationships among girls who do not know each other and to avoid the composition of unbalanced teams in terms of skills. The experience of these first two years has shown that the random choice of team members proves to be successful because nerdier girls are often joined by girls with initial marginal knowledge and skills, who can thus find help in their playmates. The top 20 teams in the final ranking were admitted to the in presence final event, organized as a jeopardy-style CTF, followed by a write-up session.

The first 3 editions of *CyberTrials* registered more than 2,050 participant girls.

In terms of institutional recognition, *CyberTrials* is recognized as part of the Italian Republic Digital initiative[11], a national strategic initiative coordinated by the Department for Digital Transformation of the Prime Minister's Office, which aims to reduce the digital divide and to promote education on future technologies, supporting the country's development process.

The initiative is included as a good practice in the publication *Overcoming the Gender Digital Divide in Digital Skills* edited by the working group consisting of civil society representatives (including the *Cybersecurity National Lab*), the Department for Digital Transformation, and the Department for Equal Opportunities of the Prime Minister's Office.

6 TeamItaly

Teamitaly - *the Italian National CyberDefender Team* - is the national team that has the task and responsibility of representing the country in the most important international competitions related to various cybersecurity sectors, including the annual European Cyber Security Challenge (ECSC)[12] organized by the European Union Agency for Cybersecurity (ENISA)[13] (see Sect. 6.1).

As of 2018, the Italian *Nucleo di Sicurezza Cibernetica* (NSC) has entrusted the *Cybersecurity National Lab* with the task of organizing and managing TeamItaly's activities and overseeing, among other things, its participation in international competitions in the sector.

On a practical level, the Lab provides for the selection of the group of "trainers", composed of the coach (coach) Mario Polino (PoliMi), the Team Manager (technical organizational contact person) Gaspare Ferraro (Cybersecurity National Lab) and a staff of experts. These have the task and responsibility of annually selecting 20 of the best participants from all editions of the training programs organized by the Cybersecurity National Lab. The participants are

---
[11] https://repubblicadigitale.innovazione.gov.it/it.
[12] https://ecsc.eu.
[13] https://www.enisa.europa.eu.

selected, at the end of the annual editions of the *CyberChallenge.IT* and *OliCyber.IT* programs, based on their achievements both during the training courses and in the various competitions, with the aim of seeking out the best talent from the different branches of cybersecurity. Specifically, following the criteria of the ECSC, the national team consists of 10 members of the Junior category, aged 14 to 19, and 10 members of the Senior category, aged 21 to 25.

In order to better prepare and measure themselves against the various types of challenges offered in the various international competitions they participate in, the team is involved in an intensive training course (*Bootcamp*), that takes place, in attendance, for an entire week.

The *Bootcamp* is aligned with national cybersecurity strategies, promoting cyber skills as an asset for the country system and subjecting the conveners to a training course of excellence, unique in Europe, with the prospect of further increasing their already high defensive and offensive capabilities both individually and, above all, as a team. With this very purpose in mind, members of the national team are trained on acquiring specific skills in numerous areas, including cryptography, web security, forensic analysis of computers and mobile devices, and hardware security. In addition, during the training, each of the team members develops the ability to expound on complex topics in a way that is understandable to an audience of non-specialists. A *Team Building* track, specifically designed for the initiative, is also an integral part of the training.

6.1 European Cyber Security Challenge (ECSC)

At the European level, ENISA, the *European Union Agency for Cybersecurity* acts as a driving force and, drawing on the experiences of individual nations, organizes the *European Cyber Security Challenge* (ECSC) each year with the aim of fostering the exchange of knowledge and talent across Europe. The competition is open to all European countries. Each nation that registers for the event participates with a team of 10 players between the ages of 14 and 25.

Among the goals of the ECSC is to put cybersecurity at the service of humanity, to promote peace, preserve democracy, dignity and freedom of thought, stimulating collaboration among players from participating countries and the importance of transparency and compliance with the rules for all phases of the competition.

Italy participated, with *TeamItaly*, in ECSC for the first time in 2017, taking third place. In 2018 it achieved sixth place, while in the 2019 edition, held in Bucharest, Romania, the team took second place. The 2020 edition was canceled due to the Covid19 restrictions. In the 2021 edition, held in Prague, Czech Republic, and the 2022 edition, held in Vienna, Austria, *TeamItaly* placed third and fourth, respectively.

6.2 Team Europe

In addition to organize ECSC, ENISA also manages *Team Europe*[14], a group of talented young individuals who are passionate about cybersecurity and represent Europe in the *International Cybersecurity Challenge*[15]. Comprised of individuals with diverse backgrounds and expertise, *Team Europe* is committed to advancing cybersecurity knowledge and skills, as well as promoting international collaboration to tackle emerging cyber threats. Through their participation in this global competition, *Team Europe* showcases the best of Europe's cybersecurity talent and contributes to shaping the future of cybersecurity.

The last 2 years of activity of *Team Europe* have seen the involvement of respectively 3 and 2 Italian players coming from *TeamItaly*, while, since its constitution, 1 out of the 5 coaches of the team is the coach of *TeamItaly*, as well.

7 CyberHighSchools

The **CyberHighSchools** program was created with the intent of activating a network among Italian High-Schools ("Istituti Superiori di II grado"), with the goal of creating an intermediate level of training and interaction with students, while at the same time fostering the growth of a community of professors increasingly aware of cybersecurity issues and interested in *Cybersecurity National Lab* programs.

By joining the program for free, the Institute becomes part of a network of schools "federated" with the Lab and is automatically considered a participant in all activities of *The Big Game* program. To date, there are more than 600 federated Italian high schools. Among the most relevant aspects as a return for teachers in a Federated School, the following should be highlighted:

- Possibility of free access to extensive and in-depth teaching materials, prepared and systematically reviewed by experts from the *Cybersecurity National Lab*;
- Opportunity to participate free of charge in targeted introductory and/or in-depth courses on cybersecurity topics (see below);
- Possibility to receive, at the end of each training courses, both *certificates of participation* issued by the *Cybersecurity National Lab* and *Open Badges*[16], usable through CINECA's Bestr[17] platform;
- Ability to access a community of professors, who will be offered the opportunity to share experiences and propose initiatives both through dedicated forums and periodic meetings;
- Ability to monitor the progress of their students within the *CyberChallenge.IT*, *OliCyber.IT* and *CyberTrials* programs.

---

[14] https://teameurope.ecsc.eu.
[15] https://icc.ecsc.eu.
[16] https://openbadges.org.
[17] https://bestr.it.

7.1 Teachers Training Courses

The program provides high-school teachers who have joined the program with the opportunity to take, free of charge, several *training courses*, upon registration on the S.O.F.I.A. platform of the Italian Ministry of Education[18]. All the course are completely free of charge and are taught by university professors and specialists in the field, pertaining to the *Cybersecurity National Lab*.

The *Basic Course* aims to raise awareness of cybersecurity issues in various aspects of daily life, through an appropriate mix of lectures and tutorials, usable remotely. The course includes 31 total hours of commitment, including 22 h of lectures (4 delivered online, through the Zoom platform and 16 usable remotely in asynchronous e-learning mode, through video-recorded lectures) and 9 h of online tutoring by the lecturer who recorded the lecture.

The *Advanced Courses* aim to delve more deeply into advanced computer security topics related to Cryptography, Web security, Network security, Software security, Hardware security, through an appropriate mix of lectures and practical exercises, all usable remotely and on official Lab platforms.

A total of 9 editions of the Basic Course and 11 editions of the Advanced ones has so far been delivered, attended globally by more than 1,550 professors.

7.2 HighSchools CTF Workshops

Starting in 2023, in order to spread the various activities of *The Big Game* program more widely, the *Cybersecurity National Lab* has initiated a series of workshops organized in various Italian cities and called **HighSchools CTF Workshops**. Organized as part of the *CyberHighSchools* program, these are hands-on introductory cybersecurity events aimed at high school students and professors from all grade levels who are interested in learning more about the basic concepts of cybersecurity. During each edition, fundamental introductory concepts related to Open Source Intelligence (OSINT), web security, network security, computer forensics, and cryptography are addressed with a hands-on approach through the presentation of tools and numerous exercises on practical cases. Each edition of the workshop includes three different sessions:

- During the morning session, a number of practical workshops introduce the basic topics of computer security, with the presentation of both the basic concepts and the main tools to be used;
- In order to gain a better understanding of the topics addressed, the afternoon session includes a computer-based computer competition, in the style of CTF competitions: participants, divided into teams of 4–6 people (composed of students and their professors), compete in a competition with hands-on challenges related to the topics presented in the morning;
- At the end of the competition, the best teams are awarded in the final closing ceremony.

Six editions of the Workshops have so far been organized in 6 different locations, globally attended by 1,200+ students and professors.

---

[18] https://sofia.istruzione.it.

8 Conclusions

In the present paper we analyzed the peculiar feature of *The Big Game*, one of the most significant and effective Italian approach to tackle the lack of workforce in different areas of cybersecurity and, at the same time, to rise the awareness w.r.t. its threads.

The main goal of the *Cybersecurity National Lab*, i.e., the program organizer and promoter of the program, is to involve a growing number of young people and make *The Big Game* a model of training on cybersecurity issues of reference, scalable, and to be proposed to other target populations, with particular reference to people with different abilities or at risk of social marginalization, including, among the others, prisoners, NEETs, unemployed, and people with disabilities.

The systematic adoption of gamification practically proved how tangible is its impact in terms of acquiring people's "defense" skills and capabilities, useful for strengthening the cybersecurity of businesses, Public Administrations and institutions, i.e., the entire country system.

References

1. Cybersecurity Skills Academy: a coordinated approach to boost the EU cyber workforce. https://digital-skills-jobs.europa.eu/en/cybersecurity-skills-academy. Accessed 10 Aug 2023
2. European Credit Transfer and Accumulation System (ECTS). https://education.ec.europa.eu/education-levels/higher-education/inclusive-and-connected-higher-education/european-credit-transfer-and-accumulation-system. Accessed 10 Aug 2023
3. European Year of Skills 2023. https://commission.europa.eu/strategy-and-policy/priorities-2019-2024/europe-fit-digital-age/european-year-skills-2023_en. Accessed 10 Aug 2023
4. Linee guida dei percorsi per le competenze trasversali e per l'orientamento. https://www.miur.gov.it/-/linee-guida-dei-percorsi-per-le-competenze-trasversali-e-per-l-orientamento. Accessed 10 Aug 2023
5. The Digital Economy and Society Index (DESI). https://digital-strategy.ec.europa.eu/en/policies/desi. Accessed 10 Aug 2023
6. The Cybersecurity Strategy (2022). https://digital-strategy.ec.europa.eu/en/policies/cybersecurity-strategy. Accessed 10 Aug 2023
7. ACN: National Cybersecurity Strategy. https://www.acn.gov.it/en/strategia/strategia-nazionale-cybersicurezza. Accessed 10 Aug 2023
8. Berra, G., Ferraro, G., Fornero, M., Maunero, N., Prinetto, P., Roascio, G.: Paideusis: a remote hybrid cyber range for hardware, network, IoT security training. In: ITASEC, pp. 284–297 (2021)
9. Caponetto, I., Earp, J., Ott, M.: Gamification and education: a literature review. In: European Conference on Games Based Learning, vol. 1, p. 50. Academic Conferences International Limited (2014)
10. Costa, G., De Francisci, S., Valiani, S., Prinetto, P.: Why Mary can hack: effectively introducing high school girls to cybersecurity. In: Proceedings of the 18th International Conference on Availability, Reliability and Security, pp. 1–8 (2023)

11. Dicheva, D., Dichev, C., Agre, G., Angelova, G.: Gamification in education: a systematic mapping study. J. Educ. Technol. Soc. **18**(3), 75–88 (2015)
12. D.L. 29 dicembre 2007, n. 262: Disposizioni per incentivare l'eccellenza degli studenti nei percorsi di istruzione (2007). https://www.normattiva.it/uri-res/N2Ls?urn:nir:stato:decreto.legislativo:2007-12-29;262!vig=
13. Nah, F.F.-H., Zeng, Q., Telaprolu, V.R., Ayyappa, A.P., Eschenbrenner, B.: Gamification of education: a review of literature. In: Nah, F.F.-H. (ed.) HCIB 2014. LNCS, vol. 8527, pp. 401–409. Springer, Cham (2014). https://doi.org/10.1007/978-3-319-07293-7_39
14. Varriale, A., Vatajelu, E.I., Di Natale, G., Prinetto, P., Trotta, P., Margaria, T.: Secube™: an open-source security platform in a single SOC. In: 2016 International Conference on Design and Technology of Integrated Systems in Nanoscale Era (DTIS), pp. 1–6. IEEE (2016)

Education and Society

Gino Yu[✉]

International Technological University, Santa Clara, CA 95054, USA
phusikoi@gmail.com

Abstract. Recent advancements in artificial intelligence (AI) and digital technologies are poised to significantly transform education and employment landscapes. This paper examines the implications of these technological shifts on educational paradigms and societal roles, emphasizing the need to reassess educational approaches in light of evolving digital environments. The analysis begins with a historical perspective on the development of knowledge, language, and functional mythologies, highlighting how early human societies used these mythologies to establish norms and values. It then explores the modern world's fragmentation of these mythologies and the impact of technological advances on our connection to nature and mystical experiences. The discussion includes the role of education in fostering self-knowledge and critical thinking, and how contemporary educational systems must adapt to the rise of AI. By integrating insights from historical, philosophical, and technological perspectives, the paper argues for a revised educational framework that addresses the challenges of the digital age and prepares students to navigate an increasingly complex world.

Keywords: Education · society · artificial intelligence · functional mythology

1 Introduction

Recent advancements in artificial intelligence threaten to disrupt our current paradigms in education and future employment opportunities for our graduates. Problems are compounded by ever shortening attention spans of students brought about by the influence of social media and the global disruption in education at all levels brought due to the COVID pandemic. While it is clear to many educators that education will undergo a dramatic change in the coming years, it is difficult to anticipate how these changes will occur due to the exponential nature of the underlying digital technologies.

Since the dawn of digital media technologies in the 1980s educators and education institutions have struggled to keep abreast with the latest advancements in technology. Now, nearly all students in first world countries use laptops, tablet computers, and smartphones instead of paper and pencil for their work. Lectures from top universities on nearly every topic are readily available via the Internet. Artificial intelligence threatens to supplant teachers by offering explanations personalized to students' individual level of understanding. As each generation of students grows up with increasingly advanced technologies, the digital culture gap between them and the ageing educator increases.

© The Author(s), under exclusive license to Springer Nature Switzerland AG 2025
M. Hinchey and B. Steffen (Eds.): Festschrift Tiziana Margaria, LNCS 15720, pp. 35–43, 2025.
https://doi.org/10.1007/978-3-031-73887-6_3

This current dilemma provides an opportunity to reassess the role of education considering the perspective of individual students as well as society at large so that educators can better craft educational experiences that incorporate the latest advances in technology. Many of the systems underpinning our modern are also facing crisis including our financial systems, our forms of governance, and the environment. It becomes increasingly imperative that our education systems produce graduates adequately prepared to address these challenges that our society faces.

2 The Role of Knowledge in Society

The realm of all knowledge can be imagined as starting from the moment the first person became self-aware. This initial spark of consciousness marked the birth of knowledge, much like an oak tree grows from an acorn. In this nascent stage, language did not yet exist, but the ability to perceive, learn, and remember experiences laid the foundation for the development of knowledge (Donald, 1991). As early humans engaged with the natural world, they began to make sense of their surroundings, developing rudimentary forms of communication through gestures, expressions, and eventually, primitive sounds (Tomasello, 2008). Over generations, these early forms of communication evolved into more complex languages, allowing humans to share their experiences, learn from one another, and build upon previous knowledge (Deacon, 1997).

The development of language and the ability to represent thoughts and experiences symbolically were pivotal in expanding human understanding and collaboration (Harari, 2014). As societies formed and cultures grew, collective knowledge increased exponentially. The process of passing down information from one generation to the next, through oral traditions and later written records, further solidified the accumulation of knowledge (Ong, 1982). Jesuit priest Pierre Teilhard de Chardin coined the term "noosphere" to describe the collective sphere of human thought, where ideas and language live, evolve, and interact (Teilhard de Chardin, 1955). The noosphere represents a new layer of existence, encompassing the shared intellectual and cultural experiences of humanity. It signifies the progressive development of human knowledge and consciousness, as each generation builds upon the discoveries and insights of those before them. This ongoing process continues to shape our understanding of the world and our place within it, highlighting the dynamic and ever-evolving nature of human knowledge.

3 Functional Mythology

The development of functional mythologies has been integral to human societies since their early formations. These mythologies often explained natural phenomena, establish societal norms and values, and provide a sense of identity and purpose to communities (Eliade, 1959; Malinowski, 1926). They helped communities understand and harmonize with their environments, fostering cohesion and stability (Durkheim, 1912). Over time, these mythologies evolved into religious beliefs, cultural practices, and narratives that continue to influence societies worldwide (Campbell, 1949; Levi-Strauss, 1962). These narratives persist as powerful tools for shaping collective identities and understanding human experiences across diverse cultures and historical contexts.

Joseph Campbell identified four primary functions of mythology that are essential to any active, living mythology. These functions provide a framework for understanding mythology from his perspective, as outlined in his works such as "Occidental Mythology" (1964). Here are the four functions:

1. **Mystical (or Metaphysical) Function:** This function inspires in the individual a sense of awe and gratitude in relation to the mystery dimension of the universe. It connects people to the profound mysteries of existence and the transcendent aspects of life, fostering a deep sense of wonder and reverence.
2. **Cosmological Function:** The cosmological function presents an image of the universe that links local knowledge and individual experience to the mystery dimension. It offers a coherent and meaningful view of the cosmos, integrating scientific and cultural understandings to situate human life within a larger context.
3. **Sociological Function:** This function validates, supports, and imprints on the individual the norms of that society. Mythology serves to reinforce the social order, promoting values, behaviours, and institutions that maintain and strengthen the community's cohesion and continuity.
4. **Pedagogical Function:** The Pedagogical function guides each individual through the stages of life within the context of that culture. Myths and rituals provide archetypes and narratives that help individuals navigate life's transitions, challenges, and milestones, offering models for personal development and self-understanding.

These four functions—mystical, cosmological, sociological, and pedogogical—are central to the role of culture in a society that is in harmony with nature.

4 The Lack of a Common Functional Mythology in the Modern World

Our modern society represents an amalgamation of the evolution of early functional mythologies that emerged with the advent of civilization. Over millennia, as societies developed and interacted, these mythological narratives evolved, transformed, and merged, influencing religious beliefs, cultural practices, and even shaping modern ideologies and worldviews (Levi-Strauss, 1966; Armstrong, 2005).

Our current understanding of reality is based upon Western science and philosophy and is predicated upon a materialistic paradigm. This framework is largely built on the need for a common semantic reference to clearly define and communicate experience. Western paradigms, particularly those influenced by Greco-Roman thought and later scientific developments, prioritize a dualistic and objective view of reality. Here, the individual is considered a separate entity, and reality is understood through empirical observation, rational analysis, and scientific inquiry.

The phusikoi (φυσικοί), also known as the Pre-Socratic philosophers, were early Greek thinkers who laid the groundwork for Western science and philosophy by exploring the nature of the cosmos and the principles governing it. The term "phusikoi" comes from the Greek word "phusis" (φύσις), meaning "nature," reflecting their primary focus on natural phenomena and the physical world. The phusikoi were careful to distinguish between "phusis" and "techne" which represent two fundamental concepts that describe different aspects of existence and knowledge. "Phusis" (φύσις), often translated as "nature," refers to the intrinsic properties and natural processes of the world, embodying the idea of growth, change, and the inherent characteristics of living things and natural phenomena. It is the natural order of things, the way they exist and develop independently of human intervention. On the other hand, "techne" (τέχνη), usually translated as "art" or "craft," denotes the skills, techniques, and knowledge used to produce artifacts and manipulate the natural world. It involves human ingenuity, creativity, and the application of practical skills to achieve specific goals. While "phusis" is associated with the organic and spontaneous unfolding of life, "techne" represents the structured, intentional efforts of humans to shape their environment and create tools, artworks, and systems. The distinction between these two concepts highlights the Greek understanding of the balance between the natural world and human agency, emphasizing the complementary roles of nature's inherent qualities and human craftsmanship in shaping reality (Heidegger, 1977; Aristotle, 1999).

Advancements in our understanding in the Universe has enabled the invention of tools or technology that amplify both intention and perception. Technological innovations, such as telescopes and the Large Hadron Collider, enhance perception by expanding our understanding of the universe and the fundamental particles of matter (Hawking, 2002; Evans, 2008). Enhanced communication tools, such as the internet and social media, allow individuals to express their ideas and intentions more broadly and effectively (Shirky, 2008). These technologies extend our sensory capabilities and influence our understanding and interpretation of reality, transforming how we perceive and interact with the world.

The convergence of scientific advancements and technologies stemming from new understandings of the universe has catalyzed clashes among traditional cultures in the era of globalization, particularly concerning the roles of functional mythologies. Scientific discoveries, serving a cosmological function, often collide with literal interpretations of religious beliefs that fulfill mystical functions. Furthermore, technological progress within civilizations frequently determines the outcomes of conflicts, providing significant advantages that empower more technologically advanced societies to dominate, defeat, or subjugate their less advanced counterparts (Diamond, 1997).

Recent technological advancements have increasingly abstracted our personal connection to nature, mediated through modern conveniences and digital interfaces. Technologies such as smartphones, virtual reality, and artificial environments can create a sense of separation, altering our perception and interaction with the natural world (Sobel, 1996; Louv, 2008). Many of our experiences are now filtered through screens and devices, making our connection to the natural world more indirect and conceptual (Kahn, 2011).

Consequently, we are increasingly losing touch with nature, the mystical, and a common functional mythology that once helped individuals and society maintain harmony with the natural world. The abstraction and mediation provided by modern technology can lead to a disconnection from the immediate and tangible experiences of the natural environment (Louv, 2008). This disconnection also diminishes our engagement with the mystical aspects of existence that traditional mythologies often encapsulated, reducing our collective sense of wonder and spirituality. Without a shared functional mythology, societies struggle to find common ground and values that promote ecological balance and a deeper connection to the world around us. The result is a growing gap between human life and the natural systems that sustain it, impacting both individual well-being and societal cohesion.

From a Western perspective, science and religion offer distinct frameworks for understanding and communicating about the world and human experience. Science employs systematic observation, experimentation, and analysis to explore the objective world, emphasizing empirical verification and precise definitions within the realm of the material and observable (Popper, 1959). This approach enables clear and widely accepted semantic references in describing physical phenomena and natural laws. However, science encounters inherent limitations in establishing a universally applicable semantic framework for subjective inner experiences like emotions, spiritual insights, and existential dilemmas (James, 1902).

In contrast, religion provides a framework grounded in faith, tradition, and spiritual experience to interpret existential questions and moral values (Durkheim, 1912). Utilizing mythology, art, and rituals as powerful tools, religion conveys and enriches inner experiences through symbolic language and communal practices that resonate with personal and collective spiritual journeys (Eliade, 1957). Nevertheless, reconciling diverse interpretations and experiences within religious contexts remains challenging, as semantic references are inherently subjective and deeply personal. Variations in the interpretation and meaning of mythology and rituals across different cultural and religious traditions underscore the complexity of establishing a singular semantic framework for communicating inner experiences (Geertz, 1973).

Eastern philosophies such as Hinduism, Buddhism, and Daoism present an alternative perspective that emphasizes a holistic and interconnected view of reality, where the self is understood as part of a larger, unified whole (Suzuki, 1956). This outlook focuses on inner experience, meditation, and the transcendence of the ego to achieve enlightenment or harmony with the universe. However, effectively conveying these deeply personal and subjective experiences poses challenges, as language and empirical frameworks often struggle to capture their essence. This dichotomy highlights the Eastern emphasis on an inner journey that is inherently subjective and challenging to articulate, contrasting with the Western emphasis on external, material understanding that is more easily communicated through observable and measurable phenomena.

Daoist philosophy, with its emphasis on aligning mind, body, and universe to achieve harmony and natural flow, shares intriguing parallels with Carl Jung's concept of synchronicity in psychology. Both challenge linear causality by suggesting that meaningful connections and events can occur beyond direct cause and effect. Daoism's principle of Wu Wei advocates for effortless action in accordance with the natural order, fostering harmonious outcomes when individuals are aligned with the Dao. Similarly, Jung's theory of synchronicity posits that meaningful coincidences arise when individuals are attuned to deeper patterns in life, suggesting a non-linear interconnectedness of events. These perspectives emphasize the importance of awareness, receptivity, and alignment with natural rhythms to perceive and engage with the world more meaningfully.

5 The Pedagogical Function in Society

Education plays a pivotal role in helping individuals understand fundamental questions about their identity, purpose, and the nature of their surroundings. Through education, individuals gain knowledge and perspectives that contribute to self-discovery and understanding. It provides frameworks for exploring personal identity, societal roles, and existential questions about existence and purpose. By learning about various subjects, cultures, and philosophies, education encourages critical thinking and reflection, enabling individuals to form informed perspectives on their place in the world and their aspirations. Thus, education serves as a pathway to gaining clarity on questions of personal identity, purpose, and the nature of reality.

Socrates famously emphasized the importance of self-knowledge. His maxim 'Know thyself' underscores the belief that self-awareness and understanding are fundamental to a meaningful and virtuous life (Plato, *Apology*, 38a). The importance of self-knowledge in education is indeed profound, as it lays the foundation for personal growth, self-awareness, and the ability to navigate life with a deeper understanding of one's values, strengths, and goals. Self-knowledge helps individuals develop a clear sense of identity and purpose, fostering confidence and resilience (McAdams, *The Psychological Self as Actor, Agent, and Author*, 2013). It encourages critical thinking and introspection, allowing people to make informed decisions and cultivate a more meaningful and fulfilling life (Flanagan, *The Geography of Morality: Diversity and Moral Understanding in the History of Ideas*, 2017). While education also serves other vital roles—such as promoting social cohesion, economic progress, and the dissemination of knowledge—self-knowledge can be seen as a central element that enhances all these aspects. By understanding themselves better, individuals are better equipped to contribute positively to society and pursue their ambitions effectively (Rogers, *On Becoming a Person: A Therapist's View of Psychotherapy*, 1961).

When each of us is born, we start out just like that first person who became self-aware. Every individual undergoes a process of development in which they are born with instinct, become encultured into their environment through the intellect, and cultivate intuition and insight (Fig. 1).

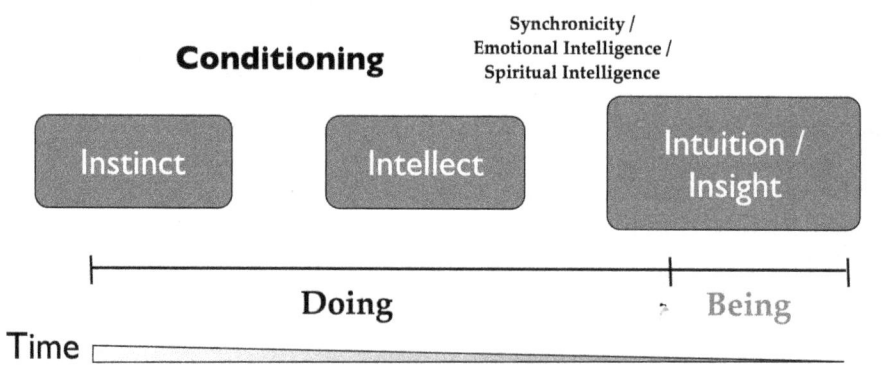

Fig. 1. Development from instincts we are born with to insights that are contextual

The progression from instinct to intellect to intuition reflects a significant aspect of human development and understanding. Our Instincts, defined as innate, primal behaviours crucial for survival and basic functioning from birth (Tinbergen, 1951), form the foundational responses in early development. As individuals grow and learn, their intellect develops, allowing for reasoning, problem-solving, and the acquisition of knowledge through education and experience (Piaget, 1970; Vygotsky, 1978). Through a process of enculturation, we are introduced to the society into which we are born, learning its language, customs, and knowledge. According to scholars such as Erik Erikson, education provides opportunities for identity formation and the exploration of personal values and beliefs (Erikson, 1950). Additionally, educational frameworks enable individuals to engage critically with philosophical and ethical inquiries, enhancing their understanding of existential concepts (Brubaker, 2015).

Drawing on Krishnamurti's perspectives on education and the significance of life, which emphasize self-inquiry, holistic learning, and the exploration of fundamental human concerns (Krishnamurti, 1953), education serves not only to impart knowledge but also to facilitate introspection and the cultivation of a deeper understanding of personal identity, purpose, and the broader human experience (Nussbaum, 1997). Intuition or insight then emerges as a deeper form of understanding that transcends mere logic and learned knowledge (Kahneman, 2011; Jung, 1971), often drawing on subconscious processes and deeper insights from lived experiences. Intelligence, when highly awakened, manifests as intuition, which Krishnamurti asserts is the only true guide in life. Creativity and intuition are seen as personal expressions of the mystical function within a functional mythology, where an individual's true nature aligns with Nature (phusis) underpinning the metaphysics of the constructed world (techne), allowing individuals to transcend conventional boundaries and contribute innovative perspectives and solutions to society. This holistic approach includes fostering greater harmony with nature as a manifestation of individuals' unique creative potential, promoting sustainable practices and a balanced coexistence with the natural world. Through this process, we make our own discoveries and contributions, advancing the collective knowledge and culture of our society. This, in turn, provides a richer foundation for the next generation, continuing the cycle of learning and growth.

6 Education in the Era of Artificial Intelligence

Education is a process of enculturation, wherein individuals are integrated into the societal framework by acquiring the necessary skills and knowledge to engage with their cultural milieu. In contemporary society, a high school education typically endows graduates with fundamental competencies in literacy, numeracy, and cultural awareness, equipping them for basic life tasks (OECD, 2019). A Bachelor's degree provides graduates with the proficiency to comprehend and engage with specialized domains of knowledge (Thelin, 2019). A Master's degree extends this capability, enabling individuals to apply their understanding creatively within their field of study (Altbach et al., 2019). A Doctorate degree signifies a level of expertise where individuals can contribute original research and generate new knowledge within their discipline (Walker et al., 2008).

Artificial Intelligence (AI) has the potential to significantly enhance the educational process by swiftly processing and presenting information tailored to the comprehension level of learners. This capability allows AI to assist students in learning, understanding, and synthesizing information based on their prior knowledge and the data on which the AI system has been trained (Holmes et al., 2019). AI can also facilitate the creation of new applications or interpretations within specific domains of knowledge (Luckin et al., 2016). However, it is important to note that AI, in its current state, lacks the capacity to create fundamentally new knowledge independent of its training data (Boden, 2016).

Enculturing individuals into functional members of society necessitates equipping them with the skills required for survival, as outlined by Maslow's hierarchy of needs (Maslow, 1943). This involves addressing physiological and safety needs, fostering a sense of belonging, and promoting self-esteem. In the contemporary context, meeting physiological and safety needs often involves securing financial stability, which can be achieved through traditional employment or innovative means such as becoming a digital nomad or utilizing AI to generate passive income streams (Reichenberger, 2018). Once these basic needs are met, individuals can leverage their insights and expertise to engage in higher cognitive processes, including the creation of new knowledge through innovative thinking and intuitive insights (Maslow, 1971).

Conflict of Interests. The author(s) has no competing interests to declare that are relevant to the content of this manuscript.

References

Altbach, P.G., Reisberg, L., Rumbley, L.E.: Trends in Global Higher Education: Tracking an Academic Revolution. UNESCO (2019)
Aristotle: Metaphysics (H. G. Apostle, Trans.). Indiana University Press (1999)
Armstrong, K.: A Short History of Myth. Canongate (2005)
Boden, M.A.: AI: Its Nature and Future. Oxford University Press (2016)
Brubaker, N.D.: Existential Foundations of Medicine and Psychology. Routledge (2015)
Campbell, J.: The Hero with a Thousand Faces. Princeton University Press (1949)
Campbell, J.: Occidental Mythology: The Masks of God. Penguin Books (1964)
Deacon, T.: The Symbolic Species: The Co-evolution of Language and the Brain. W.W. Norton & Company (1997)
Diamond, J.: Guns, Germs, and Steel: The Fates of Human Societies. W.W. Norton & Company (1997)
Donald, M.: Origins of the Modern Mind: Three Stages in the Evolution of Culture and Cognition. Harvard University Press (1991)
Durkheim, E.: The Elementary Forms of Religious Life (K. E. Fields, Trans.). Free Press (1912)
Eliade, M.: The Sacred and the Profane: The Nature of Religion (W. R. Trask, Trans.). Harcourt Brace Jovanovich (1957)
Eliade, M.: Myth and Reality (W. R. Trask, Trans.). Harper & Row (1959)
Erikson, E.H.: Childhood and Society. W. W. Norton & Company (1950)
Evans, L.: The Large Hadron Collider: The Extraordinary Story of the Higgs Boson and Other Stuff That Will Blow Your Mind. HarperCollins (2008)
Flanagan, O.: The Geography of Morality: Diversity and Moral Understanding in the History of Ideas. Oxford University Press (2017)
Geertz, C.: The Interpretation of Cultures: Selected Essays. Basic Books (1973)
Harari, Y.N.: Sapiens: A Brief History of Humankind. Harper (2014)
Hawking, S.: The Universe in a Nutshell. Bantam Books (2002)

Heidegger, M.: The Question Concerning Technology, and Other Essays (W. Lovitt, Trans.). Harper & Row (1977)

Holmes, W., Bialik, M., Fadel, C.: Artificial Intelligence in Education: Promises and Implications for Teaching and Learning. Center for Curriculum Redesign (2019)

James, W.: The Varieties of Religious Experience: A Study in Human Nature. Green, & Co., Longmans (1902)

Jung, C.G.: Psychological Types (H. G. Baynes, Trans.). Princeton University Press (1971)

Kahn, P.H.: Technological Nature: Adaptation and the Future of Human Life. MIT Press (2011)

Kahneman, D.: Thinking, Fast and Slow. Farrar, Straus and Giroux (2011)

Krishnamurti, J.: Education and the Significance of Life. Harper & Brothers (1953)

Levi-Strauss, C.: The Savage Mind. University of Chicago Press (1962)

Levi-Strauss, C.: The Raw and the Cooked: Introduction to a Science of Mythology. Harper & Row (1966)

Louv, R.: Last Child in the Woods: Saving Our Children from Nature-Deficit Disorder. Algonquin Books (2008)

Luckin, R., Holmes, W., Griffiths, M., Forcier, L.B.: Intelligence Unleashed: An Argument for AI in Education. Pearson (2016)

Malinowski, B.: Myth in Primitive Psychology. W.W. Norton & Company (1926)

Maslow, A.H.: A theory of human motivation. Psychol. Rev. **50**(4), 370–396 (1943)

Maslow, A.H.: The Farther Reaches of Human Nature. Viking Press (1971)

McAdams, D.P.: The Psychological Self as Actor, Agent, and Author. Oxford University Press (2013)

Nussbaum, M.C.: Cultivating Humanity: A Classical Defense of Reform in Liberal Education. Harvard University Press (1997)

OECD: Education at a Glance 2019: OECD Indicators. OECD Publishing (2019)

Ong, W.J.: Orality and Literacy: The Technologizing of the Word. Methuen (1982)

Piaget, J.: Science of Education and the Psychology of the Child. Viking Press (1970)

Plato. Apology. (G. M. A. Grube, Trans.). Hackett Publishing Company

Popper, K.: The Logic of Scientific Discovery. Hutchinson (1959)

Reichenberger, I.: Digital nomads – a quest for holistic freedom in work and leisure. Ann. Leisure Res. **21**(3), 364–380 (2018)

Rogers, C.R.: On Becoming a Person: A Therapist's View of Psychotherapy. Houghton Mifflin (1961)

Shirky, C.: Here Comes Everybody: The Power of Organizing Without Organizations. Penguin Books (2008)

Sobel, D.: Beyond Ecophobia: Reclaiming the Heart in Nature Education. Orion Society (1996)

Suzuki, D.T.: Zen Buddhism: Selected Writings. Doubleday (1956)

Teilhard de Chardin, P.: The Phenomenon of Man. Harper & Brothers (1955)

Thelin, J.R.: A History of American Higher Education. Johns Hopkins University Press (2019)

Tinbergen, N.: The Study of Instinct. Clarendon Press (1951)

Tomasello, M.: Origins of Human Communication. MIT Press (2008)

Vygotsky, L.S.: Mind in Society: The Development of Higher Psychological Processes. Harvard University Press (1978)

Walker, G.E., Golde, C.M., Jones, L., Conklin Bueschel, A., Hutchings, P.: The Formation of Scholars: Rethinking Doctoral Education for the Twenty-First Century. Jossey-Bass (2008)

From Otter to ISoLA

Martin Wirsing(✉)

Ludwig-Maximilians-Universität München, Munich, Germany
wirsing@lmu.de

Abstract. On the occasion of Tiziana Margaria's 60th birthday, this short paper presents my personal perspective on Tiziana's scientific achievements. Beginning with her work on hardware verification using the Otter theorem prover, I recount her arrival at the University of Passau and highlight several of her outstanding contributions to tools and methods for model-driven development, many accomplished in close collaboration with her husband, Bernhard Steffen. The paper also shortly addresses her collaboration with Mike Hinchey, her intriguing applications of digital techniques, and my involvement with the ISoLA conference series, which she co-founded with Bernhard Steffen and has chaired for the past 20 years. I conclude with my heartfelt thanks to her.

1 The Beginning: Otter and Passau

The first paper by Tiziana that I read was titled "The OTTER Environment for Resolution-Based Proof of Hardware Correctness" [7] (with Paolo Camurati and Paolo Prinetto), which detailed her experiences with the Otter theorem prover. Otter supports first-order logic with equality and is applied to the domain of hardware verification. The paper reported several successful automated verifications of the correctness of combinational circuits, both in terms of specification vs. implementation and implementation vs. implementation. I was very impressed by this young researcher who not only understood mathematical logic but also worked proficiently with formal theorem provers!

I first met Tiziana in Passau in the early nineties. I had just left the University of Passau to take a chair at LMU Munich, while her husband, Bernhard Steffen, had received an offer for my former chair. My wife, Sabine, and I were still living in Passau when Tiziana and Bernhard visited their new city and the university. Bernhard was thrilled to start his first full professorship, but the situation was different and challenging for Tiziana. To secure a position as a researcher at Passau University, one of the professors had to offer her a job. Due to conflict of interest rules, Bernhard could not offer her a position at his chair. Eventually, Christian Lengauer, the chair of Programming, employed Tiziana, allowing her and Bernhard to both work at the University of Passau.

During the next few years, I did not have much contact with Tiziana, but I followed her scientific development and achievements with great interest. In 1997,

---

A personal view of Tiziana Margaria's scientific work.

I came across her excellent paper on the MOSEL toolset for monadic second-order logic [10]. Once again, I was very impressed, particularly when I noticed the venue of the paper. It had appeared in the proceedings of the 3rd TACAS conference, and to my surprise, Tiziana and Bernhard were among the founders of the TACAS conference series in 1995 [6]. Together, they had organized the second TACAS Workshop [17] in Passau in 1996. Moreover, in 1997, she and Bernhard founded the International Journal on Software Tools for Technology Transfer STTT, where she continues to serve as the coordinating editor [1].

Tiziana also began to shift her research direction. Together with Bernhard and his team, she was developing an advanced programming environment for the creation of large programs. "METAFrame is a meta-level framework designed to offer sophisticated support for the systematic and structured computer-aided generation of application-specific complex objects from collections of reusable components" is the first sentence of her and Bernhard's seminal paper on the METAFrame environment [24]. Application development with METAFrame is model-driven: based on libraries of components, so-called Building Blocks, and constraints, programs are graphically constructed under model checking control.

Tiziana had broadened her profile from formal hardware verification to software development and had co-founded an international journal and an international workshop, which in the following years became one of Europe's top computer science conferences!

2 Tools and Methods for Model-Driven Development

At the end of the nineties, Tiziana followed Bernhard to the University of Dortmund. A few years later, she became a professor at the University of Göttingen and then the Chair of Service and Software Engineering at the University of Potsdam. This period marked a time of close collaboration with Bernhard and significant shared ideas on tools and methods for model-driven development (MDD).

Together, they founded MetaFrame Technologies Software Consulting and Design GmbH [2], with Tiziana as its first CEO. Under their leadership, the META-Frame tool evolved from a research prototype to an industrial-quality software. One of the first major applications based on METAFrame was the innovative "Electronic Tool Integration (ETI) platform [4,23]", designed for the interactive experimentation with and coordination of heterogeneous tools. This platform was associated with STTT and helped build a repository for the tools published in the journal.

Tiziana and Bernhard also developed the Application Building Center (ABC) [12], a tool for graphical, library-based application development. This was later replaced by jABC [25], a multi-purpose modular framework written in Java for modeling complex software systems. ABC and jABC became the foundations for several significant tools, including the Online Conference Service (OCS) (see [12]), generic tool integration jETI [15], and the Bio-jETI framework for semantics-based service composition in biology [11], to name a few key applications of the jABC technology.

However, Tiziana's and Bernhard's research extended beyond tool development; they also focused on improving the software development process. They designed and promoted a novel agile engineering paradigm: Extreme Model-Driven Development (XMDD) [18]. XMDD involves the application expert continuously throughout the entire systems lifecycle, placing models at the center of activities and elevating them to first-class entities in the global system design process. System developers select models from libraries and specify systems by combining these models, with system changes occurring at the model level. jABC was the ideal development environment for a variety of case studies and applications, including supply chain management, semantic web services, and an online conference system.

3 Limerick

Around 2005, Tiziana and Bernhard collaborated with Mike Hinchey from the NASA Goddard Space Flight Center to develop an automata learning-based method for mechanically transforming system requirements into running code through provably equivalent models [14]. This collaboration continued when, in 2008, Mike moved to Ireland to become a professor at the University of Limerick and, two years later, the director of Lero, the Science Foundation Ireland Research Centre for Software. At NASA, Mike was involved in the design and verification of autonomic systems, particularly the NASA Voyager. In "Component-Oriented Behavior Extraction for Autonomic System Design [13]", Tiziana, Mike, Bernhard, and their coauthors demonstrate how Tiziana's and Bernhard's game-based model checker GEAR (see Tool-supported Enhancement of Diagnosis) can be used for verifying properties of the Voyager II space mission. Additionally, Tiziana co-authored an excellent article in CACM with Mike and other renowned scientists on the importance of formal methods for software engineering, specifically focusing on software reliability [8].

In 2015, Tiziana moved to Ireland to work at Lero and to assume the Chair of Software Systems at the University of Limerick. There, she continues her successful research on methods and tools for model-driven engineering and no-code/low-code development. Additionally, she advances digital techniques in various application domains, such as digital humanities [5], smart manufacturing with digital twins [16], and blockchain and low-code/no-code development for health informatics [3,9].

As in Passau, Tiziana and I just missed each other in Limerick. From 2010 until early 2015, I collaborated with Mike on the European project ASCENS [27], where Mike was the site leader at Lero and I was the scientific coordinator. By the time Tiziana was appointed at the University of Limerick in 2015, the ASCENS project had just concluded.

However, Tiziana and Limerick are an excellent fit which inspired me to the following lines:

> There is a top woman from LERO,
> A software systems true hero.
> She builds MDD, healthcare, and digital twin,
> With low-code, no-code, she always will win,
> The amiable hero from LERO.

4 ISoLA

Although Tiziana and I missed each other in Passau and Limerick, we have met regularly at the ISoLA conferences since the ASCENS project. In 2004, she, together with Bernhard, started the ISoLA [22] conference series, which quickly became very successful. It now provides an excellent forum for scientific discussions and is a well-known platform for building a scientific community. From the beginning, Tiziana and Bernhard invited me to contribute new scientific results to ISoLA.

The opportunity came in 2008 when I was the scientific coordinator of the EU project SENSORIA [26] on service-oriented overlay computing. For the 3rd edition of ISoLA in 2008 and the 4th edition in 2010, the project contributed three papers (see [19], 155–205) and one paper (see [20], 51–65), respectively, to the tracks related to service-oriented computing. In the 6th edition, Tiziana and Bernhard invited me again, this time to organize an own track of the ASCENS project. Together with Rocco De Nicola and Matthias Hölzl, I initiated the track on rigorous engineering of autonomic ensembles (see [21], 96–198), which has since continued under the title "Rigorous Engineering of Collective Adaptive Systems" at each edition of ISoLA.

5 Thank You, Tiziana

Collaborating and discussing with Tiziana is always a very pleasant experience. I deeply admire her dedication to the scientific community, especially her commitment to the ISoLA conference series. Tiziana is not only an excellent scientist and an outstanding editor and conference chair but also a warm-hearted and kind friend and colleague. I look forward to many more inspiring exchanges with her.

References

1. International Journal on Software Tools for Technology Transfer. https://link.springer.com/journal/10009/editors. Accessed 04 Aug 2024
2. MetaFrame Technologies Software Consulting and Design GmbH. https://www.metaframe.de/management.html#founder. Accessed 05 Aug 2024

3. Brandon, C., Margaria, T.: Low-code/no-code artificial intelligence platforms for the health informatics domain. Electron. Commun. Eur. Assoc. Softw. Sci. Technol. **82** (2022)
4. Braun, V., Margaria, T., Weise, C.: Integrating tools in the ETI platform. Int. J. Softw. Tools Technol. Transf. **1**(1–2), 31–48 (1997)
5. Breathnach, C., Ibrahim, N.M., Clancy, S., Margaria, T.: Towards model checking product lines in the digital humanities: an application to historical data. In: ter Beek, M.H., Fantechi, A., Semini, L. (eds.) From Software Engineering to Formal Methods and Tools, and Back. LNCS, vol. 11865, pp. 338–364. Springer, Cham (2019). https://doi.org/10.1007/978-3-030-30985-5_20
6. Brinksma, E., Cleaveland, R., Larsen, K.G., Margaria, T., Steffen, B. (eds.): Tools and Algorithms for Construction and Analysis of Systems, First International Workshop, TACAS 1995, Aarhus, Denmark, May 19-20, 1995, Proceedings. Lecture Notes in Computer Science, vol. 1019. Springer, Heidelberg (1995). https://doi.org/10.1007/3-540-60630-0
7. Camurati, P., Margaria, T., Prinetto, P.: The OTTER environment for resolution-based proof of hardware correctness. Microprocess. Microprogram. **30**(1–5), 421–428 (1990)
8. Hinchey, M., Jackson, M., Cousot, P., Cook, B., Bowen, J.P., Margaria, T.: Software engineering and formal methods. Commun. ACM **51**(9), 54–59 (2008)
9. Javed, I., Alharbi, F., Bellaj, B., Margaria, T., Crespi, N., Qureshi, K.: Health-ID: a blockchain-based decentralized identity management for remote healthcare. Healthcare **9**, 712 (2021)
10. Kelb, P., Margaria, T., Mendler, M., Gsottberger, C.: Mosel: a flexible toolset for monadic second-order logic. In: Brinksma, E. (ed.) TACAS 1997. LNCS, vol. 1217, pp. 183–202. Springer, Heidelberg (1997). https://doi.org/10.1007/BFb0035388
11. Lamprecht, A., Margaria, T., Steffen, B.: Bio-jETI: a framework for semantics-based service composition. BMC Bioinform. **10**(S–10), 8 (2009)
12. Margaria, T.: Components, features, and agents in the ABC. In: Ryan, M.D., Meyer, J.-J.C., Ehrich, H.-D. (eds.) Objects, Agents, and Features. LNCS, vol. 2975, pp. 154–174. Springer, Heidelberg (2004). https://doi.org/10.1007/978-3-540-25930-5_10
13. Margaria, T., Bakera, M., Wagner, C., Vassev, E., Hinchey, M.G., Steffen, B.: Component-oriented behavior extraction for autonomic system design. In: Denney, E., Giannakopoulou, D., Pasareanu, C.S. (eds.) First NASA Formal Methods Symposium - NFM 2009. NASA Conference Proceedings, vol. NASA/CP-2009-215407, pp. 66–75 (2009)
14. Margaria, T., Hinchey, M.G., Raffelt, H., Rash, J.L., Rouff, C.A., Steffen, B.: Completing and adapting models of biological processes. In: Pan, Y., Rammig, F.J., Schmeck, H., Solar, M. (eds.) BICC 2006. IIFIP, vol. 216, pp. 43–54. Springer, Boston, MA (2006). https://doi.org/10.1007/978-0-387-34733-2_5
15. Margaria, T., Nagel, R., Steffen, B.: jETI: a tool for remote tool integration. In: Halbwachs, N., Zuck, L.D. (eds.) TACAS 2005. LNCS, vol. 3440, pp. 557–562. Springer, Heidelberg (2005). https://doi.org/10.1007/978-3-540-31980-1_38
16. Margaria, T., Schieweck, A.: Active behavior mining for digital twins extraction. IT Prof. **24**(4), 74–80 (2022)
17. Margaria, T., Steffen, B. (eds.): Tools and Algorithms for Construction and Analysis of Systems, Second International Workshop, TACAS 1996, Passau, Germany, March 27–29, 1996, Proceedings. Lecture Notes in Computer Science, vol. 1055. Springer, Heidelberg (1996). https://doi.org/10.1007/3-540-61042-1

18. Margaria, T., Steffen, B.: Agile IT: thinking in user-centric models. In: Margaria, T., Steffen, B. (eds.) ISoLA 2008. CCIS, vol. 17, pp. 490–502. Springer, Heidelberg (2008). https://doi.org/10.1007/978-3-540-88479-8_35
19. Margaria, T., Steffen, B. (eds.): Leveraging Applications of Formal Methods, Verification and Validation, Third International Symposium, ISoLA 2008, Porto Sani, Greece, October 13–15, 2008. Proceedings. Communications in Computer and Information Science, vol. 17. Springer, Heidelberg (2008). https://doi.org/10.1007/978-3-540-88479-8
20. Margaria, T., Steffen, B. (eds.): Leveraging Applications of Formal Methods, Verification, and Validation - 4th International Symposium on Leveraging Applications, ISoLA 2010, Heraklion, Crete, Greece, October 18–21, 2010, Proceedings, Part II. Lecture Notes in Computer Science, vol. 6416. Springer, Heidelberg (2010). https://doi.org/10.1007/978-3-642-16561-0
21. Margaria, T., Steffen, B. (eds.): Leveraging Applications of Formal Methods, Verification and Validation. Technologies for Mastering Change - 6th International Symposium, ISoLA 2014, Part I. Lecture Notes in Computer Science, vol. 8802. Springer, Heidelberg (2014). https://doi.org/10.1007/978-3-662-45234-9
22. Margaria, T., Steffen, B., Philippou, A., Reitenspieß, M. (eds.): International Symposium on Leveraging Applications of Formal Methods, ISoLA 2004, October 30 - November 2, 2004, Paphos, Cyprus. Preliminary proceedings, TR-2004-6 of Technical report. Department of Computer Science, University of Cyprus (2004)
23. Steffen, B., Margaria, T., Braun, V.: The Electronic Tool Integration platform: concepts and design. Int. J. Softw. Tools Technol. Transf. **1**(1–2), 9–30 (1997)
24. Steffen, B., Margaria, T., Claßen, A., Braun, V.: The METAFrame'95 environment. In: Alur, R., Henzinger, T.A. (eds.) CAV 1996. LNCS, vol. 1102, pp. 450–453. Springer, Heidelberg (1996). https://doi.org/10.1007/3-540-61474-5_100
25. Steffen, B., Margaria, T., Nagel, R., Jörges, S., Kubczak, C.: Model-driven development with the jABC. In: Bin, E., Ziv, A., Ur, S. (eds.) HVC 2006. LNCS, vol. 4383, pp. 92–108. Springer, Heidelberg (2007). https://doi.org/10.1007/978-3-540-70889-6_7
26. Wirsing, M., Hölzl, M.M. (eds.): Rigorous Software Engineering for Service-Oriented Systems - Results of the SENSORIA Project on Software Engineering for Service-Oriented Computing. Lecture Notes in Computer Science, vol. 582. Springer, Heidelberg (2011). https://doi.org/10.1007/978-3-642-20401-2
27. Wirsing, M., Hölzl, M.M., Koch, N., Mayer, P. (eds.): Software Engineering for Collective Autonomic Systems – The ASCENS Approach. Lecture Notes in Computer Science, vol. 8998. Springer, Heidelberg (2015). https://doi.org/10.1007/978-3-319-16310-9

A Quantum-Like Intellect: Celebrating the Profound Impact of Tiziana Margaria, Professor and Friend

Cristina Seceleanu[✉]

Mälardalen University, Västerås, Sweden
cristina.seceleanu@mdu.se

Abstract. It is not often that someone possesses qualities akin to those found in quantum phenomena, such as cleverness and quick reactions. Hence, I consider myself privileged that I have met and collaborated for many years with Tiziana Margaria, a renowed professor of Software Engineering and respected friend. This personal note that I dedicate to her tries to reflect both the professional and personal admiration that I hold for her.

1 A Short Account of Our History

In the world of academia, there are those who teach, those who inspire by their research, and those who do both with a touch of magic. Professor Tiziana Margaria belongs to the latter category. I have had the privilege of knowing her not just as a colleague but as a mentor and friend. Her remarkable journey and immense contributions to our field are well-known, but today, I want to share a more personal perspective. Few people possess qualities akin to those found in quantum phenomena, such as cleverness and quick reactions. If one asks me to select a representative human, to illustrate parallels between cognitive prowess and the fascinating world of quantum mechanics, the first who comes to mind is Tiziana: her insights are precise, her influence is far-reaching, and her contributions create ripples that extend far beyond her immediate sphere.

I first met Tiziana in 2002, at Turku Centre for Computer Science, Finland, during a Summer School in Software Verification that I was attending as a Ph.D. student. Amidst the hustle and bustle of academic presentations and lectures from reputed professors, she stood out with her infectious enthusiasm and genuine curiosity. As she engaged with each presenter and almost each student, you could see the sparks of ideas forming, her mind working at lightning speed. It was like watching a maestro at work, orchestrating a symphony of knowledge.

After my graduation, we cooperated on different fronts: we co-organized a series of workshops for the component-based design of resource-constrained systems (`CORCS`) [1–3], joint with the `IEEE CS` flagship International Conference on Computers, Software, and Applications (`COMPSAC`), Tiziana was a speaker in the

© The Author(s), under exclusive license to Springer Nature Switzerland AG 2025
M. Hinchey and B. Steffen (Eds.): Festschrift Tiziana Margaria, LNCS 15240, pp. 50–54, 2025.
https://doi.org/10.1007/978-3-031-73887-6_5

panels that I organized at **COMPSAC** 2011 and **COMPSAC** 2015, I co-organized Special Tracks at the International Symposium on Leveraging Applications of Formal Methods, Verification and Validation, **ISoLA** 2021, 2022, 2024 that Tiziana organizes together with Professor Bernhard Steffen, and Tiziana was Program Co-Chair at the 8th International Conference on Engineering of Computer-based Systems (**ECBS** 2023), which I organized at Mälardalen University in Sweden. Tiziana was the faculty opponent in the Licentiate defense of my first Ph.D. student, Dr. Aneta Vulgarakis, whom I co-supervised, and a member of the grading committee of Aneta's Ph.D. defense. Observing Tiziana's collaborative and innovative research and supervisory style, as well as her interaction with, then, my Ph.D. students Dr. Ashalatha Kunnappilly, Dr. Predrag Filipovikj, and Dr. Raluca Marinescu, have profoundly shaped my approach to research. I have embraced a more dynamic and supportive method in mentoring doctoral students, fostering a nurturing environment that encourages creativity and rigorous scientific inquiry. Together with Prof. Ivica Crnkovic, I have contributed a journal paper [4] in the special issue on "Simplicity in IT" in IEEE Computer that Tiziana co-edited [5], which appeared in November 2013. I served for five years as the appointed External Examiner for University of Limerick's programs in Computer Science, the B.Sc. (hons) in Computer Systems and the B.Sc. (hons) in Computer Games Development, Tiziana being the Chair of Software Systems at the Department of Computer Science and Information Systems during that time.

All these events were enriching for me, yet I was most overjoyed to collaborate with Tiziana and other reputed scientists, Prof. Bernhard Steffen, Prof. Axel Legay, Dr. Ashalatha Kunnappilly, Dr. Louis-Marie Traonouez, in the joint work "Analyzing Ambient Assisted Living Solutions: A Research Perspective" [6], published at the 12th International Conference on Design and Technology of Integrated Systems in Nanoscale Era (DTIS). This work delves into the integration of crucial Ambient Assisted Living features such as health monitoring, fall detection, and social inclusion. It emphasizes the significance of ensuring safe functionality and quality of service, considering timing and security requirements. By leveraging advanced tools like **DIME** [7] for model-driven design, **REMES** [8,9] for timing and resource-usage modeling and analysis, **SECube** [10] for security, and **PLASMA** [11] for statistical model-checking, we address the challenges of analyzing these complex systems. Tiziana's contributions have been pivotal in proposing high-level solutions that mitigate the issues of semantic interoperability [12] and evolving architectures.

Tiziana has a unique ability to make complex concepts seem approachable, and her passion for research is matched only by her dedication to her students and colleagues. I remember one particularly challenging point in the paper that we worked on together. The deadline was looming, and we were knee-deep in problems that seemed insurmountable. The collaboration was purely remote and we were having online meetings. While I was on the verge of pulling my hair out, Tiziana logged in with a big smile: "Let us take a break", she said, "Sometimes, all one needs is a bit of sugar and a fresh perspective". We took a break, and, true to her words, returned with renewed energy and eventually cracked the problem. That moment encapsulates who Tiziana is: someone who knows the value of hard work but also understands the importance of taking a step back and enjoying the little things in life.

Her sense of humor is another quality that makes her so special. Her witty remarks and playful banter can turn regular meetings into delightful experiences. I fondly recall a visit to Ireland for an advisory board meeting at the University of Limerick. We met at my hotel's cafe early one morning, eager to start the day with a warm beverage. When the waitress asked what we would like to start with, Tiziana, with a mischievous glint in her eye, responded, "Today we feel wild, we start with tea". It was such a simple yet charming moment, perfectly capturing her ability to find joy and whimsy in everyday situations. We smiled and enjoyed our "wild" start to the day, setting a positive tone for the rest of our meeting.

Beyond her professional achievements, Tiziana is a wonderful friend. I recall a time when I was facing a particularly tough personal decision. She listened patiently and then, in her typical fashion, offered a perspective that was both profound and humorous. "Cristina," she said, "life is like a research project. Sometimes, you need to take risks and follow your instincts, and if all else fails, there is always biscotti".

Tiziana's impact extends far beyond her academic prowess. She has created a community where collaboration and kindness are paramount. Her ability to connect with people, to bring out the best in them, and to foster an environment of mutual respect and support is truly inspirational. She has not only shaped the minds of countless students and colleagues, but has also touched their hearts. As we celebrate Tiziana's remarkable career, I find myself reflecting on the many lessons she has taught me. Her dedication to her work, her unwavering support for her students, her leadership style, and her ability to find joy during work are qualities that I strive to emulate. She has shown me that success is not just about accolades and achievements but also about the positive impact we have on others' lives.

2 Tiziana's Thinking Process: A State-Based Draft Model

Creating a formal model to express the cleverness and quantum-like thinking of Professor Tiziana Margaria can be only approached, not completed, by incorporating elements that highlight complexity, parallelism, and innovation. The model can be represented as a series of states and transitions, reflecting Tiziana's expertise in complex problem-solving and innovative thinking. The states represent different stages of thought and the transitions reflect the clever, quantum-like leaps in thinking. The components of the model are as follows:

- States:
    - Idle: Initial state representing a resting or waiting state.
    - Inspiration: State representing the moment of inspiration or idea generation.

- Analysis: State where in-depth analysis and logical reasoning occur.
- ParallelThinking: State representing simultaneous consideration of multiple ideas or solutions.
- Innovation: State where innovative and novel solutions are realized.
- Validation: State where solutions are validated and verified.
– Transitions:
  - Trigger: Transition from Idle to Inspiration, triggered by a timer or an external event.
  - Evaluate: Transition from Inspiration to Analysis, triggered by the completion of initial idea generation.
  - Parallel Process: Transition from Analysis to Parallel Thinking, showcasing quantum-like processing.
  - Synthesize: Transition from Parallel Thinking to Innovation, where multiple threads are synthesized into innovative solutions.
  - Confirm: Transition from Innovation to Validation, ensuring solutions are sound and applicable.
  - Reset: Transition from Validation back to Idle, ready for the next cycle.
– Timed Elements: Each state has a timer indicating the minimum and maximum time Tiziana might spend in that state, respectively.

Here it is a conceptual design:

State Idle{
On Timer(IdleTime) $\rightarrow$ *Inspiration*
}
State Inspiration{
On Timer(1 − 3 units) $\rightarrow$ *Analysis*
}
State Analysis{
On Timer(2 − 5 units) $\rightarrow$ *ParallelThinking*
}
State ParallelThinking{
On Timer(1 − 4 units) $\rightarrow$ *Innovation*
}
State Innovation{
On Timer(2 − 6 units) $\rightarrow$ *Validation*
}
State Validation{
On Timer(1 − 2 units) $\rightarrow$ *Idle*
}
InitialState(Idle)

3 Conclusions

In conclusion, Tiziana, thank you for being an extraordinary role model, a brilliant scholar, and, most importantly, a dear friend. Your legacy is not just in the numerous publications and awards, but in the hearts of all those who have been fortunate enough to know you. Here it is to many more years of scientific achievements, leading and influencing others, as well as unforgettable moments.

References

1. Seceleanu, C., Margaria, T., Pettersson, P.: CORCS 2012: the 4th IEEE International Workshop on Component-Based Design of Resource-Constrained Systems - Message from the Workshop Organizers. In: Proceedings of the IEEE 36th Annual Computer Software and Applications Conference Workshops (COMPSACW 2012), pg. xli–xlii. IEEE (2012)
2. Seceleanu, C., Margaria, T., Streitferdt, D., Seceleanu, T., Nenninger, P.: Message from the Workshop Organizers - CORCS-IEESD. In: Proceedings of the 38th IEEE Annual International Computer Software and Applications Conference Workshops (COMPSACW 2014), p. xxxi, IEEE (2014)
3. Seceleanu, T., Margaria, T., Subramanyan, R., Bugliesi, M., Seceleanu, C., McMillin, B.: Message from the ECPE organizing committee. In: Proceedings of the 40th IEEE Annual Computer Software and Applications Conference (COMPSAC 2016), vol. 1, pp. 281-281, IEEE (2016)
4. Seceleanu, C., Crnkovic, I.: Component models for reasoning. Computer **46**(11), 40–47 (2013)
5. Margaria, T., Hinchey, M.: Simplicity in IT: the power of less. Computer **46**(11), 23–25 (2013)
6. Kunnappilly, A., Legay, A., Margaria, T., Seceleanu, C., Steffen, B., Traonouez, L.-M.: Analyzing ambient assisted living solutions: a research perspective. In: Proceedings of the 12th International Conference on Design & Technology of Integrated Systems In Nanoscale Era (DTIS 2017), pp. 1-7. IEEE (2017)
7. Boßelmann, S., et al.: DIME: a programming-less modeling environment for web applications. In: Margaria, T., Steffen, B. (eds.) ISoLA 2016. LNCS, vol. 9953, pp. 809–832. Springer, Cham (2016). https://doi.org/10.1007/978-3-319-47169-3_60
8. Seceleanu, C., Vulgarakis, A., Pettersson, P.: REMES: a resource model for embedded systems. In: Proceedings of the 14th IEEE International Conference on Engineering of Complex Computer Systems (ICECCS 2009), pp. 84–94. IEEE (2009)
9. Ivanov, D., Orlić, M., Seceleanu, C., Vulgarakis, A.: REMES toolchain: a set of integrated tools for behavioral modeling and analysis of embedded systems. In: Proceedings of the IEEE/ACM International Conference on Automated Software Engineering, ASE 2010, pp. 361–362. ACM (2010)
10. Varriale, A., di Natale, G., Prinetto, P., Steffen, B., Margaria, T.: SEcubeTM: an open security platform: general approach and strategies. In: Margaria, T., Solo, A.M.G. (eds.) Proceedings of 2016 International Conference on Security and Management (SAM 2016), Special Track "End-to-End Security and Cybersecurity: from the Hardware to Application", pp. 131–137. CREA Press (2016)
11. Boyer, B., Corre, K., Legay, A., Sedwards, S.: PLASMA-lab: a flexible, distributable statistical model checking library. In: Joshi, K., Siegle, M., Stoelinga, M., D'Argenio, P.R. (eds.) QEST 2013. LNCS, vol. 8054, pp. 160–164. Springer, Heidelberg (2013). https://doi.org/10.1007/978-3-642-40196-1_12
12. Margaria, T., Chaudhary, H.A.A., Guevara, I., Ryan, S., Schieweck, A.: The interoperability challenge: building a model-driven digital thread platform for CPS. In: Margaria, T., Steffen, B. (eds.) ISoLA 2021. LNCS, vol. 13036, pp. 393–413. Springer, Cham (2021). https://doi.org/10.1007/978-3-030-89159-6_25

The Softer Side of a Formal Methods Researcher

Barry D. Floyd[✉]

Information Systems and Management, California Polytechnic State University,
San Luis Obispo, CA, USA
bfloyd@calpoly.edu

Abstract. In this article I present the softer side of Professor Tiziana Margaria, who is more commonly known for her work in computer science research. Focusing on Formal Methods and Software Systems, Tiziana is a highly regarded researcher and educator. She has been the highest ranking female Computer Scientist researcher in Ireland since she moved to the country, among her numerous other accomplishments. This article presents some of her professional accomplishments and collaborations concerning innovation in education, soft skills, health care, and simplicity. While my presentation covers many initiatives in which I participated and is not exhaustive, it does provide a snapshot of her broad interests and interdisciplinary accomplishments.

Keywords: Formal Methods · Learn by Doing · Soft Skills · Simplicity

1 In the Beginning

In November 2008, I met Tiziana at the 3gERP/Microsoft Convergence Conference in Denmark organized by Microsoft and by Professor Fritz Henglein from The University of Copenhagen [5]. At that time, she was a full professor and department chair of computer science at the University of Potsdam (UP) in Germany. She was attending the conference to present a talk on "Enterprise Physics" [13,17]. During her visit, Tiziana also participated as a PhD examiner for Christian Stefansen, a student of Professor Henglein: as usual, Tiziana combined her research activities, such as attending a conference, with supporting her colleagues by participating in various PhD exams and other committees.

At the time, I was a Professor of Information Systems and Management in the Orfalea College of Business at California Polytechnic State University (Cal Poly)[1] in San Luis Obispo and was a member of Microsoft's Academic Advisory Board for Microsoft's MS Dynamics ERP/CRM software package. My role at the conference was to help discuss and provide current use testimony of their software in an academic setting. Cal Poly is a university on the central coast of California with a distinction as a public, master's level educational

---
[1] Cal Poly homepage: https://www.calpoly.edu.

Fig. 1. Tiziana and family (2011): Barbara, Bernhard, Tiziana, and Bruno. (Photo by Barry Floyd)

institution that has embraced a learn-by-doing philosophy since its founding in 1901. Admission to Cal Poly is highly competitive, as Cal Poly is well-known for its polytechnic curriculum including programs in computer science, engineering, and architecture and for producing career-ready graduates who are highly sought after by industry (Fig. 1).

One of the most valuable aspects of conferences, especially those with an interdisciplinary audience, is the role of serendipity. As things go, Tiziana and I found ourselves sitting next to each other on a bus to the conference dinner. In this ride, I quickly understood that she was keenly interested in research in Computer Science and was highly regarded and well published. That said, she expressed interest in my use of ERP technologies in the classroom, and even more so, in my discussion of teaching soft skills such as leadership, conflict management, teamwork, and cross-cultural management when I took students on study abroad trips and in other teaching engagements at universities outside the USA. Tiziana commented to me that knowledge of and working practice in these skills would be enormously useful for her computer science students to learn, both at the PhD and undergraduate level. This bus ride, and the discovered common interests, led into a working relationship that has lasted 15 years.

In this article, I reflect on Tiziana's initiatives and accomplishments outside the technical realm of her traditional formal methods research and computer science teaching, however, as always with Tiziana, there is a bit of tech involved.

Importantly, I illustrate the breadth of her interdisciplinary work which may not be immediately apparent to her tribe of techies.

The article begins by discussing her interests in professional development through soft skills such as conflict management and leadership (Sect. 2). I then discuss interdisciplinary research activities (e.g., digital humanities) that she has pursued, though always with an eye on the technologies which add enormous value to her work (Sect. 3). Of interest in these discussions are her efforts and successes in building working relationships which are a cornerstone to so much of her efforts. Underpinning much of this, I find the embodied philosophy of learn-by-doing evident.

2 Education: International Business Negotiations and Building on Success for Professional Development

As is true for most of us, we meet folks who express interest in our endeavors (e.g., my discussing teaching on soft skills) and then fade away after the conversation. Perhaps they were just being polite, which is certainly ok. In the dynamics offered by the conference in Denmark, Tiziana was not just being polite: she believed there was a gap in the education of her students and thought that bringing in an external 'catalyst' would be a successful approach to filling that gap. She wrote to me shortly after the conference asking if I would be willing to conduct a full seminar course on conflict management at the University of Potsdam. She had just been co-opted into the Faculty of Economics and Social Sciences at UP, next to her Faculty of Mathematics and Natural Sciences home, and was looking for ways to contribute to interdisciplinary and transdisciplinary initiatives across the two faculties. She thought that she could put together a consortium of two to three groups at the university who could each benefit from such a seminar, and be willing to chip in the funding to make it happen. If successful, she thought that this could lead to additional educational successes on soft skills education for tech students at UP.

I accepted her offer and Tiziana followed through by working with Professor Christoph Rasche and Professor Guido Reger through Potsdam Transfer and their MBA programs *InfoTech*[2] and *MedTech*. The seminar *International Business Negotiations* was quickly organized and took place in June 2009. It included theory, practice (in-class negotiation exercises), presentation of exercise results, and discussion, all in alignment with a learn-by-doing philosophy. Participants consisted of a heterogeneous cohort of 19 executive MBA students, nine UP administrators, and four Computer Science students. The sessions were lively and the discussions an excellent recap highlighting what was learned.

As hoped, the seminar was a success and led to stronger working relationships, as well as further deliveries of the module to successive MBA cohorts. However, Tiziana remained keenly interested in improving soft skills education

---

[2] UP MBA InfoTech: https://www.up-transfer.de/en/executive-education/master-of-business-administration-mba/mba-infotech/.

for more of her technical students and considered further ways to grow this thin line of action. This led to a number of different paths including teaching opportunities at UP, bringing soft skills training to ISoLA, and later embedding soft skills/professional development on day one within an innovative Computer Science program she created at the University of Limerick (UL), Ireland.

2.1 Visiting Professor on a DAAD Grant

When a Deutscher Akademischer Austauschdienst (DAAD) call for visiting professors came out, Tiziana sponsored me as the local host in Potsdam. This grant led to spending my sabbatical in Potsdam on a joint appointment to the CS Department and the Faculty of Economic and Social Sciences for a full year. This appointment allowed Tiziana to fulfill her interest in offering soft skills courses such as Leadership and Conflict Management to students in three faculties: to her undergraduate computer science students, to students of the Business School, and to students in Sport Management. Through this appointment I also taught Database Systems, Project Management, and Lean Software Development courses.

2.2 Industry Tours

With Tiziana's passion for international exchanges and cultural/technical visits (she was also ERASMUS coordinator for the CS Department) and my close industry relationships, we decided to create an eight day industry tour to California for UP's Executive MBA students. Working again with Professor Christoph Rasche and with Potsdam Transfer, over the course of four years the industry tour module saw the first three tours take place in California (2011, 2012 and 2014). A fourth one took place in Ireland in March 2016, in perfect time for St. Patrick's Day and the Irish Republic "centenary" celebrations.

In California, the companies we visited included Apple (meeting its CIO Niall O'Connor, who is Irish), NetApp, Oracle, CISCO, Amgen, and Google where, to Tiziana's surprise, the students were welcomed by Christian Stefansen, the Danish PhD who graduated during our very first meeting. In addition, the students met with various entrepreneurs and visited the Plug N' Play center in Sunnyvale.

In 2010, the students also participated in a student-organized International Career Conference I was conducting at Cal Poly at the time[3] Tiziana then replicated this career conference as a new, hands-on and very successful module in UP the following two years.

Finding a collaborator who shares one's interests in international adventures and exchanges is personally valuable while being enormously effective and beneficial for students' education and their professional growth.

---

[3] ICC 2010: https://digitalcommons.calpoly.edu/cgi/viewcontent.cgi?article=3672&context=pao_pr.

2.3 ISoLA Professional Development Track for PhD Students

The International Symposium on Leveraging Applications of Formal Methods, Verification and Validation (ISoLA)[4] is a series of conferences created 20 years ago by Tiziana Margaria and Bernhard Steffen. Highly technical and highly regarded, it is held traditionally every two years. In 2012, working with Tiziana, a new professional development track was introduced in the STRESS Graduate School (International School on Tool-based Rigorous Engineering of Software Systems) preceding ISoLA. The track's focus was on improving PhD students' soft skill competencies by adding conflict management into their educational repertoire. This track was initially a surprise to these computer science students, but the feedback was very positive and the professional development track continued for numerous ISoLAs. In ISoLA 2021, this track was offered by Barbara Steffen, Tiziana's daughter. Barbara had spent one of her high school years summers taking classes at Cal Poly and then again traveled with an international group of students to a course I was teaching at the University of Shanghai. It was, appropriately, one on international business negotiations, where Barbara had an opportunity to negotiate with both US and Chinese students.

2.4 Immersive Software Engineering Program - University of Limerick

Immersive Software Engineering (ISE) is a new integrated BSc/MSc computer science program for which Tiziana was a key developer at the University of Limerick in 2019–2022. Launched in September 2022 and funded in large part by industry, ISE's students earn an integrated Bachelors/Masters in four years with learn-by-doing as the educational pedagogy. As expected, Tiziana included a professional development track from year one. When Tiziana and her co-director acquired donations from industry for ISE, Tiziana importantly included a research track (Research@ISE). In 2023 this became the five years R@ISE Strategic Partnership Project[5] she now leads, co-funded by industry partners, the Limerick City and County Council, and Science Foundation Ireland. Her ambition of embedding research into the undergraduate education through projects was practiced in the first year of the course while Tiziana served as the first Course Director.

In her continuous quest for research-led education, she partnered with Amazon AWS to establish a perpetual source of funding for AWS Fellowships aimed at researchers who would visit UL for a period between three weeks and six months, conducting research and contributing their expertise to the ISE program and its ecosystem. During the first year of ISE, seven international fellows brought their expertise on programming languages and software verification, compilers, programming systems, continuous software development, mathematics and statistics, and data analytics to Limerick. As the very first AWS fellow, I

---

[4] ISoLA conference series homepage: https://www.isola-conference.org/.
[5] R@ISE SPP: https://software-engineering.ie/raise/.

developed and delivered the ISE professional development track, including topics such as personal brand management, resume writing, interviewing techniques, leadership, conflict management, and cross cultural management among others (Fig. 2).

Fig. 2. Day 1 of the ISE course: Team building exercise. professional development track. (Photo by Barry Floyd)

3 Expanding the Research Boundary - Research and Leadership

The background and focus of Tiziana is traditionally very technical: her major emphasis is in Formal Methods where she continues to work. To illustrate her technical record, IEEE lists the following publication topics associated with Tiziana:

> *Blockchain Technology, Computer Science,* **Historians**, **Open Educational Resources**, *Access Control, Digital Humanities, Internet Of Things,* **Practice-based Learning**, *Web Application, Attribute-based Encryption, Blockchain Network, Data Entry, Data Management System, Data Model, Data Privacy,* **Death Registry**, *Digital Format, Domain-specific Languages, General Data Protection Regulation, Graphical User Interface, Hyperledger Fabric, Internet Of Things Devices, Key Learning, Process Model*

While these topics illustrate her technology emphasis, they also are indicative of the breadth of her work. I have highlighted in bold non-traditional topics for a computer scientist where Tiziana has made significant contributions. In the following paragraphs, three topics, simplicity, health care, and digital humanities, are discussed which reflect her breadth in interdisciplinary work.

3.1 Simplicity

IT Simply Works (ITSy) was an European Union funded Strategic Support Action led by Tiziana in 2010–12. It was focused on generating a set of innovative research topics on the concept of simplicity as a driving paradigm in ICT development, maintenance and use. Based in the USA, I was an ITSy external collaborator. The research included a literature review and a direct interaction with experts in the ICT area through focus groups held at ISoLA, ETAPS, COMPSAC, and in various other locations including NASA Ames, Brazil, Argentina, Chile, and Uruguay. These focus groups and individual interviews involved researchers and educators as well as industry representatives. The findings provided evidence that the community of researchers, adopters, and users of ICT technologies and products believed that the philosophy of simplicity is strategically important, yet still insufficiently understood. This lack of understanding seems to be true especially for the societal and technological consequences of ICT use. For example, as a strategic directive in IT development and uptake, simplicity is rarely systematically applied. This has not improved much since then, in spite of the AI and LC/NC push.

Instead, it was found that current design principles focus on increased functionality within thinly disguised complexity, often at the expense of life cycle costs and total cost of ownership issues (e.g., training, system malfunctions, system upgrades). Often designers are unaware of the tradeoffs and impacts. Researchers in fields such as Computer Science center their work on efficiencies rather than on issues that make the application of their work easier to adapt, deploy and integrate into effective use.

The ITSy initiative resulted in several publications [8,11,14,16,19], a special session at SEW 2011 [15], a special session at SDPS 2012 in Berlin followed by a special issue in the IDPT journal [9], a special issue in IEEE Computing [12] [4], and ultimately it led to the organization of ICSOB 2013 in Potsdam at UP [6]. Due to his interest in the relationship of agility and simplicity, these publications also led to Wylliams Barbosa Santos "sandwich" PhD semester in Limerick with Tiziana in 2014–15, that also resulted in several joint publications [20,23].

Thus, the findings showed that systematic knowledge gained through research on simplicity can provide the EU with a sustainable competitive advantage. Learning environments like ISE and large research projects like R@ISE, which addresses MDD based Low-Code/No-Code and has an HCI component, establish an attractive environment that constructively fosters the creation, adoption, and wider spread of simplicity-driven cultural traits and ultimately artifacts.

3.2 Health Care

Tiziana was well versed in developing case studies for her model driven development techniques in many application domains and in conjunction with various business model aspects. A specific application domain she pursued was healthcare, starting with a DAAD and CnPQ supported collaboration with the research group of Professor Marilia Cerqueira Leite Seelaender at USP (Universidade de

São Paulo) in Brazil, the top university of the country. Marilia, a physiologist, led a large-scale project investigating the effects of physical activity on inflammation with a focus on the cachexia of cancer patients. Tiziana, with Anna-Lena Lamprecht and Johannes Neubauer, visited Brazil often and established a line of research [25]. The dataset Marilia's group collected for cachexia patient classification was used as a case study leading to several publications: one at ISoLA 2014 [10] and years later to a further one concerning an MDD implementation of the evaluation processes [26].

While in Brazil, Tiziana addressed concerns about the potential expansion of dengue fever in Rio de Janeiro: the health authorities were worried that the World FIFA Cup in 2014 and later the Olympic games in 2016 would bring a higher prevalence of all possible strands of dengue during these events and extend afterwards. Tiziana worked with local representatives, such as Dr. Salete Rego and her colleagues, to design an application that would enable social workers in the favelas to detect if a resident had a potential case of dengue and its level of gravity. The app (in DyWA) was developed by a master student in Potsdam and presented at the congress of EuSEM, the European Society of Emergency Medicine, which covers public health and epidemics as part of their disaster management programs.

Subsequently, I accepted her invitation to join EuSEM's *Special Interest Group on Technology and Processes of Care in Emergency Care*. There we discussed the IT and information systems needs of triage, pediatric processes, and an emerging area of interest: telehealth for low densely populated areas. This connected very well with the situation she found in Ireland when she moved to Limerick.

Tying business, computer science, and healthcare together, Tiziana established a seminar on Quality Management for Healthcare for several years in Potsdam joining students of Computer Science, the Business School, and the course on Sports Management offered in the Faculty of Humanities. For this course, Tiziana co-opted Professor Rasche and myself to incorporate into the classroom Business Model Canvas (BMC) [21]: in 2011 it was a novel approach that simplified the understanding and representation of business models. True to a learn-by-doing approach, after learning about BMCs, students applied their knowledge and interviewed clinical and medical directors at the Charite' in Berlin, at the Asklepios Klinik in Hamburg, in smaller consortial hospitals such as Mölln-Ratzeburg, and in state controlling agencies for health insurers like the MDK in Rhenania-Palatinate. Working with those field experts, the students co-developed BMCs for their organizations. This visual tool helped the experts to see the workings of their organization with greater clarity and, thus, improve how they communicated their organization's positioning to others.

While these efforts were under NDA and never published, the insights and the way to work with health services decision makers turned out to be very useful in Tiziana's early project on personalized medicine [3]. In this project, Steve Boßelmann implemented the first cloud based "wizard" that guided health experts in personalized medicine to fill out the BMC model for their innovative business ideas in diagnostics and therapeutics [1, 18].

Tiziana's current engagements in Limerick with the Health Research Institute and the UL Cancer Research Network can be seen as long term outcomes of these diverse and interdisciplinary activities.

Similarly, her founding the IEEE International Workshop on Advanced Visual Knowledge Management Tools (AVKMT)[6] again with Professor Rasche, is a further success of having experienced and practiced the power of visual knowledge management over the previous years.

3.3 Digital Humanities and Interdisciplinary Teaching

Since 2018 Tiziana has collaborated with historians like Professor Ciara Breathnach to apply her beloved MDD and Low-Code/No-Code technology to the area of digital humanities. Tiziana spoke often of the Irish registers of the civil registration of deaths introduced by Queen Victoria in the British empire and its correlation with the Irish Census in the early 1900s. This work led to the development of a "Historians' App" [24] which was first presented at the ISoLA Doctoral Symposium 2018 [7]. The growing collaboration led to the Digital Humanities track that she co-organized with Ciara Breathnach last year at AISoLA 2023 [2].

Pursuing her goal of embedding research activities in the early education of CS students, in September 2022 Tiziana and her PhD student Amandeep Singh "reused" the ADD-Lib based classifiers created in her CRT-AI research group for the Irish civil registration data [22] as a learn-by-doing activity. In week two of the very first semester of ISE, the twenty five students of this cohort learned about boolean logic, decision trees and Binary Decision Diagrams, and applied this knowledge through the ADD-Lib tool[7] (a no-code online tool built in Dortmund) to design their own classifiers for individual columns of the historic registers' content. On top of the technical knowledge gained on boolean expressions and trees as data structure, it was exceptional that these students (not yet able to program) carried out a highly technical project in a no-code fashion, created posters for the problem and their solutions, reviewed each other's posters in the form of 'mock demos," and impressed visitors from the funding companies of the ISE program, who were eager to check out the "immersive" and "research" traits of the new program. This class project was a real world demonstration of the power of no-code Formal Methods tools based on abstractions and models, that serve a computational thinking purpose: solve the problem and understand how, without first having to be able to code. The project also included soft skills in terms of visual presentations (the posters) and oral presentations (to the company representatives) in a nurturing and safe environment while including early feedback by the teaching team and peer feedback among the student groups. This innovative and enabling pedagogy combining interdisciplinary projects with soft and hard skills for students of history as well as CS students was recognized: Professor Ciara Breathnach, Dr. Rachel Murphy, and Tiziana won the UL Team Teaching Award in 2023 (Fig. 3).

---

[6] AVKMT homepage: https://ieeecompsac.computer.org/2022/avkmt-2022/.
[7] ADD-Lib homepage: https://add-lib.scce.info.

Fig. 3. Tiziana Margaria, Ciara Breathnach and Rachel Murphy receive the UL Excellence in Teaching Team Award 2022/23 (Aug. 29th 2023), with UL Mace bearer John O'Neill. (Photo by Ita Richardson)

4 Summary

In this article, I have presented many of the "softer" initiatives that Professor Margaria has pursued with passion and success. Even though I address many of these as "soft", they all, in some manner, touch on technology foundations and are coupled with holistic critical thinking, which are both mainstays for Tiziana. I find that her success is driven by her intellect, unending curiosity, hard work, and, importantly, her ability to build strong working relationships across individuals and communities in various disciplines. She is very well respected by her technical colleagues and, I believe, even more so by the functional specialists who have collaborated with her and have experienced the power of the technologies she brings to the table as well as her interdisciplinary thinking and insights. I have also watched Tiziana in her mentoring and guiding PhD students; she lets them know she has high expectations and demands while offering attention, grace, and caring. I have been fortunate enough to have participated in many of these endeavors and have found both personal and professional success by partnering with her.

References

1. Boßelmann, S., Margaria, T.: Domain-specific business modeling with the business model developer. In: Margaria, T., Steffen, B. (eds.) ISoLA 2014, Part II. LNCS, vol. 8803, pp. 545–560. Springer, Heidelberg (2014). https://doi.org/10.1007/978-3-662-45231-8_45
2. Breathnach, C., Margaria, T.: Digital humanities and cultural heritage in AI and IT-enabled environments. In: Proceedings AISoLA 2023, Digital Humanities and Cultural Heritage in AI and IT-enabled Environments. LNCS, vol. 14129. Springer, Heidelberg (2024)
3. Eppinger, E., Halecker, B., Hölzle, K., Kamprath, M. (eds.): Dienstleistungspotenziale und Geschäftsmodelle in der Personalisierten Medizin. Springer, Heidelberg (2015). https://doi.org/10.1007/978-3-658-08403-5
4. Floyd, B.D., Bosselmann, S.: ITSy-simplicity research in information and communication technology. Computer **46**(11), 26–32 (2013). https://doi.org/10.1109/MC.2013.332
5. Henglein, F., Bjørn-Andersen, N. (eds.): Proceedings of 2nd Workshop on 3D generation Enterprise Resource Planning systems (3gERP), Convergence 2008 Copenhagen Academic Preconference, 17–18 November 2008 (2008). http://hjemmesider.diku.dk/~henglein/3gERP-workshop-2008/program.pdf
6. Herzwurm, G., Margaria, T. (eds.): Software Business. From Physical Products to Software Services and Solutions - 4th International Conference, ICSOB 2013, Potsdam, Germany, June 11–14, 2013. Proceedings. LNBIP, vol. 150. Springer, Heidelberg (2013). https://doi.org/10.1007/978-3-642-39336-5
7. Khan, R., Schieweck, A., Breathnach, C., Margaria, T.: Historical civil registration record transcription using an extreme model driven approach. Proc. Inst. Syst. Program. RAS **33**(3) (2021)
8. Margaria, T., Boßelmann, S., Kujath, B.: Simple modeling of executable role-based workflows: an application in the healthcare domain. In: Margaria, T., Steffen, B. (eds.) ISoLA 2012, Part II. LNCS, vol. 7610, pp. 70–72. Springer, Heidelberg (2012). https://doi.org/10.1007/978-3-642-34032-1_8
9. Margaria, T., Floyd, B.D.: Simplicity in IT: a chance for a new kind of design and process science. J. Integr. Des. Process. Sci. **17**(3), 1–7 (2013). https://doi.org/10.3233/JID-2013-0021
10. Margaria, T., Floyd, B.D., Gonzalez Camargo, R., Lamprecht, A.-L., Neubauer, J., Seelaender, M.: Simple management of high assurance data in long-lived interdisciplinary healthcare research: a proposal. In: Margaria, T., Steffen, B. (eds.) ISoLA 2014. LNCS, vol. 8803, pp. 526–544. Springer, Heidelberg (2014). https://doi.org/10.1007/978-3-662-45231-8_44
11. Margaria, T., Floyd, B.D., Steffen, B.: IT simply works: simplicity and embedded systems design. In: Workshop Proceedings of the 35th Annual IEEE International Computer Software and Applications Conference, COMPSAC Workshops 2011, Munich, Germany, 18–22 July 2011, pp. 194–199. IEEE Computer Society (2011). https://doi.org/10.1109/COMPSACW.2011.42
12. Margaria, T., Hinchey, M.: Simplicity in it: the power of less. Computer **46**(11), 23–25 (2013). https://doi.org/10.1109/MC.2013.397
13. Margaria, T., Steffen, B.: An enterprise physics approach for evolution support in heterogeneous service-oriented landscapes. In: Henglein, F., Bjørn-Andersen, N. (eds.) Proceedings of 2nd Workshop on 3D Generation Enterprise Resource Planning Systems (3gERP), Convergence 2008 Copenhagen Academic Preconference, 17–18 November 2008 (2008). https://tinyurl.com/msb4m9ut

14. Margaria, T., Steffen, B.: Simplicity as a driver for agile innovation. Computer **43**(6), 90–92 (2010). https://doi.org/10.1109/MC.2010.177
15. Margaria, T., Steffen, B.: Special session on "simplification through change of perspective". In: 2011 IEEE 34th Software Engineering Workshop, pp. 67–68 (2011). https://doi.org/10.1109/SEW.2011.15
16. Margaria, T., Steffen, B.: Service-orientation: conquering complexity with XMDD. In: Hinchey, M., Coyle, L. (eds.) Conquering Complexity, pp. 217–236. Springer, London (2012). https://doi.org/10.1007/978-1-4471-2297-5_10
17. Margaria, T., Steffen, B., Kubczak, C.: Evolution support in heterogeneous service-oriented landscapes. J. Braz. Comput. Soc. **16**(1), 35–47 (2010). https://doi.org/10.1007/S13173-010-0004-4
18. Margaria-Steffen, T., Boßelmann, S., Wickert, A.: Der business model developer – entwicklung eines tools zur erstellung und analyse von geschäftsmodellen. In: Eppinger, E., Halecker, B., Hölzle, K., Kamprath, M. (eds.) Dienstleistungspotenziale und Geschäftsmodelle in der Personalisierten Medizin, pp. 95–115. Springer, Wiesbaden (2015). https://doi.org/10.1007/978-3-658-08403-5_4
19. Naujokat, S., Lamprecht, A., Steffen, B., Jörges, S., Margaria, T.: Simplicity principles for plug-in development: the jABC approach. In: Garbervetsky, D., Kim, S. (eds.) Proceedings of the Second International Workshop on Developing Tools as Plug-Ins, TOPI 2012, Zurich, Switzerland, 3 June 2012, pp. 7–12. IEEE Computer Society (2012). https://doi.org/10.1109/TOPI.2012.6229816
20. Neto, G.T.G., Santos, W.B., Fagundes, R.A.A., Margaria, T.: Towards an understanding of value creation in agile software development. In: Proceedings of the XV Brazilian Symposium on Information Systems, SBSI 2019, Association for Computing Machinery, New York (2019). https://doi.org/10.1145/3330204.3330256
21. Osterwalder, A., Pigneur, Y.: Business Model Generation: A Handbook for Visionaries, Game Changers, and Challengers, vol. 1. Wiley, Hoboken (2010)
22. O'Shea, E., Khan, R., Breathnach, C., Margaria, T.: Towards automatic data cleansing and classification of valid historical data an incremental approach based on MDD. In: 2020 IEEE International Conference on Big Data (Big Data), pp. 1914–1923 (2020)
23. Santos, W.B., Cunha, J.A.O.G., Moura, H., Margaria, T.: Towards a theory of simplicity in agile software development: A qualitative study. In: 2017 43rd Euromicro Conference on Software Engineering and Advanced Applications (SEAA), pp. 40–43 (2017). https://doi.org/10.1109/SEAA.2017.38
24. Schieweck, A., Murphy, R., Khan, R., Breathnach, C., Margaria, T.: Evolution of the historian data entry application: Supporting transcribathons in the digital humanities through MDD. In: 2022 IEEE 46th Annual Computers, Software, and Applications Conference (COMPSAC), pp. 177–186. IEEE (2022)
25. Seelaender, M., Laviano, A., Busquets, S., Püschel, G., Margaria, T., Batista Jr., M.: Inflammation in cachexia (2015)
26. Wickert, A., Lamprecht, A.L., Margaria, T.: Domain-specific design of patient classification in cancer-related cachexia research. In: Proceedings of the 6th Conference on Formal Methods in Software Engineering, FormaliSE 2018, pp. 60-63. Association for Computing Machinery, New York (2018). https://doi.org/10.1145/3193992.3194002

The Power of Models for Software Engineering

Ina K. Schieferdecker

TU Berlin, Einsteinufer 25, 10587 Berlin, Germany
ina.schieferdecker@tu-berlin.de

Abstract. This paper reviews the development of Model-Driven Software Engineering (MDSE) from its origins to the present day. The paper discusses the components of models, modelling activities, and the challenges and open issues in MDSE. It reviews the adoption of modelling languages and their use in MDSE processes. Selected tool sets and frameworks are presented. The paper concludes with a review of the still unresolved relationship and implications of Artificial Intelligence (AI) for software engineering, including MDSE, and the coming developments in the Internet of Collaboration for distributed MDSE. Throughout the paper, Tiziana Margaria's research and dissemination contributions in these areas are highlighted.

Keywords: Software engineering · Modelling · Verification and Validation · Testing

1 Introduction

The global demand for complex software and software-intensive systems will continue to grow at a rate comparable to the increase in computing and communications capacity. We strive to understand the different domains well, and also to understand and apply the new possibilities associated with new technologies in the Web, the Internet of Things and the future of quantum computing. The result is software-based systems of unprecedented scale: in terms of lines of code, the sheer volume of data collected and processed, the number and variability of communication channels, the large number of network elements, servers and terminals, the variety of system purposes and objectives, the large number of (partially) automated processes and 'emergent behaviours', and the large number of people involved in one way or another.

When developing such complex software, there is often a huge gap between the original problem space and the desired software-based implementation, so that a purely code-centric approach is not sufficient. Model-Driven Software Engineering uses models, often several models, as intermediaries between the requirements and the implementation of a software-based system. Indeed, MDSE

© The Author(s), under exclusive license to Springer Nature Switzerland AG 2025
M. Hinchey and B. Steffen (Eds.): Festschrift Tiziana Margaria, LNCS 15240, pp. 67–80, 2025.
https://doi.org/10.1007/978-3-031-73887-6_7

is an umbrella term for methods that use high-level, often domain-specific models [4] for the design, implementation, integration, maintenance, testing, understanding and/or documentation of software-based systems.

[23] stated almost 20 years ago: "The software industry remains reliant on the craftsmanship of skilled individuals engaged in labor intensive manual tasks. However, growing pressure to reduce cost and time to market and to improve software quality may catalyse a transition to more automated methods. We look at how the software industry may be industrialized, and we describe technologies that might be used to support this vision. We suggest that the current software development paradigm, based on object orientation, may have reached the point of exhaustion, and we propose a model for its successor. ... We can now define a software factory as a model-driven product line - a product line automated by meta-data captured by models using domain specific modeling languages".

But, the development of MDSE began much earlier. Back in the days of the software crisis: [55] resembled that "The problems of software development during the 1960s created an awareness of how important and difficult programming was. Software was recognised not just as an appendage of hardware, but as a force in its own right. This was reflected in the commodification of software and in a growing sense of a"software crisis". This feeling of crisis gave rise to conscious attempts to provide solid theoretical foundations for the development of programming".

In this paper, we discuss the evolution of models and modelling in science and engineering in Sect. 2 before reviewing modelling in Computer Science and in software engineering in Sect. 3 leading towards MDSE. Recent developments in using MDSE for AI-based systems or using AI-methods for MDSE are finally discussed in Sect. 4.

2 The Scientific Model Concept

In this section, we we take a brief look at the concepts of scientific models and modelling. 1894 saw the birth of the concept of a (mathematical) model of the physical world in [27]:

> We make for ourselves inner illusory images or symbols of external objects, and we make them of such a kind that the logical consequences of the images are always again the images of the natural consequences of the depicted objects. In order that this requirement may be fulfilled at all, there must be certain correspondences must exist between nature and our spirit. Experience teaches us that this requirement can be fulfilled and that such correspondences do indeed exist. Once we have succeeded, from the accumulated experience, we can use them, as models, to develop in a short time the consequences which will only appear in the outer world in a longer time or as consequences of our own intervention. We are thus able to anticipate the facts and can base our present decisions on the insight we have gained. The images of which we speak are our conceptions of

things; they have one essential correspondence with things, which lies in the fulfilment of the above-mentioned requirement, but it is not necessary for their purpose that they should have any further correspondence with things. Nor, indeed, do we know nor have we any means of knowing whether our ideas of things agree with them in anything but that one fundamental relation.

[27] is not the source of the word "model" as such in a scientific context, but for the semantic meaning of a scientific model: Hertz wrote about "inner illusory images or symbols". He made clear that models are not in the realm of external objects, but to our ideas of them. Therefore, they have something arbitrary within certain limits [44].

Models provide a mental representation of our environment in everyday environment. They give us the ability to act, because models help us to (quickly) assess (new) situations. This requires biases and prejudices, which can also be seen as models. Modelling is therefore fundamental to human thinking. The ability to model is learned and can be trained for more advanced models.

In today's understanding, models are a partial/limited representation of reality or an anticipation of it. Models represent originals. Yet, originals can also be models, which in turn can be modelled. Models have a specific purpose. Their function, presentation and usability should be appropriate. Models have a context that relates to the purpose of the model. Models capture only relevant attributes of the original, embodying a particular, purposeful view of the original. This abstraction in a model involves a loss of information.

As a result, models have become an indispensable tool in many disciplines. Different disciplines use different approaches to modelling and different formalisations of models and analysis techniques. In general, models can be used to illustrate complex relationships by reducing and abstracting irrelevant details, to communicate using a standardised vocabulary corresponding to the naming of model components, or to make predictions by deriving statements from the model. These allow conclusions to be drawn about equivalent statements in reality. In addition, models support communication, ensure the consistency of artefacts, enable the automation of recurring tasks, can improve the quality of system development, and are sometimes the only option available.

The modelling process is shown in Fig. 1, which is an adaptation of the modelling cycle in [29]: Starting with a system to be referenced to or targeted, the system situation(s) must be formalised in a model, i.e. a concrete, often real-life situation is translated into the concepts and modelling languages of science or engineering. This model is further processed, e.g. by formal reasoning, simulation or other types of model analysis. The consequences of the model need to be translated again, i.e. interpreted in the context of the original system, resulting in a potential solution to the original problem. To do this, the potential solution needs to be validated to see if it is suitable for the original problem.

All four steps may need to be repeated several times. This modelling cycle is embedded in the domain of the system being analysed and the problem space being considered. Different modelling methods and frameworks may be used for

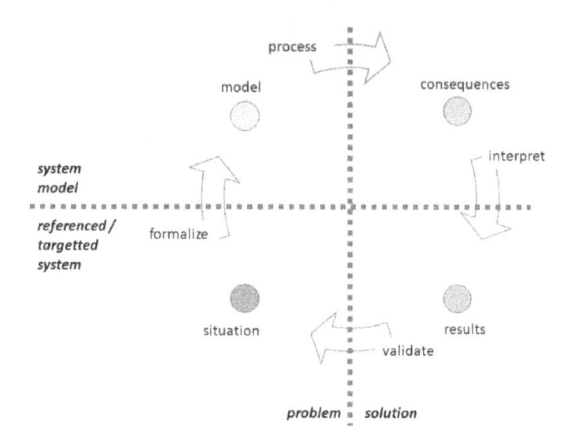

Fig. 1. Principal Process of Modelling

the modelling cycle in a given domain and problem space, but they are not predetermined in science or engineering. Although there is a wide variety of modelling methods and frameworks, there is no comprehensive and generally accepted taxonomy of models in science. For example, [19] presents an "attempt to classify the universe of models as used in various scientific and non-scientific disciplines. The taxonomy is multi-level. At the first level, models are grouped into concrete (e.g., a physical scale model such as a model air plane), abstract (e.g., an analytical formula or numerical approximation), and mimetic (e.g., a work of art or a virtual reality environment)".

With respect to modelling, it is important to understand that "the sciences do not try to explain, they hardly even try to interpret, they mainly make models. By a model is meant a mathematical construct which, with the addition of certain verbal interpretations, describes observed phenomena. The justification of such a mathematical construct is solely and precisely that it is expected to work – that is, correctly to describe phenomena from a reasonably wide area ... The ability to describe – or to predict – correctly is important in such a model, but it need not be decisive per se ... Of course, it must be correct" [43].

And, there is danger in the use of models as pointed out by Meadows in [42]: "However, and conversely, our models fall far short of representing the world fully. That is why we make mistakes and why we are regularly surprised. In our heads, we can keep track of only a few variables at one time. We often draw illogical conclusions from accurate assumptions, or logical conclusions from inaccurate assumptions. Most of us, for instance, are surprised by the amount of growth an exponential process can generate".

3 Modelling in Computer Science and Software Engineering

Models in computing and for model-driven software engineering are explored in this section. Since the advent of computers in the 1940s, modelling has been used extensively for basic research in physics, chemistry or biology, for meteorology and climate research, for economic development, transport planning, industrial production, logistics, military, etc. to gain insight through model-based analysis and simulation.

The computational power of model-based analysis and simulation has enabled or improved, for example, weather forecasting, planning with prototype demonstrations, decision making by selecting design alternatives of engineering systems, optimisation along improved workloads, or the validation of system controls.

Model-based analysis and simulation is used when reality is too complex for pure mathematical analysis, cannot withstand physical experiments (e.g. for safety reasons), is too fast (e.g. in biochemical reactions) or too slow (e.g. in the formation of icebergs). Models are also needed when physical experiments are too expensive or simply impossible because the physical systems do not yet exist.

The benefits of model-based analysis and simulation have also been applied to software engineering in response to the software crisis [55] as a solution to improve overall software quality and reliability. Since then, models have been used throughout software engineering, as shown in Fig. 2.

Without going into detail, models support all the major phases of software engineering throughout the software life cycle. Starting with analysis and design, requirements or architectural software models are used. System and product models are used during development and deployment. Runtime models and digital twins are used during operation and maintenance. In addition, various verification and validation models are used throughout the software engineering life cycle, e.g. to support formal verification or testing in the different software engineering phases.

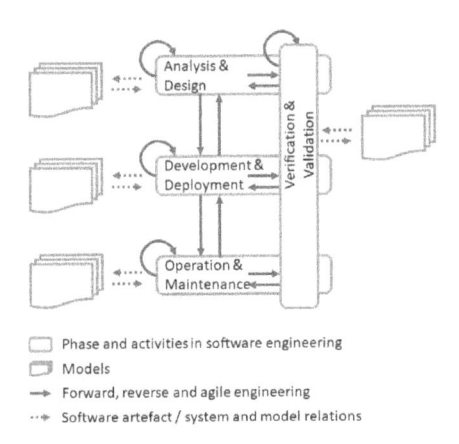

Fig. 2. Principal Use of Models in Software Engineering

Accordingly, there is a wealth of modelling techniques and languages used in software engineering, see also Fig. 3.

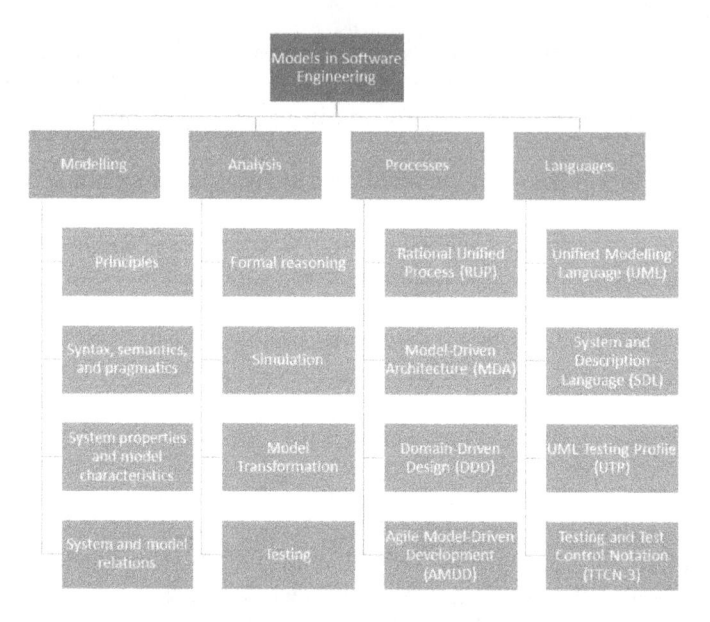

Fig. 3. Principal Overview on Models in Software Engineering

A modelling technique is constituted by its principles, i.e. the core concepts such as the definition of structure, information or behaviour, or the use in a behavioural model of a state machine based approach or a temporal logic based approach. The principles, together with semantics and pragmatics, give rise to syntaxes for formulating appropriate models. They can be used to specify system properties in models which themselves have properties/characteristics. Formal relationships between model and system reveal the fit between system and model, e.g. does the model fit the system or vice versa, or is a system correct or incorrect with respect to a given model? Models can be analysed using a variety of methods, including not only methods for analysing the models themselves, such as formal reasoning or simulation, but also methods for further processing the models through model transformation or testing approaches, including model-based testing or testing on model level, e.g. for complex models. Models in software engineering have also given rise to model-driven or model-based software development processes such as Rational Unified Process (RUP [33]), Model-Driven Architecture (MDA [51]), Domain-Driven Design (DDD [15]) or Agile Model-Driven Development (AMDD [1]), to name but a few. Such processes have been made possible by industrial-scale modelling languages that support complex modelling or analysis activities through tools or comprehensive modelling frameworks. To name but a few, there is the Unified Modelling Language (UML [5]), the Specifications and Description Language (SDL [3]), the UML Testing Profile (UTP [2]) or the Testing and Test Control Notation (TTCN-3 [22]). An elaborated discussion of today's modelling techniques is given in [6], which will be updated soon in version 4.0.

An approach for model-driven system development and testing is given in [57]. This process uses models for both system development and testing. The models support the transformation from requirements to designs to implementation. Each model can be validated and verified. Models can also be used to run against each other in test simulations at model level or test executions at system level. In this way, high levels of quality can be achieved. This approach uses Behaviour Trees (BT [14]) for requirements modelling in addition to the modelling languages mentioned above.

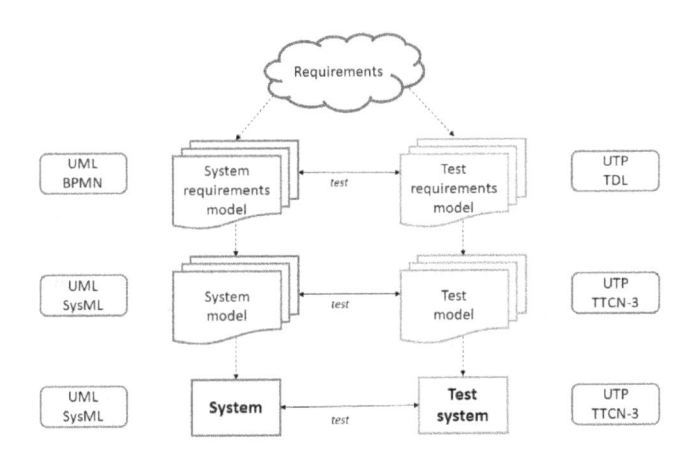

Fig. 4. Model-Driven Software Development and Testing

Nevertheless, and as early as 1987, Brooks stated [7]: "I believe the hard part of building software to be the specification, design, and testing of this conceptual construct, not the labor of representing it and testing the fidelity of the representation". There are essential and accidental difficulties in building large, complex software. In the past, the great leaps forward have been in eliminating the accidental difficulties, for example by using high-level languages. At least half of the remaining difficulties appear to be essential difficulties, due to the inherent complexity of the software-based system we are trying to build. Therefore, no method of reducing accidental difficulties would result in an order of magnitude improvement in software development. In fact, most of the "radical" improvements in software development that have been seen would only continue to address accidental difficulties.

20 years later in [17], Parnas adds "However, I object to the phrase "accidental difficulties". The word "accident" is often used in an attempt to escape blame. ... In fact, the accidents that I know about have all resulted from a combination of negligence, momentary carelessness, haste, greed, and poor training. This is also true of the many poor software products ...". And, "[t]he only solution to the never-ending software "crisis" is to try to emulate the science-based, disciplined, document based, development we see in good engineering projects.",

which in all engineering disciplines is actually a model-based approach. Let us add: "To the extent that society is increasingly dependent on autonomous, intelligent and critical software-based systems in energy supply, mobility services and production, but also in media discourses or democratic processes, new strategies must be found to ensure not only their well-understood quality characteristics such as safety, efficiency, reliability and security, but also their associated socio-technical and socio-political implications and all additional requirements in the context of human-machine interaction and collaboration" [47].

A professional MDSE process for model-driven system development and testing is shown in Fig. 4. It is a generalisation of [57] and shows a selection of commonly used modelling languages: from requirements models, through system and test models, to runtime models for both the system and the test system. The requirements for a system to be built are typically broken down into system requirements and test requirements, each of which is manually or partially automatically transformed into models from which the respective systems are built. Runtime models may also be used for the final system and/or test system to support runtime monitoring, tracing, configuration or similar.

Besides formal languages such as Z [13] or Alloy [30] and numerous domain-specific languages such as Modelica [20] or Promela [28], commonly used languages on the system side include the Unified Modelling Language (UML [5]), the Systems Modelling Language (SysML [18]) and the Business Process Modelling Notation (BPMN [10]), and on the test side the UML Testing Profile (UTP [2]), the Test Description Language (TDL [54]) and the Testing and Test Control Notation (TTCN-3 [22]). UML provides a broad set of modelling languages that offer comprehensive capabilities for modelling requirements as well as for modelling systems in the design or runtime phase. The same is true for UTP, which is a UML profile and therefore inherits these comprehensive modelling capabilities from UML for all development phases.

A more radical view of a single model in continuous model-driven engineering has been elaborated by T. Margaria in [39–41]: "Key to the One-Thing Approach (OTA) is viewing the entire development process as a cooperative hierarchical and interactive decision process, which is organized by building and refining one comprehensive model, the "one thing."". The different perspectives on this one model are similar to the different models needed at different stages of system development for different stakeholders in Fig. 4. In any case, the models, or model perspectives, need to be consistent with each other, whether they are part of one or more models. Whether a model with different perspectives or different models for different purposes is the more successful strategy may depend on the system context and domain, and may only be known in the future.

In addition, modelling languages with strong tool support for complex systems are widely used for the models along such a model-driven development process. This has always been a concern in the work of T. Margaria. In [52], the jABC framework for model-driven application development based on lightweight process coordination is presented: By "composing reusable building blocks into hierarchical (flow) graph structures that are executable models of the application", applications or services are developed. The collaborative design of complex software is supported by the ability to "animate(d), analyze(d), simulate(d), verify(ied), execute(d) and compile(d)" the jABC models. And as our take on one model versus several models in MDSE differ, so do our tooling approach differ: while jABC is based on services around one model, our ModelBus approach in [26,49] is based on services on model transformations to cope with several models. Both approaches, jABC as well as ModelBus have been successfully used in industrial applications: [31] and [46], for example and respectively. Other work by T. Margaria on strong tool support for MDSE include [37] for a model-driven digital thread platform for cyber-physical systems in Industry 4.0 environments or [38] for the integration and distributed use of tools, in particular of modelling and verification & validation tools over the Internet.

4 Model-Driven Software Engineering, AI and the Internet of Collaboration

This paper would not be complete without considering some of the implications that the capabilities of Artificial Intelligence (AI), and in particular Machine Learning (ML), are already having or may have in the near future. Their recent impressive results have stimulated both research into and application of AI-based methods in almost every area of software engineering. Overall, it is interesting to see how it will change software engineering in general and MDSE in particular, and whether the power of models and AI can be combined for the benefit of software engineering.

As early as 1998, [45] discussed the application of AI methods to software engineering and vice versa. Over the years, a whole host of AI-based methods have been developed in software engineering [24]: The use of genetic algorithms has a long tradition in software engineering [35] for genetic programming [32] and for genetic testing [53,56]. Search-based software engineering [25] developed with the advent of large software code bases on open source programming platforms such as Eclipse [58] or GitHub [11]. [59] goes further and asks "to step back (from just simply applying AI technologies) and explore instilling intelligence in software engineering solutions, with AI technologies and other technologies (such as program analysis)".

Another important question is the extent to which traditional software engineering methods are applicable to AI-based systems as a special kind of software [16]. For example in [21], T. Margaria looks for a "formal methods boost ... for explainable AI". [48] discusses the use of (model-based testing) to safeguard AI. A recent survey [36] examines the use of AI methods in model-driven software engineering: Over the last decade, the use of neural networks for MDSE has increased, but research into decision, regression and classification trees is also producing further results. Currently, research into the use of Large Language Models (LLM) in MDSE is increasing [8,9,34] and may even surpass the rise of neural networks. The papers suggest that ML methods work well with models because of their rigidity and structure, making them particularly well suited to pattern recognition. However, whether certain modelling languages, model structures or model encodings in LLMs, for example, are better suited to ML than others is an open research question.

A follow-up question is whether there will be enough models available to train LLMs well enough. This raises the question of how to promote the availability and reusability of software and system models, not only for new AI-based engineering methods, but also for existing ones in MDSE.

In this respect, an important line of research will be to extend the evolving data spaces like [12] and Industry 4.0 environments like [50] with model storage, model-driven engineering services, and lifecycle support and engineering process execution. In the coming Internet of Collaboration (IoC), see Fig. 5, model-driven software engineering will by that be possible with unprecedented levels of collaboration of people and tools, including AI, with a wide variety of distributions in space, time and development stages, as well as great flexibility in model/software/hardware co-development. The various stakeholders, from business to development and operations, will be able to collaborate dynamically, taking into account historical, simulation, monitoring and/or runtime data for the software and system being built.

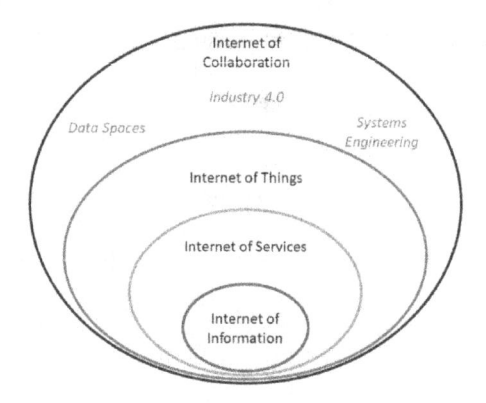

Fig. 5. MDSE in the Internet of Collaboration

5 Summary

This paper outlines the origins of scientific modelling, the use of models in software engineering in computer science, and the perspectives of model-driven software engineering with new AI methods and within the coming Internet of Collaboration, which again requires new approaches to the design, development, management and use of models for software engineering. The paper is interwoven with selected research results of T. Margaria. The ideas in Sect. 4 will be further developed in future research.

Acknowledgments. It was a great pleasure to contribute to this Festschrift for Tiziana Margaria on the combined power of research, teaching and dissemination. I have enjoyed working with Tiziana over the years, for example in the context of FMICS - the ERCIM Working Group in Formal Methods for Industrial Critical Systems, ISoLA - the International Symposium On Leveraging Applications of Formal Methods, Verification and Validation, or STTT - the Springer International Journal on Software Tools for Technology Transfer.

Let me also take this opportunity to thank my colleagues and friends at Fraunhofer FOKUS, Technische Universität Berlin, and the Weizenbaum Institute for the Networked Society, with whom I have worked for three decades on model-driven software engineering, testing, and AI. It has been a great privilege to work with all of you.

Disclosure of Interests. Ina Schieferdecker is an editorial board member of STTT, where Tiziana Margaria is coordinating editor.

Conflict of Interest. The author has no competing interests to declare that are relevant to the content of this manuscript.

References

1. Ambler, S.W.: The Object Primer: Agile Model-driven Development with UML 2.0. Cambridge University Press, Cambridge (2004)
2. Baker, P., Dai, Z.R., Grabowski, J., Schieferdecker, I., Williams, C.: Model-Driven Testing: Using the UML Testing Profile. Springer, Heidelberg (2007). https://doi.org/10.1007/978-3-540-72563-3
3. Belina, F., Hogrefe, D., Sarma, A.: SDL with Applications from Protocol Specification. Prentice-Hall, Inc. (1991)
4. Bézivin, J.: On the unification power of models. Softw. Syst. Model. **4**, 171–188 (2005). https://doi.org/10.1007/s10270-005-0079-0
5. Booch, G., Jacobson, I., Rumbaugh, J., et al.: The unified modeling language. Unix Rev. **14**(13), 5 (1996)
6. Bourque, P., Fairley, R.: Software Engineering Body of Knowledge (SWEBOK). IEEE Computer Society (2004)
7. Brooks, F.P., Bullet, N.S.: No silver bullet. Essence and accidents of software engineering. IEEE Comput. **20**(4), 10–19 (1987). https://doi.org/10.1109/MC.1987.1663532
8. Busch, D., Nolte, G., Bainczyk, A., Steffen, B.: ChatGPT in the loop: a natural language extension for domain-specific modeling languages. In: Steffen, B. (ed.) AISoLA 2023. LNCS, vol. 14380, pp. 375–390. Springer, Cham (2023). https://doi.org/10.1007/978-3-031-46002-9_24
9. Chen, K., Yang, Y., Chen, B., López, J.A.H., Mussbacher, G., Varró, D.: Automated domain modeling with large language models: A comparative study. In: 2023 ACM/IEEE 26th International Conference on Model Driven Engineering Languages and Systems (MODELS), pp. 162–172. IEEE (2023). https://doi.org/10.1109/MODELS58315.2023.00037
10. Chinosi, M., Trombetta, A.: BPMN: an introduction to the standard. Comput. Stand. Interfaces **34**(1), 124–134 (2012). https://doi.org/10.1016/j.csi.2011.06.002

11. Cosentino, V., Izquierdo, J.L.C., Cabot, J.: A systematic mapping study of software development with GitHub. IEEE Access **5**, 7173–7192 (2017). https://doi.org/10.1109/ACCESS.2017.2682323
12. Diepenbroek, M., et al.: Towards a research data commons in the german national research data infrastructure NFDI: vision, governance, architecture. In: Proceedings of the Conference on Research Data Infrastructure, vol. 1. TIB Open Publishing (2023). https://doi.org/10.52825/cordi.v1i.355
13. Diller, A.: Z: An Introduction to Formal Methods, 2nd edn. Wiley, New York (1994)
14. Dromey, R.G.: From requirements to design: Formalizing the key steps. In: 2003 Proceedings of the First International Conference on Software Engineering and Formal Methods, pp. 2–11. IEEE (2003)
15. Evans, E.: Domain-Driven Design: Tackling Complexity in the Heart of Software. Addison-Wesley Professional (2003)
16. Feldt, R., de Oliveira Neto, F.G., Torkar, R.: Ways of applying artificial intelligence in software engineering. In: Proceedings of the 6th International Workshop on Realizing Artificial Intelligence Synergies in Software Engineering, pp. 35–41 (2018). https://doi.org/10.1145/3194104.3194109
17. Fraser, S.D., etal.: No silver bullet "reloaded: Retrospective on" essence and accidents of software engineering. In: Companion to the 22nd ACM SIGPLAN Conference on Object-Oriented Programming Systems and Applications Companion, pp. 1026–1030 (2007). https://doi.org/10.1145/1297846.1297973
18. Friedenthal, S., Moore, A., Steiner, R.: A Practical Guide to SysML: The Systems Modeling Language. Morgan Kaufmann (2014)
19. Friedman, L.W., Friedman, H.H., Pollack, S.: The role of modeling in scientific disciplines: a taxonomy. Rev. Bus. **29**(1), 61–67 (2008). https://ssrn.com/abstract=2322506
20. Fritzson, P., Engelson, V.: Modelica—a unified object-oriented language for system modeling and simulation. In: Jul, E. (ed.) ECOOP 1998. LNCS, vol. 1445, pp. 67–90. Springer, Heidelberg (1998). https://doi.org/10.1007/BFb0054087
21. Gossen, F., Margaria, T., Steffen, B.: Formal methods boost experimental performance for explainable AI. IT Prof. **23**(6), 8–12 (2021). https://doi.org/10.1109/MITP.2021.3123495
22. Grabowski, J., Hogrefe, D., Réthy, G., Schieferdecker, I., Wiles, A., Willcock, C.: An introduction to the testing and test control notation (TTCN-3). Comput. Netw. **42**(3), 375–403 (2003). https://doi.org/10.1016/S1389-1286(03)00249-4
23. Greenfield, J.: Software factories: assembling applications with patterns, models, frameworks and tools. In: Karsai, G., Visser, E. (eds.) GPCE 2004. LNCS, vol. 3286, p. 488. Springer, Heidelberg (2004). https://doi.org/10.1007/978-3-540-30175-2_26
24. Harman, M.: The role of artificial intelligence in software engineering. In: 2012 First International Workshop on Realizing AI Synergies in Software Engineering (RAISE), pp. 1–6. IEEE (2012). https://doi.org/10.1109/RAISE.2012.6227961
25. Harman, M., Jones, B.F.: Search-based software engineering. Inf. Softw. Technol. **43**(14), 833–839 (2001). https://doi.org/10.1016/S0950-5849(01)00189-6
26. Hein, C., Ritter, T., Wagner, M.: Model-driven tool integration with ModelBus. In: International Workshop on Future Trends of Model-Driven Development, vol. 1, pp. 35–39. SCITEPRESS (2009). https://doi.org/10.5220/0002174800350039
27. Hertz, H.R.: Gesammelte Werke: Die Prinzipien der Mechanik in neuem Zusammenhange dargestellt/herausgegeben von Ph. Lenard, mit einem Vorwort von H. von Helmholtz. Barth (1894)

28. Holzmann, G.J.: The model checker SPIN. IEEE Trans. Softw. Eng. **23**(5), 279–295 (1997). https://doi.org/10.1109/32.588521
29. Humbert, L., Puhlmann, H.: Essential ingredients of literacy in informatics. Inform. Stud. Assess. **65**, 76 (2004)
30. Jackson, D., Schechter, I., Shlyahter, H.: Alcoa: the alloy constraint analyzer. In: Proceedings of the 22nd International Conference on Software Engineering, pp. 730–733 (2000). https://doi.org/10.1145/337180.337616
31. Jorges, S., Kubczak, C., Pageau, F., Margaria, T.: Model driven design of reliable robot control programs using the jABC. In: Fourth IEEE International Workshop on Engineering of Autonomous and Autonomous Systems (EASe 2007), pp. 137–148. IEEE (2007). https://doi.org/10.1109/EASE.2007.17
32. Koza, J.R.: Genetic programming as a means for programming computers by natural selection. Stat. Comput. **4**, 87–112 (1994). https://doi.org/10.1007/BF00175355
33. Kruchten, P.: The Rational Unified Process: An Introduction, 3rd edn. Addison-Wesley Professional (2003)
34. Kulkarni, V., Reddy, S., Barat, S., Dutta, J.: Toward a symbiotic approach leveraging generative AI for model driven engineering. In: 2023 ACM/IEEE 26th International Conference on Model Driven Engineering Languages and Systems (MODELS), pp. 184–193. IEEE (2023). https://doi.org/10.1109/MODELS58315.2023.00039
35. Mantere, T., Alander, J.T.: Evolutionary software engineering, a review. Appl. Soft Comput. **5**(3), 315–331 (2005). https://doi.org/10.1016/j.asoc.2004.08.004
36. Marcén, A.C., Iglesias, A., Lapeña, R., Pérez, F., Cetina, C.: A systematic literature review of model-driven engineering using machine learning. IEEE Trans. Software Eng. (2024). https://doi.org/10.1109/TSE.2024.3430514
37. Margaria, T., Chaudhary, H.A.A., Guevara, I., Ryan, S., Schieweck, A.: The interoperability challenge: building a model-driven digital thread platform for CPS. In: Margaria, T., Steffen, B. (eds.) ISoLA 2021. LNCS, vol. 13036, pp. 393–413. Springer, Cham (2021). https://doi.org/10.1007/978-3-030-89159-6_25
38. Margaria, T., Nagel, R., Steffen, B.: Remote integration and coordination of verification tools in JETI. In: 12th IEEE International Conference and Workshops on the Engineering of Computer-Based Systems (ECBS 2005), pp. 431–436. IEEE (2005). https://doi.org/10.1109/ECBS.2005.59
39. Margaria, T., Steffen, B.: Business process modeling in the jABC: the one-thing approach. In: Handbook of Research on Business Process Modeling, pp. 1–26. IGI Global (2009). https://doi.org/10.4018/978-1-60566-288-6.ch001
40. Margaria, T., Steffen, B.: Continuous model-driven engineering. Computer **42**(10), 106–109 (2009). https://doi.org/10.1109/MC.2009.315
41. Margaria, T., Steffen, B.: Service-orientation: conquering complexity with XMDD. In: Hinchey, M., Coyle, L. (eds.) Conquering Complexity, pp. 217–236. Springer, London (2012). https://doi.org/10.1007/978-1-4471-2297-5_10
42. Meadows, D.H.: Thinking in Systems: A Primer. Chelsea Green Publishing (2008)
43. von Neumann, J.: Method in the physical sciences. In: Leary, L. (ed.) The Unity of Knowledge, pp. 157–164. Doubleday and Company, New York (1955)
44. Ortlieb, C.P., Dresky, C.V., Gasser, I., Günzel, S.: Zur Entwicklung des Modellbegriffs. In: Ortlieb, C.P., Dresky, C.V., Gasser, I., Günzel, S. (eds.) Mathematische Modellierung: Eine Einführung in zwölf Fallstudien, pp. 1–5. Springer, Heidelberg (2009). https://doi.org/10.1007/978-3-8348-9298-0_1
45. Partridge, D.: Artificial Intelligence and Software Engineering: Understanding the Promise of the Future. Taylor & Francis (1998)

46. Sadovykh, A., et al.: Architecture driven modernization in practice - study results. In: 2009 14th IEEE International Conference on Engineering of Complex Computer Systems, pp. 50–57 (2009). https://doi.org/10.1109/ICECCS.2009.39
47. Schieferdecker, I.: Responsible software engineering. Future softw. Qual. Assur. 137–146 (2020). https://doi.org/10.1007/978-3-030-29509-7_11
48. Schieferdecker, I., Großmann, J., Schneider, M.A.: How to safeguard AI. AI Critique | Volume 245 (2019). https://doi.org/10.1515/9783839447192-015
49. Schieferdecker, I., Ritter, T.: Advanced software engineering: developing and testing model-based software securely and efficiently. Digit. Transf. 353–369 (2019) https://doi.org/10.1007/978-3-662-58134-6_21
50. Schöppenthau, F., et al.: Building a digital manufacturing as a service ecosystem for Catena-X. Sensors **23**(17), 7396 (2023). https://doi.org/10.3390/s23177396
51. Soley, R., et al.: Model driven architecture. OMG White Pap. **308**(308), 5 (2000)
52. Steffen, B., Margaria, T., Nagel, R., Jörges, S., Kubczak, C.: Model-driven development with the jABC. In: Bin, E., Ziv, A., Ur, S. (eds.) HVC 2006. LNCS, vol. 4383, pp. 92–108. Springer, Heidelberg (2007). https://doi.org/10.1007/978-3-540-70889-6_7
53. Sthamer, H.H.: The automatic generation of software test data using genetic algorithms. University of South Wales (United Kingdom) (1995)
54. Ulrich, A., Jell, S., Votintseva, A., Kull, A.: The ETSI test description language TDL and its application. In: 2014 2nd International Conference on Model-Driven Engineering and Software Development (MODELSWARD), pp. 601–608. IEEE (2014). https://doi.org/10.5220/0004708706010608
55. Valdez, M.E.P.: A gift from Pandora's box: the software crisis. Ph.D. thesis, University of Edinburgh (1988). https://era.ed.ac.uk/handle/1842/7304
56. Wappler, S., Schieferdecker, I.: Improving evolutionary class testing in the presence of non-public methods. In: Proceedings of the 22nd IEEE/ACM International Conference on Automated Software Engineering, pp. 381–384 (2007) https://doi.org/10.1145/1321631.1321689
57. Wendland, M.F., Schieferdecker, I., Vouffo-Feudjio, A.: Requirements-driven testing with behavior trees. In: 2011 IEEE Fourth International Conference on Software Testing, Verification and Validation Workshops, pp. 501–510. IEEE (2011). https://doi.org/10.1109/ICSTW.2011.25
58. Wiegand, J., et al.: Eclipse: a platform for integrating development tools. IBM Syst. J. **43**(2), 371–383 (2004). https://doi.org/10.1147/sj.432.0371
59. Xie, T.: Intelligent software engineering: Synergy between AI and software engineering. In: Proceedings of the 11th Innovations in Software Engineering Conference, p. 1 (2018). https://doi.org/10.1145/3172871.3172891

Unveiling Modeling Patterns in Workflow Sketches: Insights for Designing an Abstract Workflow Language for Scientific Computing

Anna-Lena Lamprecht

Institute of Computer Science, University of Potsdam, Potsdam, Germany
anna-lena.lamprecht@uni-potsdam.de

Abstract. Scientific workflows are structured sequences of computational or data processing steps commonly used to automate complex scientific analyses. Abstract workflows, which provide high-level representations of these processes, play a crucial role in designing, understanding, and communicating complex workflows before delving into implementation details. In this paper, we explore the modeling patterns emerging from a collection of 172 workflow sketches created by students in a beginners' course on scientific workflow management. Our aim is to understand how novice users intuitively model workflows when given the freedom to choose their own modeling styles. The study specifically focuses on graphical abstract workflow languages, which are generally perceived as more intuitive compared to their textual counterparts. The findings suggest that extending classical control-flow modeling with optionally usable data nodes can form an effective foundation for an abstract workflow specification language. These insights offer valuable guidance for designing a workflow language that aligns with the natural inclinations of users in scientific computing, enhancing both usability and functionality.

Keywords: Process Modeling · Scientific Workflows · Data Analysis Workflows · Abstract Workflows · Modeling Patterns

1 Introduction

In recent years, numerous workflow systems have emerged within the scientific community (see, e.g., [1,15]), reflecting the growing need for efficient and reproducible methods to manage complex scientific analyses. In this context, the notion of abstract workflows is gaining popularity as a requirements-capturing artefact for the early phases of workflow development: Abstract workflows help in conceptualizing and planning the processes before delving into detailed implementation [22]. Several approaches to abstract workflow modeling have been suggested in the past. Notable examples include Concept Maps by Beard et al. [6], the combination of UML Activity Diagrams with non-functional requirements as described by Pereira et al. [28], the workflow templates in WINGS [9], the loose workflows in PROPHETS [19,26], and the prototypical constraint sketcher in a web interface to APE [10,11]. All these methods use graphical notations, which seem to be more intuitive than textual representations at this stage of development. However, there is no consensus on the exact characteristics that such a language should possess.

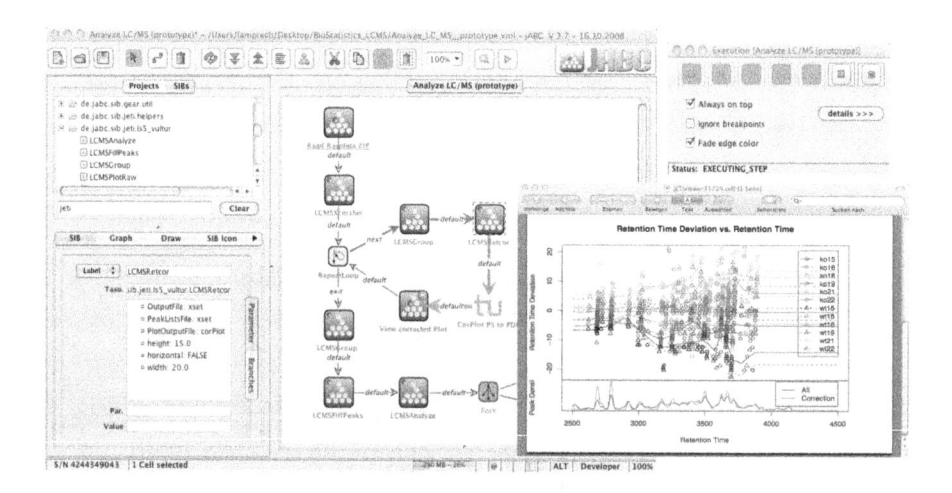

Fig. 1. Workflow modelling and execution in jABC.

Incidentally, we have an interesting source of workflow artifacts that could provide valuable insights for our search for a suitable abstract workflow language: Tiziana Margaria has worked on the paradigm of eXtreme Model-Driven Design (XMDD) [24] and the corresponding jABC modeling framework [30] over several years. Figure 1 gives an impression of the jABC's user interface. In its very basic form, it is simply a framework for "drawing" graphical workflow models consisting of nodes and directed edges connecting them. The usual interpretation that the different plugins of the standard jABC release (like the interpreter component visible in the figure) apply is to treat the models as control-flow graphs, while other interpretations are possible and for instance taken by the DBSchema and FormulaBuilder plugins. Over the years, the jABC framework has been used extensively for modeling, synthesizing, implementing, and executing scientific workflows [2–5,8,16–18,20,21,23,27,32].

Furthermore, XMDD and the jABC framework have been integrated into various courses at the University of Potsdam [7,12], where Tiziana Margaria held the Chair of Service and Software Engineering from 2006 to 2014. In some of these courses, students from computer science and other scientific disciplines received practical training in the development of scientific workflows [13,14]. As an early assignment, students used the jABC framework to create initial workflow prototypes (using a particular "Prototype" workflow building block, with which nodes and edges in the graph can essentially be labeled by arbitrary text), which they would later refine into operational workflows. Interestingly, during this initial stage, students often ignored the standard control-flow semantics of the jABC (that they had been explained) and which the framework only enforced in later stages. Instead, they used the framework intuitively, reflecting their natural approach to workflow modeling. While this led to some challenges during the courses, it now provides a valuable source of data for our quest to design an abstract workflow language. The students' intuitive use of the framework offers insights into what features and elements are most important and intuitive for users, especially those from non-computer science backgrounds, when sketching a scientific workflow.

In this paper, we describe how we analyzed 172 workflow sketches from student projects for the modeling patterns they applied. We present and discuss our results, which indicate that an extension of classical control-flow modeling with optionally usable data nodes could form an adequate basis for an abstract workflow specification language. Finally, we outline directions for future work based on our findings.

2 Analysis Method

The analysis of the workflows was carried out in two major steps. In a first, qualitative phase, the workflows were examined to determine which features could be observed and distinguished. In particular, it was important to identify the different workflow modelling styles used. They are described in Sect. 2.1. In a next, quantitatively oriented phase, all workflows were annotated with those of the features that applied to them, in order to assess how often the identified features actually occur. The annotation strategy is summarised in Sect. 2.2.

2.1 Modeling Styles

The following workflow modelling styles could be identified in the sample:

A Control flow
  Control-flow modelling appeared in three variants:
  A1 Standard control flow
    The nodes in the graph represent actions, while the edges define the flow of control between them. Data and data flow are not directly visible.
  A2 Control flow with input nodes
    Like A1, but in addition distinguished nodes are used to represent workflow input data.
  A3 Control flow with (intermediate) result nodes
    Like A1, but in addition distinguished nodes are used to represent (intermediate) results within the workflow.
B Data flow
  The nodes in the graph represent actions, while the edges define the flow of data between them. The execution order of the action is implied by the data flow definition.

C Activity flow
The nodes in the graph represent data items, while the edges represent actions. This style occurred in three variants:

C1 Activity flow (action-data)
Data nodes form a unit with an incoming action edge. Analogous to an imperative sentence (in English and German), the action on the edge is the predicate and the data at the node is the object of the thus assembled command.

C2 Activity flow (data-action)
Data nodes form a unit with an outgoing action edge, that is, the first part of the command defines the object and the second defines the predicate. Note while this is not a valid structure for an imperative sentence in English, in German it is possible to formulate commands also in this order.

C3 Activity flow (data-action-data)
The nodes in the graph represent data items, and edges between pairs of nodes denote actions that transform that data at the source of the edge into the data at its target.

D States and transitions
In a style that reminds of the Kripke Transition Systems used in formal verification (see, e.g., [25]), the nodes in the graph describe states, while the actions at the edges represent transitions between states.

E Component interactions
Taking more an architectural than a behavioural perspective, in this modelling style nodes in the graph represent components or resources in a system or network, and the edges describe interactions between them.

Z Indefinable
This category was introduced to annotate workflow models for (parts of) which no underlying modelling concept or strategy could be identified.

Being derived from what has been observed in the workflows of a concrete sample, this list is of course not complete with regard to what would principally be possible. For example, some modelling approaches that are typically dealt with in principal literature and textbooks on workflow modelling, such as Petri nets [29], are not included. The notion of modelling the activity flow, however, is none of the typically considered possible modelling approaches, and is thus particularly interesting to investigate further.

2.2 Workflow Annotation

In order to assess how often the modelling styles described above have been used and to quantify also some other features of the workflows, the following information was recorded for each workflow in the sample:

1. Course in which it was created
2. Creator (especially for being able to compare workflows of the same author between the two samples)

3. Workflow size (number of nodes)
4. Language used for labelling nodes and edges (German or English)
5. Primary workflow modelling style (the only or, if modelling is not consistent, the predominant style)
6. Additional workflow modelling styles ("none" if modelling follows one of the above styles consistently)
7. Further observations

The information for items 1 and 2 was directly available from the coursework archive. The workflow size (item 3) was computed using the corresponding functionality of the jABCstats framework for statistical analysis of jABC workflows [31]. The information for all other items was collected through manual inspection of the individual workflows.

3 Samples and Basic Results

Two sets of workflows were analysed in the scope of this study: prototypical workflow models describing cooking recipes and sketches of scientific (data analysis) workflows. They are described in the following Sects. 3.1 and 3.2, respectively, along with the major findings from the quantitative analysis of the features listed above. The workflows were created by participants of the module "Informatics for natural scientists" that we taught four times between 2011 and 2014 at the University of Potsdam in Germany. Note that there are a different number of workflows in the two samples, and in both samples there are less workflows then there were students, which is simply due to the fact that sometimes students don't do all their assignments.

3.1 Sample 1: Cooking Recipe Workflows

The first sample comprises 92 workflows that were handed in as solutions to the following assignment: *"Create a jABC process model that describes how you make your favourite dish. Simply use the Prototype-SIB (de.jabc.sib.common.basic.-Prototype) for representing the single steps of your process. Customise it as needed, and consider setting more meaningful custom icons."*

The workflows in this sample have an average size of 12.1 nodes (median: 11, standard deviation: 6.97). 79 of them (85.9%) used German language for the labelling of nodes and edges, and 13 of them (14.1%) used English.

Figure 2 shows the distribution of the primary workflow modelling styles for this sample. Control-flow oriented modelling is clearly dominating, with classical control-flow modelling (A1) being the primary modelling style in 55.5% of the workflows, and control-flow modelling with distinguished input types (A2) in another 6.5% of the workflows. Second most used are the different activity-flow modelling styles (C1, C2 and C3) which are the primary modelling style in around 29% of the workflows. One single workflow has primarily been modelled based on states and transitions (D), while for about 7.5% of the workflows

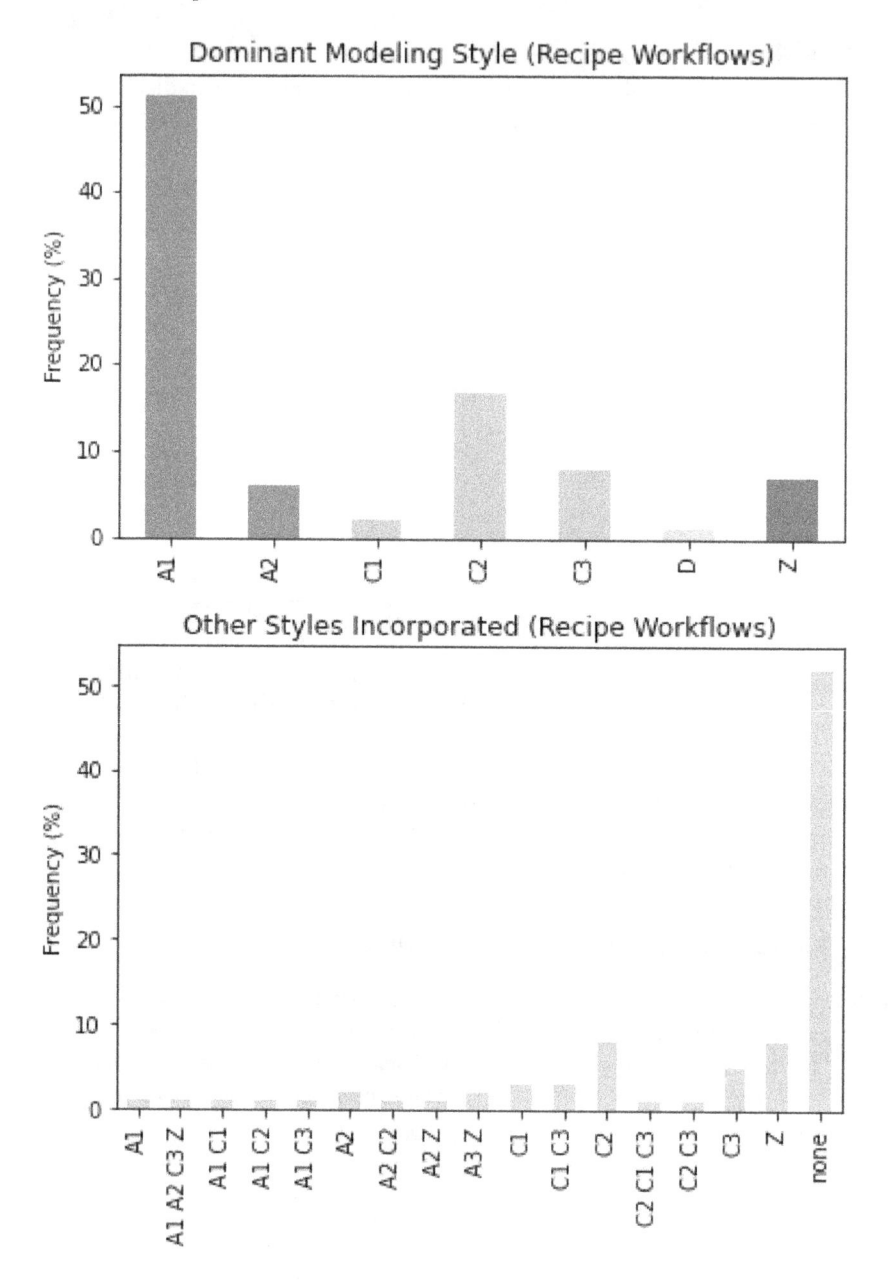

Fig. 2. Workflow modelling styles in Sample 1.

no primary modelling style could be identified. Data-flow modelling (B) and component interaction diagrams (E) were not used here at all.

Figure 2 surveys which additional modelling styles have been used in the workflows in Sample 1. More than 55% show no additional modelling styles, meaning that their primary style has been used consistently. All other combinations of styles account for less than 10% each. Interestingly, almost all styles used as primary styles also appear here, while data-flow modelling (B), states and transitions (D) and interactions diagrams (E) do not appear (either).

3.2 Sample 2: Scientific Workflows

The second sample comprises 80 workflows that were handed in as solutions to the following assignment: *"Scientific workflows define series of computation steps that tackle a scientific question. Research about typical scientific problems in your domain, and how these can be approached with software support. [...] Choose one example for closer investigation. Identify the essential computation steps [...] and create a jABC process model that describes the workflow. Again, simply use the Prototype-SIB (de.jabc.sib.common.basic.Prototype) for representing the single steps of your process."*

Very similar to what was recorded for the first sample, he workflows in this sample have an average size of 12.7 nodes (median: 11, standard deviation: 6.67). 56 of them (70%) used German language for the labelling of nodes and edges, and 24 of them (30%) used English.

Figure 3 shows the distribution of the primary workflow modelling styles for this sample. Control-flow oriented modelling is again clearly dominating, with classical control-flow modelling (A1) being the primary modelling style in about 67% of the workflows, control-flow modelling with distinguished input types (A2) in another 6.5%, and control-flow modelling with (intermediate) result nodes (A3) in another 5% of the workflows. Second most recorded were indefinable styles (Z) with 11.5% in this sample, followed by data-action-data activity flows (C3, 6.5%), component interaction diagrams (E, 2.5%), and states and transitions (D, 1.5%).

Figure 3 surveys which additional modelling styles have been used in the workflows in Sample 2. More than 65% show no additional modelling styles here. Again, all other combinations of styles account for less than 10% each. In addition to the primary modelling styles used in this sample, here also the other flavours of activity-flow modelling (C1 and C2) and data-flow modelling (B) appear in a few cases.

4 Discussion and Further Observations

The results are apparently biased towards control-flow modelling, which is not surprising as the students produced their workflow sketches using the jABC framework, in which this is the standard semantics of the graphical models. However, as mentioned in the introduction, this could be and often was ignored by the students in the assignments they were doing using the "Prototype" workflow building blocks, and this observation created the motivation for taking a closer look at how novice users describe workflows when they are basically free to choose a modelling style.

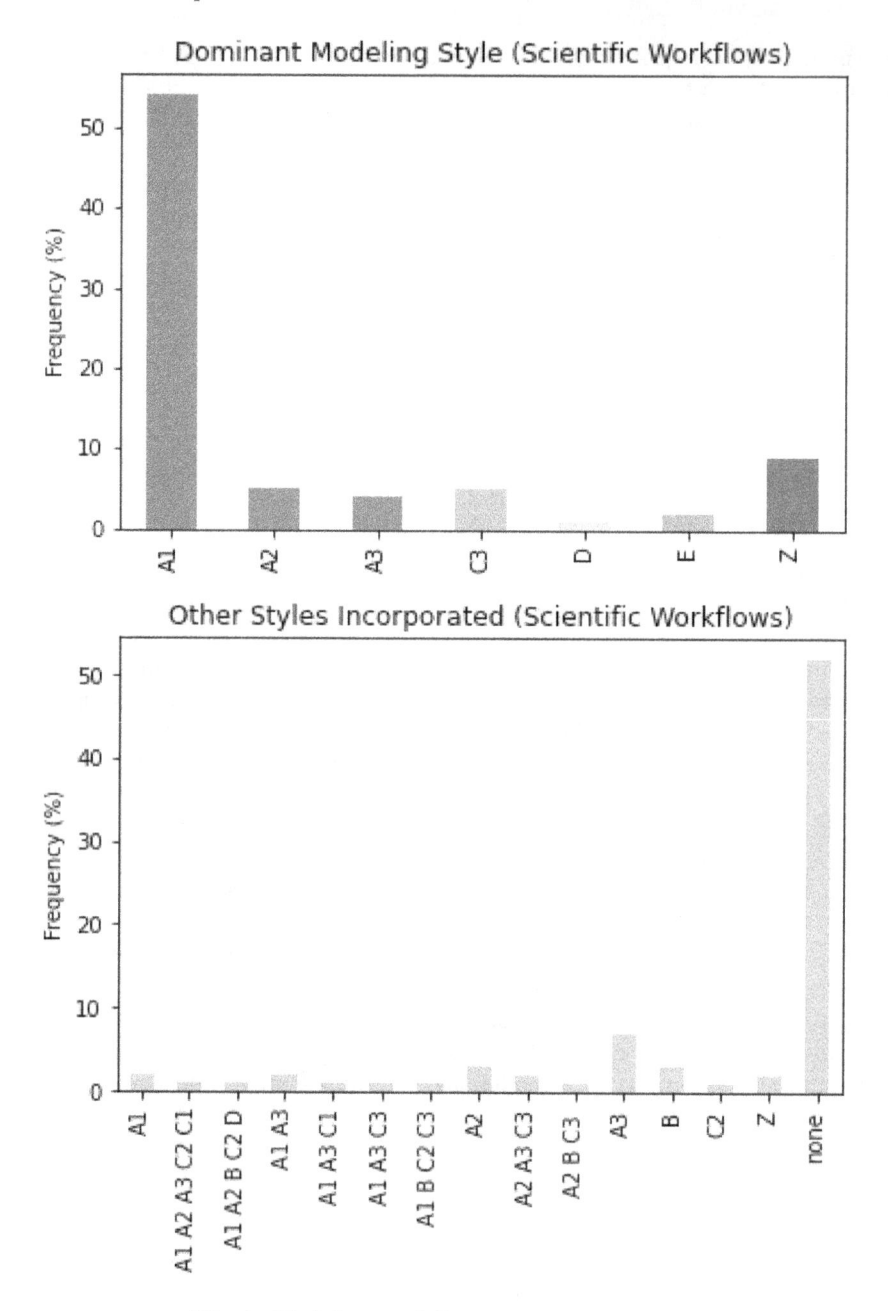

Fig. 3. Workflow modelling styles in Sample 2.

As shown in the previous section, there are many mixed representations, but most modellers were consistent in the modelling style they choose for the individual workflow model (more than 55% and 65%, respectively, who use none but the primary workflow modelling style). Interestingly, however, they did not always follow the same modelling style for all of their workflows: Of the 116 students that created the workflows of the two samples analysed, 27 (23.8%) used the same (primary) workflow modelling style in both assignments, 29 (25.00%) used different styles, and the other 60 (51.8 %) only created one workflow, so that this question does not apply. While the currently collected data is not suited to explain this observation sufficiently, the difference in the distribution of the primary workflow patterns in the two samples (cf. Figs. 2 and 3) suggests that not only the software development skills of the workflow designer play a role, but also the application domain and the background knowledge and the context that they assume. For the recipe workflows there is often quite some cooking experience assumed and required to interpret the diagrams correctly. The scientific workflows, where the modellers probably assumed much less background knowledge from the reader, the models also tend to be more precise and elaborate.

Another observation in this direction was that sometimes images were not just used to illustrate the workflow further (in jABC the icons of the workflow building blocks can be customised as well), but rather as replacements for text. In fact, this happened in the recipe workflows, probably based on the assumption that someone with cooking experience obtains enough information by this. In the scientific workflows, custom icons where used in addition to textual descriptions to provide further information or illustration, but they not as essential elements for understanding the model.

5 Conclusion

This paper has explored the modeling patterns observed in 172 workflow sketches created by students in a "Computer Science for Scientists" course. Through qualitative and quantitative analyses, we identified various workflow modeling styles that students naturally gravitate towards when given the freedom to choose their own modeling approach. The study revealed several key insights into how novice users, particularly those from non-computer science backgrounds, conceptualize and represent workflows.

Our findings show that control-flow oriented modeling is predominant among students, suggesting a natural inclination towards representing workflows as sequences of actions. Interestingly, the introduction of data nodes, whether as inputs or intermediate results, was also a common feature, suggesting that users find it beneficial to explicitly represent data alongside control flow. This aligns with the observation that an extension of classical control-flow modeling with optionally usable data nodes might form an adequate basis for an abstract workflow specification language.

Future work should focus on developing a robust and widely applicable abstract workflow language by incorporating feedback from a broader range of users and testing its applicability in various domains. Additionally, exploring ways to integrate visual aids and intuitive interfaces could further enhance the usability and adoption of the language.

References

1. Existing Workflow systems. https://github.com/common-workflow-language/common-workflow-language/wiki/Existing-Workflow-systems
2. Al-Areqi, S., Kriewald, S., Lamprecht, A.-L., Reusser, D., Wrobel, M., Margaria, T.: Towards a flexible assessment of climate impacts: the example of agile workflows for the ci:grasp platform. In: Margaria, T., Steffen, B. (eds.) ISoLA 2014. LNCS, vol. 8803, pp. 420–435. Springer, Heidelberg (2014). https://doi.org/10.1007/978-3-662-45231-8_33
3. Al-Areqi, S., Lamprecht, A.L., Margaria, T.: Automatic workflow composition in the geospatial domain: an application on sea-level rise impacts analysis. In: 19th AGILE International Conference on Geographic Information Science (2016). https://ulir.ul.ie/handle/10344/5428
4. Al-Areqi, S., Lamprecht, A.-L., Margaria, T.: Constraints-driven automatic geospatial service composition: workflows for the analysis of sea-level rise impacts. In: Gervasi, O., et al. (eds.) ICCSA 2016. LNCS, vol. 9788, pp. 134–150. Springer, Cham (2016).https://doi.org/10.1007/978-3-319-42111-7_12
5. Al-areqi, S., Lamprecht, A.L., Margaria, T., Kriewald, S., Reusser, D., Wrobel, M.: Agile workflows for climate impact risk assessment based on the ci:grasp platform and the jABC modeling framework. In: 7th International Congress on Environmental Modelling and Software, pp. 470–477, June 2014. https://scholarsarchive.byu.edu/iemssconference/2014/Stream-B/2
6. Beard, N.: Import workflows into TeSS concept maps. https://github.com/elixir-europe/BioHackathon
7. Bordihn, H., Lamprecht, A.L., Margaria, T.: Foundations of semantics and model checking in a software engineering course. In: Proceedings of the First Workshop on Formal Methods in Software Engineering Education and Training (FMSEE&T '15) (2015). http://ceur-ws.org/Vol-1385/paper4.pdf
8. Ebert, B.E., Lamprecht, A.L., Steffen, B., Blank, L.M.: Flux-P: automating metabolic flux analysis. Metabolites **2**(4), 872–890 (2012). https://doi.org/10.3390/metabo2040872, https://ncbi.nlm.nih.gov/pmc/articles/PMC3901227/
9. Gil, Y., et al.: Wings: intelligent workflow-based design of computational experiments. IEEE Intell. Syst. **26**(1), 62–72 (2011). https://doi.org/10.1109/MIS.2010.9
10. Kasalica, V., Lamprecht, A.L.: APE: a command-line tool and API for automated workflow composition. In: Proceedings of the International Conference on Computational Science (ICCS 2020). vol. to appear (2020)
11. Kasalica, V., Lamprecht, A.L.: Workflow discovery with semantic constraints: the SAT-based implementation of APE. Electron. Commun. EASST **78** (2020). https://doi.org/10.14279/tuj.eceasst.78.1092, https://journal.ub.tu-berlin.de/eceasst/article/view/1092, number: 0
12. Lamprecht, A., Margaria, T., Neubauer, J.: On the use of XMDD in software development education. In: 2015 IEEE 39th Annual Computer Software and Applications Conference, vol. 2, pp. 835–844, July 2015. https://doi.org/10.1109/COMPSAC.2015.178
13. Lamprecht, A.L., Margaria, T.: Process Design for Natural Scientists: An Agile Model-Driven Approach. Springer, Berlin, Heidelberg (2014). https://doi.org/10.1007/978-3-662-45006-2

14. Lamprecht, A.L., Margaria, T.: Scientific workflows with XMDD: a way to use process modeling in computational science education. Procedia Comput. Sci. **51**, 1927–1936 (2015). https://doi.org/10.1016/j.procs.2015.05.457, https://sciencedirect.com/science/article/pii/S187705091501265X
15. Lamprecht, A.L., Margaria, T.: Modeling of Scientific Workflows. In: Tatnall, A. (ed.) Encyclopedia of Education and Information Technologies, pp. 1–8. Springer International Publishing, Cham (2019). https://doi.org/10.1007/978-3-319-60013-0_210-1
16. Lamprecht, A.L., Margaria, T., Steffen, B.: Supporting process development in Bio-jETI by model checking and synthesis. In: SWAT4LS 2008 Proceedings, CEUR-WS.org Workshop Proceedings Service, vol. 435, January 2008
17. Lamprecht, A.L., Margaria, T., Steffen, B.: Bio-jETI: a framework for semantics-based service composition. BMC Bioinform. **10**(10), S8 (2009). https://doi.org/10.1186/1471-2105-10-S10-S8
18. Lamprecht, A.L., Margaria, T., Steffen, B., Sczyrba, A., Hartmeier, S., Giegerich, R.: GeneFisher-P: variations of GeneFisher as processes in Bio-jETI. BMC Bioinform. **9**(4), S13 (2008). https://doi.org/10.1186/1471-2105-9-S4-S13
19. Lamprecht, A.L., Naujokat, S., Margaria, T., Steffen, B.: Synthesis-based loose programming. In: 2010 Seventh International Conference on the Quality of Information and Communications Technology, pp. 262–267. IEEE, Porto, Portugal, September 2010. https://doi.org/10.1109/QUATIC.2010.53, http://ieeexplore.ieee.org/document/5655574/
20. Lamprecht, A.L., Naujokat, S., Margaria, T., Steffen, B.: Semantics-based composition of EMBOSS services. J. Biomed. Semant. **2**(1), S5 (2011). https://doi.org/10.1186/2041-1480-2-S1-S5
21. Lamprecht, A.L., Naujokat, S., Steffen, B., Margaria, T.: Constraint-guided workflow composition based on the EDAM ontology. In: Proceedings of the 3rd International Workshop on Semantic Web Applications and Tools for the Life Sciences (2010). https://doi.org/10.1038/npre.2010.5397.1, http://arxiv.org/abs/1012.1640, arXiv: 1012.1640
22. Lamprecht, A.L., et al.: Perspectives on automated composition of workflows in the life sciences. Technical report 10:897, F1000Research, September 2021. https://doi.org/10.12688/f1000research.54159.1, type: article
23. Margaria, T., Floyd, B.D., Gonzalez Camargo, R., Lamprecht, A.L., Neubauer, J., Seelaender, M.: Simple management of high assurance data in long-lived interdisciplinary healthcare research: a proposal. In: Margaria, T., Steffen, B. (eds.) Leveraging Applications of Formal Methods, Verification and Validation. Specialized Techniques and Applications. ISoLA 2014. LNCS, vol. 8803, pp. 526–544. Springer, Berlin, Heidelberg (2014). https://doi.org/10.1007/978-3-662-45231-8_44
24. Margaria, T., Steffen, B.: Service-orientation: conquering complexity with XMDD. In: Hinchey, M., Coyle, L. (eds.) Conquering Complexity, pp. 217–236. Springer, London (2012).https://doi.org/10.1007/978-1-4471-2297-5_10
25. Müller-Olm, M., Schmidt, D., Steffen, B.: Model-Checking, vol. 1694, pp. 330–354. Springer, Berlin, Heidelberg (1999).https://doi.org/10.1007/3-540-48294-6_22
26. Naujokat, S., Lamprecht, A.L., Steffen, B.: Loose Programming with PROPHETS. In: de Lara, J., Zisman, A. (eds.) Fundamental Approaches to Software Engineering, pp. 94–98. LNCS, Springer, Berlin, Heidelberg (2012).https://doi.org/10.1007/978-3-031-30826-0
27. Palmblad, M., Lamprecht, A.L., Ison, J., Schwämmle, V.: Automated workflow composition in mass spectrometry based proteomics. Bioinformatics (2018). https://doi.org/10.1093/bioinformatics/bty646

28. Pereira, W., et al.: A conception process for abstract workflows: an example on deep water oil exploitation domain (2009). https://ora.ox.ac.uk/objects/uuid:ba3b6434-f5db-4acd-af24-4f9c15cfc9b5
29. Petri, C.A., Reisig, W.: Petri net. Scholarpedia **3**(4), 6477 (2008). https://doi.org/10.4249/scholarpedia.6477, https://scholarpedia.org/article/Petri_net
30. Steffen, B., Margaria, T., Nagel, R., Jorges, S., Kubczak, C.: Model-driven development with the jABC. In: Bin, E., Ziv, A., Ur, S. (eds.) Hardware and Software, Verification and Testing. HVC 2006. LNCS, vol. 4383, pp. 92–108. Springer, Berlin, Heidelberg (2007). https://doi.org/10.1007/978-3-540-70889-6_7
31. Wickert, A., Lamprecht, A.L.: jABCstats: an extensible process library for the empirical analysis of jABC workflows. In: Margaria, T., Steffen, B. (eds.) Leveraging Applications of Formal Methods, Verification and Validation. Specialized Techniques and Applications. ISoLA 2014. LNCS, vol. 8803, pp. 449–463. Springer, Berlin, Heidelberg (2014).https://doi.org/10.1007/978-3-662-45231-8_35
32. Wickert, A., Lamprecht, A.L., Margaria, T.: Domain-specific design of patient classification in cancer-related cachexia research. In: Proceedings of the 6th Conference on Formal Methods in Software Engineering. pp. 60–63. FormaliSE '18, ACM, New York, NY, USA (2018).https://doi.org/10.1145/3193992.3194002, http://doi.acm.org/10.1145/3193992.3194002, event-place: Gothenburg, Sweden

The Isolette System: Illustrating End-to-End Artifacts for Rigorous Model-Based Engineering

John Hatcliff[(✉)] and Jason Belt

Kansas State University, Manhattan, KS 66506, USA
{hatcliff,belt}@ksu.edu

Abstract. Margaria and colleagues have emphasized a paradigm for system construction and assurance in which development is organized around building and refining one comprehensive model of the system (referred to as the "One Thing Approach" (OTA)). In this paper, we connect to several key OTA ideas by presenting an integrated collection of development artifacts for a simple safety-critical system (an Infant Incubator example called the *Isolette*). Our illustration uses AADL for defining system models, the HAMR model-driven development tool, the GUMBO model-based component contract language for specifying constraints, and the Slang/Logika framework for code-level automated property-based testing and verificationl. The artifacts illustrate a rigorous process, moving end-to-end from the concepts of operations and requirements to assurance cases and deployment on the formally verified seL4 microkernel. We describe pedagogical resources and tutorials that have been used to introduce both students and industry teams to formal-methods integrated with model based development.

1 Introduction

Many initial presentations of formal methods concepts to students or potential industry partners include an enumeration of formal methods successes in industry and/or illustrations of formal verification for a particular development artifact (e.g., a simple behavioral model or some source code with method contracts and assertions). While this can generate initial interest, at some point potential users or students need to be presented with illustrations of how formal methods can be used in an integrated fashion across the entire development process. In addition, it needs to be explained that (a) one can never have a completely formal development process (e.g., because one must always begin with a customer's initial informal ideas about how they want the system, or one must brainstorm in hazard analysis about how a system may fail), (b) effective and realistic use of formal methods always involves an integration of formal and informal steps. While there are many excellent illustrations of practical formal methods, there are far fewer illustrations of end-to-end development integrating informal and formal methods in a rigorous way.

In this paper, we present an overview of artifacts [38] that we have developed for illustrating end-to-end development with integrated formal methods. The illustration uses a simple safety-critical system – an Infant Incubator called the *Isolette* originally presented in the NASA Requirements Engineering Management Handbook (REMH) [27]). While these artifacts have been used primarily in teaching graduate courses, we also use them successfully in tutorials for our industrial collaborators.

It is fitting that we present this material in a volume of work dedicated to the work of Tiziana Margaria, because she and her colleagues have for decades championed similar themes in research, teaching, and in interactions with industry. In particular, Margaria and colleagues have emphasized a paradigm for system construction and assurance in which development is organized around building and refining one comprehensive model of the system (referred to as the "One Thing Approach" (OTA)) [31,40]. In the OTA vision, development steps are directed by enhancing the model with various forms of constraints in languages or notations that are oriented to the concerns of different stakeholders. The One Thing is considered "the single source of truth" and every other artifact (including executable implementations) is generated from that source.

Although our illustration does not capture every aspect of OTA, nor does it agree philosophically on every point, it does align on many key aspects. The artifacts illustrate end-to-end development as supported by the HAMR [15] model-driven development tool chain. Regarding the central theme of OTA, our illustration uses the AADL[1] modeling language to define a system's architecture. The system architecture is the "single source of truth", supporting visualization, analysis, code generation, and verification. Regarding OTA purpose-specific languages, our models integrate specifications in various purpose-specific languages, including specifications of hazard analysis, behavioral contracts, and timing constraints. The purpose-specific languages are presented using AADL's *property sets* and *annex languages* (the AADL annex mechanism allows the base modeling language to be extended with additional language constructs supported by accompanying modeling tool plug-ins). Regarding OTA's generation of artifacts from the single source of truth, HAMR generates real-time task skeletons, accompanying formal software contracts to support automated code-level verification of application logic, and infrastructure for automated property-based unit and system testing deployed in continuous integration environments. Regarding OTA's emphasis on practical relevance, HAMR generates deployments for the Java Virtual Machine, Linux, and the formally verified seL4 microkernel. In particular, the seL4 deployments are currently the key capability utilized in our industrial collaborations.[2]

This paper presents the goals and features for the Isolette artifact collection (Sect. 2) and summarizes the current publicly available artifacts (Sect. 3). Sections 4–11 present a high-level walkthrough of the artifacts. Section 12 provides a

---

[1] The artifacts also include a version of system models in SysMLv2, as the AADL community is currently transitioning AADL concepts into SysMLv2 libraries to support future work within the AADL community.

[2] These collaborations including teaming with Collins Aerospace and Galois on a number of US defense-related projects, including projects funded by DARPA, US Army, US Airforce, and US Department of Homeland Security.

brief Sect. 13 describes supporting pedagogical material, and Sect. 14 concludes and indicates possible future work. The complete artifacts and supporting teaching material are available on the Isolette artifacts website [38]. For future work, we recognize that the current artifacts provide only a baseline and framing into which many other interesting techniques might be integrated and illustrated.

We gratefully acknowledge the work of the original authors of the Isolette system description and requirements – David Lempia and Steven Miller – from Rockwell Collins (now Collins Aerospace) from which the artifacts presented here derive.

2 Pedagogical Goals and Features

We adopted the Isolette example for illustrating end-to-end use of formal methods in embedded systems because it has a number of desirable features for this purpose.

Large enough in scope and complexity to exhibit challenging aspects of realistic embedded system development: The example has non-trivial modal behavior implemented using six real-time tasks and an independent operator interface. It has interesting functional and non-functional properties including both timing and requirements for subsystem *independence*.

Small enough in scope and complexity to enable easy in-class explanations of the system and associated development and safety process across the entire development cycle: In our high-assurance systems course, the example is used in class to present many different topics across the development process and to support weekly homework assignments. Students then apply these concepts in the context of larger semester-long projects such as a medical device infusion pump [20, 39] or a nuclear power shutdown systems [14, 37].

Illustrates iterative refinement steps associated with realistic system development in which trade-offs and tensions between between costs, safety, and security are considered: As an example, following hazard analysis and cost considerations originally presented in the REMH, an initial simplistic design of the system is refined into two independent subsystems: a control system and a safety system. Further refinements including adding sensor redundancy with voting logic, network interfaces, and security features are introduced as student assignments.

Interesting interactions between the system and environment including sensing and actuation of physical properties as well as interactions with human operators and organizational governance policies: In addition to temperature sensing and air heating actuation, it includes system interactions with a care giver (nurse) as well as constraints associated with health care workflows.

Provides a compelling setting for introducing hazard analyses and risk management concepts within a compressed time frame in a classroom setting: The example has a few simple control loops (both automated and operator driven) to illustrate concepts related to STPA-based hazard analysis [28] as well as communication and hardware failure possibilities that enable FMEA and FTA hazard analyses [11] to be illustrated.

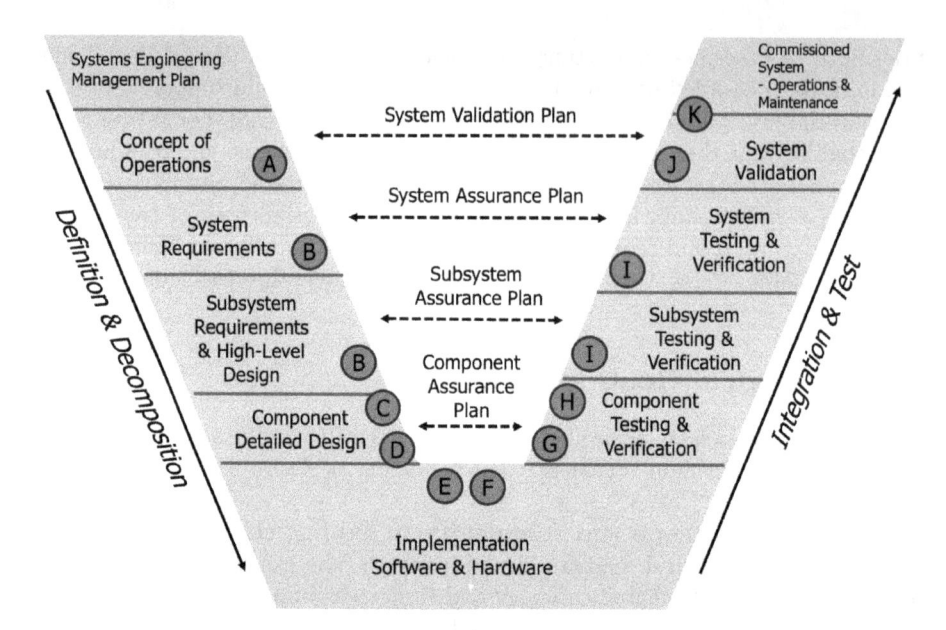

Fig. 1. Development Process Overview and Artifacts

Aligned with marketed infant incubator products: This enables students to trace the concepts from the classroom example to features of real products appearing in public product specifications, use cases, and documented workflow support.

From a regulated domain, enabling a direct and uncontrived presentation of relevant regulatory processes, industry development, and safety/security standards that form the basis of conformity assessment: The accompanying course material includes discussions of US FDA medical device regulatory submission processes as well as overviews of key international medical device standards (e.g., ISO 14971, IEC 62304).

Amenable to a variety of possible extensions of system features as well as development and assurance techniques that can form the basis of course or longer-term research projects: Example extensions include incorporating different types of temperature sensors (inspired by actual incubator products), reporting/logging/control via network interfaces, authentication/authorization of system operators.

3 Artifact Overview

Figure 1 shows an idealized development process and points at which the artifacts occur within that process.

- **Operational Concepts/Use Cases:** (Artifact A) Sect. 4 describes how operational concepts (system use cases presented in the style of Cockburn

[9]) are presented in the REMH to support system scoping, requirements elicitation, and initial system design. We supplement the REMH presentation with formalizations of the use cases in the jUCMNav use case modeling tool [1].
- **Requirements:** (Artifact B) Sect. 5 overviews of heart of the content inherited from the REMH – system and component natural language requirements that are subsequently refined to other artifacts including formal specifications and formal architecture models in subsequent sections.
- **System/Component Models:** (Artifact C) Sect. 6 provides excerpts of the Isolette AADL models (refined from informal designs) that we will use to illustrate code generation, application code development, and integrated contracts in subsequent sections.
- **Model Behavioral Specifications:** (Artifact D) Sect. 7 provides excerpts of model-level GUMBO requirements (refined from requirements) that form the basis of auto-generation of code-level verification contracts for verification and property-based testing.
- **Thread component code APIs and integrated contracts and Application Code Development:** (Artifacts E and F) Sect. 8 provides excerpts of HAMR-generated thread component skeletons and port communication APIs (with code contracts derived from GUMBO model-level contracts). Developers fill in these code skeletons with application logic. Subsequent sections show how automated property-based testing and verification demonstrates that the developer-supplied application code conforms to these contracts.
- **Automated Property-based Unit Testing for Component Implementations:** (Artifact G) Sect. 9 overviews HAMR's auto-generated infrastructure for manual and automated property-based unit testing in the GUMBOX framework. A key element of this includes auto-generation of test oracles from GUMBO contracts.
- **Automated Verification for Component Implementations:** (Artifact H) Sect. 10 overviews how developer-supplied component application code can be automatically verified to conform to HAMR-generated code-level contracts derived from model-level GUMBO contracts.
- **System Testing, Simulation, and Runtime Verification:** (Artifact I,J,K) Sect. 11 overviews HAMR's JVM-based capabilities for system testing, simulation, and runtime monitoring.

From these artifacts, the non-formalized use cases and requirements are from the REMH, and the rest of the artifacts have been developed in our course materials and research projects. In additional AADL Isolette models, we provide SysMLv2 models based on the emerging support for SysMLv2 in HAMR. The code-level artifacts and system implementations are currently developed using Slang [35] – a high-integrity subset of Scala. Slang includes an expressive contract language, and the companion Logika symbolic-execution based verifier [36] is used to verify code conformance to contracts and to also support model-level contract reasoning. Slang can be transpiled to high-quality C code that is suited for embedded systems. This gives us the ability, for example, to verify code-to-contract conformance in Slang/Logika, transpile Slang to C, compile the C code

Primary Actor: Thermostat

Precondition:

- The Isolette and Thermostat are turned on
- The Current Temperature is within the Alarm Temperature Range
- The Alarm is off

Postcondition:

- The Isolette and Thermostat are turned on
- The Current Temperature is within the Desired Temperature Range
- The Alarm is off

Main Success Scenario:

1. Current Temperature falls below or rises above the Alarm Temperature Range
2. Thermostat activates the Alarm (A.5.2.3)
3. Nurse responds to the Alarm and sees that the Display Temperature is in the Alarm Temperature Range (A.5.1.1)
4. Nurse removes Infant from the Isolette
5. Nurse corrects the problem, e.g., closing an open door (alternate course 1)
6. Nurse waits until the Display Temperature is within the Desired Temperature Range (A.2.6 and A.5.1.1)
7. Nurse places Infant back in the Isolette

Fig. 2. Exception Case: Failure to Maintain Safe Temperature

using the CompCert verified compiler, and deploy a complete system on the verified seL4 microkernel. The artifacts provide an excellent opportunity for the comparison of formal methods techniques. For example, for code-level techniques, other programming languages that have accompanying contract verification tools might be used to program and verify components. We give suggestions for a number of other exploratory comparisons in Sect. 14 and on the Isolette project web page.

4 Operational Concepts

The REMH requirements engineering process begins with building out content for a *concept of operations*. In addition to identifying stakeholders and concerns, specifying system scope, environment identities, and providing a system synopsis, the content includes use cases for both normal and exceptional situations.

Use cases are presented in a textual style advocated by Cockburn [9]. Figure 2 presents an example of this use case format for scenarios in which a visual and audible alarm is generated on the Isolette Operator Interface. The REMH advocates (a) writing use cases as part of the requirements elicitation phase, and (b)

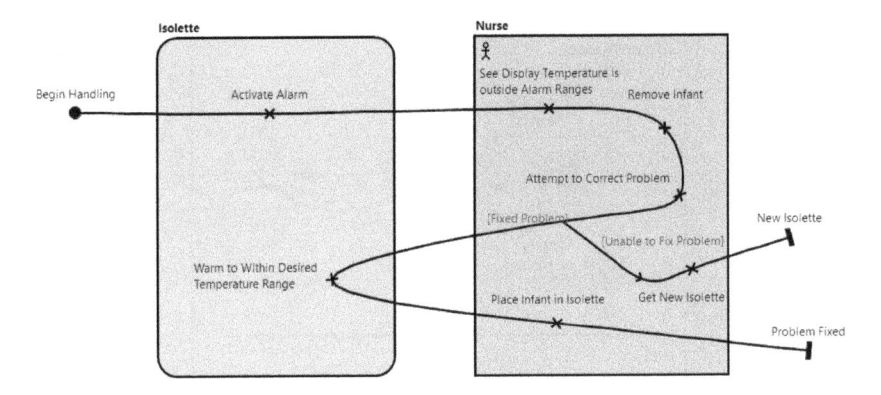

Fig. 3. jUCMNav Rendering of Exception Case: Failure to Maintain Safe Temperature

analyzing the use case actions to determine the main functions/operations of the system for which requirements will be written. In our accompanying pedagogical material, we note the connection to *user stories* emphasized, e.g., in Agile Development literature. Use cases are also identified as an example of an important *informal* artifact that can be subsequently (partially) formalized and leveraged in formal-methods based analysis, testing, simulation, and validation.

As an example of a partial but systematic formalization, we have rendered the use cases as *use case maps* in the jUCMNav tool [1,2]. As an example, Fig. 3 shows the use case map representation of the Fig. 2 use case. The jUCMNav tool allows simple formal constraints to be added to a use case and provides basic simulation capabilities. Subsequently, students use the formalization as a basis for writing system tests and designing validation activities. There are many opportunities to include additional semi-formal artifacts based on the use cases.

In the accompanying pedagogical material, we describe how documented use cases also support system test case design and validation. This is a theme emphasized by Margaria et al. for telecom systems [33] in which interactions between an environment (containing both human and machine elements) are incrementally formalized in a graphical language and then used to support model checking and system test automation.

5 Requirements

Following the presentation of uses cases, the FAA REMH presents natural language requirements for the Isolette. The requirements include environmental assumptions, system requirements, and component/function requirements.

While technical requirements typically aim to be implementation independent, it is often necessary to include some element of design in order to make reference to system inputs/outputs and to refine and allocate requirements to subsystems. The REMH provides an initial design in which the thermostat is

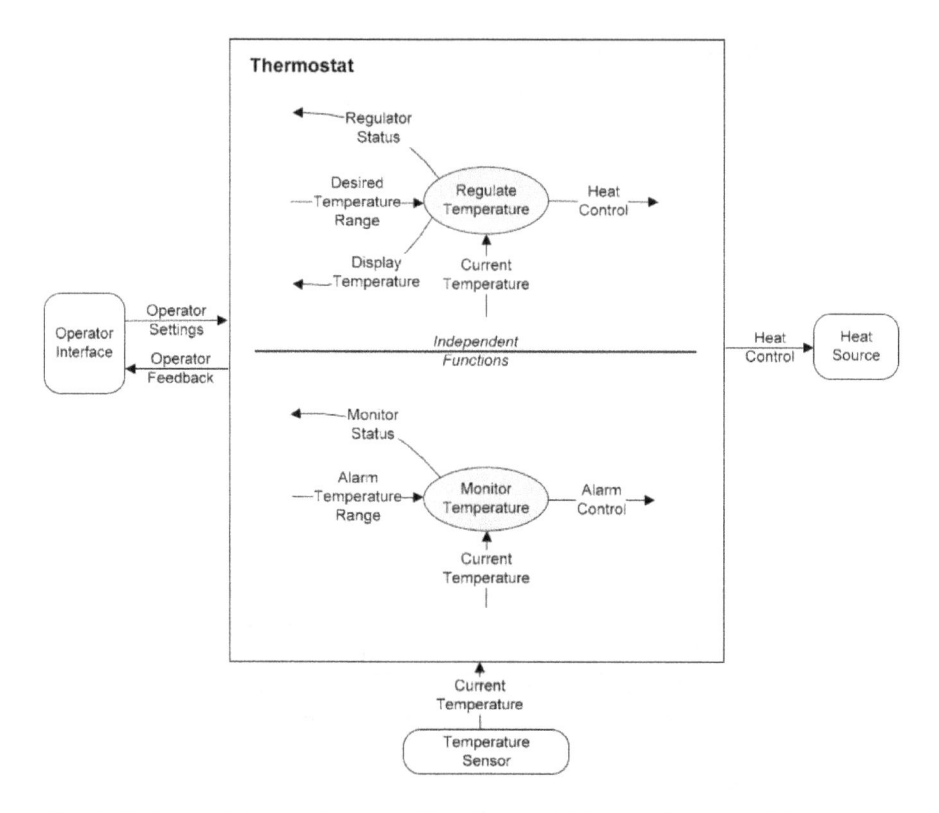

Fig. 4. Isolette - Informal Design of Regulate and Monitor Functional Separation

separated into Regulate and Monitor functions. These initial designs are stated informally in the REMH. In the HAMR vision for model-based development, initial designs are captured as abstract AADL models ("abstract" in the sense that some details needed for analysis and code generation may be omitted). Such initial design models are subsequently refined to the detailed models illustrated in Sect. 6.

Figure 4 illustrates how the REMH authors indicate their intent to have independent subsystems for the Regulate and Monitor functions. *Independence* of the subsystems forms part of the safety assurance argument for the system: if the Regulate subsystem fails, the Monitor subsystem should continue to function and notify the Nurse of a failure of the Isolette to achieve its safety function. Being able to capture such independence objectives is a key goal of AADL. Further, for software elements, it is a key goal of HAMR to be able to automatically generate seL4 kernel configuration information and appropriate scheduling to achieve spatial and temporal separation needed for partitioning (independence) of software components.

Figures 5 shows the REMH informal design of the Regulate subsystem. The REMH design aims to indicate the primary functions of each subsystem and the

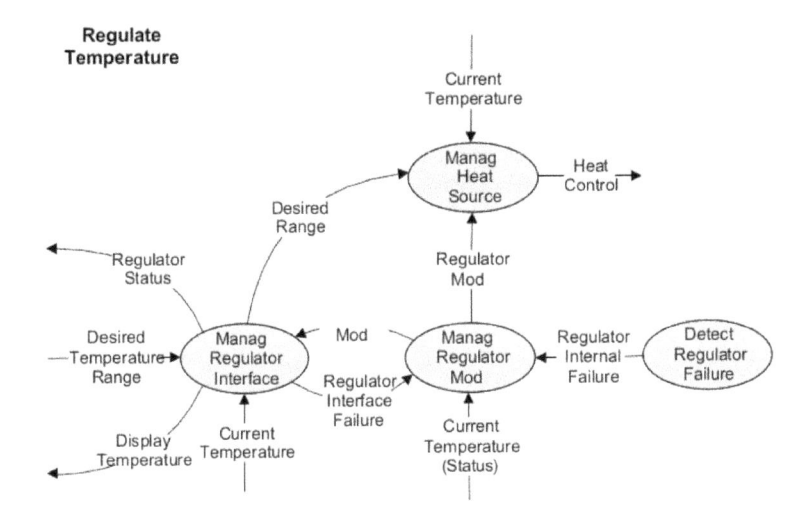

Fig. 5. Isolette - Informal Design of Regulate functions and data flows

data flows between them. This is then used to illustrate how system requirements need to be decomposed and allocated to functions/components. In the HAMR methodology, an abstract model representing the initial subsystem structure of Fig. 4 would be refined to abstract models representing the design in Figs. 5 with a similar modeling of the Monitor subsystem.

Once subsystems and components are indicated in the design, requirements can be stated at the component level. For example, the requirements for the Manage Heat Source component (which turns the Heat Source on and off to maintain the Current Temperature of the Isolette within the Desired Temperature Range) are given in Fig. 6. In total there are approximately 35 such requirements for the components in the Isolette thermostat subsystem.

Collectively, the REMH methodology illustration using the Isolette system provides excellent opportunities for class room exercises for data modeling, specification of environment constraints and environment interactions, real-time constraints, and behavior constraints. We will illustrate how the requirements of Fig. 6 can be rendered as GUMBO contracts (behavior constraints) in Sect. 7.

6 Models

In the next development steps of the Isolette artifacts, the initial abstract designs (whether abstract models in AADL or informally drawn) are refined into an AADL model that is complete enough for code generation. When aligning with the OTA concepts, AADL can be understood as a domain-specific language for specifying the software and hardware architecture of real-time embedded systems.

Figure 7 presents the AADL graphical view of the software thread components in the Regulate (controller) and Monitor (safety) subsystems as might be

- **REQ-MHS-1**: If the Regulator Mode is INIT, the Heat Control shall be set to Off.
  Rationale: A regulator that is initializing cannot regulate the Current Temperature of the Isolette and the Heat Control should be turned off.
- **REQ-MHS-2**: If the Regulator Mode is NORMAL and the Current Temperature is less than the Lower Desired Temperature, the Heat Control shall be set to On.
- **REQ-MHS-3**: If the Regulator Mode is NORMAL and the Current Temperature is greater than the Upper Desired Temperature, the Heat Control shall be set to Off.
- **REQ-MHS-4**: If the Regulator Mode is NORMAL and the Current Temperature is greater than or equal to the Lower Desired Temperature and less than or equal to the Upper Desired Temperature, the value of the Heat Control shall not be changed.
  Rationale: When the Isolette is warming towards the Upper Desired Temperature, the Heat Source should be left on until the Upper Desired Temperature is reached. In a similar fashion, if the Isolette is cooling towards the Lower Desired Temperature, the Heat Source should be left off until the Lower Desired Temperature is reached.
- **REQ-MHS-5**: If the Regulator Mode is FAILED, the Heat Control shall be set to Off. *Rationale*: In failed mode, the regulator cannot regulate the Current Temperature of the Isolette and the Heat Control should be turned off.

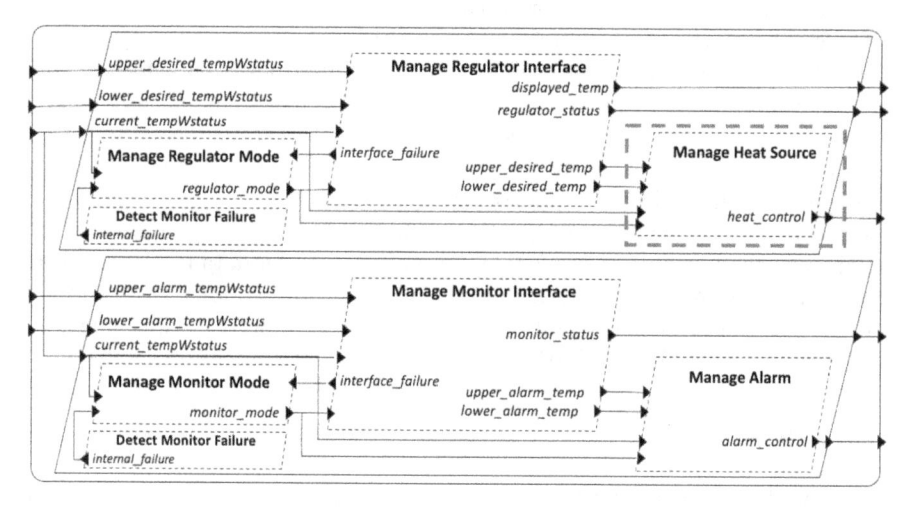

Fig. 6. REMH Component Requirements for Manage Heat Source

Fig. 7. Isolette - AADL Graphical View of Regulate and Monitor Subsystems

developed from the informal designs such as in Figs. 4 and 5. We use the Manage Heat Source (MHS) thread to illustrate framework concepts in the following discussions.

The iconography in this figure illustrates AADL's depiction of subsystems (the outer rounded corner rectangle), processes (the two solid line parallelograms), and threads (the multiple dashed line parallelograms). In the system, communication between components is realized via AADL *data ports* (represented by solid triangles on component boundaries) – unbuffered data cells. The use of connected thread/task components with well-defined interfaces is similar in spirit to the use of Service-Independent Building Blocks (SIBs) in the work of Margaria and colleagues [30]. A key insight is that the abstraction level of both AADL threads and SIBs is low enough to describe the key computation units in the system (and to support code generation) while high enough to support model checking and other forms of analysis. System definition via SIBs was also very well suited to graphical visualizations of not only system structure, but system simulations – allowing both tasking steps and relationships between tasks (leading to system topology) to be easily captured [42]. AADL's presentation of system structure is attractive for similar reasons.

```
1   thread Manage_Heat_Source
2     features
3       current_tempWstatus: in data port TempWstatus.impl;
4       lower_desired_temp: in data port Temp.impl;
5       upper_desired_temp: in data port Temp.impl;
6       regulator_mode: in data port Regulator_Mode;
7       heat_control: out data port On_Off;
8     properties
9       Dispatch_Protocol => Periodic;
10      Period => 1000ms;
11  end Manage_Heat_Source;
```

Listing 1.1. AADL specification for Manage Heat Source thread component

Listing 1.1 provides the AADL textual view of the MHS thread interface, including component ports (lines 2–7) and thread properties (lines 8–10). Excerpts of the HAMR-generated Slang thread skeleton for this thread are illustrated in Sect. 8 Listing 1.3.

7 Model-Level Behavioral Specifications

A key feature of the OTA is the emphasis on developers including "constraint-based guidance". "Application constraints are formulated and continuously validated at the meta level, the development level, and at runtime." This enables a CI/CD pipeline to "connect the meta- modeling level with the production level", and to "automatically checks all constraints, ensuring that violating systems do not reach the production platform." [40, Section 2.3]. Similar concepts appear in HAMR model-driven development. Using AADL property sets and annexes, a variety of forms of properties including behavioral constraints, timing constraints, resource utilization objectives, can also be added by developers to express their intent for both the functional and non-functional properties of the system. These constraints are then enforced via subsequent code generation, testing, verification, and run-time monitoring.

```
thread Manage_Heat_Source
  features
    current_tempWstatus: in data port TempWstatus.impl;
    lower_desired_temp: in data port Temp.impl;
    upper_desired_temp: in data port Temp.impl;
    regulator_mode: in data port Regulator_Mode;
    heat_control: out data port On_Off;
  properties
    Dispatch_Protocol => Periodic;
    Period => 1000ms;
  -- ===========================================================
  --  GUMBO contracts added to Manage Heat Source AADL Componenent Type
  --    to specify specification relevant local state and
  --    input / output behavior of the component.
  -- ===========================================================
  annex GUMBO {**
    state
      lastCmd: On_Off;

    initialize
      guarantee REQ_MHS_1 "If the Regulator Mode is
        |INIT, the Heat Control shall be set to Off":
        heat_control == On_Off.Off
        & lastCmd == heat_control;

    compute
      assume lower_is_less_than_upper_temp:
        lower_desired_temp.value < upper_desired_temp.value;
      guarantee lastCmd
        "Set lastCmd to value of output port":
        lastCmd == heat_control;

      cases
        case REQ_MHS_1
          "If the Reg Mode is INIT, the Heat Control shall be set to Off.":
          assume regulator_mode == Regulator_Mode.Init_Regulator_Mode;
          guarantee heat_control == On_Off.Off;
        case REQ_MHS_2
          "If the Reg Mode is NORMAL and the Current Tempe is less than the
            |Lower Desired Temp, the Heat Control shall be set to On.":
          assume regulator_mode == Regulator_Mode.Normal_Regulator_Mode
            & current_tempWstatus.value < lower_desired_temp.value;
          guarantee heat_control == On_Off.Onn;
        case REQ_MHS_3
          "If the Reg Mode is NORMAL and the Current Temp is greater than
            |the Upper Desired Temp, the Heat Control shall be set to Off.":
          assume regulator_mode == Regulator_Mode.Normal_Regulator_Mode
            & current_tempWstatus.value > upper_desired_temp.value;
          guarantee heat_control == On_Off.Off;
        case REQ_MHS_4
          "If the Reg Mode is NORMAL and the Current Temp is greater than or
            |equal to Lower Desired Temp and less than or equal to Upper
            |Desired Temp, the Heat Control value shall not be changed.":
          assume regulator_mode == Regulator_Mode.Normal_Regulator_Mode
            & current_tempWstatus.value >= lower_desired_temp.value
            & current_tempWstatus.value <= upper_desired_temp.value;
          guarantee heat_control == In(lastCmd);
        case REQ_MHS_5
          "If the Reg Mode is FAILED, the Heat Control shall be set to Off.":
          assume regulator_mode == Regulator_Mode.Failed_Regulator_Mode;
          guarantee heat_control == On_Off.Off;
  **};
end Manage_Heat_Source;
```

Listing 1.2. AADL specification for Manage Heat Source thread component

As an example, Sect. 6 provided in Listing 1.1 is the AADL textual definition of the MHS thread. Listing 1.2 illustrates how the developer can add behavioral constraint properties to the AADL type using the GUMBO contract language (implemented using AADL's annex mechanism). Lines 16–62 provide the GUMBO behavioral contract for the component. Like other contract languages (e.g., the `state` declarations in SPARK Ada), GUMBO contracts include declarations of local state that are relevant to the contract-specified behavior (lines 17–18). The AADL standard dictates that thread code should be structured as "entry point" methods that will be invoked by the underlying scheduling framework. GUMBO provides dedicated contracts for each thread's: (a) *initialize* entry point that is executed once in the system's initialization phase, and (b) the *compute* entry point that is executed repeatedly (either event-triggered for sporadic components or time-triggered for periodic components) during system execution. Compute entry point contracts can take multiple forms. For sporadic components, contracts clauses can be organized in sections that specify component behavior on the arrival of specific events. For periodic components (as in the MHS thread), lines 27–28 provide general pre-conditions (**assume** clauses) and post-conditions (**guarantee** clauses) which apply to every dispatch, and these can be extended with contract **cases** (e.g., as in JML [8]). A contract case applies when its **assume** clause is satisfied in the pre-state, and the associated **guarantee** clause must hold in the post-state.

The GUMBO contract language includes a number of features for specifying AADL behavioral properties (see [21] for an overview).

8 Component Development with Embedded Contracts

HAMR generates code from AADL models for multiple execution platforms [15]. The generated code includes threading, port communication, and scheduling infrastructure code that conforms to AADL run-time semantics as well as application code skeletons that engineers fill in to complete the behavior of the system.

In this section (based on the presentation in [17,18]), we illustrate how HAMR generates code skeletons in Slang and embedded contracts for Logika. One of the significant design aspects of GUMBO involves the combining and arranging of the many different forms of model-level contracts (including data invariants, integration constraints, entry point contracts, etc.) into code-level contracts appropriate for code verification or testing tools. The GUMBO contracts are automatically woven into the generated code base and appear as contracts on Slang methods and datatype declarations.

```
 1  def timeTriggered(api: Manage_Heat_Source_impl_Operational_Api): Unit = {
 2    // -- Auto-generated contract (excerpts) --
 3    Contract(
 4      Requires(
 5        // BEGIN COMPUTE REQUIRES timeTriggered
 6        //   assume lower_is_less_than_upper_temp
 7        api.lower_desired_temp.value < api.upper_desired_temp.value
 8        // END COMPUTE REQUIRES timeTriggered ),
 9      Modifies(api,lastCmd),
10      Ensures(
11        // BEGIN COMPUTE ENSURES timeTriggered
12        //   guarantee lastCmd
13        //   Set lastCmd to value of output port
14        lastCmd == api.heat_control,
15        // (...other aspect elided...)
16        // case REQ_MHS_2
17        //     If the Regulator Mode is NORMAL and the
18        //     Current Temperature is less than the
19        //     Lower Desired Temperature, the Heat
20        //     Control shall be set to On.
21        (api.regulator_mode == Regulator_Mode.Normal_Regulator_Mode &
22           api.current_tempWstatus.value < api.lower_desired_temp.value)
23           -->: (api.heat_control == On_Off.Onn),
24        // (...other aspects elided)
25        // END COMPUTE ENSURES timeTriggered
26      ))
27    // -- Developer-supplied application code here --
28    ...
```

Listing 1.3. Manage Heat Source in Slang: HAMR generated code and contracts (excerpts)

For example, for the MHS thread interface and contracts declared in Listings 1.1 and 1.2 HAMR will generate the Slang application code skeleton and Logika contract shown Listing 1.3. When coding the application logic for the thread, the developer will supply code for the timeTriggered() method, which will be invoked periodically (according to the model-declared Period property) by the underlying scheduling framework. Lines 3–26 show the HAMR auto-generated code-level contract for method The general **assume** clause in the GUMBO **compute** block (Listing 1.2, line 27) is translated to a pre-condition in the code-level Requires(..) clause (line 7), and the general **guarantee** clause (Listing 1.2, line 29) is translated to a post-condition in the code-level Ensures(..) clause (lines 14).

Note that the translation provides traceability information by embedding GUMBO clause descriptions and identifiers in the code-level contracts. In addition, HAMR includes delimiters such as those at lines 11 and 25 of auto-generated contracts. If GUMBO contracts are updated in the AADL model, HAMR can regenerate updated contracts into the same position in the code (by parsing the file to locate the delimiters), and thus can keep the code-level contracts in sync with the model contracts without clobbering the developer's application code.

```
 1  def timeTriggered(api: Manage_Heat_Source_impl_Operational_Api): Unit = {
 2    // -- Auto-generated contract (excerpts shown in listing above) --
 3    Contract(
 4      ...
 5    )
 6    // -- Developer-supplied application code --
 7    val lower = api.get_lower_desired_temp().get
 8    val upper = api.get_upper_desired_temp().get
 9    val regulator_mode = api.get_regulator_mode().get
10    val currentTemp = api.get_current_tempWstatus().get
11
12    var currentCmd = lastCmd
13    regulator_mode match {
14      case Regulator_Mode.Init_Regulator_Mode =>
15        currentCmd = On_Off.Off
16      case Regulator_Mode.Normal_Regulator_Mode =>
17        if (currentTemp.value > upper.value) {
18          currentCmd = On_Off.Off
19        } else if (currentTemp.value < lower.value) {
20          currentCmd = On_Off.Onn }
21      case Regulator_Mode.Failed_Regulator_Mode =>
22        currentCmd = On_Off.Off }
23    api.put_heat_control(currentCmd)
24    lastCmd = currentCmd }
```

Listing 1.4. Manage Heat Source in Slang: developer supplied application code.

Given the auto-generated thread compute entry point skeleton, the developer codes the application logic (e.g., for the MHS thread, lines 7–24 for the **timeTriggered** method in Listing 1.4).

The concept of realizing the definition and behavior for AADL components in HAMR (the definition as model-based, and the behavior as code-based) is similar to the approach for *Native SIBs* in Margaria et al.'s work [41] For example (following the summary in [40, Section 8.1]), in the Dime Process Model, Native SIBs are defined with a textual language, which is used to specify the structure of a SIB including its name, input ports, and output ports (similar to the AADL textual view for a thread type). The types of these ports can be one of the built-in primitive types or a referenced data type defined in a Data Model (which is almost identical to the HAMR AADL approach). The execution behavior of a Native SIB is specified by referencing a Java method that contains the actual implementation (analogous to the HAMR association of the Slang Compute Entry Point method (e.g., the **timeTriggered** method of Listing 1.4)). The motivation for this approach is again very similar between the SIB approach and AADL HAMR. As stated in [40, Section 8.1], "[the Native SIBs] help to maintain a high level of abstraction, avoiding the need to define low-level operations with high-level modeling languages when programming languages are better suited for the job. On the other hand, they facilitate service orientation at the behavioral level and enable the reuse of existing service implementations that are not based on models within the current workspace. Since the actual service implementation is not visible at the modeling level, even complex, ideally self-contained services can be integrated and used by users without programming skills." While the HAMR strategy does not necessarily aim to totally avoid programming, the idea of integrating abstract component interfaces by connecting component ports, is the same.

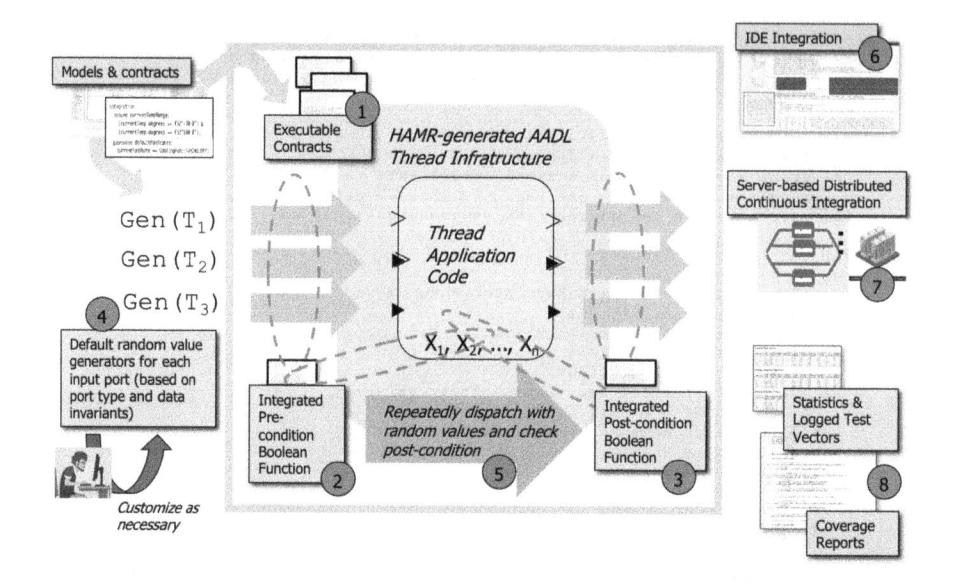

Fig. 8. GUMBO-X Property-Based Testing Framework

9 Component Testing

In recent years, there have been a number of advances in the formal methods community related to deriving unit tests for formal contracts. The Isolette artifacts have a significant emphasis on contract-based unit testing. In this section, we give a brief overview of the key capabilites (based on the discussion in [17,18], which the reader can consult for more details). In the HAMR context, "unit" corresponds to "thread component", as thread components form the "leaf nodes" of the architecture. Tests are formally grounded by generating test oracles (and a variety of forms of test automation) from AADL models and GUMBO thread component contracts. Code-level test oracles are essentially executable versions of GUMBO model-level contracts (therefore, we often refer to them as "executable contracts" or GUMBOX contracts, where "X" stands for "eXecutable"). Code-level contracts used in SMT-based verification and executable contracts are derived from exactly the same model-level GUMBO contracts, and both contract versions enforce exactly the same semantics. Thus, the developer can switch seamlessly from assurance from testing to assurance from formal verification for the same contracts/properties. Moreover, outcomes of testing and verification support the same assurance case claims (e.g., those associated with specified behavior of a particular component), and moving from testing to verification can be seen as increasing the confidence in the relevant claims.

Figure 8 graphically outlines the main elements of the GUMBOX automated property-based testing framework. The red markers indicate the different categories of artifacts and features of the framework. From AADL-based GUMBO contracts, HAMR generates executable versions of each GUMBO contract clause (called GUMBOX contracts) (A1) represented as a Slang side-effect free boolean function that takes as parameters thread port and local variable values. These contracts are emitted into a test infrastructure library separate from application code so they can easily be automatically re-generated without interfering with application code. HAMR automatically generates random value generators (A4) for each component input port and GUMBO-declared local state variable. For each user type specified in AADL's Data Modeling annex, HAMR will automatically generate an initial random value generator based on the type's structure. The goal is to get a serviceable generator for initial testing that the user can subsequently easily adapt to achieve more effective value generation and increased coverage. HAMR generates boolean-valued pre- and post- condition methods (A2,A3) for thread entry points that integrate all relevant contract clauses from data invariants, integration constraints, and entry point contracts to form the checks of the thread dispatch pre- and post-states implied by the GUMBO contract language semantics. HAMR generates test harnesses (A5) and unit tests that combine the above elements to: (a) generate vectors of random values for input ports and local variables, (b) discard test vectors that do not satisfy the generated pre-condition method and applicable invariants, (c) dispatch the thread application code, (d) retrieve output port and updated local variable values and then invoke the post condition method on (saved) input values and output values, and (e) provide a pass/fail result that is incorporated into the test reporting mechanism. The resulting test suite can be launched for a single thread or all threads in the system with a single button push in the IDE (A6).[3] HAMR generates deployment scripts for parallel/distributed execution on a family of multi-core servers (A7), enabling easy integration into a continuous integration framework. Finally, HAMR generates HTML reports (A8) of coverage statistics, source-code color-coded markups of statement/branch coverage, with integrated links to JSON representation of test vectors, etc.

In course material associated with the Isolette, students first learn to manually write unit tests for components, and different forms of code coverage are discussed. Then the capabilities of the full automated framework above are presented, along with information describing how the testing infrastructure is deployed in a continuous integration environment.

10   Component Verification

The GUMBO contract specifications illustrated in Sect. 7 are designed to enable translation of model contracts to code contracts when code is generated according to principles presented in the AADL standard (see [21] for a detailed discussion). To support this, we have extended HAMR code generation to generate Logika contracts in the Slang APIs and thread application component skeletons generated from HAMR.

---

[3] As with any testing/code-level formal method, I/O and interactions with physical devices or stateful services may need to be supported by manually crafted stubs.

Fig. 9. Logika verification of Manage Heat Source code-level contracts within the IntelliJ IDE.

Formal verification of the code is performed using Logika: the highly automated program verifier for Slang [29]. Slang's integrated contract language enables developers to formally specify method pre- and post-conditions, in line assertions, data type invariants, and global invariants for global states. In HAMR code generation for models with GUMBO contracts, these specifications are auto-generated for program artifacts related to the component interfaces and model-declared system datatypes. The developer can add additional contracts for local methods and data types not associated with interfaces. Logika verification of code conformance to contracts is performed compositionally and employs multiple back-end solvers in parallel, including Alt-Ergo [10], CVC4 [5], CVC5 [4], and Z3 [32]. Logika scalability is enhanced using incremental and parallel (distributable) verification algorithms. Verification results, developer-friendly feedback on verification results, and contract/proof editing are directly supported in the Sireum IVE – a customization of the popular IntelliJ IDE.

Figure 9 shows how the developer uses the Sireum IVE to develop, debug, and to verify that the code conforms to the model-derived contract using Logika (notice the contracts shown in Listing 1.3 translated into Slang via HAMR.) AADL's semantics for threading and port-manipulation ensure that thread implementations can be verified compositionally; abstractly, a thread's behavior is a function from its input port state and local variables to its output port state, with possibly updated local variables (see [19]).

In the teaching material associated with the Isolette, students are taught basic aspects of Logika verification using small examples, and then with the Manage Heat Source component as in Fig. 9. Then as exercises, they add contracts and perform verification for other components in the system.

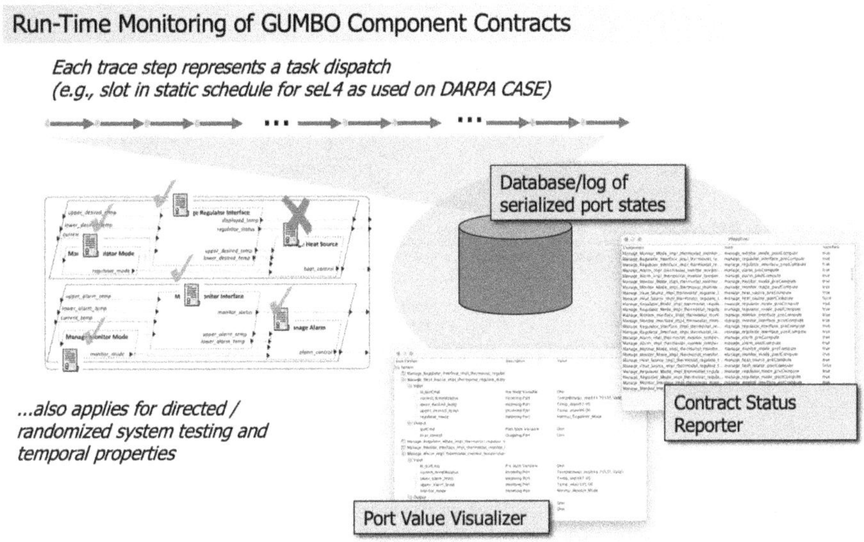

Fig. 10. HAMR Slang/JVM Simulation and Debugging Concepts

11 System Testing, Simulation, and Visualization

HAMR provides a variety of system testing, visualization, and debugging facilities for systems implemented with Slang and deployed on the JVM.

Figure 10 illustrates some key concepts of the simulation and run-time verification framework. At each slot in the static schedule, the values in the input ports and GUMBO-declared state variables of the to-be-executed thread are logged (serialized and stored in a database). After thread execution, the values of the output ports and GUMBO-declared state variables are logged. This logging can be activated during unit testing, system testing, simulation, and full execution. Logged values can be accessed dynamically (during activation) or retrieved from the database after execution completes.

These logged values can be leveraged in several ways. First, for controlled simulation and debugging, HAMR provides a UI that allows the developer to manually control stepping through thread activations in the static schedule. At each step the current values of all port states in the system can be viewed. Figure 10 illustrates a trace state in which the most recent values of the Manage Alarm thread input and output port values are being visualized.

During controlled simulation, system testing, and JVM-based execution, HAMR maintains a viewer reporting on the status of run-time verification of GUMBO contracts. Figure 10 illustrates this capability in a situation in which the Manage Heat Source post-condition has been violated. The figure also shows HAMR's ability to automatically generate a unit test for the component that illustrates the contract violation – by having the inputs of the unit test based on logged component input state whose execution led to the contract violation).

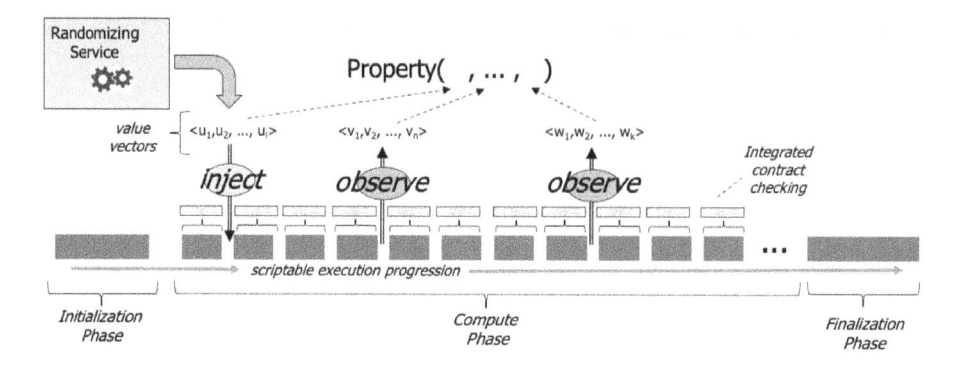

Fig. 11. HAMR System Testing Framework Concepts

More generally, HAMR can generate a unit *test suite* of unit tests for a collection (or all) components that have failing contracts. This greatly reduces the effort of developers to report and fix bugs.

For system testing, as described in [16], Fig. 11 presents the primary concepts of the framework. HAMR's infrastructure for static scheduling is extended with APIs that enable the advancing of execution to be controlled programmatically from test scripts – enabling the test engineer to move the system forward through primary phases of AADL run-time execution (e.g., the Initialization) or to step n scheduling slots, or m complete scheduling cycles (hyper-periods), etc. The scheduling control is aligned with the abstract concepts presented in the AADL standard, e.g., each schedule slot step involves a single execution of the AADL run-time service for dispatching a thread component and the dispatch executes the standard-specified thread *compute entry point*. This adherence to the abstract steps in the AADL computational model enables us to preserve the semantics of system properties and testing across deployments on different platforms and languages supported by the HAMR backends. The framework also provides support for making observations about a portion of the system's state. The engineer can declare different observations, where an observation specification includes a named set of ports whose queues/values are to be acquired in a "snapshot". A common example is the set of all output ports for a particular subsystem. For each such declaration, HAMR generates infrastructure for representing a vector of port values along with infrastructure for acquiring an observation vector. Interspersed with execution-stepping commands in the test script are calls to acquire observation vectors for possibly multiply-declared observation types. After all relevant observations have been acquired, code in the test script passes accumulated vectors to a boolean function representing a specific system property. In addition to system properties, the framework can be set to automatically check thread component pre- and post-conditions auto-generated from AADL-level GUMBO contracts.

Injections can also be declared using port set declarations similar to those for observations. A common example is the set of all input ports for a particular subsystem, or a set of ports communicating sensor values acquired from the system environment. In addition to auto-generating value vector types and infrastructure code to set ports to values from a vector, HAMR produces infrastructure code to generate a randomized vector, subject to engineer-configured constraints (e.g., range constraints on scalars). In the test script, these vectors can be acquired/pushed to the associated port set – giving the engineer the ability to force executions to states that are relevant for the property and to control the coverage associated with the tests. This facility enables engineers to flexibly control a variety of inputs to the system (or subsystem), and in many cases alleviates the need to create special-purpose stubs/mocks that generate values flowing into the unit under test.

To provide scalability and to support a continuous integration process, HAMR auto-generates infrastructure for deploying tests in a distributed fashion (e.g., using Jenkins).

12 Deployment

The Isolette repository includes artifacts for a continuous integration environment, and for final deployments for JVM, Linux, and seL4 microkernel. For Linux and seL4 deployments, Slang is transpiled to C. The generated C can optionally be compiled with the verified CompCert compiler.

While the current Isolette artifacts teaching material does not include extensive material on deployments, the availability of the material above gives the lecturer the opportunity to give overviews of CompCert and seL4 – both of which are represent some of the most signficant applications of formal methods within the last two decades.

13 Resources and Teaching Material

The Isolette website [38] provides a variety of pedagogical material including lecture slides, recorded lecture videos, guided written/video exercises, links to representative infant incubator product manuals, and relevant regulatory documents and standards.

- Lecture slides and video providing an overview of the Isolette system.
- Slides and lecture videos for eight lectures covering the NASA Requirements Engineering Management Handbook
- Slides and lecture videos for four lectures providing an overview of AADL and HAMR model-driven development.
- A set of written tutorial exercises and recorded video solution guides for basic aspects of HAMR development including creating AADL models, implementing HAMR systems using Slang, HAMR unit testing, and HAMR unit verification using Logika.
- Lecture slides for overviews of safety and risk management concepts in the medical device domain.

- Installation guides (written and videos) for HAMR and other supporting tools.

Teaching material for component implementation verification using Logika utilizes our accompanying teaching material for Logika [13] and contract-based verification of source code. Additional lectures provide an overview of safety-critical system development processes, certification concepts and challenges [23], and challenges is interoperable medical device risk management [22,24]. Also provided are suggested projects for extending the Isolette artifacts.

14 Conclusion

An overarching theme of the work of Tiziana Margaria and colleagues has been the use of lightweight and developer-friendly formal methods across the entire development process – ranging from system conception to system deployment (and even the monitoring of deployed systems). This holistic approach has had practical impacts in a number of application domains ranging from intelligent networks [6], business service modeling in hospital management [34], to product lines in the digital humanities [7]. With the Isolette artifacts, we have similarly tried to emphasize the importance of addressing the entire development processes, with an aim to understand how informal, semi-formal, and formal techniques can be effectively integrated.

The "One Thing Approach" is also key to the successes of Margaria et al. in that it provides a mechanism for *guiding/helping* developers by supplying appropriate purpose-specific abstractions while also *constraining/managing* development so that system elements can be subjected to formal analysis and also more effectively reused via clean composition. Our use of the AADL modeling language, with an accompanying formal semantics [12], and suite of purpose-specific annex languages and tools (e.g., [16,17,21]) also shares aspects of the OTA vision.

We see the current Isolette artifacts, not as a completed project, but rather a baseline that may help the community understand alternate perspectives on the OTA and can provide a starting point for others to evaluate rigorous development techniques within a complete system development context.

Our own priorities for expanding the Isolette artifacts include illustrating hazard analysis techniques in greater detail, utilizing AADL's timing properties and community-provided real-time scheduling tools to provide a more complete understanding of designing for real-time, and illustrating construction of an system assurance case. As part of our current participation with Collins Aerospace on the DARPA PROVERS project, we are (a) extending HAMR to generate Rust code that can be verified with the Verus [26] tool and (b) extending the HAMR backend to support the new seL4 microkit kernel configuration and programming framework, and (c) integrating HAMR into the Collins product group continuous integration platform and assurance dashboard. We plan to roll the publicly available artifacts that result into the Isolette artifacts repository. Taking further inspiration from the work of Margaria et al., we also see significant value in including product-line modeling techniques [25] and model-checking model-level specifications [3].

References

1. Amyot, D.: Jucmnav - eclipse plugin for the user requirements notation (2018). http://jucmnav.softwareengineering.ca/foswiki/ProjetSEG/WebHome
2. Amyot, D., Mussbacher, G.: User requirements notation: the first ten years, the next ten years (invited paper). J. Softw. **6**, 747–768 (2011). https://doi.org/10.4304/jsw.6.5.747-768
3. Bakera, M., Margaria, T., Renner, C., Steffen, B.: Tool-supported enhancement of diagnosis in model-driven verification. Innov. Syst. Softw. Eng. **5**, 211–228 (2009)
4. Barbosa, H., et al.: CVC5: a versatile and industrial-strength SMT solver. In: Fisman, D., Rosu, G. (eds.) Tools and Algorithms for the Construction and Analysis of Systems. TACAS 2022. LNCS, vol. 13243, pp. 415–442. Springer, Cham (2022). https://doi.org/10.1007/978-3-030-99524-9_24
5. Barrett, C., et al.: CVC4. In: Gopalakrishnan, G., Qadeer, S. (eds.) Computer Aided Verification. CAV 2011. LNCS, vol. 6806, pp. 171–177. Springer, Berlin, Heidelberg (2011). https://doi.org/10.1007/978-3-642-22110-1_14
6. Braun, V., Margaria, T., Steffen, B., Bruhns, F.: Service definition for intelligent networks: experience in a leading-edge technological project based on constraint techniques. In: Wallace, M. (ed.) Proceedings of the Third International Conference on the Practical Application of Constraint Technology, PACT 1997, Westminster Central Hall, London, UK, 23–25 April 1997, pp. 91–106. Practical Application Company Ltd. (1997)
7. Breathnach, C., Ibrahim, N.M., Clancy, S., Margaria, T.: Towards model checking product lines in the digital humanities: an application to historical data. In: ter Beek, M., Fantechi, A., Semini, L. (eds.) From Software Engineering to Formal Methods and Tools, and Back. LNCS, vol. 11865, pp. 338–364. Springer, Cham (2019). https://doi.org/10.1007/978-3-030-30985-5_20
8. Burdy, L., et al.: An overview of JML tools and applications. Int. J. Softw. Tools Technol. Transf. **7**(3), 212–232 (2005)
9. Cockburn, A.: Writing Effective Use Cases. Addison-Wesley, Boston, MA (2001)
10. Conchon, S., Coquereau, A., Iguernlala, M., Mebsout, A.: Alt-ergo 2.2. In: SMT Workshop: International Workshop on Satisfiability Modulo Theories (2018)
11. Ericson II, C.A.: Hazard Analysis Techniques for System Safety. John Wiley & Sons, Hoboken (2005)
12. Hallerstede, S., Hatcliff, J.: A mechanized semantics for component-based systems in the HAMR AADL runtime. In: Camara, J., Jongmans, S.S. (eds.) Formal Aspects of Component Software. FACS 2023. LNCS, vol. 14485, pp. 45–64. Springer, Cham (2024). https://doi.org/10.1007/978-3-031-52183-6_3
13. Hallerstede, S., Hatcliff, J., Robby: teaching with logika: conceiving and constructing correct software. In: Formal Methods Teaching Workshop (FMTEA 2024) (2024), to appear
14. HARDENS: high assurance rigorous digital engineering for nuclear safety (artifacts repository). https://github.com/GaloisInc/HARDENS
15. Hatcliff, J., Belt, J., Robby, Carpenter, T.: HAMR: an AADL multi-platform code generation toolset. In: Margaria, T., Steffen, B. (eds.) Leveraging Applications of Formal Methods, Verification and Validation. ISoLA 2021. LNCS, vol. 13036, pp. 274–295. Springer, Cham (2021). https://doi.org/10.1007/978-3-030-89159-6_18

16. Hatcliff, J., Belt, J., Robby, Hardin, D.: Integrated contract-based unit and system testing for component-based systems. In: Benz, N., Gopinath, D., Shi, N. (eds.) NASA Formal Methods. NFM 2024. LNCS, vol. 14627, pp. 406–426. Springer, Cham (2024). https://doi.org/10.1007/978-3-031-60698-4_25
17. Hatcliff, J., Belt, J., Robby, Legg, J., Stewart, D., Carpenter, T.: Automated property-based testing from AADL component contracts. In: Cimatti, A., Titolo, L. (eds.) Formal Methods for Industrial Critical Systems (2023)
18. Hatcliff, J., Belt, J., Robby, Legg, J., Stewart, D., Carpenter, T.: Automated property-based testing from AADL component contracts. Submitted for journal publication. (2024)
19. Hatcliff, J., Hugues, J., Stewart, D., Wrage, L.: Formalization of the AADL runtime services. In: Leveraging Applications of Formal Methods, Verification and Validation - 11th International Symposium on Leveraging Applications of Formal Methods, ISoLA 2022, Rhodes, Greece (2022)
20. Hatcliff, J., Larson, B.R., Carpenter, T., Jones, P.L., Zhang, Y., Jorgens, J.: The open PCA pump project: an exemplar open source medical device as a community resource. SIGBED Rev. **16**(2), 8–13 (2019)
21. Hatcliff, J., Stewart, D., Belt, J., Robby, Schwerdfeger, A.: An AADL contract language supporting integrated model- and code-level verification. In: Proceedings of the 2022 ACM Workshop on High Integrity Language Technology. HILT '22 (2022)
22. Hatcliff, J., Vasserman, E.Y., Carpenter, T., Whillock, R.: Challenges of distributed risk management for medical application platforms. In: 2018 IEEE Symposium on Product Compliance Engineering (ISPCE), pp. 1–14 (2018)
23. Hatcliff, J., Wassyng, A., Kelly, T., Comar, C., Jones, P.L.: Certifiably safe software-dependent systems: challenges and directions. In: Proceedings of the on Future of Software Engineering (ICSE FOSE), pp. 182–200 (2014). https://doi.org/10.1145/2593882.2593895
24. Hatcliff, J., Zhang, Y., Goldman, J.M.: Risk management objectives for distributed development of interoperable medical products. In: 2019 IEEE Symposium on Product Compliance Engineering (SPCE Austin), pp. 1–6 (2019)
25. Jörges, S., Lamprecht, A.L., Margaria, T., Schaefer, I., Steffen, B.: A constraint-based variability modeling framework. Int. J. Softw. Tools Technol. Transf. **14** (2012)
26. Lattuada, A., et al.: Verus: verifying Rust programs using linear ghost types. Proc. ACM Program. Lang. **7**(OOPSLA1), 286–315 (2023)
27. Lempia, D., Miller, S.: DOT/FAA/AR-08/32. Requirements engineering management handbook. Federal Aviation Administration (2009)
28. Leveson, N.G.: Engineering a Safer World: Systems Thinking Applied to Safety. Engineering Systems, The MIT Press, Cambridge (2012)
29. Sireum logika (2022). https://logika.sireum.org
30. Margaria, T., Meyer, D., Kubczak, C., Isberner, M., Steffen, B.: Synthesizing semantic web service compositions with jMosel and Golog. In: Bernstein, A., et al. (eds.) The Semantic Web - ISWC 2009. ISWC 2009. LNCS, vol. 5823, pp. 392–407. Springer, Berlin, Heidelberg (2009). https://doi.org/10.1007/978-3-642-04930-9_25
31. Margaria, T., Steffen, B.: Chapter i business process modelling in the jabc: the one-thing-approach. In: Handbook of Research on Business Process Modeling, January 2009

32. de Moura, L., Bjorner, N.: Z3: an efficient SMT solver. In: Ramakrishnan, C.R., Rehof, J. (eds.) Tools and Algorithms for the Construction and Analysis of Systems. TACAS 2008. LNCS, vol. 4963, pp. 337–340. Springer, Berlin, Heidelberg (2008). https://doi.org/10.1007/978-3-540-78800-3_24
33. Niese, O., Steffen, B., Margaria, T., Hagerer, A., Brune, G., Ide, H.D.: Library-based design and consistency checking of system-level industrial test cases. In: Fundamental Approaches to Software Engineering, pp. 233–248, April 2001
34. Rasche, C., Margaria, T., Floyd, B.D.: Service model innovation in hospitals: beyond expert organizations. In: Pfannstiel, M., Rasche, C. (eds.) Service Business Model Innovation in Healthcare and Hospital Management, pp. 1–20. Springer, Cham (2017). https://doi.org/10.1007/978-3-319-46412-1_1
35. Robby, Hatcliff, J.: Slang: the sireum programming language. In: Margaria, T., Steffen, B. (eds.) Leveraging Applications of Formal Methods, Verification and Validation. ISoLA 2021. LNCS, vol. 13036, pp. 253–273. Springer, Cham (2021). https://doi.org/10.1007/978-3-030-89159-6_17
36. Robby, Hatcliff, J., Belt, J.: Logika: the sireum verification framework. In: Formal Methods for Industrial Critical Systems (FMICS 2024) (2024)
37. SAnToS Laboratory: HAMR/HARDENS nuclear reactor trip system artifacts showcase (2024). https://github.com/santoslab/rts-showcase
38. SAnToS Laboratory: Isolette artifacts website – illustrating rigorous model-based development with integrated formal methods (2024). https://isolette.santoslab.org
39. SAnToS Laboratory: Open PCA Project website (2024). https://openpcapump.santoslab.org
40. Steffen, B., et al.: Language-driven engineering: an interdisciplinary software development paradigm (2024). (to appear)
41. Steffen, B., Margaria, T., Braun, V., Kalt, N.: Hierarchical service definition. Annu. Rev. Commun. **51**, 847–856 (1997)
42. Steffen, B., Margaria, T., Nagel, R., Jorges, S., Kubczak, C.: Model-driven development with the jABC. In: Bin, E., Ziv, A., Ur, S. (eds.) Hardware and Software, Verification and Testing. HVC 2006. LNCS, vol. 4383, pp. 92–108. Springer, Berlin, Heidelberg (2007). https://doi.org/10.1007/978-3-540-70889-6_7

A Case-Study on Structured Modeling with Internal Domain-Specific Languages

Steven Smyth[✉], Tim Tegeler, Daniel Busch, and Steve Boßelmann

Dortmund University, Dortmund, Germany
{steven.smyth,tim.tegeler,daniel2.busch,
steve.bosselmann}@tu-dortmund.de

Abstract. We present KTML, a Kotlin library for creating well-structured and type-safe HTML documents. KTML is entirely built within the Kotlin language set, highlighting Kotlin's suitability through language design choices to support internal DSLs. Internal DSLs are fully embedded in an existing ecosystem and can take full advantage of the host language's capabilities. Yet, they are designed for a single purpose, abstracting from otherwise cumbersome boilerplate code and other intricacies while simultaneously allowing the developer to use the tool stack they are familiar with. We exemplify KTML through the professional Tangle project, part of a conference management collection that generates different programme views during ongoing conferences.

1 Introduction

Internal DSLs have an advantage. They are fully embedded in an existing ecosystem and take full advantage of the host language and its tool stack. However, they are designed for a single purpose and abstract from otherwise cumbersome boilerplate code or other intricacies. While all programming languages provide abstractions that can be leveraged as DSL, not all languages are equally suitable as host languages. Kotlin, and similar languages for that matter, however provides a clean instantiation and expression syntax, which arguably makes the embedded DSL more readable.

KTML is a library for generating well-structured and type-safe HTML documents built in Kotlin. Unlike other HTML generation frameworks, KTML does not require a Document Object Model (DOM) to build an HTML tree. Because it is embedded in Kotlin, KTML's objects are created as usual, e.g., `Body()`. Hence, to create an HTML element, you just instantiate an object, called html in Kotlin. Unlike to other object-oriented language, the instantiation of objects does not require the new keyword, which reduces visual clutter. The main principle of KTML is the context-free creation of HTML trees and subtrees. All supported HTML elements can be created at any time in your applications' flow. While this enables the elegant construction of complex HTML trees, it also eases testing of KTML classes in an isolated environment. Secondly, leveraging

© The Author(s), under exclusive license to Springer Nature Switzerland AG 2025
M. Hinchey and B. Steffen (Eds.): Festschrift Tiziana Margaria, LNCS 15240, pp. 118–128, 2025.
https://doi.org/10.1007/978-3-031-73887-6_10

Kotlin's type system, KTML prevents the incorrect nesting of tags, e.g., nesting block elements into inline elements, such as `<p><div></div></p>`. Thirdly, KTML is deliberately only relying on plain object-oriented patterns, inspired by the book Elegant Objects [2].

```
import info.scce.ktml.impl.*

fun main() {
  print(
    Html(
      Head(
        Title(
          Text("Example")
        )
      ),
      Body(
        Text("Hello World!")
      )
    )
  )
}
```

(a) *Hello World!* in Kotlin using KTML

```
<!DOCTYPE html>
<html lang="en">
  <head>
    <title>Example</title>
  </head>
  <body>Hello World!</body>
</html>
```

(b) The KTML *Hello World!* output

Fig. 1. KTML *Hello World!* example

Tiziana's approach to teaching modeling is unique. As the initiator of the Immersive Software Engineering course at the Limerick University she has ensured that students learn to model abstract relationships. DSLs and extreme MDD [6] play an important role to using the right tools for a job, which becomes even more important when dealing with users from non-CS domains. Under her guidance, several modeling tools and analyses have been developed to help a wider audience, such as smart manufacturing [3], cancer research [1], and the analysis of historical documents [4]. Furthermore, she continuously transfers this research knowledge to the industry [5]. In this context, we were fortunate to spend some time in Ireland teaching about DevOps, compilers and modeling environments [9–12]. In our humble opinion, more experts should reach out to their colleagues in other fields to discuss and develop tools together that will take us all forward. Thank you very much, Tiziana.

In Sect. 2, we present KTML, an internal DSL implemented as Kotlin library for creating type-safe HTML documents. The section describes the idea behind KTML, how to use it in Kotlin, and how to extend the library with new and more complex constructs. Section 3 then presents a real-world case-study using KTML. The real-life project Tangle is part of a conference management collection that generates conference programmes as a service. We discuss related work in Sect. 4 and conclude in Sect. 5.

```
1 class Html(
2    private val head: HeadInterface,
3    private val body: BodyInterface,
4 ) : AbstractTagBuilder<TagInterface>(), HtmlInterface {
5    override fun build(): TagInterface {
6      return TagSequence(
7        Doctype(),
8        Tag(
9          "html",
10          TagSequence(
11            head,
12            body
13          ),
14          Attributes(
15            Attribute("lang", "en")
16          )
17        )
18      )
19    }
20
21    override fun toString(): String {
22      return this.string()
23    }
24 }
```

Fig. 2. HTML tag definition

2   KTML

HTML is a strictly structured markup language. KTML leverages Kotlin's object-oriented class paradigm to enforce a correct HTML structure. Thanks to Kotlin's non-verbose syntax, such as the missing **new** keyword that is common in other languages, the object instantiation can be used to create a clean internal DSL. Figure 1 shows an HTML *Hello World!* example using KTML. Figure 1a lists the Kotlin source code, while Fig. 1b depicts the generated output. The HTML code simply consists out of a html, title, and a body tag to create the usual HTML structure. However, due to the structure- and type-safety of KTML, this is also the only way to combine these tags. For example, to create a well-formed HTML document the html tag is preceded by the doctype and contains exactly one head and one body tag. As seen in Fig. 1a, these tags are created at the time they are needed. These tags also have children, creating their own DOM-like structure. Note that the objects could be instantiated beforehand, which makes is easier to test them independently.

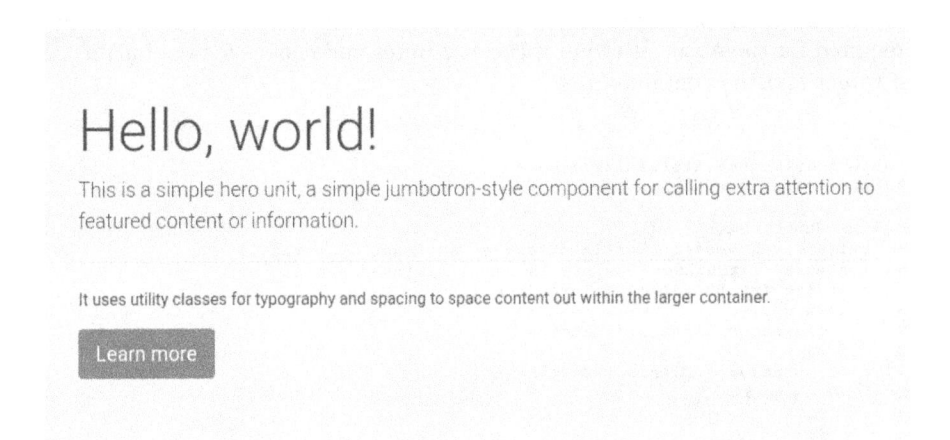

Fig. 3. Jumbotron *Hello World!*

All tags in KTML are constructed in a similar way. Figure 2 shows the definition of the Html class that defines the html tag in the KTML language. The class name is the name of the tag. This name is used in the internal DSL to construct the objects. The parameter list in the constructor defines which children can be included in the tag. The html tag requires exactly one head and one body tag. Other tags may also contain optional parameters, such as attributes or HTML classes. To keep things lean, each combination of options needs its own constructor, which can call each other to avoid duplicating code. The tag inherits the build and string functions from the AbstractTagBuilder. build constructs the result, which is a sequence of tags. In the case of html the sequence consists out of the doctype and the actual html tags. The same is done one step deeper in the tree, where a html tag consists of a TagSequence which creates the children for the head and body. In addition, the html tag gets a lang attribute set to en. Finally, the constructed tag is printed with toString, which calls the inherited string method to serialize the constructed tag. A tag constructed in this way is syntactically correct, well-structured, and type-safe.

The KTML implementation includes all common HTML tags. Furthermore, KTML is designed to support extensibility and reusability as first-class citizens following the presented schema. The following example shows how to create a reusable element, which implements Bootstrap's Jumbotron[1] component. The component can be seen in Fig. 3. The KTML code of the example is listed in Fig. 4. Similar to the definition of the html tag, a new component uses the abstract

---

[1] https://getbootstrap.com/docs/4.6/components/jumbotron.

tag builder. In this example, the div tag is extended to create the jumbotron component. The div contains a sequence of other tags, namely H1, P, Hr, P, and A. Nearly all tags contain class definitions, provided by Bootstrap. The H1 tag shows how to include other components, in this case a Text field, that are defined elsewhere, while the P tag includes the Text itself. Most of the information is required for the A tag. It requires the attributes and classes for the button, an href target and the contained text.

```
1 import info.scce.ktml.interfaces.*
2 import info.scce.ktml.util.*
3
4 class Jumbotron(
5   private val header: TextInterface = Text("Hello, world!"),
6 ) : AbstractTagBuilder<DivInterface>(), DivInterface {
7   override fun build(): DivInterface {
8     return Div(
9       classes = Classes("jumbotron"),
10      H1(
11        classes = Classes("display-4"),
12        header,
13      ),
14      P(
15        classes = Classes("lead"),
16        Text("This is a simple hero unit, a simple jumbotron-style
                component for calling extra attention to featured content or
                information."),
17      ),
18      Hr(
19        classes = Classes("my-4")
20      ),
21      P(
22        Text("It uses utility classes for typography and spacing to space
                content out within the larger container.")
23      ),
24      A(
25        attributes = Attributes(Attribute("role", "button")),
26        classes = Classes("btn", "btn-primary", "btn-lg"),
27        href = Href("#"),
28        Text("Learn more"),
29      ),
30    )
31  }
32 }
```

Fig. 4. Jumbotron KTML example

Fig. 5. Track view of the AISoLA website

3 The Tangle Case-Study

Tangle is part of a conference management collection that generates conference programmes as a web service. It supports multiple conferences and classically divides them into tracks and sessions. The web service provides overviews at different of these levels, e.g., which tracks are running simultaneously in which rooms. It also provides detailed information about the sessions. All HTML code is generated using KTML.

Its framework ensures that the generated code is well-structured and typesafe. Coincidentally, it is also being used for this very conference. Figure 5 shows the track view of the AISoLA conference[2] as a web page. Tangle's TrackView class, depicted in Fig. 6, receives a service object for further requests and the trackId of the track that should be displayed. Lines 6–10 retrieve the necessary data and store it them in local variables. Then, the HTML of the track view is generated and returned, following the same procedure of the previous example from Sect. 2. To display conference specific data, constructors, such as HeadView, also take a conferenceRecord. In the body, objects that are tied to bootstrap[3] elements for aesthetic reasons. The code constructs the conference header, a breadcrumb menu, and the *Track* title, followed by the actual title of the track and its description. Eventually, the table contains the track schedule.

KTML's expressive structure makes it easy to identify these elements in the source code. While it is still possible to re-arrange common tags and their semantic content, KTML ensures that the resulting HTML is well-formed. For example, the thead constructor expects a table row to follow and there is no other way in KTML to construct a well-formed object tree. Tangle provides similar views for sessions, rooms, and single topics. All classes for these views are constructed analogously to the TrackView class, shown in Fig. 6.

The extensibility of KTML is highlighted by Line 54. Here, the sessionTrs array is passed to the TBody constructor of the table. Each tr entry represents a row in the track view. Note that the data is collected at the beginning of the build function and does not depend on any document object as it is common in other frameworks. Figure 7 shows the SessionTr class. The constructor stores information about the session, the room, and the track, which is provided at Line 10 in the TrackView. When the table row is created, the text for the row is set depending on whether the track is divided into different types of sessions. Then the tr tag is created with cells for the date, room, and a link to the session.

---

[2] https://aisola.org.
[3] https://getbootstrap.com.

```
1 class TrackView(
2   private val services: Services,
3   private val trackId: Int,
4 ) : ViewInterface {
5   override fun build(): HtmlInterface {
6
7     val trackRecord = services.trackService.retrieve(trackId)
8     val title = trackRecord.title
9     val conferenceRecord = services.conferenceService.bySessionId(trackId)
10    val sessionRecords = services.sessionService.byTrackId(trackRecord.id)
11    val sessionTrs = sessionRecords.map { SessionTr(it, trackRecord) }.
          toTypedArray()
12    return Html(
13      HeadView(
14        "Track: $title",
15        conferenceRecord
16      ),
17      Body(
18        ContainerBootstrap(
19          ConferenceHeader(
20            conferenceRecord,
21            BreadcrumbTrack(
22              conferenceRecord,
23              trackRecord
24            )
25          ),
26          H3(
27            classes = Classes("mb-3"),
28            B(Text("Track")),
29          ),
30          H4(
31            classes = Classes("mb-3"),
32            Text(title),
33          ),
34          P(
35            classes = Classes("my-3"),
36            Text(trackRecord.description),
37          ),
38          Div(
39            classes = Classes("card", "mb-2"),
40            TableStrippedBootstrap(
41              THead(
42                Tr(
43                  Td(
44                    Text("Time"),
45                  ),
46                  Td(
47                    Text("Room"),
48                  ),
49                  Td(
50                    Text("Session")
51                  )
52                )
53              ),
54              TBody(
55                *sessionTrs
56              )
57            )
58          )
59        )
60      )
61    )
62  }
63 }
```

Fig. 6. The TrackView class that generates the track view web page in the conference programme

```
1 class SessionTr(
2   private val sessionRecord: SessionRecord,
3   private val roomRecord: RoomRecord,
4   private val trackRecord: TrackRecord,
5 ) : AbstractTagBuilder<TrInterface>(), TrInterface {
6
7   constructor(
8     sessionAndRoomRecord: Record2<SessionRecord, RoomRecord>,
9     trackRecord: TrackRecord,
10  ) : this(
11    sessionAndRoomRecord.component1(),
12    sessionAndRoomRecord.component2(),
13    trackRecord
14  )
15
16  override fun build(): TrInterface {
17    var text = Text(trackRecord.title)
18    if (SessionType.session == sessionRecord.type) {
19      text = Text(sessionRecord.title)
20    }
21    return Tr(
22      DateTimeCell(sessionRecord),
23      Td(
24        RoomA(roomRecord),
25      ),
26      Td(
27        A(
28          href = SessionHref(sessionRecord),
29          text,
30        ),
31      ),
32    )
33  }
34 }
```

Fig. 7. The SessionTr class that creates a row entry of the track view

Table 1. Size of the Tangle project

	Service	Views	KTML extensions	Overall
LoCs	963	479	983	2,425
Ratio	0.397	0.198	0.405	1

Overall, the complete Tangle generator is relatively concise. Table 1 shows an overview of the whole project and its LoCs divided into different aspects. The views make up the majority of the lines. While there is some logic necessary, e.g., shown at the beginning of the TrackView class, most of the code uses the KTML library, which is ensures well-formed HTML output.

4 Related Work

Numerous DSLs exist for a wide variety of purposes. In this section, we want to introduce some DSLs that have influenced KTML or serve similar purposes.

Kotlinx.html[4] is another framework that is designed to build DOM trees for an HTML document. Similar to KTML, one can create individual tag elements or append tags to an existing tree. While Kotlin also allows for a clean Kotlinx.html syntax, e.g., `p {+"text inside"}` and can be seen as an internal DSL, the structure is less strict and therefore less type-safe. The aim of KTML is to provide a semantic benefit for the developer that goes beyond mere structural simplification.

Other popular DSLs for generating HTML documents are Svelte[5], Elm[6], and JSX[7]. All three allow creating HTML in a DSL and add typing to it, at least when used in a TypeScript context. However, they all compile to JavaScript and therefore do not produce static HTML code. Instead, they are typically used alongside frameworks to facilitate the creation of dynamic user interfaces. Soundless[8] provides functional HTML templating in PHP. Unlike KTML, it uses pure functions and a separate generator instead of objects that all generate their own code.

A different kind of internal DSL is the Project Description Language. It is used in the CINCO workbench [7] to allow easy creation of project structures. Its main purpose is to create directories and files, specify how they are organized hierarchically, and manage dependencies to bootstrap new development projects.

Pragmatic Action Charts [8] are an internal DSL for Statecharts that allows arbitrary hostcode execution. While serving a different domain, it is an example for leveraging a given host language and providing Statecharts semantics without the need for a dedicated new language. The nature of internal DSLs, allows developers to use the languages and tools they are familiar with.

5 Conclusion

We presented the internal DSL KTML to produce well-structured and type-safe HTML documents. Due to Kotlins clean syntax, such an internal DSL can be provided, with little mental clutter. The detailed examples from Sect. 2 showed a seemingly natural way to construct the resulting DOM. Section 3 presented the professional project Tangle, which uses the KTML library. The use-case shows that KTML helps the developer to create more sophisticated views and scales well to hundredth of users. All presentation-related code is based on KTML.

Lastly, we would like to thank Tiziana once again. Your continued efforts to promote abstract and domain-specific thinking are of great benefit for us all and the next generation of computer scientists. Happy birthday, Tiziana.

---

[4] https://github.com/Kotlin/kotlinx.html.
[5] https://svelte.dev.
[6] https://elm-lang.org.
[7] https://react.dev/learn/writing-markup-with-jsx.
[8] https://gitlab.com/MazeChaZer/soundless.

References

1. Brandon, C., Margaria, T.: Low-code/no-code artificial intelligence platforms for the health informatics domain. Electron. Commun. EASST **82** (2023)
2. Bugayenko, Y.: Elegant Objects. CreateSpace Independent Publishing (2016)
3. Chaudhary, H.A.A., Margaria, T.: DSL-based interoperability and integration in the smart manufacturing digital thread (2024)
4. Doherty, A.J., Murphy, R.A., Schieweck, A., Clancy, S., Breathnach, C., Margaria, T.: CensusIRL: historical census data preparation with MDD support. In: 2022 IEEE International Conference on Big Data (Big Data), pp. 2507–2514. IEEE (2022)
5. Margaria, T., Schieweck, A.: The digital thread in industry 4.0. In: Ahrendt, W., Tapia Tarifa, S.L. (eds.) IFM 2019. LNCS, vol. 11918, pp. 3–24. Springer, Cham (2019). https://doi.org/10.1007/978-3-030-34968-4_1
6. Margaria, T., Steffen, B.: Service-orientation: conquering complexity with XMDD. In: Hinchey, M., Coyle, L. (eds.) Conquering Complexity, pp. 217–236. Springer, London (2012). https://doi.org/10.1007/978-1-4471-2297-5_10
7. Naujokat, S., Lybecait, M., Kopetzki, D., Steffen, B.: Cinco: a simplicity-driven approach to full generation of domain-specific graphical modeling tools. Int. J. Softw. Tools Technol. Transfer **20**, 327–354 (2018)
8. Smyth, S.: Pragmatic action charts. In: Proceedings of the 22th ACM-IEEE International Conference on Formal Methods and Models for System Design (MEMOCODE 2024), Raleigh, NC, USA (2024, accepted)
9. Smyth, S., et al.: Executable documentation: test-first in action. In: Margaria, T., Steffen, B. (eds.) ISoLA 2022. LNCS, vol. 13702, pp. 135–156. Springer, Cham (2022). https://doi.org/10.1007/978-3-031-19756-7_8
10. Smyth, S., Schulz-Rosengarten, A., von Hanxleden, R.: Guidance in model-based compilations. In: Proceedings of the 8th International Symposium on Leveraging Applications of Formal Methods, Verification and Validation (ISoLA 2018), Doctoral Symposium. Electronic Communications of the EASST, vol. 78. Limassol, Cyprus (2018)
11. Smyth, S., Schulz-Rosengarten, A., von Hanxleden, R.: Towards interactive compilation models. In: Margaria, T., Steffen, B. (eds.) ISoLA 2018. LNCS, vol. 11244, pp. 246–260. Springer, Cham (2018). https://doi.org/10.1007/978-3-030-03418-4_15
12. Tegeler, T., Boßelmann, S., Schürmann, J., Smyth, S., Teumert, S., Steffen, B.: Executable documentation: from documentation languages to purpose-specific languages. In: Margaria, T., Steffen, B. (eds.) ISoLA 2022. LNCS, vol. 13702, pp. 174–192. Springer, Cham (2022). https://doi.org/10.1007/978-3-031-19756-7_10

Semantic Reflection and Digital Twins: A Comprehensive Overview

Eduard Kamburjan, Andrea Pferscher, Rudolf Schlatte, Riccardo Sieve, Silvia Lizeth Tapia Tarifa, and Einar Broch Johnsen(✉)

Department of Informatics, University of Oslo, Oslo, Norway
{eduard,andreapf,rudi,riccasi,sltarifa,einarj}@ifi.uio.no

Abstract. Semantic reflection combines reflection in programming languages with semantic technologies for knowledge representation. It enables a program to represent and query its own runtime state as a knowledge graph. The knowledge graphs reflecting program states can be combined with domain knowledge which allows queries about a program to be made in terms of a given domain vocabulary, as well as with external graph data. Both extensions of the knowledge graph reflecting the runtime state are useful for digital twins. In this paper, we discuss the basic concepts of semantic reflection, its applications for digital twins, and its connections to formal methods.

1 Introduction

Digital twins propose a model-based approach to cyber-physical systems, in which a physical system (the "physical twin") is connected with a digital system (the "digital twin"). The digital twin contains models of the physical twin and connects these models with the physical twin to (a) update the models with live data and (b) enable control over the physical twin using different kinds of model-based analyses. While the exact definition of a digital twin is elusive (e.g., [11,12,44]) one important perspective in engineering is that the life-time of the digital twin goes beyond the operational phase to reflect the lifecycle of the physical twin, already starting with the requirement elicitation phase. Thus, documents and models that are collected through the different phases of the lifecycle become part of the digital twin, which, together with tools to support design, construction, and operation, are often referred to as a *digital thread* [50].

Developing such digital twins, with their inherent multidisciplinarity and their multitude of tools and data formats, is a major challenge for both software developers and system architects. One way to deal with interdisciplinarity, is through the formal representation of domain knowledge in knowledge graphs. While ontologies, knowledge graphs [25] and related semantic technologies [24] have been identified as a key technology for digital twins [41,61], their use in turn poses additional challenges to the software developer [23].

In this paper, we discuss our work on *semantic lifting* [34] in the context of digital twins. Semantic lifting is the process of (1) serializing a digital entity as

© The Author(s), under exclusive license to Springer Nature Switzerland AG 2025
M. Hinchey and B. Steffen (Eds.): Festschrift Tiziana Margaria, LNCS 15240, pp. 129–145, 2025.
https://doi.org/10.1007/978-3-031-73887-6_11

a knowledge graph, (2) connecting this knowledge graph to domain knowledge necessary to operate or interpret the digital entity, and (3) accessing this combined knowledge graph from the original digital entity. The last step is referred to as *semantic reflection*. Specifically, we consider the use of *knowledge graphs* to

1. model the architecture and configurations of digital twins during development as well as operation, and
2. enable digital twins to access their own runtime configuration in order to adapt their future behavior.

Together, these properties enable *procedural reflection* [43,58] through semantic technologies, such as ontologies and graph queries. Semantic reflection does not only enhance digital twins, but can also be used to provide tool support and integrate with formal methods. So far, semantic reflection has been used to adapt to *structural changes* in the digital twin [35,40], check structural correctness [30,32,35], interpretation of software architectures [16] and to enable new techniques for programming [33] with semantic graph data. In this paper, we show the connections and interactions between these applications.

Paper Outline. We provide an overview of our work on semantic reflection (Sect. 2), with a focus on digital twins (Sect. 3). We then discuss software development and analysis for digital twins (Sect. 4), and some perspectives on integrating formal methods into digital twins by extending our techniques (Sect. 5). Examples and content in this paper builds on previous publications, which also detail the corresponding related work; the contribution of this paper is the comprehensive overview.

2 From Semantic Lifting to Semantic Reflection

Let us illustrate the basic idea of semantic lifting of programs [34] and how semantic lifting can be used to integrate domain knowledge in programs through reflection. Throughout the paper we use as a running example a simple program of a smart house [35], written in the *Semantic Micro Object Language* (SMOL)[1]. This example will gradually become a digital twin.

Consider a smart house that consists of a sequence of rooms, each modeled by an instance of a class Room with an identifier and a target temperature for heating. The code in Fig. 1 shows an excerpt of the corresponding SMOL code. The main block instantiates a house with two rooms; we will detail its control method later.

2.1 Semantic Lifting

Semantic lifting is a procedure that generates a knowledge graph from a program state. The generated knowledge graph includes a representation of the full

---

[1] https://www.smolang.org.

```
SMOL
1  class Wall(Room left, Room right) end
2  class Room(Wall left, Wall right, Int id, Int target)
3    Unit control() ... end
4  end
5
6  main
7    Wall w1 = new Wall(null, null); Wall w2 = new Wall(null, null);
8    Wall w3 = new Wall(null, null);
9    Room r1 = new Room(w1, w2, 1, 18);
10   Room r2 = new Room(w2, w3, 2, 19);
11   w1.right = r1; w2.right = r2; w2.left = r1; w3.left = r2;
12 end
```

Fig. 1. A SMOL model for a digital twin of a smart house.

runtime state—object, variables, heap memory, call stack—but also the static information of the program, in particular the class table and the abstract syntax tree of the program.

```
RDF
1  run:obj1 a prog:Wall; prog:Wall_right run:obj4.
2  run:obj2 a prog:Wall; prog:Wall_right run:obj5;
3                        prog:Wall_left  run:obj4.
4  run:obj3 a prog:Wall; prog:Wall_left  run:obj5.
5  run:obj4 a prog:Room; prog:Room_left  run:obj1;
6                        prog:Room_right run:obj2;
7                        prog:Room_target 18;
8                        prog:Room_id 1.
9  run:obj5 a prog:Room; prog:Room_left  run:obj2;
10                       prog:Room_right run:obj3;
11                       prog:Room_target 19;
12                       prog:Room_id 2.
```

Fig. 2. A lifted final state of the program in Fig. 1 (excerpt).

To illustrate, Fig. 2 contains an excerpt of the lifting of the smart house program shown in Fig. 1, at the end of its execution, with a knowledge graph generated from the objects and parts of the class table, represented in RDF[2]. As we can see, the architectural structure of the digital twin is clearly expressed in the lifted program state—in particular, the configuration of the smart house which shows how the two rooms are connected, can be retrieved from the graph. In anticipation of the digital twin this program will become, we can already see

---
[2] Resource Description Framework, https://www.w3.org/RDF/.

```
OWL
1  Class: prog:Room SubClassOf: SMOLClass
2  Class: prog:Wall SubClassOf: SMOLClass
3  ObjectProperty: prog:Room_left Domain: prog:Room
4                                  Range: prog:Wall or {smol:null}
5  ObjectProperty: prog:Room_right Domain: prog:Room
6                                  Range: prog:Wall or {smol:null}
7  ObjectProperty: prog:Wall_left Domain: prog:Wall
8                                  Range: prog:Room or {smol:null}
9  ObjectProperty: prog:Wall_Right Domain: prog:Wall
10                                 Range: prog:Room or {smol:null}
11 DataProperty: prog:Room_id Domain: prog:Room
12                             Range: xsd:int
13                             Characteristics: functional
14 DataProperty: prog:Room_target Domain: prog:Room
15                                 Range: xsd:int
16                                 Characteristics: functional
17
18 ObjectProperty: leftOf
19    EquivalentTo: inverse(prog:Wall:right) o prog:Wall_left
20    Domain: prog:Room
21    Range: prog:Room
```

Fig. 3. Axioms for the lifted state in Fig. 2. Observe that only the last axiom is part of the external knowledge graph.

that the lifted graph expresses the architectural structure of the house *as it is modeled at a given moment*.

Merely generating the knowledge graph, which is essentially serialization, is not using the potential of knowledge graphs—but by connecting the generated knowledge graph with ontologies, we can add domain knowledge to the program state to investigate it and reason over it. We say that the lifted stated is *enriched* with information from an external knowledge graph.

For example, consider the OWL[3] axioms in Fig. 3. They express the domain and range of different relations in the knowledge graph, and declare some concepts to be OWL classes. The final axiom captures the spatial relation between two rooms. Some axioms are already part of the generated knowledge graph (the axioms concerned with range and domain, as well as the OWL classes related to the lifting of the runtime state). Remark that the knowledge graph that the lifted runtime state connects to need not necessarily be an ontology, but can also contain concrete data; we shall return to this point in later sections.

Using the generated knowledge graph and the domain ontology, we can now query the semantically lifted runtime state *in terms of the domain*. The SPARQL[4] query in Fig. 4, for example, asks for all rooms that are left of another

---

[3] Web Ontology Language, https://www.w3.org/OWL/.
[4] SPARQL RDF Query Language, https://www.w3.org/TR/sparql11-overview/.

```
SPARQL
SELECT ?obj WHERE { ?obj leftOf ?obj2.}
```

Fig. 4. A query on the lifted state from Fig. 2, using the axioms from Fig. 3. The result of the query is the node `run:obj4`.

```SMOL
1  ... // Classes as in Figure 1
2  main
3    ... // Initialization as in Figure 1
4    List<Room> rooms =
5      access("SELECT ?r WHERE {?r leftOf ?r2. ?r prog:Room_id ?id1.
6                               ?r2 prog:Room_id ?id2.
7                               FILTER(?id1 = ?id2) }");
8
9    //every result is a room that has the same id as its neighbor
10   //the following should print 'false'
11   print(rooms != nil);
12 end
```

Fig. 5. Semantic reflection for checks in terms of the domain.

(known) room. This information must be derived using the above axioms. Observe that this query abstracts from internal data structures used to organize rooms in the program.

2.2 Semantic Reflection

Building on semantic lifting, *semantic reflection* is the process of accessing the generated and enriched knowledge graph of a program state from inside the very same program (introspection) to influence its future behavior (intercession).

For this purpose, we need to execute graph queries from within the program. The queries can either return a Boolean value (denoting whether there is a result for the query) or are restricted to return representable results (for example, through a static type system [33]). A result, for the purposes of our example here, is *representable* if it is an RDF node corresponding to a SMOL object. The result of a reflective query then becomes a list of SMOL objects. Consider the variant of our smart house in Fig. 5, which queries itself to check whether the identifiers differ for all rooms such that one room is left of the other. The **access** statement executes a query on the knowledge graph with the lifted state. The result is assigned to the list **rooms**, which should be the empty list (denoted `nil`).

Semantic Reflection in Practice. A typical use case for semantic reflection is the development of domain-specific simulators. For example, the geological simulator of Qu *et al.* [55] directly integrates the GeoFault [56] and GeoCore [15] ontologies into the simulation of geological processes, thus removing most redundancy between the two modeling formalisms. By combining these ontologies into a simulator, geological deliberations that take days, can be supported with simulations that return *qualitative* results within minutes.

3 Foundations of Semantically Reflective Digital Twins

The previous section showed how programs can use domain knowledge expressed in a knowledge graph either through reflection or through access to external knowledge. We now consider how these techniques can be used to program digital twins. The main insight here is that the knowledge graph that enriches the lifted state can contain information about the physical twin, such as its architectural structure, requirements and other asset information.

3.1 Using Asset Models for Architectural Self-Adaptation

An *asset information model* is a digital description of a physical or planned asset to facilitate its design, development and operation[5]. We consider the asset information model to be a part of the digital thread related to an asset. The digital thread additionally contains information that describes the context of the asset as well as, e.g., operational logs.

An asset information model describes the architectural structure of a physical twin, including its components and their connections. We are specifically interested in this structure of the physical twin: it changes throughout the lifetime of the physical twin, and the digital twin must adapt *its own architectural structure* to reflect these changes.

The digital twin and the physical twin have different architectural structures, as they have different components and represent different abstraction levels, but there is still a relation between these structures. For example, in our running example, the digital twin will have one object that represents each room of the smart house. This Room object in the digital twin should evolve in sync with the corresponding room in the physical twin, which it can realize by monitoring the room in the physical twin. This monitoring is typically related to *requirements* connected to the physical twin (e.g., the targeted temperature for the room). If the physical twin changes, it may be necessary to adapt the digital twin, but not all changes require an adaptation. For example, adding a room to the smart house or adding additional requirements from operations would make an adaptation of the digital twin necessary, but turning on the light in a room would not.

The relationship between the physical twin and the digital twin can be seen as a *structural consistency relation*, expressing that the architectural structure of the digital twin is consistent with that of the physical twin. Semantic lifting

---

[5] Asset information models generalize the building information model (BIM) [26] to systems engineering (e.g., [14]).

can be used to formalize consistency between the architectural structures in a uniform way, despite the potentially different nature of the two architectures: As both the asset information model and the digital twin (via the semantic lifting) are part of the same knowledge graph, we can define structural consistency using queries. This has several advantages:

- The formalization of consistency is decoupled from the exact nature of the digital twin implementation. Changing from, for example, one programming language to another for the digital twin, does not require to reformulate structural consistency.
- Structural consistency can be expressed using standard semantic web technologies (concretely, SPARQL in our case), for which advanced pragmatics are developed to ease their use. In particular, structural consistency can be expressed in a formalism specifically design for *structural modeling*.
- By querying the knowledge graph, we can easily integrate consistency and self-adaptation.

Technically, we define consistency between architectural structures using *defect queries* [16]. A defect query defines *an inconsistency* and returns all instances of the inconsistency in the graph. For example, given a program, an asset information model and a set of defect queries, we consider the program and the asset information model to be structurally consistent if all the defect queries return an empty result set. Note that logical reasoning using the ontology may be needed to derive the answers (i.e., a so-called entailment regime from the query engine).

Strategies for *architectural self-adaptation* [6] can be easily expressed by means of defect queries [35], using, e.g., the MAPE-K self-adaptation loop (see, e.g., [9]). In the MAPE-K framework, a managing subsystem monitors a managed subsystem, analyzes found inconsistencies, plans their repair and executes that plan.

For architectural self-adaptation of a digital twin, the managing subsystem is an additional component in the digital twin, while the managed subsystem contains the other, original, digital twin components. As every query returns an inconsistency, the set of defect queries act as the monitoring components at the meta-level, monitoring the architectural structure of the digital twin. The analysis component than analyses query results to detect the source of the inconsistency. This can be either a more detailed query, or just some computation without referring to the knowledge graph. Planning and execution can be tailored to the defect queries and the inconsistencies that they model.

Let us now reconsider the running example of the smart house. The code in Fig. 6 illustrates how semantic reflection can be used by the digital twin to self-adapt to changes in the architectural structure of the physical twin. First, we retrieve all room identifiers in the asset model that do not have a digital twin object modeling them (Lines 6–9). This means that these rooms have been added to the physical twin recently. The **construct** creates a new object instance from retrieved data values. This general form of a defect query generalizes for this kind of constraints [35]. The next query analyses the defect and retrieves

```
1  ... //Classes as in Figure 1
2  class RoomAsrt(Int roomID) end
3  class RoomNeigh(Int leftWallId, Int rightWallId) end
4  class MAPE()
5    Unit selfAdapt()
6      List<RoomAsrt> newRooms =   // (1) Monitoring with defect query
7        construct("SELECT ?roomID
8                    { ?x asset:Room_id ?roomID.
9                      FILTER NOT EXISTS {?y prog:Room_id ?roomID}}");
10     foreach roomAsrt in newRooms do
11       List<RoomNeigh> neighbors = // (2) Analysis
12         construct("SELECT ?leftWallId ?rightWallId
13                     { ?x asset:Room_id %1;
14                       ?x asset:left  [asset:Wall_od ?leftWallId];
15                       ?x asset:right [asset:Wall_od ?rightWallId].",
16                   roomAsrt.roomId);
17      // determine whether one of the walls is known, plan and
18      // execute the creation of a new room in the digital twin
19    end
```

Fig. 6. Architectural self-adaptation in SMOL.

the wall neighboring the new room (Lines 11–16). One of these walls must be known if we assume that rooms are added one by one. SMOL allows values to be injected in the queries using % and these queries are specific to one found defect.

3.2 Beyond the Monolith

Digital twins are not in general monolithic programs, but consist of multiple models and data sources, some of which are typically (black-box) simulators. It is unrealistic to assume that all components of a digital twin are expressed in the same programming language, and numerous architectures and platforms for digital twins have been proposed [46], including one by Margaria et al. [7]. We now discuss how semantic lifting and reflection can be applied in such architectures, with a focus on the following approaches:

- **Semantically reflected orchestrators.** Orchestrators are central components of the digital twins and integrate the connection to other components. In semantically reflected orchestrators, only the orchestrator, connections and interfaces of other components are lifted into the knowledge graph.
- **Semantically reflected architectures** define their lifting not in terms of the programming language, but in terms of the components of the architecture. The system is semantically lifted (and can semantically reflected) based on a lifting of all components *with respect to the architecture*.

We now provide more detail for these two approaches.

Semantically Reflected Orchestrators. We have investigated the semantically reflected orchestrators approach in SMOL by integrating simulation units into the language and considering them as special objects in the language [32]. These objects can realize either a simulator or a connection to the physical twin, as their interface consists of only three methods: reading an object port, writing an object port and advancing the local (simulation) time of the object.

More concretely, we integrate functional mock-up units (FMUs) [5] into SMOL. An FMU is a wrapper defined by the functional mock-up interface that offers the above operations. Each FMU comes with a model description, which is part of the semantic lifting, that describes its ports, name of the model and internal details that must be exposed for co-simulation. However, it does not expose the implementation of the simulation—indeed it must not implement a simulation at all, but can connect to other temporal data sources[6]. Continuing with our running example, the code in Fig. 7 places two FMUs in each room: one FMU to simulate the behavior of the room, the other to connect to the sensors of the physical twin. The shown code uses semantic lifting to check that the correct FMUs are used; this is done by a query comparing the model name of the simulation FMU with information in the asset model. SMOL also supports a similar connection for InfluxDB[7]. A semantically reflected orchestrator, embedded into architecture that is not lifted, has been successfully demonstrated on an extensible digital twin architecture for a greenhouse [40].

Semantically Reflected Architectures. We have investigated semantically reflected architectures in a service-oriented setting for a digital twin of robotic arms [16]. The digital twin is defined by a software architecture, expressed in UML, with more than 10 different software components: databases, services, simulators and physical twin endpoints. In this architecture, there is a *lifting service* that generates a knowledge graph for the current instance of the software implementing the architecture. This means that each component implements an interface to lift itself. Instead of relying on a generic lifting function provided by the language (which is the case for SMOL), the semantic lifting must here be implemented by hand, in terms of the vocabulary defined by the architecture (such as the components and attribute names). Currently, there is on-going effort to implement semantic lifting as a service on a Digital-Twin-as-a-Service (DTaaS) platform [59]. Additional information and specification can be annotated to the architecture and then be used in the semantic lifting.

There are numerous digital twin platforms and architectures [46], and several proposals that combine digital twins with ontologies and knowledge graphs [41, 57, 61]. However, no general methodology has been developed so far to determine whether a lifted architecture or a lifted orchestrator is best suited for a given system; we consider this challenge the next step in research on semantically reflected digital twins.

---

[6] See, e.g., the RabbitMQ FMU https://into-cps-rabbitmq-fmu.readthedocs.io/en/latest/overview.html.
[7] https://www.influxdata.com/products/influxdb-overview/.

```
SMOL
1  class Room(Wall left, Wall right, Int id, Int target,
2             FMU[in Boolean switch, out Double value] room,
3             FMU[in Boolean switch, out Double value] model)
4    Unit control()
5      if /* check on room.value and model.value */ then //start heating
6          room.switch = True; model.switch = True;
7      end
8      room.tick(1.0); model.tick(1.0); //advance time
9    end
10 end
11 class ConsistencyManager()
12   List<Room> getMisconfigured() //should return nil
13     return
14     access("SELECT ?obj {?obj prog:Room_room ?fmu.
15                         ?fmu fmu:name ?fName.
16                         FILTER(?fName != 'connectionFMU')}")
17     ++ //syntactic sugar for list concatenation
18     access("SELECT ?obj {?obj prog:Room_model ?fmu.
19                         ?fmu fmu:name ?fName.
20                         FILTER(?fName != 'simulationFMU')}");
21   end
22 end
```

Fig. 7. SMOL code with integrated FMUs.

4 Analysis of Semantically Reflected Programs

At the core of semantic reflection is the ability to program with semantic graph data, a challenging task sometimes referred to as the next big topic in the semantic web [23]. It requires not only to coordinate different tools (reasoners, query endpoints, databases) and formalisms (graph shapes, ontologies, queries), but also to integrate their conceptual class models with object-oriented class models. While these two class models seem similar, they are in fact fundamentally different. Not only technical terms, but also in their very purpose: an object-oriented model is concerned with structuring data and behavior, a conceptual class model (i.e., an ontology) is concerned with the modeling of domain knowledge[8].

The semantic gap [2] between object-oriented models and knowledge representation can be addressed using semantic lifting. As semantic lifting expresses the program using an ontology, the semantic lifting process can be used to analyze the query that loads data into the program; the answer to the query must be contained in the part of the knowledge graph defined by the lifting. In fact, we have exploited this feature in the above examples.

---

[8] Remark that the Scandinavian school of object-oriented design, stemming from Simula [10], places as much weight on modeling and simulation as on code reuse in object-oriented systems [48,49].

Consider the following statement:

```SMOL
List<Room> r = access("SELECT ?obj {?obj leftOf ?obj2}"); //query Q
```

To check whether this query is type-safe, one must reason about the ontology $\mathcal{O}$ (from Fig. 3) used with the program: Is the query Q always returning a collection of Room objects *on any knowledge graph that adheres to* $\mathcal{O}$? This can be answered using *query containment* [8,54]. We have shown that SMOL is type-safe for queries that can be be reduced to concept subsumption [37]. Namely, if the query Q is contained in the query

```SPARQL
SELECT ?obj WHERE { ?obj a prog:Room. }
```

using $\mathcal{O}$, then no runtime error can be triggered by a query result that cannot be represented as a Room object. It is easy to see that this is indeed the case, from the axioms defining the leftOf relation. This idea can be further generalized to define SMOL classes not in terms of a ontology concept, but in terms of the queries that retrieve them [33], which introduces behavioral subtyping [47] for program classes interacting with ontological knowledge bases.

Formal Methods with Semantic Lifting. Semantic reflection opens for interesting questions in formal methods. We briefly describe two directions that we have started to explore. new ways of doing formal met First, semantic reflection can be used for runtime enforcement [29]. Using hypothetical execution, one can use the lifted state of a program *after* a potential step, to check for consistency with the domain knowledge. If a step would result in a inconsistent knowledge graph, then the runtime forces another step to be taken, thus ensuring that domain knowledge is adhered to during execution, even without an explicit, reflective access. Second, semantic lifting can be used for software verification, foe example by integration in Hoare logics [31] for deductive verification. While semantic reflection is so far out of reach, it enables the use of ontologies as a specification language (together with program expressions), thus opening a new line of attack to the old problem of the specification bottleneck [3].

5 Discussion: Formal Methods in Digital Twins

We now consider connections between formal methods and digital twins (a broader discussion may be found in the paper from the FMDT workshop [36]). First, observe that the semantic lifting mechanism discussed in this paper has connections to formal methods, analysis and verification for digital twins. The defect queries, discussed in Sect. 3.1, can be exploited as a mechanism for self-adaptation, in particular for structural changes. Alternatively, they can also be seen as correctness conditions that need to be monitored at runtime [30].

The orchestration and coupling of simulation units, discussed in Sect. 3.2, can be subjected to runtime monitoring to ensure the correct use of co-simulation master algorithms [18] and in changing scenarios [21]. While processes, traces and temporal properties may be challenging to model generically using ontologies, due to their dependence on a concrete application [22], this shows that temporal properties can still be used to specify correctness properties for digital twins using semantic technologies.

In addition to the use of semantic lifting and semantic reflection for verification, we briefly mention some other topics in formal methods that are relevant for digital twins.

Hybrid Systems Verification. So far in this paper, we have discussed a largely language-based approach to connect and analyze code and simulators as discrete structures. However, this impedes the formal analysis of continuous behavior and sensor streams. There are numerous languages for hybrid systems modeling, and we envision that an integration with a structured, object-oriented formalism to hybrid systems, such as hybrid active objects [28,38,39] or hybrid actors [27] can result in a holistic formal method for verification of digital twins.

Automata Learning. Automata learning [17] is a technique to automatically generate behavioral models of black-box systems. Learning algorithms have been developed to learn models describing behavioral aspects such as timed or stochastic behavior. Margaria and Schieweck [51] propose automata learning as a technique to automatically create a digital twin of cyber-physical systems. Similarly, Pferscher *et al.* [53] showed that this can be done for security-critical communication protocols. The learned models that enable further analyses, e.g., model-checking or model-based testing. Similar to our proposed technique, the learned model enables insights into the physical twin. Wallner [60] has shown that automata learning can also be used to analyze the digital twin. By applying automata learning also *to* the digital twin, the behavioral difference between the digital twin and the physical twin can be analyzed.

Runtime Enforcement and Extra-Functional Properties. The value proposition of digital twins is largely based on its ability to incorporate live data with model-based analysis to aid in decision-making. In many of these cases, this data may be *sensitive*. Data lakes [13,20] can be used to collect and organize this data space in a decentralized manner. The access to data from different sources needs to be carefully managed through fine-grained access control policies; for example, Margaria *et al.* proposed an algorithm for role-based access control in digital twins [7]. Furthermore, these data access policies can be connected with data privacy, expressing, e.g., GDPR compliance, and connected with language-based methods to enforce data privacy consent (e.g., [1,42]). It would be interesting to explore whether semantic reflection could be used for runtime enforcement of dynamic privacy policies that changes at runtime, such as data privacy consent as required by GDPR, for digital twins that need to access personal data. Going beyond the use of personal data for analysis in the digital twin, such runtime enforcement could potentially be directly related to the digital thread, thereby regulating data access throughout the digital twin lifecycle [7,45].

Concerns on Responsible Decision Making. Responsible decision support using digital twins to explore and compare hypothetical scenarios, will increasingly require solutions that take into consideration transparency, explainability, human-centric values, and the law [52]. It would be interesting to investigate whether semantic reflection, as outlined in this paper, could be used to address responsible decision-making and decision support, e.g., using knowledge graphs and runtime analyses as a means for argumentation in the decision-making process and to capture human-centric values and legal regulations; in this direction, Gruber discusses how collective intelligence can be captured via collective knowledge systems [19], while Becu *et al.* [4] explores how simulation approaches can be used for participatory decision-making, where all stakeholders' views are taken into consideration.

6 Conclusion

Semantic reflection is a language-based approach to programming with graph data and ontologies, that has proven useful in the context of digital twins. In particular, semantic reflection can be used to connect software to the digital thread and to asset models, thereby supporting a lifecycle perspective on the digital twin. In this paper, we have provided an overview of our work in this area. We further suggest how semantic reflection can be used to draw interesting connections between three different areas of computer science: programming languages, formal methods and knowledge representations. So far, the work on formal methods has been investigated less than the connection with digital twins, and we hope that the comprehensive overview and perspective given here can help foster further research on this topic.

Acknowledgments. The authors would like to thank Tiziana Margaria for many interesting discussions on digital twins. We are further grateful to all contributors to SMOL and its development. This work was partly funded by the EU project SM4RTENANCE (grant no. 101123423) and the Research Council of Norway via PeTWIN (grant no. 294600) and SIRIUS (grant no. 237898).

References

1. Baramashetru, C.P., Tapia Tarifa, S.L., Owe, O., Gruschka, N.: A policy language to capture compliance of data protection requirements. In: ter Beek, M.H., Monahan, R. (eds.) IFM 2022. LNCS, vol. 13274, pp. 289–309. Springer, Cham (2022). https://doi.org/10.1007/978-3-031-07727-2_16
2. Baset, S., Stoffel, K.: Object-oriented modeling with ontologies around: a survey of existing approaches. Int. J. Softw. Eng. Knowl. Eng. **28**(11–12), 1775–1794 (2018). https://doi.org/10.1142/S0218194018400284
3. Baumann, C., Beckert, B., Blasum, H., Bormer, T.: Lessons learned from microkernel verification – specification is the new bottleneck. In: Cassez, F., Huuck, R., Klein, G., Schlich, B. (eds.) Proceedings of the 7th Conference on Systems Software Verification (SSV 2012). EPTCS, vol. 102, pp. 18–32 (2012). https://doi.org/10.4204/EPTCS.102.4

4. Becu, N., Neef, A., Schreinemachers, P., Sangkapitux, C.: Participatory computer simulation to support collective decision-making: potential and limits of stakeholder involvement. Land Use Policy 25(4), 498–509 (2008). https://linkinghub.elsevier.com/retrieve/pii/S0264837707000877
5. Blockwitz, T., et al.: Functional mockup interface 2.0: the standard for tool independent exchange of simulation models. In: Proceedings of the 9th International Modelica Conference, vol. 76, pp. 173–184. Linköping University Electronic Press (2012). http://dx.doi.org/10.3384/ecp12076173
6. Braberman, V.A., D'Ippolito, N., Kramer, J., Sykes, D., Uchitel, S.: MORPH: a reference architecture for configuration and behaviour self-adaptation. In: Filieri, A., Maggio, M. (eds.) Proceedings of the 1st International Workshop on Control Theory for Software Engineering (CTSE@FSE 2015), pp. 9–16. ACM (2015). https://doi.org/10.1145/2804337.2804339
7. Chaudhary, H.A.A., et al.: Model-driven engineering in digital thread platforms: a practical use case and future challenges. In: Margaria, T., Steffen, B. (eds.) ISoLA 2022. LNCS, vol. 13704, pp. 195–207. Springer, Cahm (2022). https://doi.org/10.1007/978-3-031-19762-8_14
8. Chekol, M.W., Euzenat, J., Genevès, P., Layaïda, N.: SPARQL query containment under SHI axioms. In: Proceedings of the 26th AAAI Conference on Artificial Intelligence (AAAI 2012), pp. 10—16. AAAI Press (2012). https://doi.org/10.1609/aaai.v26i1.8108DOI
9. Cheng, B.H.C., et al.: Software engineering for self-adaptive systems: a research roadmap. In: Cheng, B.H.C., de Lemos, R., Giese, H., Inverardi, P., Magee, J. (eds.) Software Engineering for Self-Adaptive Systems. LNCS, vol. 5525, pp. 1–26. Springer, Heidelberg (2009). https://doi.org/10.1007/978-3-642-02161-9_1
10. Dahl, O.-J., Nygaard, K.: SIMULA - an ALGOL-based simulation language. Commun. ACM 9(9), 671–678 (1966). https://doi.org/10.1145/365813.365819
11. Dalibor, M., et al.: A cross-domain systematic mapping study on software engineering for digital twins. J. Syst. Softw. 193, 111361 (2022). https://doi.org/10.1016/J.JSS.2022.111361
12. Eramo, R., Bordeleau, F., Combemale, B., van Den Brand, M., Wimmer, M., Wortmann, A.: Conceptualizing digital twins. IEEE Softw. 39(2), 39–46 (2021). https://doi.org/10.1109/MS.2021.3130755
13. Fang, H.: Managing data lakes in big data era: what's a data lake and why has it became popular in data management ecosystem. In: Proceedings of the International Conference on Cyber Technology in Automation, Control, and Intelligent Systems (CYBER 2015), pp. 820–824. IEEE (2015). https://doi.org/10.1109/CYBER.2015.7288049
14. Fjøsna, E., Waaler, A.: READI Information modelling framework (IMF). Asset Information Modelling Framework. Technical report, READI Project (2021). https://readi-jip.org/wp-content/uploads/2021/03/Information-modelling-framework-V1.pdf
15. Garcia, L.F., Abel, M., Perrin, M., dos Santos Alvarenga, R.: The GeoCore ontology: a core ontology for general use in geology. Comput. Geosci. 135, 104387 (2020). https://doi.org/10.1016/j.cageo.2019.104387
16. Gil, S., Kamburjan, E., Talasila, P., Larsen, P.G.: An architecture for coupled digital twins with semantic lifting (2024, submitted for publication)
17. Gold, E.M.: Language identification in the limit. Inf. Control 10(5), 447–474 (1967). https://doi.org/10.1016/S0019-9958(67)91165-5

18. Gomes, C., Thule, C., Broman, D., Larsen, P.G., Vangheluwe, H.: Co-simulation: a survey. ACM Comput. Surv. **51**(3), 49:1–49:33 (2018). https://doi.org/10.1145/3179993
19. Gruber, T.: Collective knowledge systems: where the social web meets the semantic web. J. Web Semant. **6**(1), 4–13 (2008). https://doi.org/10.1016/j.websem.2007.11.011
20. Hai, R., Koutras, C., Quix, C., Jarke, M.: Data lakes: a survey of functions and systems. IEEE Trans. Knowl. Data Eng. **35**(12), 12571–12590 (2023). https://doi.org/10.1109/TKDE.2023.3270101
21. Hansen, S.T., Kamburjan, E., Kazemi, Z.: Monitoring reconfigurable simulation scenarios in co-simulated digital twins. In: ISoLA 2024. LNCS. Springer, Cham (2024, in production)
22. Harth, A., Käfer, T., Rula, A., Calbimonte, J.P., Kamburjan, E., Giese, M.: Towards representing processes and reasoning with process descriptions on the web. Trans. Graph Data Knowl. **2**(1), 1:1–1:32 (2024). https://doi.org/10.4230/TGDK.2.1.1
23. Hitzler, P.: A review of the semantic web field. Commun. ACM **64**(2), 76–83 (2021). https://doi.org/10.1145/3397512
24. Hitzler, P., Krötzsch, M., Rudolph, S.: Foundations of Semantic Web Technologies. Chapman and Hall/CRC Press (2010). http://www.semantic-web-book.org/
25. Hogan, A., et al.: Knowledge graphs. ACM Comput. Surv. **54**(4), 71:1–71:37 (2022). https://doi.org/10.1145/3447772
26. ISO: Organization and digitization of information about buildings and civil engineering works, including building information modelling (BIM). Standard, Intl. Organization for Standardization, Geneva, CH (2018). https://www.iso.org/standard/68078.html, ISO 19650-1:2018
27. Jahandideh, I., Ghassemi, F., Sirjani, M.: An actor-based framework for asynchronous event-based cyber-physical systems. Softw. Syst. Model. **20**(3), 641–665 (2021). https://doi.org/10.1007/s10270-021-00877-y
28. Kamburjan, E.: From post-conditions to post-region invariants: deductive verification of hybrid objects. In: Bogomolov, S., Jungers, R.M. (eds.) Proceedings of the 24th ACM International Conference on Hybrid Systems: Computation and Control (HSCC 2021), pp. 9:1–9:11. ACM (2021). https://doi.org/10.1145/3447928.3456633
29. Kamburjan, E., Din, C.C.: Runtime enforcement using knowledge bases. In: Lambers, L., Uchitel, S. (eds.) FASE 2023. LNCS, vol. 13991, pp. 220–240. Springer, Cham (2023). https://doi.org/10.1007/978-3-031-30826-0_12
30. Kamburjan, E., Din, C.C., Schlatte, R., Tapia Tarifa, S.L., Johnsen, E.B.: Twinning-by-construction: ensuring correctness for self-adaptive digital twins. In: Margaria, T., Steffen, B. (eds.) ISoLA 2022. LNCS, vol. 13701, pp. 188–204. Springer, Cham (2022). https://doi.org/10.1007/978-3-031-19849-6_12
31. Kamburjan, E., Gurov, D.: A Hoare logic for domain specification (full version). CoRR abs/2402.00452 (2024). https://doi.org/10.48550/arXiv.2402.00452
32. Kamburjan, E., Johnsen, E.B.: Knowledge structures over simulation units. In: Martin, C.R., Emami, N., Blas, M.J., Rezaee, R. (eds.) Proceedings of the Annual Modeling and Simulation Conference (ANNSIM 2022), pp. 78–89. IEEE (2022). https://doi.org/10.23919/ANNSIM55834.2022.9859490
33. Kamburjan, E., Klungre, V.N., Giese, M.: Never mind the semantic gap: modular, lazy and safe loading of RDF data. In: Groth, P., et al. (eds.) ESWC 2022. LNCS, vol. 13261, pp. 200–216. Springer, Cham (2022). https://doi.org/10.1007/978-3-031-06981-9_12

34. Kamburjan, E., Klungre, V.N., Schlatte, R., Johnsen, E.B., Giese, M.: Programming and debugging with semantically lifted states. In: Verborgh, R., et al. (eds.) ESWC 2021. LNCS, vol. 12731, pp. 126–142. Springer, Cham (2021). https://doi.org/10.1007/978-3-030-77385-4_8
35. Kamburjan, E., Klungre, V.N., Schlatte, R., Tapia Tarifa, S.L., Cameron, D., Johnsen, E.B.: Digital twin reconfiguration using asset models. In: Margaria, T., Steffen, B. (eds.) ISoLA 2022. LNCS, vol. 13704, pp. 71–88. Springer, Cham (2022). https://doi.org/10.1007/978-3-031-19762-8_6
36. Kamburjan, E., et al.: Emerging challenges in compositionality and correctness for digital twins. In: FMDT@FM. CEUR Workshop Proceedings, vol. 3507. CEUR-WS.org (2023). https://ceur-ws.org/Vol-3507/paper2.pdf
37. Kamburjan, E., Kostylev, E.V.: Type checking semantically lifted programs via query containment under entailment regimes. In: Homola, M., Ryzhikov, V., Schmidt, R.A. (eds.) Proceedings of the 34th International Workshop on Description Logics (DL 2021). CEUR Workshop Proceedings, vol. 2954. CEUR-WS.org (2021). https://ceur-ws.org/Vol-2954/paper-19.pdf
38. Kamburjan, E., Mitsch, S., Hähnle, R.: A hybrid programming language for formal modeling and verification of hybrid systems. Leibniz Trans. Embed. Syst. **8**(2), 04:1–04:34 (2022). https://doi.org/10.4230/LITES.8.2.4
39. Kamburjan, E., Schlatte, R., Johnsen, E.B., Tapia Tarifa, S.L.: Designing distributed control with hybrid active objects. In: Margaria, T., Steffen, B. (eds.) ISoLA 2020. LNCS, vol. 12479, pp. 88–108. Springer, Cham (2021). https://doi.org/10.1007/978-3-030-83723-5_7
40. Kamburjan, E., et al.: GreenhouseDT: an exemplar for digital twins. In: Proceedings 19th International Symposium on Software Engineering for Adaptive and Self-managing Systems (SEAMS 2024), pp. 175-181. ACM (2024). https://doi.org/10.1145/3643915.3644108
41. Karabulut, E., Pileggi, S.F., Groth, P., Degeler, V.: Ontologies in digital twins: a systematic literature review. Future Gener. Comput. Syst. **153**, 442–456 (2024). https://doi.org/10.1016/j.future.2023.12.013
42. Karami, F., Basin, D.A., Johnsen, E.B.: DPL: a language for GDPR enforcement. In: Proceedings of the 35th IEEE Computer Security Foundations Symposium (CSF 2022), pp. 112–129. IEEE (2022). https://doi.org/10.1109/CSF54842.2022.9919687
43. Kiczales, G., Rivieres, J.D.: The Art of the Metaobject Protocol. MIT Press, Cambridge (1991)
44. Kritzinger, W., Karner, M., Traar, G., Henjes, J., Sihn, W.: Digital twin in manufacturing: a categorical literature review and classification. IFAC-PapersOnLine **51**(11), 1016–1022 (2018). https://doi.org/10.1016/j.ifacol.2018.08.474. 16th IFAC Symposium on Information Control Problems in Manufacturing (INCOM 2018)
45. Kuruppuarachchi, P., Rea, S., McGibney, A.: Trust and security analyzer for digital twins. In: Chbeir, R., Benslimane, D., Zervakis, M.E., Manolopoulos, Y., Nguyen, N.T., Tekli, J. (eds.) MEDES 2023. CCIS, vol. 2022, pp. 278–290. Springer, Cham (2023). https://doi.org/10.1007/978-3-031-51643-6_20
46. Lehner, D., et al.: Digital twin platforms: requirements, capabilities, and future prospects. IEEE Softw. **39**(2), 53–61 (2022). https://doi.org/10.1109/MS.2021.3133795
47. Liskov, B., Wing, J.M.: A behavioral notion of subtyping. ACM Trans. Program. Lang. Syst. **16**(6), 1811–1841 (1994). https://doi.org/10.1145/197320.197383

48. Madsen, O.L., Møller-Pedersen, B.: What object-oriented programming was supposed to be: two grumpy old guys' take on object-oriented programming. In: Scholliers, C., Singer, J. (eds.) Proceedings of the 2022 ACM SIGPLAN International Symposium on New Ideas, New Paradigms, and Reflections on Programming and Software (Onward! 2022), pp. 220–239. ACM (2022). https://doi.org/10.1145/3563835.3568735
49. Madsen, O.L., Møller-Pedersen, B.: What your mother forgot to tell you about modeling - and programming. In: ACM/IEEE International Conference on Model Driven Engineering Languages and Systems, MODELS 2023 Companion, pp. 200–210. IEEE (2023). https://doi.org/10.1109/MODELS-C59198.2023.00049
50. Margaria, T., Schieweck, A.: The digital thread in industry 4.0. In: Ahrendt, W., Tapia Tarifa, S.L. (eds.) IFM 2019. LNCS, vol. 11918, pp. 3–24. Springer, Cham (2019). https://doi.org/10.1007/978-3-030-34968-4_1
51. Margaria, T., Schieweck, A.: Active behavior mining for digital twins extraction. IT Prof. **24**(4), 74–80 (2022). https://doi.org/10.1109/MITP.2022.3193044
52. Milosevic, Z., van Schalkwyk, P.: Towards responsible digital twins. In: Sales, T.P., de Kinderen, S., Proper, H.A., Pufahl, L., Karastoyanova, D., van Sinderen, M. (eds.) EDOC 2023. LNBIP, vol. 498, pp. 123–138. Springer, Cham (2024). https://doi.org/10.1007/978-3-031-54712-6_8
53. Pferscher, A., Wunderling, B., Aichernig, B.K., Muskardin, E.: Mining digital twins of a VPN server. In: Hallerstede, S., Kamburjan, E. (eds.) Proceedings of the Workshop on Applications of Formal Methods and Digital Twins. CEUR Workshop Proceedings, vol. 3507. CEUR-WS.org (2023). https://ceur-ws.org/Vol-3507/paper6.pdf
54. Pichler, R., Skritek, S.: Containment and equivalence of well-designed SPARQL. In: Proceedings of the 33rd ACM SIGMOD-SIGACT-SIGART Symposium on Principles of Database Systems, PODS 2014 pp. 39—50. Association for Computing Machinery (2014). https://doi.org/10.1145/2594538.2594542
55. Qu, Y., Kamburjan, E., Torabi, A., Giese, M.: Semantically triggered qualitative simulation of a geological process. Appl. Comput. Geosci. **21**, 100152 (2024). https://doi.org/10.1016/j.acags.2023.100152
56. Qu, Y., Perrin, M., Torabi, A., Abel, M., Giese, M.: GeoFault: a well-founded fault ontology for interoperability in geological modeling. Comput. Geosci. **182**, 105478 (2024). https://doi.org/10.1016/j.cageo.2023.105478
57. Singh, S., et al.: Data management for developing digital twin ontology model. Proc. Inst. Mech. Eng. Part B: J. Eng. Manuf. **235**(14), 2323–2337 (2021). https://doi.org/10.1177/0954405420978117
58. Smith, B.C.: Procedural reflection in programming languages. Ph.D. thesis. MIT (1982). http://publications.csail.mit.edu/lcs/pubs/pdf/MIT-LCS-TR-272.pdf
59. Talasila, P., Gomes, C., Mikkelsen, P.H., Arboleda, S.G., Kamburjan, E., Larsen, P.G.: Digital twin as a service (DTaaS): a platform for digital twin developers and users. In: 2023 IEEE Smart World Congress (SWC), pp. 1–8. IEEE (2023). https://doi.org/10.1109/SWC57546.2023.10448890
60. Wallner, F.: Development of a robust active automata learning algorithm for automotive measurement devices avoiding resets. Master's thesis, Graz University of Technology, Graz, Austria (2022). https://repository.tugraz.at/publications/9bn45-0d225
61. Zheng, X., Lu, J., Kiritsis, D.: The emergence of cognitive digital twin: vision, challenges and opportunities. Int. J. Prod. Res. **60**(24), 7610–7632 (2022). https://doi.org/10.1080/00207543.2021.2014591

Assessing Static and Dynamic Features for Packing Detection

Charles-Henry Bertrand Van Ouytsel, Axel Legay, Serena Lucca[✉],
and Dimitri Wauters

INGI, ICTEAM, Universite Catholique de Louvain, Place Sainte Barbe 2,
LG05.02,01, 1348 Louvain-La-Neuve, Belgium
{charles-henry.bertrand,axel.legay,serena.lucca,d.wauters}@uclouvain.be

Abstract. Packing is a widely used obfuscation technique for malware to bypass detection tools and hinder reverse engineering. Existing research has already covered methods to detect packing, both with static and dynamic analysis. These methods are based on various features: headers, entropy, API calls, section permissions, etc. While dynamic features are generally more informative, their contribution compared to static features is not always clear. This paper compares the impact of these static and dynamic features on different machine learning classifiers. We propose a study on different datasets to determine whether the information provided by dynamic analysis outweighs its significant extraction time.

Keywords: Packing · Malware · Machine Learning · Static Analysis · Dynamic Analysis · Experimental Comparison

1 Introduction

The growing number of malware discovered each year [24] requires building accurate and efficient malware detection mechanisms to protect the cyberspace. Currently, different malware detection tools available on the market use signature-based detection for their high efficiency. These signatures represent malware by syntactic properties (e.g., length, byte sequences, entropy, etc.), but they could also exploit artifacts observed during malware execution in a monitored environment (e.g., network communication, interaction with the system,...). To avoid the need to manually create such signatures, researchers developed machine learning classifiers based on the same features (i.e., byte sequence, API calls observed during monitored execution,...). However, these signatures and classifiers are vulnerable to obfuscation, which changes the syntactic properties of the malware [11]. Moreover, evasion techniques allow the malware to exhibit its malicious behavior under selected conditions (e.g., absence of sandbox, waiting for a certain day,...) that are not necessarily fulfilled during the analysis. All these techniques make malware analysis challenging and require the development of new approaches to ensure the detection of malicious behavior.

Aware of these challenges, researchers have proposed the use of symbolic execution for malware analysis. Symbolic execution is a formal verification technique that explores the different execution paths of a binary by considering all variables of the execution environment as symbolic. During symbolic execution of the binary, constraints are added to symbolic variables and the different possible execution paths are explored. A Satisfiability Modulo Theory (SMT) solver is responsible for verifying the satisfiability of the collected symbolic constraints and thus the validity of the execution path. Symbolic execution can counter evasion and obfuscation techniques [12,13] and thus ensure the triggering of the malicious behavior [11]. It has led to the development of a new set of machine learning based malware classification methods [7,18,42]. In [42], the authors have proposed to combine symbolic execution with Gspan [51], a graph mining algorithm that detects the largest common subgraphs between two graphs. They first collect API calls via symbolic execution and then connect them in a System Call Dependency Graph (SCDG), i.e., a graph that abstracts the flow of information between these calls. In the training phase, Gspan computes the largest common subgraphs between malware in a given family. These then represent the signature for the family. In the classification phase, they extract the SCDG from the binary and compare it to the signature of each family. This approach has been extended with a focus on using efficient tactics for the SMT solver [43] and path prioritization techniques to improve malware code coverage as well as more efficient classifiers than Gspan [9].

Unfortunately, symbolic execution remains expensive to apply, therefore it is generally not possible to explore all possible execution paths of the binary. In particular, the packing obfuscation technique hinders the efficiency of the symbolic engine and the scalability of this approach. Packing can obfuscate a binary with different strategies: compression, encryption, virtualization,... It directly affects the syntactic properties of the target binary, making it more difficult to analyze. While packing can be used for legitimate purposes (e.g., intellectual property protection), it is often used by malware authors to hide their code [37]. Packing detection could improve the efficiency of symbolic execution for malware analysis. If a packed sample is identified, an unpacking procedure could be used to extract the original binary. It could then be analyzed symbolically to understand its behavior.

While signatures have also been developed to detect specific packers, they are easily bypassed by unknown packers [11]. Thus, different heuristics based on syntactic properties have been proposed. The literature includes works based on the entropy of the binary [33], section names and permissions [40], IAT table [47], metrics related to section sizes [17], N-grams [49], etc. All these characteristics have been extensively used as features for supervised machine learning techniques [19]. For example, Biondi et al. [10] extract 119 features from the literature including entry bytes, entropy, imported functions, metadata, resource and sections to train their classifiers. Given that these attributes have been clearly defined in their paper and originate from a recent review of the relevant literature, they will serve as a baseline for this work.

Although such classifiers are generally efficient, recent works highlight their limitations regarding low entropy packing scheme [34] but also the overlap between classifiers to detect packing and malware [1]. Static features focus on syntactic properties of the sample and could fail to grasp the semantics of the analyzed sample (i.e., this is called the semantic gap [45]). On the other hand, features extracted dynamically could allow to discover semantic properties of the sample [25] (i.e., its behavior at run-time) but lead to high extraction cost. Unfortunately, few works propose to compare the efficiency of these two types of features. Regarding the malware detection problem [20], dynamic features show a better ability to generalize but are also more error-prone to extract.

The main contribution of this paper is the comparison of features extracted statically and dynamically to detect packing. For each static feature commonly used, the literature has been explored and equivalent features extracted dynamically have been implemented. Three sets of features are used, including either static features, dynamic features, or both. These sets are then fed to a machine learning algorithm to compare their classification performance. The individual importance of these different features are then exposed thanks to SHAP value, an explainable machine learning technique. In our experiments, we use two different datasets, one with benign samples that have been manually packed, and one composed of various malware found in the wild. These two datasets are then combined to create a third, more diverse dataset. We train Decision Trees, Random Forests, and Gradient Boosted Decision Trees with the three feature sets defined above and extracted from our datasets. These experiments will allow us to show which features and models perform best at packing detection.

This paper is divided into five sections. Section 2 introduces general background about packing, machine learning and our malware analysis workflow. Section 3 discusses the dynamic features used in this work and how they are extracted. Section 4 explains our methodology for the experiments by discussing our datasets, the feature extraction and the model training. Section 5 evaluates tree-based classifiers considering different feature sets and the individual importance of the features in the classification process. Section 6 discusses future works and concludes.

Message for Tiziana Margaria. Dear Tiziana, There are so many things to say about the relationship that binds us, but I think the best way to summarize it is in these few words: kindness, trust, dedication, and compassion. Thank you for all these years of support and for your presence and loyalty (as well as Bernhard's) during difficult times when others were no longer there. Our shared passion for formal verification research has connected us for many years. The article you are about to read represents a practical culmination of these results in the very applied field of cybersecurity. Your constant drive to engage with industry has likely influenced me. I am confident that you will appreciate the proposed results and that they will open new avenues of research for you, especially within the RAISE project.

2 Background

In this section, we present background related to packers and their influence on the characteristics of an executable. Following that, we will proceed to introduce machine learning models and the key metrics employed in their evaluation. Finally, we present our malware analysis workflow and the importance of packing detection to make it efficient.

2.1 Packing

A packer is a program designed to transform a binary input into an obfuscated binary, typically involving compression or encryption processes but also anti-analysis tricks (e.g.: erasing import, junk code,...). The resulting obfuscated binary encompasses both the concealed code and the unpacking procedure, as illustrated in Fig. 1. During runtime, the unpacking routine is executed as a preliminary step to reconstruct the original code into the process memory. Afterward, the original code is executed by means of a jump to the original entry point (OEP). Malicious actors frequently employ packers with the intent of concealing their malware from antivirus detection mechanisms.

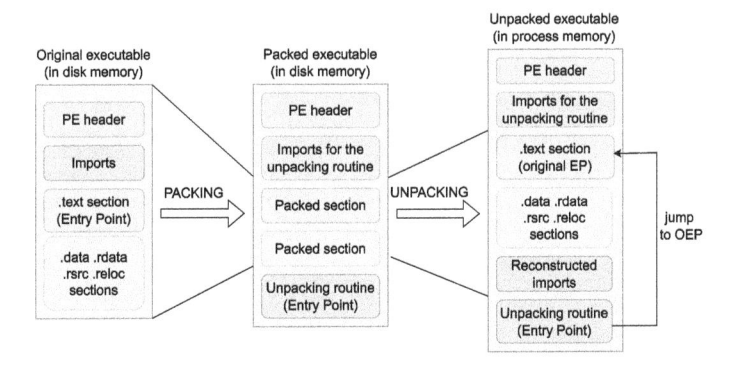

Fig. 1. Packing and unpacking process

Packers often engage in the alteration of the attributes inherent to the original executable. To illustrate, one notable change is the augmentation of entropy within a packed executable, which typically surpasses the entropy level found in the original binary. Furthermore, packed executables may exhibit non-standard section names, as multiple sections are generated to accommodate the original code segments. Another prevalent modification technique employed by packers involves the reduction of the imported functions list. In practice, the list of imported functions is often compressed alongside the original executable and subsequently replaced with a more concise set of functions, specifically tailored to the requirements of the unpacking routine.

2.2 Machine Learning

Machine Learning (ML) allows a system to learn from a dataset in order to make predictions on new data. We will use supervised machine learning which learns from a labeled dataset.

Tree based models are among the most popular models in machine learning. Decision Trees (DT) consist of branches and leaves that represent choices based on features and predicted outputs, respectively. Random Forests (RF) consist in ensembles of different DTs and are less prone to over-fitting than DTs. Finally, Gradient-Boosted Decision Trees (GBDT) are based on a set of DTs that are built sequentially to correct mistakes in previous DTs. They usually result in robust models with good accuracy. Recent research [8,10] shows that tree-based models provide good prediction performance for packing detection with low training time and memory consumption. Therefore, we choose to focus our study on these models.

Performance metrics are needed to evaluate and compare models. We will use well-known ML metrics to assess the strengths and weaknesses of our models. These metrics are computed from 4 measures: TP (True Positives, i.e.: packed classified as packed), FP (False Positives, i.e.: not packed classified as packed), TN (True Negatives, i.e.: not packed classified as not packed) and FN (False Negatives, i.e.: packed classified as not packed).

- The *balanced accuracy* is the mean between the proportion of well classified packed samples and the proportion of well classified not-packed samples. $\frac{1}{2}(\frac{TP}{TP+FN} + \frac{TN}{TN+FP})$
- The *precision* is the proportion of packed sample identifications that are actually correct. A low precision indicates that the model classifies many not packed samples as packed. $\frac{TP}{TP+FP}$
- The *recall* is the proportion of actual packed samples that were correctly identified. If this metric is low, it puts in light that many packed samples are missed by the model. $\frac{TP}{TP+FN}$
- The *F1-score* is the harmonic mean of the recall and the precision. This metric works well on imbalanced data. $\frac{2*precision*recall}{precision+recall}$

Finally, we use ROC curves to compare the tradeoffs between FP rate and TP rate with different classification thresholds on our models.

2.3 Malware Analysis Workflow

Detection of packed binaries allows malware analysis techniques to be adapted to ensure efficient detection of malicious behavior. This section describes SEMA - Symbolic Execution for Malware Analysis - and the importance of packing detection to improve its efficiency.

SEMA [6] is an open source tool for analyzing, detecting and classifying malware using symbolic execution and machine learning. It is based on the angr

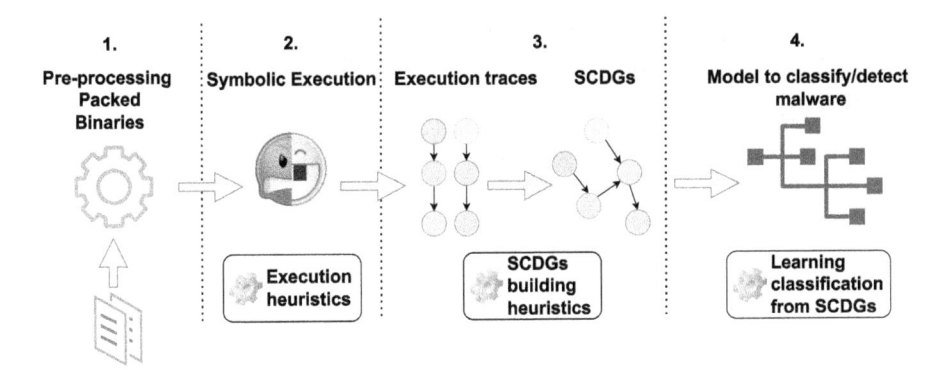

Assessing Static and Dynamic Features for Packing Detection 151

Fig. 2. Malware analysis workflow with SEMA

symbolic execution framework and implements different strategies to improve binary code coverage: path prioritization strategies, loop handling, optimized SMT solver strategies,... The general SEMA workflow is illustrated in Fig. 2 and relies on the following key building blocks. The first step, which is the focus of this paper, is to identify packed binaries using packing detection models. The packed binaries are further analyzed to identify the packer and a possible unpacking procedure. We then use symbolic execution on non-packed (or unpacked) binaries from different malware families. During each symbolic execution, we record the API calls and their arguments according to their respective execution paths to create execution traces. These execution traces are used to build the binary's SCDG - System Call Dependency Graph of the binary. Multiple SCDGs built from different binaries are then used to train machine learning algorithms to either distinguish a malicious file from a benign one, or to identify the malware family. When a new binary needs to be classified, we build its SCDG and use the previously trained classifier to output a decision.

To illustrate the importance of packing detection, consider the simple program introduced in [6] and shown in Listing 1.1. This program prints the message "I'm evil!!" as its malicious behavior. While static analysis is bypassed by splitting the string (Lines 13 and 14), dynamic analysis is bypassed when using a debugger (Line 4) or not updating the tick count (Line 4) to simulate a sleep of 500000 s (Line 2). SEMA successfully builds an SCDG representing the entire binary behavior in a few seconds. We use UPX [39] to pack this example and observe the effect on symbolic execution. It appears that SEMA is unable to record any API call, even with a 15 min timeout, because the symbolic execution is slowed down by the unpacking routine. This observation may generalize to other packers. Therefore, it is essential to detect packing to pre-process the binary before applying symbolic execution to improve its scalability.

```
1  ULONGLONG uptime = GetTickCount();
2  Sleep(500000);
3  ULONGLONG uptimeBis = GetTickCount();
```

```
 4   if ((uptimeBis - uptime)<500000 || IsDebuggerPresent())
 5       {MessageBox(NULL,"Hello world!","", MB_OK);}
 6   else
 7       {char message[20] = "";
 8       HINSTANCE hlib = LoadLibrary("msvcrt.dll");
 9       MYPROC func = (MYPROC) GetProcAddress(hlib,"strcat");
10       (func) (message, "I'm ");
11       (func) (message, "evil!!");
12       MessageBox(NULL, message, "", MB_OK);}
```

Listing 1.1. Malware code toy example from [6]

Packing detection based on static features has been widely studied in the literature [13,38,47]. While these features are fast to extract, they are easily modified [8,46] and thus their efficiency is limited for packing detection to support symbolic execution. Recent studies suggest the use of features extracted from dynamic analysis [5,8,25,34], as they should improve the efficiency and robustness of machine learning models for packing detection. However, a comprehensive evaluation of the benefits associated with these dynamic features is lacking in the literature. Therefore, we propose to explore and evaluate these features to observe if they can really improve the efficiency of packing detection despite the higher extraction time.

3 Dynamic Features

This section describes in details the dynamic features which have been investigated for packing detection.

Entropy. This method measures the statistical variation of a byte sequence in an executable. Lyda and al. [33] were the first to use entropy to detect packing since packed binaries have generally a higher entropy than a normal executable due to the encryption/compression. Static analysis could only gather entropy of the sample before the execution of the sample and the deployment of the payload. It should be noted that some packers will enforce a low entropy for their sections [34], hindering entropy measures based on static analysis. Dynamic analysis could measure the entropy multiple times through the execution of the sample and expose a more detailed representation.

Bat-Erdene M. et al. [5] identify multiple classes of patterns that can be extracted from the entropy of executable section:

- *Increasing class*
  The section that will contain the unpacked code initializes its memory to 0, setting the entropy close to 0 as well. When the section will be populated with the unpacked executable, the entropy will increase as illustrated in Fig. 3.
- *Decreasing class*
  Contrary to the increasing class, the section of this class will not be initialized to 0 and left with the random bytes present when the memory was allocated.

Therefore, the initial entropy of the section will be high as the distribution of the bytes will be close to random. Once the section is populated, the entropy will decrease a little as the bytes will represent assembly instructions as illustrated in Fig. 4.
- *Combination class*
  This class combines the entropy increase/decrease with a constant class. The initial entropy of this class will either be low, increasing to a maximum, or high, decreasing to a minimum. After those maximum and minimum, the entropy will almost stay constant as illustrated in Fig. 5.
- *Constant class*
  The last observed class of entropy is the constant class. In this class, the entropy does not variate and stays constant for the whole execution. Therefore, we can assume that the sample is not packed.

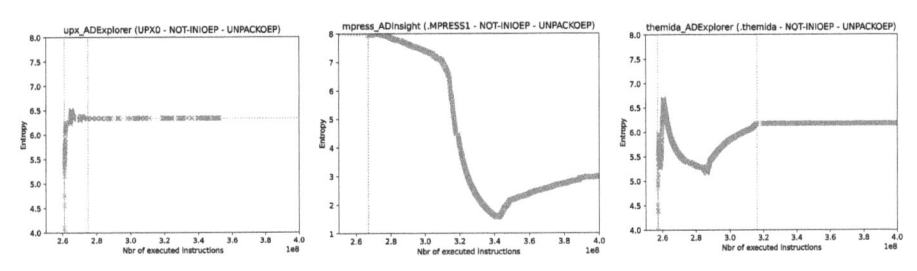

Fig. 3. Increasing class (Packer: UPX)

Fig. 4. Decreasing class (Packer: MPRESS)

Fig. 5. Combination class (Packer: THEMIDA)

These classes are useful for packing detection since non-packed executable have generally an almost constant entropy. In this implementation, the value of the entropy is computed with a fixed granularity. Meaning that a fixed number of basic blocks will be skipped between every computation to reduce the overhead of this technique. The obtained basic block count and entropy values allow to extract features used by machine learning to deduce if the sample is packed. Those features include statistics such as `maximum`, `minimum`, `delta`, `mean`, `median`, `variance` and `standard deviation` of the recovered entropy points.

IAT Functions. The Import Address Table (IAT) of a PE executable contains multiple imported Windows functions. These functions may originate either from internal Windows Dynamic Link Libraries (DLLs), such as `kernel32.dll`, or external DLL sources.

From the IAT, static analysis could extract features for packing detection by recovering the number and names of imported functions [53]. However, it is not able to consider dynamically loaded function since they do not appear in the IAT. A dynamically loaded function is a function that is loaded during the execution of the binary thanks to specific functions present in the IAT (e.g.: `GetProcAddress`). Even though the IAT is empty, the executable can recover the functions needed to reconstruct it. For example, it could manually compute the address of the functions [27].

This obfuscation can be counteracted with dynamic analysis: before the execution the addresses of each memory-loaded functions is recovered and saved by looking into the memory mappings of the sample. With this pre-processing, the addresses of these functions are easily recognizable during the execution. Moreover, every call to `GetProcAddress` is monitored and saved (i.e.: the function name and its address). As illustrated in Fig. 6, this monitoring offers more information than simple static analysis.

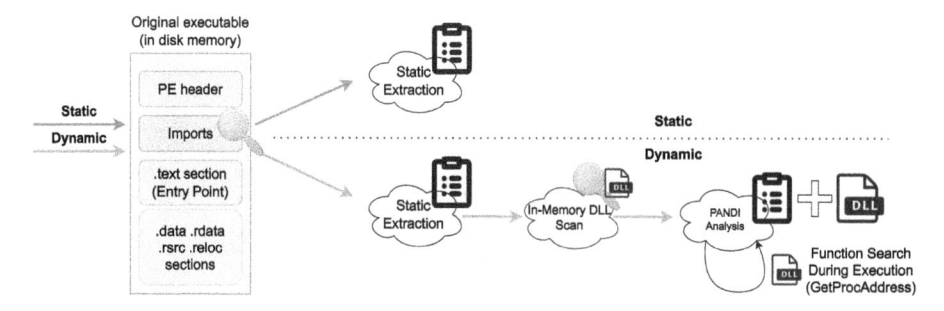

Fig. 6. Representation of IAT static and dynamic analysis workflow

First Bytes. In signature based approach (e.g.: YARA rules), it is common to examine the first bytes at the entry point of an executable (i.e.: corresponding to the first instructions executed). These features have also been used in machine learning approaches [26]. However, is not always the real entry point of the executable [52]. For example, Thread Local Storage (TLS) callback is a piece of code usually used to initiate threads and called before instructions at the entry point. Code executed by TLS callbacks are not caught by debuggers and a malicious actor could use this anti-debugging technique to bypass signatures [47]. Other techniques [50] such as trampoline (i.e.: creating a new entry point which immediately jumps to the original entry point) could hinder this feature extraction. Dynamic analysis allows to extract first bytes which are effectively executed [5,30,38] by the sample.

Executable Sections Permission. After the execution of the unpacking routine, the original code is written in memory and executed. Since proper section permissions are required to write and execute the code, those have been used as features to detection packing [2,49]. There are three possible values for the permissions indicated in the PE header: `read`, `write` and `execute`. The most common permission is `read` and the most suspicious pair of permissions regarding packing detection is `write-execute`. While static analysis could extract permissions from the PE header, it has no means to detect a permission change at runtime.

In our dynamic analysis approach, we extract permissions from the PE header and follow permissions modifications during the execution. New memory regions could be allocated with API calls like `LocalAlloc` and their permissions modified with calls like `VirtualProtect`. We monitor these memory regions by following such API calls and monitoring the memory mapping of the sample to verify its permissions. If a memory write occurs in a region initially read-only, it is logged. OmniUnpack [35] followed a similar approach by monitoring suspicious calls and memory access. Note that in our approach, monitoring memory read/write implies a high overhead regarding feature extraction time.

Memory write-then-executed. A technique widely used in literature [34,35,48] to detect packing is to monitor *write-then-executed* instructions. This provides a simple and more fine-grained solution to detect packing than memory permissions. Each memory write address is registered in a list. Then, if the currently executed instruction is in the list, it is moved to a *write-then-executed* list. When this second list goes beyond a defined threshold (i.e.: to reduce the false-positives), the sample is considered packed. By design, this technique requires dynamic analysis and is resource intensive (i.e.: regarding execution time and memory). Moreover, a non-packed executable may still be detected in the case of a manual DLL loading and execution, making this technique not totally reliable.

This method is popular to detect packing with dynamic analysis as it does not need a second phase of machine learning, the result is usable directly. This is not the case of the other options proposed for this contribution, they will need another layer to be able to answer to the "packed or not" question. In return, the other options are quicker to execute and need much less resources as they (almost) never observe the memory.

4 Methodology

This section details our experimental setup: the datasets, the feature extraction process and the complete machine learning workflow.

Datasets. We use three datasets. The first dataset CLEANPACK [14] consists of 1863 packed and 335 not packed cleanware. The packed samples have been manually packed with known packers: Alienyze, Amber, ASPack, BeRoEXEPacker, EnigmaVirtualBox, EronanaPacker, Exe32pack, EXpressor, FSG, JDPack, MEW, Molebox, MPRESS, Neolite, NSPack, Packman, PECompact, PEtite, RLPack, TELock, Themida, UPX, WinUpack, Yoda-Crypter, Yoda-Protector. The second dataset WILDPACK comes from Aghakhani et al. [1]. The files have been gathered in the wild around 2017. They have already been labeled as packed or not packed. For our use case, we selected 5728 samples (4953 packed and 775 not packed) from their wild dataset. It includes benign and malicious packed samples alongside benign not packed samples. Finally, we combined the CLEANPACK and the WILDPACK datasets to create the MIXPACK dataset. Both datasets have a similar proportion of packed samples. By merging these datasets, we hope to create more diversity since samples come from different sources (manual packing and wild collection).

Feature Extraction. The dynamic features used by our models are extracted with our tool PANDI [32]. This tool is built on top of PANDA [41], a platform for architecture-neutral dynamic analysis, that is used to perform the execution in a virtual environment. The purpose of PANDI is to handle the executable file that will be analyzed by feeding it to PANDA. Once the execution is finished, PANDA will save the execution workflow to be able to replay it later [23]. PANDI replays this execution workflow to analyze the sample thanks to the API made available by PANDA. This API can trigger callbacks that will be caught by PANDI. The callbacks can be, for example, when the sample writes something to memory or when the sample executes a system call. While malware could detect the sandbox used, we limit this possibility by not implementing any detection mechanism directly in the sandbox. Nevertheless, a malware can still implement some more complex techniques to detect the sandbox, like waiting for user input or analyzing the uptime of the machine before extracting the packed executable.

Fig. 7. Representation of the interactions between PANDI and PANDA

Initially, 110 dynamic features were gathered. They represent entropy values (16 features), first few executed bytes (64 features), permissions changes (2 features), write-then-execute sequence (1 feature), imported functions (3 features) and functions calls (24 features). We decided to not include the features linked to permission changes and write-then-execute due to their high extraction cost. We end up with 107 dynamic features. In addition to the dynamic features, a static feature set is extracted thanks to PeLib library [4]. This set is made of 119 features [10] grouped into different categories: metadata, sections, entropy, entry bytes, imported functions and resources.

Figure 8 illustrates the time taken to collect data from each group of features across 1000 samples. Measurements were performed on an 8-cores KVM virtual machine (1 sample per core concurrently) and based on Ubuntu 22.04 with 32 GB of RAM. Regarding static features, Biondi et al. [10] have already discussed their extraction time. Showing extraction costs of metadata, section and entry bytes were negligible; extraction costs of entropy and resources were dependent of file size and properties; and extraction cost of imported functions was the

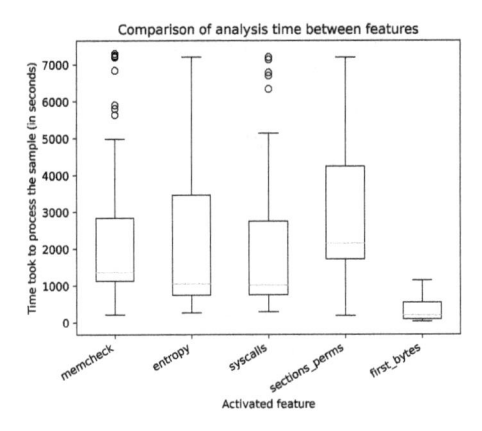

Fig. 8. Time comparison of the extraction for each type of feature

most important. Nonetheless, all extraction costs related to static features are negligible compared to extraction costs of dynamic features.

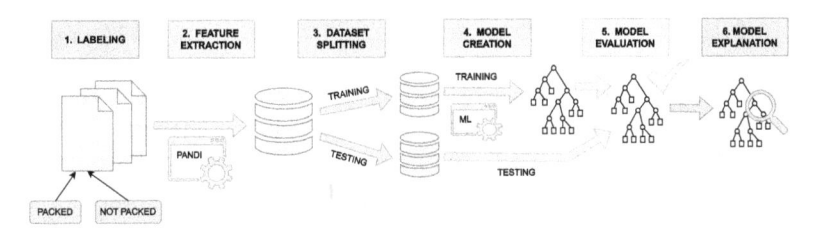

Fig. 9. Machine Learning Workflow

Machine Learning Pipeline. We use the scikit-learn 1.3.0 library during our experiments and follow the workflow depicted in Fig. 9.

1. Labeling The datasets that we use are already labeled. The CLEANPACK dataset is composed of cleanware that are manually packed. Hence, the labeling is straightforward. The binaries of WILDPACK dataset has been labeled as packed or not packed using multiple dynamic and static techniques such as deep packer inspection, sandbox execution, signatures and heuristics (Manalyze [29], Exeinfo PE, Yara rules, PEiD [21], and F-Prot) as explained in [1]. A sample from this dataset is labeled as packed if at least one of the detection techniques considers it to be packed.

2. Feature Extraction We mentioned previously the methods used to extract the static and dynamic features. Each experiment will be performed using the set of dynamic features, then the static features and finally using the combination of both feature sets. This will allow to compare the dynamic approach to the more classical static approach and their combination.

3. Dataset Splitting We split the datasets into a training and a test set. The training set is only used for the model creation (step 4) while the test set will only intervene for the evaluation of the model (step 5). We choose to keep 70% of the data for training and the remaining 30% for testing. Moreover, we shuffle the datasets and split them with a stratified sampling method.

4. Model Creation The performances of the different ML models depend greatly on their hyper-parameters. We use a grid search to evaluate different hyper-parameters combinations and build the best models for packing detection. The hyper-parameters grid tested for each algorithm is depicted in Table 1. In our experiment, we use the stratified 10-fold cross-validation on the training set and the balanced accuracy scoring method to evaluate each combination of hyper-parameters.

Table 1. Hyper-parameters for each type of model

DT			
RF			
GBDT			
criterion	min_sample_leaf	max_depth	n_estimators
gini/entropy	2-12	2-12	10-39

5. Model Evaluation Using the best hyper-parameters found with the training set, we evaluate the models on the test set. We use different metrics: the balanced accuracy, the precision, the recall, the F1-score and the ROC curve.

6. Model Explanation Finally, we use explainable artificial intelligence methods (XAI) to analyse our classifiers and their decision with SHAP values (SHapley Additive exPlanations). This technique, which comes from the game theory field, determines the individual contribution of each feature on the predictions made by the model. Analyzing models with these techniques is good practice to avoid spurious correlation [3] and better understand our models.

5 Experiments and Results

This section presents the different experiments with dynamic features extracted thanks to PANDI [32] and static features already explored in literature [10].

Training on the CleanPack Dataset. The results of the models trained on the CLEANPACK dataset are presented in Table 2. This dataset is classified with high accuracy by all models. The ROC curves of the 9 models are depicted in Fig. 10. The DT models are slightly less efficient than the RF and GBDT models as we can see from their AUC values.

These excellent results are likely linked to the simplicity of the dataset with well-known packers. The samples have been manually packed, likely resulting in a substantial degree of commonality among them, thereby rendering their classification more straightforward.

We evaluate these models on the WILDPACK dataset to see if they generalize to more complex datasets. Unfortunately, the results were not satisfactory. The recall scores were very low which indicates that many packed samples were misclassified. This is likely due to the variety and complexity of packers that appear in the WILDPACK dataset. Moreover, the CLEANPACK dataset is solely composed of cleanware while the WILDPACK dataset mostly comprises malware.

Table 2. Metrics for the models trained on the CLEANPACK dataset

		BA	P	R	F1
dynamic	DT	0.97	0.99	1.0	0.99
	RF	0.99	0.99	1.0	1.0
	GBDT	0.98	0.99	1.0	1.0
static	DT	0.99	1.0	1.0	1.0
	RF	0.99	0.99	1.0	1.0
	GBDT	1.0	1.0	1.0	1.0
both	DT	0.99	0.99	1.0	1.0
	RF	0.99	1.0	1.0	1.0
	GBDT	0.99	1.0	1.0	1.0

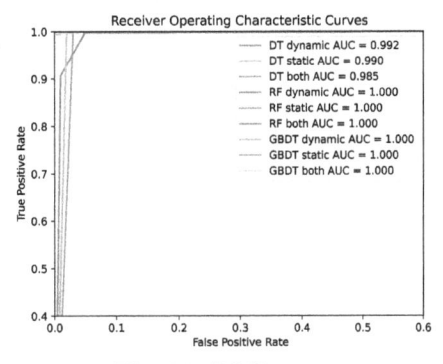

Fig. 10. ROC curves

Training on the **WildPack** ***Dataset.*** The metrics of the models on the second dataset are listed in Table 3. We notice that the precision, recall and F1-scores are high for most models. The best performing models are the RF and the GBDT trained on the combination of both feature sets (as we can see in Table 3 and Fig. 11). The high recall but lower balanced accuracy put into light that the models detect the packed samples better than the not packed samples. In the context of a malware analysis toolchain, it is important to have a high recall to detect packing and perform a correct analysis of the sample (even at the cost of a few false positives).

Table 3. Metrics for the models trained on the WILDPACK dataset

		BA	P	R	F1
dynamic	DT	0.87	0.97	0.93	0.95
	RF	0.86	0.96	0.98	0.97
	GBDT	0.88	0.97	0.98	0.97
static	DT	0.83	0.96	0.93	0.94
	RF	0.77	0.93	0.98	0.95
	GBDT	0.83	0.95	0.98	0.96
both	DT	0.89	0.97	0.95	0.96
	RF	0.91	0.97	0.98	0.98
	GBDT	0.91	0.98	0.98	0.98

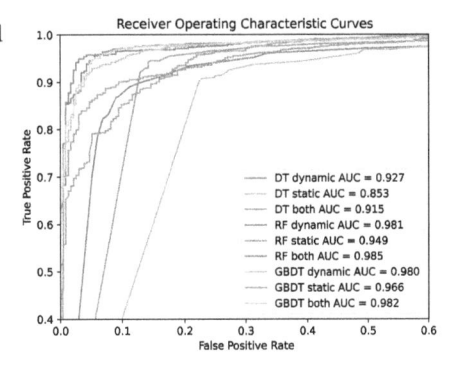

Fig. 11. ROC curves

Training on the MixPack Dataset. We notice that metrics in Table 4 slightly improve compared to Table 3. The AUC values improve as well, as we can see by comparing the ROC curves from Figs. 11 and 12.

However, when we analyze in detail the results of the classification on the test set, we notice that the CLEANPACK part of the test set is much better classified than the WILDPACK part. If we test the models exclusively on the WILDPACK part of the dataset, we find that the scores are nearly identical to those from the previous experiment. Therefore, including manually packed samples in the training set does not seem to improve the performance of our classifiers.

Table 4. Metrics for the models trained on the MIXPACK dataset

		BA	P	R	F1
dynamic	DT	0.90	0.97	0.96	0.97
	RF	0.90	0.97	0.98	0.98
	GBDT	0.91	0.97	0.98	0.98
static	DT	0.87	0.96	0.95	0.96
	RF	0.85	0.96	0.98	0.97
	GBDT	0.86	0.96	0.98	0.97
both	DT	0.91	0.98	0.96	0.97
	RF	0.92	0.98	0.98	0.98
	GBDT	0.93	0.98	0.98	0.98

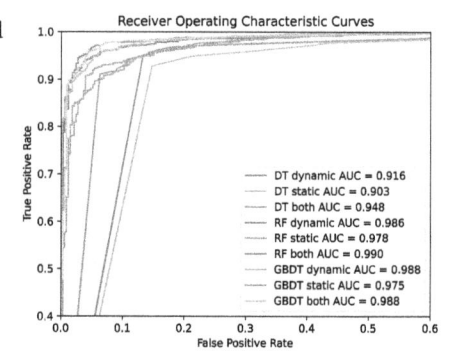

Fig. 12. ROC curves

Interpretable Machine Learning. Analyzing the SHAP values of our models allows us to understand the features that influence their decisions [36]. We investigate our Random Forest models on the different datasets because they perform best in our experiments. We chose to focus on models trained on dynamic features and on the combination of static and dynamic features since models based only on static features have already been studied in the literature [8]. The SHAP values of the top 10 features for each of our 6 models are shown in Fig. 13. Figures 13 (a), (c) and (e) represent models trained on the dynamic feature set while Figs. 13 (b), (d) and (f) represent models trained on the static and dynamic feature sets. We highlight the dynamic features in pink.

The classification of each sample is visualized as a dot on the graph. Dots located on the left side of the graph indicate a decision towards the *not packed* label. Conversely, dots located on the right side of the graph indicate a decision towards the *packed* label. Red dots indicate high feature values for the given sample, while blue dots indicate low feature values.

In Fig. 13(a), the CLEANPACK dataset is classified using many features related to executed bytes. Furthermore, in Fig. 13(b), we see that static features play an important role in the classification of the CLEANPACK dataset, while dynamic features have more influence on the classification of the WILDPACK dataset (Fig. 13(d)). These observations are consistent because the CLEANPACK dataset represents a more restricted set of packers than the WILDPACK dataset. Therefore, it is more suitable for classification by patterns and signatures. The WILDPACK dataset requires broader and more robust features because it consists of a wider variety of packers.

The features max_total_entropy and max_oep_section_entropy represent the maximum entropy that can be obtained from the whole binary and the section containing the OEP, respectively. As we can see, a low entropy value influences the classification towards the *not packed* result and vice versa.

Other important features are related to entropy: number_total_entropy and number_oep_section_entropy. These represent the number of entropy points collected during the execution and are directly related to the number of blocks executed. The classifier tends to consider a sample as packed when these values are high. We can explain this tendency by the fact that the unpacking routine usually implies that many blocks are executed and many entropy points generated.

The reconstructed_iat_suspicious_func feature represents the number of suspicious functions retrieved by the GetProcAddress function. A high number of these indicates that the sample may be packed.

The number of functions called by the original IAT are represented by the features initial_iat_called_generic_func and initial_iat_called_all_func. A low value for these features pushes the classification towards the *packed* result. In fact, a packed sample will only use the original IAT to decompress and reconstruct its original IAT. The majority of calls will be made from the reconstructed IAT.

Finally, the API calls used are represented by discovered_called_suspicious_func, discovered_called_generic_func and discovered_called_all_func. They seem to take higher values for not packed samples than for packed samples. This may be because malicious samples call native windows functions directly instead of using high level API calls (i.e.: a high-level API is usually based on lower-level API that we all record).

Observing our results, we could conclude that dynamic features have a high impact on machine learning algorithms, improving their accuracy and appearing more robust. In particular, entropy features seem to be selected as an influential feature by all the different models studied. However, extracting dynamic features is costly and it could be interesting to extend PANDI to directly detect the original entry point when a sample is detected as packed. This will further improve our malware analysis workflow while maintaining a similar overhead.

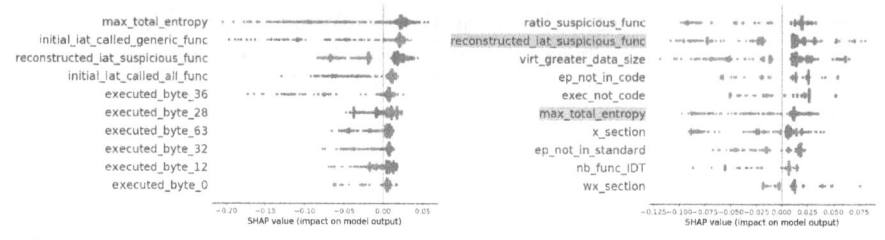

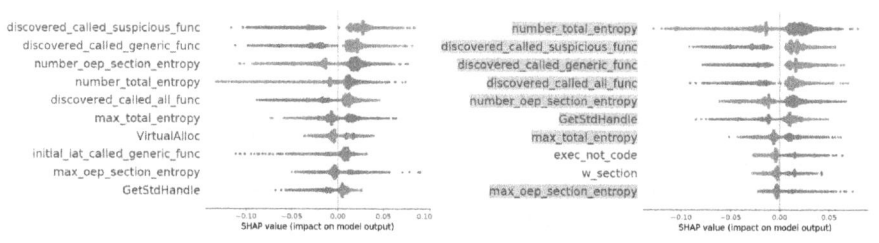

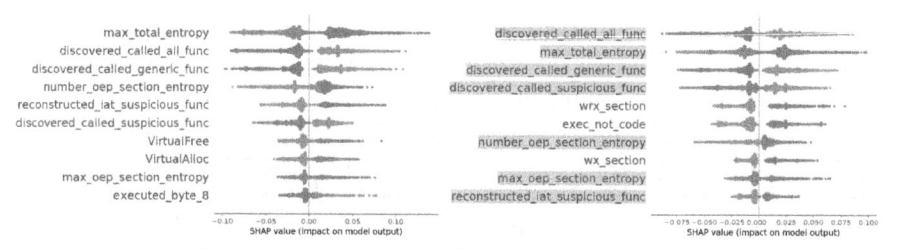

(a) trained on CLEANPACK with dynamic features
(b) trained on CLEANPACK with dynamic and static features
(c) trained on WILDPACK with dynamic features
(d) trained on WILDPACK with dynamic and static features
(e) trained on MIXPACK with dynamic features
(f) trained on MIXPACK with dynamic and static features

Fig. 13. SHAP values

Limitations. Our approach faces different limitations related to PANDI and our experimental setup. While PANDI takes some time to analyze, it allows us to extract extensive information about system calls and memory writes. However, we do not have access to the sample's execution state and use a timer to terminate the virtual machine after a certain period of time and then analyze the replay. This method avoids the need for direct feedback from the virtual machine, but could interrupt the execution of the sample before it finishes. As noted by Kuchler et al. [28], the vast majority of malicious activity of a malware is observed within the first two minutes of its execution. Moreover, we focus on the unpacking part of the execution and not the full malicious behavior, which may include more evasion techniques. Therefore, the impact on our results should be limited.

As discussed by Arp et al. [3], the dataset used by machine learning for cybersecurity tasks is difficult to construct without biases. First, the labeling process of the dataset is generally difficult and should rely on other techniques (antivirus, heuristics, manual inspection, ...) with their own biases and errors. This problem could be solved by the Packing Box [22] as discussed in the next section. Datasets could also be subject to temporal shift, i.e. the distribution and characteristics of the packed samples could change over time. While we do not consider this type of evaluation, the dataset obtained from [1] already provides a good representation of the packing ecosystem.

6 Conclusion and Future Work

We have studied several methods in the literature that are based on dynamic analysis. Our research shows that the use of dynamic features within a machine learning framework can yield impressive results, matching or even exceeding those achieved with static features. However, their significant extraction cost should also be considered when designing an efficient malware analysis toolchain. There is still room for improvement in several aspects.

We can use feature selection to extract only the more important features (e.g., $max\_total\_entropy$), thus reducing the extraction cost. Further exploration of the effectiveness of dynamic features in classifying different types of packers would be an interesting prospect. The machine learning approach could help in identifying the type of packer (protector, compressor, etc.) and/or the complexity of the packer [48]. However, creating ground truth with sufficient information for such experiments is challenging. Contributing to the Packing Box [22] by adding information about packing complexity and packing type for each packer would help our future research as well as other studies. In addition, the ability to pack malware samples could be added to this tool to improve dataset diversity and help our models to generalize to real-world scenarios.

Moreover, it is imperative to address adversarial aspects when applying machine learning to a cybersecurity problem [3]. First, the sandbox used by PANDI should be improved to minimize the risk of malware evasion (e.g., adding automatic mouse movements, launching other processes in the background, etc.). We could generate adversarial examples based on static features using tools such as MAB-malware [46], but the task becomes significantly more challenging when using dynamic features [44]. Finally, since malware and packers evolve over time, it seems necessary to analyze the performance of our models on an evolving real-world dataset. As a result of this evolution, the need and cost of retraining our models should be studied [8]. We hope that dynamic features would be more robust to temporal evolution, since it is harder to change semantic properties than syntactic properties of a binary.

In addition, our approach could be extended to include unpacking capabilities. Specifically, machine learning algorithms can be used to trigger a memory dump when a sample is identified as unpacked during execution replay. This would require defining features that characterize the end of the unpacking process and the beginning of the execution of the original executable. Existing techniques ([15,16,31,35]) could be adapted to our dynamic analysis and machine learning approach to efficiently detect the original entry point.

Finally, investigating unsupervised machine learning algorithms could help us overcome the lack of information about the samples [38]. This would regroup samples with high similarity. The resulting clusters could then be examined to identify common patterns. Dynamic features would certainly provide new insights into the behavioral similarities of packers. The information identified by this method could be used to develop customized unpacking strategies.

Acknowledgments. This research is supported by the Walloon region's CyberExcellence program (grant #2110186).

Conflict of Interest. The author(s) has no competing interests to declare that are relevant to the content of this manuscript.

References

1. Aghakhani, H., et al.: When malware is packin'heat; limits of machine learning classifiers based on static analysis features. In: NDSS 2020 (2020)
2. Ahmadi, M., Ulyanov, D., Semenov, S., Trofimov, M., Giacinto, G.: Novel feature extraction, selection and fusion for effective malware family classification. In: Proceedings of the Sixth ACM Conference on Data and Application Security and Privacy, pp. 183–194 (2016)
3. Arp, D., et al.: Dos and don'ts of machine learning in computer security. In: USENIX Security 22, pp. 3971–3988 (2022)
4. Avast: Pelib (2023). https://github.com/avast/pelib
5. Bat-Erdene, M., Park, H., Li, H., Lee, H., Choi, M.S.: Entropy analysis to classify unknown packing algorithms for malware detection. Int. J. Inf. Secur. **16**, 227–248 (2017)
6. Bertrand Van Ouytsel, C.-H., Crochet, C., Dam, K.H.T., Legay, A.: Tool Paper - SEMA: symbolic execution toolchain for malware analysis. In: Kallel, S., Jmaiel, M., Zulkernine, M., Hadj Kacem, A., Cuppens, F., Cuppens, N. (eds.) CRiSIS 2022. LNCS, vol. 13857, pp. 62–68. Springer, Cham (2023). https://doi.org/10.1007/978-3-031-31108-6_5
7. Bertrand Van Ouytsel, C.H., Dam, K.H.T., Legay, A.: Symbolic analysis meets federated learning to enhance malware identifier. In: Proceedings of the 17th International Conference on Availability, Reliability and Security, pp. 1–10 (2022)
8. Bertrand Van Ouytsel, C.H., Dam, K.H.T., Legay, A.: Analysis of machine learning approaches to packing detection. Comput. Secur. 103536 (2023)
9. Bertrand Van Ouytsel, C.H., Legay, A.: Malware analysis with symbolic execution and graph kernel. In: Reiser, H.P., Kyas, M. (eds.) Secure IT Systems. NordSec 2022. LNCS, vol. 13700, pp. 292–310. Springer, Cham (2022). https://doi.org/10.1007/978-3-031-22295-5_16
10. Biondi, F., Enescu, M.A., Given-Wilson, T., Legay, A., Noureddine, L., Verma, V.: Effective, efficient, and robust packing detection and classification. Comput. Secur. **85**, 436–451 (2019)

11. Biondi, F., Given-Wilson, T., Legay, A., Puodzius, C., Quilbeuf, J.: Tutorial: an overview of malware detection and evasion techniques. In: Margaria, T., Steffen, B. (eds.) Leveraging Applications of Formal Methods, Verification and Validation. Modeling. ISoLA 2018. LNCS, vol. 11244, pp. 565–586. Springer, Cham (2018). https://doi.org/10.1007/978-3-030-03418-4_34
12. Biondi, F., Josse, S., Legay, A.: Bypassing malware obfuscation with dynamic synthesis. ERCIM News (106) (2016)
13. Biondi, F., Josse, S., Legay, A., Sirvent, T.: Effectiveness of synthesis in concolic deobfuscation. Comput. Secur. **70**, 500–515 (2017)
14. packing box: dataset-packed-pe (2023). https://github.com/packing-box/dataset-packed-pe
15. Cheng, B., et al.: Towards paving the way for large-scale windows malware analysis: generic binary unpacking with orders-of-magnitude performance boost. In: Proceedings of the 2018 ACM SIGSAC Conference on Computer and Communications Security, pp. 395–411 (2018)
16. Cheng, B., et al.: {Obfuscation-Resilient} executable payload extraction from packed malware. In: 30th USENIX Security Symposium (USENIX Security 21), pp. 3451–3468 (2021)
17. Choi, Y.S., Kim, I.K., Oh, J.T., Ryou, J.C.: PE file header analysis-based packed PE file detection technique (PHAD). In: International Symposium on Computer Science and its Applications, pp. 28–31. IEEE (2008)
18. Dam, K.H.T., Given-Wilson, T., Legay, A.: Unsupervised behavioural mining and clustering for malware family identification. In: Proceedings of the 36th Annual ACM Symposium on Applied Computing, pp. 374–383 (2021)
19. Dam, K.H.T., Given-Wilson, T., Legay, A., Veroneze, R.: Packer classification based on association rule mining. Appl. Soft Comput. **127**, 109373 (2022)
20. Dambra, S., et al.: Decoding the secrets of machine learning in malware classification: a deep dive into datasets, feature extraction, and model performance. arXiv preprint arXiv:2307.14657 (2023)
21. D'Hondt, A.: Peid (2023). https://github.com/packing-box/peid
22. D'Hondt, A., Van Ouytsel, C.H.B., Legay, A.: Experimental toolkit for manipulating executable packing. arXiv preprint arXiv:2302.09286 (2023)
23. Dolan-Gavitt, B., Hodosh, J., Hulin, P., Leek, T., Whelan, R.: Repeatable reverse engineering with panda. In: Proceedings of the 5th Program Protection and Reverse Engineering Workshop, pp. 1–11 (2015)
24. ENISA: Threat landscape report 2022 (2022). https://www.enisa.europa.eu/publications/enisa-threat-landscape-2022
25. Islam, R., Tian, R., Batten, L.M., Versteeg, S.: Classification of malware based on integrated static and dynamic features. J. Netw. Comput. Appl. **36**(2), 646–656 (2013)
26. Kancherla, K., Donahue, J., Mukkamala, S.: Packer identification using byte plot and Markov plot. J. Comput. Virol. Hacking Tech. **12**, 101–111 (2016)
27. Kotov, V., Wojnowicz, M.: Towards generic deobfuscation of windows API calls (2018). arXiv preprint arXiv:1802.04466
28. Küchler, A., Mantovani, A., Han, Y., Bilge, L., Balzarotti, D.: Does every second count? time-based evolution of malware behavior in sandboxes. In: NDSS (2021)
29. Kwiatkowski, I.: Manalyze (2023). https://github.com/JusticeRage/Manalyze
30. Li, X., Shan, Z., Liu, F., Chen, Y., Hou, Y.: A consistently-executing graph-based approach for malware packer identification. IEEE Access **7**, 51620–51629 (2019)
31. Lim, C., Ramli, K., Kotualubun, Y.S., et al.: Mal-Flux: rendering hidden code of packed binary executable. Digit. Investig. **28**, 83–95 (2019)

32. Lucca, S., Wauters, D.: Pandi (2023). https://github.com/dimitriwauters/PANDI
33. Lyda, R., Hamrock, J.: Using entropy analysis to find encrypted and packed malware. IEEE Secur. Priv. **5**(2), 40–45 (2007)
34. Mantovani, A., Aonzo, S., Ugarte-Pedrero, X., Merlo, A., Balzarotti, D.: Prevalence and impact of low-entropy packing schemes in the malware ecosystem. In: NDSS (2020)
35. Martignoni, L., Christodorescu, M., Jha, S.: Omniunpack: fast, generic, and safe unpacking of malware. In: ACSAC. IEEE (2007)
36. Molnar, C.: Interpretable machine learning. Lulu. com (2020)
37. Muralidharan, T., Cohen, A., Gerson, N., Nissim, N.: File packing from the malware perspective: techniques, analysis approaches, and directions for enhancements. ACM Comput. Surv. **55**(5), 1–45 (2022)
38. Noureddine, L., Heuser, A., Puodzius, C., Zendra, O.: SE-PAC: a self-evolving packer classifier against rapid packers evolution. In: CODASPY (2021)
39. Oberhumer, M., Molnar, L., Reiser, J.: UPX, the Ultimate Packer for eXecutables. https://upx.github.io/
40. Perdisci, R., Lanzi, A., Lee, W.: Classification of packed executables for accurate computer virus detection **29**(14), 1941–1946
41. panda re: Panda (2023). https://github.com/panda-re/panda
42. Said, N.B., et al.: Detection of mirai by syntactic and behavioral analysis. In: ISSRE, pp. 224–235. IEEE (2018)
43. Sebastio, S., et al.: Optimizing symbolic execution for malware behavior classification. Comput. Secur. 101775 (2020)
44. Shafiei, A., Rimmer, V., Tsingenopoulos, I., Desmet, L., Joosen, W.: Position paper: on advancing adversarial malware generation using dynamic features. In: Proceedings of the 1st Workshop on Robust Malware Analysis, pp. 15–20 (2022)
45. Smith, M.R., et al.: Mind the gap: on bridging the semantic gap between machine learning and malware analysis. In: Proceedings of the 13th ACM Workshop on Artificial Intelligence and Security, pp. 49–60 (2020)
46. Song, W., Li, X., Afroz, S., Garg, D., Kuznetsov, D., Yin, H.: Mab-malware: a reinforcement learning framework for attacking static malware classifiers. arXiv preprint arXiv:2003.03100 (2020)
47. Treadwell, S., Zhou, M.: A heuristic approach for detection of obfuscated malware. In: IEEE International Conference on Intelligence and Security Informatics, ISI 2009, Dallas, Texas, USA, 8–11 June 2009, Proceedings, pp. 291–299. IEEE (2009)
48. Ugarte-Pedrero, X., Balzarotti, D., Santos, I., Bringas, P.G.: Sok: deep packer inspection: a longitudinal study of the complexity of run-time packers. In: 2015 IEEE Symposium on Security and Privacy, pp. 659–673. IEEE (2015)
49. Ugarte-Pedrero, X., Santos, I., García-Ferreira, I., Huerta, S., Sanz, B., Bringas, P.G.: On the adoption of anomaly detection for packed executable filtering. Comput. Secur. **43**, 126–144 (2014)
50. Wu, C., Shi, J., Yang, Y., Li, W.: Enhancing machine learning based malware detection model by reinforcement learning. In: Proceedings of the 8th International Conference on Communication and Network Security, pp. 74–78 (2018)
51. Yan, X., Han, J.: Gspan: graph-based substructure pattern mining. In: 2002 IEEE International Conference on Data Mining, 2002, pp. 721–724. IEEE (2002)
52. Yason, M.V.: The art of unpacking. Retrieved Feb **12**, 2008 (2007)
53. Zakeri, M., Faraji Daneshgar, F., Abbaspour, M.: A static heuristic approach to detecting malware targets. Secur. Commun. Netw. **8**(17), 3015–3027 (2015)

Towards a Framework for Transitioning from Monolith to Serverless

Giuseppe De Palma[1,2], Saverio Giallorenzo[1,2], Jacopo Mauro[3(✉)], Matteo Trentin[1,2,3], and Gejsi Vjerdha[1]

[1] Alma Mater Studiorum - Università di Bologna, Bologna, Italy
[2] OLAS team INRIA, Biot, France
[3] University of Southern Denmark, Odense, Denmark
mauro@imada.sdu.dk

Abstract. Serverless programming revolutionises the implementation of cloud architectures by allowing developers to deploy stateless functions without managing server infrastructure, enabling efficient scaling and resource usage. Serverless shifts to the cloud provider the burden of managing servers and scaling, enabling developers to focus solely on writing the code for the functionalities specific to a given architecture.

In this paper, we introduce Fenrir, a programming framework designed to facilitate the transition from monolithic programming to serverless. Fenrir enables developers to write applications in a monolithic style. Using annotation, users specify which components of the monolith shall implement separate serverless functions. Given these annotations, Fenrir generates a deployable serverless codebase, facilitating quick development and testing cycles while ensuring the alignment of the execution semantics between monolithic and serverless code.

1 Introduction

The landscape of Cloud architectures includes microservices [15] and serverless functions [23]. Each approach offers unique advantages and trade-offs regarding management and operational efficiency.

The microservices style advocates for the decomposition of applications into loosely-coupled services, each internally cohesive to encapsulate a specific business functionality—thus, microservices are usually "small" if compared to monolithic software that implements multiple, loosely-related functionalities. These stateful processes expose multiple operations to users and developers, affording granular control over individual components of an application. In the microservices paradigm, developers take responsibility for provisioning the servers that host these services and managing their scalability to accommodate fluctuations in user demand or traffic spikes. This approach necessitates a comprehensive understanding of the underlying infrastructure and entails proactive monitoring and adjustment of resources to maintain optimal performance.

Conversely, serverless functions, also called Function as a Service (FaaS), represent a departure from the traditional server-based approach to application deployment. In this paradigm, developers assemble a cloud application from the composition of stateless functions, each designed to execute a specific operation or task. Developers leverage cloud platforms to deploy these functions without the need to manage underlying servers or infrastructure explicitly. Indeed, programmers delegate the responsibility of scaling their architectures and managing server resources to the serverless platform provider. This abstraction of infrastructure management enables developers to focus exclusively on writing and deploying the code of functions, thereby streamlining the development process and reducing operational overhead. While microservices offer fine-grained control over resource allocation and performance optimisation, they may entail higher operational complexity and overhead due to the need for infrastructure management. Serverless architectures abstract away the complexities of infrastructure management, offering a pay-as-you-go model where the provider bills developers only for the resources consumed by their functions. However, this abstraction may introduce limitations on performance tuning and resource customisation, particularly for applications with stringent latency and resource requirements.

No matter what style is chosen, the growing number of functions or microservices found in cloud architectures causes an exponential explosion of the possible interactions a system can experience. This interaction explosion makes it hard for programmers to reason on the correctness of their implementations against their expected behaviour. In contrast, the experience of programming traditional monolithic software is much more "linear". In this style, programmers usually build their applications as a comprehensive codebase that includes all the logic into a single model. In this way, both static reasoning on the code and following the steps of execution are much simpler tasks than for the microservices and serverless cases.

Looking at recent advancements in the development of distributed systems, the paradigm of choreographic programming [10,13,18,32] uses choreographies as "monolithic" artifacts/models that specify the distributed logic of the system, relying on compilation to generate sets of components (e.g., connectors [7,17]). Like for model-driven engineering [24], the code automatically generated correctly implements the properties of the model (in this case, the distributed logic of the system) and possibly mediates the interaction with the existing components (e.g., microservices).

Inspired by choreographic programming and model-driven engineering, we aim to support programmers in building serverless applications. For this reason, in this paper, we present the design and implementation of Fenrir, a programming framework that facilitates the transition between monolithic and serverless programming. In Fenrir, developers write applications in a monolithic style. Then, they annotate which parts of the artefact shall be deployed as separate serverless functions, along with their respective call events (e.g., via external HTTP invocations, time-scheduled, etc.). Given the annotated codebase, as it happens in choreographic programming, Fenrir generates a correct-by-construction deployable serverless codebase following the annotations. Hence, Fenrir helps programmers achieve quick development and testing cycles, making sure that the execution semantics of the generated serverless application follow the one defined by the source program. Fenrir is available as an open-source project at https://www.github.com/Gejsi/fenrir.

Lessons Learned from Tiziana Margaria. We present this contribution in honor of Tiziana on the occasion of her 60th birthday. Tiziana Margaria's career has significantly shaped the field of programming safe and formally verified systems and her work has been instrumental in bridging the gap between theoretical foundations and practical applications in software engineering and many other domains such as healthcare [40], agriculture [20], and history [8]. Starting from her work in the telecommunication services [43] and later on Service-Oriented design [30] and Web-Service Construction [25], she always advocates for a "divide and conquer" approach where initial prototypes are successively modified until each component satisfies the requirements, paying attention to the fact that the generation of services is constantly accompanied by verification of the validity of the required features. Key to her approach is the notion of Model and Model-Driven Engineering [12,28] that allows at the same time to describe the behaviour of the program, reason on the correctness of the system, and generate the code that correctly implements it. Talking to her, it is easy to see that Tiziana is an energetic and keen believer in using Model-Driven Engineering to lower the entry barriers for software development, always recommending involving all the stakeholders in the design process [29] and more recently even pushing the boundaries with low-code/no-code approaches [11,34].

This proposal integrates some of Tiziana's ideas applied to the domain of cloud application development. Indeed, Fenrir follows a Model-Driven development approach in which developers write a model of the system, delegating the generation of the code to a tool that exploits annotations to correctly implement architecture components on serverless platforms. We hope that this work can contribute to the lowering of the entry barriers for developing correct-by-constructions serverless applications.

Structure of the Paper. In Sect. 2, we start by introducing Fenrir using a running example. In Sect. 3, we present an overview of serverless programming. We introduce in Sect. 4 the main features of Fenrir, namely, its annotation constructors and its pipeline. In Sect. 5, we show how Fenrir works with a more elaborate example. We conclude by commenting on related and future work in Sect. 6.

2 Introductory Example

We start by introducing the experience of using Fenrir with a running example (expanded and explained in detail in Sect. 5) of a monolithic JavaScript codebase with a pair of illustrative functions that transform into a serverless architecture. In the codebase, one function, called `processOrd`, retrieves orders (e.g., via a database query). The other function, called `generateRep`, produces reports based on the retrieved orders.

```
1  export async function processOrd(orderId) {
2  // ... processing logic ...
3    return order
4  }
5  export async function generateRep() {
6    //... report generation logic ...
7  }
```

Given the code above, we introduce annotations for the processOrd and generateRep functions to make them separate serverless functions via the Fenrir code generator. Specifically, we annotate the first function to make it callable from clients via HTTP requests. The second is instead a backend batch function that shall run every two hours. We report below the except of the code above with the Fenrir annotations of the two functions.

```
1  /**
2   * $Fixed
3   * $HttpApi(method: "GET", path: "/orders/report")
4   */
5  export async function processOrd(orderId) {
6    ...
7  }
8  /** $Scheduled(rate: "2 hours") */
9  export async function generateRep() {
10   ...
11 }
```

Briefly, we annotate processOrd as $Fixed to mean it is a fixed-size serverless function—the fixed-size attribute means that the resources assigned to the function (e.g., CPU, RAM) are constant and statically determined regardless of the workload or input size—and that it must be exposed as an $HttpApi reachable through the GET HTTP method at the URL /orders/report (the annotation abstracts away the address of the server hosting the function, bound at deployment time). Similarly, we annotate generateRep to be $Scheduled at a rate of once every "2 hours".

Concentrating, for brevity, on the result of the process of processOrd (the results for the other function are similar), we obtain two artefacts. The first is the JavaScript code of the serverless implementation of processOrd, reported below on the left. The most notable traits of the translation regard the transformation of the input of processOrd to match the expected signature for functions of the serverless platform, i.e., an event e that carries, among other content, the invocation parameters of the function, which are automatically assigned to local counterparts at the beginning of the function body. Complementarily, we also find the return value changed to match the shape of the response expected by the platform, where we create a JSON object with a status code and a body that contains a serialised version of the value held by the variable order, which carried the returned output of the function in the source codebase. The second artefact generated by the code generator is the YAML code found on the right, which contains the information that the serverless platform needs to deploy the function, i.e., the type of invocation (HTTP, with method and path) for the processOrd function.

```
1  export async function processOrd(e){
2      const orderId = e.orderId
3      // ... processing logic ...
4      return {
5          statusCode: 200,
6          body: JSON.stringify(order)
7      }
8  }
```

```
1  processOrd:
2      handler: output.
             processOrd
3      events:
4          - httpApi:
5              method: GET
6              path: /orders/
                      report
```

3 Preliminaries

In this section, we provide a brief overview of serverless computing and the platforms that support it.

Modern cloud applications have access to a plethora of services that allow them to scale and be more resilient. As they can scale more, their complexity and usage increases, leading to the need to be efficiently (and automatically) managed. Serverless computing was born to respond to these needs by offering a kind of service that abstracts away the underlying infrastructure, and allows an application to be built as a composition of stateless, event-driven functions that can automatically scale up and down.

A serverless application is written via software units called functions, which are run in short-lived environments triggered by some kind of event. When a function invocation is triggered by an event such as HTTP requests, database changes, file uploads, scheduled intervals or various other triggers, the provider runs the code after initializing an execution environment, a secure and isolated context that manages all the resources needed for the function lifecycle. Execution environments are technically handled differently by the platform providers, e.g. Virtual Machines (VMs), μVMs or Docker containers, etc.

Figure 1 presents the typical architecture of a serverless platform. The main components are the controllers and the workers. The controller receives requests from external sources, such as users or other systems. It handles scaling decisions based on incoming traffic and system load, orchestrates the allocation of worker nodes for function execution and manages the overall system coordination and monitoring. The scheduler in particular determines which worker node should execute each function based on factors such as current load, function requirements, and resource availability. Worker nodes then execute the actual functions requested by the controller node, handling the execution environment lifecycle, including provisioning, scaling, and teardown.

Serverless platforms usually adopt a communication layer that facilitates communication between the controller node and worker nodes, handling messages and data transfer between components. In particular, message queues or event brokers (e.g., RabbitMQ [?], Kafka [5]) are used for asynchronous communication between components, allowing decoupling and scalability. Internal APIs

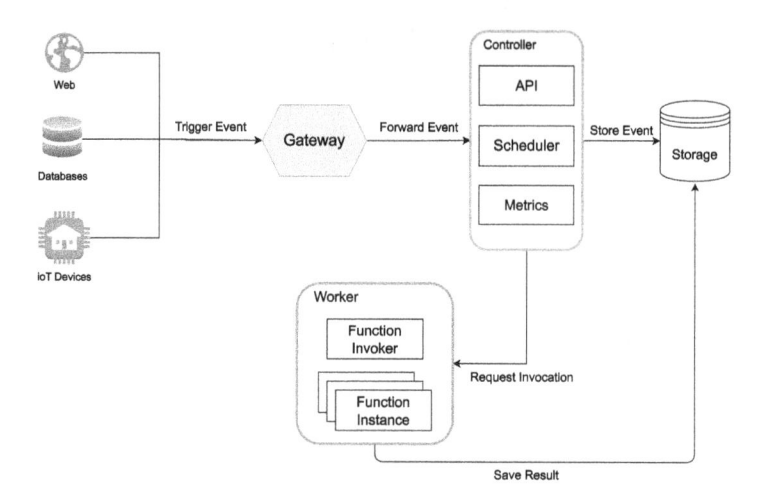

Fig. 1. Typical serverless platform architecture.

or RPC facilitate synchronous communication for tasks such as function deployment, status updates, and resource allocation. Monitoring tools are also used to collect metrics on resource usage, function execution times, and error rates. Metrics provide visibility into system performance, function execution, and overall health and enable debugging, troubleshooting, and performance optimization.

In serverless platforms, events play a crucial role in triggering function executions and driving the serverless architecture. Platforms often support a variety of events ranging from HTTP requests for handling webhooks and web-based interactions, cloud storage events (e.g., creation, deletion, or modification of an object in the cloud storage system or database activities such as inserts, updates, or deletions of records), events triggered at predefined intervals or specific times, events triggered by messages arriving in a message queue or streams, and events generated by custom sources or external systems via integrations or APIs.

Among the leading providers of serverless computing platforms, Amazon Web Services (AWS) Lambda [4] stands out as a pioneer in the field. AWS Lambda was the first publicly available serverless platform, allowing developers to pay only for the compute time consumed by their functions. Other platforms followed suit, offering similar capabilities, such as Microsoft Azure Cloud Functions [31] and Google Cloud Platform (GCP) Cloud Functions [19].

A number of open-source serverless platforms have also emerged, such as OpenWhisk [6], Knative [44], and OpenFaaS [35]. These platforms can be deployed on-premises or on the cloud, and offer a more flexible and customizable solution compared to the proprietary platforms.

4 The Fenrir Framework

The idea behind Fenrir is to use annotations as an abstraction layer that the developers can unobtrusively use to apply code transformations and metadata generation to a given application, to deploy it on a serverless platform. Here, we focus on concrete annotations built for the popular AWS Lambda platform [4], but the concepts directly translate to similar serverless platforms, both private [19,31] and open-source [6,16,21,35].

Fenrir's Annotations. Fenrir relies on standard JSDoc comments, on which it introduces annotations as new special keywords that follow the pattern `/** $AnnotationName(param:"foo") */` . That pattern shows a crucial feature of Fenrir, i.e., users can *pass parameters to annotations*. This means that the user can customise how annotations define the translation process of a specific piece of the monolithic codebase. Besides primitive values (strings, numbers, etc.), annotation parameters are full-fledged JavaScript objects, such as arrays that carry multiple values or functions that specify custom behaviour used in the code generation process. Another important feature supported by Fenrir is the *composition* of annotations so that users can specify sequences of transformation steps, essentially defining compilation pipelines for each piece of the monolithic codebase.

Practically, each annotation corresponds to a code transformer, which is a visitor function that works on the annotated piece of source code to generate a modified version of it and/or related metadata. Core annotations supported by Fenrir are (we report their signature using TypeScript's syntax):

- `$Fixed(memorySize?: number, timeout?: number, ...)` converts monolithic functions into fixed-size serverless functions, whose resources are statically determined and remain constant regardless of the workload or input size. The annotation works by transforming the parameters and parts of the body of the functions (`return`/`throw` statements) to make them follow the platform's function signature (e.g., they are unary functions with an `event` parameter that carries the actual invocation parameters along with other runtime values). Note that functions without the `$Fixed` annotation are considered local functions and are included in the body of other annotated functions.
- `$TrackMetrics(namespace: string, metricName: string, metricValue?: ts.Expression, ...)` generates code that monitors and logs the functions' resource usage—the annotation automatically imports the necessary dependencies, e.g., for AWS it uses and injects the CloudWatch [3]. dependency. The optional `metricValue` accepts any TypeScript expression, which is added to the function's body in a context-aware manner (e.g., if the expression feeds some data to a variable to monitor some measure, the monitoring code executes only after the expression);
- `$HttpApi(method: string, path: string, ...)` makes the function available at an HTTP endpoint through a set HTTP method;
- `$Scheduled(rate: string, ...)` makes the function run at specific dates or periodic intervals.

Besides the above annotations, Fenrir supports custom annotations, which let developers create their own transformers. Developers can publish their annotations/transformers and import them in a given codebase to assemble the compilation pipelines that best fit their deployment scenarios.

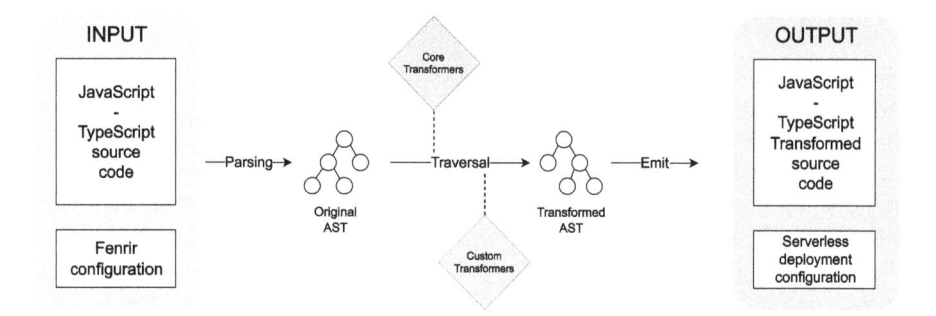

Fig. 2. Fenrir's annotation-driven pipeline.

Fenrir's Workflow. Fenrir parses (user-written) annotations, builds the related pipeline of code transformers, and then processes each piece of annotated source code to generate its output. From the implementation standpoint, Fenrir performs the parsing and the transformations through the TypeScript compiler API, making the framework compatible with both TypeScript and JavaScript codebases—TypeScript codebases enjoy additional guarantees thanks to the type checker of the language, which is also used to check user-defined transformers.

We complete our overview of Fenrir by looking at its pipeline, depicted in Fig. 2. Starting from the left, after annotating their monolithic codebase, developers can use Fenrir's console interface to start the code generation process. The tool provides step-by-step instructions to set up the code generation (initialising the file `fenrir.config.json`) and handle the subsequent deployment.

The pipeline starts with the parsing of the input source code through the TypeScript compiler API, which produces AST nodes with their related annotations. Then, each annotation induces the application of its related transformation step, whose output is fed into the next transformer, if any. During the transformation steps, Fenrir reports possible errors by gracefully stopping the process and indicating the offending instructions. Once the transformations have taken place without any errors, Fenrir saves the output source code, and it also appends the related metadata to a `serverless.yml` file—the latter specifies function deployment properties, e.g., the address to invoke a given function; specifically, the `serverless.yml` file makes the generated functions deployable through the Serverless framework [42].

5 From a Monolith to Serverless, by Example

To better visualise the developer's programming tasks, in this section, we exemplify how Fenrir could be used to transform an application written as a monolith into a serverless cloud application.

Let's consider a subset of an example e-commerce application. We want this application to, at least:

1. allow for the insertion of a new order, representing the purchase of an item by a specific user;
2. allow for the retrieval of information about an order, given its identifier;
3. generate a report of all processed orders periodically

Such functionalities would interact directly with an underlying storage (e.g. a database), to retrieve and insert the required orders. In Listing 1.1, we show these three basic features, in the form of functions taken from a monolithic codebase.

One function, called `insertOrder`, receives in input the ID of the product being purchased, its amount, and the ID of the user making the purchase; it then generates an ID for the corresponding order, stores the data in a database, and returns the ID to the caller. The `retrieveOrder` function performs the inverse operation: given the ID of an order, it retrieves the related information from storage, and returns it to the caller. Finally, the `generateReport` function produces reports based on the processed orders. Since we want both `insertOrder` and `retrieveOrder` to be invocable by clients and not treated as local functions, we annotate them as `$Fixed` , and we specify their HTTP endpoints and methods with the `$HttpApi` annotation (POST and GET respectively, reflecting their behaviour). The `generateReport` function, however, is a backend functionality that does not require (nor expect) user interaction; instead, we want it to run at pre-established intervals. To obtain this behaviour, we use the `$scheduled` annotation to specify that it shall be run every two hours.

Using Fenrir, we translate the code of Listing 1.1 into the serverless codebase of Listings 1.2 and 1.3.

In Listing 1.2, we find all three functions ready to be deployed on the serverless platform. In particular, notice that the input of both `insertOrder` and `retrieveOrder` changed to match the expected signature for functions of the serverless platform, i.e., an `event` that carries, among other content, the invocation parameters of the function, which are automatically assigned to local counterparts at the beginning of the function body. Complementarily, we also find the return values changed to match the shape of the response expected by the platform—at lines 5–8 and 18–21 of Listing 1.2, we create a JSON object with a status code and a body that contains a serialised version of the value held by the return variable in the source codebase (i.e. `orderId` for `insertOrder`, `order` for `retrieveOrder`). As for `generateReport`, the function's body is unchanged, given that it doesn't take any inputs and doesn't return any outputs, so from Fenrir's point of view, it is comprised only of its internal logic. The other notable element is the YAML code found in Listing 1.3, which contains the information that the serverless platform needs to deploy the three functions, e.g., the type of invocation for the `processOrder` function (HTTP) and its invocation address and the call schedule of the `generateReport` function.

```
1   /**
2    * $Fixed
3    * $HttpApi(method: "GET", path: "/orders/retrieve")
4    */
5   export async function retrieveOrder(orderId) {
6     console.log(`Retrieving order ${orderId}`)
7     // ... retrieve order from database ...
8     return order
9   }
10
11  /**
12   * $Fixed
13   * $HttpApi(method: "POST", path: "/orders/insert")
14   */
15  export async function insertOrder(productId, amount, userId) {
16    // ... processing logic ...
17    console.log(`Order ${orderId} inserted`)
18    return orderId
19  }
20
21  /** $Scheduled(rate: "2 hours") */
22  export async function generateReport() {
23    console.log("Generating report")
24    // get the processed data and generate report
25  }
```

Listing 1.1. Source code.

6 Discussion and Conclusion

We presented Fenrir, a programming framework that aims to make the development of serverless applications as seamless as possible by letting developers write serverless architectures as traditional, monolithic programs. Fenrir's annotations let developers mark monolithic codebases to indicate what parts shall be deployed as serverless functions. Then, Fenrir applies annotation-induced transformations on the source code to generate an architecture amenable to serverless deployment. In doing so, Fenrir also promotes the incremental adoption of the serverless paradigm and supports developers in gradually learning serverless deployment patterns.

Works closely related to Fenrir include similar tools that make a given codebase amenable to serverless deployment; so-called "FaaSifiers". The work closest to Fenrir are FaaSFusion, DAF, and M2FaaS [27,39,41]. The main difference between Fenrir and these proposals is in the objective behind the tools. Fenrir aims to build a serverless architecture starting from a monolithic codebase, which provides a more cohesive and responsive experience for developers, thanks to the consolidated techniques and set of tools available to programmers. The goal of FaaSifiers is that of offloading parts of the computation of a monolith to a serverless runtime, which is (intended to be) controlled and accessible only by the monolith itself. FaaSFusion and Fenrir are close also from the ergonomics

```
 1  export async function retrieveOrder(event) {
 2      const orderId = event.orderId
 3      console.log(`Retrieving order ${orderId}`)
 4      // ... processing logic ...
 5      return {
 6          statusCode: 200,
 7          body: JSON.stringify(order), }}
 8
 9  export async function insertOrder(event) {
10      const productId = event.productId
11      const amount = event.amount
12      const userId = event.userId
13
14      // ... processing logic ...
15      console.log(`Order ${orderId} inserted`)
16      return {
17          statusCode: 200,
18          body: JSON.stringify(orderId) }}
19
20  export async function generateReport() {
21      // get the processed data and generate report
22      console.log("Generating report") }
```

Listing 1.2. Generated code.

standpoint since they block support function-level annotations. Contrarily, DAF and M2FaaS intersperse annotations within the code, to indicate which arbitrary lines of the monoliths shall become serverless units, including which values should be forwarded to functions, the dependencies that should be included, and which values should be returned to the monolith.

Another example is Node2FaaS [14], which is one of the earliest proposals in the field and, like Fenrir, targets JavaScript codebases. The main difference with Fenrir is that Node2FaaS deploys all functions of the monolith as separate serverless functions, providing no control over the many aspects of the deployment, like what functionalities are exposed by the serverless platform and which invocation modalities they accept (time-scheduled, via HTTP hooks).

Kallas et al. [26] recently presented mu2sls, a framework for transforming microservice applications into serverless ones; mu2sls uses a variant of Python with two extra primitives (transactions and asynchronous calls) to provide a formally-proven, correct-by-construction translation.

We deem Fenrir a valid prototype to showcase the promising approach of building serverless architectures out of a monolithic codebase. However, we see interesting future directions that pose challenges to both research and development for overcoming the limitations of the current implementation. Firstly, Fenrir cannot handle global mutable variables within functions' bodies or perform filesystem operations. In a monolithic approach, global variables and files

```
 1  retrieveOrder:
 2    handler: output.retrieveOrder
 3    events:
 4      - httpApi:
 5          method: GET
 6          path: /orders/retrieve
 7  insertOrder:
 8    handler: output.insertOrder
 9    events:
10      - httpApi:
11          method: POST
12          path: /orders/insert
13  generateReport:
14    handler: output.generateReport
15    events:
16      - schedule:
17          rate: 2 hours
```

Listing 1.3. Generated code, deployment configuration.

can be used to store information such as the state of the application. However, since Fenrir transforms functions to be executed in a fully distributed system, it becomes impossible to use the filesystem or global state for storing information, as these are not available in a fully distributed environment. Developers can achieve the same functionalities by refactoring global mutable variables to be passed as parameters to functions and returned as results, avoiding the often-considered bad practice of using global variables [38]. Developers also need to translate operations using the file system to add calls to external storage services, as functions do not share memory (rendering mutable global variables unusable) or a common persistent filesystem.

While annotated functions can call non-annotated functions by including them as local function calls, another missing feature is that, in Fenrir, annotated functions cannot invoke other annotated functions. This cross-function calls restriction is to prevent an antipattern where serverless functions call each other through their respective endpoints. While in a monolithic approach this function-to-function call style is the norm—where any procedure call will simply add a frame on the stack in the server memory without big overheads—such calls would significantly increase latency in a serverless setting. The invoked functions would indeed need to pass through the serverless platform's entry point and load balancer repeatedly. New proposals of serverless frameworks such as the one by Jia and Witchel [22] are trying to reduce the overhead of cross-function calls, e.g., optimising internal function calls locally on the same worker without going through the API gateway, for the time being, we decided to enforce this constraint.

Related to the previous point, Fenrir does not support higher-order annotated functions. Implementing higher-order functions, i.e., functions that take other functions as arguments or return them as results, in a distributed setting can be challenging because these functions often involve passing other functions as arguments or returning them as results. In particular, closures, which capture the local state of a function, are difficult to manage in a distributed environment because the captured state must be serialised and transferred across nodes. Hence, supporting this feature would require maintaining function references and states across different nodes in the distributed system, which can introduce significant complexity.

Additionally, Fenrir currently implements coarse-grained error handling: when the runtime detects an exception in an annotated function it transforms it into a 400 HTTP response, similar to how Fenrir transforms the returns found in the source code into 200 HTTP responses. We plan to consider a more fine-grained approach in the future, e.g., using annotations to refine what kind of HTTP error exceptions shall transform into.

Finally, looking at scheduling policies, Fenrir could provide insights on how much cold starts affect the serverless function due to its external dependencies. Cold starts can introduce latency because the serverless platform needs to initialise the function's runtime environment, which includes loading any required libraries and dependencies. Hence, developers must consider the size and complexity of their functions' dependencies to minimise the impact on deployment performance. Since Fenrir has (at least part) of the information needed to provide insight on this issue, future work can develop tools that, starting from Fenrir's annotations can help the developers in devising the architectural division and implement the optimisations needed to ensure that their functions will be lightweight and efficient.

Future directions for Fenrir include the automatic support for closures (which one can implement as session-based calls to external databases) and the formalisation of the annotations and transformations performed to prove the correctness of the generated serverless code w.r.t. its source code, similar to the work conducted by Kallas et al. [26]. Moreover, we are interested in exploring how using choreographic languages, like Choral [18], can allow us to specify the interactions and behaviour of serverless functions. In particular, we conjecture that a choreographic language would allow us to express the patterns of interaction among the functions, e.g., supporting analyses such as finding the communication schemes that minimise the exchanges among the functions, to reduce the coordination overhead, and identifying/preventing possible antipatterns, e.g., due to an under- or over-granularisation of the logic of functions—an antipattern seen also in microservices, called mega-/nano-services [33,45].

Another interesting line of work regards the possibility of optimising the workflow of the generated FaaS application. Indeed, a recent trend of FaaS is the definition/handling of the composition/workflows of functions, like AWS step-functions [2] and Azure Durable functions [9]. The main idea behind these works is to allow users to define workflows as the composition of functions with their branching logic, parallel execution, and error handling. The orchestrator/controller of the platform then uses the workflow to manage function executions and handle retries, timeouts, and errors. Similarly, recent work [1,36,37] used optional opaque parameters or scheduling constraints in function invocations to inform the load balancer on the affinity with previous invocations and the data they produced or to control where the functions need to be run. Following this direction, one could extend Fenrir's annotation to incorporate also this information, thus allowing the final serverless application to be more efficient, robust, and reliable.

Conflict of Interest. The author(s) has no competing interests to declare that are relevant to the content of this manuscript.

References

1. Abdi, M., et al.: Palette load balancing: locality hints for serverless functions. In: Proceedings of the Eighteenth European Conference on Computer Systems, pp. 365–380 (2023)
2. Amazon Web Services. AWS Step Functions (2023). https://aws.amazon.com/step-functions/. Accessed July 2024
3. Amazon Web Services. Amazon CloudWatch (2024). https://aws.amazon.com/it/cloudwatch/. Accessed July 2024
4. Amazon Web Services. Introducing AWS Lambda (2024). https://aws.amazon.com/about-aws/whats-new/2014/11/13/introducing-aws-lambda/. Accessed July 2024
5. Apache Software Foundation. Apache Kafka (2024). https://kafka.apache.org/. Accessed July 2024
6. Apache Software Foundation. Apache OpenWhisk (2024). https://openwhisk.apache.org/. Accessed July 2024
7. Autili, M., Di Ruscio, D., Di Salle, A., Inverardi, P., Tivoli, M.: A model-based synthesis process for choreography realizability enforcement. In: Cortellessa, V., Varró, D. (eds.) FASE 2013. LNCS, vol. 7793, pp. 37–52. Springer, Heidelberg (2013). https://doi.org/10.1007/978-3-642-37057-1_4
8. Breathnach, C., Murphy, R., Schieweck, A., O'Shea, E., Clancy, S., Margaria, T.: Curating history datasets and training materials as OER: an experience. In: Shahriar, H., et al. (eds.) IEEE Annual Computers, Software, and Applications Conference, COMPSAC, pp. 1570–1575. IEEE (2023)
9. Burckhardt, S., Gillum, C., Justo, D., Kallas, K., McMahon, C., Meiklejohn, C.S.: Durable functions: semantics for stateful serverless. Proc. ACM Program. Lang. 5(OOPSLA), 1–27 (2021)
10. Carbone, M., Montesi, F.: Deadlock-freedom-by-design: multiparty asynchronous global programming. ACM SIGPLAN Not. **48**(1), 263–274 (2013)
11. Chaudhary, H., Margaria, T.: Integration of micro-services as components in modeling environments for low code development. In: Proceedings of the Institute for System Programming of the RAS (ISP RAS), vol. 33, pp. 19–30 (2021)
12. Chaudhary, H.A.A., et al.: Model-driven engineering in digital thread platforms: a practical use case and future challenges. In: Margaria, T., Steffen, B. (eds.) ISoLA 2022. LNCS, vol. 13704, pp. 195–207. Springer, Cham (2022). https://doi.org/10.1007/978-3-031-19762-8_14

13. Dalla Preda, M., Gabbrielli, M., Giallorenzo, S., Lanese, I., Mauro, J.: Dynamic choreographies: theory and implementation. Log. Methods Comput. Sci. **13**, 1–57 (2017)
14. de Carvalho, L.R., de Araújo, A.P.F.: Framework Node2FaaS: automatic NodeJS application converter for function as a service. In: CLOSER, pp. 271–278 (2019)
15. Dragoni, N., et al.: Microservices: yesterday, today, and tomorrow. In: Mazzara, M., Meyer, B. (eds.) Present and Ulterior Software Engineering, pp. 195–216. Springer, Cham (2017). https://doi.org/10.1007/978-3-319-67425-4_12
16. Fission Project. Fission (2024). https://fission.io/. Accessed July 2024
17. Giallorenzo, S., Lanese, I., Russo, D.: ChIP: a choreographic integration process. In: Panetto, H., Debruyne, C., Proper, H.A., Ardagna, C.A., Roman, D., Meersman, R. (eds.) OTM 2018. LNCS, vol. 11230, pp. 22–40. Springer, Cham (2018). https://doi.org/10.1007/978-3-030-02671-4_2
18. Giallorenzo, S., Montesi, F., Peressotti, M., Richter, D., Salvaneschi, G., Weisenburger, P.: Multiparty languages: the choreographic and multitier cases (pearl). In: Møller, A., Sridharan, M. (eds.) 35th European Conference on Object-Oriented Programming, ECOOP. LIPIcs, vol. 194, pp. 22:1–22:27. Schloss Dagstuhl - Leibniz-Zentrum für Informatik (2021)
19. Google. Google Cloud Functions (2024). https://cloud.google.com/functions/. Accessed July 2024
20. Guevara, I., Ryan, S., Singh, A., Brandon, C., Margaria, T.: Edge IoT prototyping using model-driven representations: a use case for smart agriculture. Sensors **24**(2), 495 (2024)
21. Hendrickson, S., Sturdevant, S., Harter, T., Venkataramani, V., Arpaci-Dusseau, A.C., Arpaci-Dusseau, R.H.: Serverless computation with OpenLambda. In: 8th USENIX Workshop on Hot Topics in Cloud Computing (HotCloud 2016) (2016)
22. Jia, Z., Witchel, E.: Nightcore: efficient and scalable serverless computing for latency-sensitive, interactive microservices. In: Sherwood, T., Berger, E.D., Kozyrakis, C. (eds.) ASPLOS 2021: 26th ACM International Conference on Architectural Support for Programming Languages and Operating Systems, pp. 152–166. ACM (2021)
23. Jonas, E., et al.: Cloud programming simplified: a berkeley view on serverless computing. arXiv preprint arXiv:1902.03383 (2019)
24. Jörges, S., Margaria, T., Steffen, B.: Assuring property conformance of code generators via model checking. Formal Aspects Comput. **23**(5), 589–606 (2011)
25. Jung, G., Margaria, T., Nagel, R., Schubert, W., Steffen, B., Voigt, H.: SCA and jABC: bringing a service-oriented paradigm to web-service construction. In: Margaria, T., Steffen, B. (eds.) ISoLA 2008. CCIS, vol. 17, pp. 139–154. Springer, Heidelberg (2008). https://doi.org/10.1007/978-3-540-88479-8_11
26. Kallas, K., Zhang, H., Alur, R., Angel, S., Liu, V.: Executing microservice applications on serverless, correctly. Proc. ACM Program. Lang. **7**(POPL), 367–395 (2023)
27. Klingler, R., Trifunovic, N., Spillner, J.: Beyond @cloudfunction: powerful code annotations to capture serverless runtime patterns. In: Proceedings of the Seventh International Workshop on Serverless Computing (WoSC7) 2021, pp. 23–28 (2021)
28. Margaria, T., Steffen, B.: Service-orientation: conquering complexity with XMDD. In: Hinchey, M., Coyle, L. (eds.) Conquering Complexity, pp. 217–236. Springer, London (2012). https://doi.org/10.1007/978-1-4471-2297-5_10
29. Margaria, T., Steffen, B.: eXtreme Model-Driven Development (XMDD) technologies as a hands-on approach to software development without coding. In: Tat-

nall, A. (ed.) Encyclopedia of Education and Information Technologies, pp. 1–19. Springer, Cham (2020). https://doi.org/10.1007/978-3-319-60013-0_208-1
30. Margaria, T., Steffen, B., Reitenspieß, M.: Service-oriented design: the roots. In: Benatallah, B., Casati, F., Traverso, P. (eds.) ICSOC 2005. LNCS, vol. 3826, pp. 450–464. Springer, Heidelberg (2005). https://doi.org/10.1007/11596141_34
31. Microsoft. Microsoft Azure Functions (2024). https://azure.microsoft.com/. Accessed July 2024
32. Montesi, F.: Introduction to Choreographies. Cambridge University Press, Cambridge (2023)
33. Neri, D., Soldani, J., Zimmermann, O., Brogi, A.: Design principles, architectural smells and refactorings for microservices: a multivocal review. SICS Softw.-Intensive Cyber-Phys. Syst. **35**, 3–15 (2020)
34. University of Limerick. Raise project (2024). https://software-engineering.ie/raise/. Accessed July 2024
35. OpenFaaS Ltd. OpenFaaS (2024). https://www.openfaas.com/. Accessed July 2024
36. Palma, G.D., Giallorenzo, S., Mauro, J., Trentin, M., Zavattaro, G.: A declarative approach to topology-aware serverless function-execution scheduling. In: IEEE International Conference on Web Services, ICWS, pp. 337–342. IEEE (2022)
37. De Palma, G., Giallorenzo, S., Mauro, J., Zavattaro, G.: Allocation priority policies for serverless function-execution scheduling optimisation. In: Kafeza, E., Benatallah, B., Martinelli, F., Hacid, H., Bouguettaya, A., Motahari, H. (eds.) ICSOC 2020. LNCS, vol. 12571, pp. 416–430. Springer, Cham (2020). https://doi.org/10.1007/978-3-030-65310-1_29
38. Parkhe, R.: Global variables are bad (2024). https://wiki.c2.com/?GlobalVariablesAreBad. Accessed July 2024
39. Pedratscher, S., Ristov, S., Fahringer, T.: M2FaaS: transparent and fault tolerant FaaSification of Node.js monolith code blocks. Future Gener. Comput. Syst. **135**, 57–71 (2022)
40. Rehman, M., Javed, I.T., Qureshi, K.N., Margaria, T., Jeon, G.: A cyber secure medical management system by using blockchain. IEEE Trans. Comput. Soc. Syst. **10**(4), 2123–2136 (2023)
41. Ristov, S., Pedratscher, S., Wallnoefer, J., Fahringer, T.: DAF: Dependency-Aware FaaSifier for Node.js monolithic applications. IEEE Softw. **38**(1), 48–53 (2020)
42. Serverless Inc. Serverless (2024). https://www.serverless.com/. Accessed July 2024
43. Steffen, B., Margaria, T., Claßen, A., Braun, V., Nisius, R., Reitenspieß, M.: A constraint-oriented service creation environment. In: Margaria, T., Steffen, B. (eds.) TACAS 1996. LNCS, vol. 1055, pp. 418–421. Springer, Heidelberg (1996). https://doi.org/10.1007/3-540-61042-1_63
44. The Knative Authors. Knative (2024). https://knative.dev/docs/. Accessed July 2024
45. Tighilt, R., et al.: On the study of microservices antipatterns: a catalog proposal. In: Proceedings of the European Conference on Pattern Languages of Programs 2020, pp. 1–13 (2020)

Computing Inflated Explanations for Boosted Trees: A Compilation-Based Approach

Alnis Murtovi[✉], Maximilian Schlüter[iD], and Bernhard Steffen[iD]

TU Dortmund University, Dortmund, Germany
{alnis.murtovi,maximilian.schlueter,bernhard.steffen}@tu-dortmund.de

Abstract. Explaining a classification made by tree-ensembles is an inherently hard problem that is traditionally solved approximately, without guaranteeing sufficiency or necessity. *Abductive explanations* were the first attempt to provide concise sufficient information: Given a sample, they consist of the minimal set of features that are relevant for the outcome. Inflated explanations are a refinement that additionally specify how much at least one feature must be altered in order to allow a change of the prediction. In this paper, we present the first algorithm for generating inflated explanations for gradient boosted trees, today's de facto standard for tree-based classifiers. Key to our algorithm is a compilation approach based on algebraic decision diagrams. The impact of our approach is illustrated along a number of popular data sets.

Keywords: Tree Ensemble · Boosted Trees · Explainable AI · Algebraic Decision Diagrams · Abductive Explanation · Inflated Explanation

1 Introduction

Over the past decade, machine learning has become increasingly popular. While deep learning dominates the fields of natural language processing, computer vision, and speech recognition, tree-based models, such as *Random Forests* [5] and *gradient boosted trees* [9], can still outperform deep learning based models on tabular data [4,14,30]. Tree ensemble models consist of a multitude of decision trees. While individual decision trees are usually considered to be interpretable [15], tree ensemble models, consisting of dozens or hundreds of decision trees, are not.

Much research has been conducted on making tree ensembles and their predictions explainable. Popular are model-agnostic approaches like LIME [28] and SHAP [24] that only observe the input-output relationship of a model to generate an explanation. By their nature, these approaches only provide approximate information, in the sense that they are neither necessary nor sufficient for the considered outcome.

In contrast, approaches that formally analyze the structure of the model aim at provable guarantees. This allows, e.g., to determine abductive explanations [18]: Given a sample and the prediction of a classifier for this sample, an abductive explanation is a *minimal subset* of the features, such that it is impossible to change the prediction without altering the value of at least one feature of this subset. Approaches for generating abductive explanations are based on solvers designed for problems such as SAT [22], SMT [19] or MaxSAT [1,17].

Inflated (abductive) explanations are a refinement of abductive explanations that additionally specify how much a feature must be altered in terms of maximal intervals. More concretely each feature of the underlying abductive explanation F is given an interval such that:

- The prediction is not changed, as long as all features of F have values of their corresponding interval, and
- Enlarging the interval of any other the features of F allows one to construct a sample with a different outcome.

Determining inflated explanation subsumes determining abductive explanations and has, to our knowledge, only be done for Random Forests [21] using SAT solving. In particular, it has never been done for boosted trees, today's de facto standard for tree-based classifiers.

In this paper, we present a compilation-based approach to, for the first time, generate inflated explanations for boosted trees. In particular, we show (Fig. 1)

1. how to transform boosted trees into semantically equivalent Algebraic Decision Diagrams (ADDs) [2] and
2. how existing algorithms for decision graphs can be used to generate abductive and inflated explanations for ADDs.

For the first step, we adapt the approach presented in [13] for compiling Random Forests into semantically equivalent ADDs to boosted trees, while we generalize an SMT-based algorithm [21] for inflated explanation to work for ADDs in the second step. In order to explore the impact of this approach, we consider the following three research questions:

RQ1 Can we compile boosted trees into ADDs in a reasonable amount of time?
RQ2 Can we generate abductive/inflated explanations faster than other state-of-the-art approaches?
RQ3 How does the size of our explanations compare to explanations from other state-of-the-art approaches?

We will see that, as expected, the compilation of the boosted models is the bottleneck (cf. Table 1). Please note, however, that this step has only to be done once for a boosted tree whose outcomes can, subsequently, be rapidly be explained as discussed in the answer to the second research question which shows performance gains of several orders of magnitude (cf. Table 2). Finally, as shown in Table 3, our approach typically also provided more concise explanations.[1]

---
[1] Neither abductive nor inflated explanations are unique in general (cf. [3]).

This paper is dedicated to Tiziana Margaria as part of her Festschrift. She has worked on related topics, in particular, exploiting the power of compilation and domain-specific languages (DSLs). The development framework jABC [32] was based on full code generation and followed a dedicated model-driven compilation approach [23]. Moreover, she used monadic second-order logic over strings for circuit verification [25,33] and planning [26]. In both cases, binary decision diagrams (BDDs) were used as internal DSLs for efficiency reason. This idea was generalized in [31], which proposes to use multiple DSLs for system construction. Most similar to our approach are, however, [10,11], which translate Random Forests into algebraic decision diagrams for performance reasons.

The paper is structured as follows: Sect. 2 introduces boosted trees, abductive and inflated explanations, and ADDs. In Sect. 3, we explain our transformation from boosted trees to ADDs. Given the ADD, we then discuss an approach for generating abductive and inflated explanations efficiently in Sect. 4. We evaluate our approach in Sect. 5 by comparing it with other state-of-the-art tools and we conclude this paper in Sect. 6.

2 Background

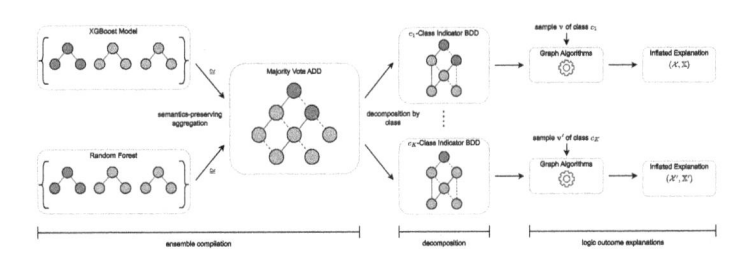

Fig. 1. Overview of the compilation and explanation process. Starting at tree ensemble methods, such as XGBoost models or Random Forests, one can aggregate these distributed structures into a single (algebraic) decision tree while preserving semantics. Based on this single representation of the semantics, one can derive a set of (binary) decision diagram for each class, where each BDD is a concise representation of predicates that have to hold for the specific class. From these one can generate different kinds of outcome explanations using graph algorithms. This includes especially logic explanations like path, abductive, and inflated explanations.

In this section, we introduce the relevant concepts similar to previous work in this area [17]. For some natural number $n \in \mathbb{N}$, let $[n] := \{1, \ldots, n\}$ be the set of all natural numbers less than or equal to n.

2.1 Classification Problems

In this paper, we are concerned with classification problems where $\mathcal{F} = \{1, \ldots, m\}$ denotes the set of features and $\mathcal{C} = \{1, \ldots, K\}$ the set of classes.

Each feature $j \in \mathcal{F}$ is characterized by a domain D_j. The feature space is defined as $\mathbb{F} := D_1 \times D_2 \times \cdots \times D_m$. A *sample* or an *instance* is a specific point $\boldsymbol{v} = (v_1, \ldots, v_m) \in \mathbb{F}$ in the feature space. We use $\boldsymbol{x} = (x_1, \ldots, x_m) \in \mathbb{F}$, for an arbitrary point in the feature space. The value of a feature $j \in \mathcal{F}$ is denoted as x_j where $x_j \in D_j$. In general, when referring to the value of a feature $j \in \mathcal{F}$, we will use a variable x_j, with x_j taking values from D_j. A classifier implements a total classification function $\tau \colon \mathbb{F} \to \mathcal{C}$.

2.2 XGBoost Models

Decision trees are a widely used method for classification and regression tasks. Each internal node in the tree represents a test on a feature j and has two branches representing the outcome of the test. One type of decision tree is the *gradient boosted tree* [9], where each leaf contains a real-valued weight $w \in \mathbb{R}$. In this paper, we only deal with gradient-boosted trees whose internal nodes compare the value of a feature $j \in \mathcal{F}$ with a threshold[2] $d \in D_j$, i.e., internal nodes are of the form $x_j < d$. One disadvantage of decision trees is that they are likely to *overfit*. In contrast, tree ensembles, such as *XGBoost models* [7] (and Random Forests [5]), typically outperform single decision trees in terms of accuracy, while also being less susceptible to overfitting.

In this paper, we are interested in XGBoost models, where the decision trees are gradient-boosted trees, that are learned sequentially such that each tree attempts to correct the errors of the previously learned trees. We are not concerned with the details of the training procedure of an XGBoost model, but we will go over how an XGBoost model makes its prediction.

Consider a multiclass classification problems, i.e. $K > 2$, and let $\mathfrak{E}$ be an ensemble of boosted trees. An ensemble $\mathfrak{E}$ computes a classification function $\tau(\boldsymbol{x})$. Each class $i \in [K]$ in $\mathfrak{E}$ is represented by $n \in \mathbb{N}_{>0}$ trees $T_i^1, \ldots, T_i^n$. Each decision tree is associated with a specific class i and contributes to the weight of that class. An XGBoost model makes its decision by evaluating the total weight assigned by the trees for each class and selecting the class with the largest total weight. For each $i \in [K]$ let $w_i \colon \mathbb{F} \to \mathbb{R}$ denote the total weight of class i computed by ensemble $\mathfrak{E}$ for instance $\boldsymbol{x} \in \mathbb{F}$. Each individual tree $T_i^j \colon \mathbb{F} \to \mathbb{R}$ ($j \in [n]$) contributes to the total weight of class i as follows

$$w_i(\boldsymbol{x}) := \sum_{j \in [n]} T_i^j(\boldsymbol{x}) \ .$$

2.3 Logic Explanations

In this paper, we deal with types of explanations that have to satisfy certain *logic requirements*. In contrast to many other forms of explanations, which are

---

[2] All of our techniques in this paper can also be applied to decision trees learned on categorical features.

usually of heuristic nature, these have an exact formal definition allowing to reason about them using mathematical rigor.

One type of formal explanations are *abductive explanations* (AXps) [18].[3] An AXp for a sample $v \in \mathbb{F}$ is an *inclusion-minimal* set of feature-value pairs that are sufficient for the prediction.

Definition 1 (Abductive Explanation [18]). *For an instance $v \in \mathbb{F}$, an abductive explanation (AXp) is a minimal subset $\mathcal{X} \subseteq \mathcal{F}$ such that:*

$$\forall \boldsymbol{x} \in \mathbb{F}. \ \left(\bigwedge_{j \in \mathcal{X}} (x_j = v_j) \right) \implies \tau(\boldsymbol{x}) = \tau(\boldsymbol{v}) \ .$$

Abductive definitions are not unique, i.e., given a fixed sample v there can exist multiple $\mathcal{X}$ satisfying the above equation.

Recently, abductive explanations were extended to *inflated explanations* which do not only provide information about which features are sufficient, but also a subset of the domain for each feature that it can take on without changing the prediction.

Definition 2 (Inflated Explanation [21]). *For an instance $v \in \mathbb{F}$ with AXp $\mathcal{X} \subseteq \mathcal{F}$, an inflated (abductive) explanation (iAXp) is a tuple $(\mathcal{X}, \mathbb{X})$, where $\mathbb{X}$ contains for each feature $j \in \mathcal{X}$ a set $\mathbb{E}_j \subseteq D_j$ with $v_j \in \mathbb{E}_j$, satisfying:*

$$\forall \boldsymbol{x} \in \mathbb{F}. \ \left(\bigwedge_{j \in \mathcal{X}} (x_j \in \mathbb{E}_j) \right) \implies \tau(\boldsymbol{x}) = \tau(\boldsymbol{v}) \tag{1}$$

When j is a numerical feature, $\mathbb{E}_j$ must be an interval. Additionally, each $\mathbb{E}_j$ must be inclusion-maximal in the sense that any trivial extension of $\mathbb{E}_j$ within the allowed bounds $\mathbb{E}_j \subseteq D_j$ violates (1).

2.4 Algebraic Decision Diagrams

Algebraic Decision Diagrams (ADDs) [2] generalize Binary Decision Diagrams (BDDs) [6] from the boolean to any algebraic co-domain. ADDs represent functions $\mathbb{F} \to A$ where A is the carrier set of an algebraic structure (A, O) with operations O.[4]

Definition 3 (Binary Aggregation [6]). *Given a binary operation $\bullet \in O$, it is possible to lift this operation on the ADD level such that for ADDs $f, g \colon \mathbb{F} \to A$ and all inputs $\boldsymbol{x} \in \mathbb{F}$ the following holds*

$$(f \bullet_A g)(\boldsymbol{x}) := f(\boldsymbol{x}) \bullet g(\boldsymbol{x})$$

---

[3] These are also known as *PI explanations* [29] and *sufficient reasons* [8].
[4] This is an extension of classic ADDs which are defined over a domain $\{0,1\}^n$. By allowing predicates over $\mathbb{F}$ we extend the expressiveness of ADDs at the cost of semantic dependencies along paths [13].

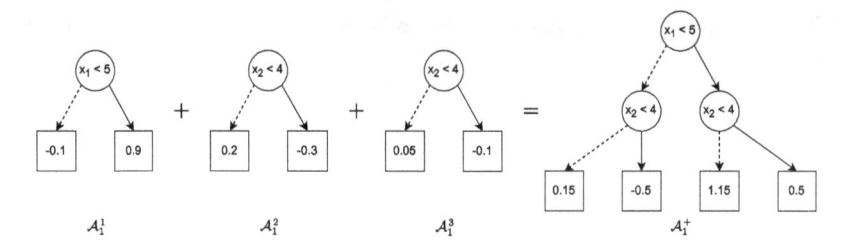

Fig. 2. ADD aggregation with shared predicate $x_2 < 4$.

Just like binary operations, monadic operations can also be lifted to ADDs.

Definition 4 (Monadic Aggregation [6]). *Given a unary operation* $\bullet \in O$, *it is possible to lift this operation on the ADD level such that for an ADD* $f \colon \mathbb{F} \to A$ *and all inputs* $\boldsymbol{x} \in \mathbb{F}$ *the following holds*

$$\big(\bullet_A(f)\big)(\boldsymbol{x}) := f\big(\bullet(\boldsymbol{x})\big)$$

Binary and monadic aggregation are the main drivers behind our compilation approach.

Traditionally, ADDs operate on Boolean variables instead of predicates that are required in this case. We will first treat predicates as Boolean variables and in Sect. 3.3 discuss how we deal with dependencies that may arise between predicates. For a detailed overview of how to use ADDs with predicates, see [13], who also show how to transform Random Forests into ADDs.

3 Compiling Boosted Trees To Algebraic Decision Diagrams

Our approach compiles a XGBoost model $\mathfrak{E}$ consisting of n trees $T_i^1, \ldots, T_i^n$ for each class $i \in [K]$ into an ADD by performing the following four steps:

1. For each class $i \in [K]$, we transform all individual trees T_i^j to ADDs $\mathcal{A}_i^j$.
2. For each class $i \in [K]$, we aggregate the ADDs $\mathcal{A}_i^1, \ldots, \mathcal{A}_i^n$ to a single ADD $\mathcal{A}_i^+$, that given a sample $\boldsymbol{x}$, returns $w_i(\boldsymbol{x})$, i.e., the sum of weights of all trees for that class.
3. We then aggregate the ADDs $\mathcal{A}_1^+, \ldots, \mathcal{A}_K^+$ for all classes into a single ADD $\mathcal{A}^K$ that is semantically equivalent to the XGBoost model $\mathfrak{E}$. That is, given a sample $\boldsymbol{x}$, $\mathcal{A}^K$ returns the predicted class $\arg\max_{i \in [K]} w_i(\boldsymbol{x})$.
4. Finally, we construct for each class i one BDD $\mathcal{B}^{c_i}$ that indicates whether an input will be classified as class i or not.

3.1 Decision Trees to ADDs

Generally, the transformation of an individual decision tree T_i^j to an ADD $\mathcal{A}_i^j$ is straightforward and can be performed as described in [13]. Though, there are two properties of ADDs that have to be kept in mind:

1. All isomorphic subgraphs in ADDs are merged. In a single boosted tree with real-valued leaves, there are rarely isomorphic subgraphs, but if there are, these will be merged in the ADD.
2. ADDs have a fixed variable order while boosted trees do not. This can lead to the ADD evaluating the predicates in a different order, although the semantics are unchanged.

3.2 Class-Weight ADDs

Now, we want to create one ADD $\mathcal{A}_i^+$ per class i that returns the sum of weights w_i of the trees $T_i^1, \ldots, T_i^n$. That is, for each class $i \in [K]$ an ADD $\mathcal{A}_i^+$ such that for all $\boldsymbol{x} \in \mathbb{F}$

$$\mathcal{A}_i^+(\boldsymbol{x}) = w_i(\boldsymbol{x}) = \sum_{j=1}^{n} T_i^j(\boldsymbol{x}) \ .$$

Building on the previous transformation, the function $+_A$ that lifts standard addition to the ADDs [2] can be used to construct $\mathcal{A}_i^+$ as follows:

$$\mathcal{A}_i^+ \simeq \mathcal{A}_i^1 +_A \mathcal{A}_i^2 +_A \cdots +_A \mathcal{A}_i^n \ .$$

Example 1. Consider Fig. 2, which shows three ADDs $\mathcal{A}_1^1$, $\mathcal{A}_1^2$ and $\mathcal{A}_1^3$ and their aggregation $\mathcal{A}_1^+ = \mathcal{A}_1^1 +_A \mathcal{A}_1^2 +_A \mathcal{A}_1^3$. Given a sample $\boldsymbol{x} = (x_1 = 4, x_2 = 3)$, to calculate $w_i(\boldsymbol{x})$ without $\mathcal{A}_1^+$, we would have to traverse all 3 trees and sum up their leaf values, i.e., $0.9 + (-0.3) + (-0.1) = 0.5$. In contrast, with $\mathcal{A}_1^+$ we only have to traverse one DAG and can immediately return the leaf value. $\mathcal{A}_1^+$ avoids having to evaluate the truth value of predicate $x_2 < 4$ twice because on a path from a root to a leaf, a predicate is visited at most once.

3.3 Infeasible Path Elimination

As mentioned in Sect. 2.4, ADDs are typically based on Boolean variables, whereas in our setting, we need predicates of the form $x_i < d$. Until now, our aggregation is symbolic and does not consider that the truth value of one predicate may influence the truth value of another predicate.

Example 2. Figure 3 shows two ADDs $\mathcal{A}_2^1$ and $\mathcal{A}_2^2$ as well as their aggregation $\mathcal{A}_2^+$. Considering $\mathcal{A}_2^+$, when we follow the false edge (dotted) of $x_1 < 5$, we know that $x_1 \geq 5$ must hold. Then, when we encounter the next predicate $x_1 < 4$ along that path, we can infer that it can never hold. Thus, the path $\neg(x_1 < 5) \land (x_1 < 4)$ cannot be traversed by any input, it is *infeasible*. After pruning it from the tree, we receive the optimized ADD $\psi(\mathcal{A}_2^+)$.

We can filter such infeasible paths using the techniques described in [13,27]. We denote the function that eliminates all infeasible paths with ψ.

As each application of $+_A$ can introduce new infeasibilities, the elimination of infeasible paths is applied after every application of $+_A$. The ADD $\mathcal{A}_i^+$ can then be constructed as follows

$$\mathcal{A}_i^+ := \psi\Big(\psi(\psi(\mathcal{A}_i^1 +_A \mathcal{A}_i^2) +_A \cdots) +_A \mathcal{A}_i^n\Big)$$

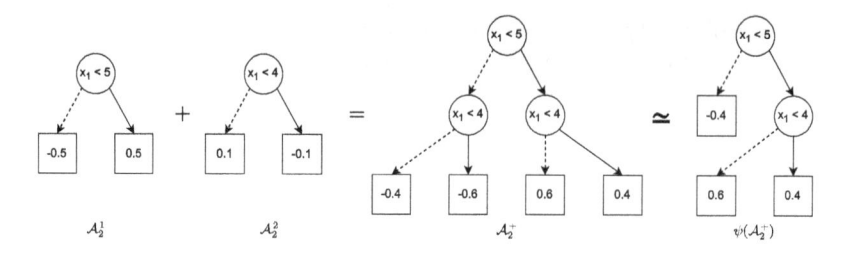

Fig. 3. ADD aggregation with infeasible path $\neg(x_1 < 5) \wedge (x_1 < 4)$.

The infeasible path elimination is a powerful transformation for optimizing predicate-based ADDs.

3.4 Majority Vote ADD

Finally, we want to create a single ADD $\mathcal{A}^K$ such that

$$\mathcal{A}^K(\boldsymbol{x}) = \mathfrak{E}(\boldsymbol{x}) = \arg\max_{i \in [K]} w_i(\boldsymbol{x}) .$$

We can easily adapt $\mathcal{A}_i^+$ to not only return the weight, but also the class associated with that weight. This adaption will allow us to perform an 'on-the-fly' argmax by lifting the function $\circ$ to the ADDs

$$\circ\big((w_1, c_1), (w_2, c_2)\big) = \begin{cases} (w_1, c_1) & \text{if } w_1 \geq w_2 \\ (w_2, c_2) & \text{otherwise} \end{cases}$$

We can then construct an ADD, $\mathcal{A}^{wK}$, that returns both the maximal weight and the class associated with that weight, as follows:

$$\mathcal{A}^{wK} \simeq \mathcal{A}_1^+ \circ_A \mathcal{A}_2^+ \circ_A \ldots \circ_A \mathcal{A}_K^+$$

Given a sample $\boldsymbol{x}$, $\mathcal{A}^{wK}(\boldsymbol{x})$ returns not only the predicted class, but also the weight. Here, the application of the infeasible path elimination is also crucial to keep the size of the intermediate results small. So, we instead construct $\mathcal{A}^{wK}$ as follows:

$$\mathcal{A}^{wK} := \psi\Big(\psi(\psi(\mathcal{A}_1^+ \circ_A \mathcal{A}_2^+) \circ_A \ldots) \circ_A \mathcal{A}_K^+\Big)$$

As we are only interested in the predicted class but not the weight, when we generate an explanation, we can create one final ADD, whose leaves contain only the predicted class. We define $\mathbf{0}((w, c)) = c$ and lift this operation to the ADD. We can now construct $\mathcal{A}^K$ as follows:

$$\mathcal{A}^K = \mathbf{0}_A(\mathcal{A}^{wK})$$

By leaving out the weight and only keeping the class in the leaf nodes, the size of the ADD is reduced significantly as certain internal nodes exist only to differentiate between different weights of the same class.

3.5 Class Characterizations

For boosted trees learned on datasets with more than 2 classes we can further reduce the size of the ADD. The ADD $\mathcal{A}^K$ differentiates between K different classes. Some predicates in $\mathcal{A}^K$ may only be needed to differentiate between class c_1 and c_2 but be unnecessary for class c_3. If we are interested in generating an explanation for a class c_i, we only need to be able to differentiate between class c_i and all other classes c_j with $c_j \neq c_i$.

We can construct a Binary Decision Diagram that is used only to differentiate between class c_i and all other classes c_j, $i \neq j$ by lifting the following monadic function to $\mathcal{A}^K$

$$\delta_{c_i}(c) = \begin{cases} 1 & \text{if } c = c_i \\ 0 & \text{otherwise} \end{cases}$$

The BDD $\mathcal{B}^{c_i}$ constructed by applying δ_{c_i} on $\mathcal{A}^K$ is called the *class characterization* for class c_i. The class characterization has already been introduced in [13] and has several advantages:

1. Its size can be significantly smaller than that of $\mathcal{A}^K$ as predicates that are only needed to differentiate between other classes are eliminated.
2. A size reduction simplifies the generation of abductive/inflated explanations.

4 Generating Inflated Explanations from BDDs

By transforming an XGBoost model to a single ADD, we only need to consider a single decision diagram and therefore enable the application of algorithms that generate explanations for decision diagrams.

4.1 Generating Abductive Explanations

To generate an inflated explanation, we start with generating an abductive explanation. In this subsection we briefly present how the technique presented in [16] can be adopted to the setting of ADDs.

Given a sample v, one can determine its classification $\mathfrak{E}(v)$ by traversing $\mathcal{A}^K$ from the root to the leaf to obtain the prediction c_i. The features that are referenced in the predicates along this path are the *path explanation* [20] of v. A more concise path explanation is given when instead considering the path taken by v in $\mathcal{B}^{c_i}$, as it contains only the predicates that are necessary to distinguish elements of class i from all others.

For decision graphs, [16] describe how one abductive explanation can be computed in polynomial time. Since the ADD constructed by our approach is a decision graph, the application of their approach is straightforward. Their approach requires a starting seed, i.e., a set of variables $A \subseteq \mathcal{F}$ and respectively a set $C = \mathcal{F} \setminus A$ of unset variables. While $\mathcal{F}$ is a safe choice for the initial starting seed A, we set A to the path explanation as it is typically shorter and serves as a more efficient seed, although it can, in the worst case, be as large as $\mathcal{F}$.

4.2 Generating Inflated Explanations

Now we adjust the SMT-based approach of [21] over tree ensembles for generating inflated explanations to ADDs. We assume that the class characterizations $\mathcal{B}^{c_i}$ for all classes $i \in [K]$ have already been constructed as outlined in Sect. 3. For an instance $\boldsymbol{v} \in \mathbb{F}$, where $c_i = \tau(\boldsymbol{v})$, based on $\mathcal{B}^{c_i}$, we compute an AXp as described in Sect. 4.1, which gives us a set of necessary features $\mathcal{X} \subseteq \mathcal{F}$. Now, we compute the interval $\mathbb{E}_j$ for each feature $j \in \mathcal{F}$ in some fixed order. Let $d_1, \ldots, d_m$ be the enumeration of all thresholds in ascending order of the XGBoost model concerning feature j. These thresholds partition the value domain D_j into the following intervals

$$(d_0, d_1), [d_1, d_2), \ldots, [d_m, d_{m+1})$$

where $d_0 = -\infty$ and $d_{m+1} = \infty$. By construction of the decision trees, values of the same interval are indistinguishable by the trees. We start by initializing each $\mathbb{E}_j$ for $j \in \mathcal{F} \setminus \mathcal{X}$ to (d_0, d_{m+1}), and each $\mathbb{E}_j$ for $j \in \mathcal{X}$ to the unique interval $[d_k, d_{k+1})$ that contains the value of v_j. This is always a valid choice given that $\mathcal{X}$ is an AXp for $\boldsymbol{v}$. Now, one can simply join the intervals that are below (resp. above) of $\mathbb{E}_j$, one after another, until $\mathbb{E}_j$ does no longer satisfy Equation (1). We use the BDD $\mathcal{B}^{c_i}$ to efficiently decide if property (1) holds. By this process, any resulting interval $\mathbb{E}_j$ satisfies (1) and cannot be trivially extended, and therefore satisfies Definition 2.

Checking the Validity of Eq. (1). Algorithm 1 can be used to check whether Eq. (1) holds for the given tuple $(\mathcal{X}, \mathbb{X})$. The algorithm checks whether there exists a path to a leaf with the value 0^5 through a simple depth-first search. If there exists a path to a leaf labeled 0, Eq. (1) does not hold as it is possible the XGBoost model will predict a different class for a sample in the given intervals. We keep track of nodes that have already been visited, as we know that, if a node has already been visited, there exists no path to a 0 leaf. If we know that $x_j < d$ must be true, or false, we only continue with the true-, respectively false-successor of the current node. Otherwise, we traverse both successors.

Inflating Explanations. Algorithm 2 shows how to inflate a given AXp $\mathcal{X}$. For each feature, we first try to find a smaller lower bound by considering all thresholds that are smaller than the initial lower bound d_k. Algorithm 3 stops as soon as replacing the lower bound makes it possible to reach a path to a 0 leaf. After finding the smallest lower bound, the same is done for the upper bound (see Algorithm 4). Finding the smallest lower bound, and largest upper bound could of course also be done through a binary search. While a binary search is better in the worst-case, a linear search can in the best case terminate already after trying out one threshold.

---

[5] Based on the class characterization the value 0 represents any class different from c_i.

Algorithm 1 Checking the validity of equation (1)

1: **procedure** PATHTOZERO($\mathcal{B}^{c_i}$, ($\mathcal{X}, \mathbb{X}$), visited)
2:     **if** $\mathcal{B}^{c_i} \in$ visited **then**
3:         **return** false
4:     **end if**
5:     visited $\leftarrow$ visited $\cup$ $\{\mathcal{B}^{c_i}\}$
6:     **if** isLeaf($\mathcal{B}^{c_i}$) **then**
7:         **return** isZero($\mathcal{B}^{c_i}$)
8:     **end if**
9:     $j \leftarrow$ feature($\mathcal{B}^{c_i}$)
10:    $d \leftarrow$ threshold($\mathcal{B}^{c_i}$)
11:    $[d_l, d_u] \leftarrow \mathbb{E}_j$
12:    $\mathcal{B}^{c_i}_t \leftarrow$ TrueSuccessor($\mathcal{B}^{c_i}$)
13:    $\mathcal{B}^{c_i}_f \leftarrow$ FalseSuccessor($\mathcal{B}^{c_i}$)
14:    **if** $d_l \leq d < d_u$ **then**
15:        **return** PathToZero($\mathcal{B}^{c_i}_t$, ($\mathcal{X}, \mathbb{X}$), visited) **OR**
16:                 PathToZero($\mathcal{B}^{c_i}_f$, ($\mathcal{X}, \mathbb{X}$), visited)
17:    **else if** $d \leq d_l$ **then**
18:        **return** PathToZero($\mathcal{B}^{c_i}_f$, ($\mathcal{X}, \mathbb{X}$), visited)
19:    **else**
20:        **return** PathToZero($\mathcal{B}^{c_i}_t$, ($\mathcal{X}, \mathbb{X}$), visited)
21:    **end if**
22: **end procedure**

5 Evaluation

In this section, we evaluate our approach by compiling XGBoost models learned on a variety of datasets from the UCI Machine Learning Repository to ADDs. Following the compilation, we then generate abductive, and inflated explanations as described in Sect. 4.

5.1 Hardware, Software Setup and Benchmarks

We evaluated our approach on a machine with an Intel(R) Xeon(R) Gold 6152 CPU 2.10 GHz with 502 GB of RAM. We use the decision diagram library *ADD-Lib* [12] for the construction of the ADDs. We compare our approach with the SMT-based [19] and MaxSAT-based [17] approaches to generate abductive explanations for XGBoost models[6]. We also use their implementation to verify the correctness of the abductive explanations generated by our approach. We are not aware of any approaches that can construct inflated explanations for XGBoost models, so we compare the time it takes for our approach to generate an inflated

---

[6] While there are also other approaches to generating abductive explanations such as [1] that is able to achieve slight performance improvement over [17], our approach remains significantly faster by several orders of magnitude compared to [17]. Moreover, our primary contribution lies in the generation of inflated explanations, that neither [17] nor [1] can handle.

Algorithm 2 Inflating explanations

1: **procedure** INFLATEINTERVALS($\mathcal{B}^{c_i}, \boldsymbol{v}$)
2:    $\mathcal{X} \leftarrow AbductiveExplanation(\mathcal{B}^{c_i}, \boldsymbol{v})$
3:    $\mathbb{X} \leftarrow \emptyset$
4:    **for** $j \in \mathcal{F} \setminus \mathcal{X}$ **do**
5:       $\mathbb{E}_j \leftarrow [d_0, d_{m+1})$
6:       $\mathbb{X} \leftarrow \mathbb{X} \cup (j, \mathbb{E}_j)$
7:    **end for**
8:    **for** $j \in \mathcal{X}$ **do**
9:       $\mathbb{E}_j \leftarrow [d_k, d_{k+1})$
10:      $\mathbb{X} \leftarrow \mathbb{X} \cup (j, \mathbb{E}_j)$
11:   **end for**
12:   **for** $j \in \mathcal{X}$ **do**
13:      $k_0 \leftarrow InflateLowerBound(\mathcal{B}^{c_i}, (\mathcal{X}, \mathbb{X}), \mathbb{E}_j)$
14:      $\mathbb{E}_j \leftarrow [d_{k_0}, d_{k+1})$
15:      $k_1 \leftarrow InflateUpperBound(\mathcal{B}^{c_i}, (\mathcal{X}, \mathbb{X}), \mathbb{E}_j)$
16:      $\mathbb{E}_j \leftarrow [d_{k_0}, d_{k_1})$
17:   **end for**
18: **end procedure**

Algorithm 3 Find smallest lower bound

1: **procedure** INFLATELOWERBOUND($\mathcal{B}^{c_i}, (\mathcal{X}, \mathbb{X}), \mathbb{E}_j = [d_k, d_{k+1})$)
2:    **for** $k' = k - 1$ **down to** 0 **do**
3:       $\mathbb{E}_j \leftarrow [d_{k'}, d_{k+1})$
4:       **if** $PathToZero(\mathcal{B}^{c_i}, (\mathcal{X}, \mathbb{X}), \emptyset)$ **then**
5:          **return** $k' + 1$
6:       **end if**
7:    **end for**
8:    **return** 0
9: **end procedure**

explanation with the time it takes the other approaches to generate an abductive-based explanation. Note that generating inflated explanations is a harder problem than generating abductive explanations. The XGBoost models are exactly those that are used for the evaluation in [17]. For the models in [17], the training procedure was initialized with 50 trees per class to be learned[7]. The models are learned using 80% of the dataset as the train set while 20% of the data is used as the test set. The maximum depth is set to 3–4 for all models.

5.2 Experimentation Results

With this evaluation, we want to answer the following research questions:

---

[7] Note that (1) the learning process can terminate early which results in less than 50 trees and (2) for 2 classes it is sufficient to learn 50 trees in total.

RQ1 Can we compile XGBoost models into ADDs in a reasonable amount of time?

Algorithm 4 Find largest upper bound

1: **procedure** INFLATEUPPERBOUND($\mathcal{B}^{c_i}$, $(\mathcal{X}, \mathbb{X})$, $\mathbb{E}_j = [d_{k'}, d_{k+1})$)
2:     **for** $k'' = k+2$ **to** $m+1$ **do**
3:        $\mathbb{E}_j \leftarrow [d_{k'}, d_{k''})$
4:        **if** $PathToZero(\mathcal{B}^{c_i}, (\mathbb{X}, \mathcal{X}), \emptyset)$ **then**
5:           **return** $k'' - 1$
6:        **end if**
7:     **end for**
8:     **return** $m+1$
9: **end procedure**

Table 1. Overview of datasets and the compiled ADD $\mathcal{A}^K$ (#F = Number of features, #C = Number of classes, #N = Number of nodes in the tree ensemble, #P = Number of unique predicates in the tree ensemble, D = Maximum depth, %A = Accuracy on test set, #N ADD = Number of nodes in the ADD, ADD C. = ADD construction time in seconds).

Dataset	#F	#C	#N	#P	D	%A	#N ADD	ADD C.
ann-thyroid	21	3	1302	113	3	100	162 055	4470.00
appendicitis	7	2	328	48	3	91	8 287	8.57
divorce	54	2	88	16	3	100	332	0.08
ecoli	7	5	2370	184	3	85	102 640	3346.00
glass2	9	2	540	107	4	88	312 644	1092.00
promoters	58	2	39	1	3	100	3	0.02
shuttle	9	7	2026	143	3	100	60 251	755.00
threeOf9	9	2	72	3	3	100	3	0.02
wine-recog.	13	3	552	76	3	97	29 742	131.00
zoo	16	7	772	16	4	83	290	0.11

RQ2 Can we generate abductive/inflated explanations faster than other state-of-the-art approaches?

RQ3 How does the size of our explanations compare to explanations from other state-of-the-art approaches?

RQ1: Can we compile XGBoost models into ADDs in a reasonable amount of time? Table 1 gives an overview of the datasets used to evaluate our approach and the time it takes to compile the XGBoost model to the ADD $\mathcal{A}^K$ and its size. For 5 out of 10 datasets, the compilation process takes less than 10 seconds. For 2 out of 10 datasets, *ann-thyroid* and *ecoli*, the highest compilation time can be observed with around 1 h. For the remaining three datasets, the XGBoost models can be compiled in around 2, 12 and 18 min. The largest ADD

Table 2. Overview of the time it takes to generate explanations in milliseconds, excluding compilation time (#inst. = Number of instances).

Dataset	#inst.	SMT max.	SMT min.	SMT avg.	MaxSAT max.	MaxSAT min.	MaxSAT avg.	ADD (Abductive Expl.) max.	min.	avg.	Speedup	ADD (Inflated Expl.) max.	min.	avg.	Speedup
ann-thyroid	7200	1700	21.5	70	3833.0	38.1	78.4	2.384	0.003	0.018	4355×	34.86	0.006	0.139	564×
appendicitis	106	457	17.9	60	97.2	20.4	34.0	0.237	0.012	0.039	871×	0.668	0.021	0.087	390×
divorce	170	79	24.1	40	14.4	2.5	8.4	0.459	0.009	0.023	365×	0.390	0.026	0.045	186×
ecoli	327	5814	67.5	490	1078.0	254.4	692.4	0.612	0.023	0.086	8051×	57.07	0.035	1.350	512×
glass2	163	1583	24.1	210	260.3	115.6	179.8	0.500	0.037	0.097	1853×	2.996	0.068	0.352	510×
promoters	106	102	20.0	40	0.7	0.3	0.4	0.090	0.006	0.016	25×	0.246	0.024	0.040	10×
shuttle	58000	9159	131.0	450	1436.0	75.7	236.1	12.810	0.005	0.019	12426×	22.56	0.026	0.379	622×
threeOf9	512	89	5.8	10	1.1	0.3	0.4	0.111	0.001	0.004	100×	0.229	0.004	0.013	30×
wine-recog.	178	194	35.2	60	129.4	34.9	66.6	1.499	0.017	0.253	137×	3.873	0.076	0.737	47×
zoo	101	1403	119.0	340	58.4	7.6	16.9	0.515	0.019	0.053	318×	0.678	0.033	0.075	225×

size can be observed for *glass2* with a size of 312644 nodes. While it takes some time to construct the ADDs, this construction has to be performed only once per model.

RQ2: Can we generate abductive/inflated explanations faster than other state-of-the-art approaches? Table 2 gives an overview of how long it takes to generate abductive and inflated explanations with our approach compared with other state-of-the-art approaches. We repeated a subset of the experiments from [17] on our own machine to get a fair comparison with the times we obtained with our approach. The samples for which the explanations were generated include the entire dataset. The speedups gained by using our approach to generate abductive explanations range from 25× to 12426× over the MaxSAT approach. For all datasets, except for *wine-recognition*, it takes less than 0.1 ms on average to generate an explanation and even for *wine-recognition* it takes only 0.253ms on average.

Since the *SMT* and *MaxSAT* approaches are not able to generate inflated explanations for XGBoost models, we compare the time it takes for us to generate an inflated explanation with the time it takes the SMT and MaxSAT approaches to generate an abductive explanation. Although the task of generating an inflated explanation is harder than that of generating an abductive explanation, our approach is still able to achieve speedups of 10× to 622×. Despite the ADD consisting of up to 312645 nodes, our approach is still able to generate abductive and inflated explanations extremely fast.

RQ 3: How does the size of our explanations compare to explanations from other state-of-the-art approaches? Finally, we compare the size of explanations generated by our approach with the sizes of the explanations of the *SMT* and *MaxSAT* approaches. We also compare the number of features that can be found from the root to the leaf to the size of the abductive explanation. Table 3 shows the average size of an explanation by the different approaches and it also shows how many features are seen along the path from the root to the leaf in the ADD.

Table 3. Overview of the average size of the generated abductive explanations.

Dataset	SMT	MaxSAT	ADD	ADD Path
ann-thyroid	1.52	1.42	1.42	2.64
appendicitis	3.61	3.48	3.54	5.43
divorce	5.41	4.38	3.99	4.72
ecoli	3.40	3.40	3.38	4.77
glass2	4.66	4.64	4.34	7.15
promoters	1.00	1.00	1.00	1.00
shuttle	3.70	3.28	3.21	4.37
threeOf9	1.00	1.00	1.00	1.00
wine-recog.	3.47	3.50	2.93	6.79
zoo	4.14	3.74	4.11	10.00

For most datasets, the sizes of the abductive explanations of the MaxSAT approach and our approach are similar. In general, the sizes of the explanations generated by the MaxSAT approach seem to be smaller than those generated by the SMT approach. For *divorce*, *glass2*, and *wine-recognition* the explanations generated by our approaches are 8.9%, 6.4%, and 16% smaller compared to the MaxSAT approach. For *zoo*, the MaxSAT-based explanations are 9% smaller than those generated by our approach.

The size of the path explanation shows that there are often features on the path that are not part of the abductive explanation. For *wine-recognition* and *zoo* only half of the features, that are seen on the part, are actually needed for the abductive explanation. As the features seen on the path depend on the variable order of the ADD, one could try to apply reordering heuristics to reduce the number of redundant features that are seen along the path.

Many abductive explanations can exist for one prediction. The abductive explanation generated by our approach is determined by the order in which the features are processed. As our approach is extremely fast, one could also generate many different explanations by processing the features in different orders and returning the smallest one.

6 Conclusions and Future Work

In this paper, we have presented an approach for compiling boosted trees to semantically equivalent ADDs in order to efficiently generate abductive and, for boosted trees for the first time, inflated explanations. The power of our compilation-based approaches is a result of ADDs being a representation tailored for analysis and explanation. The comparison of our corresponding prototype implementation with the state of the art shows performance gains of several orders of magnitude for the explanation steps. These results pave the way for inflated explanations to become a convenient and efficient way to establish trust for tree ensemble-based classifications by equipping each classification with a corresponding inflated explanation in real-time.

Besides preparing an open-source release of our implementation, we are currently developing a browser-based tool even for non-experts to experience the power of our technology either via replaying prepared case studies or to design own ones.

References

1. Audemard, G., Lagniez, J., Marquis, P., Szczepanski, N.: Computing abductive explanations for boosted trees. In: Ruiz, F.J.R., Dy, J.G., van de Meent, J. (eds.) International Conference on Artificial Intelligence and Statistics, 25–27 April 2023, Palau de Congressos, Valencia, Spain. Proceedings of Machine Learning Research, vol. 206, pp. 4699–4711. PMLR (2023). https://proceedings.mlr.press/v206/audemard23a.html
2. Bahar, R.I., et al.: Algebraic decision diagrams and their applications. Form. Methods Syst. Des. **10**, 171–206 (1997)
3. Biradar, G., Izza, Y., Lobo, E., Viswanathan, V., Zick, Y.: Axiomatic aggregations of abductive explanations. In: Wooldridge, M.J., Dy, J.G., Natarajan, S. (eds.) Thirty-Eighth AAAI Conference on Artificial Intelligence, AAAI 2024, Thirty-Sixth Conference on Innovative Applications of Artificial Intelligence, IAAI 2024, Fourteenth Symposium on Educational Advances in Artificial Intelligence, EAAI 2014, 20–27 February 2024, Vancouver, Canada, pp. 11096–11104. AAAI Press (2024). https://doi.org/10.1609/AAAI.V38I10.28986
4. Borisov, V., Leemann, T., Seßler, K., Haug, J., Pawelczyk, M., Kasneci, G.: Deep neural networks and tabular data: a survey. IEEE Trans. Neural Netw. Learn. Syst. 1–21 (2022). https://doi.org/10.1109/TNNLS.2022.3229161
5. Breiman, L.: Random forests. Mach. Learn. **45**(1), 5–32 (2001). https://doi.org/10.1023/A:1010933404324
6. Bryant: Graph-based algorithms for Boolean function manipulation. IEEE Trans. Comput. **C-35**(8), 677–691 (1986). https://doi.org/10.1109/TC.1986.1676819
7. Chen, T., Guestrin, C.: Xgboost: a scalable tree boosting system. In: Krishnapuram, B., Shah, M., Smola, A.J., Aggarwal, C.C., Shen, D., Rastogi, R. (eds.) Proceedings of the 22nd ACM SIGKDD International Conference on Knowledge

Discovery and Data Mining, San Francisco, CA, USA, 13–17 August 2016, pp. 785–794. ACM (2016). https://doi.org/10.1145/2939672.2939785
8. Darwiche, A., Hirth, A.: On the reasons behind decisions. In: Giacomo, G.D., et al. (eds.) ECAI 2020 - 24th European Conference on Artificial Intelligence, 29 August–8 September 2020, Santiago de Compostela, Spain, August 29 - September 8, 2020 - Including 10th Conference on Prestigious Applications of Artificial Intelligence (PAIS 2020). Frontiers in Artificial Intelligence and Applications, vol. 325, pp. 712–720. IOS Press (2020). https://doi.org/10.3233/FAIA200158
9. Friedman, J.H.: Greedy function approximation: a gradient boosting machine. Ann. Stat. 1189–1232 (2001)
10. Gossen, F., Margaria, T., Steffen, B.: Towards explainability in machine learning: the formal methods way. IT Prof. **22**(4), 8–12 (2020). https://doi.org/10.1109/MITP.2020.3005640
11. Gossen, F., Margaria, T., Steffen, B.: Formal methods boost experimental performance for explainable AI. IT Prof. **23**(6), 8–12 (2021). https://doi.org/10.1109/MITP.2021.3123495
12. Gossen, F., Murtovi, A., Zweihoff, P., Steffen, B.: Add-lib: decision diagrams in practice. CoRR **abs/1912.11308** (2019). http://arxiv.org/abs/1912.11308
13. Gossen, F., Steffen, B.: Algebraic aggregation of random forests: towards explainability and rapid evaluation. Int. J. Softw. Tools Technol. Transf. 1–19 (2021)
14. Grinsztajn, L., Oyallon, E., Varoquaux, G.: Why do tree-based models still outperform deep learning on typical tabular data? In: NeurIPS (2022). http://papers.nips.cc/paper_files/paper/2022/hash/0378c7692da36807bdec87ab043cdadc-Abstract-Datasets_and_Benchmarks.html
15. Guidotti, R., Monreale, A., Ruggieri, S., Turini, F., Giannotti, F., Pedreschi, D.: A survey of methods for explaining black box models. ACM Comput. Surv. **51**(5), 93:1–93:42 (2019). https://doi.org/10.1145/3236009
16. Huang, X., Izza, Y., Ignatiev, A., Marques-Silva, J.: On efficiently explaining graph-based classifiers. In: Bienvenu, M., Lakemeyer, G., Erdem, E. (eds.) Proceedings of the 18th International Conference on Principles of Knowledge Representation and Reasoning, KR 2021, Online event, 3–12 November 2021., pp. 356–367 (2021). https://doi.org/10.24963/KR.2021/34
17. Ignatiev, A., Izza, Y., Stuckey, P.J., Marques-Silva, J.: Using maxsat for efficient explanations of tree ensembles. In: Thirty-Sixth AAAI Conference on Artificial Intelligence, AAAI 2022, Thirty-Fourth Conference on Innovative Applications of Artificial Intelligence, IAAI 2022, The Twelveth Symposium on Educational Advances in Artificial Intelligence, EAAI 2022 Virtual Event, February 22–1 March 2022, pp. 3776–3785. AAAI Press (2022). https://doi.org/10.1609/AAAI.V36I4.20292
18. Ignatiev, A., Narodytska, N., Marques-Silva, J.: Abduction-based explanations for machine learning models. In: The Thirty-Third AAAI Conference on Artificial Intelligence, AAAI 2019, The Thirty-First Innovative Applications of Artificial Intelligence Conference, IAAI 2019, The Ninth AAAI Symposium on Educational Advances in Artificial Intelligence, EAAI 2019, Honolulu, Hawaii, USA, January 27–1 February 2019, pp. 1511–1519. AAAI Press (2019). https://doi.org/10.1609/AAAI.V33I01.33011511
19. Ignatiev, A., Narodytska, N., Marques-Silva, J.: On validating, repairing and refining heuristic ML explanations. CoRR **abs/1907.02509** (2019). http://arxiv.org/abs/1907.02509

20. Izza, Y., Ignatiev, A., Marques-Silva, J.: On tackling explanation redundancy in decision trees. J. Artif. Intell. Res. **75**, 261–321 (2022). https://doi.org/10.1613/JAIR.1.13575
21. Izza, Y., Ignatiev, A., Stuckey, P.J., Marques-Silva, J.: Delivering inflated explanations. CoRR **abs/2306.15272** (2023). https://doi.org/10.48550/ARXIV.2306.15272
22. Izza, Y., Marques-Silva, J.: On explaining random forests with SAT. In: Zhou, Z. (ed.) Proceedings of the Thirtieth International Joint Conference on Artificial Intelligence, IJCAI 2021, Virtual Event / Montreal, Canada, 19–27 August 2021, pp. 2584–2591. ijcai.org (2021). https://doi.org/10.24963/IJCAI.2021/356
23. Jörges, S., Margaria, T., Steffen, B.: Genesys: service-oriented construction of property conform code generators. Innov. Syst. Softw. Eng. **4**(4), 361–384 (2008). https://doi.org/10.1007/S11334-008-0071-2
24. Lundberg, S.M., Lee, S.: A unified approach to interpreting model predictions. In: Guyon, I., et al. (eds.) Advances in Neural Information Processing Systems 30: Annual Conference on Neural Information Processing Systems 2017, 4–9 December 2017, Long Beach, CA, USA, pp. 4765–4774 (2017). https://proceedings.neurips.cc/paper/2017/hash/8a20a8621978632d76c43dfd28b67767-Abstract.html
25. Margaria, T.: Fully automatic verification and error detection for parameterized iterative sequential circuits. In: Margaria, T., Steffen, B. (eds.) TACAS 1996. LNCS, vol. 1055, pp. 258–277. Springer, Heidelberg (1996). https://doi.org/10.1007/3-540-61042-1_49
26. Margaria, T., Meyer, D., Kubczak, C., Isberner, M., Steffen, B.: Synthesizing semantic web service compositions with jMosel and Golog. In: Bernstein, A., et al. (eds.) ISWC 2009. LNCS, vol. 5823, pp. 392–407. Springer, Heidelberg (2009). https://doi.org/10.1007/978-3-642-04930-9_25
27. Murtovi, A., Bainczyk, A., Nolte, G., Schlüter, M., Steffen, B.: Forest GUMP: a tool for verification and explanation. Int. J. Softw. Tools Technol. Transf. **25**(3), 287–299 (2023). https://doi.org/10.1007/S10009-023-00702-5
28. Ribeiro, M.T., Singh, S., Guestrin, C.: Why should I trust you?': explaining the predictions of any classifier. In: Krishnapuram, B., Shah, M., Smola, A.J., Aggarwal, C.C., Shen, D., Rastogi, R. (eds.) Proceedings of the 22nd ACM SIGKDD International Conference on Knowledge Discovery and Data Mining, San Francisco, CA, USA, 13–17 August 2016, pp. 1135–1144. ACM (2016). https://doi.org/10.1145/2939672.2939778
29. Shih, A., Choi, A., Darwiche, A.: A symbolic approach to explaining Bayesian network classifiers. In: Lang, J. (ed.) Proceedings of the Twenty-Seventh International Joint Conference on Artificial Intelligence, IJCAI 2018, 13–19 July 2018, Stockholm, Sweden, pp. 5103–5111. ijcai.org (2018). https://doi.org/10.24963/IJCAI.2018/708
30. Shwartz-Ziv, R., Armon, A.: Tabular data: deep learning is not all you need. Inf. Fusion **81**, 84–90 (2022). https://doi.org/10.1016/J.INFFUS.2021.11.011
31. Steffen, B., Gossen, F., Naujokat, S., Margaria, T.: Language-driven engineering: from general-purpose to purpose-specific languages. In: Steffen, B., Woeginger, G. (eds.) Computing and Software Science. LNCS, vol. 10000, pp. 311–344. Springer, Cham (2019). https://doi.org/10.1007/978-3-319-91908-9_17
32. Steffen, B., Margaria, T., Nagel, R., Jörges, S., Kubczak, C.: Model-driven development with the jABC. In: Bin, E., Ziv, A., Ur, S. (eds.) HVC 2006. LNCS, vol. 4383, pp. 92–108. Springer, Heidelberg (2007). https://doi.org/10.1007/978-3-540-70889-6_7

33. Topnik, C., Wilhelm, E., Margaria, T., Steffen, B.: jMosel: a stand-alone tool and jABC plugin for M2L(Str). In: Valmari, A. (ed.) SPIN 2006. LNCS, vol. 3925, pp. 293–298. Springer, Heidelberg (2006). https://doi.org/10.1007/11691617_18

The AI Act and Some Implications for Developing AI-Based Systems

Martin Leucker[✉][iD]

Institute for Software Engineering and Programming Languages,
University of Lübeck, Lübeck, Germany
leucker@isp.uni-luebeck.de

Abstract. This paper presents several challenges when developing AI-based software systems for potentially safety-critical domains in the European jurisdiction. Starting with the legal developments in the European Union, especially the so-called AI act, we recall the idea of the risk-based approach and its implications for the software engineering development process. We state the benefits of using formal methods for supporting the design and analysis steps in a corresponding development process. We identify research challenges, especially when aiming to build trustworthy AI based systems.

Keywords: AI Act · Trustworthy AI · SE4AI

1 Introduction

Artificial intelligence is currently attracting a lot of attention and is considered a disruptive technology that can change large parts of modern life. In a variety of domains, it is expected that processes can be significantly improved and optimized by using systems that work using artificial intelligence techniques. In the medical field, for example, in addition to making it easier to find new drugs, it is expected to support medical diagnoses or help with day-to-day patient care. In the automotive sector, autonomous driving is one of the main fields of application for artificial intelligence. The use of artificial intelligence and robots that build on it are expected to lead to significant cost and time savings in industrial production. In addition, systems for communicating with customers, but also for monitoring people or assessing people's creditworthiness, for example, are areas of application for artificial intelligence. While artificial intelligence can be used to perform many tasks with higher quality, more efficiently, more cost-effectively and therefore better, there are also numerous problems if artificial intelligence is used incorrectly or improperly.

This observation has led to intensive scientific and popular scientific discussions about possible future scenarios for artificial intelligence, ranging from dystopian to utopian [18]. See [33] for notes on extensive discussions on the benefits and risks of AI.

Whenever there is potential harm of a system or technology, it may become subject to regulation. For example, a medical device may do potential harm to patients, so for the European jurisdiction the Medical Device Regulatory (MDR, [27]) has been passed regulating under which conditions a medical device may be placed on the market. In a similar manner, the potential benefit but also potential harm of AI has prompted the EU to work on the regulation for the development of AI-based systems. The so-called AI Act [7,8] defines a legal framework that must be taken into account when developing AI-based systems. In this paper, we take up elementary points of the AI Act and discuss the implications for the development of AI-based systems. The aim is not to provide a well-founded, complete treatment of the topic, which is not possible at the present time due to evolving laws and standards, but to present some main ideas and implications.

This article is dedicated to Tiziana Margaria, who is one of the leading scientists in Software Engineering, especially from a formal methods perspective. Her work also covers regulatory affairs, for example, when building dedicated solutions for the medical domain. She also studies the use of artificial intelligence techniques for developing systems solutions. In [3], Tiziana et al. have worked out several challenges for AI in healthcare systems, while this article focuses mainly on the regulatory aspects imposed by the AI act.

2 The AI Act

Before turning to a more detailed definition of AI, let us consider AI as some form of a program and let us recall some fundamental insights.

In essence, a program is a computable mathematical function providing output for given inputs. A (mathematical) function or generally a piece of software computes outputs for given inputs. It does not (directly) interact with its environment and thus cannot be safe or unsafe, cannot be fair or unfair, cannot protect or leak private information, cannot be good or bad, etc. It is the system that is build using the software that may lead to unsafe situations, that may be used in an unfair manner, may leak personal information, may be considered bad, etc. As such, when considering potential *harm* when using AI, it is important to look at the whole system interacting in its environment. Similar observations have already been made when, for example, developing medical systems. The software of a medical device can never be safe or unsafe, but when employing software within a medical device, the whole system may become unsafe.

Systems may be distinguished based on their potential harm. A hammer is a tool that is generally considered harmless and there are limited restrictions for producing and using hammers. A fork lift is a potentially dangerous system. It is heavy by itself and steering it may hurt people, the goods transported may hurt people, the oil pressure pipes of the lift might hurt people when leaking. As such, the use of the lift is restricted to trained people, the lift is restricted for lifting goods that fit to its forks, and the lift is designed with all state of the art methods to ensure its safety and is continuously monitored and checked by authorities. In simple words, the potentially harmful forklift has to be well-designed and developed, continuously monitored, and used only for the intended use (trained people lifting heavy but stackable goods). Given these measure, it is considered safe to use fork lifts. Note that a fork lift is all of a mechanical system, an electrical system, a tool for employees, etc. and many different aspects have to be considered when discussing safety.

Let us now turn our attention to AI. We do not give a precise definition of artificial intelligence but follow Russel and Norvig that "the field of artificial intelligence, or AI, is concerned with not just understanding but also building intelligent entities-machines that can compute how to act effectively and safely in a wide variety of novel situations" [29]. The EU AI act defines an AI system as follows: "An AI system is a machine-based system designed to operate with varying levels of autonomy and that may exhibit adaptiveness after deployment and that, for explicit or implicit objectives, infers, from the input it receives, how to generate outputs such as predictions, content, recommendations, or decisions that can influence physical or virtual environments." [20]. As such, the AI act (similar as the scientific definition) talks of systems rather than programs and algorithms, following the insight that only systems can be harmful and need potential regulation. At the same time, the distinction between AI software and traditional software is fuzzy and it is unclear when the AI act has to be applied. However, the commission plans to develop guidelines for concretization. Moreover, the AI act also introduces the notion of general purpose artificial intelligence (GPAI) models, which we will discuss further below.

When discussing safety of a system and the potential harm it can cause, it is essential to understand relevant of safety measures to be taken to reduce potential harm. A system might never be completely safe, but for practical means, it suffices to ensure that the *risk* of a potential problem is minimized. It is economically as well as ecologically meaningful to take as many measures that are needed but not more to ensure the safety of the system. Risk is typically defined as a combination (often the product) of the harm the a problem in the system can do and the probability of the problem to occur. These kinds of principles have made their way into norms for medical devices as well as airplanes. Norms for the automotive domain additionally consider controllability of problematic situations as a further factor to estimate the risk of a potential problem. In the end, several risk classes or criticality levels are obtained for which different kind of measures have to be taken to control the corresponding risks. The risk level for (a component of) a system identifies the risk level of the software employed in this component. In the avionics domain, for example, four risk levels for software (from Class A (catastrophic) to Class D (minor)) have been defined in the norm DO-178B and different kind of coverage metrics for testing the corresponding software are required to be fulfilled to assure that corresponding risk measures have been taken.

Practically, AI is considered a powerful tool that may be applied in many areas by assisting in daily work activities. It may run as a standalone system, for example a chat-bot, or be part of a larger system, like a medical device. To ensure that the right measures are taken to reduce any kind of harm, the AI act has been defined and must be followed when building an AI-based system, except if the AI system is for military, defense or national security, or scientific research and development purposes. Depending of the system, e.g., a medical device, also further laws and directives have to respected, like the medical device regulatory. But let us concentrate on the AI act for the moment.

The AI act defines four different risk levels depending on the harm of the system (see Fig. 1). The levels range from *unacceptable risk*, over *high-risk* and *transparency risk* to *minimal risk*.

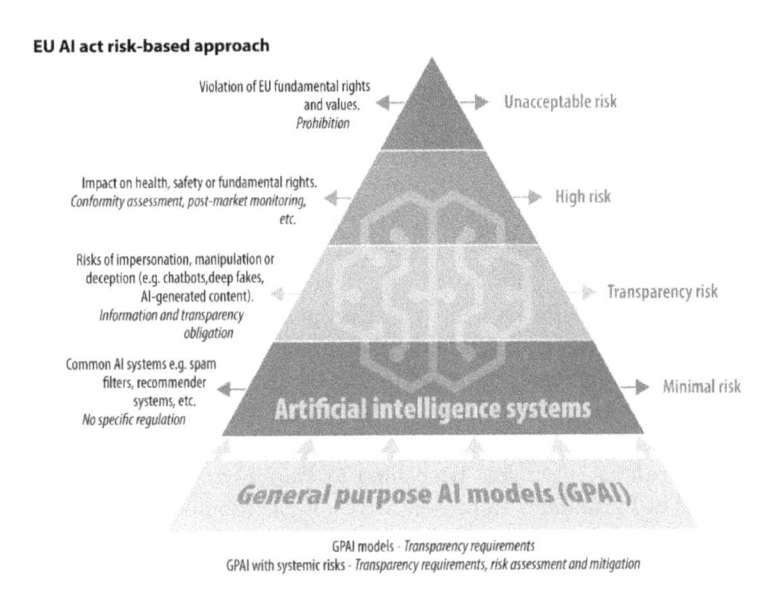

Fig. 1. The risks levels of the AI act [20]

Unaccaptable and therefore *prohibited AI uses* are those that potentially create an adverse impact on people's health, safety or their fundamental rights. Examples range from social screening of society for law enforcement or influencing people's decision making harmfully.

The EU AI Act defines certain AI systems as *high-risk* based on their potential to harm people. Risk depends on purpose: The type of job the AI does and how it's used determine if it's high-risk. There are two categories of high-risk AI:

- Built-in risk: These AI systems are inherently risky because they are used in sensitive areas like medical devices or for profiling people.
- Use-case risk: Some AI systems are only high-risk when used in specific situations, outlined in an EU database.

The AI act enforces strict rules for high-risk AI: Providers need to go through a testing and approval process to ensure their AI is safe and legal. This may involve internal checks or using a certified body. Moreover, also after approval, providers must pursue a an after market surveillance, e.g. monitor their AI and fix any problems. We discuss these checks in more detail in Sect. 4

The EU AI Act tackles *transparency risks* from AI interacting with people or creating content. This applies even to non-high-risk AI. People interacting with chatbots must be informed they are re talking to a machine, and creators of deepfakes or other manipulated content (text, audio, video) must disclose it is artificial, with some exceptions. Providers of large amounts of synthetic content must also include methods to identify it as AI-generated. Finally, employers using AI in the workplace need to inform their staff. There are, however, some exceptions, see [20] for details.

AI with *minimal risk*, like spam filters, does not need additional rules beyond existing laws (like GDPR).

When the AI act is applicable, it addresses providers and deployers including any company, organization, or individual that creates or uses AI systems and high-risk AI models (General Purpose AI or GPAI) within the EU. This applies regardless of their physical location, as long as their AI system is used in the EU.

All of the European Parliament, the European Commission, as well as the European Council have been studying the impact of AI since the mid of the 2010s. The AI Act has first been proposed by the European Commission in April 2021 [8], following the call of the European Parliament. After consultations by European national governments, further consultations in the European parliament, a draft (AI) act has been filed in December 2023 and endorsed by the Committee of Permanent Representatives of EU Member States and by Parliament's two lead committees [35]. The Parliament's plenary voted on the final agreement on March 13, 2024 in its plenary session [36] and the agreement was finally endorsed by the EU Council in May 2024 [22]. Once it is published in the EU's Official Journal it will enter into force.

3 Implementing the AI Act

To conform to the AI act, one first has to check whether it applies at all, and, if so, in which risk class the intended system falls. For the high risk and transparency classes, suitable measures have to be taken. This is typically done following two steps:

1. Risk management and
2. following further dedicated norms.

To understand the risk of a certain application, one typically performs a risk analysis and subsequent risk management activities aiming to mitigate potential risk.

3.1 Risk Management and FMEA

Risk management is the process of anticipating potential problems and taking steps to minimize their impact. It involves identifying hazards, assessing their likelihood and severity, and then developing strategies to avoid them, reduce their impact, or transfer the risk altogether.

Failure Mode and Effects Analysis (FMEA) [19] is a systematic approach to identifying, evaluating, and prioritizing potential failures in a system, product, or process. It is a qualitative method that assigns scores to each potential failure based on its severity, likelihood of occurrence, and detectability, which is used for risk assessment. These scores are then used to prioritize corrective actions and allocate resources to address the most critical risks, thus managing the risk. Powerful tools such as Peak Avenues (former Plato) e1ns support risk management based on FMEA.[1]

FMEA greatly benefits from available blue prints and/or FMEA tailored for specific application domains. While there is a vast of literature explaining FMEA e.g. for the automotive domain, not many examples exist on how to apply FMEA for AI-based systems.

3.2 Norms for Certification

First of all, a distinction must be made between binding and non-binding norms or standards. In the EU, there are so-called *harmonized norms*, which are quasi-legal and must be complied with when placing products on the market. Harmonized norms that refine the requirements of the AI Act more precisely are currently being drafted, and will therefore represent a binding specification for corresponding AI-based systems in the future.

Even if non-binding standards are not mandatory, they are a good way of demonstrating to third parties that your system has been developed as state of the art. Showing conformity to standards is therefore an important tool to enable certification. In order to prove that a system meets the potentially high requirements of the AI act, it is helpful to demonstrate conformity with relevant standards. However, many of these standards are currently under development. An overview of the relevant activities is provided by the so-called Standardization Road Map [1], which lists the challenges of standardizing individual aspects of AI-based systems and describes the efforts to establish corresponding norms and standards.

With more than 116 identified standardizations and standardization needs, the road map shows concrete potential in all core topics and formulates six key recommendations for action [1]:

- Development, validation and standardization of a horizontal conformity assessment and certification program for certification program for trustworthy AI systems
- Establishment of data infrastructures and development of data quality standards for the development and validation of AI systems
- Consideration of humans as part of the system in all phases of the AI life cycle

---

[1] https://www.peakavenue.de/software/e1ns-engineering/e1ns-uebersicht.

- Development of specifications for the conformity assessment of continuously or incrementally learning systems in the field of medicine
- Development and use of secure and trustworthy AI applications in mobility through best practices and security
- Development of comprehensive data standards and dynamic modeling methods for the efficient and sustainable design of AI systems.

Another supporting activity that has been incorporated into the formulation of the AI Act and into the formulation of various standards is the development of fundamental requirements for trustworthy AI-based systems. The so-called AI expert group of the EU has drawn up a comprehensive document on Ethics guidelines for trustworthy AI, which has identified key criteria for trustworthy systems. It serves to understand the concept of trustworthiness more precisely and to categorize it on the basis of various attributes. It lists the following key requirements [31]:

- Human agency and oversight: AI systems should empower human beings, allowing them to make informed decisions and fostering their fundamental rights. At the same time, proper oversight mechanisms need to be ensured, which can be achieved through human-in-the-loop, human-on-the-loop, and human-in-command approaches
- Technical Robustness and safety: AI systems need to be resilient and secure. They need to be safe, ensuring a fall back plan in case something goes wrong, as well as being accurate, reliable and reproducible. That is the only way to ensure that also unintentional harm can be minimized and prevented.
- Privacy and data governance: besides ensuring full respect for privacy and data protection, adequate data governance mechanisms must also be ensured, taking into account the quality and integrity of the data, and ensuring legitimised access to data.
- Transparency: the data, system and AI business models should be transparent. Traceability mechanisms can help achieving this. Moreover, AI systems and their decisions should be explained in a manner adapted to the stakeholder concerned. Humans need to be aware that they are interacting with an AI system, and must be informed of the system's capabilities and limitations.
- Diversity, non-discrimination and fairness: Unfair bias must be avoided, as it could have multiple negative implications, from the alization of vulnerable groups, to the exacerbation of prejudice and discrimination. Fostering diversity, AI systems should be accessible to all, regardless of any disability, and involve relevant stakeholders throughout their entire life circle.
- Societal and environmental well-being: AI systems should benefit all human beings, including future generations. It must hence be ensured that they are sustainable and environmentally friendly. Moreover, they should take into account the environment, including other living beings, and their social and societal impact should be carefully considered.
- Accountability: Mechanisms should be put in place to ensure responsibility and accountability for AI systems and their outcomes. Auditability, which enables the assessment of algorithms, data and design processes plays a key

role therein, especially in critical applications. Moreover, adequate an accessible redress should be ensured.

Accordingly, such attributes shall be analyzed in order to classify an AI-based system as trustworthy.

As summary, individual measures are necessary to demonstrate conformity with standards. As many of the standards for AI-based systems are still in the development stage, it is unclear how exactly conformity to these standards can be demonstrated. We therefore take out individual aspects that are mentioned in the current proposals for norms and discuss them from the perspective of formal methods in the next section.

4 Challenges of the AI-Act from a Formal Methods Point of View

The quite vague statements on the subject of standards and fundamental work on trustworthy AI suggest that, in addition to the aspects typically considered in computer science, such as safety and security, a large number of further criteria must be met in order to classify an AI-based system as trustworthy and, in particular, to get a high-risk AI-based system approved in the sense of the AI act.

A mathematical characterization and, if possible a specification, of the corresponding quality attributes is essential in order to be able to prove the corresponding criteria. On the basis of a precise formalization of corresponding quality attributes, analysis methods can then be developed that can contribute to a qualitative or quantitative proof of corresponding attributes. Accordingly, the requirements of the AI Act indirectly result in a road map for the development of corresponding formal methods that shall be useful for proving the conformity of corresponding high-risk based systems.

Let us go through the individual aspects in a detailed manner and point out challenges and possible approaches:

Risk Management. We have already identified FMEA as one popular approach to analyse risk for systems. However, not many works on risk analysis and management are know in the field of AI. However, to make it applicable questions have to be answered: What is a suitable notion of failure for identifying risks of AI-based systems? How to identify the potential failures of AI-based systems? How do exemplifying FMEA analysis for AI-bases system look like?

Data and Data Governance. The use of data is essential for machine learning in particular. Not only for accountability (see next paragraph), the (training) data must be stored in a tamper-proof manner [13,23]. Besides the AI act, also GDPR has to be followed [2]. The data has to meet certain quality aspects [32]. At the same time, privacy of the data must be taken into account. Anonymization procedures often only achieve insufficient privacy. When linking different data sources, clear data can often be generated from presumed annonymized data. Approaches such as federated learning enable machine learning without disclosing the locally available data, but are fundamentally similarly susceptible to de-anonymization attacks. Approaches using differential privacy can provide a possible remedy here. Methods such as homomorphic encryption also allow computations to be performed on encrypted data and increase the privacy of the data. Current projects are investigating the use of these techniques in various application domains, see https://anomed.de. While individual methods are developed, a clear recipe on which data governance measures to apply for which application is missing.

Accountability. An essential point for the safety and security of AI-based systems is the traceability of the system's operation, especially in the event of a safety or security problem. Appropriate logging measures are therefore necessary to show who initiated what in the system at what time. Corresponding mechanisms are necessary for both during the development and operation phase of the system. Logging mechanisms must contain precise information about the observed system. From the point of view of formal methods, corresponding log information can also be analyzed at runtime in order to identify system errors directly and to react to them if necessary. Runtime verification is the formal method of choice here [17].

Explainability. Explainable artificial intelligence (XAI) deals with AI algorithms that can show their internal process and explain how they made decisions. It is essential for covering aspects of accountability, transparency and human oversight. There are several approaches for explainable AI, see [26] for an overview. Formal methods is often building models of the artifact to analyze for further investigation [6]. It may be expected that building so-called surrogate models of the underlying AI-components tailored for explaining certain aspects of the underlying system may be beneficial. For example, one may represent decisions of an underlying net used for classifications by decision trees [14] or learn surrogate models in forms of automata [4,15]. For approaches on using formal methods for explainability can be found in [10,11].

Transparency and Information for Users. The required information for the user regarding the use of artificial intelligence is easy to implement from a software engineering perspective. However, for certification, it is important to develop reliable methods that detect the use of artificial intelligence methods in a system in order to be able to effectively check the declaration of the developer. See [21] for some methods on identifying AI-based attacks that may be used to identify AI-based sub-systems.

Human Oversight. With high-risk AI-based systems, it is mandatory that final decisions are left to a humans. Methods of program analysis are helpful in order to be able to pursue an influence analysis of the partial results of a system obtained using AI. A corresponding flow of information diagram throughout the system can be used to prove that important decisions are only used after approval by an appropriate user. Furthermore, it seems advisable to use workflow description and analysis methods to model and analyze the user interaction with the underlying system [5,9,25].

In addition, it is important that any unsafe AI-based solutions are safeguarded by understood or formally verified procedures. Examples of the use of corresponding formal methods include the use of the simplex architecture, which monitors an AI-based component and switches to a verified component in the event of a potential problem. Corresponding approaches are used in control systems for the automation of systems. [28,30]

Accuracy Specifications for AI Systems. The traditional approach to software development goes from requirements via specification to the actual system. The specification is the central artifact for verifying the system with regard to the requirements. In other words, precise specifications are mandatory to verify systems. However, it has been noted [16] that at least machine learning is especially used in settings where examples are much easier to provide than formal specifications. As such, coming up with accurate specifications is inherently difficult.

On the other hand, a specification can also be seen as one form of representation of the system to develop, as described in the requirements. The realization of the system is another form of representation of the system requirements. In this view, verification answers the question of whether the system and the specification are in a required relationship. Ultimately, it is irrelevant whether the specification is done during the development process before the actual system is realized or afterwards, or, completely independently of it. One approach to obtaining concrete specifications could therefore be to generate specifications from requirements (or examples). These could then be compared with an implementation that was obtained using machine learning, for example. The rational behind this approach is that coming up to the same solution using two different methods indicates that the result is of high value. However, it has to be seen to which extend such an approach is applicable.

Robustness Specifications for AI Systems. Robustness aims for ensuring that a system behaves similarly under small environmental changes. Often it is understood as small changes of the underlying input yield only to small changes in the output. The rational is that, for example, a raod sign should be perceived correctly in different weather conditions. Several approaches to analyzing robustness have been developed, see [34] for an overview. Also first formal analysis algorithms are available [15].

Cybersecurity Specifications for AI Systems. While safety typically involves checking a system for the desired use cases, security involves checking the usage of the system by potential attackers. It is of high practical interest [24]. In this respect, the analysis of systems especially in borderline cases is necessary. The extent to which machine-learned artifacts can be analyzed with regard to security is the subject of research. See [12] for an overview on this topic.

5 Conclusion

In this paper, we have examined the key aspects of the AI Act in more detail and in particular highlighted the challenges for high-risk AI-based systems in terms of approval. In parallel to the legal requirements, further, directly binding, harmonized standards are being developed that must be taken into account for the approval of corresponding systems. In addition, numerous individual standards have already been developed or are still under development. Ultimately, various aspects of AI-based systems must be analyzed in order to demonstrate conformity with the standards or laws. We have shown that formal methods could make a contribution here. However, a systematic road map of formal methods for conformity assessment to the regulatory affairs is still a work in progress.

Conflict of Interest. The author(s) has no competing interests to declare that are relevant to the content of this manuscript.

References

1. Adler, R., et al.: Deutsche normungsroadmap künstliche intelligenz ausgabe 2. Technical report, December 2022. https://doi.org/10.13140/RG.2.2.12632.78089
2. Alamri, B., Javed, I.T., Margaria, T.: A GDPR-compliant framework for IoT-based personal health records using blockchain. In: 2021 11th IFIP International Conference on New Technologies, Mobility and Security (NTMS), pp. 1–5. IEEE (2021)
3. Bertl, M., et al.: Challenges for AI in healthcare systems. In: Steffen, B. (ed.) Bridging the Gap Between AI and Reality - First International Conference, AISoLA 2023, Crete, Greece, 23–28 October 2023, Post-Proceedings (2024), to appear
4. Bork, A., Chakraborty, D., Grover, K., Kretínský, J., Mohr, S.: Learning explainable and better performing representations of POMDP strategies. In: Finkbeiner, B., Kovács, L. (eds.) Tools and Algorithms for the Construction and Analysis of Systems - 30th International Conference, TACAS 2024, Held as Part of the European Joint Conferences on Theory and Practice of Software, ETAPS 2024, Luxembourg City, Luxembourg, 6–11 April 2024, Proceedings, Part II. LNCS, vol. 14571, pp. 299–319. Springer, Berlin, Heidelberg (2024). https://doi.org/10.1007/978-3-031-57249-4_15
5. Brandon, C., et al.: Cinco de bio: a low-code platform for domain-specific workflows for biomedical research. BioMedInformatics 4(3) (2024)
6. Brandon, C., Singh, A., Margaria, T.: Model driven development for AI-based healthcare systems: a review. In: Steffen, B. (ed.) Bridging the Gap Between AI and Reality - First International Conference, AISoLA 2023, Crete, Greece, 23–28 October 2023, Post-Proceedings (2024), to appear
7. Commission, E.: Ai act. https://digital-strategy.ec.europa.eu/en/policies/regulatory-framework-ai
8. Commission, E.: Proposal for a regulation of the European Parliament and of the Council laying down harmonised rules on artificial intelligence (artificial intelligence act). https://digital-strategy.ec.europa.eu/en/library/proposal-regulation-laying-down-harmonised-rules-artificial-intelligence, 2021/0106 (COD)

9. Esparza, J., Leucker, M., Schlund, M.: Learning workflow petri nets. Fundam. Inform. **113**(3–4), 205–228 (2011). https://doi.org/10.3233/FI-2011-607
10. Gossen, F., Margaria, T., Steffen, B.: Towards explainability in machine learning: the formal methods way. It Prof. **22**(4), 8–12 (2020)
11. Gossen, F., Margaria, T., Steffen, B.: Formal methods boost experimental performance for explainable AI. It Prof. **23**(6), 8–12 (2021)
12. Hu, Y., et al.: Artificial intelligence security: threats and countermeasures. ACM Comput. Surv. **55**(1) (2021). https://doi.org/10.1145/3487890
13. Javed, I.T., Alharbi, F., Margaria, T., Crespi, N., Qureshi, K.N.: Petchain: a blockchain-based privacy enhancing technology. IEEE Access **9**, 41129–41143 (2021)
14. Jüngermann, F., Kretínský, J., Weininger, M.: Algebraically explainable controllers: decision trees and support vector machines join forces. Int. J. Softw. Tools Technol. Transf. **25**(3), 249–266 (2023). https://doi.org/10.1007/S10009-023-00716-Z
15. Khmelnitsky, I., et al.: Property-directed verification and robustness certification of recurrent neural networks. In: Hou, Z., Ganesh, V. (eds.) ATVA 2021. LNCS, vol. 12971, pp. 364–380. Springer, Cham (2021). https://doi.org/10.1007/978-3-030-88885-5_24
16. Leucker, M.: Formal verification of neural networks? In: Carvalho, G., Stolz, V. (eds.) SBMF 2020. LNCS, vol. 12475, pp. 3–7. Springer, Cham (2020). https://doi.org/10.1007/978-3-030-63882-5_1
17. Leucker, M., Schallhart, C.: A brief account of runtime verification. J. Log. Algebr. Methods Program. **78**(5), 293–303 (2009). https://doi.org/10.1016/j.jlap.2008.08.004
18. Lewis, T.: Don't Let Artificial Intelligence Take Over, Top Scientists Warn. https://www.livescience.com/49419-artificial-intelligence-dangers-letter.html
19. Lipol, L.S., Haq, J.: Risk analysis method: FMEA/FMECA in the organizations. Int. J. Basic Appl. Sci. **11**(5), 74–82 (2011)
20. Madiega, T.: Artificial intelligence act (2024). https://www.europarl.europa.eu/RegData/etudes/BRIE/2021/698792/EPRS_BRI(2021)698792_EN.pdf, bRIEFING, EU Legislation in Progress, consulted June 2024
21. Malatji, M., Tolah, A.: Artificial intelligence (AI) cybersecurity dimensions: a comprehensive framework for understanding adversarial and offensive AI. AI Ethics (2024). https://doi.org/10.1007/s43681-024-00427-4
22. Mammonas, D.: Artificial intelligence (AI) act: council gives final green light to the first worldwide rules on AI. https://www.consilium.europa.eu/en/press/press-releases/2024/05/21/artificial-intelligence-ai-act-council-gives-final-green-light-to-the-first-worldwide-rules-on-ai/, press release of the European Council
23. Margaria, T., Floyd, B.D., Gonzalez Camargo, R., Lamprecht, A.-L., Neubauer, J., Seelaender, M.: Simple management of high assurance data in long-lived interdisciplinary healthcare research: a proposal. In: Margaria, T., Steffen, B. (eds.) ISoLA 2014. LNCS, vol. 8803, pp. 526–544. Springer, Heidelberg (2014). https://doi.org/10.1007/978-3-662-45231-8_44
24. Margaria, T., Schieweck, A.: The digital thread in industry 4.0. In: Ahrendt, W., Tapia Tarifa, S.L. (eds.) IFM 2019. LNCS, vol. 11918, pp. 3–24. Springer, Cham (2019). https://doi.org/10.1007/978-3-030-34968-4_1
25. Margaria, T., Steffen, B.: Business process modeling in the jabc: the one-thing approach. In: Handbook of Research on Business Process Modeling, pp. 1–26. IGI Global (2009)

26. Minh, D., Wang, H.X., Li, Y.F., Nguyen, T.N.: Explainable artificial intelligence: a comprehensive review. Artif. Intell. Rev. **55**(5), 3503–3568 (2022). https://doi.org/10.1007/s10462-021-10088-y
27. Parliament, E., of the European Union, C.: Regulation (EU) 2017/745 of the European Parliament and of the Council of 5 April 2017 on medical devices, amending Directive 2001/83/EC, Regulation (EC) No 178/2002 and Regulation (EC) No 1223/2009 and repealing Council Directives 90/385/EEC and 93/42/EEC (Text with EEA relevance.). https://eur-lex.europa.eu/legal-content/EN/TXT/?uri=CELEX
28. Phan, D.T., Grosu, R., Jansen, N., Paoletti, N., Smolka, S.A., Stoller, S.D.: Neural simplex architecture. In: Lee, R., Jha, S., Mavridou, A., Giannakopoulou, D. (eds.) NFM 2020. LNCS, vol. 12229, pp. 97–114. Springer, Cham (2020). https://doi.org/10.1007/978-3-030-55754-6_6
29. Russell, S., Norvig, P.: Artificial Intelligence: A Modern Approach (4th Edition). Pearson, London (2020). http://aima.cs.berkeley.edu/
30. Seto, D., Krogh, B., Sha, L., Chutinan, A.: The simplex architecture for safe online control system upgrades. In: Proceedings of the 1998 American Control Conference. ACC (IEEE Cat. No. 98CH36207), vol. 6, pp. 3504–3508 (1998). https://doi.org/10.1109/ACC.1998.703255
31. Sharkov, G., Commission, A.: Ethics guidelines for trustworthy AI. Technical report, April 2019. https://doi.org/10.2759/346720
32. Singh, A., Minguett, O., Margaria, T.: Binary decision diagrams and composite classifiers for analysis of imbalanced medical datasets. Electron. Commun. EASST **82** (2023)
33. Steffen, B., Steffen, B., Lee, E. (eds.): Let's talk AI. Springer (2024). to appear
34. Tocchetti, A., et al.: A.I. Robustness: a human-centered perspective on technological challenges and opportunities. ACM Comput. Surv. (2024). https://doi.org/10.1145/3665926, just Accepted
35. Yakimova, Y., Ojamo, J.: Artificial intelligence act: deal on comprehensive rules for trustworthy AI. https://www.europarl.europa.eu/news/en/press-room/20231206IPR15699/artificial-intelligence-act-deal-on-comprehensive-rules-for-trustworthy-ai, press release of the European Commission
36. Yakimova, Y., Ojamo, J.: Artificial intelligence act: meps adopt landmark law. https://www.europarl.europa.eu/news/en/press-room/20240308IPR19015/artificial-intelligence-act-meps-adopt-landmark-law, press release of the European Commission

Recognizing Hand-Based Micro Activities Using Wrist-Worn Inertial Sensors: A Zero-Shot Learning Approach

Fadi Al Machot[1], Habib Ullah[1], and Florenc Demrozi[2](✉)

[1] Department of Data Science, Norwegian University of Life Sciences, Ås, Norway
{fadi.al.machot,habib.ullah}@nmbu.no
[2] Department of Electrical Engineering and Computer Science, University of Stavanger, Stavanger, Norway
florenc.demrozi@uis.no

Abstract. Zero-shot learning (ZSL) is a machine learning paradigm that enables models to recognize and classify data from classes they have not encountered during training. This approach is particularly advantageous in recognizing activities where labeled data is limited, allowing models to identify new, unseen activities by leveraging semantic knowledge from seen activities. In this paper, we explore the efficacy of ZSL for activity recognition using Sentence-BERT (S-BERT) for semantic embeddings and Variational Autoencoders (VAE) to bridge the gap between seen and unseen classes. Our approach leverages wrist-worn inertial sensor events to capture activity data and employs S-BERT to generate semantic embeddings that facilitate the transfer of knowledge between seen and unseen activities. The evaluation is conducted on datasets containing three seen and three unseen activity classes with an average duration of 2 s, as well as three seen and three unseen activity classes with an average duration of 7 s. The results demonstrate promising performance in recognizing unseen activities, with an accuracy of 0.84 for activities with an average duration of 7 s and 0.66 for activities with an average duration of 2 s. This highlights the potential of ZSL for enhancing activity recognition systems which is crucial for applications in fields such as healthcare, human-computer interaction, and smart environments, where recognizing a wide range of activities is essential.

Keywords: Zero-Shot Learning · Human Activity Recognition · Micro activities · Hand movements

1 Introduction

Zero-shot learning (ZSL) for Human Activity Recognition (HAR) has garnered significant attention due to its potential to classify activities without prior labeled examples [1,10,31,38]. This capability is crucial for applications in healthcare, assistive technologies, smart environments, and human-computer interaction [7,14]. HAR systems aim to quantify, classify, and interpret human activities using sensor data from wearable devices, smartphones, or environmental sensors, employing both classic Machine Learning (ML) and Deep Learning (DL) algorithms [4,7,15].

ZSL is particularly important in smart home environments, where the range of possible activities is vast and constantly evolving. Traditional HAR systems focus on broad activities such as walking, sitting, and standing but often overlook subtle hand-based micro activities that are crucial for understanding daily routines and independence [14,16]. Micro activities include tasks like brushing hair, washing hands, and chopping vegetables, which are essential for personal hygiene, food preparation, and household chores [7,8] as shown in Fig. 1. Recognizing these activities is vital for assessing individuals' functional capabilities and their ability to live independently [2,20,21]. In addition, HAR is applied in the research field related to healthcare [2,24] and Industry 4.0 regarding the safety/security of workers and production monitoring [4].

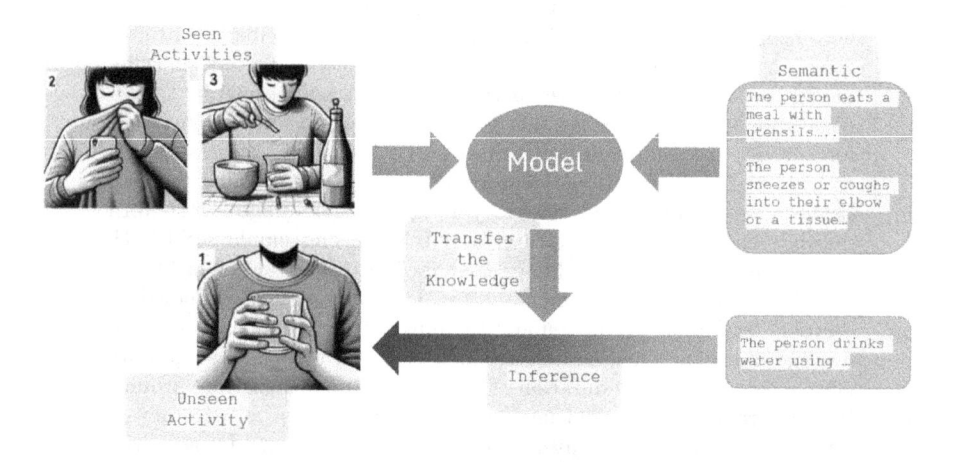

Fig. 1. An example of ZSL-based human micro activity recognition.

The primary challenge with traditional Activities of Daily Living (ADL) recognition systems is the extensive effort and cost required to collect and annotate training data for these micro activities [17]. Given the vast number of potential activities in a smart home environment, it is impractical to gather labeled examples for every possible action. These systems typically rely on predefined algorithms tailored to specific activities, which may not generalize well across different individuals or variations in movement patterns [9]. Additionally, the subjective nature of hand-based micro activities complicates the data collection and annotation process, making it difficult to develop robust models that accurately capture the nuances of human behavior.

Moreover, the varying durations of activities, such as washing hands versus opening a bottle, add to the complexity of accurate recognition [20,30]. This diversity in activity durations necessitates the development of sophisticated algorithms capable of handling these variations effectively.

This paper introduces a ZSL approach to recognize six hand-based micro ADLs. By leveraging semantic information and transfer learning, the proposed approach can generalize to new, unseen activities without requiring labeled examples. This approach addresses the limitations of existing HAR systems and enhances the recognition of micro ADLs in real-world settings. We demonstrate effective performance on six different classes (three seen and three unseen) for training and testing, using activity segments of 2 s and 7 s duration.

Sensor data is first aggregated, reshaped, and differentiated to compute the derivatives. We then calculate statistical features from the original, and the first order derivative data, forming an aggregated feature set. In addition, descriptions of actions are encoded into embeddings using the Sentence-BERT (S-BERT) model [35]. Our model architecture comprises a Variational Autoencoder (VAE) [22] that encodes the input features into a latent space and decodes them back to the original feature space. The latent space is then mapped to the S-BERT embedding space using a regressor. For zero-shot learning, we use the latent space of the VAE and the regressor to predict embeddings for unseen activities and perform nearest neighbor classification to assign action labels based on the closest S-BERT embeddings.

The main features of the proposed ZSL approach are:

- Incorporation of zero-shot learning to enable recognition of unseen micro ADLs based on semantic information and transfer learning.
- Demonstration of effective performance on six different classes (three seen and three unseen) for training and testing, using activity segments of 2 s and 7 s duration.

The paper is organized as follows: Sect. 2 provides background information, Sect. 3 outlines the HAR pipeline, Sect. 4 presents experimental findings, Sect. 5 analyzes state-of-the-art research, and Sect. 6 offers concluding remarks and outlines future work.

2 Preliminaries

In this section, we outline the data collection methodology used in our study, detailing the sensors utilized, their placement on the subjects' bodies, the data collection protocol, and specifics about the dataset.

Sensors: For data collection, we used an STM Nucleo LR103FB board along with an STM X-Nucleo-IKS01A3 sensor board, which includes both inertial and environmental sensors. Figure 2a shows the STM boards used in our study, and Fig. 2b illustrates their positioning on the subjects' wrists. These inertial sensors provide a dependable way to capture motion data crucial for recognizing hand-based micro ADLs.

Cohort of Studied Subjects: Data was gathered from a cohort of 30 subjects, including 12 females and 18 males. The females had an average age of 24.3 years

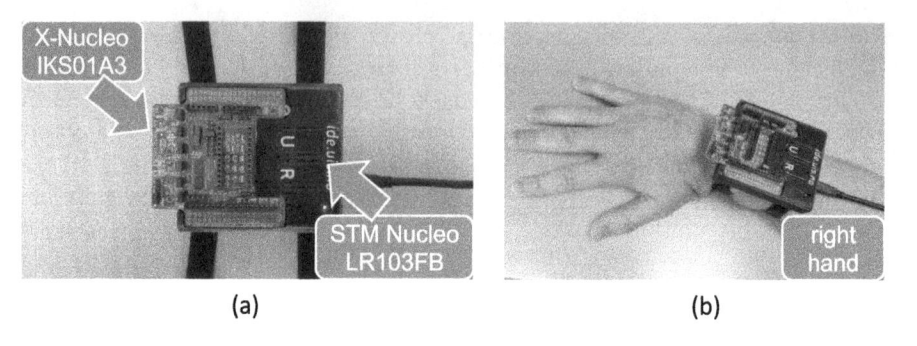

Fig. 2. Data collection device: a) board, b) on body position.

(±4.9), an average height of 167.2 cm (±7), and an average weight of 61.9 kg (±13). The males had an average age of 27.5 years (±7.2), an average height of 179.4 cm (±6.9), and an average weight of 84.4 kg (±17.3).

Data Collection Process: Subjects were asked to perform 24 different hand-based micro ADLs, each repeated 3 to 5 times. They conducted the data collection independently in their home environments without external supervision or training. Subjects were instructed to carry out the specified micro ADLs as they normally would in their daily routines. Figure 3 offers a detailed overview of the data collection setup used in our study, which incorporated three different sensors (accelerometer, gyroscope, and magnetometer) integrated into the STM X-Nucleo-IKS01A3 sensor board.

The sensor data was perceived at a frequency of 100 Hz, ensuring high temporal resolution and capturing subtle variations in hand movements during micro ADL performance. This sampling frequency balances data granularity and computational efficiency, enabling effective analysis of hand motion patterns while minimizing computational overhead.

Besides the raw sensor data, various derived features were generated to enhance the analysis of hand movements. These features included:

- **Pitch, Roll, and Yaw**: These angles represent the orientation of the sensor relative to a fixed reference frame and provide insights into the orientation of the subject's wrist during micro ADL performance.
- **Quaternions (Q_1, Q_2, Q_3, and Q_4)**: Quaternions offer an alternative representation of orientation, providing a compact and computationally efficient way to represent rotations in three-dimensional space.
- **Linear Acceleration**: This acceleration component excludes gravity's contribution and provides a measure of the subject's acceleration in the absence of gravitational effects, offering insights into the subject's movement dynamics.
- **Gravity Vector**: The gravity vector represents the direction and magnitude of gravitational acceleration acting on the sensor, aiding in estimating the sensor's orientation relative to the Earth's gravity field.

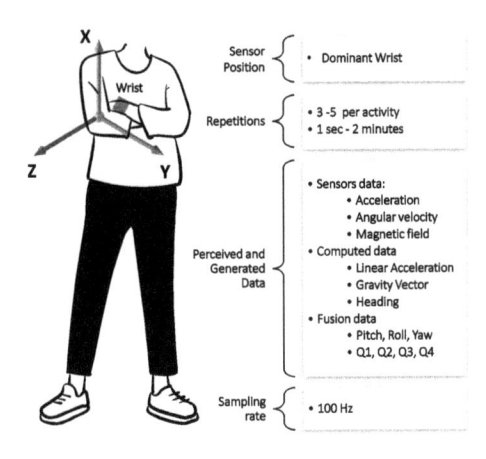

Fig. 3. Data collection setup.

- **Heading**: Heading refers to the direction in which the sensor points relative to the magnetic north and provides information about the subject's orientation in space.

Overall, the dataset is composed of a total of 24 features/columns, namely 1) timestamp, 2–4) accelerometer_xyz, 5–7) gyroscope_xyz, 8–10) magnetometer_xyz, 11–13) linear_accelerometer_xyz, 14–16) pitch, roll, yaw, 17–20) Q1, Q2, Q3, Q4, 21–23) gravity_xyz, and 24) heading, for a total of 10.78 h (aka., 3882540 samples) collected activity data.

Data Characteristics: Table 1 offers a thorough summary of the micro ADLs, detailing their descriptions, the number of repetitions requested from each participant, and statistics on the duration of each activity in seconds (minimum, maximum, mean, standard deviation, 25%, 50%, 75% quantiles). It also includes the total collected data for each activity in terms of 1-s segments. Additionally, Table 2 illustrates the distribution of each activity in 1-s segments for each subject. This detailed segmentation facilitates a granular analysis of activity patterns and durations among different individuals.

The data in Tables 1 and 2 reveal significant variations between different activities and subjects, highlighting the challenges in recognizing hand-based micro ADLs. These variations emphasize the subjective nature of performed micro ADLs and the complexity involved in capturing and analyzing such data.

Uniqueness of This Data: Unlike many existing datasets, such as those in [8] and [19], our data collection is unsupervised, without video/audio recording, and weakly annotated. This distinctive method ensures our dataset genuinely reflects everyday reality, capturing all the complexities and subtleties of human movement. The lack of supervision during data collection allows participants to interact with their environment and perform activities naturally, free from external influence or guidance. Consequently, this dataset encompasses human movements' authentic variability and complexity in real-life contexts.

Table 1. Studied ADLs with Duration Statistics in seconds: in RED/BLUE the statistics lowest/highest values

Nr	ADLs	Basic info on dataset description — Description	Repeat	Statistics on ADLs duration in seconds — mean	std	min	25%	50%	75%	max	1 S segments
1	drink water	Drink from a glass, cup, or bottle	5	8.8	11.3	2.0	4.2	5.8	9.4	70.8	1223
2	eat meal	Perform the gesture of eating, using a fork, a spoon, or the hands	3	32.6	10.6	1.5	27.6	29.5	34.0	73.6	2941
3	open bottle	Open a bottle (uncap it)	5	7.1	4.7	1.6	4.2	5.3	9.0	35.5	1023
4	open box	Open a food container (e.g., Tupperware)	5	5.5	3.7	1.4	3.0	4.2	6.5	17.4	790
5	brush teeth	Brush teeth for approximately 20 s	5	22.3	5.4	10.7	19.3	20.9	24.2	45.1	3216
6	brush hair	Brush hair for 10 s (using a comb, or the hands)	5	13.2	4.5	4.4	10.2	11.6	15.0	26.9	1903
7	take off jacket	Take off a jacket by undoing the buttons or zip	3	8.1	5.2	2.0	4.6	5.8	11.4	27.1	721
8	put on jacket	Put on a jacket and optionally do the buttons or zip	3	9.6	6.3	2.8	5.2	7.3	13.4	36.2	836
9	put on shoe	Put on a shoe, doing the laces, zip, etc. (if available)	3	9.5	4.8	1.8	6.2	8.4	11.0	31.9	864
10	take off shoe	Take off a shoe, by optionally undoing the laces/zip	3	6.7	4.0	0.3	4.2	5.6	8.4	19.9	589
11	put on glasses	Put on (sun)glasses	5	4.9	3.7	1.5	2.5	3.6	5.4	23.5	697
12	take off glasses	Take off (sun)glasses	5	4.5	3.5	1.3	2.5	3.2	5.0	15.6	648
13	sit down	Sit down on an chair/sofa/high stool	3	4.1	2.9	1.6	2.3	3.1	4.6	13.8	584
14	stand up	Stand up	5	3.9	2.9	1.1	1.9	2.9	4.6	14.4	597
15	writing	Write (by hand) for 15 to 20 s	5	19.5	7.9	9.4	14.7	17.5	22.1	63.3	2687
16	phone call	Pick up the (mobile) phone once (bring to ear)	5	5.9	7.2	1.3	2.7	3.3	5.9	48.7	852
17	type on keyboard	Type on a computer/laptop keyboard for 15–20 s	5	19.5	7.8	8.7	14.5	16.6	21.6	56.6	2715
18	salute (wave hand)	Wave the hand for 10 s	5	12.3	4.7	5.4	10.0	10.8	12.7	39.4	1713
19	sneeze cough	Sneeze or cough once	5	4.1	3.6	1.3	2.1	2.8	4.0	17.6	384
20	blow nose	Blow nose	5	5.2	4.1	1.0	2.5	3.6	6.1	21.2	743
21	washing hands	Wash hands: apply soap, rub hands together, and rinse	5	11.4	6.0	3.7	6.5	9.5	14.9	28.0	1649
22	dusting	Dust a surface with a rag/cloth for some time (15–20 s)	5	18.8	5.8	6.6	15.3	16.5	22.3	34.5	2577
23	ironing	Iron (a garment) for 15–20 s	5	18.6	5.6	10.5	14.5	16.6	21.5	36.2	2565
24	washing dishes	Scrub/scour a plate, cup/glass, or fork/knife/spoon; and rinse	5	12.9	8.6	3.1	7.3	10.1	15.6	51.2	1850

Table 2. Summary of ADLs Total Counts and Percentages per Subject

Subject	0000	1125	1279	1313	1324	1358	1390	1396	1405	1435	1453	1505	1570	1697	1735
1 S	2255	1247	1013	1068	1343	1069	1691	649	2300	1144	1017	649	1418	1248	918
segments (%)	(6%)	(3%)	(3%)	(3%)	(3%)	(3%)	(4%)	(2%)	(6%)	(3%)	(3%)	(2%)	(4%)	(3%)	(2%)

Subject	1751	1777	1803	1825	1975	1978	2045	2056	2097	2115	2116	2136	2155	2159	2160
1 S	2598	1121	872(	1718	1126	1011	784	1219	1091	2220	1056	1281	863	1496	1325
segments (%)	(7%)	(3%)	2%)	(4%)	(3%)	(3%)	(2%)	(3%)	(3%)	(6%)	(3%)	(3%)	(2%)	(4%)	(3%)

Additionally, the weak annotation in our dataset mirrors the inherent subjectivity and ambiguity in human activity labeling. This provides a more realistic representation of the challenges in activity recognition, such as variations in movement patterns, participant compliance, and annotation inconsistencies.

3 Methodology

3.1 Problem Definition

ZSL aims to develop a predictive model capable of understanding sensors readings and semantic indicators to classify unseen activities. Generative ZSL becomes crucial when there are no labeled examples for all classes (activities) in question. Consequently, the micro-activity dataset is divided into a training set with seen classes denoted as $Y_{seen} = y_{seen}^1, y_{seen}^2, \ldots, y_{seen}^n$ and a testing set with unseen classes represented as $Y_{unseen} = y_{unseen}^1, y_{unseen}^2, \ldots, y_{unseen}^n$. It is critical to ensure that $Y_{seen} \cap Y_{unseen} = \emptyset$. The challenge lies in constructing a function $\mathbb{R}^d \rightarrow Y_{unseen}$, which learns to predict the unseen classes using the training set and subsequently tests its efficacy on the unseen class data, maintaining the condition $Y_{seen} \cap Y_{unseen} = \emptyset$. ZSL aspires to mimic human adaptability to novel scenarios by leveraging models that can anticipate without prior examples.

3.2 Data Preparation

The principle of data split follows the principle of sharing contextual similarities between seen and unseen activities, enabling the model to leverage learned features from the seen classes to recognize the unseen ones. Detailed semantic descriptions are provided in the appendix. The seen classes, which the model was trained on, include activities such as "Washing hands," "Writing," and "Brushing teeth" for the 7-s duration, and "Open a bottle," "Take off a jacket," and "Put on glasses" for the 2-s duration as shown in Table 3. The unseen classes, which the model had to generalize to, are "Washing dishes," "Typing on a keyboard," and "Brushing hair" for the 7-s duration, and "Open a box," "Take off a shoe," and "Take off glasses" for the 2-s duration. In addition, the sensor readings were downsampled from 100 Hz to 50 Hz.

Table 3. Seen and unseen Classes for Different Durations.

Duration	Seen Classes	Unseen Classes
7 s	Washing hands	Washing dishes
	Writing	Typing on a keyboard
	Brushing teeth	Brushing hair
2 s	Open a bottle	Open a box
	Take off a jacket	Take off a shoe
	Put on glasses	Take off glasses

Semantic Embedding. S-BERT, or Sentence-BERT [35], is a modification of the BERT (Bidirectional Encoder Representations from Transformers) architecture [18] that is designed to generate sentence embeddings. The goal of S-BERT is to produce meaningful sentence representations that can be compared using cosine similarity for tasks like semantic textual similarity, clustering, and information retrieval. Traditional BERT models are computationally expensive for pairwise sentence comparisons because they require passing both sentences together through the model. S-BERT, however, fine-tunes BERT using a siamese and triplet network structure to derive semantically significant sentence embeddings, enabling efficient similarity comparisons.

The key improvements of S-BERT include: (a) By processing sentences independently through a shared BERT model, it generates fixed-sized sentence embeddings and (b) Uses supervised data with sentence pairs to fine-tune the model, optimizing it for tasks requiring semantic similarity. This approach significantly reduces computation time while maintaining high performance in various sentence similarity and clustering tasks.

Sensor Data Aggregation. In this process, we are dealing with sensor data represented by $X \in \mathbb{R}^{N \times M}$, where N denotes the number of samples, and M indicates the number of sensor readings (measurements) per sample. To capture the dynamic changes in the sensor data, we calculate the first derivatives along the measurement axis (i.e., the time axis, assuming measurements are taken sequentially over time). The first derivative X_{diff1} is computed as:

$$X_{\text{diff1}} = \frac{\partial X}{\partial t}$$

This derivative provides insight into the rate of change of sensor readings over time, highlighting trends and variations that may not be evident from the raw data alone. For both the original sensor data X and the derived data X_{diff1}, a variety of statistical features are extracted. These features are intended to summarize key characteristics of the data distributions. The statistical features calculated include the mean (the average value of the data), standard deviation (a measure of the amount of variation or dispersion in the data), minimum (the smallest value in the data set), maximum (the largest value in the data set), median (the middle value when the data is sorted), variance (the expectation of the squared deviation of the data from its mean), range (the difference between the maximum and minimum values), interquartile range (the range within which the central 50% of the data lies, i.e., the difference between the 75th and 25th percentiles), root mean square (the square root of the mean of the squares of the data values), signal magnitude area (the sum of the absolute values of the data divided by the number of samples), and median absolute deviation (the median of the absolute deviations from the median of the data). These features can be represented as:

$$\text{features}(X) = \begin{bmatrix} \text{mean}(X) \\ \text{std}(X) \\ \text{min}(X) \\ \text{max}(X) \\ \text{median}(X) \\ \text{var}(X) \\ \text{range}(X) \\ \text{iqr}(X) \\ \text{rms}(X) \\ \text{sma}(X) \\ \text{mad}(X) \end{bmatrix}$$

To form a comprehensive feature set, we aggregate the statistical features derived from both the original sensor data X and its first derivative X_{diff1}. The aggregated feature matrix $X_{\text{aggregated}}$ is constructed as:

$$X_{\text{aggregated}} = [\text{features}(X_{\text{reshaped}}), \text{features}(X_{\text{diff1}})]$$

This combined feature set includes both the original statistical features and those computed from the first derivatives, providing a rich and informative representation of the sensor data. By preparing the data in this manner, we ensure that the most pertinent characteristics of the sensor readings are captured and ready for subsequent analysis, such as machine learning or statistical modeling. This process enhances the ability to detect patterns, trends, and anomalies within the sensor data, ultimately leading to more accurate and insightful conclusions.

3.3 Model Architecture

The Variational Autoencoder (VAE) is used as our generative model. It learns to encode data into a latent space and then decodes it back to the original space. The architecture consists of an encoder, a latent space representation, and a decoder [22].

Given the input $X_{\text{aggregated}}$, the encoder consists of dense layers with ReLU activation, batch normalization, and dropout to prevent overfitting. Specifically, the input passes through three dense layers with 512, 256, and 128 units respectively, each followed by batch normalization and dropout (0.1). The encoder outputs the mean and log variance of the latent space z, each of dimension latent_dim.

The decoder mirrors the encoder, decoding the latent variable z back to the input space through three dense layers with 128, 256, and 512 units respectively, each followed by batch normalization and dropout.

Additionally, the latent space is projected to an embedding dimension:

$$z_{\text{projected}} = \text{Dense}_{\text{embedding\_dim}}(z).$$

The total loss for the VAE combines the reconstruction loss and the KL divergence. The reconstruction loss L_{recon} measures how well the decoder reconstructs the input:

$$L_{\text{recon}} = \frac{1}{N} \sum_{i=1}^{N} \|x_{\text{aggregated},i} - x_{\text{recon},i}\|^2,$$

while the KL divergence L_{KL} regularizes the distribution of the latent variables:

$$L_{\text{KL}} = \frac{1}{2} \sum_{i=1}^{n} \left(\sigma_i^2 + \mu_i^2 - \log(\sigma_i^2) - 1\right),$$

where μ_i is the mean of the latent variable z_i and σ_i^2 is the variance of z_i.

The total VAE loss is:

$$L_{\text{VAE}} = \frac{1}{N} \sum_{i=1}^{N} (L_{\text{recon}} + \beta L_{\text{KL}}),$$

where β is a weighting factor.

After training the VAE, a regression model g is trained which is a neural network that maps latent representations obtained from the encoder to S-BERT embeddings. The purpose of this regressor is to translate the latent space representations, which capture the underlying structure of the input data, into the S-BERT embedding space, which is used for zero-shot learning. The regressor is trained using the Adam optimizer to minimize the mean squared error (MSE) loss between the predicted embeddings and the true S-BERT embeddings of the seen classes. Formally, the regressor model is defined as:

$$y_{\text{pred}} = g(z),$$

where z is the latent representation from the encoder, and y_{pred} is the predicted S-BERT embedding.

The regression model designed to map the latent space representations to S-BERT embeddings consists of a sequential neural network. This regressor begins with an input layer that matches the dimension of the latent space, followed by a dense layer with 256 units and ReLU activation to introduce non-linearity. To mitigate overfitting, a dropout layer with a dropout rate of 0.1 is applied, and batch normalization is used to stabilize and accelerate training. This structure is repeated in subsequent layers: a dense layer with 128 units, followed by dropout and batch normalization, and then a dense layer with 64 units, again followed by dropout and batch normalization. The final output layer is a dense layer with a number of units equal to the embedding dimension, using a linear activation function to produce the final embeddings.

3.4 Zero-Shot Learning

Embedding Prediction. Once the regressor is trained, it is used to predict the S-BERT embeddings for the unseen classes data. The latent representations z_{unseen} of the unseen classes data are first obtained using the encoder. These latent representations are then passed through the regressor to generate the predicted embeddings:

$$y_{pred} = g(z_{unseen})$$

This step translates the latent space of unseen classes data to the S-BERT embedding space, enabling the comparison with the embeddings of unseen classes.

Nearest Neighbor Classification. After obtaining the predicted embeddings y_{pred} for the unseen classes data, the next step is to classify these embeddings. This is done using a nearest neighbor search in the S-BERT embedding space. The embeddings of the unseen classes $y_{unseen}(k)$ are precomputed using S-BERT. For each predicted embedding, the nearest neighbor among the unseen class embeddings is found by minimizing the Euclidean distance:

$$\hat{y} = \arg\min_{k} \|y_{pred} - y_{unseen}(k)\|$$

where $\hat{y}$ is the predicted label for the unseen classes data, and k indexes the unseen class embeddings. The nearest neighbor search effectively assigns the activity labels to the test data based on the closest S-BERT embeddings, leveraging the semantic similarity captured by S-BERT.

4 Results

The performance metrics for the selected activities demonstrate the effectiveness and limitations of the ZSL approach in recognizing both seen and unseen activities. Table 4 evaluates activities "washing hands," "typing on a keyboard," and "brushing hair". For "washing hands," the activity shows a precision of 0.72, recall of 0.91, and F1-score of 0.80, indicating high sensitivity but slightly lower precision. "Typing on a keyboard" exhibits excellent performance with a precision of 0.94, recall of 0.98, and F1-score of 0.96, showcasing the model's accuracy in recognizing this activity. "Brushing hair" demonstrates lower performance with a precision of 0.87, recall of 0.57, and F1-score of 0.69, highlighting the challenges in recognizing this unseen activity. Overall, the model achieves an accuracy of 0.85, a macro average F1-score of 0.82, and a weighted average F1-score of 0.84.

Table 4. Performance Metrics for Selected Activities. Seen classes: washing hands, writing, brushing teeth. Unseen classes: washing dishes, typing on a keyboard, brushing hair (7 s).

Activity	Precision	Recall	F1-Score	Support
Washing hands	0.72	0.91	0.80	195
Typing on a keyboard	0.94	0.98	0.96	311
Brushing hair	0.87	0.57	0.69	190
Accuracy			0.85	
Macro avg	0.84	0.82	0.82	696
Weighted avg	0.86	0.85	0.84	696

Table 5 focuses on the activities "open a box," "take off a shoe," and "take off glasses". "Open a box" shows moderate performance with a precision of 0.70, recall of 0.60, and F1-score of 0.64, indicating balanced but not outstanding recognition capability. "Take off a shoe" achieves a precision of 0.85, recall of 0.48, and F1-score of 0.61, suggesting high precision but lower recall, likely due to variability in how this activity is performed. "Take off glasses" presents a precision of 0.58, recall of 0.92, and F1-score of 0.71, revealing high recall but lower precision. The overall accuracy for this set of activities is 0.66, with a macro average F1-score of 0.66 and a weighted average F1-score of 0.66. These results reflect the challenges in recognizing activities with high variability and those that were unseen during training.

The analysis reveals that the zero-shot learning model demonstrates the ability to generalize to new, unseen activities, although with varying degrees of success.

These results emphasize the importance of continuous improvement in zero-shot learning techniques to enhance the recognition of diverse and subtle activities in smart home environments. The current data is limited, focusing on a small set of activities, and should be extended to include more classes to improve the model's generalization capabilities. The ability to accurately recognize a wide range of human activities is crucial for applications in healthcare, assistive technologies, and beyond, where understanding and adapting to a wide range of human activities is essential. Expanding the dataset to include more activities with varying contexts and semantics will further enhance the robustness and applicability of the ZSL approach in real-world settings.

Table 5. Performance Metrics for Selected Activities. Seen classes: open a bottle, take off a jacket, put on glasses. Unseen classes: open a box, take off a shoe, take off glasses (2 s).

Activity	Precision	Recall	F1-Score	Support
Open a box	0.70	0.60	0.64	324
Take off a shoe	0.85	0.48	0.61	253
Take off glasses	0.58	0.92	0.71	262
Accuracy			0.66	
Macro avg	0.71	0.67	0.66	839
Weighted avg	0.71	0.66	0.66	839

5 Related Work

5.1 Non-ZSL Approaches

In this section, to conduct a thorough review of the literature, we employed a systematic approach utilizing the research query shown in Table 6 on Scopus. The query is specifically designed to capture relevant studies that a) focus on accelerometers, gyroscopes, magnetometers, or inertial measurement unit (IMU) sensors, b) mounted on the wrist, and c) aim to recognize a set of micro ADLs.

Table 6. Defined Research Query (2015–2024)

Operator	Keywords
	(accelerometer OR gyroscope OR magnetometer OR IMU)
AND	(wrist-mounted OR wrist)
AND	(drink water OR eat meal OR open a bottle OR open a box OR brush teeth OR brush hair OR take off a jacket OR put on a jacket OR put on a shoe OR take off a shoe OR put on glasses OR take off glasses OR sit down OR stand up OR writing OR phone call OR type on a keyboard OR salute OR wave hand OR sneeze cough OR blow nose OR washing hands OR dusting OR ironing OR washing dishes)

Through this approach, 30 relevant studies were identified discussing the challenges of recognizing micro ADLs using wearable sensors and proposing potential solutions. Out of these studies, only 12 delve into the recognition of hand-related micro-ADLs. In particular, they are linked to the PAAL-ADL (Performance in an Active and Assisted Living-ADL) dataset [8] and the HTAD (Home-Tasks Activities Dataset) dataset [19]. The methodologies related to PAAL-ADL, such as those outlined in [7] and [3], propose HAR methodologies achieving accuracies of nearly 86% and 91%, respectively, in recognizing the 24 ADLs[1] within

---
[1] The PAAL-ADL and our dataset present the same ADLs.

the PAAL-ADL dataset. Both methods employ data filtering, feature extraction in both time and frequency domains, and the utilization of different algorithms, precisely the Nondominated Sorting Genetic Algorithm III (NSGA-III) [7] and Locally Weighted Random Forest (LWRF) [3].

On the other hand, the methodology [19] investigates the recognition of 7 activities (i.e., eating chips, mopping the floor, sweeping, brushing teeth, washing hands, typing on the keyboard, and watching TV) using data from a wrist accelerometer and audio stream provided in the HTAD dataset. The methodology proposes a Multilayer Perception (MLP) approach that takes as input a set of 16 statistical features related to acceleration and 36 Mel Frequency Cepstral Coefficients (MFCCs) related to audio, achieving an F1-Score of 0.91.

However, in [3,7,19], during the training and testing phases, the authors apply a classic k-fold approach over the dataset. This implies that the proposed method includes data from the same subject and the same data collection session of that subject in both the training and testing phases, thereby posing a potential risk of overfitting to specific individuals and sessions, which may limit the generalization capability of the model to broader populations or different contexts.

In [11], the authors presented a multi-level segmentation approach for recognizing a set of 24 hand-related micro activities, achieving higher accuracy results for activities longer than 7 s of average duration.

In [36], authors present a transfer learning methodology that recognizes seven toilet-related activities (i.e., dressing, undressing, brushing teeth, using the toilet, washing face, and washing hands), achieving an F1-Score of 0.84. Other hand-related micro-activities recognition includes digit recognition [23,34], handwritten signature [33,39], finger movements [5], and hand washing [40] through wrist movements. Moreover, from the grey literature, various approaches were proposed during the *IEEE COINS 2023 Contest for In Sensor Machine Learning Computing* [32]. However, regardless of the highly accurate results achieved, the details of the proposed methods are missing.

5.2 ZSL Approaches

Finally, by updating the Scopus research query from Table 6 to include an element related to ZSL (see Table 7), it was revealed that no prior work on hand-related micro ADL has been proposed in the literature. This makes the present work the first of its kind.

Table 7. Updated Research Query (2015–2024)

Operator	Keywords
AND	(zsl OR zero shot learning OR zero-shot learning OR zero-shot OR zero shot)

Based on our analysis, the existing literature mainly concentrates on: *a)* reduced sets of hand-based ADLs presenting similar temporal and functional characteristics, *b)* data collection performed in a laboratory environment, undergoing strict constraints, *c)* testing approaches that are not subject-independent, and *d)* to the best of our knowledge, recognizing hand-based micro activities using wrist-worn inertial sensors with ZSL has not been proposed in the state-of-the-art.

6 Conclusions

This study focused on recognizing 12 hand-based Activities of Daily Living (ADLs) using inertial sensor data, introducing a two-level segmentation strategy.

We examined the efficacy of Zero-Shot Learning (ZSL) for activity recognition, using Sentence-BERT (S-BERT) for semantic embeddings and Variational Autoencoders (VAE) to link seen and unseen classes. Our approach leveraged sensor data and S-BERT-generated embeddings to transfer knowledge effectively between seen and unseen activities. Future work will focus on expanding the number of recognized activities beyond the current 12, ensuring that seen and unseen classes share contextual semantic similarities to facilitate a more effective transfer learning process. We will also explore the use of large language models to represent the semantic space, potentially enhancing the accuracy and robustness of the ZSL framework.

7 Celebrating Prof. Tiziana Margaria

Tiziana has been a pivotal figure in my (Florenc Demrozi's) academic journey, as well as that of my colleague, Fadi al Machot. Our collaboration spans various research activities, project involvements, and organizational endeavors, all of which have been profoundly enriching.

We indirectly met in 2022 when my paper [13] and her paper [6] were the best paper candidates at the IFIP International Internet of Things Conference. After that, we meet within the IFIP Working Group 10.5 and the AWS Fellowship context. This collaboration has led to notable contributions in the fields of Human Activity Recognition (HAR) and educational methodologies in software engineering, as well as a three-month visiting period at the Immersive Software Engineering (ISE) program at the University of Limerick. During this visiting period, we started our collaboration, which led to the first two joint publications. In our paper *Experiences from the First Delivery of a New Immersive Software Engineering Course: Mathematical Foundations and Data Analytics* [12], we explore the integration of mathematical foundations and data analytics into the ISE course. This work underscores the transformative potential of innovative teaching methodologies in software engineering education.

Another notable contribution is our research on *CNN-based HAR on Edge Computing Devices* [37]. This study delves into the application of Convolutional Neural Networks (CNN) for HAR on edge computing devices. It highlights the potential of edge computing in enhancing real-time data processing and activity recognition accuracy, paving the way for more efficient and effective HAR systems. My collaboration with Tiziana also extends to organizing significant conferences, such as Very Large Scale Integration - System on Chip (VLSI-SoC 2026), and prolific discussions towards European projects focused on predictive health technologies dedicated to developing a human digital twin for health status prediction and Alzheimer's disease prevention. These endeavors showcase our collective commitment to advancing research and development in crucial areas of technology and health. Looking ahead, we are excited about potential future collaborations in the context of the Research at Immersive Software Engineering (R@ISE) project. This initiative, along with similar projects [29], promises to further our exploration into immersive and practical aspects of software engineering education. The R@ISE project exemplifies our forward-thinking approach to integrating immersive technologies into educational frameworks, enhancing the learning experience, and preparing students for the evolving demands of the software engineering industry. Additionally, the philosophy of simplicity [27,28] underpins our methodologies, as articulated in several influential publications. This philosophy advocates for streamlined, efficient approaches to complex problems, ensuring that solutions are both effective and accessible. The foundational concepts of Low-Code/No-Code (LCNC) [25] development have been a cornerstone of our research, fostering innovative approaches to software and HAR model creation. These concepts promote the use of visual development environments and pre-built components, enabling faster and more flexible software development processes [26].

It is essential to highlight the academic journey of Fadi Al Machot, a former student of Tiziana at Potsdam University. Under her mentorship, Fadi developed a deep understanding of software engineering and cyber-physical systems. He created the Machine Learning and Neurocomputing group as an Associate Professor at the Norwegian University of Life Sciences, where he applies his expertise to advance the field and mentor the next generation of researchers. Tiziana's mentorship has been instrumental in shaping Fadi's career, and her influence is evident in the quality and impact of his work. Our collaboration with Tiziana has shaped our research directions and achievements. Her mentorship and contributions have left an indelible mark on our professional paths, and we look forward to continuing this fruitful partnership in future endeavors. Prof. Margaria's unwavering commitment to advancing the field of software engineering, combined with her innovative approach to research and education, makes her a truly remarkable and inspirational figure in our academic community.

Conflict of Interest. The author(s) has no competing interests to declare that are relevant to the content of this manuscript.

Appendix: Detailed Descriptions (Semantics) of Seen and Unseen Activities Used for ZSL

Seen Classes

1. The person washes their hands with soap and water for hygiene, typically in a bathroom or kitchen. This involves rubbing their hands together with soap under running water, often for at least 20 s to ensure cleanliness and reduce the risk of infection.
2. The person writes notes or a letter using a pen or pencil, typically at a desk or table. This involves holding the writing instrument and making marks on paper, often focusing on conveying thoughts clearly and legibly.
3. The person brushes their teeth with a toothbrush and toothpaste, typically in a bathroom. This involves applying toothpaste to the brush and moving it back and forth against the teeth, aiming to remove plaque and maintain oral hygiene, and often results in a fresh minty taste in their mouth.
4. The person opens a plastic bottle by unscrewing the cap, typically to drink or pour the contents. This involves gripping the bottle with one hand and twisting the cap with the other, sometimes hearing a popping sound as the seal breaks.
5. The person removes a jacket they are wearing by pulling it off, usually when entering a warm indoor space. This involves unzipping or unbuttoning the jacket and sliding it off their arms, often feeling relief from the heat as they do so.
6. The person puts on glasses to improve their vision, typically done in a well-lit area. This involves lifting the glasses and positioning them on their nose and ears, allowing them to see more clearly and reduce eye strain.

Unseen Classes

1. The person washes dishes in the sink or a dishwasher after a meal, typically in a kitchen. This involves scrubbing dishes with a sponge or loading them into a dishwasher, often ensuring that all food residue is removed and the dishes are clean and ready for future use.
2. The person types on a keyboard of a computer or laptop, typically sitting at a desk. This involves pressing keys to input text or commands, often focusing on accuracy and speed to complete a task or communicate online.
3. The person brushes their hair using a hairbrush or a comb, usually in front of a mirror. This involves running the brush or comb through their hair to detangle and smooth it, often making their hair look neat and presentable.
4. The person opens a cardboard box to retrieve an item inside, usually by cutting or tearing the tape. This involves pulling open the flaps and reaching inside the box, often feeling a sense of anticipation and curiosity about the contents.
5. The person takes off a shoe they are wearing by pulling it off, often when returning home. This involves loosening any laces or straps and sliding the

shoe off their foot, often feeling a sense of relief and comfort as their feet are freed.
6. The person removes glasses they were wearing to see better, usually to clean them or switch to contact lenses. This involves taking hold of the frames and lifting them off their face, often feeling a temporary blur in their vision.

References

1. Al Machot, F., Elkobaisi, M.R., Kyamakya, K.: Zero-shot human activity recognition using non-visual sensors. Sensors **20**(3), 825 (2020)
2. Ali, M.T., Turetta, C., Demrozi, F., Pravadelli, G.: ICT-based solutions for Alzheimer's disease care: a systematic review. IEEE Access **12**, 13944–13961 (2024). https://doi.org/10.1109/ACCESS.2024.3356348
3. Aşuroğlu, T.: Complex human activity recognition using a local weighted approach. IEEE Access **10**, 101207–101219 (2022)
4. Boldo, M., et al.: Integrating wearable and camera based monitoring in the digital twin for safety assessment in the industry 4.0 era. In: Margaria, T., Steffen, B. (eds.) ISoLA 2022. LNCS, vol. 13704, pp. 184–194. Springer, Cham (2022). https://doi.org/10.1007/978-3-031-19762-8_13
5. Chandel, V., Ghose, A.: Demo abstract - NNTrak: real-time wrist tracking using smartwatch with CNN. In: SenSys 2022 - Proceedings of the 20th ACM Conference on Embedded Networked Sensor Systems, pp. 754–755 (2022). https://doi.org/10.1145/3560905.3568047
6. Chaudhary, H.A.A., Guevara, I., John, J., Singh, A., Margaria, T., Pesch, D.: Low-code Internet of Things application development for edge analytics. In: Camarinha-Matos, L.M., Ribeiro, L., Strous, L. (eds.) IFIPIoT 2022. IFIPAICT, vol. 665, pp. 293–312. Springer, Cham (2022). https://doi.org/10.1007/978-3-031-18872-5_17
7. Climent-Pérez, P., Florez-Revuelta, F.: Privacy-preserving human action recognition with a many-objective evolutionary algorithm. Sensors **22**(3), 764 (2022)
8. Climent-Pérez, P., Muñoz-Antón, Á.M., Poli, A., Spinsante, S., Florez-Revuelta, F.: Dataset of acceleration signals recorded while performing activities of daily living. Data Brief **41**, 107896 (2022)
9. Compagnon, P., Lefebvre, G., Duffner, S., Garcia, C.: Learning personalized ADL recognition models from few raw data. Artif. Intell. Med. **107**, 101916 (2020)
10. Deelaka, P.N., De Silva, D.Y., Wickramanayake, S., Meedeniya, D., Rasnayaka, S.: TEZARNet: temporal zero-shot activity recognition network. In: Luo, B., Cheng, L., Wu, Z.G., Li, H., Li, C. (eds.) ICONIP 2023. CCIS, vol. 1969, pp. 444–455. Springer, Cham (2023). https://doi.org/10.1007/978-981-99-8184-7_34
11. Demrozi, F., Al Machot, F.: An enhanced subject-independent approach for hand-based micro activities recognition. In: 2024 IEEE International Conference on Omni-layer Intelligent Systems (COINS), pp. 1–4 (2024)
12. Demrozi, F., Marchisio, M., Margaria, T., Sacchet, M.: Experiences from the first delivery of a new immersive software engineering course: mathematical foundations and data analytics. In: 2023 IEEE 47th Annual Computers, Software, and Applications Conference (COMPSAC), pp. 1576–1581. IEEE (2023)
13. Demrozi, F., Pravadelli, G.: SHPIA: a low-cost multi-purpose smart home platform for intelligent applications. In: Camarinha-Matos, L.M., Ribeiro, L., Strous, L. (eds.) IFIPIoT 2022. IFIPAICT, vol. 665, pp. 217–234. Springer, Cham (2022). https://doi.org/10.1007/978-3-031-18872-5_13

14. Demrozi, F., Pravadelli, G., Bihorac, A., Rashidi, P.: Human activity recognition using inertial, physiological and environmental sensors: a comprehensive survey. IEEE Access **8**, 210816–210836 (2020)
15. Demrozi, F., Serlonghi, N., Turetta, C., Pravadelli, C., Pravadelli, G.: Exploiting Bluetooth low energy smart tags for virtual coaching. In: 2021 IEEE 7th World Forum on Internet of Things (WF-IoT), pp. 470–475. IEEE (2021)
16. Demrozi, F., et al.: A low-cost wireless body area network for human activity recognition in healthy life and medical applications. IEEE Trans. Emerg. Top. Comput. **11**(4), 839–850 (2023)
17. Demrozi, F., Turetta, C., Machot, F.A., Pravadelli, G., Kindt, P.H.: A comprehensive review of automated data annotation techniques in human activity recognition. arXiv preprint arXiv:2307.05988 (2023)
18. Devlin, J., Chang, M.W., Lee, K., Toutanova, K.: BERT: pre-training of deep bidirectional transformers for language understanding. arXiv preprint arXiv:1810.04805 (2018)
19. Garcia-Ceja, E., et al.: HTAD: a home-tasks activities dataset with wrist-accelerometer and audio features. In: Lokoč, J., et al. (eds.) MMM 2021. LNCS, vol. 12573, pp. 196–205. Springer, Cham (2021). https://doi.org/10.1007/978-3-030-67835-7_17
20. Ishihara, Y., et al.: Association between daily physical activity and locomotive syndrome in community-dwelling Japanese older adults: a cross-sectional study. Int. J. Environ. Res. Public Health **19**(13), 8164 (2022)
21. Issa, M.E., et al.: Human activity recognition based on embedded sensor data fusion for the internet of healthcare things. In: Healthcare, vol. 10, p. 1084. MDPI (2022)
22. Kingma, D.P., Welling, M., et al.: An introduction to variational autoencoders. Found. Trends® Mach. Learn. **12**(4), 307–392 (2019)
23. Leong, L., Wiere, S.: Digit recognition from wrist movements and security concerns with smart wrist wearable IOT devices. In: Proceedings of the Annual Hawaii International Conference on System Sciences, pp. 6448–6455 (2020)
24. Mantovani, E., et al.: Wearables, sensors, and smart devices for the detection and monitoring of chemotherapy-induced peripheral neurotoxicity: systematic review and directions for future research. J. Peripheral Nerv. Syst. **27**(4), 238–258 (2022)
25. Margaria, T.: Knowledge management for inclusive system evolution. In: Steffen, B. (ed.) Transactions on Foundations for Mastering Change I. LNCS, vol. 9960, pp. 7–21. Springer, Cham (2016). https://doi.org/10.1007/978-3-319-46508-1_2
26. Margaria, T., Chaudhary, H.A.A., Guevara, I., Ryan, S., Schieweck, A.: The interoperability challenge: building a model-driven digital thread platform for CPS. In: Margaria, T., Steffen, B. (eds.) ISoLA 2021. LNCS, vol. 13036, pp. 393–413. Springer, Cham (2021). https://doi.org/10.1007/978-3-030-89159-6_25
27. Margaria, T., Floyd, B.D.: Simplicity in it: a chance for a new kind of design and process science. J. Integr. Des. Process. Sci. **17**(3), 1–7 (2013)
28. Margaria, T., Hinchey, M.: Simplicity in it: the power of less. Computer **46**(11), 23–25 (2013). https://doi.org/10.1109/MC.2013.397
29. Margaria, T., Steffen, B.: eXtreme Model-Driven Development (XMDD) technologies as a hands-on approach to software development without coding. In: Tatnall, A. (ed.) Encyclopedia of Education and Information Technologies, pp. 732–750. Springer, Cham (2020). https://doi.org/10.1007/978-3-030-10576-1_208
30. Martins, L.M., Ribeiro, N.F., Soares, F., Santos, C.P.: Inertial data-based AI approaches for ADL and fall recognition. Sensors **22**(11), 4028 (2022)

31. Matsuki, M., Lago, P., Inoue, S.: Characterizing word embeddings for zero-shot sensor-based human activity recognition. Sensors **19**(22), 5043 (2019)
32. Pau, D., Korobitsyn, A., Proshin, D., Zherebtsov, D., Bianco, M.: IEEE COINS 2023 contest for in sensor machine learning computing. Authorea Preprints (2023)
33. Ramachandra, R., Venkatesh, S., Raja, K., Busch, C.: Handwritten signature and text based user verification using smartwatch. In: Proceedings - International Conference on Pattern Recognition, pp. 5099–5106 (2020). https://doi.org/10.1109/ICPR48806.2021.9412048
34. Rattray, J.M., Ujhazy, M., Stevens, R., Etienne-Cummings, R.: Assistive multimodal wearable for open air digit recognition using machine learning. In: International IEEE/EMBS Conference on Neural Engineering, NER (2023). https://doi.org/10.1109/NER52421.2023.10123870
35. Reimers, N., Gurevych, I.: Sentence-BERT: sentence embeddings using siamese BERT-networks. arXiv preprint arXiv:1908.10084 (2019)
36. Shang, M., Zhang, Y., Ali Amer, A.Y., D'Haeseleer, I., Vanrumste, B.: Bathroom activities monitoring for older adults by a wrist-mounted accelerometer using a hybrid deep learning model. In: Proceedings of the Annual International Conference of the IEEE Engineering in Medicine and Biology Society, EMBS, pp. 7112–7115 (2021). https://doi.org/10.1109/EMBC46164.2021.9630659
37. Singh, A., Margaria, T., Demrozi, F.: CNN-based human activity recognition on edge computing devices. In: 2023 IEEE International Conference on Omni-Layer Intelligent Systems (COINS), pp. 1–4 (2023). https://doi.org/10.1109/COINS57856.2023.10189270
38. Wang, W., Li, Q.: Generalized zero-shot activity recognition with embedding-based method. ACM Trans. Sens. Netw. **19**(3), 1–25 (2023)
39. Xu, C., Pathak, P.H., Mohapatra, P.: Finger-writing with smartwatch: a case for finger and hand gesture recognition using smartwatch. In: HotMobile 2015 - 16th International Workshop on Mobile Computing Systems and Applications, pp. 9–14 (2015). https://doi.org/10.1145/2699343.2699350
40. Zhang, Y., Xue, T., Liu, Z., Chen, W., Vanrumste, B.: Detecting hand washing activity among activities of daily living and classification of who hand washing techniques using wearable devices and machine learning algorithms. Healthc. Technol. Lett. **8**(6), 148–158 (2021). https://doi.org/10.1049/htl2.12018

A Modal Logic Analysis of the MUTEX Variable Coverage Theorem

Michael Mendler[✉]

Faculty of Information Systems and Applied Computer Sciences, Bamberg University, Bamberg, Germany
michael.mendler@uni-bamberg.de

Abstract. A striking aspects in the theory of shared-memory distributed systems is that the existence of algorithms depends on subtle assumptions at the level of granularity of interaction, both regarding scheduling and memory models. A central result in this context is the Variable Coverage Theorem (VC Theorem): *"Any n-processor no-deadlock mutual exclusion algorithm using only read/write registers must use at least n shared variables."* The traditional textbook proofs of this result are informal and based on different operational models of shared-memory systems involving a detailed combinatorial analysis of the scheduling in the chosen model. In these notes, we revisit the VC Theorem from an axiomatic perspective. We transcribe the proofs into a strict formal argument using modal logic. Thus abstracting from the concrete operational setting, we are able to separate the purely combinatorial parts of the proofs from those aspects that pertain to the read/write interaction architecture and those that relate to the concrete mutex synchronisation problem. Specifically, we characterise the key limitation of the read/write memory model from which the impossibility result ultimately stems, in a single closure axiom, the Variable Cover Axiom. This axiom plays a role akin to the Pumping Lemma for regular or context-free languages.

Keywords: Mutual Exclusion · Read/Write Memory · Modal Logic

The Variable Coverage Theorem (VC Theorem) (see, e.g., Thm 4.18 [1], Thm. 10.33 [8]) is a basic impossibility result for distributed computations. It is a striking result whose educational value lies in the fact that it highlights a fundamental trade-off in synchronisation. When concurrent threads must cooperate to achieve a globally consistent functionality based on local communications, they need to synchronise. Yet, the level of granularity must be chosen judiciously as synchronisation (mutexes, locks, atomic regions, etc.) may sometimes be beneficial and sometimes detrimental to the solvability of a problem: Fine-grained asynchronous interaction increases decoupling and improves scalability, but introduces the risk of data races, non-determinism and unfairness. Large-grained synchronised transactions, on the other hand, avoid data races but introduce the risk of deadlocks and run-time overhead.

The VC Theorem is likely the first instance of such a situation that students will encounter in distributed system theory. They learn that for concurrent threads to safely share distributed data structures, they must synchronise their accesses to avoid data corruption, arising from fine-grained scheduling and data races. Mutual exclusion algorithms are then proposed to implement atomic access to memory. However, so the lecturer admits, when distributed, these mutex algorithms must themselves use shared memory. But then, how is this auxiliary memory safe-guarded from corruption? It is readily understood that if the memory already permits atomic *read-modify-write*[1] accesses to registers, then the mutex problem is trivial to solve. A single, read-modify-write control register suffices to synchronise arbitrarily many processors to share an arbitrary data structure. But mutex with read-modify-write feels like cheating, so the students wonder, because it implements atomic access to one data structure by assuming atomic access to another.

Clearly, distributed mutex algorithms are interesting only if they bootstrap atomic access from non-atomic *read/write* registers[2]. These are registers that can be read and written but not in a single atomic transaction, like read-modify-write registers. The import of the VC Theorem now is that with such weak memory, mutex is possible but only if we employ a minimum number of registers to decouple the processes. Otherwise, by the VC Theorem, our mutex algorithm must deadlock or fail to protect against data races. So, if we bundle the weak read-/write memory cells into a single composite cell we do not strengthen but weaken their power to synchronise, so it seems. To this author, this always looked like a paradox and teaching the VC Theorem from the standard textbook felt like presenting a magician's trick. The standard proofs involve extended combinatorial arguments that appear to entangle "accidental" aspects of the detailed operational simulation of a mutex algorithm. In order to persuade students (and himself) that the arguments are intrinsically more algebraic and more generic than they appear, the author found it useful to translate the informal proofs into formal modal logic. This transcription is presented here, in an extended form, for the first time.

As a transcription of a long-known result, these notes may offer only modest scientific insights. The main contribution is on the didactical side. It is useful to revisit the VC Theorem as one of the first results in the theory of distributed algorithms and change the methodological perspective, away from the standard operational model to an axiomatic point of view. By expressing the argument in terms of axiomatic logic, the VC Theorem can be appreciated as a fundamental result on the limits of synchronisation. It is then less likely misunderstood as

---

[1] A read-modify-write register [8] allows a process to read the register's content and overwrite it with a new value that is computed from the value that was read, in a single non-interruptible ("atomic") method call.

[2] A read/write register [8] only offers separate read and write methods. Thus, a process reading the register's content may be interrupted before it can overwrite it with a new value.

exposing merely an accidental artefact of the read/write model for a singular problem called mutual exclusion.

A Personal Note Motivating This Contribution to the Festschrift
The author is convinced that the methodological and didactical value of formal logic in an engineering context cannot be overstressed. It has been on this very mission that the author first met Tiziana Margaria, at a conference, sometime around 1989–1991. At that time, as part of her doctoral studies, Tiziana was exploring the application of automatic theorem proving for the formal verification of digital hardware. This innovative technology had just been created a couple of years before and generated an excitement of activities in the academic world. The author, also a PhD student at the same time, was on a similar trip. He fondly remembers heated discussions with Tiziana on the advantages of first-order automatic theorem-proving (Tiziana was using the Otter theorem prover by William McCune, Argonne National Laboratory, USA) versus higher-order interactive theorem proving (the author was using the LAMBDA prover by Mike Fourman et al., Abstract Hardware Limited, UK). There could not be any agreement, of course. Yet, as it happened, a couple of years after submission of their PhD theses, both researchers met again, this time on a middle ground. Tiziana was the among the first to recognise and exploit the potentials of restricted second-order logic (Weak MSO) as a specification language and automatic decision procedure for the verification of digital systems. The Mosel Project, directed by Tiziana, produced an efficient implementation of Weak MSO (Mona Tool) and exploited it for automatic verification of parameterised sequential circuits. The author had the pleasure to join Tiziana's research group as a postdoc at Passau University between 1995–1998. This was an equally enjoyable as fruitful collaboration producing exciting results [5,6,9]. The author is greatful for the opportunity and support he received during that time.

1 Shared Memory Mutual Exclusion

Figure 1 illustrates Peterson's Algorithm for the mutual exclusion problem for two processes, see, e.g., [8][Sec. 10.5.1]. The processes use three read/write registers, two boolean cells flag$_i$ ($i \in \{1,2\}$) and a binary cell turn, carrying values 1 or 2. The initial value of the latter is irrelevant. The flag$_i$ registers are assumed to be initialised 0.

The two processes p_1 and p_2 cycle through their code, repeatedly to access shared data during their *critical* regions, illustrated by the crit state. The looping transition at the crit state, labelled cont, indicates possibly repeated use of the shared data during the critical section. When a process does not need access to the critical data structure, it operates in the *remainder* section. This is represented in Fig. 1 by the abstract state rem. Again, the cont loop indicates that the process can stay there for an arbitrary amount of time. In order to progress from the rem to the crit state, a process must pass through the *trying* region, consisting of the three states set_flag, set_turn and check_flag. In this region the process p_i first sets its flag$_i$ to 1 and turn to i (write operations). Once in state

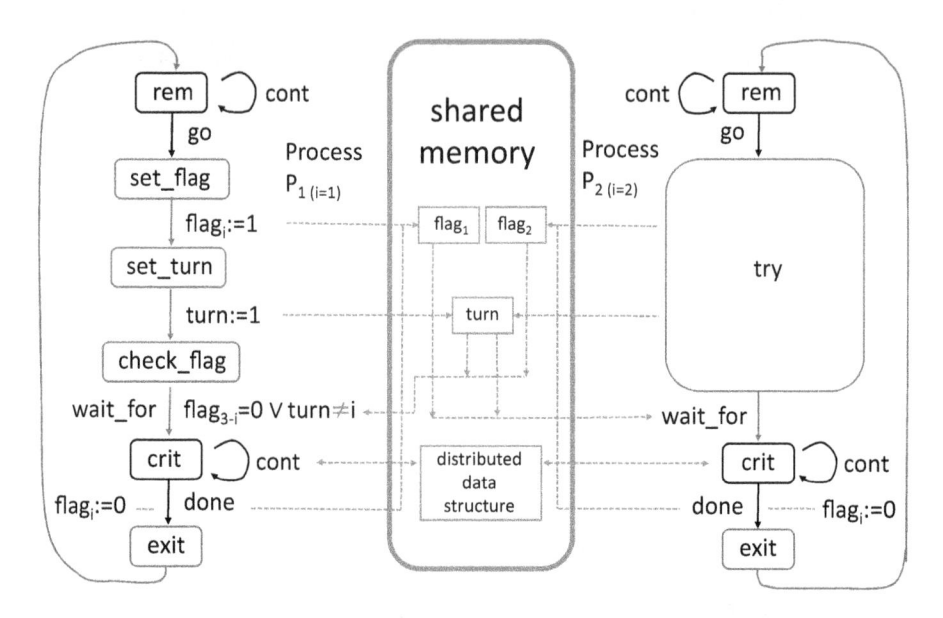

Fig. 1. Peterson's Algorithm for Mutual Exclusion. The control-flow graphs on both sides of the shared memory are the processes p_1 and p_2 to be synchronised. The shared memory in the center contains the control registers turn, $flag_1$, $flag_2$ through which mutual exclusion is achieved, but also all the data structures that are accessed during the critical section.

check_flag, it must wait for one of the conditions $flag_{3-i} = 0$ or $turn \neq i$ to become true (read operations). Then it can proceed to state crit. When done, the process moves to the *exit* region, abstracted as the state exit, in which it can perform internal clean-up, if necessary, whereupon it resets $flag_i$ to 0 and returns to the remainder section rem.

The properties of mutex algorithms are stated in slightly differing forms in the literature, yet the following conditions are typically imposed for every admissible (fair) execution schedule:

MUTEX: No two processors are in their critical section at any time.
NO DEADLOCK: If some processor is in its trying section, then some processor must become critical some time later.
NO LOCKOUT: If some processor is in its trying section, this processor must become critical eventually.
UNOBSTRUCTED EXIT: No processor remains in its exit region, forever.

The algorithm in Fig. 1 has been verified correct many times over, and we do not need to repeat this here, again. While the correctness argument for a fixed given algorithm is useful for practical applications, the scientific investigation starts when we try to understand the problem by challenging the role of the structural assumptions for the possibility of a solution.

One natural variation concerns the granularity of the memory model. The algorithm in Fig. 1 uses two binary-valued memory registers, flag_1, flag_2 and a binary register turn. This is no accident. For instance, consider what happens if we implemented all the three variables by a single array reg that is read/write and contains the values of flag_1, flag_2 and turn bundled together. Then the assignment $\mathsf{flag}_1 := 1$ would have to implemented by a reading $(f_1, f_2, t) := \mathsf{reg}$ followed by a write-back $\mathsf{reg} := (1, f_2, t)$ where we overwrite the flag_1 attribute of the vector but restore the values f_2 and t of the components flag_2 and turn, because they are not supposed to be altered. The corresponding symmetric write-back on the side of p_2 would be $\mathsf{reg} := (f_1, 1, t)$. This, however, breaks the algorithm in the write/read model. It can happen (from the initial configuration) that both processors p_1 and p_2 execute the reading $(0, 0, t) := \mathsf{reg}$ in their try state simultaneously and then execute their write-backs $\mathsf{reg} := (1, 0, t)$ and $\mathsf{reg} := (0, 1, t)$ in some order immediately afterwards. Say, $\mathsf{reg} := (1, 0, t)$ by p_1 is first and then $\mathsf{reg} := (0, 1, t)$ by p_2 second. But now, instead of setting both flag_i to 1, as in the original algorithm, flag_1 is overwritten by the "old" value 0. This is unavoidable as p_2 cannot know that p_1 also entered into trying region at the same time. Since $\mathsf{flag}_1 = 0$, the door is open for process p_2 to traverse the wait_for condition in state check_flag. At the same time, when this happens, p_2 will have set turn to value 2 which opens the door for p_1, too. Thus, both enter into the critical region and MUTEX is violated.

Hence, the separation of the memory registers is essential to the solvability of the problem. This is a well-known limitation of read/write registers. The VC Theorem states that every correct mutual exclusion algorithm for n processors that uses only read/write registers must necessarily use at least n shared variables. However, the universality of the limitation, reaching beyond the specific problem at hand (mutual exclusion), is hidden in the standard textbook arguments [1,8], which are based on tangled combinatorial arguments that are not easy to grasp. Ideally, we would like to understand the VC Theorem as a form of "Pumping Lemma" for read/write variable architectures, though we do not know of such a characterisation. However, we can make some progress by employing an axiomatic approach, transcribing the argument into a modal logic formalism. In doing so, we can clearly separate those parts of the argument that are due to universal logic from those which reflect the underlying memory architecture, and finally from those which pertain to the specific application problem. Also, by formalising precisely all assumptions and mathematical statements, we remove much of the room for misinterpretation that might arise from the informal language used in the textbooks.

2 Read/Write Dynamics in Modal Logic

A shared memory system [1] with read/write registers consists of a finite set *Proc* of *processes* and a finite set *Var* of *memory variables* or *registers*. The operational semantics associates with each $v \in Var$ a *domain* $\mathbb{D}_v$ of *values* that are stored at reference v, and with each $p \in Proc$ a set $\mathbb{S}_p$ to model the *program states* and local memory of each process p. A system *configuration* $C = (Glob, Loc) \in \mathbb{C}$ then consists of a global memory $Glob$ mapping each $v \in Var$ to a value $Glob(v) \in \mathbb{D}_v$ and local process states Loc, mapping each $p \in Proc$ to $Loc(p) \in \mathbb{S}_p$. As in [1,8] we adopt an interleaving model of concurrency, where the operational behaviour of the processes is modelled as a deterministic labelled transition system

$$(Glob, Loc) \xrightarrow{\alpha} (Glob', Loc') \tag{1}$$

on configurations, modelling an atomic execution step with actions

$$\alpha \in Act = Proc \times Op \times Var$$

where $\alpha = (p, o, v)$ means that process p executes operation o on variable v, which we also write as $\alpha = p : v.o$. In the case of read/write process systems, like we are interested in here, we distinguish two types of operations $Op = \{\text{wr}, \text{rd}\}$, where wr codes a *write* and rd codes a *read* operation.

There are natural constraints on the transition system (1) expressing the locality of the actions, such as that the effect of an action $p : v.o$, for $o \in Op$, depends only on the local state $Loc(p)$ of the process p taking the step; that it can change only the local state $Loc'(p)$ of p or the memory register $Glob'(v)$. We are going express these coherence constraints using the axiomatic method, in the language of propositional multi-modal logic. We will need only the most elementary constructions, as would be treated in an introductory class to basic modal logic. In particular, the following does not depend on knowledge of specialised temporal logics such has PLTL, CTL, CTL*. Any introduction to basic modal logic should be sufficient such as provided by [2,3]. For multi-modal logics the reader is referred to [7,10]. Readers interested in taking our case study further, might find the work on propositional (or first-order) dynamic logic [4] inspiring.

2.1 Modal Syntax and Semantics

Our modal specifications for configurations are built with the following propositional syntax

$$\phi ::= a \mid \bot \mid \phi \land \phi \mid \phi \lor \phi \mid \phi \to \phi \mid K_P \phi \mid M_P \phi \mid \forall_P^X \phi \mid \exists_P^X \phi \mid \text{Wr}_P^X \phi$$

where $a \in Atom$ ranges over a set of atomic propositions, $P \subseteq Proc$ is a subset of processes and $X \subseteq Var$ a subset of variables. The model-theoretic semantics is given in terms of a *satisfaction* relation

$$C \models \phi \tag{2}$$

expressing that formula ϕ is satisfied at configuration $C \in \mathbb{C}$. In these notes, like in the original proofs [1,8] that we are transcribing, we will assume that the set $\mathbb{C}$ only contains the *reachable* configurations of our process system, i.e., the configurations that can be obtained from some admissible initial configurations by scheduling the processes in arbitrary ways. Given a set of formulas Φ and a formula ψ, the *semantic entailment*

$$\Phi \models \psi \tag{3}$$

states that in all reachable configurations $C \in \mathbb{C}$, it is the case that if $C \models \phi$ for all $\phi \in \Phi$, then also $C \models \psi$. Note that $\models \phi$ means $C \models \phi$ for all $C \in \mathbb{C}$, i.e., that ϕ is a tautology on reachable configurations. Our plan is to transcribe the arguments given in Sec. 4.1.1 and Sec. 4.4.4 of [1] and Sec. 10.8 of [8] into modal logic syntax, using semantic statements of form (2) and (3).

The classical operators are understood as usual: The logical constant $\bot$ denotes falsity, and the binary operators $\wedge$, $\vee$ and $\rightarrow$ are logical conjunction, disjunction and implication, all with their standard classical boolean semantics. The power of the formalism comes from the *modal operators* K_P, M_P, $\forall_P^X \phi$, $\exists_P^X \phi$ and $\mathsf{Wr}_P^X \phi$. These encapsulate different forms of first-order quantification over specific *accessibility relations* between configurations which are derived from the structure of configurations and basic action steps (1). Specifically, K_P and M_P embody *epistemic* modalities, $\forall_P^X \phi$ and $\exists_P^X \phi$ *temporal* modalities and $\mathsf{Wr}_P^X \phi$ is a special form of *covering* modality, whose interconnection with the epistemic and temporal modalities is the Variable Cover Axiom. We first introduce these relations in the following, and then interpret the modalities associated with them.

Epistemic Modalities
The fact that processes only have a local view of the global configuration is captured by an equivalence relation

$$C \sim_P D,$$

expressing that configurations $C, D \in \mathbb{C}$ are indistinguishable for a coalition of processes $P \subseteq Proc$, in the sense that they differ at most in the local states of the remaining processes $Proc \backslash P$.

Definition 1. *Let* $C = (Glob_C, Loc_C)$ *and* $D = (Glob_D, Loc_D)$ *be reachable configurations. Then,*
$$C \sim_P D$$
iff $Glob_C = Glob_D$ *and* $Loc_C(q) = Loc_D(q)$ *for all* $q \in P$. □

Quantification over $\sim_P$ from Definition 1 as a labelled accessibility relation over $\mathbb{C}$ gives rise to epistemic modalities of knowledge:

$C \models M_P \phi$ iff there *exists* a reachable configuration D with $C \sim_P D$ and $D \models \phi$;
$C \models K_P \phi$ iff for *all* reachable configurations D with $C \sim_P D$ it follows $D \models \phi$.

Considering that a process can access the global memory but not the local state of the other processes, the statement $K_P \phi$ expresses that the processes P *jointly know* that ϕ is true. The modality $M_P \phi$ is the classical dual, $M_P \phi \leftrightarrow \neg K_P \neg \phi$, which may be read as saying that processes P consider it plausible that ϕ might hold.

Temporal Modalities

The next pair of modalities arises by quantifying over execution schedules that involve pre-specified processes and variable writing. Consider the reflexive and transitive relation
$$C \leadsto_P^X D$$
stating that there is an execution schedule from $C \in \mathbb{C}$ to reach $D \in \mathbb{C}$ in which only processes in P are executed and at most the variables in X are written. This is also called a *P-only* schedule. When $P = \{p\}$ contains only a single process p we also talk about a *p-only* schedule.

Definition 2. *Let $C, D \in \mathbb{C}$ be reachable configurations, $X \subseteq Var$ and $P \subseteq Proc$. Then,*
$$C \leadsto_P^X D$$
iff there exist $n \geq 0$ and $C_0, C_1, \ldots, C_n \in \mathbb{C}$ such that
$$C = C_0 \xrightarrow{p_0:x_0.o_0} C_1 \xrightarrow{p_1:x_1.o_1} C_2 \quad \cdots \quad C_{n-1} \xrightarrow{p_{n-1}:x_{n-1}.o_{n-1}} C_n = D$$
and $\{p_i \mid 0 \leq i \leq n-1\} \subseteq P$ and $\{x_i \mid o_i = \mathsf{wr}, 0 \leq i \leq n-1\} \subseteq X$. □

Quantifying over the labelled accessibility relation from Definition 2 induces the following canonical temporal modalities:

$C \models \exists_P^X \phi$ iff there exists $D \in \mathbb{C}$ such that $C \leadsto_P^X D$ and $D \models \phi$;
$C \models \forall_P^X \phi$ iff for all $D \in \mathbb{C}$ with $C \leadsto_P^X D$ we have $D \models \phi$.

The modality $\forall_P^X \phi$ is the standard temporal statement that ϕ remains "always" true, while $\exists_P^X \phi$ states that ϕ will become "eventually" true. They are typically abbreviated by the symbols F and G, or $\square$ and $\diamond$, respectively. The special nature of our modalities $\forall_P^X$ and $\exists_P^X$ is that they quantify over a restricted set of schedules captured by their labels P and X, which make them a parametrised family of modalities.

In the special case where we do not want to restrict the variable accesses, we simplify notation and write $\exists_P \phi$ and $\forall_P \phi$ for $\exists_P^{Var} \phi$ and $\forall_P^{Var} \phi$, respectively. Also, if $P = \{p\}$ and $X = \{v\}$ are singleton sets, we write $\exists_p^v \phi$ and $\forall_p^v \phi$ instead of $\exists_P^X \phi$ and $\forall_P^X \phi$.

Covering Modality

We now come to the last family of modalities, expressing a configuration-dependent *covering* relation between processes and variables. The basic definition given in Definition 4.4, p. 81 [1] is as follows:

> "A processor covers a variable in a configuration if it is about to write it (according to its state in the configuration)."

However, as it turns out, a generalisation is more convenient for the proof, which expresses that some *set* of variables X are covered by some *set* of processes P, meaning that for each $v \in X$ there is some process in $p \in P$ that will overwrite v immediately as its first step, when it is executed. This is a modal quantification over a multi-step relation.

Definition 3. *Let $C, D \in \mathbb{C}$, $P \subseteq Proc$ and $X \subseteq Var$ with $|X| = m$. Then,*

$$C \Rightarrow_P^X D$$

iff there exist $C_0, C_1, \ldots, C_m \in \mathbb{C}$ such that

$$C = C_0 \xrightarrow{p_0 : x_0 . \mathsf{wr}} C_1 \xrightarrow{p_1 : x_1 . \mathsf{wr}} C_2 \quad \cdots \quad C_{m-1} \xrightarrow{p_{m-1} : x_{m-1} . \mathsf{wr}} C_m = D$$

and $\{p_i \mid 0 \leq i \leq m-1\} \subseteq P$ and $\{x_i \mid 0 \leq i \leq m-1\} = X$. □

The accessibility relation of Definition 3 again induces two dual modalities, but we are only interested in the existential form:

$$C \models \mathsf{Wr}_P^X \phi \text{ iff there exists } D \in \mathbb{C} \text{ such that } C \Rightarrow_P^X D \text{ and } D \models \phi.$$

A special case arises for singletons $P = \{p\}$ and $X = \{v\}$. Since processes are deterministic, the statement $C \models \mathsf{Wr}_p^v \phi$ means (i) that the current active statement of p is a write on v and (ii) after it is executed from C, we reach a configuration where proposition ϕ holds. Here the universal and existential quantification over the first step of p are identical, by determinism, i.e., $\neg \mathsf{Wr}_p^v \neg \phi \leftrightarrow \mathsf{Wr}_p^v \phi$. For general $|P| \geq 2$, however, there is a difference between $\mathsf{Wr}_P^v \phi$ and $\neg \mathsf{Wr}_P^v \neg \phi$. Note that we have $\mathsf{Wr}_P^Y \phi \to \mathsf{Wr}_P^X \phi$ whenever $X \subseteq Y$.

2.2 Frame Axioms

Abstractly speaking, we may think of our specification language as a modal logic over the logical signature $(Proc, Var)$ that is interpreted over *Kripke frames*

$$\mathfrak{F} = (\mathbb{C}, \sim_P, \xrightarrow{\alpha} \mid P \subseteq Proc, \alpha \in Act)$$

where $\sim$ and $\to$ are indexed families of binary relations over $\mathbb{C}$. They generate derived accessibilities as per Definitions 1–3 to interpret the modal operators.

The *frame axioms* of a modal theory are those axioms that are independent of the particular interpretation of the atomic propositions *Atom*. They express universal properties of the accessibility relations that make up the frame $\mathfrak{F}$. Some frame axioms are independent of the special properties of the accessibilities and reflect general laws of basic modal logic. Other frame axioms are specific coherence laws that capture the special nature of the accessibility relations and their interactions. In the following we will introduce the most important frame axioms sufficient for the application at hand. We do not claim semantic completeness or even aim to be complete. Since the modalities are entirely standard, complete axiom systems (semantically as well as proof-theoretically) can be obtained using the standard techniques found in textbooks (specifically, see [7]). In the sequel we will also tacitly assume all laws of classical propositional logic (and classical first-order logic at the meta level) without mentioning them. Our focus is on the part that involves modalities, as it is here where we wish to gain notational precision over the reference textbooks [1,8].

Frame Axioms for Basic Modal Logic K

The most basic laws are those of System K for each of K_P and $\forall_P^X$. They simply arise from the nature of universal quantification expressed by these modalities. The key rule is the Rule of Necessitation:

$$\text{If } \models \phi, \text{ then } \models \forall_P^X \phi \text{ and } \models K_P \phi. \tag{4}$$

The Normality Axioms express the distribution of K_P and $\forall_P^X$ over finite conjunctions:

$$\models (\forall_P^X \phi \wedge \forall_P^X \psi) \rightarrow \forall_P^X (\phi \wedge \psi) \tag{5}$$
$$\models (K_P \phi \wedge K_P \psi) \rightarrow K_P(\phi \wedge \psi) \tag{6}$$
$$\models \forall_P^X \top \tag{7}$$
$$\models K_P \top \tag{8}$$

and the Shifting Axioms permit us to move universal statements K_P and $\forall_P^X$ under existential ones M_P, $\exists_P^X$ and Wr_P^X:

$$\models (\forall_P^X \phi \wedge \exists_P^X \psi) \rightarrow \exists_P^X (\phi \wedge \psi) \tag{9}$$
$$\models (K_P \phi \wedge M_P \psi) \rightarrow M_P(\phi \wedge \psi) \tag{10}$$
$$\models \forall_P^X \phi \wedge \mathsf{Wr}_P^X \psi \rightarrow \mathsf{Wr}_P^X (\phi \wedge \psi). \tag{11}$$

Finally, the Duality Axioms

$$\models M_P \phi \leftrightarrow \neg K_P \neg \phi \tag{12}$$
$$\models \exists_P^X \phi \leftrightarrow \neg \forall_P^X \neg \phi \tag{13}$$

make universal and existential modalities interdefinable. Obviously, from Duality, the validities $\neg \exists_P^X \bot$ and $\neg M_P \bot$ can be derived from (7) and (6). An important consequence of these laws is the Extensionality Principle:

Proposition 1 (Extensionality Principle). *Let θ be a formula in which some propositional variable a only occurs in positive position, i.e., in the scope of an even number of negations. Then $\models \phi \rightarrow \psi$ implies $\models \theta[\phi/a] \rightarrow \theta[\psi/a]$. Further, $\models \phi \leftrightarrow \psi$ implies $\models \theta[\phi/a] \leftrightarrow \theta[\psi/a]$, even without the restriction on the positive occurrence of a.*

The second important admissible rule that we are going to use extensively is the Deduction Principle:

Proposition 2 (Deduction Principle). $\Theta, \phi \models \psi$ iff $\Theta \models \phi \to \psi$.

The are also the obvious structural laws to do with the label sets, such as $\models \forall_P^X \phi \to \forall_Q^Y \phi$ for all $P \supseteq Q$ and $X \supseteq Y$. We do not aim to be complete, however, and so we leave this to the interested reader.

Frame Axioms for Epistemic Logic S5

The relation $\sim$ is reflexive, transitive and symmetric, which is captured by the standard axioms (14), (15) and (16), respectively:

$$\models K_P \phi \to \phi \tag{14}$$
$$\models K_P \phi \to K_P K_P \phi \tag{15}$$
$$\models \phi \to K_P M_P \phi. \tag{16}$$

These are the well-known axioms of the modal theory S5 for knowledge.

Frame Axioms for (Temporal) Logic S4

The reflexivity and transitivity of $\rightsquigarrow$ comes down to the axioms

$$\models \phi \to \exists_P^X \phi \tag{17}$$
$$\models \exists_P^X \exists_P^X \psi \to \exists_P^X \psi \tag{18}$$

expressed in terms of the existential modality $\exists_P^X$.

Finally we come to expose the coherence laws governing the interaction of the modalities. These reflect the locality properties inherent in the operational semantics of our shared read/write process system. These laws of local observability and controllability impose part of the limitations of expressiveness from which the VC Theorem will ultimately derive. In the following we will only state the frame axioms, relying on standard techniques (specifically see [10]) for the technical justifications.

Frame Axioms for Locality

Since a process can only change its own local control state but not the control state of all the other processes, on each schedule $C \rightsquigarrow_P^X D$ (see Definition 2), where only processes from P are scheduled, the control states of processes $Proc \setminus P$ must remain constant. Moreover, the execution of P only depends on the local control states of P (and the global memory) not on the states of processes $Proc \setminus P$. This means that the relations $\sim_P$ and $\rightsquigarrow_P^X$ commute. Specifically, we have the frame property[3]

$$\sim_P ; \rightsquigarrow_P^X = \rightsquigarrow_P^X ; \sim_P$$

which gives rise to the frame axioms (notice that $\sim_P$ is symmetric)

---

[3] The notation $R; S$ expresses the sequential composition of relation R before S, i.e., $(x, z) \in R; S$ iff there is y with $(x, y) \in R$ and $(y, z) \in S$.

$$\models \exists_P^X K_P \phi \leftrightarrow K_P \exists_P^X \phi \qquad (19)$$
$$\models \forall_P^X K_P \phi \leftrightarrow K_P \forall_P^X \phi \qquad (20)$$

and, of course, the duals of (19) and (20), i.e., with M_P instead of K_P.
Another form of coupling between $\sim_P$ and $\leadsto_P^X$ is the inclusion

$$\leadsto_P^\emptyset \subseteq \sim_{Proc \setminus P}$$

which states that if processes P do not write to any variable, then the configurations reached can differ at most in the local states of P, i.e., they must be $\sim_{Proc \setminus P}$ indistinguishable from each other. This is captured by the frame axiom

$$\models K_{Proc \setminus P} \phi \rightarrow \forall_P^\emptyset \phi. \qquad (21)$$

Proposition 3. *In the presence of the other laws, the axiom (21) is interderivable with the axiom*

$$\models \phi \rightarrow \forall_P^\emptyset M_{Proc \setminus P} \phi \qquad (22)$$

The law (22) can be read as follows: If a set P of processes is executed so that none of them writes to the global memory, then the resulting configuration coincides with the initial configuration, except for changes in the local states of these processes.

Proof. We can derive (22) from (21) as follows: First, $\models \phi \rightarrow K_{Proc \setminus P} M_{Proc \setminus P} \phi$ by (16) and further $\models K_{Proc \setminus P} M_{Proc \setminus P} \phi \rightarrow \forall_P^\emptyset M_{Proc \setminus P} \phi$ as an instantiation of (21). The result (22) follows from this by standard propositional logic. Vice versa, we instantiate (22) to obtain $\models K_{Proc \setminus P} \phi \rightarrow \forall_P^\emptyset M_{Proc \setminus P} K_{Proc \setminus P} \phi$. By dualising (16) we have $M_{Proc \setminus P} K_{Proc \setminus P} \phi \rightarrow \phi$. Now we exploit Extensionality Proposition 1 and conclude $\models K_{Proc \setminus P} \phi \rightarrow \forall_P^\emptyset \phi$ as desired. □

Frame Axioms for Write Abstraction
The multi-step relation $\leadsto_P^X$ is the (conditional) reflexive transitive closure of the single-step action transitions $\xrightarrow{\alpha}$. For instance, given $p \in P$ and $x \in X$, by definition, we have the inclusion

$$\xrightarrow{p:x.\mathsf{wr}} \subseteq \leadsto_P^X$$

whenever $p \in P$ and $x \in X$. This inclusion gives rise to the axiom schemes

$$\models \mathsf{Wr}_Q^Y \phi \rightarrow \exists_P^X \phi \qquad (23)$$
$$\models \mathsf{Wr}_p^x \exists_P^X \phi \rightarrow \exists_P^X \phi \qquad (24)$$

under the condition $Y \subseteq X$ and $Q \subseteq P$. We also have the obvious aggregation, that

$$\models (\mathsf{Wr}_p^v \top \wedge \mathsf{Wr}_P^U \top) \to \mathsf{Wr}_{P \cup \{p\}}^{U \cup \{v\}} \top. \tag{25}$$

where $p \notin P$.

Frame Axiom for Variable Coverage
Finally, we come to identify the crucial coherence law that is characteristic of read/write systems as opposed to stronger memory models such as read-modify-write.

Let $p \neq q$ be distinct processes. Given a configuration C where q covers v, i.e., is about to overwrite v. Since we do not permit atomic *read-modify-write* operations, the new memory value of v depends only on the local state of q in C. This means that if we let process p execute before, $C \leadsto_p^v C'$ so that it writes at most to v, the process q will behave from C' exactly as from original C. It will immediately overwrite the only variable v that p might have changed. The local state of q has not changed and the new value will be the very same value that q would write in C. Hence, every configuration D reachable from C by executing q, $C \leadsto_q D$, can be reached from C', too, modulo changes to the local state of p. Technically, this is the inclusion[4]

$$(\leadsto_p^v)^{-1} ; \xrightarrow{q:v.\mathsf{wr}} \subseteq \xrightarrow{q:v.\mathsf{wr}} ; \leadsto_q$$

which is captured by the Variable Cover Axiom (VC Axiom)

$$\models \mathsf{Wr}_q^v K_q \phi \to \forall_p^v \mathsf{Wr}_q^v \phi$$

for a single covering process and

$$\models \mathsf{Wr}_P^W K_{Proc \setminus Q} \phi \to \forall_Q^W \mathsf{Wr}_P^W \phi \tag{26}$$

for the general case, where $Q \cap P = \emptyset$. It will turn out that is the crucial axiom that forces the number of variables match the number the processes in deadlock-free mutual exclusion algorithms. Note that the axiom (26) will not hold for read-modify-write actions.

2.3 Model Axioms

The frame axioms are still independent of the application scenario, i.e., they are valid under arbitrary substitution of formulas for propositional variables. When we come to model a specific process system, such as one that implements mutual exclusion, we need to introduce specific propositional constants, to express properties on the state of processes (and possibly memory content). Fixing the valuation of the propositional atoms as constants turns the frame into a *model*

$$\mathfrak{M} = (\mathfrak{F}, V)$$

---
[4] The relation R^{-1} denotes the reverse of R, i.e., $(x, y) \in R^{-1}$ iff $(y, x) \in R$.

where V is a valuation that maps each atom $a \in \mathit{Atom}$ to a set of configurations $V(a) \subseteq \mathbb{C}$ where a holds true.

The *model axioms* are now all the additional axioms that we get because of the specific valuation V on the concrete set of propositional atoms

$$\mathit{Atom} = \{\mathit{Rem}_P, \mathit{Try}_P, \mathit{Crit}_P, \mathit{Exit}_P \mid P \subseteq \mathit{Proc}\}.$$

They fix the assumptions of the concrete application context, i.e., relationships and properties of the primitive propositional symbols. Formally, they reflect a fixed truth valuation of the symbols on the frame of configurations. Instead of defining the valuation function V we list the model axioms that we want V to satisfy. It is important to keep in mind that the signature of processes $\mathit{Proc} = \{p_0, p_1, \ldots, p_{n-1}\}$ and variables $\mathit{Var} = \{v_0, v_1, \ldots, v_m\}$ is now also assumed to be fixed and finite.

The atomic propositions are used to express the specific control-flow of our application:

$C \models \mathit{Rem}_P$ All $p \in P$ are in their remainder section in C;
$C \models \mathit{Try}_P$ All $p \in P$ are in their trying section in C;
$C \models \mathit{Crit}_P$ All $p \in P$ are in their critical section in C;
$C \models \mathit{Exit}_P$ All $p \in P$ are in their exit section in C.

A reachable configuration satisfying $\mathit{Rem}_{\mathit{Proc}}$ stating that all processes are in their remainder section is called *idle*. Accordingly, we use Idle to abbreviate $\mathit{Rem}_{\mathit{Proc}}$. Obviously, we have $\models \mathit{Idle} \to \mathit{Rem}_P$ for all $P \subseteq \mathit{Proc}$. The literature always tacitly assumes that there is a reachable idle configuration in $\mathbb{C}$, i.e., that $\not\models \neg \mathit{Idle}$.

Invariances

First, we need to state that every process must be in one of the regions, for every $p \in \mathit{Proc}$:

$$\models \mathit{Rem}_p \vee \mathit{Crit}_p \vee \mathit{Try}_p \vee \mathit{Exit}_p \tag{27}$$

The usual assumption that the regions are exclusive, e.g., $\models \neg(\mathit{Rem}_p \wedge \mathit{Crit}_p)$, are not relevant for our proofs, so we ignore them. What is more pertinent is that the region atoms are properties that refer only to the local state of a process rather the local state of other processes and global memory. These obviously remain invariant under execution of the other processes, as well as changes to the local states of the other processes. Specifically, for $Q \cap P = \emptyset$:

$$\models \mathit{Rem}_Q \to (\forall_P^X \mathit{Rem}_Q \wedge K_Q \mathit{Rem}_Q) \tag{28}$$
$$\models \mathit{Crit}_Q \to (\forall_P^X \mathit{Crit}_Q \wedge K_Q \mathit{Crit}_Q) \tag{29}$$
$$\models \mathit{Try}_Q \to (\forall_P^X \mathit{Try}_Q \wedge K_Q \mathit{Try}_Q) \tag{30}$$
$$\models \mathit{Exit}_Q \to (\forall_P^X \mathit{Exit}_Q \wedge K_Q \mathit{Exit}_Q). \tag{31}$$

Notice that from (29), axiom (14) and the fact that $\models K_q \phi \to K_Q \phi$, where $q \in Q$, we can derive the equivalence

$$\models \bigvee_{q \in Q} \mathit{Crit}_q \leftrightarrow K_Q \bigvee_{q \in Q} \mathit{Crit}_q. \tag{32}$$

Further note that we have

$$\models \mathit{Idle}_P \to K_Q\, \mathit{Idle}_P \tag{33}$$

$$\models \mathsf{Wr}_P^U \top \to K_Q\, \mathsf{Wr}_P^U \top \tag{34}$$

where $P \subseteq Q$.

Mutual Exclusion Axioms

The VC lower bound result on the number of read/write registers does not depend on any liveness assumptions. Specifically, we do not require that the scheduling is fair. Hence, it suffices to treat the axioms as safety conditions on the Kripke model of reachable configurations of a process system that implements a mutual exclusion scenario, just like done in [1,8].

MUTEX. The requirement of mutual exclusion is a conjunction that covers all possible pairs of processes: For any pair $p, q \in \mathit{Proc}$ with $p \neq q$, no reachable configuration must satisfy $\mathit{Crit}_p \wedge \mathit{Crit}_q$. For a fixed finite set Proc of processor, we can state this with a propositional formula as follows:

$$\models \bigwedge_{p \neq q} \neg(\mathit{Crit}_p \wedge \mathit{Crit}_q) \tag{35}$$

In this way, we keep the combinatorics on processes and variables outside the formalised object-logic which remains purely propositional. Alternatively, we could extend our specification language to first-order modal logic and formalise the argument in full.

NO-DEADLOCK. The requirement of deadlock-freedom can be expressed by a propositional formula, assuming that all processes are explicitly named:

$$\models (\mathit{Try}_P \wedge \mathit{Rem}_{\mathit{Proc}\backslash P}) \to \exists_P \bigvee_{p \in P} \mathit{Crit}_p \tag{36}$$

This says that if some processes P are all trying while all the other processes are in their remainder section, then the trying processes can be executed so that at least one of them becomes critical.

Note that for a given trying process $p \in P$, this condition does not require that the process becoming critical is actually the process p. It could be any other process $q \neq p$ and even infinitely often a different one. To exclude such a form of starvation, practical algorithms need to satisfy a stronger condition of NO-LOCKOUT: If all processes always eventually return to their remainder region then any trying process must eventually become critical. This is a liveness condition that is not expressible in our formalism.

NON-BLOCKING. The only place where we permit a process to get stuck is in the trying section. A process always needs the context to cooperate in order to be able to advance from trying into the critical section. The progress from trying is governed by the NO-DEADLOCK condition above. In all other sections Rem,

Crit, Exit we assume that is always possible for a process to make progress by itself in a single-threaded execution:

$$\models Rem_p \rightarrow \exists_p Try_p \quad (37)$$
$$\models Crit_p \rightarrow \exists_p Exit_p \quad (38)$$
$$\models Exit_p \rightarrow \exists_p Rem_p \quad (39)$$

A simple consequence of NO-DEADLOCK and NON-BLOCKING is that if a set of processes P is in the remainder section, we can always execute the other processes to make some of them become critical and all of them idle.

Proposition 4 (NO-OBSTRUCTION). *Let $P \subseteq Proc$ and $Q = Proc \setminus P$. Then, $Rem_P \models \exists_Q Idle$ and $Rem_P \models \exists_Q \bigvee_{q \in Q} Crit_q$.*

Proof. Each processes from Q must be in one of the regions Rem_q, Try_q, $Crit_q$ or $Exit_q$ by (27). Those in regions $Crit_q$ or $Exit_q$ can be scheduled (NON-BLOCKING) to enter into Rem_q by (38) and (39) as necessary. Formally, we use the Extensionality Principle Proposition 1 and (18). For the remaining processes $Q' \subseteq Q$ in region $Try_{Q'}$ we can then apply NO-DEADLOCK (36) to force at least one of them $q' \in Q'$ into $Crit_{q'}$. At this point we have achieved the second part of the Proposition 4, $Rem_P \models \exists_Q \bigvee_{q \in Q} Crit_q$. For the first part, $Rem_P \models \exists_Q Idle$, we continue to let q' progress into $Rem_{q'}$ by NON-BLOCKING, and repeat the process with the remaining $Q' \setminus \{q'\}$ in the trying region. In the end, we have a configuration satisfying *Idle*. □

3 Derivations for Main Theorem

With the specification language and its semantics in place, we can now begin our formalisation. The fact that the informal expositions in [1,8] are detailed and carefully phrased, makes the transcription a relatively easy exercise. Here is the main VC Theorem that we are after:

Theorem 5 (Variable Cover (VC) Theorem; Thm 4.18 [1], Thm. 10.33 [8]). *Any no-deadlock mutual exclusion algorithm with $|Proc| = n$ that uses only read/write registers must use at least n shared registers, i.e., $|Var| \geq n$.*

A central concept in the proof is the notion of a *quiescent* or an *idle* configuration. The informal definition of "quiescence" by Attiya and Welch:

> *A configuration of a mutual exclusion algorithm is quiescent if all processors are in the remainder section.* [Definition 4.3, p. 71 [1]]

as well as the analogous notion of an "idle" configuration by Lynch:

> *[...] we define a system state s to be idle if all processes are in their remainder regions in s.* [p. 300 [8]].

are somewhat misleading. They can be misread to suggest that these properties are properties of the local state of the processors only. But in fact, as it transpires in the course of the proofs in [1,8], "idling" must also involve a constraint on the global memory, namely to be actually *reachable*. This important side condition is rendered explicit in our formalisation, by making all statements be properties of a modal model, i.e., the restriction to the frame configurations $\mathbb{C}$ induced by the global algorithm.

Definition 4 (Quiescence). *A configuration $C \in \mathbb{C}$ is quiescent if $C \models Idle$.* □

A related derived notion is the notion of *P-quiescence*. It selects those reachable configurations C that appear to be quiescent to a set P of processes, i.e., there is a *reachable* configuration C' which is quiescent and differs from C only in the local states of processes $Proc \backslash P$.

Definition 5 (Def. 4.5 [1]). *A configuration $C \in \mathbb{C}$ is P-quiescent, for $P \subseteq Proc$, if $C \models M_P\, Idle$.* □

In the sequel we will abbreviate the statement $M_P\, Idle$ for P-quiescence as $Idle_P$. The proposition $M_P\, Idle$ says that by changing only the local states of processes $Proc \backslash P$, we can obtain an idle (and reachable) configuration. Note that and $\models Idle_P \rightarrow Rem_P$ and $\models Idle_P \rightarrow Idle_Q$ for all $Q \subseteq P$.

The key difference between $C \models Idle_P$ and $C \models Rem_P$ is that in the former case (P-quiescence) we can force any process $p \in P$ to become critical, simply by scheduling p alone (see Lemma 7 below). In the latter case, we have no such guarantee. When $C \models Rem_P$ all we know is that the processes in P are in their remainder section, but have no control of the global memory. To make the way free for P, we must first bring all other processes back to their remainder sections, generating an idle configuration where the memory is cleared. So, when $C \models Rem_P$ then we need the cooperation of the other processes $Q \backslash P$ to make any $p \in P$ become critical. When $C \models Idle_P$, for contrast, then we do not need this cooperation.

In the sequel we will present the arguments leading to the VC Theorem 5 in the same sequence of steps as in [1] and [8] but transcribed into modal logic.

3.1 From a Quiescent Configuration Each Process Can Become Critical by a Single-Threaded Execution

We start from a configuration C which is globally quiescent, i.e., where $C \models Idle$ holds. The first observation, captured by the following Lemma 6, is that any process p can become critical by a p-only schedule.

Lemma 6 (Lem. 10.29 of [8]). *For all $p \in Proc$, $\models Idle \rightarrow \exists_p\, Crit_p$.*

Proof. Let $p \in Proc$ and $Q = Proc \backslash \{p\}$. Here and in the following we make extensive use of Extensionality Proposition 1. Since $Idle \models Rem_p \wedge Rem_Q$ we get

$$\begin{aligned}
Idle &\models Rem_p \wedge Rem_Q & \text{Def. of } Idle \\
&\models \exists_p\, Try_p \wedge \forall_p\, Rem_Q & \text{by NON-BLOCKING (37) and (28)} \\
&\models \exists_p(Try_p \wedge Rem_Q) & \text{by (9)} \\
&\models \exists_p \exists_p\, Crit_p & \text{by (36)} \\
&\models \exists_p\, Crit_p. & \text{by (18)}
\end{aligned}$$

By the Deduction Principle Proposition 2 it follows that $\models Idle \to \exists_p\, Crit_p$, which completes the proof of Lemma 6. $\square$

Lemma 6 guarantees that if all processes are quiescent, then each process can be scheduled to reach its critical section. In the next Lemma 7 we strengthen this to show that it suffices that the process p itself is quiescent, i.e., we can get $\exists_p\, Crit_p$ from the weaker assumption $Idle_p$.

Lemma 7 (Lem. 10.30 of [8]). *For every $p \in Proc$ we have $\models Idle_p \to \exists_p\, Crit_p$.*

Proof.

$$\begin{aligned}
Idle_p &\models M_p Idle & \text{Def. of } Idle_p \\
&\models M_p\, \exists_p\, Crit_p. & \text{by Lemma 6} \\
&\models M_p\, \exists_p\, K_p\, Crit_p & \text{by (29)} \\
&\models M_p\, K_p\, \exists_p\, Crit_p & \text{by (19)} \\
&\models \exists_\mathsf{p}\, Crit_\mathsf{p} & \text{by Dualisation (12) of (16)}
\end{aligned}$$

$\square$

The path property $\exists_p\, Crit_p$ derived in Lemma 6 and Lemma 7 only states that there is a schedule making p critical. It does not imply that p must necessarily write any variable in order to achieve that.

3.2 In Order to Become Critical Each Process Must Write at Least One Variable

Intuitively, it seems clear that a process p, when starting from the remainder region, must write to some variable if it wants to become critical at all. The reason is that in order to avoid collision with the other processes, i.e., violation of MUTEX, p must communicate its intentions before it can enter the critical section. This happens in the trying region. The subtle point is that this writing requirement only holds for p-only schedules. For p does not necessarily need to write anything, if the schedule that makes p critical involves also the other processes $Q \backslash \{p\}$. In a schedule in which they write to memory first, indicating that they will wait to let p go ahead, p only needs to read this information in order to advance to the critical region. This could be an algorithm where processes pass a token that schedules the critical regions in a round-robin fashion. In Peterson's algorithm (Fig. 1) this does not happen, though. Every process p_i writes flag_i and turn on the way from the remainder to the critical section, whether it is interleaved with p_{3-i} or runs on its own.

We express the writing condition indirectly: Every p-only execution schedule without variable writing cannot lead to a critical state, i.e., $C \models \forall_p^\emptyset \neg Crit_p$.

Lemma 8 (Lem. 10.31 [8]). *For all $p \in Proc$, $Rem_p \models \forall_p^\emptyset \neg Crit_p$.*

Proof. By duality, $\forall_p^\emptyset \neg Crit_p \leftrightarrow \neg \exists_p^\emptyset Crit_p$, so we prove Lemma 8 by assuming Rem_p and $\exists_p^\emptyset Crit_p$, and obtaining a contradiction from MUTEX. In the proof, again, let $Q = Proc \backslash \{p\}$.

$$\begin{aligned}
Rem_p, \exists_p^\emptyset Crit_p &\models (\exists_Q \bigvee_{q \in Q} Crit_q) \wedge \exists_p^\emptyset Crit_p & \text{by Proposition 4 and assumption}\\
&\models (\forall_p^\emptyset M_Q \exists_Q \bigvee_{q \in Q} Crit_q) \wedge \exists_p^\emptyset Crit_p & \text{by (22)}\\
&\models \exists_p^\emptyset ((M_Q \exists_Q \bigvee_{q \in Q} Crit_q) \wedge Crit_p) & \text{by (9)}\\
&\models \exists_p^\emptyset ((M_Q \exists_Q K_Q \bigvee_{q \in Q} Crit_q) \wedge Crit_p) & \text{by (32)}\\
&\models \exists_p^\emptyset ((M_Q K_Q \exists_Q \bigvee_{q \in Q} Crit_q) \wedge Crit_p) & \text{by (19)}\\
&\models \exists_p^\emptyset ((\exists_Q \bigvee_{q \in Q} Crit_q) \wedge \forall_Q Crit_p) & \text{by Dualisation (12) of (16)}\\
&\models \exists_p^\emptyset \exists_Q (\bigvee_{q \in Q} (Crit_q \wedge Crit_p)) & \text{by (9) and distributivity}\\
&\models \exists_p^\emptyset \exists_Q \bot & \text{by MUTEX (35) since } p \neq q\\
&\models \bot. & \text{by Dualisation (13) of (7)}
\end{aligned}$$

Since the assumptions Rem_p and $\exists_p^\emptyset Crit_p$ entail a contradiction, we have $Rem_p \models \neg \exists_p^\emptyset Crit_p$, which proves Lemma 8. □

Let us summarise what we have achieved in our axiomatic analysis, so far. Assuming that p is quiescent, Lemma 7 gives $\exists_p Crit_p$ and Lemma 8 gives $\neg \exists_p^\emptyset Crit_p$. Together, they imply that there must be at least one $x \in Var$ that is written on the path to a critical region, in any p-only schedule. This would be the formal statement $C \models \exists_p Wr_p^x \exists_p Crit_p$. However, in our further analysis it will be important that we identify the *first* occurrence of a writing to some variable. This is done by quantifying over subsets as follows: There is a non-empty subset $\emptyset \neq W \subseteq Var$ of variables (each of which is written on some path from C) and for each strict subset $U \subsetneq W$ there is $x \in W \backslash U$ such that $C \models \exists_p^U Wr_p^x \exists_p^W Crit_p$. This expresses that there is a schedule

$$C \rightsquigarrow_p^U C' \xrightarrow{p:x.\text{wr}} C'' \rightsquigarrow_p^W D \text{ and } D \models Crit_p,$$

where the write action $p : x.\text{wr}$ is the first writing to any variable $x \in W$ outside of U. As a special case, with $U = \emptyset$ this is $C \models \exists_p^\emptyset Wr_p^x \exists_p^W Crit_p$ stating that the writing to x is the first writing to any variable in W. Thus, we have the following refinement from the combination of Lemma 7 and Lemma 8:

$$\begin{aligned}
Idle_p &\models \exists_p Crit_p \wedge \neg \exists_p^\emptyset Crit_p \\
&\models \bigvee_{\emptyset \neq W \subseteq Var} \bigwedge_{U \subsetneq W} \bigvee_{x \in W \backslash U} \exists_p^U Wr_p^x \exists_p^W Crit_p & (40)\\
&\models \bigvee_{x \in Var} \exists_p^\emptyset Wr_p^x \exists_p Crit_p. & (41)
\end{aligned}$$

Note that this does not claim that the set of written variables W is unique. It may well depend on the particular configuration C that satisfies the precondition $Idle_p$.

254   M. Mendler

3.3 Distinct Processes Must Cover Distinct Variables

We now strengthen Lemma 8 to show that for a process p to leave the remainder section and become critical, all by itself, it must write to a register that is not covered by any other process at that moment. The intuition is that if it only uses variables that are already covered by the other processes, these will not take any notice, because they are bound to overwrite the information communicated by p, anyway. In our axiomatics this is manifest in the Variable Cover Axiom (26).

Formally, we start from a configuration $C \models Rem_p$ and assume that the other processes $Q = Proc\backslash\{p\}$ are covering some set $U \subseteq Var$ of variables, which is expressed by $C \models \mathsf{Wr}_Q^U \top$. From there we show that in all p-only executions in which p merely writes a subset $W \subseteq U$ of these variable, it cannot become critical, i.e., $\forall_p^W \neg Crit_p$.

Lemma 9 (Lem. 10.36 [8]). *For all $p \in Proc$, $Q = Proc\backslash\{p\}$ and $W \subseteq U \subseteq Var$ we have $Rem_p, \mathsf{Wr}_Q^U \top \models \forall_p^W \neg Crit_p$.*

Proof. Let $Q = Proc\backslash\{p\}$ and $q \in Q$ and $W \subseteq U \subseteq Var$. We prove the statement of Lemma 9 by contraposition, assuming the negation $\exists_p^W Crit_p$ of $\forall_p^W \neg Crit_p$ and derive a contradiction. Let us abbreviate $Crit_Q = \bigvee_{q \in Q} Crit_q$. Then,

$$
\begin{aligned}
Rem_p, \mathsf{Wr}_Q^W \top, \exists_p^W Crit_p &\models \forall_Q^W Rem_p \wedge \mathsf{Wr}_Q^W \top && \text{by (28) and assumption} \\
&\models \mathsf{Wr}_Q^W Rem_p && \text{by (11)} \\
&\models \mathsf{Wr}_Q^W \exists_Q Crit_Q && \text{by Proposition 4} \\
&\models \mathsf{Wr}_Q^W \exists_Q K_Q Crit_Q && \text{by (32)} \\
&\models \mathsf{Wr}_Q^W K_Q \exists_Q Crit_Q && \text{by (19)} \\
&\models \forall_p^W \mathsf{Wr}_Q^W \exists_Q Crit_Q && \text{by VC Axiom (26)} \\
&\models \exists_p^W Crit_p \wedge \forall_p^W \mathsf{Wr}_Q^W \exists_Q Crit_Q && \text{by assumption} \\
&\models \exists_p^W (Crit_p \wedge \mathsf{Wr}_Q^W \exists_Q Crit_Q) && \text{by (9)} \\
&\models \exists_p^W (Crit_p \wedge \exists_Q Crit_Q) && \text{by (23) and (18)} \\
&\models \exists_p^W (\forall_Q Crit_p \wedge \exists_Q Crit_Q) && \text{by (29)} \\
&\models \exists_p^W \exists_Q (Crit_p \wedge Crit_Q) && \text{by (9)} \\
&\models \exists_p^W \exists_Q \bot && \text{by MUTEX (35) since } p \notin Q \\
&\models \bot. && \text{by (18), Dualisation (13) of (7)}
\end{aligned}
$$

□

3.4 Basic Covering Lemma

We now bring together the existence of a successful schedule to the critical region writing at least one variable from (41) and the guarantee that this variable cannot be covered by the other processes from Proposition 9. The statement that $p \in Proc$ can be scheduled to reach a critical section by writing a variable v is captured by $\exists_p \mathsf{Wr}_p^v \exists_p Crit_p$. The strengthening that the other processes $Q = Proc\backslash\{p\}$ do not cover variable v is formalised as $\neg \mathsf{Wr}_Q^v \top$.

Lemma 10 (Lem. 4.16 [1]). $Idle_p \models \bigvee_{v \in Var}((\exists_p \mathsf{Wr}_p^v \exists_p Crit_p) \wedge \neg \mathsf{Wr}_Q^v \top)$

Proof. The proof is by contraposition. We assume $C \models \mathit{Idle}_p$ and the invalidity $C \not\models \bigvee_{v \in \mathit{Var}}((\exists_p \mathsf{Wr}_p^v \exists_p \mathit{Crit}_p) \land \neg \mathsf{Wr}_Q^v \top)$ and then derive a contradiction. The invalidity is the statement that for all $v \in \mathit{Var}$, one of $C \not\models \exists_p \mathsf{Wr}_p^v \exists_p \mathit{Crit}_p$ or $C \models \mathsf{Wr}_Q^v \top$ must hold. Intuitively, this says that every variable that is written by p during an execution that leads to Crit_p, is actually covered by Q. Since by assumption $C \models \mathit{Idle}_p$, we conclude from (40) that there is a non-empty subset $\emptyset \neq W \subseteq \mathit{Var}$ of variables such that $C \models \exists_p^{W \setminus \{w\}} \mathsf{Wr}_p^w \exists_p^W \mathit{Crit}_p$ for all $w \in W$. In particular, both

$$C \models \exists_p^W \mathit{Crit}_p \text{ and } C \models \exists_p \mathsf{Wr}_p^w \exists_p \mathit{Crit}_p.$$

Since by assumption, for each variable v we have $C \not\models \exists_p \mathsf{Wr}_p^v \exists_p \mathit{Crit}_p$ or $C \models \mathsf{Wr}_Q^v \top$, it follows that for all these written variables $w \in W$ in fact we have $C \models \mathsf{Wr}_Q^w \top$. But this means $C \models \mathsf{Wr}_Q^W \top$. But now, overall, $C \models \mathit{Rem}_p$, $C \models \exists_p^W \mathit{Crit}_p$ and $C \models \mathsf{Wr}_Q^W \top$, which leads to a contradiction by Lemma 9. □

The formalisation of the arguments in [1,8] reveals that the main induction proof leading to the VC Theorem 5 needs a stronger statement than Lemma 10. We need a formulation that exposes the first writing occurrence of a fresh variable v relative to what the context already covers. Specifically, we want to be sure that all variables that p writes before, are already covered by processes Q. Our refined version of Lemma 10 is the following Basic Covering Lemma 11.

Lemma 11 (Basic Covering Lemma). *Let $Q \subseteq \mathit{Proc}$, $p \in \mathit{Proc} \setminus Q$ and $U \subseteq \mathit{Var}$. Then,*

$$\mathit{Idle}_p, \mathsf{Wr}_Q^U \top \models \bigvee_{v \in \mathit{Var} \setminus U} (\exists_p^U \mathsf{Wr}_p^v \exists_p \mathit{Crit}_p).$$

Proof. The proof is by contraposition. We assume $C \models \mathit{Idle}_p$ and $C \models \mathsf{Wr}_Q^U \top$. From Lemma 10 there is a variable $v \in \mathit{Var}$ such that $C \models \exists_p \mathsf{Wr}_p^v \exists_p \mathit{Crit}_p$ and $C \not\models \mathsf{Wr}_Q^v \top$. Since, $C \models \mathsf{Wr}_Q^U \top$ we conclude $v \notin U$, because of the monotonicity $\models \mathsf{Wr}_Q^Y \top \rightarrow \mathsf{Wr}_Q^X \top$, whenever $X \subseteq Y$. The satisfaction $C \models \exists_p \mathsf{Wr}_p^v \exists_p \mathit{Crit}_p$ says there is a schedule $C \rightsquigarrow_p D \xrightarrow{p:v.\mathsf{wr}} E \rightsquigarrow_p F$ during which this variable $v \in \mathit{Var} \setminus U$ is written and $F \models \mathit{Crit}_p$. Without loss of generality we may assume that this is the first writing of a variable outside of U, i.e., that in fact $C \rightsquigarrow_p^U D$. But this means that $C \models \exists_p^U \mathsf{Wr}_p^v \exists_p \mathit{Crit}_p$ which is what we need. □

3.5 Main Lemma

By the Basic Covering Lemma 11, every process that wants to become critical must write a variable that is not covered by any other process. Since all processes can become critical from a quiescent configuration, incrementally, it follows that we need at least as many distinct variables as there are distinct processes. We now formalise the induction step in this argument, as the Main Lemma in the analysis of [1,8]. To this end, we fix a finite set of processes $P = \{p_0, p_1, \ldots, p_{n-1}\}$ indexed by natural numbers, for an inductive argument. Informally, the Main Lemma is the following:

> "For all k, $1 \leq k \leq n$, and for all reachable quiescent configurations C, there exists a configuration D reachable from C by a $\{p_0, \ldots, p_{k-1}\}$-only schedule such that $p_0, \ldots, p_{k-1}$ cover k distinct variables in D and D is $\{p_k, \ldots, p_{n-1}\}$-quiescent." [1][p. 83].

To express this in modal logic, let $P_k = \{p_0, p_1, \ldots, p_{k-1}\}$ and $Q_k = \{p_k, \ldots, p_{n-1}\}$. The statement that the processes P_k cover k distinct variables at D is the same as saying that there is $U \subseteq Var$ with $|U| = k$ such that $D \models \mathsf{Wr}_{P_k}^U \top$. That D is Q_k-quiescent is captured by the proposition $D \models Idle_{Q_k}$. Finally, to say that from C there is a P_k-only schedule to reach such a D is $C \models \exists_{P_k}(\mathsf{Wr}_{P_k}^U \top \wedge Idle_{Q_k})$.

Lemma 12 (Main Lemma). *For every $1 \leq k \leq n$, we have*

$$Idle \models \bigvee_{U \subseteq Var, |U|=k} \exists_{P_k}(Idle_{Q_k} \wedge \mathsf{Wr}_{P_k}^U \top).$$

It is easy to see that Lemma 12 implies the VC Theorem 5. For suppose $|Var| < n$. Then, choosing $k = n$, we would have $Idle \models \bot$ because the disjunction over $U \subseteq Var$ with $|U| = n$ in Lemma 12 would be empty. But this implies $Idle \models \bot$ or, equivalently, $\models \neg Idle$ which contradicts the assumption that there is at least one reachable idle configuration.[5]

Proof. The proof of Lemma 12 is by induction on $1 \leq k \leq n$. Since our modal logic is propositional, we develop the induction argument at the meta-level, but of course nonetheless formally. The induction proof also involves the Pigeonhole Principle which also lies outside of the propositional formalism.

Base Case $k = 1$

$$\begin{aligned}
Idle &\models \bigvee_{x \in Var} \exists_{p_0}^\emptyset \mathsf{Wr}_{p_0}^x \exists_{p_0} Crit_{p_0} & \text{by (41)} \\
&\models \bigvee_{x \in Var} \exists_{p_0}^\emptyset \mathsf{Wr}_{p_0}^x \top & \text{by property abstraction } \exists_{p_0} Crit_{p_0} \to \top \\
&\models \bigvee_{x \in Var} (\exists_{p_0}^\emptyset \mathsf{Wr}_{p_0}^x \top \wedge Idle) & \text{by assumption and distributivity} \\
&\models \bigvee_{x \in Var} (\exists_{p_0}^\emptyset \mathsf{Wr}_{p_0}^x \top \wedge \forall_{p_0}^\emptyset Idle_{Q_1}) & \text{by (22)} \\
&\models \bigvee_{x \in Var} \exists_{p_0}^\emptyset (\mathsf{Wr}_{p_0}^x \top \wedge Idle_{Q_1}) & \text{by (9).}
\end{aligned}$$

Step Case $k \mapsto k+1$
We assume by induction hypothesis that

$$Idle \models \bigvee_{U \subseteq Var, |U|=k} \exists_{P_k}(Idle_{Q_k} \wedge \mathsf{Wr}_{P_k}^U \top) \tag{42}$$

---

[5] This assumption is hidden in the textbook proofs.

Note that in any configuration in which the processes Q_k are quiescent it is possible by NO-OBSTRUCTION Proposition 4 to advance the other processors to reach a globally idle configuration again: $\models Rem_{Q_k} \to \exists_{P_k} Idle$. Also, note that $\models Idle \to \forall_{P_k} Rem_{Q_k}$ by definition of $Idle$ and (28). So, in total, $\models Idle \to \forall_{P_k} \exists_{P_k} Idle$.

We first strengthen the induction hypothesis to a stronger form of "repeated coverage":

$$Idle \models \bigvee_{U \subseteq Var, |U|=k} \exists_{P_k}(Idle_{Q_k} \wedge \mathsf{Wr}^U_{P_k} \exists_{P_k}(Idle_{Q_k} \wedge \mathsf{Wr}^U_{P_k} \top)) \tag{43}$$

We do not prove this here, but refer to [1,8] for the combinatorial argument that involves the Pigeonhole Principle.

Let $C \models Idle$, then by (43) there is a set $U \subseteq Var$ with $|U| = k$ and a reachable configuration $C \leadsto_{P_k} D$ such that

$$D \models Idle_{Q_k} \wedge \mathsf{Wr}^U_{P_k} \exists_{P_k}(Idle_{Q_k} \wedge \mathsf{Wr}^U_{P_k} \top). \tag{44}$$

Since this implies $D \models Idle_{p_k}$ and $D \models \mathsf{Wr}^U_{P_k} \top$ with $p_k \notin P_k$, we can employ Lemma 11 to obtain a new variable $v \in Var \setminus U$ such that $D \models \exists^U_{p_k} \mathsf{Wr}^v_{p_k} \top$. Now we calculate the following facts for configuration D, in a purely propositional manner inside the modal formalism:

$$
\begin{array}{lll}
D \models \exists^U_{p_k} \mathsf{Wr}^v_{p_k} \top \wedge \mathsf{Wr}^U_{P_k} \exists_{P_k}(Idle_{Q_k} \wedge \mathsf{Wr}^U_{P_k} \top) & & \text{by (44)} \\
\models \exists^U_{p_k} \mathsf{Wr}^v_{p_k} \top \wedge \mathsf{Wr}^U_{P_k} \exists_{P_k}(Idle_{Q_{k+1}} \wedge \mathsf{Wr}^U_{P_k} \top) & & \text{by Def. of } Idle_Q \\
\models \exists^U_{p_k} \mathsf{Wr}^v_{p_k} \top \wedge \mathsf{Wr}^U_{P_k} \exists_{P_k}(K_{Proc \setminus \{p_k\}} Idle_{Q_{k+1}} \wedge K_{Proc \setminus \{p_k\}} \mathsf{Wr}^U_{P_k} \top) & & \text{by (29), (33), (34)} \\
\models \exists^U_{p_k} \mathsf{Wr}^v_{p_k} \top \wedge \mathsf{Wr}^U_{P_k} \exists_{P_k} K_{Proc \setminus \{p_k\}}(Idle_{Q_{k+1}} \wedge \mathsf{Wr}^U_{P_k} \top) & & \text{by (6)} \\
\models \exists^U_{p_k} \mathsf{Wr}^v_{p_k} \top \wedge \mathsf{Wr}^U_{P_k} K_{Proc \setminus \{p_k\}} \exists_{P_k}(Idle_{Q_{k+1}} \wedge \mathsf{Wr}^U_{P_k} \top) & & \text{by (19)} \\
\models \exists^U_{p_k} \mathsf{Wr}^v_{p_k} \top \wedge \forall^U_{P_k} \mathsf{Wr}^U_{P_k} \exists_{P_k}(Idle_{Q_{k+1}} \wedge \mathsf{Wr}^U_{P_k} \top) & & \text{by VC Axiom (26)} \\
\models \exists^U_{p_k}(\mathsf{Wr}^v_{p_k} \top \wedge \mathsf{Wr}^U_{P_k} \exists_{P_k}(Idle_{Q_{k+1}} \wedge \mathsf{Wr}^U_{P_k} \top)) & & \text{by (9)} \\
\models \exists^U_{p_k}(\mathsf{Wr}^v_{p_k} K_{P_k} \top \wedge \exists_{P_k}(Idle_{Q_{k+1}} \wedge \mathsf{Wr}^U_{P_k} \top)) & & \text{by (8) and (24)} \\
\models \exists^U_{p_k}(\forall_{P_k} \mathsf{Wr}^v_{p_k} \top \wedge \exists_{P_k}(Idle_{Q_{k+1}} \wedge \mathsf{Wr}^U_{P_k} \top)) & & \text{by VC Axiom (26)} \\
\models \exists^U_{p_k} \exists_{P_k}(\mathsf{Wr}^v_{p_k} \top \wedge Idle_{Q_{k+1}} \wedge \mathsf{Wr}^U_{P_k} \top) & & \text{by (9)} \\
\models \exists^U_{p_k} \exists_{P_k}(Idle_{Q_{k+1}} \wedge \mathsf{Wr}^{U \cup \{v\}}_{P_{k+1}} \top) & & \text{by Def. } \mathsf{Wr}^X_P \\
\models \exists_{P_{k+1}}(Idle_{Q_{k+1}} \wedge \mathsf{Wr}^{U \cup \{v\}}_{P_{k+1}} \top). & & \text{by Def. } \exists^W_P \text{ and (18)}
\end{array}
$$

Coming back to the point of view of configuration C, we have proven the induction step, viz.

$$Idle \models \bigvee_{U \subseteq Var, |U|=k+1} \exists_{P_{k+1}}(Idle_{Q_{k+1}} \wedge \mathsf{Wr}^U_{P_{k+1}} \top) \tag{45}$$

This completes the proof of Lemma 12. □

4 Conclusion

These notes present a transcription of the standard informal textbook proofs of the VC Theorem for mutual exclusion algorithms to propositional modal logic.

We use elementary techniques from modal logic, such as covered in a basic undergraduate course. The transcription identifies the Variable Cover Axiom $\models \mathsf{Wr}_q^v K_q \phi \to \forall_p^v \mathsf{Wr}_q^v \phi$ as the central closure property on the configuration of shared memory process systems that encapsulates the key limitation of the read-/write memory model. Our transcription is not complete, for some combinatorial arguments for VC Theorem require quantification over subsets of processes and subsets of variables, and combinatorial principles such as the Pigeonhole Principle, which lie outside of propositional logic. These could be formalised in a second-order extension of our modal specification language. We leave this to future work.

Acknowledgements. The author would like to thank the anonymous reviewers for comments and suggestions to improve this paper.

Conflict of Interest. The author(s) has no competing interests to declare that are relevant to the content of this manuscript.

References

1. Attiya, H., Welch, J.: Distributed Computing: Fundamentals, Simulations and Advanced Topics. McGraw Hill (1998)
2. Bull, R., Segerberg, K.: Basic modal logic. In: Gabbay, D.M., Guenthner, F. (eds.) Handbook of Philosophical Logic, vol. 3, pp. 1–81. Springer, Dordrecht (2001). https://doi.org/10.1007/978-94-017-0454-0_1
3. Fitting, M.: Basic modal logic. In: Handbook of Logic in Artificial Intelligence. Oxford University Press (1993)
4. Harel, D., Kozen, D., Tiuryn, J.: Dynamic Logic. MIT Press, Cambridge (2000)
5. Kelb, P., Margaria, T., Mendler, M., Gsottberger, C.: Mosel: a flexible toolset for monadic second-order logic. In: Brinksma, E. (ed.) TACAS 1997. LNCS, vol. 1217, pp. 183–202. Springer, Heidelberg (1997). https://doi.org/10.1007/BFb0035388
6. Kelb, P., Margaria, T., Mendler, M., Gsottberger, C.: MOSEL: a sound and efficient tool for M2L(Str). In: Grumberg, O. (ed.) CAV 1997. LNCS, vol. 1254, pp. 448–451. Springer, Heidelberg (1997). https://doi.org/10.1007/3-540-63166-6_45
7. Kurucz, A., Wolter, F., Zakharyashev, M., Gabbay, D.M.: Many-Dimensional Modal Logics: Theory and Applications. North Holland (2003)
8. Lynch, N.: Distributed Algorithms. Morgan Kaufmann Publishers (1996)
9. Margaria, T., Mendler, M.: Model-based automatic synthesis and analysis in second-order monadic logic. In: ACM SIG-PLAN Workshop on Automated Analysis of Software, AAS 1997, pp. 99–112 (1997)
10. Popkorn, S.: First Steps in Modal Logic. Cambridge University Press, Cambridge (1994)

Timing is All You Need

Susanne Graf[1,2(✉)], Bengt Jonsson[1], Behnam Khodabandeloo[1], Chengzi Huang[1], Nikolaus Huber[1], Philipp Rümmer[1,3], and Wang Yi[1]

[1] Uppsala University, Uppsala, Sweden
`susanne.graf@imag.fr`
[2] Univ. Grenoble Alpes, CNRS, Grenoble INP, VERIMAG, Grenoble, France
[3] University of Regensburg, Regensburg, Germany

Abstract. Deterministic models play a crucial role in computer system development, enabling the simulation and verification of system behaviors before Model-Driven Development (MDD) tools transform and compile these models into final implementations. Ensuring determinism is essential to guarantee that the behaviors of the implemented system maintain the properties analyzed in the models.

This paper investigates the semantics of deterministic models for data-flow networks, where systems consist of components that compute functions on streams. While Kahn Process Networks (KPN) serve as a well-established semantic theory for time-insensitive deterministic systems, it proves inadequate for systems with time dependent components. To address this limitation, we use the concept of timed streams and develop a fixed-point theory tailored for time-sensitive systems in the style of KPN. This theory serves as the foundation for the MDD tool-chain, known as MIMOS, currently under development in Uppsala.

1 Introduction

Model-Driven Development (MDD) is a software-engineering paradigm, which applies models to raise the level of abstraction at which software is developed and maintained. The use of models can serve many purposes, including to simplify development by abstracting from complexity, to support modularization through a component-based approach, to allow formal analysis supported by a formal semantics of models, to support reliability guarantees, documentation, and others. There are numerous concrete frameworks for MDD in various application domains. In the spectrum of MDD frameworks, one can discern a tradeoff between generality and effectiveness for various tasks such as analysis and code-generation. At one end of the spectrum is the Model-Driven Architecture by OMG, centering around the UML language; its aspiration for generality makes it difficult to provide effective automated support for tasks such as formal verification. At the other end are various domain-specific frameworks that have been developed for a certain application domain, thereby allowing the definition of a precise formal semantics, support efficient code generation, etc. In this spectrum, an interesting framework is the jABC (Java Application Building Center) framework by Tiziana Margaria and Bernhard Steffen [21], which has been developed over the last 30 years. Its original predecessors have been used in a domain-specific fashion to design telecommunication services, decision support systems, and test automation environments. In jABC, models of services and applications are constructed by composing reusable building blocks (components) into graph structures, which are digested by supporting tools for animation, prototyping, verification, code generation, and so on. Since its presentation in [21], the versatility of this approach has been demonstrated by applications of jABC and its successors (e.g., XMDD [12]) in a vast number of different applications; a recent example is agriculture [2].

For embedded systems, MDD is particularly suitable: one reason being that modeling facilitates verification and validation of systems that interact with their physical environment. A wide range of MDD frameworks focus on embedded systems design in the synchronous design paradigm, Simulink/Stateflow, and Scade. Simulation is maybe the most important verification technique for V&V of Embedded system designs: therefore deterministic execution semantics is important. Since timing is important for embedded systems, time determinism is also important. This holds true even in the presence of concurrency. For instance, the execution semantics of Simulink/Stateflow is completely time deterministic, even though Stateflow has concurrency-like constructs.

Notably, most of the existing approaches are to perform mathematical simulation based on the synchronous hypothesis where software components implement mathematical functions and the computations of functions take zero-time. The recent work on MIMOS [25] attempts to break the synchronous assumption which is not suitable for performance-demanding and predictable applications on complex platforms such as heterogeneous multi-core processors. The goal of MIMOS is to develop an asynchronous design paradigm for building embedded systems, that remain functional- and timing-deterministic as in the synchronous paradigm and in addition, performance- and resource-ware, and also composable, enabling dynamic software updates after deployment.

This paper considers the problem of providing a time deterministic execution semantics to modeling languages for embedded systems. We focus only on data-flow languages despite of the synchronous or asynchronous paradigm. There is a variety of such languages: Lustre, Esterel, Signal, Simulink/Stateflow and also MIMOS, that are all in this category. The focus of Data-flow languages on data computations makes it easy to model algorithms in signal processing, control, etc. Different languages can be equipped with models of timing in many different ways, where the timing model can be tailored to the specific desiderata of an application domain.

The problem of providing a suitable semantic model for data-flow languages has been given some attention in the research community. The starting point for (almost) all such models is the model by Kahn [4], which provides an elegant model of dataflow networks where nodes are used to implement functions on streams, and links to buffer input and output data among functions. Kahn embedded his model in an elegant CPO structure, allowing us to derive the semantics of cyclic networks from semantics of its nodes.

Kahns semantics works for functionally deterministic networks. It cannot be applied out-of-the box to functionally non-deterministic models. One central stumbling block is the non-deterministic merge node. A number of suggestions for generalizing Kahn's model have appeared. One class of model adds explicit timing to data items in streams, resulting in various suggestions for timed streams. It might seem that moving to timed streams trivially results in a deterministic semantics in the domain of timed streams, under the assumption that nodes themselves are "time deterministic". Intuitively, this means that if the exact timing of all input is given, then the behavior of a time deterministic node is completely determined, and results in a uniquely defined output. This impression is true, but only up to some limit, and under some mildly restrictive assumptions. For instance, Yates [24] produces such a model under the assumption that there is a minimal time quantity, which bounds the delay between reading input and producing output for any node. Such an assumption may be true in the physical world, assuming a minimal size of components and speed-of-light-like arguments. But some languages have a conceptual semantics not conforming to this. For instance, Simulink allows components with instantaneous output, and even allows zero-delay-cycles under some restrictions.

In this paper, we look at some of these border phenomena, and discuss how various proposals for timed stream models can or cannot cope with them. We also propose a new variation of such a time stream model, and discuss its merits and shortcomings. The main guiding principles as proposed in the work on MIMOS, include:

- Main desiderata: functional determinism and time determinism.
- The model is asynchronous to allow flexibility for dynamic software updates.
- The move from synchronous to asynchronous paradigm enables pipeline-parallelism, "faster is generally better" instead of "you must respect a static schedule".

2 Informal Motivation

The non-timed model of Kahn Networks, and the way in which it guarantees determinism is well-known [4], However, the determinism of such Networks is destroyed as soon as nodes can have time dependent behavior, where the time dependency translates into functional non-determinism, e.g. merging two streams. In an untimed setting, we could try to define a merge function recursively by something like:

$$\begin{aligned} f^{try}_{merge}(\varepsilon,\varepsilon) &= \varepsilon \\ f^{try}_{merge}(a \bullet s_1, s_2) &= a \bullet f^{try}_{merge}(s_1, s_2) \\ f^{try}_{merge}(s_1, b \bullet s_2) &= b \bullet f^{try}_{merge}(s_1, s_2) \end{aligned}$$

However, this definition does not give a unique value for $f^{try}_{merge}(\langle a \rangle, \langle b \rangle)$. We can stay in an untimed setting by making the merge unfair, e.g., defining $f^{try}_{merge}(\langle a \rangle, \langle b \rangle) = \langle ab \rangle$. But by monotonicity, we must then define $f^{try}_{merge}(\varepsilon, \langle b \rangle) = \varepsilon$, and in fact $f^{try}_{merge}(\varepsilon, s_2) = \varepsilon$ for any stream s_2. Intuitively, this function waits for input in its first input stream, regardless of what input appears in its second input stream. In order to define a reasonably fair version of the merge, one then resorts into a timed model. For such a model, there are some alternatives:

- One alternative is to model streams as timed signals over the non-negative reals, i.e., as functions $\mathbb{T} \to \mathbb{D}$ for some time domain $\mathbb{T}$ (e.g., the non-negative reals) and

data domain $\mathbb{D}$. This has been done for example in [24]. This model seems fine for modeling physical processes that operate in continuous time, and possibly also hardware components at the physical level of electric signal, but not for modeling controllers or other components at the software level, which we would like to model as observing their input only at specific time points.
- Another alternative is the approach of MIMOS [25,26] for modeling of software components such as controllers as well as complex software architecture. MIMOS allows input reading and output writing of software components only at specific time points, namely the start and end of their computation periods. This results in a model of streams as (finite or infinite) sequences of timed tokens. Each timed token is a pair $\langle d,t \rangle$, consisting of a data value $d \in \mathbb{D}$ and a time point $t \in \mathbb{T}$, sometimes referred to as a *time stamp*. Time stamping input and output is also the approach chosen in the framework of Lingua Franca [11].
The non-negative time domain allows the definition of a CPO on timed streams, in a similar way as the original model by Kahn and McQueen. It seems reasonable to require that the time stamps in a stream are (not necessarily strictly) increasing. As we will see, this type of model still allows some important design decisions that may be important for being able to model a wide class of systems.

We take the second approach and base our model on the idea of viewing streams as sequences of timed tokens. We would like such a model to be able to capture as general a class of phenomena as possible, maybe including zero-delay-cycles, timeouts, and the like. We assume nodes to be fully time deterministic. This means that they follow a completely deterministic program/code. This program may use timers, and may also have access to a precise clock for wall-clock time. In each of its behaviors, a node reads inputs at precise time points. These time points may be different from behavior to behavior, but should be uniquely determined by the sequence of inputs received upto then.

In order to allow a general class of policies for how to receive inputs buffered in e.g. FIFO or unordered sets etc., we may want, when considering the input at a specified time t, to allow nodes to oversee the complete state of input ports, implying that they can see how many timed tokens have appeared up to time t including to detect absence of input, and also in which sequence they have been produced. For instance, a node may decide at time t to read all timed tokens available at time t, or all tokens up to a maximal number. In addition, we may likely want to include the possibility to read or send a sequence of tokens with the same time stamp but with a causality or priority order.

An example of a type of component that we may want to model, is a so-called *register*. One way to model a register is as a source of streams of timed tokens, where the time stamps are determined autonomously by the register. One could also envisage a model of registers, that are "polled", which can be modeled as having a stream of input tokens that are requests for register values, and which respond to each input by a register value after some delay (which can also be 0).

After these preliminary elaborations, let us try to define a general computation model, which can capture the semantics of a very general class of time deterministic nodes, including registers. In such a model, nodes have input and output ports. Each port can be an output port of at most one node, but can be an input port of several nodes. Each port sees a stream of timed tokens produced by the node which has this port as an output port. If the port is an input of the system, the stream is an arbitrary timed stream.

Let us now return to the model of streams of timed tokens. It turns out that out-of-the-box, it cannot model the full generality of time deterministic systems. Let us show this by the following example.

Example 1. Consider a node which outputs a token at time 2 if no input has appeared up to time 1, whereas it does not output anything at all if input appears at or before time 1. If we try to model this as a function f on timed streams, then this function would have to satisfy the following equations:

$$\begin{aligned} f(\varepsilon) &= \langle b, 2 \rangle \\ f(\langle a, 1 \rangle) &= \varepsilon \end{aligned}$$

To be used in the denotational semantics setting outlined above, the function f should be *continuous* (and therefore, in particular, *monotonic*), which means that prefixes of input streams should be mapped to prefixes of output streams. The function f defined here is obviously not monotonic. On the other hand, there is no question that the node is time deterministic in an intuitive sense. □

One way to understand this example is to acknowledge that streams of timed tokens by themselves do not show one important "input" to a node, which is time. We assume that nodes have access to the current (wall-clock) time, and this "input" can also influence the behavior of a node. In Example 1, the passage of time triggers a timeout, which in its turn causes output tokens to be emitted. From this understanding, we can extend the "streams of timed tokens" model by also letting the passage of time be an input to a network, and to each of its nodes. We can see (at least) two ways in which this can be done:

- We can let time be an additional "input stream": each network has an additional time input, which is read by all its nodes. In Example 1, the function f would output $\langle b, 2 \rangle$ if its input is empty *and* its time output is more than 1. We can make f monotonic be requiring that any extension of the empty input can only add tokens with time stamps at least the corresponding time input, i.e., (strictly) larger than 1.
- We can let time be an additional "token" in each input stream. Such a token would be significant only to mark how far time has progressed for the receiver of the stream, implying that all time tokens except the last can be ignored. We thus represent this token by equipping each input stream with a "length" value Δ, indicating how far time has progressed in the reception of the stream. In Example 1, the function f would output $\langle b, 2 \rangle$ for inputs $\langle \varepsilon, \Delta \rangle$ such that $\Delta > 1$. To recover monotonicity, $\langle \varepsilon, \Delta \rangle$ cannot be extended by timed tokens with time stamps smaller than Δ.

In Sect. 4, we work out this model of timed streams and illustrate some trade-offs using examples. The guiding principle is that the resulting model should retain the machinery of the original Kahn untimed model of streams of data items. The preservation of this principle imposes some constraints on the mathematical machinery, which we aim to illustrate.

3 Related Work

For modeling timed computation, in the literature, there are two primary approaches. The first one uses ordered sets, continuous (or monotonic) functions, and Tarski's fixed-point theorem. The second utilizes metric spaces, contraction mappings, and Banach's contraction principle.

The first category of models proposed in [1,8,9,23,25,26] is essentially using complete partial orders and least fixed-points as models of timed systems. In [23], Yates and Gao tackle the fixed-point problem for systems with components constrained by bounded reaction times (referred to as "Δ-causal"). They transform this problem into one involving a suitably constructed Scott-continuous function, thus extending the Kahn principle to networks of real-time processes. In [8,9], Liu et al. simplify the use of complete partial orders with a prefix order for timed systems. They introduce a special value to mark the absence of events and define signals on lower sets of the tag set to ensure time progression in the semantics of systems. Strictly causal functions, which extend signal domains monotonically, are shown to have unique fixed-points where time diverges if they are also Scott-continuous. This method relaxes the bounded-reaction-time constraint, allowing components with locally bounded reaction times. However, it does not fully address systems with more complex, varying reaction times, like those exhibiting non-trivial Zeno behaviors. The approach in [1] models components as Scott-continuous functions based on the prefix relation on signals. They note that in many practical scenarios, simplifying assumptions could be made: (1) the tag set is a total order, and (2) the values of a signal can be indexed in non-decreasing order. This allows signals to be viewed as streams, reducing the theory to the standard Kahn semantics. Moreover, heterogeneity (managing different tag sets) and distribution are addressed within the generalized Kahn semantics. In [25,26], streams are modeled as sequences of timed tokens, where each token is described by a value and a time stamp. They represent software components as functions that read timed input streams and generate outputs at specific time points, subsequently presenting a fixed-point semantics for this model in the Kahn style.

The second category of models is proposed in other works, e.g. [3,5–7,10,13, 14,16–20,24]. These models are based on metric spaces, contraction mappings, and Banach's contraction principle. Reed and Roscoe are the first to apply this framework in a real-time extension of CSP [19,20]. Yates extends this approach to create the first extensional model of timed computation with a real-time extension of Kahn's process networks [24]. Müller and Scholz introduce another such extension in [16], adopting metric spaces of dense signals rather than timed streams. A uniform framework combining these models is presented in [5–7]. Building on the generalization of bounded reaction times, Portmann et al. [18] introduce a causality function to capture a more general form of strict causality. However, existing models [5–7,16,18–20,24] require a positive lower bound on the reaction time of system components, which ensures that the functions are contraction mappings and allows the use of Banach's fixed-point theorem. This requirement prevents the modeling of non-trivial Zeno phenomena and rigid time divergence. Additionally, these approaches typically use an unbounded subset of real numbers as the tag set, excluding other options like super dense time, thus limiting their applicability to a broader range of systems.

Naundorf [17] removes the bounded-reaction-time constraint and allows for arbitrary tag sets, defining strictly causal functions with a non-constructive proof for unique fixed-points. His approach is valid under a totally ordered tag set but remains incomplete (see Example 3.9 in [14]). An interesting generalization of Naundorf's theorem is proven in [3], aiming to remove references to generalized distances, though the proof remains non-constructive. Naundorf's proposal is also rephrased in [10], using a generalized distance function to identify strictly causal functions as strictly contracting ones, facilitating access to the fixed-point theory of generalized ultra metric spaces. Matsikoudis and Lee [13, 14] further develop this concept by presenting a constructive fixed-point theorem for strictly contracting functions. They show that this theorem arises from a more intuitive concept of strict causality, where outputs are affected only by inputs that occur strictly before them, provided that the input ordering is well-founded.

4 Formal Definition of (Timed) Streams and Continuous Functions

Complete Partial Orders. We start with some of the basic definitions required in our setting. A *chain-Complete Partial Order* (CPO) is a pair $\langle A, \sqsubseteq \rangle$, where A is a set and $\sqsubseteq$ is a partial order on A such that any increasing chain $a_1 \sqsubseteq a_2 \sqsubseteq a_3 \sqsubseteq \cdots$ in A has a least upper bound, denoted $\lim_{n \to \infty} a_n$. A *continuous function* $f : A \to A$ on a CPO $\langle A, \sqsubseteq \rangle$ is a monotonic function such that $f(\lim_{n \to \infty} a_n) = \lim_{n \to \infty} f(a_n)$ for any increasing chain $a_1 \sqsubseteq a_2 \sqsubseteq \cdots$ in A. By Kleene's fixed-point theorem, every continuous function f on a CPO $\langle A, \sqsubseteq \rangle$ with a least element $\bot \in A$ has a least fixed-point, which can be constructed as $\lim_{n \to \infty} f^n(\bot)$. More generally, if $\langle A, \sqsubseteq_A \rangle$ and $\langle B, \sqsubseteq_B \rangle$ are CPOs, then we call a function $f : A \to B$ *continuous* if f is monotonic and $f(\lim_{n \to \infty} a_n) = \lim_{n \to \infty} f(a_n)$ for any increasing chain $a_1 \sqsubseteq_A a_2 \sqsubseteq_A \cdots$ in A (see, e.g., [15]).

In denotational semantics (e.g., [22]), the construction of a fixed-point can be seen as building the result of a computation through successive approximations. If f models a program or program fragment that uses input, part of which comes from previously computed output, successive approximations $f^n(\bot)$ can be interpreted as the output obtained after n applications of f.

Streams. Assume a data domain $\mathbb{D}$. Let $\langle \mathbb{D}^\infty, \sqsubseteq \rangle$ be the set of finite and infinite sequences of elements (i.e., "streams") in $\mathbb{D}$ with $\sqsubseteq$ being the prefix ordering on sequences. Then $\langle \mathbb{D}^\infty, \sqsubseteq \rangle$ is a CPO. When describing the behavior of networks, we associate streams with ports. For a set of ports P, this association is represented by a *valuation* $V : P \to \mathbb{D}^\infty$. The set of valuations $P \to \mathbb{D}^\infty$ is turned into a CPO, as follows: For $V : P \to \mathbb{D}^\infty$ and $V' : P \to \mathbb{D}^\infty$, we define $V \sqsubseteq V'$ if $V(p) \sqsubseteq V'(p)$ for all p in P. The limit $\lim_{n \to \infty} V_n$ of an increasing chain $V_1 \sqsubseteq V_2 \sqsubseteq \cdots$ in $P \to \mathbb{D}^\infty$ is the function $V_{lim} : P \to \mathbb{D}^\infty$ defined by $V_{lim}(p) = \lim_{n \to \infty} V_n(p)$ for all p in P.

Timed Streams. Let $\mathbb{T}$ be a totally ordered time domain with ordering relation $\leq$. For the time being, let $\mathbb{T}$ be the set $\mathbb{R}^{\geq 0}$ of real numbers (later, we might also let it be the set $\mathbb{N}^{\geq 0}$ of natural numbers). A *timed stream* is a finite or infinite stream of pairs in $\mathbb{D} \times \mathbb{T}$, in which the time stamps are non-decreasing. There are two possible choices for the non-decreasingness restriction: (i) A *strict timed stream* is a timed stream in which the time stamps are strictly increasing. (ii) A *non-strict timed stream* is a timed stream in which the time stamps are non-decreasing. We consider for now non-strict timed streams, so that no restrictions are imposed that are stronger than necessary. Let *TS* be the set of streams in $(\mathbb{D} \times \mathbb{T})^\infty$ in which successive time stamps are non-decreasing. The set *TS* with prefix ordering is a CPO, in the same way as $\langle \mathbb{D}^\infty, \sqsubseteq \rangle$ is a CPO. For a set P of ports, the domain $\langle (P \to TS), \sqsubseteq \rangle$ is a CPO, which we denote by TS_P.

Functions over Timed Streams. Let us consider a node N with input ports I and output ports O. Let us try to represent its semantics as a function $f_N : TS_I \to TS_O$, We could then try to model, for instance, a (timed) merge node, which merges input streams on ports i_1 and i_2 to an output stream on port o, as a function $merge : TS_{\{i_1,i_2\}} \to TS_{\{o\}}$, defined through $merge(V_{\{i_1,i_2\}})(o) = f_{merge}(V(i_1), V(i_2))$, where f_{merge} satisfies the equations

$$\begin{aligned} f_{merge}(\varepsilon, \varepsilon) &= \varepsilon \\ f_{merge}(\langle a, t_1 \rangle, \varepsilon) &= \langle a, t_1 \rangle \\ f_{merge}(\varepsilon, \langle b, t_2 \rangle) &= \langle b, t_2 \rangle \ . \end{aligned}$$

However, if we want f_{merge} to be monotonic, we quickly run into a problem when defining $f_{merge}(\langle a, t_1 \rangle, \langle b, t_2 \rangle)$, since by monotonicity, the result of this merge must extend both $\langle a, t_1 \rangle$ and $\langle b, t_2 \rangle$. This is clearly impossible in general. A similar problem is revealed by Example 1. Looking closer at these examples, the problem seems to be that timed streams on their own do not show one important "input" to a node, which is passage of time.

We therefore have to assume that nodes have access to the current (wall-clock) time, and this "input" can also influence the behavior of a node. In a model with just timed streams, this input is invisible, even if it can trigger behavior of a node, either by making clear that it is "safe" to forward data from one of the inputs in the case of f_{merge} (since earlier input can no longer appear), or by triggering a timeout which induces subsequent output (as in Example 1). As a remedy to the problem, let us model the "passage of time" input simply as a time point t in $\mathbb{T}$. The idea of this "passage of time" input is to represent how far time has progressed in the execution of a node or network. By assuming the existence of a maximal element $\infty \in \mathbb{T}$, we obtain a CPO $\mathbb{T}$ with the ordering $\sqsubseteq$ being the standard relation $\leq$.

When extending the modeling framework with a "passage of time" input, we can see (at least) two ways in which this can be done.

1. We can let time be an additional "input stream": each network has an additional time input, which is read by all its nodes. In Example 1, the function f would output $\langle b, 2 \rangle$ if its input is empty *and* its time input is more than 1. We can make f monotonic be requiring that any extension of the empty input can only add tokens with time stamps at least the corresponding time input, i.e., (strictly) larger than 1.
2. We can let time be an additional "token" in each input stream. Such a token would mark how far time has progressed in that particular stream. We note that it is safe to ignore all time tokens except the last one. We thus represent this token by equipping each input stream with a "length" value, indicating how far time has progressed in the reception or output of the stream. In Example 1, the function f would output

$\langle b,2 \rangle$ for inputs $\langle \varepsilon, \Delta \rangle$ such that $\Delta > 1$. To recover monotonicity, an extended timed stream $\langle s, \Delta \rangle$ cannot be extended by timed tokens with time stamps smaller than Δ.

We work out alternative 1 in Sect. 4.1, and alternative 2 in Sect. 4.2. We use the timed merge as an illustrating function, since it exhibits several of the problems and features of the two solutions.

4.1 Timed Streams with Global Time

In this section, we work out in more detail alternative 1, in which each node and network have access to an additional time input, modeled simply as a value in $\mathbb{T}$, representing the "current time". We assume that nodes have access to the current (wall-clock) time, and this "input" can also influence the behavior of a node. As discussed above, we turn $\mathbb{T}$ into a CPO by adding ∞ as a maximal element. Let us preliminarily represent a node or network N with input ports I and output ports O as a function $f_N : TS_I \times \mathbb{T} \to TS_O$.

As a first illustration, we model the node in Example 1 as a function $f_{ex1} : TS_{\{i\}} \times \mathbb{T} \to TS_{\{o\}}$ through $f_{ex1}(V_{\{i\}}, t)(o) = f_t(V(i), t)$, where f_t is defined by

$$f_t(s,t) = \varepsilon \qquad \text{if } t \leq 1$$
$$f_t(s,t) = \langle b,2 \rangle \qquad \text{if } mint(s) > 1 \text{ and } t > 1$$
$$f_t(s,t) = \varepsilon \qquad \text{if } mint(s) \leq 1 \text{ and } t > 1$$

Here and in the following, for a non-empty timed stream s, we define $mint(s)$ as the smallest time stamp in s, and define $mint(\varepsilon) = \infty$. In the following, we often abuse notation, and do not distinguish between the function representing the node (which maps valuations and time points to valuations, which is f_{ex1} in the example) and the same function defined directly on timed streams (f_t) in the example.

From this illustration, we make some observations.

- We cannot define $f_t(\varepsilon, 1)$ as $\langle a, 2 \rangle$: continuity w.r.t. the time input dictates $f_t(\varepsilon, 1) = \varepsilon$. Thus, a timeout which depends on the absence of input can trigger subsequent output only when the time input has progressed past the timeout value. This is natural, since the absence of input at a time point t can only be determined after the time point t has passed.
- We cannot turn $TS_{\{i\}} \times \mathbb{T}$ into a CPO simply by component-wise extension of the orders on $TS_{\{i\}}$ and $\mathbb{T}$. Namely, if we would do so, then we would have:

$$(\varepsilon, 2) \sqsubseteq (\langle a,1 \rangle, 2) \qquad \text{but} \qquad f_t(\varepsilon, 2) \not\sqsubseteq f_t(\langle a,1 \rangle, 2) \ .$$

The problem here is that in allowing $(\varepsilon, 2) \sqsubseteq (\langle a,1 \rangle, 2)$ we allow timed tokens in an input stream to be extended with time tokens that appeared earlier than the "current time" (2 in this case). We must therefore be careful in the definition of our CPO, and only allow the input timed streams to be extended by tokens with time stamps at least being the time value. One could lament that this detracts slightly from the elegance of the original Kahn model, but it seems to be an unavoidable consequence of the fact that time is a global parameter.

- The time input can be thought of as the "current wall-clock time" of the node. If t is the current time input, then the output is the result of what the node commits to outputting at time t (which can include future outputs), given that the input streams up to t (i.e., ignoring larger time stamps) are as in the timed stream inputs.

After these observations, let us provide the formal definitions.

Definition 1 (Domain of Timed Streams with Global Time). *Let P be a set of ports. Let the domain TS_P^G consist of the set $TS_P \times \mathbb{T}$ with the ordering $\sqsubseteq$ defined by $(V,t) \sqsubseteq (V',t')$ if*

- *$t \leq t'$, and*
- *for each $p \in P$ there is a (possibly empty) timed stream s'' such that $V'(p) = V(p) \bullet s''$, and such that s'' contains no time stamp smaller than t.*

Using this definition, we model the behavior of a network with input ports I and output ports O by a continuous function from TS_I^G to TS_O. The least function from TS_I^G to TS_O is the function $\bot : TS_I^G \to TS_O$ defined by $\bot(V_I,t)(o) = \varepsilon$ for each o in O.

For the node in Example 1, the function f_t becomes continuous.

We now use these definitions to model a timed merge node. The function $f_{merge}^g : TS_{\{i_1,i_2\}}^G \to TS_{\{o\}}$ (using the previously mentioned abuse of notation) can be defined by recursion :

$$
\begin{aligned}
f_{merge}^g(\langle a,t_1\rangle \bullet s_1, \langle b,t_2\rangle \bullet s_2, t) &= \langle a,t_1\rangle \bullet f_{merge}^g(s_1, \langle b,t_2\rangle \bullet s_2, t) &\text{if } t_1 \leq t_2 \\
f_{merge}^g(\langle a,t_1\rangle \bullet s_1, \langle b,t_2\rangle \bullet s_2, t) &= \langle b,t_2\rangle \bullet f_{merge}^g(\langle a,t_1\rangle \bullet s_1, s_2, t) &\text{if } t_2 < t_1 \\
f_{merge}^g(\langle a,t_1\rangle \bullet s_1, \varepsilon, t) &= \langle a,t_1\rangle \bullet f_{merge}^g(s_1, \varepsilon, t) &\text{if } t_1 \leq t \\
f_{merge}^g(\varepsilon, \langle b,t_2\rangle \bullet s_2, t) &= \langle b,t_2\rangle \bullet f_{merge}^g(\varepsilon, s_2, t) &\text{if } t_2 < t \\
f_{merge}^g(s_1, s_2, t) &= \varepsilon &\text{otherwise.}
\end{aligned}
$$

This makes the function f_{merge}^g continuous if allowing s_1 and s_2 above to be infinite timed streams. We observe that in order to make f_{merge}^g a function, one needs to define a priority when two inputs with the same time stamp appear. In the above definition, f_{merge}^g gives priority to the first input. The input i_2 can only be forwarded when time has progressed so that one can be sure that no more inputs arrive on i_1. As an illustration, $f_{merge}^g(\langle a,1\rangle, \langle b,1\rangle, 1) = \langle a,1\rangle$; the second output cannot be forwarded at time 1, since it is still possible for input to arrive on the first input port at time 1.

The unfairness of f_{merge}^g gives rise to an unfairness in the limit, namely if an infinite stream of tokens appear at one time instant: $f_{merge}^g((\langle a,1\rangle)^\omega,(\langle b,1\rangle)^\omega,2) = (\langle a,1\rangle)^\omega$, and even $f_{merge}^g((\langle a,1\rangle)^\omega,\langle b,1\rangle,2) = (\langle a,1\rangle)^\omega$. This effect presupposes that no port can carry more than an ω-infinite long stream of tokens[1]. We can avoid such unfairness at each time point, by letting the merge switch priorities after each received token:

---

[1] We could maybe experiment with a solution like $f_{merge}((\langle a,1\rangle)^\omega,\langle b,1\rangle,2) = (\langle a,1\rangle)^\omega \langle b,1\rangle$, allowing streams that are longer than ω, but this would be beyond the scope of this paper.

$$\begin{aligned}
f^g_{merge}(\langle a,t_1\rangle \bullet s_1 \,,\, \langle b,t_2\rangle \bullet s_2 \,,\, t) &= \langle a,t_1\rangle \bullet g^g_{merge}(s_1 \,,\, \langle b,t_2\rangle \bullet s_2 \,,\, t) \quad \text{if } t_1 \leq t_2\\
f^g_{merge}(\langle a,t_1\rangle \bullet s_1 \,,\, \langle b,t_2\rangle \bullet s_2 \,,\, t) &= \langle b,t_2\rangle \bullet g^g_{merge}(\langle a,t_1\rangle \bullet s_1 \,,\, s_2 \,,\, t) \quad \text{if } t_2 < t_1\\
f^g_{merge}(\langle a,t_1\rangle \bullet s_1 \,,\, \varepsilon \,,\, t) &= \langle a,t_1\rangle \bullet g^g_{merge}(s_1 \,,\, \varepsilon \,,\, t) \quad \text{if } t_1 \leq t\\
f^g_{merge}(\varepsilon \,,\, \langle b,t_2\rangle \bullet s_2 \,,\, t) &= \langle b,t_2\rangle \bullet g^g_{merge}(\varepsilon \,,\, s_2 \,,\, t) \quad \text{if } t_2 < t\\
f^g_{merge}(s_1 \,,\, s_2 \,,\, t) &= \varepsilon \quad \text{otherwise.}\\
g^g_{merge}(\langle a,t_1\rangle \bullet s_1 \,,\, \langle b,t_2\rangle \bullet s_2 \,,\, t) &= \langle a,t_1\rangle \bullet f^g_{merge}(s_1 \,,\, \langle b,t_2\rangle \bullet s_2 \,,\, t) \quad \text{if } t_1 < t_2\\
g^g_{merge}(\langle a,t_1\rangle \bullet s_1 \,,\, \langle b,t_2\rangle \bullet s_2 \,,\, t) &= \langle b,t_2\rangle \bullet f^g_{merge}(\langle a,t_1\rangle \bullet s_1 \,,\, s_2 \,,\, t) \quad \text{if } t_2 \leq t_1\\
g^g_{merge}(\langle a,t_1\rangle \bullet s_1 \,,\, \varepsilon \,,\, t) &= \langle a,t_1\rangle \bullet f^g_{merge}(s_1 \,,\, \varepsilon \,,\, t) \quad \text{if } t_1 < t\\
g^g_{merge}(\varepsilon \,,\, \langle b,t_2\rangle \bullet s_2 \,,\, t) &= \langle b,t_2\rangle \bullet f^g_{merge}(\varepsilon \,,\, s_2 \,,\, t) \quad \text{if } t_2 \leq t\\
g^g_{merge}(s_1 \,,\, s_2 \,,\, t) &= \varepsilon \quad \text{otherwise.}
\end{aligned}$$

Note here that the priority is defined for the cases that the time stamps of the input streams are equal.

Deriving the Model of Networks from Models of Nodes. Let us now define the mathematical machinery for deriving the model of a network from the models of its nodes. Assume a network consisting of nodes $N_1,\ldots,N_k$. Each node N_i has input ports I_i and output ports O_i. Each port can be an output port of at most one node, i.e., $O_i \cap O_j = \emptyset$ for $i \neq j$. The composition of $N_1,\ldots,N_k$ is a network N with output ports $O = \cup_{i=1}^{k} O_i$ and input ports $I = (\cup_{i=1}^{k} I_i) \setminus O$. Each node N_i is modeled by a continuous function $f_i : TS^G_{I_i} \to TS_{O_i}$. From the disjointness of the sets O_i, we can decompose the functions f_i into one function $f_{o_j} : TS^G_{I_i} \to TS_{\{o_j\}}$ for each output port $o_j \in O$. For each output port $o_j \in O$ this produces an equation of form

$$V(o_j) = f_{o_j}(V(i_1),\ldots V(i_m),t) \tag{1}$$

From these equations, we would like to obtain a function $f_N : TS^G_I \to TS_O$, which represents the behavior of the entire network. The problem is that the Eqs. (1) are recursive in that the output ports may appear on both sides of the equations. Moreover, for a given t, we cannot directly derive a least solution to (1) by fixed-point iteration, since the ordering $\sqsubseteq$ on $TS^G_{\{o_j\}}$ does not allow us to extend $V(o_j)$ by time stamps smaller than t, thereby preventing a step-by-step construction of $V(o_j)$. To illustrate this, assume that a port o_1 is both an input and output port of a node N_1 and is connected back to itself when forming the network. Suppose further that the node first outputs a token a at time 1, and thereafter (including at time 1) copies input to output with no delay. The resulting network then produces an infinite timed stream $(\langle a,1\rangle)^\omega$ on o_1. This stream should be constructed step-by-step by iteration, but for time 2 (say), in the equation $V(o_1) = f_{o_1}(V(o_1),2)$ we have $f_{o_1}(s,2) = \langle a,1\rangle \bullet s$. If we try to produce $(\langle a,1\rangle)^\omega$ by the usual fixed-point iteration, as the limit of the sequence $f_{o_1}(\varepsilon,2), f_{o_1}(\langle a,1\rangle,2), f_{o_1}(\langle a,1\rangle \bullet \langle a,1\rangle,2),\ldots$, then we run into the problem that $(\varepsilon,2) \not\sqsubseteq (\langle a,1\rangle,2)$ etc. To resolve this issue we need to perform the fixed-point iteration at time 1, thereby exploiting that $(\varepsilon,1) \sqsubseteq (\langle a,1\rangle,1) \sqsubseteq (\langle a,1\rangle \bullet \langle a,1\rangle,1) \sqsubseteq \cdots$.

This means that before solving the system (1) for time t, we need solve it for all time points $t' < t$, and use the supremum of these solutions as a starting approximation at time t. Let us collect this into a definition.

Definition 2. *Let a network be formed as above yielding Eqs. (1). In order to derive the function defining network behavior, we reformulate (1) by replacing V by a time dependent valuation* $V^* : O \times \mathbb{T} \to TS$ *which satisfies*

$$V^*(o_j,t) = f_{o_j}(V^*(i_1,t),\ldots V^*(i_m,t),t) \qquad (2)$$

for all time points $t \in \mathbb{T}$. *Let then* V^* *be the valuation such that for each* $t \in \mathbb{T}$, *the valuation* $\lambda o_j.V^*(o_j,t)$ *is the smallest valuation (in the domain* TS_O*) such that for each* $o_j \in O$ *we have* $V^*(o_j,t') \sqsubseteq V^*(o_j,t)$ *for all* $t' < t$. *The function defining network behavior is then given by* $f_N(V_I,t)(o_j) = V^*(o_j,t)$.

Returning to the example before this definition, we first construct the solution $V^*(o_1,1) = (\langle a,1 \rangle)^\omega$. Since $(\langle a,1 \rangle)^\omega$ is a maximal element, it follows that $V^*(o_1,t) = (\langle a,1 \rangle)^\omega$ for all $t \geq 1$.

4.2 Timed Streams with Individual End Times

In this section, we define a semantic domain in which time has a more local character. We extend the domain of timed streams by adding, to each timed stream, an *end time*, which is a non-negative real number representing the time up to which the timed stream has been observed. The notion of stream end times leads to a somewhat richer model of node behavior than the global time model. Since end times are associated both with input and output streams, durations enable nodes to communicate not only data items with time stamps, but also at which point in time the next output can occur, and they give us more freedom in modeling networks. Maybe more importantly, streams with end times make it possible to preserve the decentralized nature of execution in Kahn networks: nodes communicate exclusively through channels, and as long as communication semantics is preserved the different parts of a network can execute completely independently. End times correspond to an implementation of timed systems in which nodes, when not producing any data, still output some form of empty data frames ("stuttering") to communicate the absence of output to subsequent nodes.

As before, we assume that the time domain $\mathbb{T}$ contains a maximal element $\infty \in \mathbb{T}$, and thus forms a CPO.

Definition 3. *The set TSE of* timed streams with end times *consists of pairs* $\langle s,\Delta \rangle$ *of a timed stream s and an end time* Δ *that is at least as large as all time stamps in s:*

$$TSE = \{\langle s,\Delta \rangle \in TS \times \mathbb{T} \mid \Delta \geq maxt(s)\}.$$

Here, we define $maxt(s)$ as the largest time stamp occurring in s, with $maxt(s) = \infty$ if there is no largest time stamp and $maxt(\varepsilon) = 0$. We can turn the set *TSE* into a CPO in a similar way as in the global time setting: timed streams with end times can be extended to longer streams by adding further elements, but only if the time stamps of the new elements are at least as large as the previous end time:

Definition 4. *For* $\langle s,\Delta \rangle, \langle s',\Delta' \rangle \in TSE$, *we define* $\langle s,\Delta \rangle \sqsubseteq \langle s',\Delta' \rangle$ *if and only if* $\Delta \leq \Delta'$ *and* $s' = s \bullet s''$ *for some stream* s'' *with* $mint(s'') \geq \Delta$.

We can observe that the limit of an increasing chain $\langle s_0, \Delta_0 \rangle \sqsubseteq \langle s_1, \Delta_1 \rangle \sqsubseteq \cdots$ is the timed stream with end time $\langle \lim_{n \to \infty} s_n, \lim_{n \to \infty} \Delta_n \rangle$. A node or network N with input ports I and output ports O is represented as a function $f_N : TSE_I \to TSE_O$, where $TSE_P = P \to TSE$ is the CPO that associates a timed stream with end time with each element of P, with point-wise extension of the ordering relation.

Modeling Timeouts. For illustration, let us return to Example 1. We can model the timeout node using the following function f_t. As mentioned in the beginning of the section, our model of the timeout node is able to explicitly state at which points in time the node can produce data. Since the earliest output can occur at time point 2, for input stream duration $\Delta \leq 1$ the function can be defined as $\langle \varepsilon, 2 \rangle$. This output can then be extended to either $\langle \langle b, 2 \rangle, \infty \rangle$ or $\langle \varepsilon, \infty \rangle$, depending on whether input data is observed at some time $t \leq 1$ or not:

$$\begin{aligned} f_t(\langle s, \Delta \rangle) &= \langle \varepsilon, 2 \rangle & \text{if } \Delta \leq 1 \\ f_t(\langle s, \Delta \rangle) &= \langle \langle b, 2 \rangle, \infty \rangle & \text{if } \Delta > 1 \text{ and } mint(s) > 1 \\ f_t(\langle s, \Delta \rangle) &= \langle \varepsilon, \infty \rangle & \text{if } \Delta > 1 \text{ and } mint(s) \leq 1 \end{aligned} \quad (3)$$

We can verify that this function is indeed a continuous function in our CPO.

Deriving Models of Networks from Models of Nodes. Like in Sect. 4.1, we discuss how the functions associated with network nodes give rise to behavior of a network as a whole. For this, assume again a network consisting of nodes $N_1, \ldots, N_k$, where each node N_i has input ports I_i and output ports O_i. Each port can be an output port of at most one node, i.e., $O_i \cap O_j = \emptyset$ for $i \neq j$. The composition of $N_1, \ldots, N_k$ is a network N with output ports $O = \bigcup_{i=1}^k O_i$ and input ports $I = \bigcup_{i=1}^k I_i \setminus O$. Each node N_i is modeled by a continuous function $f_i : TSE_{I_i} \to TSE_{O_i}$.

To execute the network, each of the nodes has to process its inputs; since the output of some of the nodes is used as input of other nodes, and since there might be feedback loops, execution has to be repeated until a fixed-point is reached. For this, consider the CPO TSE_O that associates a timed stream with end time with each output port. Each element of TSE_O can be considered as a possible internal state of the network. To run the network to completion, we start from the state $\bot \in TSE_O$ that assigns the smallest element (empty stream with end time 0) to each output port, and then repeatedly update all output streams to the values computed by the nodes.

More formally, for some set P of ports, some element $a \in TSE_P$, and some subset $P' \subseteq P$, we write $a|_{P'} \in TSE_{P'}$ for the restriction of a to P'. We define the update function of the network as the function $F_{step}(in) : TSE_O \to TSE_O$ from internal states to internal states, taking the (fixed) inputs $in \in TSE_I$ of the network into account:

$$F_{step}(in)(out) = \bigcup_{i \in \{1, \ldots, k\}} f_i((in \cup out)|_{I_i})$$

The function $F_{step}(in)$ is continuous, and its least fixed-point $F(in) = \lim_{n \to \infty} F_{step}(in)^n(\bot)$ corresponds to the outputs of the networks when run to completion.

From Denotation to Implementation. Since functions in our new model not only *receive*, but also *return* end times of streams, a discussion is necessary whether all continuous functions model nodes that could exist in the real world. Consider the following three functions for copying data from input to output:

$$f_{1/2}(\langle\langle a_1,t_1\rangle,\langle a_2,t_2\rangle,\langle a_3,t_3\rangle,\ldots,\Delta\rangle) = \langle\langle a_1,\tfrac{1}{2}t_1\rangle,\langle a_2,\tfrac{1}{2}t_2\rangle,\langle a_3,\tfrac{1}{2}t_3\rangle,\ldots,\tfrac{1}{2}\Delta\rangle$$
$$f_1(\langle\langle a_1,t_1\rangle,\langle a_2,t_2\rangle,\langle a_3,t_3\rangle,\ldots,\Delta\rangle) = \langle\langle a_1,t_1\rangle,\langle a_2,t_2\rangle,\langle a_3,t_3\rangle,\ldots,\Delta\rangle$$
$$f_2(\langle\langle a_1,t_1\rangle,\langle a_2,t_2\rangle,\langle a_3,t_3\rangle,\ldots,\Delta\rangle) = \langle\langle a_1,2t_1\rangle,\langle a_2,2t_2\rangle,\langle a_3,2t_3\rangle,\ldots,2\Delta\rangle$$

All three functions are continuous, but they differ in the time points and end time of the generated output streams. Function $f_{1/2}$ outputs every item received at time point t at the time $\tfrac{1}{2}t$, i.e., possibly at an earlier time than t; function f_1 keeps all time stamps, while function f_2 outputs at time $2t$, possibly at a later time than t. Although all three functions are meaningful in our semantic framework, function $f_{1/2}$ is an impossibility from an operational point of view: a node implementing this function would output (or forward) data before it has received the data. Assuming that time progresses equally fast on all streams of the network, no such node can exist. Functions f_1 and f_2, in contrast, could be implemented; a node for f_2 would require unbounded memory, however, since it has to store data incoming at time t until it can be output at time $2t$.

In order to talk about implementability, we introduce a general notion of causality. We first introduce the notion of cause, which is the minimal input producing a given output. Then, given a cause $\langle s', \Delta'\rangle$, we ask for a minimal extension $\langle s'', \Delta''\rangle$ of $\langle s', \Delta'\rangle$ such that $f(\langle s', \Delta'\rangle \bullet \langle s'', \Delta''\rangle)$ is an extension of $f(\langle s', \Delta'\rangle)$. For readability, the following definition only consider the case of unary functions, the extension to input tuples is straightforward.

Definition 5 (Notion of cause). *Consider a continuous function $f_N : TSE \to TSE$. We say that*

- $\langle s', \Delta'\rangle$ *is the* cause *for $\langle s, \Delta\rangle$ for f_N if $\langle s', \Delta'\rangle$ is the smallest stream such that $f_N(\langle s', \Delta'\rangle) = \langle s, \Delta\rangle$. That is, if for all $\langle s'', \Delta''\rangle \sqsubset \langle s', \Delta'\rangle$, $f_N(\langle s'', \Delta''\rangle) \sqsubset \langle s, \Delta\rangle$ (where $\sqsubset$ stands naturally for strictly smaller, that is, strictly smaller stream or end time).*
- *if $\langle s', \Delta'\rangle$ is the* cause *for $\langle s, \Delta\rangle$ for f_N, and $\langle s, \Delta\rangle$ is of the form $\langle s^* \bullet x, \Delta\rangle$ for some stream x (not necessarily a single item), then $\langle s', \Delta'\rangle$ causes the extension $\langle s^*, \Delta^*\rangle \to \langle s^* \bullet x, \Delta\rangle$ if for all $\langle s'', \Delta''\rangle \sqsubset \langle s', \Delta'\rangle$, $f_N(\langle s'', \Delta''\rangle) \sqsubseteq \langle s^*, \Delta^*\rangle$. Note that the extension x is minimal.*
- *if $\langle s', \Delta'\rangle$ causes the extension $\langle s^*, \Delta^*\rangle \to \langle s^* \bullet x, \Delta\rangle$, then the* cause *for the extension $\langle s^*, \Delta^*\rangle \to \langle s^* \bullet x, \Delta\rangle$ is Δ' if for any $\Delta'' < \Delta'$, $f_N(\langle s', \Delta''\rangle) \sqsubseteq \langle s^*, \Delta^*\rangle$, and there exists such a Δ''. That is, it is the time progress to Δ' (e.g. a timeout) that causes the extension $\langle s^*, \Delta^*\rangle \to \langle s^* \bullet x, \Delta\rangle$.*

We have now defined the cause for an extension of the output $\langle s^*, \Delta^*\rangle$ to a larger output $\langle s^* \bullet x, \Delta\rangle$. Now, we define define causality as a constraint on the time stamps of the output extension x, such that we can show (conjecture) that causal functions are implementable, possibly by infinitely powerful machines.

Definition 6 (Causality). *Consider a continuous function $f_N : TSE \to TSE$. Then, every $\langle s, \Delta'' \rangle$ in the image of f_N with $\langle \varepsilon, 0 \rangle \sqsubset \langle s, \Delta'' \rangle$ can be written in the form $\langle s^* \bullet x, \Delta'' \rangle$, such that there is a $\langle s', \Delta' \rangle$ which causes the extension $\langle s^*, \Delta^* \rangle \to \langle s^* \bullet x, \Delta \rangle$ for some $\Delta \leq \Delta''$. The function f_N is causal if*

- *whenever $\langle s', \Delta' \rangle$ is the cause for the extension $\langle s^*, \Delta^* \rangle \to \langle s^* \bullet x, \Delta \rangle$ and $\varepsilon \sqsubset x$, then, if $s' = \varepsilon$ then $mint(x) \geq 0$ else $mint(x) \geq maxt(s')$.*
- *if, in addition, Δ' is the cause for the extension $\langle s^*, \Delta^* \rangle \to \langle s^* \bullet x, \Delta \rangle$ (and $\varepsilon \sqsubset x$), then $mint(x) \geq \Delta'$. The time stamp of x must be at least as large as its cause, and here the cause is Δ'.*

This definition extends to tuples in a straightforward manner: in both cases the time of the effect must be greater than the maximal time of its cause.

Now, we can formulate our conjecture on the requirements for a function to be implementable.

Conjecture 1 (Timing consistency postulate). A continuous function $f_N : TSE_I \to TSE_O$ is implementable, if

(1) it is causal in the sense of Definition 6, and
(2) for every chain of input tuples with diverging end times, that is,

$$(\langle s_1^1, \Delta_1^1 \rangle, \ldots, \langle s_n^1, \Delta_n^1 \rangle) \sqsubseteq (\langle s_1^2, \Delta_1^2 \rangle, \ldots, \langle s_n^2, \Delta_n^2 \rangle) \sqsubseteq \cdots \quad \text{with} \quad \forall k. \lim_{j \to \infty} \Delta_k^j = \infty$$

also the end times of each output stream tend to infinity:

$$\text{if } f_N(\langle s_1^j, \Delta_1^j \rangle, \ldots, \langle s_n^j, \Delta_n^j \rangle) = (\langle r_1^j, \bar{\Delta}_1^j \rangle, \ldots, \langle r_m^j, \bar{\Delta}_m^j \rangle) \quad \text{then} \quad \forall k. \lim_{j \to \infty} \bar{\Delta}_k^j = \infty$$

(the function does not block time).

Monotonicity of f_N guarantees that the output produced for an extension of a previous input can only extend the previously computed output; it may depend on the previous output (its potentially unbounded memory). Causality (condition 1) implies timing consistency. If the interpretation of time stamps is the time at which its data item is written (or delivered), then it is guaranteed that every cause is written not later than its corresponding effect. We may still need an infinitely fast machine. Finally, condition (2) guarantees that for every input chain that does not block time (the end times of all input streams diverge), output approximations with diverging end times are produced. That is f_n does not block time progress (not for more than a finite number of steps).

Modeling Timed Merge. As a second example of using our model of timed streams with end times, we show how timed merge can be captured. The following definition corresponds to the "unfair" version of merge from Sect. 4.1, i.e., the function prefers data arriving at input 1 over the one from input 2. We use an auxiliary function g to model the interleaving of data items from the two input streams. In the first equation, defining the actual function f_{merge}^{et}, we need to set the end time of the output stream to

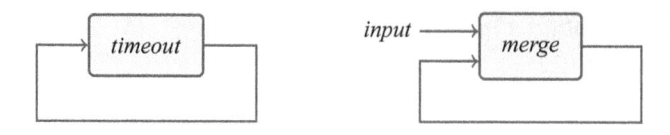

Fig. 1. Feedback loops with timeout and timed merge nodes

the minimum end time $\min\{\Delta_1, \Delta_2\}$ of the input streams, since additional data arriving through the input streams can lead to further output at time $\min\{\Delta_1, \Delta_2\}$ or later.

$$f_{merge}^{et}(\langle s_1, \Delta_1 \rangle, \langle s_2, \Delta_2 \rangle) = \langle g(\langle s_1, \Delta_1 \rangle, \langle s_2, \Delta_2 \rangle), \min\{\Delta_1, \Delta_2\}\rangle$$

$$g(\langle\langle a, t_1\rangle \bullet s_1, \Delta_1\rangle, \langle s_2, \Delta_2\rangle) = \langle a, t_1\rangle \bullet g(\langle s_1, \Delta_1\rangle, \langle s_2, \Delta_2\rangle) \quad \text{if } t_1 \leq \min(mint(s_2), \Delta_2)$$
$$g(\langle s_1, \Delta_1\rangle, \langle\langle b, t_2\rangle \bullet s_2, \Delta_2\rangle) = \langle b, t_2\rangle \bullet g(\langle s_1, \Delta_1\rangle, \langle s_2, \Delta_2\rangle) \quad \text{if } t_2 < \min(mint(s_1), \Delta_1)$$
$$g(\langle\langle a, t_1\rangle \bullet s_1, \Delta_1\rangle, \langle \varepsilon, \Delta_2\rangle) = \varepsilon \quad \text{if } \Delta_2 < t_1 \text{ lacks input from inp1}$$
$$g(\langle \varepsilon, \Delta_1\rangle, \langle\langle b, t_2\rangle \bullet s_2, \Delta_2\rangle) = \varepsilon \quad \text{if } \Delta_1 \leq t_2 \text{ lacks input from inp2}$$
$$g(\langle \varepsilon, \Delta_1\rangle, \langle \varepsilon, \Delta_2\rangle) = \varepsilon$$

4.3 On Networks with Feedback Loops

As a litmus test for our semantic models, we consider the handling of nodes that do not consume any computation time (zero delay), and of networks that contain zero-delay feedback loops. A zero-delay loop is a feedback loop that can produce output without any time passing, i.e., output is produced at the same time point as input entering the loop. Although it can be argued that actual implementations of networks cannot contain zero-delay steps, such computations are an important abstraction when modeling systems; it is therefore desirable that denotational semantics are able to capture computation that is instantaneous.

Simple Feedback Networks

Timeout with Feedback. We consider networks with feedback loops, shown in Fig. 1. The first example is a timeout node, which is a node that outputs data with delay: if no data has been received before or at time 1, then a data item is output at time 2. As a thought experiment, we investigate the effect of applying this timeout node in a direct feedback loop, shown on the left-hand side of Fig. 1.

In the global-time model, the network defines a continuous function from $\mathbb{T}$ to $TS_{\{o\}}$. We can compute the output as a fixed-point for each time point t in $\mathbb{T}$ from the definition in the beginning of Sect. 4.1. As a result, the port contains ε if $t \leq 1$ and $\langle b, 2 \rangle$ if $t > 1$.

In the model of timed streams with end time, using definition (3), the output produced by the left network is the limit of the sequence

$$\langle \varepsilon, 0 \rangle \sqsubseteq \langle \varepsilon, 2 \rangle \sqsubseteq \langle \langle b, 2 \rangle, \infty \rangle$$

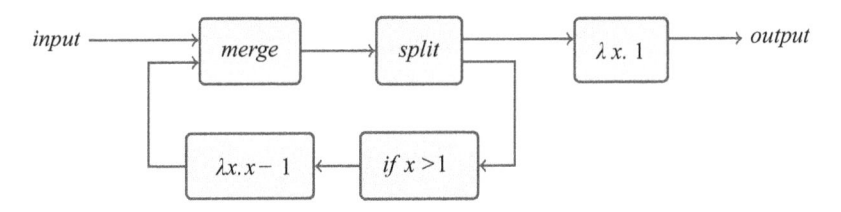

Fig. 2. Repetition network with zero-delay loop: for each timed data item $\langle k,t \rangle$ that is received, the network is supposed to output k times the item $\langle 1,t \rangle$.

which coincides with the last timed stream $\langle\langle b,2\rangle,\infty\rangle$. Arguably, this corresponds to our intuition about timeout node run in a feedback loop. It should be noted that the "passing" of time in this example is the result of the timeout node specifying an output stream end time that is greater than the end time of the input stream; intuitively, the node itself is making time pass.

Merge with Feedback. An example of zero-delay computation is the timed merge function, shown on the right-hand side of Fig. 1 and discussed for the global-time model in Sect. 4.1 and for the model of timed streams with end times in Sect. 4.2. Both of our models of timed merge (f^g_{merge} and f^{et}_{merge}) forward data received on the input streams without delay to the output stream. Both models moreover work in case of an infinite number of data items arriving at the same point in time. This situation can lead to an unfair selection of data, as discussed in Sect. 4.1, where also a possible fix to ensure fairness is provided.

In the global-time model, the first external input is copied into an infinite stream on the internal channel, but only after time has advanced from the time of that input, because of the priority given to the external input. This priority also lets a stream of external input that appears with the same time stamp on the first channel be repeated infinitely on the output channel. Denoting the whole network by $f_{mergefb}$, we have, for instance

$$
\begin{aligned}
f_{mergefb}(\langle a,t_1\rangle \bullet s_1\,,\,t) &= \varepsilon && \text{if } t_1 > t \\
f_{mergefb}(\langle a,t_1\rangle \bullet s_1\,,\,t) &= \langle a,t_1\rangle && \text{if } t_1 = t < mint(s_1) \\
f_{mergefb}(\langle a,t_1\rangle \bullet s_1\,,\,t) &= (\langle a,t_1\rangle)^\omega && \text{if } t_1 < \min(t, mint(s_1)) \\
f_{mergefb}(\langle a,t_1\rangle\langle b,t_1\rangle \bullet s_1\,,\,t) &= (\langle a,t_1\rangle\langle b,t_1\rangle)^\omega && \text{if } t_1 < \min(t, mint(s_1))
\end{aligned}
$$

In the model of timed streams with end times, the zero-delay feedback loop shown in Fig. 1 has a less obvious effect. Given input streams with end times Δ_1 and Δ_2, respectively, the function f^{et}_{merge} produces a stream with end time $\min\{\Delta_1,\Delta_2\}$ as output. This implies that the fixed-point of the feedback loop in Fig. 1 has end time 0, i.e., the feedback loop makes time stop at point 0. The node can still produce output at time point 0, provided that input occurs at time 0 on the first input, but the end time of the output stream never advances beyond 0, hence the same holds for the second output.

Repetition Network. As a somewhat more complicated example, consider now the network with zero-delay feedback of Fig. 2. For each $\langle k,t\rangle$ received from the external

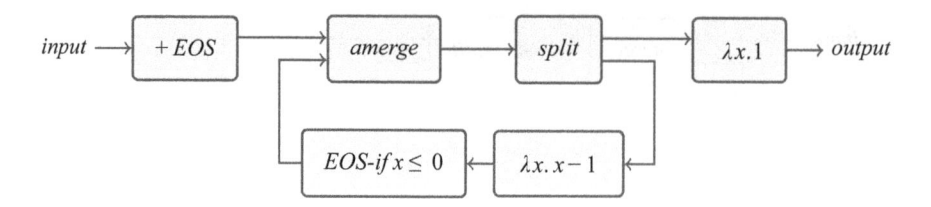

Fig. 3. Improved repetition network with zero-delay loop, using timed merge *amerge* with flow arbitration.

input, $k-1$ items $\langle i,t \rangle$ are fed back to the second input of the merge node and for each element $\langle i,t \rangle$ received by the merge node an item $\langle 1,t \rangle$ is sent to the global output. The other nodes used in the network have semantics as follows: the nodes containing λ-expressions apply a function to each element of a stream ("*map*"); the *if*-nodes remove all data elements from a stream that do not satisfy the given predicate ("*filter*"); and the *split*-node copies all data that it receives to multiple output streams. Functions modeling those nodes can be defined easily in our framework.

Sadly, the network shown in Fig. 2 does not work, showcasing the limitations of timed merge. There are two issues:

1. The unfair timed merge has to prioritize one of its two input streams, which prevents the input data and the data flowing back through the feedback loop from being merged correctly. If priority is given to the input to the network, the feedback data is blocked (since further input could arrive at the same time); if priority is given to the feedback data, the input data is blocked. In particular, in the global time model, if priority is given to the input to the network, all elements $\langle k,t_1 \rangle$ present can be read at time t_1. But the feedback input is blocked at time t_1. If the external input progresses beyond t_1, one cannot extend the feedback input with elements at t_1. Giving priority to the feedback input has a similar effect.
2. When using the model of timed streams with end times, the feedback loop gets stuck at time 0; time never progresses beyond time 0.

In Fig. 3, we show one possible way to fix the repetition network. As we want to suppose asynchronous independent execution of the nodes, we need an explicit termination signal, at least from the second input, after which time may progress and the next item from the external input can be consumed. For this, the network in Fig. 3 uses a timed merge node *amerge* that requires an explicit signal to switch between the two input streams. For this, we assume a special data item *EOS* ("end-of-stride") that can occur on the streams. The intended semantics of the node *amerge* is as follows:

– Initially, *amerge* forwards data items from the first input to its output stream. Data items arriving on the second input are not forwarded and remain in the input channel.
– Once an *EOS* is received on the first input stream, the *amerge* switches to the second input, and now copies data from the second input to the output stream, including all items that were previously queued. No data is read from the first input channel.
– Once an *EOS* is received on the second input stream, the nodes switches back to the first input, etc.

To define a complete network, we introduce two further nodes: the node $+EOS$ copies data from the input to the output, but adds an EOS after each item; the node EOS-if replaces every data item for which the given predicate holds with EOS. The definition of the three new nodes in the global-time model and the model of timed streams with end time is straightforward.

5 Conclusion and Discussion

In this paper, we have studied the problem of defining deterministic execution semantics of asynchronous data-flow languages in the presence of time. By designing appropriate complete partial orders of timed streams, we are able to define the semantics in denotational style, staying close to the original definitions for Kahn process networks, yet are able to handle zero-delay feedback loops. The research has been inspired by the (ongoing) work on the MIMOS model [26] of computation for embedded systems.

There are several avenues of future work. We can extend our notion of *timed stream with end time* by distinguishing a *weak* and a *strong* notion of end time. This extension might be useful to model zero-delay loops (see Sect. 4.3) in a more direct fashion. With the *weak* interpretation of end time Δ, any extension of the timed stream can add items with time stamps $\geq \Delta$ (as we have considered so far in Definition 4), whereas with a *strong* interpretation of end time Δ, any extension of the timed stream can only add items with time stamps $> \Delta$. This allows us to write more natural definitions, for example of the merge function: we never need to suppose an end time beyond the time point of interest, but only need to distinguish between streams with weak and strong end points.

Another extension is an alternative notion of external time: it is defined by a sequence of time points at which a function may look at its input and extend the previously computed output. This variant can be expressed within the framework of external time defined here by requiring that every output produced has a time stamp not smaller than the time point at which it is read, meaning that our versions of merge cannot forward their initial time stamps in all cases. These external computation time points may be defined per node (then it comes very close to a model for MIMOS) or for an entire network.

Conflict of Interest. The author(s) has no competing interests to declare that are relevant to the content of this manuscript.

References

1. Caspi, P., Benveniste, A., Lublinerman, R., Tripakis, S.: Actors without directors: a Kahnian view of heterogeneous systems. In: Majumdar, R., Tabuada, P. (eds.) HSCC 2009. LNCS, vol. 5469, pp. 46–60. Springer, Heidelberg (2009). https://doi.org/10.1007/978-3-642-00602-9_4
2. Guevara, I., Ryan, S., Singh, A., Brandon, C., Margaria, T.: Edge IoT prototyping using model-driven representations: a use case for smart agriculture. Sensors **24**(2), 495 (2024). https://doi.org/10.3390/s24020495

3. Hesselink, W.H.: A generalization of Naundorf's fixpoint theorem. Theor. Comput. Sci. **247**(1–2), 291–296 (2000). https://doi.org/10.1016/S0304-3975(00)00202-4
4. Kahn, G.: The semantics of a simple language for parallel programming. In: IFIP 1974, pp. 471–475. North-Holland (1974)
5. Lee, E., Sangiovanni-Vincentelli, A.: A framework for comparing models of computation. IEEE Trans. Comput. Aided Des. Integr. Circ. Syst. **17**(12), 1217–1229 (1998)
6. Lee, E.A.: Modeling concurrent real-time processes using discrete events. Ann. Softw. Eng. **7**(1), 25–45 (1999)
7. Liu, J., Lee, E.A.: On the causality of mixed-signal and hybrid models. In: Maler, O., Pnueli, A. (eds.) HSCC 2003. LNCS, vol. 2623, pp. 328–342. Springer, Heidelberg (2003). https://doi.org/10.1007/3-540-36580-X_25
8. Liu, X.: Semantic foundation of the tagged signal model. University of California, Berkeley (2005)
9. Liu, X., Lee, E.A.: CPO semantics of timed interactive actor networks. Theor. Comput. Sci. **409**(1), 110–125 (2008). https://doi.org/10.1016/j.tcs.2008.08.044
10. Liu, X., Matsikoudis, E., Lee, E.A.: Modeling timed concurrent systems. In: Baier, C., Hermanns, H. (eds.) CONCUR 2006. LNCS, vol. 4137, pp. 1–15. Springer, Heidelberg (2006). https://doi.org/10.1007/11817949_1
11. Lohstroh, M., Menard, C., Soroush, B., Lee, E.A.: Toward a lingua franca for deterministic concurrent systems. ACM Trans. Embed. Comput. Syst. **20**(4), 1–27 (2021)
12. Margaria, T., Steffen, B.: Service-orientation: conquering complexity with XMDD. In: Hinchey, M., Coyle, L. (eds.) Conquering Complexity, pp. 217–236. Springer, London (2012). https://doi.org/10.1007/978-1-4471-2297-5_10
13. Matsikoudis, E., Lee, E.A.: On fixed points of strictly causal functions. In: Braberman, V., Fribourg, L. (eds.) FORMATS 2013. LNCS, vol. 8053, pp. 183–197. Springer, Heidelberg (2013). https://doi.org/10.1007/978-3-642-40229-6_13
14. Matsikoudis, E., Lee, E.A.: The fixed-point theory of strictly causal functions. Theor. Comput. Sci. **574**, 39–77 (2015). https://doi.org/10.1016/j.tcs.2015.01.036
15. Matt, C., Maurer, U., Portmann, C., Renner, R., Tackmann, B.: Toward an algebraic theory of systems. Theor. Comput. Sci. **747**, 1–25 (2018). https://www.sciencedirect.com/science/article/pii/S0304397518304092
16. Müller, O., Scholz, P.: Functional specification of real-time and hybrid systems. In: Maler, O. (ed.) HART 1997. LNCS, vol. 1201, pp. 273–285. Springer, Heidelberg (1997). https://doi.org/10.1007/BFb0014732
17. Naundorf, H.: Strictly causal functions have a unique fixed point. Theor. Comput. Sci. **238**(1–2), 483–488 (2000). https://doi.org/10.1016/S0304-3975(99)00165-6
18. Portmann, C., Matt, C., Maurer, U., Renner, R., Tackmann, B.: Causal boxes: quantum information-processing systems closed under composition. IEEE Trans. Inf. Theory **63**(5), 3277–3305 (2017)
19. Reed, G.M., Roscoe, A.W.: A timed model for communicating sequential processes. In: Kott, L. (ed.) ICALP 1986. LNCS, vol. 226, pp. 314–323. Springer, Heidelberg (1986). https://doi.org/10.1007/3-540-16761-7_81
20. Reed, G.M., Roscoe, A.W.: Metric spaces as models for real-time concurrency. In: Main, M., Melton, A., Mislove, M., Schmidt, D. (eds.) MFPS 1987. LNCS, vol. 298, pp. 331–343. Springer, Heidelberg (1988). https://doi.org/10.1007/3-540-19020-1_17
21. Steffen, B., Margaria, T., Nagel, R., Jörges, S., Kubczak, C.: Model-driven development with the jABC. In: Bin, E., Ziv, A., Ur, S. (eds.) HVC 2006. LNCS, vol. 4383, pp. 92–108. Springer, Heidelberg (2007). https://doi.org/10.1007/978-3-540-70889-6_7
22. Tennent, R.: The denotational semantics of programming languages. Commun. ACM **19**, 437–453 (1976)

23. Yates, R.K., Gao, G.R.: A Kahn principle for networks of nonmonotonic real-time processes. In: Bode, A., Reeve, M., Wolf, G. (eds.) PARLE 1993. LNCS, vol. 694, pp. 209–227. Springer, Heidelberg (1993). https://doi.org/10.1007/3-540-56891-3_17
24. Yates, R.K.: Networks of real-time processes. In: Best, E. (ed.) CONCUR 1993. LNCS, vol. 715, pp. 384–397. Springer, Heidelberg (1993). https://doi.org/10.1007/3-540-57208-2_27
25. Yi, W., et al.: MIMOS in a nutshell (in preparation) (2024)
26. Yi, W., Mohaqeqi, M., Graf, S.: MIMOS: a deterministic model for the design and update of real-time systems. In: ter Beek, M.H., Sirjani, M. (eds.) COORDINATION 2022. LNCS, vol. 13271, pp. 17–34. Springer, Cham (2022). https://doi.org/10.1007/978-3-031-08143-9_2

Three Ways of Proving Termination of Loops

Krzysztof R. Apt[1,2](✉), Frank S. de Boer[1](✉), and Ernst-Rüdiger Olderog[3](✉)

[1] CWI, Amsterdam, The Netherlands
{apt,F.S.de.Boer}@cwi.nl
[2] MIMUW, University of Warsaw, Warsaw, Poland
[3] Carl von Ossietzky University of Oldenburg, Oldenburg, Germany
olderog@informatik.uni-oldenburg.de

Abstract. We investigate three proof rules for proving termination of **while** programs and show their proof-theoretic equivalence. This involves a proof-theoretic analysis of various auxiliary proof rules in Hoare's logic. By discussing representations of proofs in the form of proof outlines, we reveal differences between these equivalent proof rules when used in practice. We also address applications in the context of the paradigm of design by contract.

1 Introduction

In his seminal paper [12], Hoare introduced an axiomatic method of reasoning about correctness of **while** programs, now called Hoare's logic. It is based on correctness formulas $\{p\}\ S\ \{q\}$, where S is a program and p and q are assertions (logical formulas), with the interpretation

"If the assertion p is true before initiation of a program S, then the assertion q will be true on its completion."

In this context p is referred to as a *precondition* and q as a *postcondition* of S.

However, in contrast to Floyd's earlier paper [11] that dealt with correctness of flowchart programs, program termination was not addressed. To stress this difference one distinguishes now between *partial correctness* that only focuses on the delivery of correct results, and *total correctness*, that in addition stipulates that the program terminates. So the original proposal of Hoare dealt with partial correctness.

All approaches to proving program termination within Hoare's logic formalize Floyd's [11] observation that

"Proofs of termination are dealt with by showing that each step of a program decreases some entity which cannot decrease indefinitely."

The first extension of Hoare's logic to deal with total correctness is due to [14]. Since then substantially simpler proof rules were proposed. In these proof rules variables that range over natural numbers are used. An appropriate relative completeness result, see for example [4], shows that variables ranging over more general well-founded orderings are not needed.

Termination continues to be a relevant and vibrant topic in program analysis, see for example [7] and the Annual International Termination Competition[1]. The latter comprises various competition categories, for instance proving termination of C programs, Java bytecode programs, logic programs, functional programs, and term rewriting systems. Here we focus on the shape of termination proofs in the context of Hoare's logic. To this end, we investigate three natural proof rules from the proof-theoretic point of view. More specifically, we study **while** programs with Hoare's original proof system for program correctness, in which the well-known proof rule for partial correctness of the **while** loops, which we call the LOOP I rule, is replaced by a suitable proof rule for establishing total correctness. We analyze three versions of such a proof rule:

- The LOOP II rule achieves a separation of the reasoning about the invariant and the bound function.
- The LOOP III rule allows us to document proofs as *proof outlines*, which is in particular useful when arguing about the interference freedom of component proofs in the context of parallel programs.
- The LOOP IV rule is particularly well-suited when dealing with nested loops because it modularizes the correctness proof of the outer loop from the ones of the inner loops. It is a *hybrid* proof rule with premises referring to proof systems for both partial and total correctness.

Depending on the choice of the loop rule, we obtain proof systems that we refer to by II, III, and IV, respectively. We show that these three proof systems are equivalent in the sense that every proof of a correctness formula $\{p\}\ S\ \{q\}$ carried out in one of these systems can be effectively transformed into a correctness proof in any other of these proof systems. This result is obtained by a detailed proof-theoretic analysis of the three loop rules in the context of these proof systems. To structure the proof well, we make use of auxiliary proof rules, which we show to be admissible in the proof systems.

Even though Hoare's logic has been extensively studied (see for example our survey [5]), little work has been done on the analysis of proofs in Hoare's logic. We are familiar with only three references, [2,8], and [18], in which transformations of proofs in a Hoare logic are discussed.

While these proof rules are equivalent, their use and representation in the form of proof outlines, which are programs annotated by assertions, differs. We illustrate this by analyzing a termination proof of a program with nested loops. We also address applications in the context of assertions used as annotations in the design by contract paradigm.

Dedication. We dedicate our paper to Tiziana Margaria on the occasion of her 60th birthday given that her interest in software engineering includes also meth-

---

[1] https://termination-portal.org/wiki/Termination_Competition.

ods for verification of software. The third author recalls various pleasant meetings at conferences and in Bremen, Passau, and Dortmund.

2 Preliminaries

Assume a given language that is determined by its set of formulas. In what follows we assume that all considered axioms, proof rules, and proof systems are concerned with the same language.

Given a proof system PR and two sequences of formulas $\phi_1, \ldots, \phi_m$ and $\varphi_1, \ldots, \varphi_n$ we write
$$\phi_1, \ldots, \phi_m \vdash_{PR} \varphi_1, \ldots, \varphi_n$$
to denote the fact that each formula φ_i can be proved in PR using as additional axioms the formulas $\phi_1, \ldots, \phi_m$. We also use this notation when the sequence $\phi_1, \ldots, \phi_m$ is empty and when PR is a set of proof rules.

A proof rule
$$(R) \quad \frac{\varphi_1, \ldots, \varphi_k}{\varphi}$$
is called **admissible in** PR if
$$\vdash_{PR} \varphi_1, \ldots, \vdash_{PR} \varphi_k \text{ implies } \vdash_{PR} \varphi.$$

Intuitively, if a rule is admissible in PR it does not increase the power of the proof system PR [18], but it serves as a lemma that simplifies proofs in PR by condensing a detailed proof argument into one application of (R).

We say that two proof systems PR_1 and PR_2 are **equivalent** if for all formulas φ
$$\vdash_{PR_1} \varphi \text{ iff } \vdash_{PR_2} \varphi.$$

From now on we shall be concerned with the language, the formulas of which are either first-order formulas, called **assertions**, or **correctness formulas**, which are constructs of the form $\{p\} S \{q\}$, where p and q are assertions and S is a **while** program. Below we denote by $free(p)$ the set of free variables of the assertion p and by $var(t)$, $var(B)$, and $var(S)$ the set of variables that appear in the expression t, the Boolean expression B, and the program S, respectively.

We shall consider four proof systems concerned with the correctness formulas. They only differ in the used LOOP rule.

Proof system I denotes the customary proof system allowing us to prove partial correctness of **while** programs. Its axioms and proof rules, taken from our book [4], are listed in the Appendix. Its LOOP rule has the following form:

RULE LOOP I
$$\frac{\{p \wedge B\} S \{p\}}{\{p\} \text{ while } B \text{ do } S \text{ od } \{p \wedge \neg B\}}$$

In the proof system II this rule is replaced by

RULE LOOP II

$$\frac{\{p \wedge B\} \ S \ \{p\}, \\ \{p \wedge B \wedge t = z\} \ S \ \{t < z\}, \\ p \rightarrow t \geq 0}{\{p\} \ \textbf{while} \ B \ \textbf{do} \ S \ \textbf{od} \ \{p \wedge \neg B\}}$$

where t is an integer expression such that $var(t) \subseteq var(B) \cup var(S)$ and z is an integer variable that does not appear in p, B, t or S.

In the context of the LOOP rules discussed here, the assertion p is called the **loop invariant** and the expression t is called the **bound function**. It provides an estimate how many iterations the loop will still perform before termination. The restriction $var(t) \subseteq var(B) \cup var(S)$ is added to simplify the subsequent proofs.

In the proof system III the LOOP I rule is replaced by

RULE LOOP III

$$\frac{\{p \wedge B \wedge t = z\} \ S \ \{p \wedge t < z\}, \\ p \rightarrow t \geq 0}{\{p\} \ \textbf{while} \ B \ \textbf{do} \ S \ \textbf{od} \ \{p \wedge \neg B\}}$$

where t and z are as above.

Finally, we shall consider the following hybrid rule that combines provability in two proof systems.

RULE LOOP IV

$$\frac{\vdash_I \{p \wedge B\} \ S \ \{p\}, \\ \vdash_I \{p \wedge B \wedge t = z\} \ S \ \{t < z\}, \\ \{p \wedge B\} \ S \ \{\textbf{true}\}, \\ p \rightarrow t \geq 0}{\{p\} \ \textbf{while} \ B \ \textbf{do} \ S \ \textbf{od} \ \{p \wedge \neg B\}}$$

where t and z are as above.

Proof system IV is obtained from proof system I by replacing the LOOP I rule by the LOOP IV rule. The use of two forms of provability in the premises of this rule can be circumvented by the following modification of the notation. Denote the correctness formulas in the sense of partial correctness by $\{p\} \ S \ \{q\}$ and in the sense of total correctness by $[p] \ S \ [q]$. Then combine the proof system I with the proof system in which the axioms and proof rules of I except the LOOP I rule are rewritten using the $[p] \ S \ [q]$ syntax. Finally, add to this proof system the LOOP IV rewritten as follows:

$$\frac{\begin{array}{l}\{p \wedge B\}\ S\ \{p\},\\ \{p \wedge B \wedge t = z\}\ S\ \{t < z\},\\ [p \wedge B]\ S\ [\textbf{true}],\\ p \rightarrow t \geq 0\end{array}}{[p]\ \textbf{while}\ B\ \textbf{do}\ S\ \textbf{od}\ [p \wedge \neg B]}$$

where t and z are as above.

In what follows we use the original formulation of this rule, as it will not lead to any ambiguities.

The LOOP II rule was introduced in [16]. It corresponds to Dijkstra's modification of his weakest precondition semantics proposed in [9] and reproduced as [10]. It is difficult to determine where the LOOP III rule was introduced first. We mentioned it in [3]. It also appears in [17] on page 64 and in [1] on page 151.

The LOOP IV rule is new. It formalizes the following intuition. In order to prove the termination of a **while** loop it suffices to find a loop invariant and a bound function such that

(i) the loop invariant is maintained by each loop body execution, in the sense of partial correctness,
(ii) each loop body execution decreases the bound function, also in the sense of partial correctness,
(iii) the loop body terminates, and
(iv) the loop invariant implies that the bound function remains non-negative.

This rule supports modular reasoning about program correctness by separating the premises into partial correctness and termination properties. This is of particular relevance in the presence of nested loops, i.e., when the loop body contains inner loops. Then (i) establishes only the partial correctness of the loop body, whereas its termination is relegated to (iii). That the loop body can be iterated only finitely often is established in (ii) in combination with (iv). Note that for loop bodies without inner loops, partial and total correctness coincide. In this case the third premise, $\{p \wedge B\}\ S\ \{\textbf{true}\}$, can then be dropped, and we arrive at the LOOP II rule. So the hybrid form of this rule arises only for nested loops.

Note that the LOOP III rule resulted from combining the first two premises of the LOOP II into one. An analogous modification can be carried out in the case of the LOOP IV rule. In what follows we disregard this possibility, given that the resulting analysis is analogous to the one concerning the LOOP II and LOOP III rules.

In the proof-theoretic analysis of the LOOP II and III rules, we make use of the following two auxiliary rules, see also [4].

RULE CONJUNCTION

$$\frac{\{p_1\}\ S\ \{q_1\}, \{p_2\}\ S\ \{q_2\}}{\{p_1 \wedge p_2\}\ S\ \{q_1 \wedge q_2\}}$$

RULE ∃-INTRODUCTION

$$\frac{\{p\}\ S\ \{q\}}{\{\exists x : p\}\ S\ \{q\}}$$

where x does not occur in S or in $\textit{free}(q)$.

To reason about the LOOP IV rule we shall consider the following auxiliary rule that combines provability in two proof systems.

RULE HYBRID CONJUNCTION

$$\frac{\vdash_I \{p_1\}\ S\ \{q_1\},\ \{p_2\}\ S\ \{q_2\}}{\{p_1 \wedge p_2\}\ S\ \{q_1 \wedge q_2\}}$$

A special case of this rule is the following rule from [4].

RULE DECOMPOSITION

$$\frac{\vdash_I \{p\}\ S\ \{q\},\ \{p\}\ S\ \{\textbf{true}\}}{\{p\}\ S\ \{q\}}$$

3 Admissible Rules

The LOOP II and LOOP III rules look very much the same and it is obvious that they are in some sense equivalent. The following main theorem, that also discusses the LOOP IV rule, states this claim in the strongest way.

Theorem 1. *The loop rules are admissible in the other proof systems as follows:*

(i) The LOOP II rule is a admissible rule in the proof system III.
(ii) The LOOP III rule is a admissible rule in the proof system II.
(iii) The LOOP IV rule is a admissible rule in the proof system II.
(iv) The LOOP II rule is a admissible rule in the proof system IV.

The next lemma refers to the premises of the LOOP II and LOOP III rules. The names of the rules are abbreviated in the obvious way.

Lemma 1. *Suppose that z is an integer variable that does not appear in p, B, t or S. Then*

(i) $\{p \wedge B\}\ S\ \{p\},\ \{p \wedge B \wedge t = z\}\ S\ \{t < z\}$
$\vdash_{\{\text{CONJ, CONS}\}}$
$\{p \wedge B \wedge t = z\}\ S\ \{p \wedge t < z\}$.

(ii) $\{p \wedge B \wedge t = z\}\ S\ \{p \wedge t < z\}$
$\vdash_{\{\exists-\text{INTRO, CONS}\}}$
$\{p \wedge B\}\ S\ \{p\},\ \{p \wedge B \wedge t = z\}\ S\ \{t < z\}$.

Proof. (*i*) Immediate.

(*ii*) First note that by the CONSEQUENCE rule we can derive from

$$\{p \wedge B \wedge t = z\} \ S \ \{p \wedge t < z\}$$

both

$$\{p \wedge B \wedge t = z\} \ S \ \{p\}$$

and

$$\{p \wedge B \wedge t = z\} \ S \ \{t < z\}.$$

Next, by the ∃-INTRODUCTION rule, we derive from $\{p \wedge B \wedge t = z\} \ S \ \{p\}$

$$\{\exists z : p \wedge B \wedge t = z\} \ S \ \{p\}.$$

By the assumption about the variable z,

$$p \wedge B \to (p \wedge B \wedge \exists z : t = z) \to (\exists z : p \wedge B \wedge t = z),$$

so by the CONSEQUENCE rule, we derive $\{p \wedge B\} \ S \ \{p\}$, as desired. □

Next, we show how to dispense with the auxiliary rules. We shall need the following result, the proof of which we delay until Sect. 4.

Theorem 2. *The auxiliary rules are admissible in the following proof systems:*

(*i*) *The* ∃-INTRODUCTION *rule is admissible in the proof system* II.
(*ii*) *The* ∃-INTRODUCTION *rule is admissible in the proof system* III.
(*iii*) *The* CONJUNCTION *rule is admissible in the proof system* III.
(*iv*) *The* HYBRID CONJUNCTION *rule is admissible in the proof system* II, *that is,*
if $\vdash_\mathrm{I} \{p_1\} \ S \ \{q_1\}$ *and* $\vdash_\mathrm{II} \{p_2\} \ S \ \{q_2\}$, *then* $\vdash_\mathrm{II} \{p_1 \wedge p_2\} \ S \ \{q_1 \wedge q_2\}$.

We are now prepared for the proof of our main result.

Proof of Theorem 1.

(*i*) Suppose
$$\vdash_\mathrm{III} \{p \wedge B\} \ S \ \{p\},$$
$$\vdash_\mathrm{III} \{p \wedge B \wedge t = z\} \ S \ \{t < z\},$$
and that $p \to t \geq 0$ holds. By Lemma 1(*i*),
$$\vdash_{\mathrm{III} \cup \{\mathrm{CONJ, CONS}\}} \{p \wedge B \wedge t = z\} \ S \ \{p \wedge t < z\}.$$
By Theorem 2(*iii*) $\vdash_\mathrm{III} \{p \wedge B \wedge t = z\} \ S \ \{p \wedge t < z\}$, so by the LOOP III rule $\vdash_\mathrm{III} \{p\}$ **while** B **do** S **od** $\{p \wedge \neg B\}$.

(ii) Suppose
$$\vdash_{II} \{p \wedge B \wedge t = z\} \; S \; \{p \wedge t < z\}$$
and that $p \to t \geq 0$ holds. By Lemma 1(ii),
$$\vdash_{II \cup \{\exists\text{-INTRO, CONS}\}} \{p \wedge B\} \; S \; \{p\}$$
and
$$\vdash_{II \cup \{\exists\text{-INTRO, CONS}\}} \{p \wedge B \wedge t = z\} \; S \; \{t < z\}.$$
By Theorem 2(i) $\vdash_{II} \{p \wedge B\} \; S \; \{p\}$ and $\vdash_{II} \{p \wedge B \wedge t = z\} \; S \; \{t < z\}$, so by the LOOP II rule $\vdash_{II} \{p\}$ **while** B **do** S **od** $\{p \wedge \neg B\}$.

(iii) Suppose
$$\vdash_I \{p \wedge B\} \; S \; \{p\},$$
$$\vdash_I \{p \wedge B \wedge t = z\} \; S \; \{t < z\},$$
$$\vdash_{II} \{p \wedge B\} \; S \; \{\mathbf{true}\},$$
and that $p \to t \geq 0$ holds. By Theorem 2(iv) applied twice $\vdash_{II} \{p \wedge B\} \; S \; \{p\}$ and $\vdash_{II} \{p \wedge B \wedge t = z\} \; S \; \{t < z\}$.
So by the LOOP II rule $\vdash_{II} \{p\}$ **while** B **do** S **od** $\{p \wedge \neg B\}$.

(iv) Suppose
$$\vdash_{II} \{p \wedge B\} \; S \; \{p\},$$
$$\vdash_{II} \{p \wedge B \wedge t = z\} \; S \; \{t < z\},$$
and that $p \to t \geq 0$ holds. By omitting everywhere in these two proofs the second premise of the LOOP II rule whenever this rule is applied, we get $\vdash_I \{p \wedge B\} \; S \; \{p\}$ and $\vdash_I \{p \wedge B \wedge t = z\} \; S \; \{t < z\}$. Further, by the CONSEQUENCE rule $\vdash_{II} \{p \wedge B\} \; S \; \{\mathbf{true}\}$.
So by the LOOP IV rule $\vdash_{IV} \{p\}$ **while** B **do** S **od** $\{p \wedge \neg B\}$. □

Corollary 1. *The proof systems II, III, and IV are equivalent.*

Assume now that some notion of semantics of programs and assertions is given that includes the concept of a state, execution of a program, the notion of a state satisfying an assertion, and the truth of an assertion. We write then $\models \{p\} \; S \; \{q\}$ to denote the fact that every execution of S that starts in a state satisfying p terminates in a state satisfying q and say then that $\{p\} \; S \; \{q\}$ is **true**. (Thus we are referring to **total correctness**.) Next, we say then that a proof rule

$$\frac{\varphi_1, \ldots, \varphi_k}{\varphi}$$

is **sound** if $\models \varphi_1, \ldots, \models \varphi_k$ implies $\models \varphi$.

In [4] we proved that the LOOP II rule is sound, while in [17] it was proved that the LOOP III is sound. A natural question arises whether soundness of one of these rules can be directly deduced from the soundness of the other rule. This can be accomplished by modifying the claims of Lemma 1 as follows.

Lemma 2. *Suppose that z is an integer variable that does not appear in p, B, t or S. Then*

(i) *If $\models \{p \wedge B\}\ S\ \{p\}$ and $\models \{p \wedge B \wedge t = z\}\ S\ \{t < z\}$,
then $\models \{p \wedge B \wedge t = z\}\ S\ \{p \wedge t < z\}$.*
(ii) *If $\models \{p \wedge B \wedge t = z\}\ S\ \{p \wedge t < z\}$,
then $\models \{p \wedge B\}\ S\ \{p\}$ and $\models \{p \wedge B \wedge t = z\}\ S\ \{t < z\}$.*

Proof. It is a direct consequence of the fact that the proof rules used in Lemma 1 are sound. Thus each time one of these rules is applied, truth of the correctness formulas is preserved. □

Suppose now that the LOOP II rule is sound. To prove the soundness of the LOOP III rule assume that its premises are true. Then by Lemma 2(ii) the premises of the LOOP II rule are true, so by its soundness the conclusion of both rules is true. The same argument shows that soundness of the LOOP III rule implies soundness of the LOOP II rule.

We conclude this discussion by two remarks. First, notice that the last premise of each of the LOOP rules II, III and IV can also be modified, by considering in each case the implication $p \wedge B \to t \geq 0$ instead of $p \to t \geq 0$. It is easy to see that such a modification does not affect provability in the considered proof systems II, III, and IV. Indeed, an application of the original rule with a bound function t is also a valid application of the modified rule and an application of the modified rule with a bound function t can be replaced by an application of the original rule with the bound function **if B then t else 0 fi**.

Finally, for the rules LOOP II–IV we assumed that the bound function t satisfies the restriction $var(t) \subseteq var(B) \cup var(S)$. This allows for the proof of admissibility of the ∃-INTRODUCTION rule in Theorem 2, which in turn is used via Lemma 1 in the proof of Theorem 1 and thus in the proof of the equivalence result stated in Corollary 1. In future we will investigate how to avoid this restriction. We see that the equivalence of the different proof systems for total correctness depends very subtly on the intricate interplay of the loop rules with the admissibility of standard auxiliary rules of Hoare's logic, which requires further investigation.

4 Proof of Theorem 2

To prove this theorem we first establish two lemmas that provide additional information about the proofs in the considered proof systems.

Lemma 3. *Let PR be one of the proof systems I, II, III, or IV. If $PR \vdash \varphi$, there exists a proof of φ in PR with exactly one final application of the CONSEQUENCE rule.*

Proof. Since implication → is reflexive, we can always add to a given proof in PR one final application of the CONSEQUENCE rule. Since implication is transitive, successive applications of the CONSEQUENCE rule in a proof in PR can be condensed into one application. □

Lemma 4. *Let PR be one of the proof systems I, II, III, or IV.*

(i) Suppose that $\vdash_{PR} \{p\} S_1; S_2 \{q\}$. Then for some assertion r

$$\vdash_{PR} \{p\} S_1 \{r\} \text{ and } \vdash_{PR} \{r\} S_2 \{q\}.$$

(ii) Suppose that $\vdash_{PR} \{p\}$ if B then S_1 else S_2 fi $\{q\}$. Then

$$\vdash_{PR} \{p \wedge B\} S_1 \{q\} \text{ and } \vdash_{PR} \{p \wedge \neg B\} S_2 \{q\}.$$

Proof. (i) By Lemma 3, the considered correctness formula was proved using the COMPOSITION rule followed by a single application of the CONSEQUENCE rule. So for some assertions p_1, r, q_1, we have

$$\vdash_{PR} \{p_1\} S_1 \{r\} \text{ and } \vdash_{PR} \{r\} S_2 \{q_1\}$$

and the implications $p \to p_1$ and $q_1 \to q$ hold. We now get the claim by the CONSEQUENCE rule.

(ii) The argument is analogous as in (ii). □

We now turn to the proof of Theorem 2, repeating the four statements at the beginning of each proof part.

Proof. (i) The ∃-INTRODUCTION rule is admissible in the proof system II.

We proceed by induction on the structure of S and consider a proof of $\{p\} S \{q\}$ in the proof system II, where the last two steps involve an axiom or a rule of the proof system II for the top-level operator of the program S, followed by one final application of the CONSEQUENCE rule according to Lemma 3. In all cases we assume that $x \notin var(S) \cup free(q)$.

- Case $S \equiv u := t$. Thus suppose $\vdash_{II} \{p\} S \{q\}$. Then for some assertion q_1,

$$\vdash_{II} \{q_1[u := t]\} S \{q_1\}$$

by the ASSIGNMENT axiom, and the implications $p \to q_1[u := t]$ and $q_1 \to q$ hold. We assumed that $x \notin var(S)$, so $x \not\equiv u$. By the assignment axiom, also

$$\{(\exists x : q_1)[u := t]\} S \{\exists x : q_1\}.$$

Note that the implications $\exists x : p \to \exists x : (q_1[u := t])$ and $\exists x : q_1 \to \exists x : q$ hold. Since $x \not\equiv u$ and $x \notin free(q)$, also the implications

$$\exists x : (q_1[u := t]) \to (\exists x : q_1)[u := t] \text{ and } (\exists x : q) \to q$$

hold. So the CONSEQUENCE rule yields $\vdash_{II} \{\exists x : p\} S \{q\}$, as desired.

- *Case* $S \equiv S_1; S_2$. Thus suppose $\vdash_{II} \{p\} S \{q\}$. By Lemma 4(*i*) for some assertion r,
$$\vdash_{II} \{p\} S_1 \{r\} \text{ and } \vdash_{II} \{r\} S_2 \{q\}.$$
Since $r \to \exists x : r$, the CONSEQUENCE rule yields $\vdash_{II} \{p\} S_1 \{\exists x : r\}$. Since $x \notin \textit{free}(\exists x : r)$, the induction hypothesis yields $\vdash_{II} \{\exists x : p\} S_1 \{\exists x : r\}$. Since $x \notin \textit{free}(q)$, by the induction hypothesis, also $\vdash_{II} \{\exists x : r\} S_2 \{q\}$. Thus by the COMPOSITION rule, $\vdash_{II} \{\exists x : p\} S \{q\}$, as desired.

- *Case* $S \equiv$ **if** B **then** S_1 **else** S_2 **fi**. Thus suppose $\vdash_{II} \{p\} S \{q\}$. Then by Lemma 4(*ii*),
$$\vdash_{II} \{p \wedge B\} S_1 \{q\} \text{ and } \vdash_{II} \{p \wedge \neg B\} S_2 \{q\}.$$
By the induction hypothesis,
$$\vdash_{II} \{\exists x : (p \wedge B)\} S_1 \{q\} \text{ and } \vdash_{II} \{\exists x : (p \wedge \neg B)\} S_2 \{q\}.$$
Since $x \notin \textit{var}(B)$, the CONSEQUENCE rule yields
$$\vdash_{II} \{(\exists x : p) \wedge B\} S_1 \{q\} \text{ and } \vdash_{II} \{(\exists x : p) \wedge \neg B\} S_2 \{q\}.$$
By the CONDITIONAL rule, $\vdash_{II} \{\exists x : p\} S \{q\}$, as desired.

- *Case* $S \equiv$ **while** B **do** S_0 **od**. Thus suppose $\vdash_{II} \{p\} S \{q\}$. By the assumption about t, we have $x \notin \textit{var}(t)$ and without loss of generality we can assume $x \neq z$. Then for some assertion p_0 and an appropriate bound function t and variable z,
$$\vdash_{II} \{p_0 \wedge B\} S_0 \{p_0\},$$
$$\vdash_{II} \{p_0 \wedge B \wedge t = z\} S_0 \{t < z\},$$
and the implications $p \to p_0$, $p_0 \to t \geq 0$, $(p_0 \wedge \neg B) \to q$ hold. Since $p_0 \to \exists x : p_0$, the CONSEQUENCE rule yields
$$\vdash_{II} \{p_0 \wedge B\} S_0 \{\exists x : p_0\}.$$
By the induction hypothesis, the assumption about x, and the CONSEQUENCE rule both
$$\vdash_{II} \{(\exists x : p_0) \wedge B\} S_0 \{\exists x : p_0\}$$
and
$$\vdash_{II} \{(\exists x : p_0) \wedge B \wedge t = z\} S_0 \{t < z\}.$$
So the LOOP II rule yields
$$\vdash_{II} \{\exists x : p_0\} S \{(\exists x : p_0) \wedge \neg B\}.$$

Further, since $(p_0 \land \neg B) \to q$ holds and $x \notin (\mathit{free}(q) \cup \mathit{var}(B))$, also the implication $((\exists x : p_0) \land \neg B) \to q$ holds. So a final application of the CONSEQUENCE rule yields $\vdash_{II} \{\exists x : p\}\ S\ \{q\}$, as desired.

(ii) The ∃-INTRODUCTION rule is admissible in the proof system III.
Again, we proceed by induction on the structure of S, but now consider a proof of $\{p\}\ S\ \{q\}$ in the proof system III, where the last two steps involve the axiom or rule of the proof system III for the top-level operator of the program S, followed by one final application of the CONSEQUENCE rule according to Lemma 3.
Except for the **while** statement, all cases are analogous, with $\vdash_{II}$ replaced by $\vdash_{III}$. The case of the **while** statement differs from (i) only in that one now considers just one correctness formula in the premise of the LOOP III rule instead of two. Since the details are the same, we omit them.

(iii) The CONJUNCTION rule is admissible in the proof system III.
We proceed by induction on the structure of S and for $i = 1, 2$ consider proofs of $\{p_i\}S\{q_i\}$ in the proof system III, where the last two steps involve the axiom or rule of the proof system III for the top-level operator of the program S, followed by one final application of the CONSEQUENCE rule according to Lemma 3.

- *Case* $S \equiv u := t$. Thus suppose $\vdash_{III} \{p_1\}\ S\ \{q_1\}$ and $\vdash_{III} \{p_2\}\ S\ \{q_2\}$. Then for some assertions q_{01} and q_{02}, by the ASSIGNMENT axiom, both

$$\vdash_{III} \{q_{01}[u := t]\}\ S\ \{q_{01}\} \quad \text{and} \quad \vdash_{III} \{q_{02}[u := t]\}\ S\ \{q_{02}\},$$

and the implications $p_1 \to q_{01}[u := t]$, $q_{01} \to q_1$ and $p_2 \to q_{02}[u := t]$, $q_{02} \to q_2$ hold. The ASSIGNMENT axiom also yields

$$\{q_{01}[u := t] \land q_{02}[u := t]\}\ S\ \{q_{01} \land q_{02}\}.$$

By the implications $(p_1 \land p_2) \to (q_{01}[u := t] \land q_{02}[u := t])$ and $(q_{01} \land q_{02}) \to (q_1 \land q_2)$, the CONSEQUENCE rule yields

$$\vdash_{III} \{p_1 \land p_2\}\ S\ \{q_1 \land q_2\},$$

as desired.

- *Case* $S \equiv S_1;\ S_2$. Thus suppose $\vdash_{III} \{p_1\}\ S\ \{q_1\}$ and $\vdash_{III} \{p_2\}\ S\ \{q_2\}$. Then by Lemma 4(i) for some assertions r_1 and r_2

$$\vdash_{III} \{p_1\}\ S_1\ \{r_1\} \quad \text{and} \quad \vdash_{III} \{r_1\}\ S_2\ \{q_1\},$$

$$\vdash_{III} \{p_2\}\ S_1\ \{r_2\} \quad \text{and} \quad \vdash_{III} \{r_2\}\ S_2\ \{q_2\}.$$

By the induction hypothesis,

$$\vdash_{III} \{p_1 \land p_2\}\ S_1\ \{r_1 \land r_2\} \quad \text{and} \quad \vdash_{III} \{r_1 \land r_2\}\ S_1\ \{q_1 \land q_2\},$$

so by the COMPOSITION rule,

$$\vdash_{III} \{p_1 \wedge p_2\} \; S_1; \; S_2 \; \{q_1 \wedge q_2\},$$

as desired.

- *Case* $S \equiv$ **if** B **then** S_1 **else** S_2 **fi**. Thus suppose $\vdash_{III} \{p_1\} \; S \; \{q_1\}$ and $\vdash_{III} \{p_2\} \; S \; \{q_2\}$. Then by Lemma 4(*ii*),

$$\vdash_{III} \{p_1 \wedge B\} \; S_1 \; \{q_1\} \quad \text{and} \quad \vdash_{III} \{p_1 \wedge \neg B\} \; S_2 \; \{q_1\},$$

$$\vdash_{III} \{p_2 \wedge B\} \; S_1 \; \{q_2\} \quad \text{and} \quad \vdash_{III} \{p_2 \wedge \neg B\} \; S_2 \; \{q_2\}.$$

By the induction hypothesis,

$$\vdash_{III} \{p_1 \wedge p_2 \wedge B\} \; S_1 \; \{q_1 \wedge q_2\}$$

and

$$\vdash_{III} \{p_1 \wedge p_2 \wedge \neg B\} \; S_2 \; \{q_1 \wedge q_2\}.$$

So by the CONDITIONAL rule,

$$\vdash_{III} \{p_1 \wedge p_2\} \; \textbf{if } B \textbf{ then } S_1 \textbf{ else } S_2 \textbf{ fi } \{q_1 \wedge q_2\},$$

as desired.

- *Case* $S \equiv$ **while** B **do** S_0 **od**. Suppose $\vdash_{III} \{p_1\} \; S \; \{q_1\}$ and $\vdash_{III} \{p_2\} \; S \; \{q_2\}$. Then for some assertions p_{01}, p_{02}, appropriate bound functions t_1, t_2 and variables z_1, z_2,

$$\vdash_{III} \{p_{01} \wedge B \wedge t_1 = z_1\} \; S_0 \; \{p_{01} \wedge t_1 < z_1\},$$

$$\vdash_{III} \{p_{02} \wedge B \wedge t_2 = z_2\} \; S_0 \; \{p_{02} \wedge t_2 < z_2\},$$

the implications $p_{01} \to t_1 \geq 0$, $p_1 \to p_{01}$, $(p_{01} \wedge \neg B) \to q_1$ and $p_{02} \to t_2 \geq 0$, $p_2 \to p_{02}$, $(p_{02} \wedge \neg B) \to q_2$ hold.
Without loss of generality we can assume that $z_2 \notin \{z_1\} \cup \mathit{free}(p_{01})$. By the induction hypothesis,

$$\vdash_{III} \{p_{01} \wedge p_{02} \wedge B \wedge t_1 = z_1 \wedge t_2 = z_2\} \; S_0 \; \{p_{01} \wedge p_{02} \wedge t_1 < z_1 \wedge t_2 < z_2\}.$$

It suffices to consider one bound function, say t_1. Formally, we show this as follows. By the CONSEQUENCE rule,

$$\vdash_{III} \{p_{01} \wedge p_{02} \wedge B \wedge t_1 = z_1 \wedge t_2 = z_2\} \; S_0 \; \{p_{01} \wedge p_{02} \wedge t_1 < z_1\}.$$

Now, an application of the ∃-INTRODUCTION rule, which is admissible in the proof system III according to part (*ii*) of this theorem, followed by an application of the CONSEQUENCE rule yields

$$\vdash_{III} \{p_{01} \wedge p_{02} \wedge B \wedge t_1 = z_1 \wedge \exists z_2 : t_2 = z_2\} \; S_0 \; \{p_{01} \wedge p_{02} \wedge t_1 < z_1\}.$$

A further application of the CONSEQUENCE rule yields

$$\vdash_{III} \{p_{01} \wedge p_{02} \wedge B \wedge t_1 = z_1\} \; S_0 \; \{p_{01} \wedge p_{02} \wedge t_1 < z_1\}.$$

Then by the LOOP III rule,

$$\vdash_{III} \{p_{01} \wedge p_{02}\} \textbf{ while } B \textbf{ do } S_0 \textbf{ od } \{p_{01} \wedge p_{02} \wedge \neg B\}.$$

The implications above yield $(p_1 \wedge p_2) \to (p_{01} \wedge p_{02})$ and $(p_{01} \wedge p_{02} \wedge \neg B) \to (q_1 \wedge q_2)$. Thus by the CONSEQUENCE rule,

$$\vdash_{III} \{p_1 \wedge p_2\} \textbf{ while } B \textbf{ do } S_0 \textbf{ od } \{q_1 \wedge q_2\},$$

as desired.

(iv) The HYBRID CONJUNCTION rule is admissible in the proof system II, that is, if $\vdash_I \{p_1\} \; S \; \{q_1\}$ and $\vdash_{II} \{p_2\} \; S \; \{q_2\}$, then $\vdash_{II} \{p_1 \wedge p_2\} \; S \; \{q_1 \wedge q_2\}$. The proof is analogous to the proof of (iii). The only case that is somewhat different is the one concerned with the **while** statement. So we only deal with

- *Case* $S \equiv$ **while** B **do** S_0 **od**. Suppose $\vdash_I \{p_1\} \; S \; \{q_1\}$ and $\vdash_{II} \{p_2\} \; S \; \{q_2\}$. Then for some assertions p_{01}, p_{02} and an appropriate bound function t and variable z,

$$\vdash_I \{p_{01} \wedge B\} \; S_0 \; \{p_{01}\},$$
$$\vdash_{II} \{p_{02} \wedge B\} \; S_0 \; \{p_{02}\},$$
$$\vdash_{II} \{p_{02} \wedge B \wedge t = z\} \; S_0 \; \{t < z\},$$

and the implications

$$p_1 \to p_{01}, \; (p_{01} \wedge \neg B) \to q_1, \; p_{02} \to t \geq 0, \; p_2 \to p_{02}, \; (p_{02} \wedge \neg B) \to q_2$$

hold. By the induction hypothesis,

$$\vdash_{II} \{p_{01} \wedge p_{02} \wedge B\} \; S_0 \; \{p_{01} \wedge p_{02}\},$$

and by the induction hypothesis combined with the CONSEQUENCE rule,

$$\vdash_{II} \{p_{01} \wedge p_{02} \wedge B \wedge t = z\} \; S_0 \; \{t < z\}.$$

So by the LOOP II rule,

$$\vdash_{II} \{p_{01} \wedge p_{02}\} \textbf{ while } B \textbf{ do } S_0 \textbf{ od } \{p_{01} \wedge p_{02} \wedge \neg B\}.$$

The implications above yield $(p_1 \wedge p_2) \to (p_{01} \wedge p_{02})$ and $(p_{01} \wedge p_{02} \wedge \neg B) \to (q_1 \wedge q_2)$. Thus by the CONSEQUENCE rule,

$$\vdash_{II} \{p_1 \wedge p_2\} \textbf{ while } B \textbf{ do } S_0 \textbf{ od } \{q_1 \wedge q_2\},$$

as desired.

□

5 Representing Proofs

5.1 Proof Outlines

Even though the LOOP rules II, III, and IV are equivalent in the sense of Theorem 1 or Corollary 1, they lead to different proofs of total correctness of **while** programs. The idea behind the LOOP II rule is to establish that p is a loop invariant and t is a bound function separately, while in the LOOP III rule both facts are established simultaneously. So the LOOP II rule looks more convenient when we want to strengthen a proof of partial correctness to a proof of total correctness: it suffices to establish two new premises concerned with the bound function t. In turn, the LOOP IV rule allows us to split the proof obligations even further, by identifying the property actually needed to be proved in terms of total correctness. This, as already mentioned, allows one to support modular reasoning.

However, matters change when we want to represent the proofs in the resulting proof systems II, III, and IV in a convenient form. Given that these proofs deal with structured programs, their most natural representation consists of so-called ***proof outlines***, a notion introduced in [16]. Informally, it is a proof representation in the form of a program annotated by the assertions arising from the appropriate rule applications. Such a representation is possible thanks to the fact that the proof rules are syntax directed. Proof outlines were introduced in [16] in order to reason about correctness of parallel programs, where they served to establish so-called interference freedom among the proofs of the component programs. However, they are also very useful as a representation of correctness proofs of sequential programs and, when some obvious assertions are deleted, as a program documentation.

Now, given that the LOOP II and IV rules have more than one premise consisting of a correctness formula, it is difficult to employ a single proof outline to represent a proof involving any of these rules. This is not the case with the LOOP III rule. To illustrate this point recall first that the proof outlines are defined by induction on the program structure. We only focus on the crucial formation rule concerned with the **while** statement. For the proof system I the following formation rule was used in [4]:

$$\frac{\{p \wedge B\}\ S^*\ \{p\}}{\{\mathbf{inv}: p\}\ \mathbf{while}\ B\ \mathbf{do}\ \{p \wedge B\}\ S^*\ \{p\}\ \mathbf{od}\ \{p \wedge \neg B\}}$$

where S^* is the program S annotated with some assertions.

For the proof system II we used in [4] the following formation rule:

$$\frac{\{p \wedge B\}\ S^*\ \{p\},\ \{p \wedge B \wedge t = z\}\ S^{**}\ \{t < z\},\ p \to t \geq 0}{\{\mathbf{inv}:p\}\{\mathbf{bd}:t\}\ \mathbf{while}\ B\ \mathbf{do}\ \{p \wedge B\}\ S^*\ \{p\}\ \mathbf{od}\ \{p \wedge \neg B\}}$$

where S^* and S^{**} are annotations of the program S with some assertions, t is an integer expression and z is an integer variable not occurring in p, t, B or S^*.[2]

Finally, for the proof system III we introduce the following formation rule:

$$\frac{\{p \wedge B \wedge t = z\}\ S^*\ \{p \wedge t < z\},\ p \to t \geq 0}{\{\mathbf{inv}:p\}\{\mathbf{bd}:t\}\ \mathbf{while}\ B\ \mathbf{do}\ \{p \wedge B \wedge t = z\}\ S^*\ \{p \wedge t < z\}\ \mathbf{od}\ \{p \wedge \neg B\}}$$

where t and z are as above.

For a moment we defer the discussion of proof outlines for the proof system IV. One can easily prove by induction that each proof outline for the proof system I corresponds to a proof in this proof system. For example, if by the induction hypothesis the proof outline $\{p \wedge B\}\ S^*\ \{p\}$ corresponds to a proof of $\{p \wedge B\}\ S\ \{p\}$ in I, then the proof outline

$$\{\mathbf{inv}:p\}\ \mathbf{while}\ B\ \mathbf{do}\ \{p \wedge B\}\ S^*\ \{p\}\ \mathbf{od}\ \{p \wedge \neg B\}$$

corresponds to a proof of $\{p\}\ \mathbf{while}\ B\ \mathbf{do}\ S\ \mathbf{od}\ \{p \wedge \neg B\}$ in I, which is obtained by applying to $\{p \wedge B\}\ S\ \{p\}$ the LOOP I rule.

However, this property fails to hold for the proof outlines for the proof system II, because the second proof outline used in the premise of the formation rule is dropped. As a consequence, the proof outline for the **while** statement does not allow one to reconstruct the proof of $\{p\}\ \mathbf{while}\ B\ \mathbf{do}\ S\ \mathbf{od}\ \{p \wedge \neg B\}$ in the proof system II.

5.2 Proofs Using the LOOP III Rule

By contrast, each proof outline for the proof system III involving the LOOP III rule does correspond to a proof in this proof system, because all assertions used are retained. In other words, from each proof outline for the proof system III a proof in this system can be extracted.

To illustrate this point consider the following program S_N involving nested loops, suggested to us by Tobias Nipkow (private communication):

$$S_N \equiv \mathbf{while}\ i < n\ \mathbf{do}$$
$$\quad j := i;$$
$$\quad \mathbf{while}\ 0 < j\ \mathbf{do}$$
$$\quad\quad j := j - 1$$

---

[2] In [4], in contrast to [3], there is a typo and S^{**} is mentioned here instead of S^*.

$$\textbf{od} ;$$
$$i := i+1$$
$$\textbf{od}$$

where i, j, n are integer variables.

We would like to prove that it terminates for all initial states. To this end, we prove the correctness formula $\{\textbf{true}\}\ S_N\ \{\textbf{true}\}$ in the proof system III. In Fig. 1, we show the proof in the form of a proof outline, instantiating the corresponding formation rule for the **while** statement in proof system III with the following loop invariants and bound functions for the outer and the inner loop, respectively:

$$p \equiv \textbf{true} \text{ and } t \equiv max(n-i, 0) ,$$

$$p \equiv n - i = z_1 \wedge z_1 > 0 \text{ and } t \equiv max(j, 0) .$$

Note that in a proof outline adjacent assertions stand for implications according to an application of the CONSEQUENCE rule. For instance, the assertion in line 3 implies that of line 4. Assignments are treated by backward substitution according to the ASSIGNMENT axiom. For instance, the assignment $i := i+1$ in line 18 is dealt with by substituting i by $i+1$ in the assertion in line 19, yielding the assertion in line 17.

```
1       {inv : true} {bd : max(n − i, 0)}
2       while i < n do
3           {true ∧ i < n ∧ max(n − i, 0) = z₁}
4           {n − i = z₁ ∧ z₁ > 0}
5           j := i;
6           {n − i = z₁ ∧ z₁ > 0}
7           {inv : n − i = z₁ ∧ z₁ > 0} {bd : max(j, 0)}
8           while 0 < j do
9               {n − i = z₁ ∧ z₁ > 0 ∧ 0 < j ∧ max(j, 0) = z₂}
10              {n − i = z₁ ∧ z₁ > 0 ∧ j = z₂ ∧ z₂ > 0}
11              {n − i = z₁ ∧ z₁ > 0 ∧ j − 1 < z₂ ∧ z₂ > 0}
12              j := j − 1
13              {n − i = z₁ ∧ z₁ > 0 ∧ j < z₂ ∧ z₂ > 0}
14              {n − i = z₁ ∧ z₁ > 0 ∧ max(j, 0) < z₂}
15          od;
16          {n − i = z₁ ∧ z₁ > 0 ∧ ¬(0 < j)}
17          {n − (i + 1) < z₁ ∧ z₁ > 0}
18          i := i + 1
19          {n − i < z₁ ∧ z₁ > 0}
20          {true ∧ max(n − i, 0) < z₁}
21      od
22      {true ∧ ¬(i < n)}
23      {true}
```

Fig. 1. Proof outline for $\{\textbf{true}\}\ S_N\ \{\textbf{true}\}$ in the proof system III. The line numbers have been added for reference only.

5.3 Proofs Using the LOOP IV Rule

Let us now move on to a discussion of the proofs involving the LOOP IV rule. This rule, just like the LOOP II rule, uses more than one correctness formula as a premise. As a result, it shares with the LOOP II rule the problem that it is not clear how to faithfully represent correctness proofs using a single proof outline. Indeed, each of the first three premises calls for a separate proof outline.

But it is not difficult to see that this would give rise to largely overlapping proof outlines. So, instead, we propose an alternative approach in which we replace these overlapping proof outlines referring to the proof system IV by an interrelated *set* of proof outlines in the sense of *partial correctness*, so referring to the proof system I.

For a given correctness formula $\{p\}\ S\ \{q\}$ to be proved in the proof system IV this set is defined as follows. First, we have a proof outline $\{p\}\ S^*\ \{q\}$ that employs the first formation rule given above and thus represents a proof of partial correctness of $\{p\}\ S\ \{q\}$ in I.

Next, for each occurrence of a loop **while** B **do** S_0 **od** in S, we have a proof outline $\{p_0 \wedge B \wedge t = z\}\ S_0^*\ \{t < z\}$, which represents a proof of partial correctness of $\{p_0 \wedge B \wedge t = z\}\ S_0\ \{t < z\}$ in I. Here p_0 is the invariant associated with the occurrence of the loop **while** B **do** S_0 **od** in the above proof outline $\{p\}\ S^*\ \{q\}$ and t is some bound function t such that $p_0 \to t \geq 0$. We omit the proof that existence of such a set of proof outlines in the sense of partial correctness ensures a proof of the corresponding correctness formula in the proof system IV. Intuitively, the use of the above proof outlines for *each* loop occurrence in S ensures by structural induction the third premise of the LOOP IV rule, so $\{p \wedge B\}\ S\ \{\mathbf{true}\}$ in the sense of total correctness.

We illustrate how such a set of proof outlines can be used to establish the proof of the correctness formula $\{\mathbf{true}\}\ S_N\ \{\mathbf{true}\}$ for Nipkow's program S_N in the proof system IV. We skip the trivial proof outline $\{\mathbf{true}\}\ S_N^*\ \{\mathbf{true}\}$, which corresponds to a proof of partial correctness of $\{\mathbf{true}\}\ S_N\ \{\mathbf{true}\}$. Let S_0 denote the body of the outer loop of S_N. Given the bound function $max(n-i, 0)$, Fig. 2 shows the proof outline which corresponds to a proof of partial correctness of

$$\{\mathbf{true} \wedge i < n \wedge max(n-i, 0) = z\}\ S_0\ \{max(n-i, 0) < z\},$$

assuming that the trivial invariant **true** is associated with this loop in the proof outline $\{\mathbf{true}\}\ S_N^*\ \{\mathbf{true}\}$. Note that $\mathbf{true} \to max(n-i, 0) \geq 0$.

Finally, the LOOP IV rule requires us to prove termination of S_0. This boils down to establish the termination of the inner loop. To this end, we introduce the bound function $max(j, 0)$. Note that $\mathbf{true} \to max(j, 0) \geq 0$. Figure 3 shows the proof outline which corresponds to a proof of partial correctness of

$$\{\mathbf{true} \wedge 0 < j \wedge max(j, 0) = z\}\ j := j - 1\ \{max(j, 0) < z\}.$$

6 Practical Applications

Research on program verification has entered practice most visibly by the use of assertions as annotations of programs and program interfaces that remain to be

$$\{\text{true} \wedge i < n \wedge max(n-i,0) = z\}$$
$$\{n - i = z \wedge z > 0\}$$
$$j := i;$$
$$\{n - i = z \wedge z > 0\}$$
$$\{\text{inv} : n - i = z \wedge z > 0\}$$
$$\quad \text{while } 0 < j \text{ do}$$
$$\quad\quad \{n - i = z \wedge z > 0\}$$
$$\quad\quad j := j - 1$$
$$\quad\quad \{n - i = z \wedge z > 0\}$$
$$\text{od};$$
$$\{n - i = z \wedge z > 0 \wedge \neg(0 < j)\}$$
$$\{n - (i+1) < z \wedge z > 0\}$$
$$i := i + 1$$
$$\{n - i < z \wedge z > 0\}$$
$$\{max(n - i, 0) < z\}$$

Fig. 2. Proof outline for $\{\text{true} \wedge i < n \wedge max(n-i,0) = z\}$ S_0 $\{max(n-i,0) < z\}$ in the proof system I.

$$\{\text{true} \wedge 0 < j \wedge max(j,0) = z\}$$
$$\{j - 1 < z \wedge z > 0\}$$
$$j := j - 1$$
$$\{j < z \wedge z > 0\}$$
$$\{max(j, 0) < z\}$$

Fig. 3. Proof outline for $\{\text{true} \wedge 0 < j \wedge max(j,0) = z\}$ $j := j - 1$ $\{max(j,0) < z\}$ in the proof system I.

implemented. This can be seen in the paradigm of *design by contract* introduced by Bertrand Meyer for his object-oriented programming language Eiffel [15]: program design starts with a specification in terms of assertions, the contract, against which the program is to be checked either statically by means of a proof or dynamically at runtime.

This paradigm has been adopted and extended to other programming languages, in particular to Java. The *Java Modeling Language* (JML) enriches Java with facilities for writing assertions (pre- and postconditions as well as class invariants) but also with a concept of abstract state space (using so-called model variables) [13][3]. For assertions, JML uses Java's Boolean expressions extended by universal and existential quantifiers. They are directly written into the Java source code in the form of comments starting with the symbols //@ (so that the annotated source code may be processed by both an ordinary Java compiler and a specialized JML tool).

JML is designed to deal with the specification of Java classes, but here we focus on loops. JML provides the designated keywords **requires** for specifying the precondition, **ensures** for the postcondition, **loop_invariant**, and

---

[3] See also https://www.cs.ucf.edu/$\sim$leavens/JML/index.shtml.

loop_decreases for the bound function. To enhance readability, the pre- and postcondition as well as the loop invariant may be split into several assertions, each one stated after a separate repeated keyword[4]. An annotated Java program corresponds to a proof outline as discussed here, but restricted to the essential assertions for each loop (pre- and postcondition, loop invariant and bound function).

Also for the programming language C, a standardized specification language for C programs, called ACSL and inspired by JML, has been designed, see for instance [6][5].

In this paper, we have shown that the rules LOOP II-IV for proving termination of loops are equivalent. With respect to the number of premises LOOP III is clearly the simplest rule for proving termination. However, a proof using this rule in general requires more complex assertions because of the accumulation of the specifications of the bound functions of inner loops. This can be seen in the proof outline given in Fig. 1, in which the assertions inside the inner loop refer to both z_1 and z_2, where z_1 is the variable freezing the value of the bound function $max(n-i, 0)$ of the outer loop and z_2 is the variable freezing the value of the bound function $max(j, 0)$ of the inner loop. The reason is that in this proof outline we need to establish that the value of the bound function of the outer loop is not affected by the inner loop and that the value of the other bound function decreases.

The LOOP IV rule allows for a separate proof of termination of each loop, which does not require the specification of bound functions for the inner loops. Thus we have a trade off between a single complex proof and a number of simpler proofs, where complexity is measured by the size of the assertions. What works best in practice depends on the particular program structure.

Conflict of Interest. The author(s) has no competing interests to declare that are relevant to the content of this manuscript.

Appendix

The proof system I consists of the following axioms and rules:

AXIOM SKIP
$$\{p\}\ skip\ \{p\}$$

AXIOM ASSIGNMENT
$$\{p[u := t]\}\ u := t\ \{p\}$$

RULE COMPOSITION
$$\frac{\{p\}\ S_1\ \{r\}, \{r\}\ S_2\ \{q\}}{\{p\}\ S_1;\ S_2\ \{q\}}$$

---

[4] For an example, see https://www.openjml.org/examples/binary-search.html.
[5] See also https://frama-c.com/download/acsl-1.20.pdf.

RULE CONDITIONAL

$$\frac{\{p \wedge B\}\ S_1\ \{q\}, \{p \wedge \neg B\}\ S_2\ \{q\}}{\{p\}\ \textbf{if}\ B\ \textbf{then}\ S_1\ \textbf{else}\ S_2\ \textbf{fi}\ \{q\}}$$

RULE LOOP I

$$\frac{\{p \wedge B\}\ S\ \{p\}}{\{p\}\ \textbf{while}\ B\ \textbf{do}\ S\ \textbf{od}\ \{p \wedge \neg B\}}$$

RULE CONSEQUENCE

$$\frac{p \to p_1, \{p_1\}\ S\ \{q_1\}, q_1 \to q}{\{p\}\ S\ \{q\}}$$

Additionally, given an interpretation $\mathcal{I}$ for the underlying first-order language, we use as axioms all assertions that are true in $\mathcal{I}$. These assertions are used as premises in the CONSEQUENCE rule.

References

1. Almeida, J.B., Frade, M.J., Pinto, J.S., de Sousa, S.M.: Rigorous Software Development: An Introduction to Program Verification. Springer, London (2011). https://doi.org/10.1007/978-0-85729-018-2
2. Apt, K.R.: Recursive assertions and parallel programs. Acta Informatica **13**, 219–232 (1981)
3. Apt, K.R., de Boer, F.S., Olderog, E.-R.: Proving termination of parallel programs. In: Feijen, W.H.J., van Gasteren, A.J.M., Gries, D., Misra, J. (eds.) Beauty is Our Business: A Birthday Salute to Edsger W. Dijkstra, pp. 1–6. Springer, New York (1990). https://doi.org/10.1007/978-1-4612-4476-9_1
4. Apt, K.R., de Boer, F.S., Olderog, E.-R.: Verification of Sequential and Concurrent Programs, 3rd edn. Springer, New York (2009). https://doi.org/10.1007/978-1-84882-745-5
5. Apt, K.R., Olderog, E.-R.: Fifty years of Hoare's logic. Formal Aspects Comput. **31**(6), 751–807 (2019)
6. Baudin, P., et al.: The dogged pursuit of bug-free C programs: the Frama-C software analysis platform. Commun. ACM **64**(8), 56–68 (2021)
7. Cook, B., Podelski, A., Rybalchenko, A.: Proving program termination. Commun. ACM **54**(5), 88–98 (2011)
8. de Gouw, S., Rot, J.: Effectively eliminating auxiliaries. In: Ábrahám, E., Bonsangue, M., Johnsen, E.B. (eds.) Theory and Practice of Formal Methods. LNCS, vol. 9660, pp. 226–241. Springer, Cham (2016). https://doi.org/10.1007/978-3-319-30734-3_16
9. Dijkstra, E.W.: A great improvement (1976). http://www.cs.utexas.edu/users/EWD/ewd05xx/EWD573.PDF. Published as [10]
10. Dijkstra, E.W.: A great improvement. In: Dijkstra, E.W. (ed.) Selected Writings on Computing: A Personal Perspective. MCS, pp. 217–219. Springer, New York (1982). https://doi.org/10.1007/978-1-4612-5695-3_37
11. Floyd, R.: Assigning meaning to programs. In: Schwartz, J.T. (ed.) Proceedings of Symposium on Applied Mathematics 19. Mathematical Aspects of Computer Science, pp. 19–32. American Mathematical Society, New York (1967)

12. Hoare, C.A.R.: An axiomatic basis for computer programming. Commun. ACM **12**, 576–580, 583 (1969)
13. Leavens, G.T., Cheon, Y., Clifton, C., Ruby, C., Cok, D.R.: How the design of JML accommodates both runtime assertion checking and formal verification. Sci. Comput. Program. **55**, 185–208 (2005)
14. Manna, Z., Pnueli, A.: Axiomatic approach to total correctness of programs. Acta Informatica **3**, 253–263 (1974)
15. Meyer, B.: Object-Oriented Software Construction, 2nd edn. Prentice Hall (1997)
16. Owicki, S., Gries, D.: An axiomatic proof technique for parallel programs. Acta Informatica **6**, 319–340 (1976)
17. Reynolds, J.C.: Theories of Programming Languages. Cambridge University Press, Cambridge (1998)
18. Tiuryn, J.: Hoare logic: from first-order to propositional formalism. In: Schwichtenberg, H., Steinbrüggen, R. (eds.) Proof and System-Reliability, pp. 323–340. Kluwer Academic Publishers (2002)

Formal Verification of BDI Agents

Thomas Wright[1], Louise A. Dennis[2], Jim Woodcock[4,1,3](✉),
and Simon Foster[3]

[1] DIGIT, Department of Engineering, Aarhus University, Aarhus, Denmark
thomas.wright@ece.au.dk
[2] Department of Computer Science, University of Manchester, Manchester, UK
louise.dennis@manchester.ac.uk
[3] Department of Computer Science, University of York, York, UK
jim.woodcock@york.ac.uk
[4] School of Computer and Information Science, Southwest University,
Chongqing, China

Abstract. This paper presents a formal modelling approach for Belief-Desire-Intention (BDI) agents using Isabelle/HOL and Z-Machines. The BDI architecture is widely used for modelling intelligent agents, where agents possess beliefs about the environment, desires or goals to achieve, and intentions to execute plans for goal attainment. The paper introduces a general-purpose model of the BDI architecture using Z-Machines. The modelling framework includes specifications for beliefs, actions, rules, plans, pattern matching, and rule applications. The proposed model can be used to formally verify BDI agents' behaviour using Hoare Logic and Isabelle/Z-Machines. This framework then contributes to advancing formal modelling and verification of agent-based systems, showing how we can integrate automated reasoning to establish invariant properties of agents with compositional techniques to prove more significant properties of BDI systems. We demonstrate the effectiveness of our approach through a case study of a nuclear inspector robot, showing how we can verify invariants and uncover bugs in the system's behaviour.

Keywords: BDI · agent verification · theorem proving · Isabelle/HOL · Z-Machines · model checking

1 Dedication. The Thrill of ISoLA: Where Innovation Meets Excellence

This paper is dedicated to Professor Tiziana Margaria.

Tiziana has been instrumental in founding and developing the ISoLA conference series. The International Symposium on Leveraging Applications of Formal Methods, Verification, and Validation (ISoLA) is not just another academic

---

Thomas Wright, Louise A. Dennis, and Jim Woodcock gratefully acknowledge the support of the UK EPSRC for grant EP/V026801/1, UKRI Trustworthy Autonomous Systems Node in Verifiability. Thomas Wright and Jim Woodcock also acknowledge the RoboSAPIENS project, funded by the European Commission's Horizon Europe programme under grant agreement number 101133807.

conference; it is a dynamic nexus where the brightest minds in computer science and engineering converge to ignite innovation and push the boundaries of what is possible. Usually held biennially, ISoLA is a beacon of interdisciplinary collaboration, high-impact research, and groundbreaking technological advances.

ISoLA is a crossroads of disciplines and a must-attend event. Its interdisciplinary approach combines diverse fields such as formal methods, software engineering, cyber-physical systems, and model-driven development. This melting pot of ideas sparks creativity and leads to pioneering solutions that shape the future of technology. Its proceedings are featured in Springer's *Lecture Notes in Computer Science* series, ensuring that the cutting-edge research presented reaches a global audience. It has a lasting impact on the academic and professional communities. It is a catalyst for innovation. ISoLA is about discussing theories and showcasing transformative research with real-world applications. From enhancing the reliability of healthcare systems to revolutionising smart manufacturing, the innovations presented at ISoLA can potentially change the world. Attendees can network with leading researchers, industry experts, and academic luminaries. These interactions often lead to collaborations that drive significant technological advances and breakthroughs.

Tiziana Margaria's involvement with ISoLA is nothing short of remarkable. Her contributions as a researcher, organiser, and thought leader have significantly shaped the conference and its impact on the field. In vital organisational roles, Tiziana has been instrumental in steering ISoLA towards new heights. Her editorial work for the conference proceedings has maintained and enhanced the quality and relevance of the research presented. She has given nearly 40 pivotal papers at ISoLA, highlighting her research on formal methods, model-driven engineering, and cyber-physical systems. For JCPW, our collaboration on digital twins has been a standout feature, illustrating the transformative potential of the research.

Tiziana's research does not confine itself to theoretical advances; it translates into practical applications that revolutionise industries. For example, her work on digital twins offers new ways to ensure reliability and efficiency in critical systems, from healthcare to manufacturing. Through her contributions, Tiziana has inspired countless researchers and practitioners to explore new frontiers in formal methods and system verification. Her influence extends beyond her work, driving the entire field forward.

ISoLA stands as a testament to what can be achieved when innovation meets collaboration. With contributions from visionaries like Tiziana Margaria, the conference showcases cutting-edge research and sets the stage perfectly for the next wave of technological breakthroughs. As ISoLA continues to evolve, it remains a crucial platform for those who dare to dream big and turn their innovative ideas into reality.

Tiziana Margaria has been a trailblazer in verifying agents, the broad topic of this paper, bringing innovative methods and frameworks to ensure the correctness and reliability of software agents within complex systems. See, for example, [26,27]. With a keen emphasis on formal methods, Tiziana provides rock-solid mathematical guarantees for agent correctness. She uses formal languages to define agent behaviours and cutting-edge automated tools to validate these specifications, pushing the boundaries of reliability. Her expertise in service-oriented architectures (SOAs) applies sophisticated verification techniques to ensure seamless interactions between agents and services. Her work ensures that every component within these architectures performs flawlessly, fulfilling their intended functions.

Tiziana's innovative approach to component-based systems treats agents as integral components, developing methods to verify their interactions and integrations. Her work ensures that every piece of the puzzle fits perfectly, guaranteeing system reliability. Always at the forefront of technology, Tiziana has spearheaded the development of tools and frameworks that revolutionise the verification process. These tools automate complex verification tasks, making them more accessible and practical for real-world applications. Tiziana has extended her verification techniques to the dynamic collaborative and autonomous systems world. This ensures that multiple agents can work together harmoniously or operate independently, all while meeting specified goals and constraints with impeccable accuracy.

Tiziana's versatile verification techniques are used in diverse domains, from robotics to telecommunications and web services. Her work's broad applicability underscores its critical importance and transformative impact. She has advanced the field of agent verification by developing robust methods and tools that ensure the correctness and reliability of even the most complex software systems, setting new standards and inspiring future innovations.

Thanks, Tiziana, for your inspirational contributions!

2 Introduction

Intelligent agent systems are vital in various domains, from autonomous robots to virtual characters in simulation environments. These systems exhibit complex behaviours by reasoning about their beliefs, desires, and intentions (BDI). The BDI architecture, inspired by philosophical theories like Bratman's work [8] on practical reasoning, provides a theoretical framework for modelling intelligent agents' beliefs about the world, desires or goals they want to achieve, and intentions or plans for realising those desires. This paper presents a general-purpose model to formalise the behaviour of BDI agents.

The BDI architecture operates based on beliefs and actions. Beliefs represent the agent's understanding of the world, including goals, locations, and potential dangers, while actions encompass the agent's possible behaviours, such as moving, inspecting, or awaiting decontamination. Plans in the BDI architecture define how agents react to their beliefs, specifying rules for belief updates and actions to be taken based on the agent's internal state and environmental stimuli.

Formal methods are essential for specifying and verifying BDI-based systems, ensuring correctness, safety, and reliability. Techniques like model checking, theorem proving, simulation, and runtime monitoring are commonly employed to analyse agents' behaviour and validate their adherence to specified properties or requirements. See Woodcock et al. [43] for a discussion on formal methods practice and experience.

This paper contributes to formally verifying BDI-based systems by presenting a detailed model of the BDI architecture using Z-Machines [46]. By formalising the behaviour of BDI agents and providing mechanisms for verifying their properties, this work enhances the trustworthiness and applicability of intelligent agent systems in real-world scenarios. In particular, this approach focuses on providing techniques that can complement model-checking and runtime verification approaches by explicitly being able to handle the infinite state aspects of interactions with the real world.

With Isabelle/HOL [32], we can model the state space of a system symbolically instead of enumerating all states explicitly, which allows us to overcome the state explosion problem. With Z-Machines, we can verify invariant properties and deadlock-freedom, aided by Isabelle's powerful proof automation in tools like the simplifier, classical reasoner, and *Sledgehammer* [28].

The rest of the paper is structured as follows. In Sect. 3 on the background to our work, we discuss cognitive agents and the BDI model, emphasising beliefs, desires, and intentions as critical components in decision-making. We highlight research focusing on BDI programming languages, particularly SimpleBDI, for high-level decision-making in autonomous systems. We note various approaches to verifying multi-agent systems, including model-checking technologies. Limitations in establishing properties using model-checking methods, such as the necessity for finite state-based representations, are also addressed.

In Sect. 4 on related work, we overview key research areas within the agent paradigm, focusing on beliefs, desires, and intentions. It discusses the BDI architecture's theoretical framework, applications in various domains, formal methods for specification and verification, and hybrid approaches combining BDI with other paradigms. Additionally, we outline standard verification techniques such as formal specification, model checking, theorem proving, simulation and testing, runtime monitoring, and tool support, emphasising the importance of ensuring correctness, safety, and reliability in agent-based systems.

In Sect. 5 on Isabelle and Z-Machines, we describe Isabelle, an interactive theorem prover used for structured proofs and proof automation, particularly in modelling and verifying software systems. It introduces the Z-Machine language, built on Isabelle, for expressing programs as action systems [4]. This enables verification using Isabelle's features. It provides access to Isabelle theories, including Hoare logic [20] and *Circus* [19,39], for specifying and verifying system behaviour, ensuring specification invariance throughout the Z-Machine's operation.

In Sect. 6, we describe the SimpleBDI language, which focuses on simplicity while encompassing the core features of more complex BDI languages. It uses ground terms for expressing beliefs and actions, extended to include variables for matching against an agent's belief base, facilitating compositional verification. Program execution in SimpleBDI progresses through perception, plan selection, and plan execution stages, each characterised by distinct actions and updates to the agent's internal state and beliefs, ultimately guiding its behaviour in response to environmental changes.

In Sect. 7 on modelling the BDI architecture, we provide a general-purpose model using Z-Machines. We cover beliefs, actions, rules and plans. We describe pattern matching and rule application and how this enables our Z-Machine model to execute plans.

In Sect. 8, we discuss how to build upon our Z-Machine model to verify the properties of plans. We introduce several tactics enabling the compositional verification of plans. We then apply these techniques to verify an essential nuclear inspector robotic system invariant.

Finally, in Sect. 9, we reflect on our work, draw general conclusions, and propose some future work.

3 Background

Cognitive agents [8,33,44] possess explicit rationales for their decision-making processes. The most common justification is in terms of the agent's *beliefs* and *goals*, which, in turn, shape the agent's *intentions*. This conceptualisation of cognitive agents is Rao's *beliefs-desires-intentions* model [33,34]. *Beliefs* denote the agent's information about itself, other agents, and the environment, acknowledging the potential for incompleteness or inaccuracy. *Desires* represent the agent's enduring objectives, and *intentions* signify the goals actively pursued by the agent. The representation of intentions often includes partially instantiated or executed plans, combining the goal with its intended means.

Our research is on cognitive agents programmed in a BDI language designed for high-level decision-making within autonomous systems, as elucidated in work by Rao [33] and the practical considerations discussed in Dennis [16]. Our starting point is the SimpleBDI language introduced by Oren and Dennis [16]. While SimpleBDI prioritises simplicity in operational semantics, sacrificing some programmer convenience, it is an appealing foundation for projects focusing on analysing programs at the operational semantics level. SimpleBDI encompasses the fundamental constructs found in more intricate BDI languages, positioning it as a suitable underlying representation for various languages of this nature.

Many approaches to verifying multi-agent systems exist in studies by, among others, Alechina et al. [2], Dastani et al. [11], Lomuscio et al. [24], and Choi et al. [10]; see [5] for a systematic review. Most of these approaches are not tailor-made for BDI-style agents but offer more generalised tools for comprehensively analysing diverse multi-agent systems.

Several frameworks use model-checking technologies to analyse BDI programs, as shown by Jongmans et al. [23], Hunter et al. [21], Stocker et al. [38], Bordini et al. [6], Dennis and Fisher [13] and Yang and Holvoet [47]. While these approaches have demonstrated success, there are inherent limitations in establishing properties using this method. Notably, the necessity for a finite state-based representation of the interaction between the environment and the agent program can restrict the generality of the properties that can be verified.

For example, as discussed in a case study in [13, Chapter 11], the verification of a goal reasoning agent tasked with selecting a location with the highest heat signature in a search and rescue scenario involved constructing a finite state simulation of the environment with specific values for heat signature locations and strengths. Consequently, no general result was established regarding the agent always choosing the location with the highest signature.

4 Related Work

Rouf et al. [35] edit a collection of papers in the book *Agent Technology from a Formal Perspective*. Contributions include the following. Luck and d'Inverno present agent-based systems [35, pp. 65–96] using the Z notation [42], whilst Esterline et al. present a process-algebraic agent abstraction [35, pp. 99–137]. Hustadt et al. discuss verification within the KARO agent theory [35, pp. 193–225]. Pecheur et al. show how to verify models of autonomy in space-flight applications using SMV [35, pp. 311–339].

Research on the agent paradigm with beliefs, desires, and intentions falls within the field of artificial intelligence and multi-agent systems. Here is a brief overview of some of the key research in this area:

BDI Architecture. The BDI architecture draws inspiration from the philosophical theories of Bratman [8], who argues that intentions play a significant and distinct role in practical reasoning and cannot be reduced to beliefs and desires. The BDI architecture provides a theoretical framework for modelling intelligent agents. Agents are equipped with beliefs about the world, desires or goals they want to achieve, and intentions, which are plans or strategies for realising their desires.

Applications. Research in this area has explored various applications of BDI-based agents, including autonomous robots, intelligent software agents, and virtual characters in simulation environments (see de Silva et al. [37]). These agents can exhibit complex behaviours by reasoning about their beliefs, desires, and intentions.

Formal Methods. Formal methods are often used to specify and verify properties of BDI-based systems, such as correctness, safety, and liveness. Model checking and theorem-proving techniques can be applied to analyse agents' behaviour in different scenarios. See Archibald et al. [3].

Hybrid Approaches. Some research combines the BDI model with other paradigms, such as machine learning or game theory, to create more adaptive and robust agent systems (see, for example, Bosello [7]). These hybrid approaches can combine the strengths of different techniques to address the limitations of individual models.

Research on the agent paradigm with beliefs, desires, and intentions continues to advance our understanding of how intelligent agents can be designed, implemented, and deployed in real-world applications. This interdisciplinary research draws from computer science, cognitive science, philosophy, and other fields.

Verifying the BDI agent paradigm involves ensuring that agents' behaviour conforms to specific properties or requirements. This verification process guarantees agent-based systems' correctness, safety, and reliability. Here are some common approaches and techniques used in research for verifying the agent paradigm:

Formal Specification. Researchers often start by formally specifying agents' behaviour using formal languages or logic. For example, they may use modal logic to determine properties such as knowledge, belief, and obligation. These formal specifications serve as a basis for verification (for example, Zhu [48]).

Model Checking. Model checking is a formal verification technique used to exhaustively check whether a model of the system satisfies a given property. See Dennis et al. [14]. In the context of agent-based systems, model checking can verify properties such as the reachability of goals, absence of deadlocks, and consistency of beliefs.

Theorem Proving. Theorem proving involves proving mathematical assertions about agents' behaviour using formal logic and deduction rules. See, for example, Jensen et al. [22]. Researchers may use theorem-proving techniques to verify the properties of agent systems, such as the correctness of communication protocols or consistency of agent beliefs.

Simulation and Testing. Simulation and testing techniques validate agents' behaviour against expected outcomes or specifications. See, for example, Davoust et al. [12]. Researchers may develop simulation environments where agents can interact with each other and the environment to observe their behaviour and validate their beliefs, desires, and intentions.

Runtime Monitoring. Runtime monitoring involves monitoring the execution of agent-based systems in real time to detect violations of desired properties. See, for example, Engelmann et al. [17]. Researchers may develop monitoring tools that continuously observe agents' behaviour and raise alarms when deviations from expected behaviour occur.

Tool Support. Tools and frameworks are available to verify agent-based systems. They often provide automated support for model checking, theorem proving, simulation, and runtime monitoring. See, for example, Xu et al. [45].

By applying these verification techniques, researchers can ensure that agent-based systems behave correctly and reliably, thus increasing their trustworthiness and applicability in real-world settings.

However, the vast majority of research in this area has focused on techniques based on model-checking. This requires the problem to be stated in a finite state form. Typically, this is done by abstracting the environment into a finite set of perceptions available to the agent and, in many cases, restricting to specific combinations of perceptions that are assumed to be the only ones possible. Users of these systems are also encouraged to express properties regarding safety (this will never happen) or liveness (eventually, this will happen). As we will see, our approach, which encourages a user to think in terms of infinite states and invariants, can complement these approaches in assuring correct programs.

5 Isabelle and Z Machines

Isabelle [32] is a general-purpose interactive theorem prover. It supports structured proofs via the Isar language and proof automation, combining automated proof search (via *Sledgehammer* [28]) with custom solver integrations. Whilst Isabelle has been used extensively for modelling and verifying the behaviour of software systems, its general purpose nature requires careful consideration when modelling particular systems to capture their problem domain and enable compositional verification.

The Z-Machine language [46] builds on Isabelle to provide a language for expressing programs as an action system. Similar to dedicated software verification tools such as Z [42] and B [1], a Z-Machine defines a store containing a system's data, whilst several operations mutate the state of the system when their preconditions are met. Operations consist of (1) several parameters for inputs and outputs, (2) preconditions on the store variables and parameters, and (3) updates to the variables, which are applied when the operation is executed. Updates are written using the notation $[x_1 \leadsto e_1, x_2 \leadsto e_2, \cdots, x_n \leadsto e_n]$, which corresponds to a simultaneous assignment of n variables to n expressions. The Z-Machine language allows Isabelle data types to specify the stored data, whilst Isabelle's full power can be used to verify their behaviour.

Z-Machines are given semantics within Isabelle using *Circus* [18,39], which combines CSP-style concurrency and Z-style mutable state.[1] Then verification is supported via a form of Hoare logic [20], where Hoare triples $\{P\}\,\text{Op}\,\{Q\}$ can be used to specify that applying the operation Op to a zstore satisfying the precondition P results in a store satisfying the postconditions Q. Specifically, these include a specification that a Z-Machine's initialisation *establishes* a given specification S ($\{\text{true}\}\,\text{Init}\,\{S\}$), and that each operation Op_i of a Z-Machine *preserves* S ($\{S\}\,\text{Op}_i\,\{S\}$). The zpog proof method translates each such claim into several proof obligations, which may be discharged in Isabelle. Once proven, these claims collectively establish that a specification S is invariant throughout the operation of the Z-Machine.

6 SimpleBDI

The SimpleBDI language was introduced by Dennis and Oren in [15] and refined in [16]. It was designed to have simple semantics while containing the core constructs at the heart of more complex BDI languages. Indeed, Dennis and Oren [16] argue that many more advanced features can be captured in SimpleBDI at the expense of making programs more complex. As presented in [16], SimpleBDI considers only ground terms in expressing beliefs and actions in plans. We have extended these to allow these terms to contain variables that can be matched against the agent's belief base using unification. We present this extended semantics here.

---

[1] *Circus* has formal semantics [30,40] and a refinement theory [9,36]. Both are mechanised in the ProofPowerZ [31] and Isabelle [41] theorem provers.

A SimpleBDI program consists of a set of plans Π of the form $B \to_n I$ where n is an integer indicating the *priority* of the plan (lower is better). B (the plan's *guard*) is a set of atomic formulas in some first-order language $\mathcal{L}$, and I is a $[U, \text{do}(a)]$ pair. In turn, U is a set of *belief updates* of the form $+b, -b$ where b is a formula in $\mathcal{L}$, and a is an action, a term in $\mathcal{L}$. b, a and all the formulas in B may contain free variables. Since some plans may only update beliefs rather than execute an action, we introduce a special symbol null to denote the lack of action. In addition, we assume the existence of an *empty plan* $\pi_{\text{null}} = [] \to [[], \text{do}(\text{null})]$. If multiple plans can be executed, then plans with a lower priority number are selected over plans with a higher priority number[2]. We assume the empty plan has a higher priority number than all other plans.

SimpleBDI programs execute plans based on beliefs and percepts (environmental changes). The latter is captured by an *input trace* τ_e of events external to the agent. Each event is a list of belief updates, V, of the form $+b$ or $-b$ containing a single ground atomic formula in $\mathcal{L}$. The list of belief updates for a single event cannot contain contradictory belief updates, i.e., $+b, -b \notin V$.

The executor of a SimpleBDI program maintains a set of internal beliefs—denoted $\mathcal{B}$—encoded as a set of ground first-order predicates and is formally represented at a point in time as a tuple

$$E = \langle \mathcal{B}, \Pi, \pi, \tau_e, a_{\text{ex}}, \text{stage} \rangle$$

$\mathcal{B}$ is a set of the executor's beliefs; Π is its plan library; π the current plan selected for execution; τ_e is the input trace, and a_{ex} the (external) action executed by the executor agent at that time. $\text{stage} \in \{\mathtt{s}, \mathtt{p}, \mathtt{e}\}$ captures the current state of the executor; SimpleBDI programs run through repeated perception ($\mathtt{p}$), plan selection ($\mathtt{s}$), and plan execution ($\mathtt{e}$) stages. Given a set of plans Π representing a SimpleBDI program and an input trace τ_e, the initial state of the executor is

$$E = \langle [], \Pi, \text{null}, \tau_e, \text{null}, \mathtt{p} \rangle$$

Figure 1 summarises the semantics of SimpleBDI, describing how the tuple representing the executor evolves as a transition system (i.e., if $E_i \to E_{i+1}$ in Fig. 1 then E_i becomes E_{i+1} as the system executes). A *program execution trace* is then the sequence of tuples $[E_1, \ldots, E_n]$ where E_{i+1} is obtained by executing a program over the input trace found in E_i until the input trace is empty; the $\emptyset$ symbol denotes the end of program execution.

In the perception phase ($\mathtt{p}$), the top of the input trace (τ_e) is consumed, updating the set of beliefs $\mathcal{B}$. The update itself is done through the update function, which takes a set of belief updates and a set of beliefs as input and returns an updated set of beliefs. Note that no beliefs are consumed during the remaining phases; therefore, a null perception is consumed during these phases.

The plan selection phase ($\mathtt{s}$) proceeds by selecting an *applicable* plan using the select, gather and applicable functions respectively. The applicable function

---

[2] We note that this differs from other presentations of SimpleBDI, which treat lower numbers as lower priorities, since it simplifies reasoning about rule selection.

$$\langle \mathcal{B}, \Pi, \pi, [], a_{\text{ex}}, \mathbf{p}\rangle \to \emptyset$$
$$\langle \mathcal{B}, \Pi, \pi, [V|\tau_e], a_{ex}, \mathbf{p}\rangle \to \langle \text{update}(V, \mathcal{B}), \Pi, \pi, \tau_e, \text{null}, \mathbf{s}\rangle$$
$$\langle \mathcal{B}, \Pi, \pi, [\text{null}|\tau_e], a_{\text{ex}}, \mathbf{s}\rangle \to \langle \mathcal{B}, \Pi, \text{select}(\mathcal{B}, \Pi), \tau_e, \text{null}, \mathbf{e}\rangle$$
$$\langle \mathcal{B}, \Pi, B \to [U, \text{do}(a)], [\text{null}|\tau_e], a_{\text{ex}}, \mathbf{e}\rangle \to \langle \text{update}(U, \mathcal{B}), \Pi, \text{null}, \tau_e, a, \mathbf{p}\rangle$$

$$\text{update}([], \mathcal{B}) = \mathcal{B}$$
$$\text{update}([+b|B], \mathcal{B}) = \text{update}(B, \mathcal{B} \cup \{b\})$$
$$\text{update}([-b|B], \mathcal{B}) = \text{update}(B, \mathcal{B} \setminus \{b\})$$

$$\text{select}(\mathcal{B}, \Pi) = \text{an element of gather}(\mathcal{B}, \Pi, \{\})$$

$$\text{gather}(\mathcal{B}, \Pi, G) = \begin{cases} \{\pi_{\text{null}}\} & \text{if } \forall n.\ \text{applicable}(n, \Pi) = \{\} \\ \text{applicable}(n, \Pi) & \text{for the least } n \text{ s.t. applicable}(n, \Pi) \neq \{\} \\ & \text{otherwise} \end{cases}$$

$$\text{applicable}(n, \Pi) = \{B\theta \to_n I\theta | B \to_n I \in \Pi \wedge \text{bel\_pattern}(B\theta, \mathcal{B})\}$$
$$\text{bel\_pattern}([], \mathcal{B}) = \top$$
$$\text{bel\_pattern}([b|B], \mathcal{B}) = b \in \mathcal{B} \wedge \text{bel\_pattern}(B, \mathcal{B})$$
$$\text{bel\_pattern}([\neg b|B], \mathcal{B}) = b \notin \mathcal{B} \wedge \text{bel\_pattern}(B, \mathcal{B})$$

Fig. 1. SimpleBDI semantics. $\emptyset$ denotes termination of execution.

determines whether a plan is applicable by checking whether the plan's beliefs can or can not be unified with beliefs in the belief base. This process results in a set of *applicable plans* where the free variables in B and I have been instantiated via a substitution, θ.

All most preferred applicable plans are collected using the gather function, and a plan is selected from these (via select). With no generality loss, we assume this plan is chosen randomly. If no applicable plan exists, then the empty plan π_{null} is returned. The selected plan is recorded and used in the next phase.

Finally, the plan execution phase (e) takes the selected applicable plan and updates the belief base according to the plan's effects. Any action a executed due to the plan is recorded. The cycle then repeats with a new perception phase.

Example (Nuclear Inspector). We introduce a running example of a SimpleBDI program. The program is the high-level decision-making component in a robotic system performing an inspection process in a Nuclear facility. It is based on a cognitive agent programmed in the GWENDOLEN language previously verified using model-checking in a process described by Luckcuck et al. in [25].

```
1  goal_inspect(Loc), location_coordinate(Loc, X, Y),
2      ¬ danger_red, ¬ danger_orange,
3      ¬ going(door)
4      →2 +going(Loc), -goal_inspect(Loc), do(move(X, Y))
5
6  arrived, going(door) →1
```

```
7      −going(door), do(await_decontamination)
8      arrived , going(OldLoc), next_location(OldLoc, NewLoc)
9         →₁ −going(OldLoc), +goal_inspect(NewLoc), −arrived ,
10          do(inspect(OldLoc))
11     arrived , ¬ going(OldLoc) →₁ −arrived , do(null)
12
13     move_failure →₂ do(null)
14
15     danger_red , ¬ going(door), location(door, X, Y) →₁
16          +going(door), move(X, Y)
17     danger_orange, ¬ going(door), location(door, X, Y) →₁
18          +going(door), move(X, Y)
```

This agent has four sets of plans. The first plans handle the goal to inspect a location goal_inspect(Loc). This plan is activated if there are no danger signals and the agent is not going to the door. It retrieves the coordinates for the desired location from its belief base, adds a belief that it is going to that location, removes the goal to inspect the location and then performs a move action to the location's coordinates. The next set of plans defines how the agent behaves when it receives an arrived belief—it perceives this through the agent's interactions with sensors and motion planner. There are four plans here depending upon whether it was heading for the door (this plan has the highest priority of the three), was heading for a location (in which case it gets to the next location and does an inspection), or was not heading for a location. There is a plan for handling a move_failure. There are four plans with high priority for handling danger signals. In all cases, the agent goes to the door for decontamination, though it also removes relevant existing beliefs about where it was previously heading or its inspection goals. There are two plans with high priority for handling danger signals. In both cases, the agent proceeds to the door for decontamination while removing relevant existing beliefs about where it was previously heading.

Given a program and an initial state—which includes an input trace—the state of the executor at each step of the program execution trace describes the executor's internal state and its effects (actions) on the environment.

7 Modelling the BDI Architecture

We present a general-purpose model of the BDI architecture using Z-Machines. Whilst we present the key definitions and theory here, the complete formalisation is available in the accompanying Isabelle theory available at[3].

---
[3] https://github.com/twright/bdi-utp.

7.1 Beliefs and Actions

We assume the base alphabet for valid beliefs and actions is provided using Isabelle types. For example, in the nuclear reactor, the names of the possible actions are defined via the datatype Action,

datatype Action
  = move
  | await_decontamination
  | inspect
  | null
  | impossible_action

whilst the possible belief names are defined via the datatype Belief,

datatype Belief =
    goal_inspect
  | location_coordinate
  | danger_red
  | danger_orange
  | going
  | arrived
  | next_location
  | location
  | move_failure

However, we must also deal with parametric actions such as move(X, Y), which are defined via the type

type_synonym ParamBelief = "Belief × Value list"

as well as parametric beliefs such as location_coordinate(Loc, X, Y) which are defined by

type_synonym ParamBelief = "Belief × Value list"

where in both cases, the values are defined by

datatype Value = Atom Name | Nat nat

We assume that values are either named atomic tokens or natural numbers for simplicity.

7.2 Rules and Plans

BDI plans consider rules, which are specified using patterns where the parameters of a belief are variables that are matched at runtime, such as location(door, X, Y) that specifies a concrete door location name, but leaves the abstract coordinates X and Y to be instantiated when the pattern is matched. To implement such patterns, we first define symbolic parameters via the type

datatype Symbol = Var Name | Val Value

We also define belief signs, which define whether a belief should be should or must not be held

enumtype BelSign = pos | neg

Then, the rules specify the beliefs via patterns of the form

datatype AbstPat =
    pat BelSign Belief "Symbol list"
  | patlist "AbstPat list"

whilst the resulting action is specified via a pattern of the form

type_synonym AbstParamAction = "Action × Symbol list"

The overall shape of a SimpleBDI plan is then

type_synonym Plan = "(nat × AbstPat × AbstPat × AbstParamAction) set"

The components represent the rule's priority, the patterns of beliefs that must be held for the rule to be applied, the belief update resulting from the rule, and the action triggered by the rule. Then, for example, the rule

```
1  goal_inspect(Loc), location_coordinate(Loc, X, Y),
2     ¬ danger_red, ¬ danger_orange, ¬ going(door)
3     →₂ +going(Loc), −goal_inspect(Loc), do(move(X, Y))
```

is represented by the 4-tuple

```
(
  2,
  patlist [pat pos goal_inspect [Var ''Location''],
          pat pos location_coordinate [Var ''Location'',
                                        Var ''X'', Var ''Y''],
          pat neg danger_red [],
          pat neg danger_orange [],
          pat neg going [Val (Atom ''door'')]],
  patlist [pat pos going [Var ''Location''],
          pat neg goal_inspect [Var ''Location'']],
  (move, [Var ''X'', Var ''Y''])
)
```

and the rest of the plan for the nuclear inspector may be encoded similarly.

7.3 Pattern Matching and Rule Applications

The pattern-matching process behind the BDI-rule application consists of selecting an instantiation of each of the unbound beliefs in an abstract pattern from an agent's current beliefs set.

This is implemented using contexts that assign concrete beliefs to variables.

type_synonym Ctx = "string ⇒ Value"

Contexts are used to evaluate symbolic variable names using the function

fun eval_name :: "Ctx ⇒ Symbol ⇒ Value"   **where**
"eval_name C (Var x) = C x"|
"eval_name C (Val y) = y"

We can then define the instantiation of a belief pattern by

"instantiate_pat C (pat s b xs) = (cpat s b (map (eval_name C) xs))"|
"instantiate_pat C (patlist xs) = (cpatlist (map (instantiate_pat C) xs))"

whilst the instantiation of an action pattern is defined by

fun instantiate_act :: "Ctx ⇒ AbstParamAction ⇒ ConcParamAction"
where
"instantiate_act C (act, xs) = (act, map (eval_name C) xs)"

We now define the `matches_pat` function, which is whether an abstract pattern matches against a given belief set B given context C.

fun matches_pat :: "AbstPat ⇒ ParamBelief set ⇒ Ctx ⇒ bool"
where
"matches_pat (patlist []) B C = True"|
"matches_pat (patlist (x#xs)) B C = (matches_pat x B C
                                    ∧ matches_pat (patlist xs) B C)"|
"matches_pat (pat pos b xs) B C = ((b, map (eval_name C) xs) ∈ B)"|
"matches_pat (pat neg b xs) B C = ((b, map (eval_name C) xs) ∉ B)"

This allows us to define the set of all contexts that establish a match of a given pattern against a belief set, as follows:

fun pat_matches :: "AbstPat ⇒ ParamBelief set ⇒ Ctx set"   **where**
"pat_matches p B = { C | C . matches_pat p B C }"

7.4 Priorities and Transitions

We now proceed to how transitions are implemented based on pattern-matching results, using rule priorities to select the highest priority match. We first specify the `next_step_pri` function, which computes the set of all pattern matches from a given plan against a given belief set for a given priority n,

fun next_steps_pri :: "nat ⇒ Plan ⇒ ParamBelief set ⇒ PlanAct set"
where
"next_steps_pri pri pla B = {
  (update_seq (instantiate_pat C r), instantiate_act C a)
  | p r a C . (pri, p, r, a) ∈ pla ∧ C ∈ pat_matches p B
}"

fun min_priority :: "Plan ⇒ ParamBelief set ⇒ nat option"   **where**
"min_priority p B = (
  if ∃i . next_steps_pri i p B ≠ {}
  then Some (Least (λ n . next_steps_pri n p B ≠ {}))
  else None)"

We can also find the minimum priority for which some rules match,

```
fun min_priority :: "Plan ⇒ ParamBelief set ⇒ nat option"      where
"min_priority p B = (
  if ∃i . next_steps_pri i p B ≠ {}
  then Some (Least (λ n . next_steps_pri n p B ≠ {}))
  else None)"
```

and then compute all of the admissible minimum-priority rule applications as follows,

```
fun next_steps :: "Plan ⇒ ParamBelief set ⇒ PlanAct set"      where
"next_steps p B = (case min_priority p B of
  Some n ⇒ next_steps_pri n p B |
  None   ⇒ {null_plan_act}
)"
```

This **next_steps** function thus admits any matching rule application given the current belief set unless there is an alternative rule application with a lower priority. Alternatively, the null plan application, **null_plan_act**, is returned if there is no match.

7.5 BDI Z-Machines

We first define the Z-Machine store **BDI_st**, which represents the state needed by a BDI system.

```
zstore BDI_st =
  beliefs :: "ParamBelief set"
  pl :: "PlanAct"
  phase :: Phase
  act_tr :: "ConcParamAction list"
```

The **zstore** command creates a new store type, with the declared variables inside, in this case, **beliefs**, **pl**, **phase**, and **act_tr**. We now define the BDI Z-Machine as comprising the following operations:

```
zoperation Perceive =
  params bel_up ∈ "belief_updates perceptibles"
  pre "phase = perceive"
  update "[phase ⤳ select, beliefs ⤳ upd beliefs bel_up]"

zoperation Select =
  params pl' ∈ "next_steps plan beliefs"
  pre "phase = select ∧ beliefs ≠ {}"
  update "[phase ⤳ exec, pl ⤳ pl']"

zoperation NullSelect =
  pre "phase = select ∧ beliefs = {}"
  update "[phase ⤳ perceive]"

zoperation Execute =
```

```
    pre "phase = exec"
    update "[beliefs ↝ upd beliefs (fst pl), phase ↝ perceive,
             act_tr ↝ act_tr @ [snd pl]]"
```

The **zoperation** command creates an operation with specified set of parameters (`params`), preconditions (`pre`), and a variable `update`. For example, the `Perceive` operation has a single parameter `bel_up` drawn from the set of belief updates. It has a single precondition, `phase = perceive`, and it updates `phase` to become `select`, and `beliefs` using the `upd` function.

These operations implement the different phases of the BDI architecture:

- `Perceive(bel_up)`: this operation updates the belief set of the agent based on a belief update `bel_up` provided by the environment. This belief update is restricted to be compatible with the set `perceptibles` of beliefs that the agent can perceive.
- `Select(pl')`: this operation selects a plan action `pl'` from the plan, using the function `next_steps` to select a minimum-priority rule which is compatible with the agent's current beliefs. This is stored in `pl`.
- `Execute()`: This updates the agent's belief set based on the selected plan operation `pl`.

The additional `NullSelect` operation is used to skip the select phase and move back to perceive if the system has no beliefs (this is necessary to ensure deadlock-freedom). After each phase, the `phase` variable is updated to reflect the next phase of the system.

We also need the following initialisation operation, which sets the initial state of the BDI system.

```
    definition BDI_init :: "BDI_st subst"       where
    "BDI_init = [beliefs ↝ {}, pl ↝ ([], (null, [])), phase ↝ perceive,
                 act_tr ↝ []]"
```

Then, finally, the overall Z-Machine is defined as follows:

```
zmachine BDI_Machine =
  over BDI_st
  init BDI_init
  operations Perceive Select NullSelect Execute
```

The **zmachine** command creates a Z-Machine based on the given initialisation (`init`), and a set of `operations`.

This schema allows us to translate arbitrary BDI systems to Z-Machines. For example, the nuclear inspector can be encoded as a BDI system with the beliefs and actions defined in Sect. 7.1, and the plan translated to an Isabelle data structure as in Sect. 7.2.

8 Compositional Verification of BDI Systems

We now move on to verifying BDI systems using the Z-Machine framework. We first show how to verify the BDI system's plans and then apply this to verify a complex invariant of the nuclear inspector system. Throughout this section, we include the high-level lemmas that make up these compositional proofs whilst linking to the complete proofs in the accompanying Isabelle theory to this paper.

8.1 Verifying Plans

We now build upon Z-Machines [46] and Hoare Logic [20] to provide a compositional strategy for proving invariant properties.

As a first example, we first prove some BDI systems' meta-properties: imperceptible beliefs (as defined by the **perceptibles** set of a BDI Z-Machine) can never be believed. To this end, we show the crucial step, that disbelief in a given belief is preserved by the **Perceive(xs)** Z-Machine operation.

lemma perceive_preserves_nonperceptibles:
  assumes "b ∉ perceptibles"
  shows "Perceive(xs) preserves (b, ns) ∈ beliefs"

Here, the notation **C preserves I** is shorthand for the Hoare triple {I} C {I}. This approach can be generalised to show that any property not containing perceivable beliefs is preserved by the **Perceive(xs)** operation. The impact of this depends crucially on the sets of perceivable beliefs which is defined for a particular BDI system; in the case of the nuclear inspector, this set is

definition "perceptibles = {move_failure, location_coordinate, arrived, next_location, danger_red, danger_orange}"

We can also consider the following expression, which characterises the next steps at each stage of the Z-Machine's execution.

zexpr exec_next_steps   **is** "phase = Phase.exec
                    ⟶ pl ∈ next_steps plan beliefs"

This is defined using the **zexpr** command, which declares a named expression and is used to express and name important properties of a Z-Machine. In this case, we can show that this is an invariant of the BDI system: it preserves the BDI Z-Machine's operation at this stage. We prove the invariance of this expression via the following proofs that each operation of the Z-Machine preserves it.

lemma "BDI_init establishes exec_next_steps"
  by zpog_full

lemma "Perceive(bel_up) preserves exec_next_steps"
  by zpog_full

lemma "NullSelect() preserves exec_next_steps"
  by zpog_full

lemma "Select(pl') preserves exec_next_steps"
  by zpog_full

lemma "Execute() preserves exec_next_steps"
  by zpog_full

Formal Verification of BDI Agents   319

We note that each of these proofs is completed automatically using the **zpog_full** method provided by the Isabelle Z-Machines framework, which applies the weakest precondition calculus to calculate a set of proof obligations for invariant preservation and then applies a variety of automated proof tactics to attempt to discharge the goal. If residual proof obligations remain, we can either apply **sledgehammer** or a counterexample generator (such as **nitpick**) to refute the goal.

To define a generic proof strategy for verifying plans, we first define a type synonym for belief set properties, predicates over a BDI system's belief set.

type_synonym Belief_Set_Prop = "ParamBelief set ⇒ bool"

then, we can characterise whether a given plan preserves a belief set property via the following boolean function,

fun preserves_belief_set_prop :: "Plan ⇒ Belief_Set_Prop ⇒ bool"   where
"preserves_belief_set_prop pla bsp = (∀ bs.
                    ∀ (up, a) ∈ next_steps pla bs.
                    bsp bs ⟶ bsp(upd bs up))"

This can be used to prove that a given belief set property is preserved by the execute phase of a Z-Machine, based on the following lemma,

lemma exec_prop_preservation:
  assumes "preserves_belief_set_prop plan prop"
  shows "Execute(xs) preserves prop beliefs under exec_next_steps"

To prove belief set properties compositionally, we can characterise conditional belief set preservation as follows,

fun conditionally_preserves_belief_set_prop :: "Plan ⇒ Belief_Set_Prop
                                ⇒ Belief_Set_Prop ⇒ bool"   where
"conditionally_preserves_belief_set_prop pla prebsp bsp =
 (∀ bs. ∀ (up, a) ∈ next_steps pla bs. prebsp bs ∧ bsp bs
                    ⟶ bsp(upd bs up))"

Then, the following lemma allows us to prove invariants of the **Execute()** phase of a BDI system.

lemma exec_prop_preservation:
  assumes "preserves_belief_set_prop plan prop"
  shows "Execute(xs) preserves prop beliefs under exec_next_steps"

Such lemmas correspond to a Hoare triple of the form

$$\{\texttt{prop beliefs} \wedge \texttt{exec\_next\_steps}\} \texttt{ Execute() } \{\texttt{propbeliefs}\}$$

which make use of our existing knowledge that

$$\{\texttt{exec\_next\_steps}\} \texttt{ Execute() } \{\texttt{exec\_next\_steps}\}$$

to strengthen the preconditions available for proving the invariance of **prop beliefs**. This demonstrates how our approach combines the reasoning power of Z-Machines and Isabelle to prove individual invariants with Hoare logic-style assume-guarantee reasoning to prove more complex properties.

Now we have strategies to verify the `Perceive(bel_up)` and `Execute()` phases; the other phases of the Z-Machine are much more straightforward since they do not depend on the current plan or the environment, and hence can usually be discharged by the `zpog_full` tactic.

We can also use tactics supplied by Isabelle Z-Machines to verify the deadlock-freedom of plans. In the context of a Z-Machine, at any time, at least one of the operations is enabled since its precondition is true. For example, we have proof that the nuclear inspector Z-Machine is deadlock-free.

lemma "deadlock_free BDI_Machine"

We note that such deadlock-freedom proofs can be constructed semi-automatically by applying the `deadlock_free` tactic supplied by the Isabelle Z-Machines framework. This requires us to show that the disjunction of all operation preconditions is a tautology. As with invariant generation, residual proof obligations can be discharged by a combination of methods suggested by `sledgehammer`.

8.2 Full Example: Nuclear Inspector Verification

We now review a complete case study proving the high-level properties of a BDI system, such as the nuclear inspector.

The main property we are interested in showing is that the nuclear inspector is always going to a unique goal. This property type is difficult to verify using model-checking approaches since it requires reasoning about the unbounded evolution of the system's state in unanticipated scenarios. Still, it is crucial to verify the correctness of its long-term behaviour at runtime.

Our initial attempt at formalising this property resulted in the following belief set property,

```
fun unique_going_location_prop :: "Belief_Set_Prop"    where
"unique_going_location_prop bs = (∀ X1 X2 . (going, [X1]) ∈ bs
                                  ∧ (going, [X2]) ∈ bs
                                  ⟶ X1 = X2)"
```

Whilst it was possible to show that each of the Z-Machine preserved this property, it was not possible to show that it was preserved by the `Execute(p)` phase in a compositional way. This is because the definition of this property is not well-suited for use as an inductive invariant of the belief set since, as we move through the plan, we shift from a belief `going(X)` that we are going to a location X, and a belief `goal_inspect(X)` that our goal is to go to inspect X. That is, whilst our property should be invariant, it is not strong enough to be proven inductively on its own, given its inductive dependence on the goal of the BDI system. To remedy this issue, we strengthen the property to the following belief set property,

definition unique_target **where**
"unique_target B = ((∀ X.
                    (goal_inspect, [X]) ∈ B
              ⟶ ((∀ Y. (going, [Y]) ∉ B)
                    ∧ (∀ Y. (goal_inspect, [Y]) ∈ B ⟶ X = Y)))
              ∧ (∀ X.
                    (going, [X]) ∈ B
              ⟶ ((∀ Y. (goal_inspect, [Y]) ∉ B)
                    ∧ (∀ Y. (going, [Y]) ∈ B ⟶ X = Y))))"

This property requires that if the belief set contains a belief that it is going to a location, it does not believe it is going to any other location or has a goal to inspect any location. Conversely, if the belief set contains a goal to inspect any location, it does not have a goal to inspect any other location or a belief that it is going to any location. We can prove the following lemma that this property is a strengthening of our original property,

lemma "unique_target B ⟶ unique_going_location_prop B"
  by (auto simp add: unique_target_def)

We can apply our compositional proof strategy to prove the invariance of this property under most of the BDI operations.

lemma "BDI_init establishes unique_target beliefs"
  by (zpog_full add: unique_target_def)

lemma "NullSelect() preserves unique_target beliefs"
  by zpog_full

lemma "Select(xs) preserves unique_target beliefs"
  by zpog_full

lemma "Perceive(xs) preserves unique_target beliefs"

The first three of these proofs are completed automatically via `zpog_full`, whilst the proof for `Perceive` extends the logic of the `perceive_preserves _nonperceptibles` lemma since the definition of `unique_target` refers exclusively to non-perceivable beliefs.

However, we still failed to prove that this property was preserved by the `Execute(p)` phase. This time, this revealed *a bug in the underlying BDI model* of the nuclear inspector, which had escaped previous model-checking-based verification attempts. Within the model, the following two rules,

1   danger_red, ¬going(door), location(door, X, Y) →₁
2   +going(door), move(X, Y)
3   danger_orange, ¬going(door), location(door, X, Y) →₁
4   +going(door), move(X, Y)

which handles potential dangers by triggering a move to the door when danger is detected. These rules can, however, violate our invariant either directly by adding a duplicate **going** belief or indirectly by introducing a **going** belief when the agent already has a goal to inspect another location. To remedy this, we replaced these rules with the following four rules,

```
1   danger_red,    ¬ going(door),
2       location(door, X, Y), going(Loc)
3       →₁ +going(door), −going(Loc), do(move(X, Y))
4   danger_orange, ¬ going(door),
5       location(door, X, Y), going(Loc)
6       →₁ +going(door), −going(Loc), do(move(X, Y))
7   danger_red,    ¬ going(door),
8       location(door, X, Y), goal_inspect(Loc)
9       →₁ +going(door), −goal_inspect(Loc), do(move(X, Y))
10  danger_orange, ¬ going(door),
11      location(door, X, Y), goal_inspect(Loc)
12      →₁ +going(door), −goal_inspect(Loc), do(move(X, Y))
```

which explicitly remove any existing conflicting beliefs before adding the new belief that the agent is going to the door. With this revised model, we can prove that **unique_target** is an invariant of the **Execute(p)** phase as follows,

lemma "preserves_belief_set_prop plan (unique_going_location_prop)"

lemma "Execute() preserves unique_target beliefs under exec_next_steps"
  using exec_prop_preservation preserves_belief_set   **by** blast

This showcases the ability of theorem proving to identify and resolve subtle bugs in the design of BDI systems and how defining suitable invariants can improve the design of BDI systems by forcing system designers to determine how rules update the system's belief set to achieve its desired goals.

9 Conclusion

Intelligent agent systems, grounded in Beliefs, Desires, and Intentions (BDI), play a crucial role across various domains, from autonomous robots to virtual characters in simulation environments. This paper contributes to the formalisation and verification of BDI-based systems by presenting a detailed model of the BDI architecture using Z-Machines, enhancing the trustworthiness and applicability of such systems in real-world scenarios.

The BDI architecture provides a theoretical framework for modelling intelligent agents' beliefs, desires, and intentions. Plans within the BDI architecture define how agents react to their beliefs, specifying rules for belief updates and actions based on the agent's internal state and environmental stimuli.

Formal methods, including model checking, theorem proving, simulation, and runtime monitoring, are essential for specifying and verifying BDI-based systems, ensuring correctness, safety, and reliability. Researchers can use these techniques to analyse agents' behaviour and validate their adherence to specified properties or requirements.

We use Isabelle and Z-Machines to present a detailed model of the BDI architecture as embodied in the SimpleBDI language. Our novel contributions are:

- A general-purpose model of the BDI architecture and the SimpleBDI language using Isabelle and Z-Machines.
- A compositional theorem-proving approach to invariant properties of BDI systems, with automation enabled through Isabelle and Z-Machines.
- A case study demonstrating the application of our technique to a BDI model of a Nuclear inspector robot shows its effectiveness in proving invariant properties of BDI systems and uncovering bugs in the agent's behaviour.

Overall, this provides a novel approach to connecting the agent-based modelling capabilities of BDI with the power theorem-proving capabilities of Isabelle and the Z-Machines framework to provide a capable theorem-proving framework for multiagent systems.

9.1 Future Work

One strand of future work will focus on extending our model from SimpleBDI to more expressive BDI languages, such as GWENDOLEN. Whilst SimpleBDI captures the core features of the BDI architecture and can encode other features, such as goals, extending our encoding to support these additional features explicitly may reveal further verification challenges or the need for additional proof automation techniques. Similarly, we can extend our approach to proving a wider range of properties, such as liveness or timed properties, which play a key role in many real agent-based systems.

Another strand of future work is to investigate the application of our model to systems featuring self-adaptive behaviour. Self-adaptive systems can modify their behaviour in response to changes in their environment or requirements and are vital for designing robust autonomous systems. BDI agents are a natural platform for modelling self-adaptive systems [29]. We hope to extend our approach to verifying self-adaptive systems within the BDI by identifying patterns characterising self-adaptive BDI systems (as encoded within Z-Machines) and identifying proof tactics for verifying the correctness of their self-adaptive behaviour (for example, that adaptations are triggered when suitable conditions are met, and that suitable invariants are preserved after adaptation).

References

1. Abrial, J.-R.: The B-Book-Assigning Programs to Meanings. Cambridge University Press, Cambridge (1996)
2. Alechina, N., Logan, B., Nga, N.H., Rakib, A.: Verifying time, memory and communication bounds in systems of reasoning agents. Synthese **169**(2), 385–403 (2009)
3. Archibald, B., Calder, M., Sevegnani, M., Xu, M.: Probabilistic BDI agents: actions, plans, and intentions. In: Calinescu, R., Păsăreanu, C.S. (eds.) SEFM 2021. LNCS, vol. 13085, pp. 262–281. Springer, Cham (2021). https://doi.org/10.1007/978-3-030-92124-8_15

4. Back, R.-J., Kurki-Suonio, R.: Decentralization of process nets with centralized control. In: Probert, R.L., Lynch, N.A., Santoro, N., (eds.) Proceedings of the Second Annual ACM Symposium on Principles of Distributed Computing, Montreal, Quebec, Canada, 17–19 August 1983, pp. 131–142. ACM (1983)
5. Bakar, N.A., Selamat, A.: Agent systems verification: systematic literature review and mapping. Appl. Intell. **48**(5), 1251–1274 (2018)
6. Bordini, R.H., Fisher, M., Visser, W., Wooldridge, M.J.: Verifying multi-agent programs by model checking. Auton. Agents Multi Agent Syst. **12**(2), 239–256 (2006)
7. Bosello, M.: Integrating BDI and reinforcement learning: the case study of autonomous driving. Master thesis, Department of Computer Science and Engineering, Università di Bologna, Cesena Campus (2020)
8. Bratman, M.: Intention, Plans, and Practical Reason. Harvard University Press, Cambridge (1987)
9. Cavalcanti, A., Sampaio, A., Woodcock, J.: A refinement strategy for *Circus*. Formal Aspects Comput. **15**(2–3), 146–181 (2003)
10. Choi, J., Kim, S., Tsourdos, A.: Verification of heterogeneous multi-agent system using MCMAS. Int. J. Syst. Sci. **46**(4), 634–651 (2015)
11. Dastani, M., Hindriks, K.V., Meyer, J.-J.: Specification and Verification of Multi-Agent Systems. Springer, New York (2010). https://doi.org/10.1007/978-1-4419-6984-2
12. Davoust, A., et al.: An architecture for integrating BDI agents with a simulation environment. In: Dennis, L.A., Bordini, R.H., Lespérance, Y. (eds.) EMAS 2019. LNCS (LNAI), vol. 12058, pp. 67–84. Springer, Cham (2020). https://doi.org/10.1007/978-3-030-51417-4_4
13. Dennis, L.A., Fisher, M.: Verifiable Autonomous Systems: Using Rational Agents to Provide Assurance about Decisions Made by Machines. Cambridge University Press, Cambridge (2023)
14. Dennis, L.A., Fisher, M., Webster, M.P., Bordini, R.H.: Model checking agent programming languages. Autom. Softw. Eng. **19**(1), 5–63 (2012)
15. Dennis, L.A., Oren, N.: Explaining BDI agent behaviour through dialogue. In: Dignum, F., Lomuscio, A., Endriss, U., Nowé, A. (eds.) AAMAS 2021: 20th International Conference on Autonomous Agents and Multiagent Systems, Virtual Event, United Kingdom, 3–7 May 2021, pp. 429–437. ACM (2021)
16. Dennis, L.A., Oren, N.: Explaining BDI agent behaviour through dialogue. J. Auton. Agents Multi-Agent Syst. **36**(2), 29 (2022)
17. Engelmann, D.C., Ferrando, A., Panisson, A.R., Ancona, D., Bordini, R.H., Mascardi, V.: RV4JaCa-towards runtime verification of multi-agent systems and robotic applications. Robotics **12**(2), 49 (2023)
18. Foster, S., Hur, C.-K., Woodcock, J.: Formally verified simulations of state-rich processes using interaction trees in Isabelle/HOL. In: 32nd International Conferences on Concurrency Theory (CONCUR). LIPIcs, vol. 203. Schloss Dagstuhl - Leibniz-Zentrum für Informatik (2021)
19. Foster, S., Zeyda, F., Woodcock, J.: Unifying heterogeneous state-spaces with lenses. In: Sampaio, A., Wang, F. (eds.) ICTAC 2016. LNCS, vol. 9965, pp. 295–314. Springer, Cham (2016). https://doi.org/10.1007/978-3-319-46750-4_17
20. Hoare, C.A.R.: An axiomatic basis for computer programming. Commun. ACM **12**(10), 576–580 (1969)
21. Hunter, J., Raimondi, F., Rungta, N., Stocker, R.: A synergistic and extensible framework for multi-agent system verification. In: Gini, M.L., Shehory, O., Ito, T.,

Jonker, C.M. (eds.) International Conference on Autonomous Agents and Multi-Agent Systems, AAMAS 2013, Saint Paul, MN, USA, 6–10 May 2013, pp. 869–876. IFAAMAS (2013)
22. Jensen, A.B., Hindriks, K.V., Villadsen, J.: On using theorem proving for cognitive agent-oriented programming. In: Rocha, A.P., Steels, L., van den Herik, H.J. (eds.) Proceedings of the 13th International Conference on Agents and Artificial Intelligence, ICAART 2021, 4–6 February 2021, vol. 1, pp. 446–453. SCITEPRESS (2021)
23. Jongmans, S.-S.T.Q., Hindriks, K.V., van Riemsdijk, M.B.: Model checking agent programs by using the program interpreter. In: Dix, J., Leite, J., Governatori, G., Jamroga, W. (eds.) CLIMA 2010. LNCS (LNAI), vol. 6245, pp. 219–237. Springer, Heidelberg (2010). https://doi.org/10.1007/978-3-642-14977-1_17
24. Lomuscio, A., Hongyang, Q., Raimondi, F.: MCMAS: an open-source model checker for the verification of multi-agent systems. Int. J. Softw. Tools Technol. Transf. **19**, 9–30 (2017)
25. Luckcuck, M., Farrell, M., Ferrando, A., Cardoso, R.C., Dennis, L.A., Fisher, M.: A compositional approach to verifying modular robotic systems. arxiv.org/abs/2208.05507 (2023)
26. Margaria, T.: Components, features, and agents in the ABC. In: Ryan, M.D., Meyer, J.-J.C., Ehrich, H.-D. (eds.) Objects, Agents, and Features. LNCS, vol. 2975, pp. 154–174. Springer, Heidelberg (2004). https://doi.org/10.1007/978-3-540-25930-5_10
27. Margaria, T., Steffen, B.: Run-time agents as a means of reconciling flexibility and scalability of services. In: Hinchey, M.G., Rago, P., Rash, J.L., Rouff, C.A., Sterritt, R., Truszkowski, W. (eds.) WRAC 2005. LNCS (LNAI), vol. 3825, pp. 257–268. Springer, Heidelberg (2006). https://doi.org/10.1007/11964995_23
28. Meng, J., Quigley, C., Paulson, L.C.: Automation for interactive proof: first prototype. Inf. Comput. **204**(10), 1575–1596 (2006)
29. Morandini, M., Penserini, L., Perini, A.: Towards goal-oriented development of self-adaptive systems. In: Proceedings of the 2008 International Workshop on Software Engineering for Adaptive and Self-Managing Systems, SEAMS 2008, Leipzig, Germany, pp. 9–16. Association for Computing Machinery (2008)
30. Oliveira, M., Cavalcanti, A., Woodcock, J.: A denotational semantics for *Circus*. In: Aichernig, B.K., Boiten, E.A., Derrick, J., Groves, L. (eds.) Proceedings of the 11th Refinement Workshop, Refine@ICFEM 2006. Electronic Notes in Theoretical Computer Science, Macao, 31 October 2006, vol. 187, pp. 107–123. Elsevier (2006)
31. Oliveira, M., Cavalcanti, A., Woodcock, J.: A UTP semantics for *Circus*. Formal Aspects Comput. **21**(1–2), 3–32 (2009)
32. Paulson, L.C.: Natural deduction as higher-order resolution. J. Log. Program. **3**(3), 237–258 (1986)
33. Rao, A.S., Georgeff, M.P.: An abstract architecture for rational agents. In: Proceedings of the International Conference on Knowledge Representation and Reasoning (KR&R), pp. 439–449. Morgan Kaufmann (1992)
34. Rao, A.S., Georgeff, M.P.: Modeling agents within a BDI-architecture. In: Proceedings of the 2nd International Conference on Principles of Knowledge Representation and Reasoning (KR&R), pp. 473–484. Morgan Kaufmann (1991)
35. Rouff, C.A., Hinchey, M., Rash, J., Truszkowski, W., Gordon-Spears, D. (eds.): Agent Technology from a Formal Perspective. NASA Monographs in Systems and Software Engineering, p. 354. Springer, London (2006). https://doi.org/10.1007/1-84628-271-3

36. Sampaio, A., Woodcock, J., Cavalcanti, A.: Refinement in *Circus*. In: Eriksson, L.-H., Lindsay, P.A. (eds.) FME 2002. LNCS, vol. 2391, pp. 451–470. Springer, Heidelberg (2002). https://doi.org/10.1007/3-540-45614-7_26
37. de Silva, L., Meneguzzi, F., Logan, B.: BDI agent architectures: a survey. In: Bessiere, C. (ed.) Proceedings of the Twenty-Ninth International Joint Conference on Artificial Intelligence, IJCAI 2020, pp. 4914–4921. ijcai.org (2020)
38. Stocker, R., Dennis, L., Dixon, C., Fisher, M.: Verifying Brahms human-robot teamwork models. In: del Cerro, L.F., Herzig, A., Mengin, J. (eds.) JELIA 2012. LNCS (LNAI), vol. 7519, pp. 385–397. Springer, Heidelberg (2012). https://doi.org/10.1007/978-3-642-33353-8_30
39. Woodcock, J., Cavalcanti, A.: A concurrent language for refinement. In: Butterfield, A., Strong, G., Pahl, C. (eds.) Proceedings of the 5th Irish Workshop on Formal Methods (IWFM). Workshops in Computing. BCS (2001)
40. Woodcock, J., Cavalcanti, A.: The semantics of *Circus*. In: Bert, D., Bowen, J.P., Henson, M.C., Robinson, K. (eds.) ZB 2002. LNCS, vol. 2272, pp. 184–203. Springer, Heidelberg (2002). https://doi.org/10.1007/3-540-45648-1_10
41. Woodcock, J., Cavalcanti, A., Foster, S., Oliveira, M., Sampaio, A., Zeyda, F.: UTP, *Circus*, and Isabelle. In: Bowen, J.P., Li, Q., Xu, Q. (eds.) Theories of Programming and Formal Methods. LNCS, vol. 14080, pp. 19–51. Springer, Cham (2023). https://doi.org/10.1007/978-3-031-40436-8_2
42. Woodcock, J., Davies, J.: Using Z-Specification, Refinement, and Proof. International Series in Computer Science. Prentice Hall (1996)
43. Woodcock, J., Larsen, P.G., Bicarregui, J., Fitzgerald, J.S.: Formal methods: practice and experience. ACM Comput. Surv. **41**(4), 19:1–19:36 (2009)
44. Wooldridge, M., Rao, A. (eds.): Foundations of Rational Agency. Applied Logic Series. Kluwer Academic Publishers (1999)
45. Xu, M., Rivoalen, T., Archibald, B., Sevegnani, M.: CAN-VERIFY: a verification tool for BDI agents. In: Herber, P., Wijs, A. (eds.) iFM 2023. LNCS, vol. 14300, pp. 364–373. Springer, Cham (2023). https://doi.org/10.1007/978-3-031-47705-8_19
46. Yan, F., Foster, S., Habli, I.: Automated compositional verification for robotic state machines using Isabelle/HOL. In: 2023 27th International Conference on Engineering of Complex Computer Systems (ICECCS). IEEE Computer Society, pp. 167–176 (2023)
47. Yang, Y., Holvoet, T.: Safe autonomous decision-making with *vGOAL*. In: Mathieu, P., Dignum, F., Novais, P., de la Prieta, F. (eds.) PAAMS 2023. LNCS, vol. 13955, pp. 388–400. Springer, Cham (2023). https://doi.org/10.1007/978-3-031-37616-0_32
48. Zhu, H.: Formal specification of evolutionary software agents. In: George, C., Miao, H. (eds.) ICFEM 2002. LNCS, vol. 2495, pp. 249–261. Springer, Heidelberg (2002). https://doi.org/10.1007/3-540-36103-0_28

Formal Methods for Industrial Critical Systems
30 Years of Railway Applications

Maurice H. ter Beek[1], Alessandro Fantechi[1,2], and Stefania Gnesi[1]

[1] Formal Methods and Tools Lab, CNR–ISTI, Pisa, Italy
{maurice.terbeek,stefania.gnesi}@isti.cnr.it
[2] University of Florence, Florence, Italy
alessandro.fantechi@unifi.it

Abstract. This paper, written in honour of Tiziana Margaria, aims to provide a comprehensive presentation of where mainstream formal methods are currently used for modelling and analysis of railway applications.

1 Introduction

Our collaboration with Tiziana Margaria has a long history, which is part of the history of the Working Group on Formal Methods for Industrial Critical Systems (FMICS)[1] of the European Research Consortium for Informatics and Mathematics (ERCIM)[2], the oldest active working group in this consortium. The FMICS WG, founded in 1996, focuses on the development of formal verification techniques and leads activities, such as joint international projects, related to verification and other formal aspects of software, with a keen eye to industrial applicability. The authors share with Tiziana that they have all chaired this WG.

The annual FMICS conference, first organised in 1996, has held its 29th edition in September 2024. Tiziana chaired the 2005 edition of this conference series [73], whose proceedings are published by Springer in its LNCS series since 2006 (cf., e.g., [14,17,28]), while special issues with extended version of selected conference contributions have regularly appeared in prestigious formal methods journals (cf., e.g., [30,52,54–56,74]; for many years now, these special issues are published in the *International Journal on Software Tools for Technology Transfer* (cf., e.g., [15,16,42]), of which Tiziana is Coordinating Editor and Editor-in-Chief of the thematic theme Foundations for Mastering Change (FoMaC).

The activities of the FMICS WG have stimulated an ongoing scientific discussion on identifying the most efficient formal development and verification techniques, with industrial applicability in mind. Most members of the FMICS community have strong links with the industry and have thus directly contributed to the slow but constant introduction of formal methods in the development cycle of industrial critical systems witnessed during the last decades [13,71].

---

[1] https://fmics.inria.fr.
[2] https://www.ercim.eu.

© The Author(s), under exclusive license to Springer Nature Switzerland AG 2025
M. Hinchey and B. Steffen (Eds.): Festschrift Tiziana Margaria, LNCS 15240, pp. 327–344, 2025.
https://doi.org/10.1007/978-3-031-73887-6_21

In 2013, as a follow-up of an FMICS workshop held in Aix-les-Bains in 2004, Tiziana and Stefania edited a book [57] (cf. Fig. 1) to provide a comprehensive presentation of the mainstream formal methods that were used at that time for designing industrial critical systems. The purpose of this book was threefold: (i) to reduce the learning effort of formal methods, which is typically seen as a major drawback for their industrial dissemination; (ii) to help designers adopt the formal methods that are most appropriate for their systems; and (iii) to offer state-of-the-art techniques and tools for analyzing critical systems. All authors contributed to this book. Tiziana has also been involved in other joint efforts by FMICS members [4,66,72,75].

Fig. 1. Covers of the FMICS Working Group book [57] edited by Tiziana and Stefania

Nowadays, the necessity of formal methods as an essential step in the design process of industrial safety-critical systems is widely recognized. In its more general definition, the term *formal methods* encompasses all notations that have a precise mathematical semantics, together with their associated analysis tools, and which describe the behavior of a system in a formal manner [51]. Many formal methods have emerged during the last few decades. Although the benefits of using these formal methods are undeniable, practical experience shows that each particular method is suitable for handling specific aspects of a system. Therefore, the design of a complex industrial system ideally requires expertise in several formal methods to describe and analyze different views of the system.

Successful applications of formal methods in industry (in particular in the transport domain) have demonstrated these benefits to varying degrees, and have shown that the number of defects in the code can be significantly reduced [13,33]. However, formal methods as yet do not pervade the critical software industry, and this happens also in the railway domain, that is by far the domain in which, for several decades now, most success stories have been reported [10,11,39,40, 46,49]. These success stories are also due to the fact that formal methods are highly recommended by the CENELEC standards [38] for the development of the most critical software for use in the railway industry.

The high expectations concerning safety, but also concerning availability and performance, of advanced future computer-based railway signalling systems, which are large geographically distributed computing systems, can only be successfully addressed by a systematic adoption of formal methods in their definition and development [43,44,80]. This view has been shared by numerous projects within the Shift2Rail Joint Undertaking (JU) such as X2Rail, ASTRail, 4SECU-Rail, PerformingRail, etc.[3] (more below in Sect. 2.4). Although it is not possible to exhaustively cite the success stories of formal methods adoption in railways here, we refer to the vast literature on the theme through some relevant surveys that have recently been published [6,11,46,47].

This paper aims to provide a comprehensive presentation of where mainstream formal methods are currently used for designing railway applications, as well as pointers for their application to future railways systems.

2 Survey on Railway Systems and Related Applications of Formal Methods

Modern railways are in most cases controlled by real-time computer-based systems. Those systems feature embedded, cyber-physical, distributed and heterogeneous architectures, which are increasingly large and complex. To fulfil the safety requirements, railway control systems must undergo extensive verification and validation, which is typically rather time-consuming when conducted by intensive software testing. Model-based analyses and formal methods promise to make such verification activities less error-prone, therefore increasing the effectiveness and efficiency of the overall process.

The main safety-critical railway signalling equipment can roughly be classified in two large classes of applications, excluding just a few future innovations:

1. train movement and distancing control systems, including three subsystems:
   ATC – Automatic Train Control
   ATP – Automatic Train Protection
   ATO – Automatic Train Operation
2. **IXL** – interlocking (Input and eXit Locking) systems
3. other equipment and future advancements

---

[3] https://projects.shift2rail.org/s2r_projects.aspx.

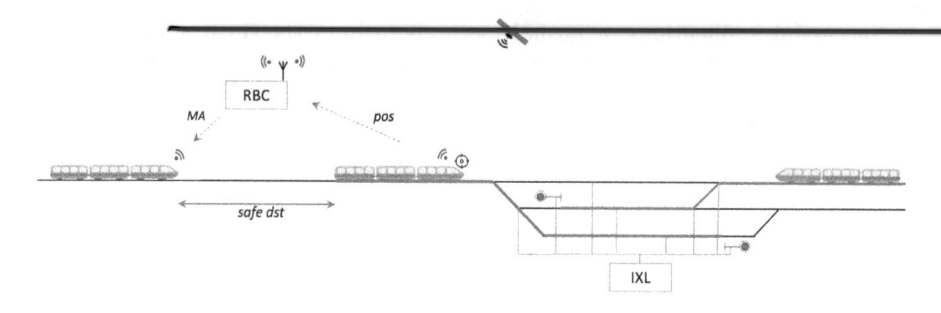

Fig. 2. Main classes of railway signalling systems

Figure 2 provides a broad outline of the purpose of the two classes. On the left, it showcases a train control system based on the communication between trains and a central controller—a so-called Radio Block Centre (RBC), according to ETCS terminology. On the right, it showcases an IXL system controlling the routing of trains inside a station. The drawing also hints at future innovations, among which the use of GPS/GNSS-based satellite positioning of trains [7,70].

2.1 Automatic Train Control and Other Subsystems

ATC subsystems are complex *systems of systems*, made of distributed equipment located on the ground (a.k.a. wayside or trackside) and on board the trains. The main objective of the on-board ATC subsystem is to elaborate and apply the so-called 'dynamic speed profile' (a.k.a. *braking curve*) to control the maximum train speed and automatically brake in case of need (i.e., in case of a risk of collision). To this aim, the on-board ATC subsystem receives the necessary information on the allowed maximum speed and on the status of the line from trackside subsystems: in current ATC subsystems, trains typically receive *Movement Authority* (MA) messages via radio from a monitoring centre that computes related information based on knowledge of the position of the trains along the line. The safety-critical enforcement of emergency braking is also called Automatic Train Protection (ATP).

Modern driverless ATC subsystems have Automatic Train Operation (ATO) functionalities, often used in metro railways, allowing the train to automatically accelerate and decelerate to respect the speed profile and even stop in stations for passenger service whenever required. ATC subsystems may also feature auxiliary control functionalities (e.g., control of pantographs, train integrity check).

The main representatives of ATC/ATP/ATO subsystems respect international standards to ensure interoperability between the different subsystems described. These include ERTMS/ETCS (European Rail Traffic Management Systems/European Train Control System), its Chinese counterpart CTCS (Chinese Train Control System), both focusing on interoperability for passenger, high speed and freight lines, and CBTC (Communication-Based Train Control) systems, mainly aimed at the automatic operation of high capacity metro lines.

The main characteristic of CBTC, shared with ERTMS/ETCS level 3, is the concept of *moving block* signalling (more below in Sect. 2.3). In a nutshell, it consists of computing the safety distance between trains by considering the exact position of each train rather than considering the segment of the line occupied by the train as its position. The wayside ATP for CBTC systems is typically called Zone Controller.

These classes of subsystems have been subject to formal specification and verification for several decades now, as witnessed by the success stories of the application of the B method to many cases, which include the verification of the ATP system for the RER Line A of Paris [59], the Subway Speed Control System (SSCS) of the subway of Calcutta [32], and Line 14 of the Paris Metro [35], as well as derivatives thereof, like line 1 or the NY Canarsie line [37], or the driverless Paris–Roissy Airport shuttle [18]; B was also used for an industrial scale analysis of Alstom's U400 system [29], which is in operation in about 100 metro lines worldwide. Further success stories of applications of formal methods include the metro control system of Rio de Janeiro, with the support of Simulink/Stateflow [48], ERTMS/ETCS with NuSMV [26] and, in [2], the MA scenario of CTCS level 3 modelled in the Architectural Analysis and Design Language (AADL) and in Hybrid CSP and verified with the Hybrid Hoare Logic (HHL) Prover based on Isabelle/HOL.

2.2 Interlocking Systems

A railway *interlocking* (IXL) system is responsible for guiding trains safely through a given railway network made of track devices such as junctions and crossings, providing exclusive access to the requested routes. Once a route is set for a train, all movable devices belonging to the route are set in a locked position and a signal to proceed over that route is given; when the train has passed beyond the section of the track involved, the section and the route are released for successive reservations by other trains. The IXL safety logic is mostly realised through control tables, a set of rules/constraints that must be observed and that are an abstract specification for the area under the IXL responsibility. The IXL control tables are designed such that it is impossible to display a signal to proceed unless the route to be used is proven safe. In this way, no other train is allowed to enter a conflicting route until it is released by the IXL system.

The equation-based tabular nature of the IXL systems, and the fact that their safety requirements can easily be expressed in temporal logic, makes them particularly amenable for formal verification employing model checking or SMT solving. However, these verification tasks share the combinatorial state-space explosion problem, due to the high number of Boolean variables involved, especially in the case of IXL systems controlling large stations: the first applications of model checking, tracing back to the late nineties, have addressed portions of an IXL system (cf., e.g., [20,27,58]); later studies have benefited from the more powerful verification engines powered by SMT solvers [22,64], and focused on the use of specific abstractions [21,65] or of compositional reasoning [61,68] to address the state-space explosion problem.

2.3 Other Equipment and Future Advancements

The classification presented in the beginning of this section excludes a number of other railway equipment that has nevertheless captured the interest of the formal methods community due to the high degree of responsibility for software to ensure safety. These include safety-critical systems that are ancillary to the previous ones (such as the control of level crossings or platform screen doors), systems focused on traffic management/supervision, or envisioned future advances in train control policies. We mention some of these systems in this section.

Level Crossings. Level crossing control has been used as a case study in several studies on the use of formal methods in railways, due to the high safety concerns generated by the intersection of road and rail traffic. A notable example is the use of validation of model checking with UPPAAL of a novel design of a level crossing protection system [53].

Platform Screen Doors. In automated metros, typically operating in a closed environment, platform screen doors are adopted to avoid users to enter or to fall on the tracks. A platform screen door controller has the responsibility of opening only when the train's doors are perfectly aligned with the platform doors. It is worth mentioning that the software of several such installations around the world was developed with the help of the B method [67].

ATS (Automatic Train Supervision). ATS systems aim to supervision the railway system for all those high-level monitoring, track optimisation and maintenance operations not addressed by the other subsystems. While many tasks related to ATS systems (e.g., remote route lock/unlock command) cannot be considered as safety critical since other subsystems will provide the necessary protection against hazards, there are situations in which a certain level of criticality is assigned to those systems as well, for instance when they can be used to activate rescue interventions in case of anomalies requiring feedback from train operators. An ATS system typically acts by issuing route requests to an IXL system; doing so, it can easily incur in deadlocks due to the IXL constraints. Deadlock avoidance can be tackled by model checking, as shown in [76,77].

Moving Block. The ERTMS/ETCS standard considers different levels of operation for compliant ATC systems. In the most advanced one, ERTMS/ETCS level 3, there are no track occupancy sensors and it is the responsibility of an on-board odometry system to keep track of the train's position, as well as to compute the current train speed. The on-board computer of each train periodically sends to the RBC a position report and the results of a train integrity check. In turn, the RBC sends the MA back to each train. The MA is computed by considering the minimum safe rear end of the foregoing train (*moving block* signalling), further improving a line's throughput and reducing maintenance costs.

The absence of track circuits as safe train detection and localisation mechanism, and the difficulty of computing the exact train position, have so far prevented the actual deployment of ETCS level 3 systems, due to safety concerns.

Nevertheless, ETCS level 3 is currently the most promising level of operation in terms of safety increase, capacity gains and maintenance cost reduction. As such it provides a challenging case study; in particular, there is a rich literature on the application of a variety of formal methods and tools to a downsized version named ERTMS/ETCS Hybrid L3 [1,3,5,7,24,31,34,60,69,81].

Satellite Positioning. The localisation of trains along a line is currently detected by specific trackside sensors (such as track circuits or axle counters) that are able to detect the occupancy of a track section. More precise computation of the current position of a train, required by moving block signalling systems, can be achieved by on-board odometry, accelerometers and other sensors. Satellite positioning promises to become an absolute positioning system, significantly reducing the need and cost of trackside sensing equipment. The statistical nature of positioning information given by GPS/GNSS sensors requires a paradigm shift from qualitative formal verification of safety towards quantitative evaluation aimed at the validation of probabilistic safety requirements. In this regard, UPPAAL's statistical model-checking features were considered in [62,63] for the evaluation of GNSS localisation in the context of ETCS level 3.

The same choice was followed for the safety verification of the satellite-based Autonomous Positioning System (APS) of the Florence tramways in [9].

Virtual Coupling. Further challenges arise from visionary advances of the moving block concept. Indeed, the availability of safe information concerning the position, speed, acceleration and deceleration of the preceding train, like that used in level 3 of ERTMS/ETCS, has inspired the idea of an innovative method of train formation, called Virtual Coupling (VC). The concept, which resembles the platooning concept studied in the automotive domain, is based on the idea of multiple trains that run one behind the other without physical contact but at a distance comparable to mechanical coupling. The strict real-time control of the dynamic parameters of the following train with respect to those of the preceding train, allows the distance between trains to be minimised, thus allowing high flexibility, for instance in forwarding the different segments of a train to different destinations through composition and decomposition during the run. Notably, VC is one of the challenges addressed in the Multiannual Programme of the Shift2Rail JU Initiative and its potential has been studied in [50,78] in the context of the Shift2Rail project PERFORMINGRAIL (more below in Sect. 2.4).

Standard Interfaces. When all subsystems described above, which are typically validated separately, interact with each other—as is the case in all modern settings—it becomes essential to also validate the interfaces between these subsystems. The reason is that some hazards might possibly be generated at the inter-communication protocol level. Formal methods are among the methods specifically adopted for this purpose (cf., e.g., [8,19]), since they are suitable to detect anomalies in the specification and implementation of communication protocols.

2.4 International Projects on Formal Methods and Railways

With no claim to completeness, we briefly describe some international projects on applying formal methods in the railway domain.

EuroInterlocking This project of the International Union of Railways (UIC) aimed at the harmonisation, joint development, and standardisation of IXL and signalling systems in Europe. In particular, it has contributed to the development of standardised file formats for IXL data exchange, and to the construction of a generic simulation tool (exploiting the project-defined location and IXL file formats) for the verification and validation of IXL rules.

EuRailCheck[4] (European Railway Formalization and Validation): This was a project of the European Railway Agency (ERA). The objective of this project was the development of a methodology and supporting tools for the formalisation and validation of (a subset of) the ETCS specifications. Within the project, three main results were achieved: a methodology for the formalisation and validation of the ETCS specifications that goes from the informal analysis of the requirements to their formalisation and validation; a set of support tools, covering the various phases of the methodology; and a realistic subset of the formalised specifications.

INESS[5] (INtegrated European Signalling System): The main goal of this EU FP7 project was to extend and enhance the standardisation process defining and developing specifications for a new generation of IXL systems. One of its tasks was to identify safety requirements of the IXL model and their representation in a formal format, as invariant state properties (using UML-B). A prototypical tool for the verification of these invariants was developed.

EULYNX[6] (European Initiative Linking Interlocking Subsystems): This was an initiative of European Infrastructure Managers. The project aspired to a mutually shared vision toward harmonisation of railway signalling systems, their technical architecture, functions and interfaces. The project includes items like system architecture, modelling and testing, data preparation, interfaces between IXL systems, interfaces to track vacancy detection and adjacent IXL or signalling subsystems: requirement management tools, UML (Unified Modelling Language) and SysML (Systems Modelling Language) modelling techniques were used to formalise unambiguous requirements.

ASTRail[7] (SAtellite-based Signalling and Automation SysTems on Railways along with Formal Method and Moving Block validation): This EU H2020 Shift2Rail project included (i) an analysis phase, dedicated to the comparison and evaluation of the main formal methods and tools that were being

---

[4] https://es-static.fbk.eu/projects/eurailcheck/.
[5] https://www.iness.eu.
[6] https://eulynx.eu.
[7] http://www.astrail.eu.

used at that time in the railway industry to guarantee that software design and implementation criticalities do not jeopardise the safety, as well as (ii) an application phase, in which selected formal methods were used to model and analyse two main goals addressed by the project, namely moving block distancing and automatic driving. The aim was to validate that the formal methods are not only able to guarantee safety issues, but also—more in general—the long term reliability and availability of the software.

X2RAIL-2[8] (Enhancing Railway Signaling Systems): This EU H2020 Shift2-Rail project carried out a survey to identify the railway signalling industry's expectations of formal methods and tools, in terms of their most important characteristics, benefits and challenges. This survey [83] showed that formal methods can provide significant benefits to railway signalling system development in terms of improved safety, better requirement quality and reliability and, finally, reduced time-to-market and cost. However, the survey indicated that there are also significant obstacles increasing to the widespread use of formal methods to gain such benefits. The main obstacle is the high learning curve and indeed formal methods have the image of being too difficult to apply for "ordinary engineers". This survey moreover showed that the use of formal methods would be helped by more standardised interfaces.

4SECURail[9] (FORmal Methods and CSIRT for the RAILway sector): This EU H2020 Shift2Rail project addressed the development of a demonstrator for the use of formal methods in the railway environment. This project provided a demonstrator of state-of-the-art formal methods and tools to evaluate the learning curve and to perform a cost-benefit analysis of the adoption of formal methods in the railway industry. The demonstrator has been applied to a railway signalling subsystem described using standard interfaces aimed at illustrating some usable state-of-the-art techniques for rigorous standard interface specification, as well as at supporting a cost-benefit analysis to back this strategy with sound economic arguments.

PERFORMINGRAIL[10] (PERformance-based Formal modelling and Optimal tRaffic Management for movING-block RAILway signalling): This EU H2020 Shift2Rail project aimed to deliver formal modelling and optimal traffic management of a moving block railway signalling system using advanced train positioning approaches that mitigate potential hazards in the diverse market segments. It implemented a holistic system approach to address the open challenges for the moving block and VC concepts in terms of safe operational principles and specifications, reliable TIM technologies, high-accuracy train localisation and optimised moving block traffic management algorithms. The main objectives were to enhance and verify existing specifications for moving block signalling, while developing formal models, algorithms and proof-of-concepts to test and validate an integrated future mov-

---

[8] https://projects.shift2rail.org/s2r_ip2_n.aspx?p=X2RAIL-2.
[9] http://www.4securail.eu.
[10] https://www.performingrail.com.

ing block system architecture that will provide safe and effective operational performance.

X2RAIL-5[11] (Advanced Traffic Management & Control Systems): This EU H2020 Shift2Rail project had the objective to improve the standardisation and integration of formal methods application in the development of Europe's rail control systems while reducing time to market and improving effectiveness in the introduction of new signalling and supervision systems. A particular project output was to propose and apply a methodology and toolchain to automate the transformation of semi-formal (specification) models into models suitable for formal verification. The objective was to create a tool that can automatically translate the semi-formal SysML models into a formal model, to obtain a more precise and rigorous representation of the system, and to apply formal verification to prove properties against the formal model. According to this, two toolchains were proposed for the automated transformation of EULYNX SysML models into formal models.

3 ISoLA: Leveraging Applications of Formal Methods, Verification and Validation

ISoLA is a highly successful symposium series[12], currently at its 12th edition, for developers, users and researchers to discuss issues related to the adoption and use of rigorous tools, based on formal methods, for the specification, analysis, verification, certification, construction, testing and maintenance of systems from the perspective of their different application domains, instituted by Tiziana and Bernhard Steffen.

The adoption of formal methods in railway signalling has been the subject of specific tracks at ISoLA conferences for over a decade now. The "Formal Methods for Intelligent Transportation Systems" track, held at ISoLA 2012 [41], focused on railway applications, as a recognition of how much the railway signalling sector has been a source of success stories on the adoption of formal methods. The "Formal Methods and Safety Certification: Challenges in the Railways Domain" track, held at ISoLA 2016 [40], addressed the many challenges posed by the increasing scale and complexity of railway systems.

In 2019, a workshop colocated with the DisCoTec federated conference on distributed computing techniques, coined DisCoRail ("Formal methods for DIStributed COmputing in future RAILway systems"), was initiated. The aim of this workshop series is to discuss how distributed computing is affecting the railway signalling domain, given that the new technologies being applied in this domain (with a main example represented by the wide deployment of ERTMS/ETCS systems on high-speed lines as well as on freight corridors) have transformed railways in a very large geographic distributed computing system.

It thus appeared evident that the high expectations on safety, but also on availability and performance of future railway signalling systems, in the presence

---

[11] https://verkehrsforschung.dlr.de/en/projects/x2rail-5.
[12] https://www.isola-conference.org.

of a high degree of distribution, can only be addressed by the systematic adoption of formal methods in the definition and development of such systems. This view was shared by several projects within the Shift2Rail JU, which were represented in the successive editions of the DisCoRail workshop, held at ISoLA 2020/21 [43] as a track on "Formal methods for DIStributed COmputing in future RAILway systems", replicated at the ISoLA 2022 and 2024 editions [44,45].

4 Conclusion

The use of formal methods and tools is an essential step in the design process of industrial safety-critical systems. Their successful application in the transport domain has demonstrated several benefits, showing that the number of defects in the code can be significantly reduced. The aim of this paper is to provide a comprehensive presentation of where mainstream formal methods are currently being used for designing railway applications, as well as future advanced railway systems where their application might turn out useful. Yet there are significant obstacles that hinder a greater use of formal methods to achieve benefits.

Presumably the greatest obstacle is the steep learning curve. A recent survey among 130 experts in formal methods (including—next to Tiziana—3 Turing Award winners[13], all 5 FME Fellowship Award winners[14], 17 CAV Award winners[15]) investigated the factors limiting the uptake of formal methods in industry [51, Section 5: Formal Methods in Industry]. These experts recognised several limiting factors: "academic tools have limitations and are not professionally maintained" (66.9%), formal methods "are not properly integrated in the industrial design life cycle" (66.9%) and "have a steep learning curve" (63.8%). Moreover, 62.3% of the respondents indicated that "developers are reluctant to change their way of working." Alas, formal methods have the image of being too difficult. Yet, according to this expert survey, the key *limiting factor for a wider adoption of formal methods by industry*, identified by 71.5% of the respondents, is that "engineers lack proper training in formal methods".

This conclusion is shared by numerous experts. A recent white paper [25], which presents the outcome of a Workshop on Formal Methods, advocates "the inclusion of a compulsory formal methods course in Computer Science (CS) and software engineering curricula" based on the observation that "there is a lack of CS graduates who are qualified to apply formal methods in industry".

In the context of safety- and mission-critical applications, a very recent paper recognises "an urgent need to emphasize and integrate formal methods into the undergraduate curriculum in CS in the United States", since "the lack of a well-structured exposure to formal methods is a serious shortcoming in our computing curricula" [79]: "We cannot expect graduates to become experts in program verification as professionals if they never encountered the ideas as students".

---

[13] https://amturing.acm.org/byyear.cfm.
[14] https://www.fmeurope.org/awards/.
[15] http://i-cav.org/cav-award/.

Finally, [12] advocates a prominent role of formal methods in the ACM/IEEE-CS/AAAI CS2023 curriculum and provides concrete suggestions for educators to incorporate formal methods into CS education without displacing other engineering aspects of CS that are already widely accepted as essential. This paper is based on three accompanying papers which underline (i) the importance of formal methods *thinking* in CS education [36], since it provides the necessary rigour in reasoning about correctness which is a fundamental skill for future software developers; (ii) that every computer scientist needs to *know* formal methods [23], since the skills and knowledge acquired from studying formal methods provide the indispensable solid foundation that forms the backbone of CS practice; and (iii) the increasing *use* of formal methods in industry [13], not limited to safety-critical domain, which demonstrates that formal methods have wide-ranging practical value in a in a society that increasingly relies on software.

Other significant obstacles to further adoption of formal methods in the railway domain include the fact that applicable standards (such as CENELEC EN 50128 [38]) are not sufficiently clear on how to actually use formal methods cost-effectively and the lack of a clear picture of what can be achieved by using formal methods (in terms of benefits, both technical and economical; even though a recent study reports promising cost savings [19, Section 3: Cost-Benefit Analysis]. This leads management to deem formal methods too risky. The aforementioned survey among 130 experts in formal methods also contained a question that asked the respondents to make an informal cost-benefit analysis over time [51, Section 5.3: Return on Investment]. A small majority of 58.5% of the respondents answered that the application of formal methods is *profitable in medium and long terms*; 15% that they are *immediately profitable* and 12.3% answered that they are *profitable in the long term only*, while 2.3% answered that there is *no return on investment* and 11.5% had *no opinion*.

Another obstacle to the widespread use of formal methods is the current lack of commercial formal tools, easy to integrate in the software development process and working on open standard formats [49]. The state-of-the-art of the development tools market apparently sees either the offer of industry-ready, well-maintained, and supported tools working on closed proprietary formats, or open-source tools working on standard open format but offering a low level of support and maintenance.

But the future is bright! The formal methods community recently received support from The White House [82, Part II: Securing the Building Blocks of Cyberspace—Formal Methods]: "Given the complexities of code, testing is a necessary but insufficient step in the development process to fully reduce vulnerabilities at scale. If correctness is defined as the ability of a piece of software to meet a specific security requirement, then it is possible to demonstrate correctness using mathematical techniques called *formal methods*. [...] While formal methods have been studied for decades, their deployment remains limited; further innovation in approaches to make formal methods widely accessible is vital to accelerate broad adoption."

Acknowledgements. This paper is dedicated to Tiziana Margaria to celebrate her diamond jubilee (never mention a lady's age!). While none of us ever wrote a paper with Tiziana, we all have many fond memories of meetings (in particular within the FMICS WG), dinners (never in Italian restaurants outside Italy!) and conferences (in particular at the ενήλιος ISoLA series, *the place* for networking on formal methods!). *Buon compleanno, Tiziana!*

Part of this study was carried out within the MUR PRIN 2022 PNRR P2022A492B project ADVENTURE (ADVancEd iNtegraTed evalUation of Railway systEms) and the MOST – Sustainable Mobility National Research Center and received funding from the European Union NextGenerationEU (PIANO NAZIONALE DI RIPRESA E RESILIENZA (PNRR) – MISSIONE 4, COMPONENTE 2, INVESTIMENTO 1.4 – D.D. 1033 17/06/2022, CN00000023. This manuscript reflects only the authors' views and opinions, neither the European Union nor the European Commission can be considered responsible for them.

Conflicts of interest. The author(s) has no competing interests to declare that are relevant to the content of this manuscript.

References

1. Abrial, J.: The ABZ-2018 case study with Event-B. Int. J. Softw. Tools Technol. Transf. **22**(3), 257–264 (2020). https://doi.org/10.1007/s10009-019-00525-3
2. Ahmad, E., Dong, Y., Larson, B.R., Lü, J., Tang, T., Zhan, N.: Behavior modeling and verification of movement authority scenario of Chinese train control system using AADL. Sci. China Inf. Sci. **58**(11), 1–20 (2015). https://doi.org/10.1007/s11432-015-5346-2
3. Arcaini, P., Kofroň, J., Ježek, P.: Validation of the hybrid ERTMS/ETCS level 3 using SPIN. Int. J. Softw. Tools Technol. Transf. **22**(3), 265–279 (2020). https://doi.org/10.1007/s10009-019-00539-x
4. Arenas, A.E., Bicarregui, J., Margaria, T.: The FMICS view on the verified software repository. J. Integr. Des. Process. Sci. **10**(4), 47–54 (2006)
5. Bartholomeus, M., Luttik, B., Willemse, T.: Modelling and analysing ERTMS hybrid level 3 with the mCRL2 toolset. In: Howar, F., Barnat, J. (eds.) FMICS 2018. LNCS, vol. 11119, pp. 98–114. Springer, Cham (2018). https://doi.org/10.1007/978-3-030-00244-2_7
6. Basile, D., et al.: On the industrial uptake of formal methods in the railway domain. In: Furia, C.A., Winter, K. (eds.) IFM 2018. LNCS, vol. 11023, pp. 20–29. Springer, Cham (2018). https://doi.org/10.1007/978-3-319-98938-9_2
7. Basile, D., ter Beek, M.H., Ferrari, A., Legay, A.: Exploring the ERTMS/ETCS full moving block specification: an experience with formal methods. Int. J. Softw. Tools Technol. Transf. **24**(3), 351–370 (2022). https://doi.org/10.1007/s10009-022-00653-3
8. Basile, D., Fantechi, A., Rosadi, I.: Formal analysis of the UNISIG safety application intermediate sub-layer. In: Lluch Lafuente, A., Mavridou, A. (eds.) FMICS 2021. LNCS, vol. 12863, pp. 174–190. Springer, Cham (2021). https://doi.org/10.1007/978-3-030-85248-1_11
9. Basile, D., Fantechi, A., Rucher, L., Mandò, G.: Analysing an autonomous tramway positioning system with the Uppaal statistical model checker. Form. Asp. Comput. **33**(6), 957–987 (2021). https://doi.org/10.1007/s00165-021-00556-1

10. ter Beek, M.H.: Formal methods and tools applied in the railway domain. In: Bonfanti, S., Gargantini, A., Leuschel, M., Riccobene, E., Scandurra, P. (eds.) ABZ 2024. LNCS, vol. 14759, pp. 3–21. Springer, Cham (2024). https://doi.org/10.1007/978-3-031-63790-2_1
11. ter Beek, M.H., et al.: Adopting formal methods in an industrial setting: the railways case. In: ter Beek, M.H., McIver, A., Oliveira, J.N. (eds.) FM 2019. LNCS, vol. 11800, pp. 762–772. Springer, Cham (2019). https://doi.org/10.1007/978-3-030-30942-8_46
12. ter Beek, M.H., Broy, M., Dongol, B.: CS2023: The role of formal methods in computer science education. ACM InRoads (2024)
13. ter Beek, M.H., et al.: Formal Methods in Industry. Form. Asp, Comput (2024). https://doi.org/10.1145/3689374
14. ter Beek, M.H., Gnesi, S., Knapp, A. (eds.): FMICS/AVoCS 2016. LNCS, vol. 9933. Springer, Cham (2016). https://doi.org/10.1007/978-3-319-45943-1
15. ter Beek, M.H., Gnesi, S., Knapp, A.: Formal methods and automated verification of critical systems. Int. J. Softw. Tools Technol. Transf. **20**(4), 355–358 (2018). https://doi.org/10.1007/s10009-018-0494-5
16. ter Beek, M.H., Gnesi, S., Knapp, A.: Formal methods for transport systems. Int. J. Softw. Tools Technol. Transf. **20**(3), 237–241 (2018). https://doi.org/10.1007/s10009-018-0487-4
17. ter Beek, M.H., Ničković, D. (eds.): FMICS 2020. LNCS, vol. 12327. Springer, Cham (2020). https://doi.org/10.1007/978-3-030-58298-2
18. Behm, P., Benoit, P., Faivre, A., Meynadier, J.-M.: Météor: a successful application of B in a large project. In: Wing, J.M., Woodcock, J., Davies, J. (eds.) FM 1999. LNCS, vol. 1708, pp. 369–387. Springer, Heidelberg (1999). https://doi.org/10.1007/3-540-48119-2_22
19. Belli, D., et al.: The 4SECURail case study on rigorous standard interface specifications. In: Cimatti, A., Titolo, L. (eds.) FMICS 2023. LNCS, vol. 14290, pp. 22–39. Springer, Cham (2023). https://doi.org/10.1007/978-3-031-43681-9_2
20. Bernardeschi, C., Fantechi, A., Gnesi, S., Larosa, S., Mongardi, G., Romano, D.: A formal verification environment for railway signaling system design. Form. Methods Syst. Des. **12**(2), 139–161 (1998). https://doi.org/10.1023/A:1008645826258
21. Bonacchi, A., Fantechi, A., Bacherini, S., Tempestini, M.: Validation process for railway interlocking systems. Sci. Comput. Program. **128**, 2–21 (2016). https://doi.org/10.1016/j.scico.2016.04.004
22. Borälv, A.: Interlocking design automation using Prover Trident. In: Havelund, K., Peleska, J., Roscoe, B., de Vink, E. (eds.) FM 2018. LNCS, vol. 10951, pp. 653–656. Springer, Cham (2018). https://doi.org/10.1007/978-3-319-95582-7_39
23. Broy, M., et al.: Does every computer scientist need to know formal methods? Form. Asp. Comput. (2024). https://doi.org/10.1145/36707
24. Butler, M., Hoang, T.S., Raschke, A., Reichl, K.: Introduction to special section on the ABZ 2018 case study: hybrid ERTMS/ETCS Level 3. Int. J. Softw. Tools Technol. Transf. **22**(3), 249–255 (2020). https://doi.org/10.1007/s10009-020-00562-3
25. Cerone, A., et al.: Rooting formal methods within higher education curricula for computer science and software engineering — a white paper —. In: Cerone, A., Roggenbach, M. (eds.) FMFun 2019. CCIS, vol. 1301, pp. 1–26. Springer, Cham (2021). https://doi.org/10.1007/978-3-030-71374-4_1
26. Chiappini, A., et al.: Formalization and validation of a subset of the European Train Control System. In: ICSE 2010, pp. 109–118. ACM (2010). https://doi.org/10.1145/1810295.1810312

27. Cimatti, A., Giunchiglia, F., Mongardi, G., Romano, D., Torielli, F., Traverso, P.: Formal verification of a railway interlocking system using model checking. Form. Asp. Comput. **10**(4), 361–380 (1998). https://doi.org/10.1007/S001650050022
28. Cofer, D., Fantechi, A. (eds.): FMICS 2008. LNCS, vol. 5596. Springer, Heidelberg (2009). https://doi.org/10.1007/978-3-642-03240-0
29. Comptier, M., Leuschel, M., Mejia, L.-F., Perez, J.M., Mutz, M.: Property-based modelling and validation of a CBTC zone controller in Event-B. In: Collart-Dutilleul, S., Lecomte, T., Romanovsky, A. (eds.) RSSRail 2019. LNCS, vol. 11495, pp. 202–212. Springer, Cham (2019). https://doi.org/10.1007/978-3-030-18744-6_13
30. Cuéllar, J., Gnesi, S., Latella, D.: FMICS special issue. Sci. Comput. Program. **36**(1), 1–3 (2000). https://doi.org/10.1016/S0167-6423(99)00014-3
31. Cunha, A., Macedo, N.: Validating the hybrid ERTMS/ETCS level 3 concept with Electrum. Int. J. Softw. Tools Technol. Transf. **22**(3), 281–296 (2020). https://doi.org/10.1007/s10009-019-00540-4
32. DaSilva, C., Dehbonei, B., Mejia, F.: Formal specification in the development of industrial applications: subway speed control system. In: Diaz, M., Groz, R. (eds.) FORTE 1992. IFIP, vol. C-10, pp. 199–213. North-Holland (1992)
33. Davis, J.A., et al.: Study on the barriers to the industrial adoption of formal methods. In: Pecheur, C., Dierkes, M. (eds.) FMICS 2013. LNCS, vol. 8187, pp. 63–77. Springer, Heidelberg (2013). https://doi.org/10.1007/978-3-642-41010-9_5
34. Dghaym, D., Dalvandi, M., Poppleton, M., Snook, C.: Formalising the hybrid ERTMS level 3 specification in iUML-B and Event-B. Int. J. Softw. Tools Technol. Transf. **22**(3), 297–313 (2020). https://doi.org/10.1007/s10009-019-00548-w
35. Dollé, D., Essamé, D., Falampin, J.: B dans le transport ferroviaire: L'expérience de Siemens transportation systems. Tech. Sci. Inf. **22**(1), 11–32 (2003). https://doi.org/10.3166/tsi.22.11-32
36. Dongol, B., et al.: On formal methods thinking in computer science education. Form. Asp. Comput. (2024). https://doi.org/10.1145/36704
37. Essamé, D., Dollé, D.: B in large-scale projects: the Canarsie line CBTC experience. In: Julliand, J., Kouchnarenko, O. (eds.) B 2007. LNCS, vol. 4355, pp. 252–254. Springer, Heidelberg (2006). https://doi.org/10.1007/11955757_21
38. European Committee for Electrotechnical Standardization: CENELEC EN 50128: Railway applications – Communication, signalling and processing systems – Software for railway control and protection systems (2011). https://standards.globalspec.com/std/1678027/cenelec-en-50128
39. Fantechi, A.: Twenty-five years of formal methods and railways: what next? In: Counsell, S., Núñez, M. (eds.) SEFM 2013. LNCS, vol. 8368, pp. 167–183. Springer, Cham (2014). https://doi.org/10.1007/978-3-319-05032-4_13
40. Fantechi, A., Ferrari, A., Gnesi, S.: Formal methods and safety certification: challenges in the railways domain. In: Margaria, T., Steffen, B. (eds.) ISoLA 2016. LNCS, vol. 9953, pp. 261–265. Springer, Cham (2016). https://doi.org/10.1007/978-3-319-47169-3_18
41. Fantechi, A., Flammini, F., Gnesi, S.: Formal methods for intelligent transportation systems. In: Margaria, T., Steffen, B. (eds.) ISoLA 2012. LNCS, vol. 7610, pp. 187–189. Springer, Heidelberg (2012). https://doi.org/10.1007/978-3-642-34032-1_19
42. Fantechi, A., Flammini, F., Gnesi, S.: Formal methods for railway control systems. Int. J. Softw. Tools Technol. Transf. **16**(6), 643–646 (2014). https://doi.org/10.1007/s10009-014-0342-1

43. Fantechi, A., Gnesi, S., Haxthausen, A.E.: Formal methods for distributed computing in future railway systems. In: Margaria, T., Steffen, B. (eds.) ISoLA 2020. LNCS, vol. 12478, pp. 389–392. Springer, Cham (2020). https://doi.org/10.1007/978-3-030-61467-6_24
44. Fantechi, A., Gnesi, S., Haxthausen, A.E.: Formal methods for distributed control systems of future railways. In: Margaria, T., Steffen, B. (eds.) ISoLA 2022. LNCS, vol. 13704, pp. 243–245. Springer, Cham (2022). https://doi.org/10.1007/978-3-031-19762-8_19
45. Fantechi, A., Gnesi, S., Haxthausen, A.E.: Formal methods for DIStributed COmputing in future RAILway systems. In: Margaria, T., Steffen, B. (eds.) ISoLA 2024. Springer, LNCS (2024)
46. Ferrari, A., ter Beek, M.H.: Formal methods in railways: a systematic mapping study. ACM Comput. Surv. **55**(4), 69:1–69:37 (2023). https://doi.org/10.1145/3520480
47. Ferrari, A., et al.: Survey on formal methods and tools in railways: the ASTRail approach. In: Collart-Dutilleul, S., Lecomte, T., Romanovsky, A. (eds.) RSSRail 2019. LNCS, vol. 11495, pp. 226–241. Springer, Cham (2019). https://doi.org/10.1007/978-3-030-18744-6_15
48. Ferrari, A., Fantechi, A., Magnani, G., Grasso, D., Tempestini, M.: The Metrô Rio case study. Sci. Comput. Program. **78**(7), 828–842 (2013). https://doi.org/10.1016/j.scico.2012.04.003
49. Ferrari, A., Mazzanti, F., Basile, D., ter Beek, M.H.: Systematic evaluation and usability analysis of formal methods tools for railway signaling system design. IEEE Trans. Softw. Eng. **48**(11), 4675–4691 (2022). https://doi.org/10.1109/TSE.2021.3124677
50. Flammini, F., Marrone, S., Nardone, R., Vittorini, V.: Compositional modeling of railway virtual coupling with stochastic activity networks. Form. Asp. Comput. **33**(6), 989–1007 (2021). https://doi.org/10.1007/S00165-021-00560-5
51. Garavel, H., Beek, M.H., Pol, J.: The 2020 expert survey on formal methods. In: ter Beek, M.H., Ničković, D. (eds.) FMICS 2020. LNCS, vol. 12327, pp. 3–69. Springer, Cham (2020). https://doi.org/10.1007/978-3-030-58298-2_1
52. Garavel, H., Gnesi, S., Schieferdecker, I.: Special issue on FMICS 2000. Sci. Comput. Program. **46**(3), 195–196 (2003). https://doi.org/10.1016/S0167-6423(02)00091-6
53. Ghazel, M.: A control scheme for automatic level crossings under the ERTMS/ETCS level 2/3 operation. IEEE Trans. Intell. Transp. Syst. **18**(10), 2667–2680 (2017). https://doi.org/10.1109/TITS.2017.2657695
54. Gnesi, S., Latella, D.: Special issue on FMICS 1996. Form. Methods Syst. Des. **12**(2), 123–124 (1998). https://doi.org/10.1023/A:1008669025349
55. Gnesi, S., Latella, D.: Special issue on FMICS 1997. Form. Asp. Comput. **10**(4), 311–312 (1998). https://doi.org/10.1007/s001650050019
56. Gnesi, S., Latella, D.: Special issue on FMICS 1999. Form. Methods Syst. Des. **19**(2), 119–120 (2001). https://doi.org/10.1023/A:1011279615774
57. Gnesi, S., Margaria, T.: Formal Methods for Industrial Critical Systems: A Survey of Applications. Wiley, Hoboken (2013). https://doi.org/10.1002/9781118459898
58. Groote, J.F., van Vlijmen, S.F.M., Koorn, J.W.C.: The safety guaranteeing system at station Hoorn-Kersenboogerd. In: COMPASS 1995, pp. 57–68 (1995). https://doi.org/10.1109/CMPASS.1995.521887
59. Guiho, G., Hennebert, C.: SACEM Software validation. In: ICSE 1990, pp. 186–191. IEEE (1990)

60. Hansen, D., et al.: Validation and real-life demonstration of ETCS hybrid level 3 principles using a formal B model. Int. J. Softw. Tools Technol. Transf. **22**(3), 315–332 (2020). https://doi.org/10.1007/s10009-020-00551-6
61. Haxthausen, A.E., Fantechi, A.: Compositional verification of railway interlocking systems. Form. Asp. Comput. **35**(1), 4:1–4:46 (2023). https://doi.org/10.1145/3549736
62. Himrane, O., Beugin, J., Ghazel, M.: Toward formal safety and performance evaluation of GNSS-based railway localisation function. IFAC-Pap. **54**(2), 159–166 (2021). https://doi.org/10.1016/j.ifacol.2021.06.049. Proceedings CTS 2021
63. Himrane, O., Beugin, J., Ghazel, M.: Implementation of a model-oriented approach for supporting safe integration of GNSS-based virtual balises in ERTMS/ETCS Level 3. IEEE Open J. Intell. Transp. Syst. **4**, 294–310 (2023). https://doi.org/10.1109/OJITS.2023.3267142
64. Hong, L.V., Haxthausen, A.E., Peleska, J.: Formal modelling and verification of interlocking systems featuring sequential release. Sci. Comput. Program. **133**, 91–115 (2017). https://doi.org/10.1016/j.scico.2016.05.010
65. James, P., Moller, F., Nga, N.H., Roggenbach, M., Schneider, S., Treharne, H.: Techniques for modelling and verifying railway interlockings. Int. J. Softw. Tools Technol. Transf. **16**(6), 685–711 (2014). https://doi.org/10.1007/S10009-014-0304-7
66. Kubczak, C., Margaria, T., Nagel, R., Steffen, B.: Plug and play with FMICS-jETI: beyond scripting and coding. ERCIM News **73**, 41–42 (2008). http://ercim-news.ercim.eu/plug-and-play-with-fmics-jeti-beyond-scripting-and-coding
67. Lecomte, T.: Safe and reliable metro platform screen doors control/command systems. In: Cuellar, J., Maibaum, T., Sere, K. (eds.) FM 2008. LNCS, vol. 5014, pp. 430–434. Springer, Heidelberg (2008). https://doi.org/10.1007/978-3-540-68237-0_32
68. Limbrée, C., Pecheur, C.: A framework for the formal verification of networks of railway interlockings - application to the Belgian railway. Electron. Commun. EASST **76** (2018). https://doi.org/10.14279/TUJ.ECEASST.76.1077
69. Mammar, A., Frappier, M., Tueno Fotso, S.J., Laleau, R.: A formal refinement-based analysis of the hybrid ERTMS/ETCS level 3 standard. Int. J. Softw. Tools Technol. Transf. **22**(3), 333–347 (2020). https://doi.org/10.1007/s10009-019-00543-1
70. Marais, J., Beugin, J., Berbineau, M.: A survey of GNSS-based research and developments for the European railway signaling. IEEE Trans. Intell. Transp. Syst. **18**(10), 2602–2618 (2017). https://doi.org/10.1109/TITS.2017.2658179
71. Margaria, T., Kiniry, J.: Welcome to formal methods in industry. IT Prof. **22**(1), 9–12 (2020). https://doi.org/10.1109/MITP.2020.2968715
72. Margaria, T., Kubczak, C., Steffen, B., Naujokat, S.: The FMICS-jETI platform: status and perspectives. In: ISoLA 2006, pp. 402–407. IEEE (2006). https://doi.org/10.1109/ISOLA.2006.50
73. Margaria, T., Massink, M.: FMICS 2005. ACM (2005). https://doi.org/10.1145/1081180
74. Margaria, T., Massink, M.: Special section on FMICS 2005. Int. J. Softw. Tools Technol. Transf. **11**(5), 355–357 (2009). https://doi.org/10.1007/S10009-009-0121-6
75. Margaria, T., Raffelt, H., Steffen, B., Leucker, M.: The LearnLib in FMICS-jETI. In: ICECCS 2007, pp. 340–352. IEEE (2007). https://doi.org/10.1109/ICECCS.2007.43

76. Mazzanti, F., Ferrari, A., Spagnolo, G.O.: Experiments in formal modelling of a deadlock avoidance algorithm for a CBTC system. In: Margaria, T., Steffen, B. (eds.) ISoLA 2016. LNCS, vol. 9953, pp. 297–314. Springer, Cham (2016). https://doi.org/10.1007/978-3-319-47169-3_22
77. Mazzanti, F., Spagnolo, G.O., Della Longa, S., Ferrari, A.: Deadlock avoidance in train scheduling: a model checking approach. In: Lang, F., Flammini, F. (eds.) FMICS 2014. LNCS, vol. 8718, pp. 109–123. Springer, Cham (2014). https://doi.org/10.1007/978-3-319-10702-8_8
78. Meo, C.D., Di Vaio, M., Flammini, F., Nardone, R., Santini, S., Vittorini, V.: ERTMS/ETCS virtual coupling: proof of concept and numerical analysis. IEEE Trans. Intell. Transp. Syst. **21**(6), 2545–2556 (2020). https://doi.org/10.1109/TITS.2019.2920290
79. Ramnath, S., Walk, S.: Structuring formal methods into the undergraduate computer science curriculum. In: Benz, N., Gopinath, D., Shi, N. (eds.) NFM 2024. LNCS, vol. 14627, pp. 399–405. Springer, Cham (2024). https://doi.org/10.1007/978-3-031-60698-4_24
80. Seisenberger, M., et al.: Safe and secure future AI-driven railway technologies: challenges for formal methods in railway. In: Margaria, T., Steffen, B. (eds.) ISoLA 2022. LNCS, vol. 13704, pp. 246–268. Springer, Cham (2022). https://doi.org/10.1007/978-3-031-19762-8_20
81. Tueno Fotso, S.J., Frappier, M., Laleau, R., Mammar, A.: Modeling the hybrid ERTMS/ETCS level 3 standard using a formal requirements engineering approach. Int. J. Softw. Tools Technol. Transf. **22**(3), 349–363 (2020). https://doi.org/10.1007/s10009-019-00542-2
82. The White House: Back to the Building Blocks: A Path Toward Secure and Measurable Software. Tech. rep., White House Office of the National Cyber Director (ONCD) (2024). https://www.whitehouse.gov/wp-content/uploads/2024/02/Final-ONCD-Technical-Report.pdf
83. X2Rail-2 – Deliverable D5.1, Formal Methods (Taxonomy and Survey), Proposed Methods and Applications (2018). https://projects.shift2rail.org/download.aspx?id=b4cf6a3d-f1f2-4dd3-ae01-2bada34596b8

A Manifesto 4 Longevity as a Biomedical Paradigm Shift - Challenging Entrenched Wisdoms in Healthcare Economics

Christoph Rasche[1]([✉]), Andrea Braun von Reinersdorff[2], and Andreas Bertram[2]

[1] University of Potsdam, Potsdam, Germany
christoph.rasche@uni-potsdam.de
[2] University of Applied Sciences Osnabrück, Osnabrück, Germany
{a.braun,a.bertram}@hs-osnabrueck.de

Abstract. Health should be regarded as an asset and a value dimension and not as a liability or a burden, as it is often the case. This article argues for a paradigm shift towards the longevity framework, taking on increasing significance not only due to demographic changes, but also because of transformed mind maps of aging societies. Paradoxically, our hospital and welfare systems incorporate the features of 'sick care', while neglecting or ignoring the value of healthcare and lifecare. Longevity resonates with the idea of a 360-degree One-Health-Concept (OHC). Instead of expanding the market for sick care, we must invest in healthcare and lifecare as strategic assets from the micro-, meso- and macro-level to overcome the obstacles and constraints of sick caring institutions.

1 Sick Welfare Systems and Hospital Landscapes: The Self-created Market for Sickness

Highly industrialized and advanced societies capitalize on skills, competences, and human assets. Put bluntly, the heralded and acclaimed war for talent reflects the increasing dominance of peopleware, brainware, and software as opposed to sheer hardware in the sense of crude natural resources. For sure, the latter are important if they are in fixed supply, but oil, gas or minerals will only unfold their usefulness if they are transformed into problem solutions by the human factor [11]. And even artificial intelligence is the outcome of bright minds, acumen, and astute knowledge application. The COVID-19 pandemic evidences that natural resources and physical value chains are anything but devaluated assets. Instead, they are the ingredients and bedrock factors of products, solutions to problems and benefit bundles. Moreover, physical assets, irrespective of their constitution, only contribute to value creation if aligned with the human factor end ensuing competences, skills, or the merits of talent. In the long run freewheeling meritocracies will outperform command and order autocracies as they reach the critical mass of creativity, competence, capital, and coordination by means of entrepreneurial markets. People and their health fuel the power of postmodern economies facing severe socio-demographic shifts towards an aging society. Demographic shifts challenge the financial resilience of many welfare systems that rely on a generation deal [6] when many young people take responsibility for a few old. Many young workers are taking on the responsibility of funding and financing the pensions of a few old people with an average life expectancy of 75 years. Thanks to medical progress, safe labor conditions, and better compliance with healthcare recommendations peoples' average life expectancy is likely to increase dramatically - perhaps even to 100 years.

But how to deal with such a disruptive demographic shift from a medical, managerial, and moral perspective? On one hand, longevity is a gift, asset, and source of value. On the other hand, it poses a burden for our entrenched welfare system that stems from an era of short and often harmful lives [5]. This era was driven by the industrialization of labor and employed workforces as input factors for the sake of value creation on behalf of stockholders and target groups. Minimum labor safety and poor labor conditions led to a philosophy of avoiding sickness and maintaining work ability to assure that labor is available, productive, and disposable. Hospital and healthcare institutions placed special emphasis on interventions, therapies, and medications to recreate decompensated human resources to be used in industrial workflows. They are the epitomes of interventional repair institutions when it comes to shock rooms, acute areas, or chronic diseases.

Referring to the Red Ocean and Blue Ocean framework of strategy contrasting selective red alert markets with prospective future markets [4], red medicine resembles the old normal of healing, helping, and handling patients in need. We must pay a substantial tribute to evidence-based medicine because of fencing off the risks of dying, suffering from severe injuries. But we should make the point that longevity extends red medicine insofar as it incorporates the seeds of blue ocean healthcare as opposed to sick care [1,12]. Ironically, the latter is a highly political issue, because red care resembles a huge business model when states handle the decompensation. Red medicine is struck by the notion of fixing the problem while not coming up with fundamental solutions to patient-centered and value-driven healthcare [6]. Red ocean care is provided by top-down driven expert organizations adopting an inside-out position making patients endure a predetermined medication regimen. In a similar vein, compliance is deduced to the acceptance of prescribed medication for the sake of evidence-based outcomes. Medical consultants capitalize on their expert status causing information and competence asymmetries between sickness professionals on the one hand and sickness amateurs on the other hand. Professionals are often reluctant to jeopardize their competence monopoly by means of information disclosure, communication, and education. Moreover, medical experts are inclined to create an aseptic atmosphere of professionalism that lacks empathy and value co-creation possibilities with committed and trained patients [11]. The latter shy away from paternalistic sick care when challenging entrenched wisdoms of service delivery according to the red medicine doctrine. Target groups such as the LOHAS-customers (Lifestyle of Health and Sustainability) spearhead the longevity movement because they command a return on health rather than discounts on sickness. While the return on health equation stands for emancipated and empowered patients actively contributing to their well-being, the discount on sickness resembles a state of pain and agony alleviation by means of straightforward intervention [3]. The motto: Treat first, what kills first! Irrespective of the undisputable merits of high-end emergency medicine and intensive care, blue ocean healthcare significantly increases the value of longevity healthcare and lifecare.

2 Longevity: Blue Ocean Healthcare and Lifecare Instead of Red Ocean Sick Care

Longevity is about quality of life and not about procrastination of death. For sure, most of us are eager to enjoy a long and healthy life that is a function of endogenous and exogenous factors to be managed in a self-conscious fashion. Evidence based medicine adopts the role of a healthcare companion with respect to AI options providing us with personalized, individualized, and localized information under real-time conditions [10]. The quantified-self movement makes passive patients erupt as active healthcare experts that are increasingly accompanied by accompanied by remote AI solutions as well as hands-on medication. The longevity framework is anything but disruptive because it serves as a complementary asset and contributes substantial value to the red medicine doctrine which is still valid in many instances. Nevertheless, red medicine should be levelled-up by means of the longevity approach. The following cornerstones foreshadow the future of longevity healthcare [1,12]:

Training and Physical Activity: One of the most effective and cost-efficient anti-aging programs implies regular exercising. A mixture of cardio, muscle, mobility, and coordination training is far more effective than pure cardio fitness as favored by many elderly people when moderately cycling or nordic walking. As body strength and muscle mass decrease by 5 percent per decade when reaching the age of 30, holistic muscle training (not bodybuilding) may contribute substantially to physical and mental health. Disciplines such as CrossFit or High Intensity Interval Training (HITT) incorporate the best of all worlds because cardio, coordination, and muscle power are trained simultaneously due to complex body movements. Bodyweight training for instance can be practiced whenever you want with minimum equipment such as elastic bands or TRX-trainers. It is worth mentioning that the battle against age cannot be won with soft fitness such as aqua fitness of walking, alone. Body challenges and stretch goals make you leave your comfort zone often causing a fitness and health stalemate. But for motivational reasons a tiny fraction of fitness and exercising is better than degenerating in the comfort zone. Physical progress hinges in the principles of stressing the organism to provoke adaptation und super-compensation. Balancing physical stress and relaxation is core to sustainable health and fitness.

Nutrition and Healthy Food Access: Chronic diseases, obesity, and the metabolic syndrome are often a function of bad food and nutrition habits. In other words, the effects of hard training can be destroyed by idle calory consumption, drug abuse or non-sustainable products in a biological way. In a broader sense, the betterment of the world in a sustainable way makes us enter a world of circularity avoiding waste of fast-moving consumer goods, fostering animal well-being, and replacing animal-based products by vegan alternatives. In a nutshell, the food industry witnesses substantial changes with respect to compliance with ESG standards. ESG calls for addressing ecological, social, and governmental issues when it comes to the new design of the food value chain reflecting not only the position of the end consumer but also the labor conditions of all involved parties. Holistic longevity on the macro-level shares many common ideas with the Club of Rome, the World Health Organization or the United Nations when placing special emphasis on three-dimensional health: Health of mankind, health of animals, and health of nature.

Stress Resilience, Robustness, and Mental Agility: Longevity is also connected to coping strategies as physical and mental burdens cannot always be anticipated or avoided. People often lack the constitution and coping strategies for managing stressful and unpleasant constellations in their professional lives. In some cases, pattern recognition capabilities support a valid forecasting of critical incidents to be managed in a predictive and preventive way. But VUCA-constellations being volatile, uncertain, complex, and ambiguous imply that the only constant is change. For this reason, we are forced to think the unthinkable to be prepared for risks, options, and imponderables of any kind. This can inflict stress, pain, and unease on people who are not equipped with high resilience, agility, smart decision making with only few information, and open to constant routine disruption. Many studies evidence that physical and mental stamina represent a self-enforcing system to be established as a stress protection shield.

Social Bonding and Emotional Capital: The pandemic caused states of sickness not only because of serious infections. It also disrupted social bonding by means of regulation forbidding or inhibiting physical face to face contacts. As a consequence, digitalization had to fill the social gap in a rather aseptic way. The pitfalls of digitalization and remote work can be seen in soaring psychological diseases ranging from digital dementia to digital addiction, and depression. Mental health hinges on stable social landscapes of empathy, courtesy, and real-life affections going beyond emojis. Real-life social bonding contributes to the establishment of emotional capital serving as the glue for affective networking among peer groups and friends. Loneliness or hazardous social bonds with sinister milieus and criminal minds may lead to pathologic social structures. The latter are harmful in a physical and/ or psychological way when disbalancing people and patients. Poor social, infrastructural, and emotional living conditions are closely related to disease, disbalance, and discomfort.

Avoidance of Drugs and Harmful Substances: Longevity is severely hampered by false medication, drug abuse, and the over-consumption of harmful substances such as salt, sugar, or fat. On the one hand, public health makes it a point of its honor to prevent citizens and societies from becoming addicted to harmful substances. On the other hand, sustainable therapies must be employed as means to make substance junkies either completely clean or support a conscious consumption of drugs, pharmaceuticals, or other potentially harmful substances. Beyond public campaigning and strict control of drug availability people must gain the insight that a drug-free life outweighs the short-term gains of substance-induced fun and stress relief. Drug-free societies are desirable but difficult to achieve through sanctions and incentives alone.

Self-empowerment and Health Motivation: The value of longevity cannot be imposed on people in a clear-cut command and order fashion. Intrinsic motivation in accordance with self-empowerment, self-efficacy, and self-consciousness are the core ingredients of the longevity degustation. Personal traits, intelligence, and smartness decisively contribute to a long and healthy high-quality life because they enable permanent self-reflections and a wide-range capability set of doing the right things right in a highly professional way. The knowing-doing-gap is all-pervading causing a state of action paralysis despite knowing everything about health, fitness, and longevity. The missing link is motivation, self-empowerment, and commitment to health and life. Without compliance, commitment, and control healthcare ambitions become suffocated and run dry. Frustration tolerance is not a burden or an obstacle. It represents the capacity to endure harmful and uncomfortable instances without losing control of life.

Genetic and Epigenetic Factors: The fate of genetic endowment cannot be neglected as an endemic health factor. But genetic heritage is not everything since individual lifestyle and commitment to health may have strong bearing on genetics. Epigenetic factors reflect our habits, routines, and behavioral traits with respect to health and correspond with genetic constituencies that are - as opposed to former assumptions - transmutable and anything but a stable system of ingrained body features. When lifestyles are translated into health styles, genetic deficits may be partially compensated by epigenetic benefits of high health compliance, commitment, and control. The relevance of epigenetics for health and wellbeing deserves more research and competence building.

Access to and Benefit from Healthcare: Having direct and easy access to healthcare is of great benefit for patients suffering from acute or chronic diseases. Rationing, rationalization, and prioritization are omni-present in healthcare systems that have to effectively manage constraints such as scarce resources in fixed supplies. The four asset categories of hardware, software, brainware, and peopleware are critical to service delivery in healthcare and must be available and accessible in terms of quality, cost, and time. In many countries, healthcare readiness does not exist yet, leaving the vast majority of people without access to quality healthcare and sanitation resources.

Socioeconomic Status and Competence Level: Referring to the aforementioned healthcare assets peopleware and brainware may extend the value of sheer hardware and software, because the three Cs competence, commitment, and (self)-control go in line with personal qualifications and the socioeconomic status as reflected by academic status or degree of professionalism. The socioeconomic status and the educational level are often highly correlated giving rise to the assumption that longevity is a matter of advanced factors having been accumulated by long-term trajectories of learning, competence building, and on the job experiences. Healthcare alertness and smartness are no inherited assets, they must be gained and sustained by means of personal investments in knowledge and competence. Poor, less educated, and non-committed people die earlier and are often sick, even with non-discriminatory access to healthcare, because they lack the complementary capabilities to take full advantage of well-established welfare systems.

Precision Medicine and AI: Last but not least, artificial intelligence turns out as a truly disruptive technology causing a paradigm shift in many industries. In sharp contrast to the analog age AI provides us with the opportunity to send and receive individualized, personalized, and localized information generated by deep-learning machines such as MedBots to arrive at conclusions and (autonomous) decisions outperforming healthcare professionals. We cannot yet fully rely on AI in healthcare at the moment and hand over much of decision making to autonomous systems and algorithms, but in predictable times, IT-induced support solutions will evolve from augmenting and adjuvant second options to options of first choice. Machines replace manmade service in healthcare pertaining standard operation procedures and even non-routine challenges. AI-supported patients and healthcare customers can highly benefit from realtime high-precision information availability and access. Wearables and external diagnostics gadgets will evolve as micro-implantables such as sensors, intelligent pills, or chip-supported nano devices [10].

Mindful and Healthy Leadership: If companies want to win the war for talent and human capital they not only have to invest in people, but in healthy and welcoming working conditions. This goes beyond risk avoidance, job safety, and a protective work climate. Mental health is a function of mindful and healthy leadership when paying respect to employees irrespective of ranks and files. Pathologic leadership traits are all-pervading and one of the main causes of inner immigration, frustration, and psychological decompensation having a strong negative effect on productivity and economic key performance indicators. The idea of corporate fitness denotes that competitive fitness and labor fitness are different sides of the same medal. How to achieve and sustain superior financial results considering pathologic leadership, devaluating people, and worshipping (short-term) numbers? Servant leadership insinuates a state of mind that nurtures and promotes the development of talents and young professionals by confronting them with inspiring challenges and ambitious stretch goals. To make things clear, mindful leadership is anything but esoteric management. It calls the attention to persons, personalities, and people as strategic assets and preconditions for value creation and competitiveness.

Digital Transformation of Healthcare: Digitalization is all-pervading and contributing to pathbreaking changes in a wide range of industries and professional service sectors. Margaria's seminal work on the One Thing Approach (OTA) and user driven software engineering paved the way for a paradigm shift in healthcare with respect to seamless workflows and interconnected technology integration into patient-centered workflows [9]. In opposition to evidence and expert driven healthcare this approach places special emphasis on the user, the customer or the patient evolving into co-value creators by means of digital options and devices. Margaria's OTA approach is a plea for patient emancipation because he or she is given the opportunity to control for health issues independently thanks to the access to advanced quantified self-technologies empowering and enabling healthcare customers. Data and information can be shared easily and disseminated within the accepted and complied boundaries of trustworthy IT regimes [8,10]. Ever since, the future of healthcare is dominated by smart technologies and med-tech ventures employing a proposal 2 profit approach to bridge the gap between design thinking and idea monetarization. It can be expected that the market for longevity services will be strongly influenced by start-ups entering the entrenched healthcare market from outside [7].

3 Holistic Longevity: Health of People, Animals, and Nature

Longevity in a broader sense encompasses health of people, health of animals, and health of nature, because sustainable one-world concepts acknowledge that the three dimensions are closely intertwined. The simple logic: One planet = One Health [3].

Health of People, Patients, and Mankind: In a narrow sense, longevity sharpens our senses for aging societies, demographic shifts, and changed mindsets with respect to health and sickness. Not the sheer absence of sickness is relevant, but also life quality, happiness, and conscious consumption with respect to externalization of negative effects and full compliance with ESG standards. The health-happiness-tandem stands for a mental, physical, economic, ecological, and economic ecosystem of balance. A balanced longevity lifestyle is inspired by the notion that aging is no disease, but an incident of life providing many opportunities and options if people comply with a masterplan of demographic challenges. Many of the baby boomers are eager to win two decades of highest life quality and health status by taking full advantage of medical options on the one hand and a commitment to preventive and predictive health on the other hand. Predictive and AI induced precision medicine may provide aging target groups with tailormade real-time information to delay states of decompensation and assure that the latter can be managed through assisted ambient living and health concepts when benefiting from complementary health-tech-solutions.

Health of Animals: Many pandemic incidents stem from zoonosis because mankind all too often does not respect "animal rights" when invading and exploiting their ecosystems leading to a reduction of biodiversity, disbalance of species, and infectious diseases being transferred from animals to people. Moreover, industrialized meat production not only leads to tremendous carbo-emissions but also to land-grabbing, monocultures, and harmful animal medication having severe side-effects in its track such as the frequent (mis-)use of antibiotics, growth hormones or steroids evidence. Additionally, massive meat consumptions are held responsible for many chronic diseases that could be avoided through vegetarian or vegan diets and nutrition concepts. Adopting a legislative standpoint, respect for animal rights challenges constitutional regulation, which must pay attention to the well-being of nature and animals for the sake of mankind. The contamination of lakes, rivers, and oceans also contributes to harmful food chains in the face of the profit boosting doctrine of the fast-moving consumer goods industry. On the one hand animals, species die out or face extinction and on the other hand, eco-systems are endangered by invasive species such as hippos in Columbia, rabbits in Australia or raccoons in Germany.

Health of Nature: Protecting biodiversity is a strategic goal because degraded ecosystems deprive mankind of significant medical and pharmaceutical opportunities. The precious asset of biodiversity provides scientists with untapped access to promising substances, genetic varieties, and therapeutical knowledge of first nation people. The latter increasingly command a fair share of value of their ecodiversity and knowledge about plants and substances. From an ESG perspective, fair trade implies a sharing economy logic that we must arrive at a new normal of property rights to honor the value of healthcare for inhabitants. The one-world and one-health-approach places special emphasis on complex dynamics because both hemispheres of the world represent a dynamically connected system with respect to global climate change, global migration, and migration of microorganisms. Health and quality of life are highly dependent on impeccable ecosystems that may be explored in a sustainable und humble manner but should not be exploited as has happened from the onset of colonization until now. The so-called critical industries are those sectors that place the burdens of value generation on nature, nations, and natives when exploiting resources efficiently and paying adequately for the negative external effects. Longevity of mankind and generations depends on a deal with nature to use it without exploiting it for economic reasons.

4 AMLEGA-Framework: 360-Degree Longevity Navigation

The one-planet-approach is a plea for 360-healthcare when mastering the present and preempting the future [3]. The AMLEG-framework stands for administration, management, leadership, entrepreneurship, and governance of healthcare and ensuing longevity. From a political and institutional point of view, healthcare and longevity can only be achieved if carefully navigated and directed [13].

Longevity Administration: Healthcare institutions often lack a smart, lean, and digitalized administration that is a precondition resource disposition, service delivery, and patient-centered healthcare. Administrative professionalism corresponds with hospital and healthcare processes beyond paper and pencil work as often prevalent in conservative and path dependent industries. Digital healthcare files and condensed status reports about patients, therapies, and medication in conjunction with many other data may contribute reduced transaction costs, smarter communication, and better decisions.

Longevity Management: Longevity is dependent on professional and circular management as epitomized by the PDCA model. Demographic change and transformation from disease repair to preventive and predictive health maintenance challenge entrenched wisdoms of the path-dependent hospital system. It is overadministrated but under-managed when it comes to opportunities offered by digitalization and AI. Management is not only about key performance indicators, continuous improvement, and an all-pervading more-for-less attitude. It is also about forecasting, trend recognition as well as coaching and consulting.

Longevity Leadership: Path-breaking transformation processes and paradigm shifts are more a function of leadership than of management and administration. Longevity means a paradigm shift for the diagnostics, therapy, and medication industry because the old normal of sickness is replaced by the new normal lifestyle of health and sustainability. Healthcare providers must be braced for an aging population of involved longevity customers claiming perceived value instead of paternalistic treatments. Leadership extends the aseptic management because of its explicit focus on culture, communication, and commitment. Longevity conveys vibrations and emotions and not only an evidence-based facts and figures.

Longevity Entrepreneurship: Adopting a start-up and business development standpoint, longevity provides us with a variety of sound investment options when aligning health and healing with digital options as reflected by MedTech-unicorns and platform-based healthcare solutions employing deep learning, algorithms, and artificial intelligence. The entrenched incumbents must be aware of disruptors from outside who define the landscape of medicine, care giving, and service delivery in an innovative way. The digital tycoons and many unicorns are challenged to establish innovative longevity platforms to capitalize on healthcare data when applying advanced AI technologies to them. They address the market for sickness as well as the market for health, fitness, vitality, and sports.

Longevity Governance: The future of healthcare hinges on governance, regulation, and legislation calling for political impact management to push new ideas and concepts against all odds. Aging societies must challenge sickness governance to arrive at a new level of holistic healthcare navigation. Governance systems are forced to change the incentive schemes with respect to payments and renumeration to avoid sickness administration instead of healthcare navigation. Emergency medicine and acute interventions are options of last resort and not standard operation procedures of problem fixing. In the long run, the longevity issue will appear on the agenda of upper echelons and board members such as ESG calling for positions and professionals who take care of longevity on the C-level of institutions.

Longevity Ambassadorship: The transformation process from sick care systems to longevity landscape is anything but easy due to dependencies and legacies of the 'old normal'. Switching towards a new normal longevity healthcare placing higher emphasis on early-stage diagnosis, illness prevention as well as compliant, committed, and competent patients automatically devaluates established service regimes of best practice. Longevity ambassadorship means assuming the political role of stakeholder management to convince critical bodies of the value longevity regimes with respect to medical, economic and welfare outcomes. Barriers of acceptance and implementation concerning the longevity approach have been reduced or removed by means political ambassadorship.

The AMLEGA-framework reflects the options of 360-degree healthcare navigation and represents a self-enforcing system of supporting and promoting longevity aspirations [13]. Referring to the balanced hospital management concept [2], 360-degree navigation is based on the notion that the six dimensions should be harmonized for the purpose of achieving operative and strategic alignment (Fig. 1).

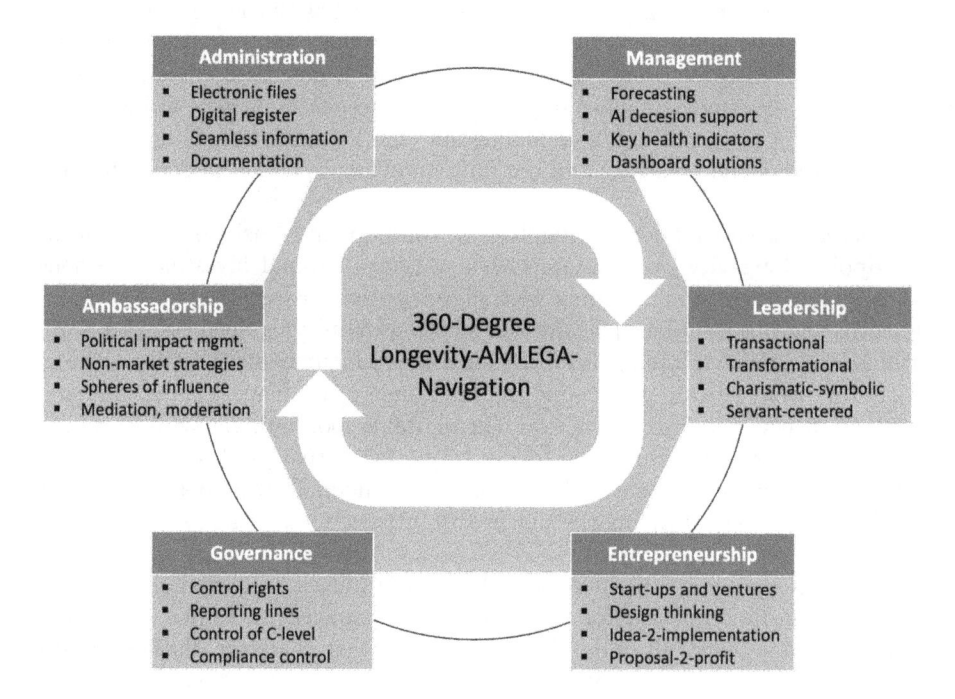

Fig. 1. The Longevity AMLEGA-Framework

5 Longevity Economics: Smart Asset Management 4 Value Creation

Challenging Entrenched Wisdoms. As we witness a debate about managing bottlenecks and constraints in healthcare at both the macro and micro levels, too often resources are poured into the 'market for sickness' when practicing red-flag medicine to save lives through acute or elective interventions. Patients are decompensated and medicine must fix the problem in the short term through therapy and technology recruitment to help and heal. Needy patients are eligible for 'sick services' to stop the progression of sickness and achieve a state of improvement. With a fixed supply of healing resources and escalating patient expectations, the widening service gap poses a challenge to healthcare asset management. To close the service gap, many healthcare managers are turning to the RRP approach, which stands for rationalization, rationing, and prioritization. In short, RRP reflects an efficient, effective, sufficient, and economically feasible process of resource deployment to achieve a high healthcare value in constrained contexts.

Rationalization aims to mobilize scarce resources through digitalization, automation, parallelization, delegation, or substitution to achieve a high return on healthcare spending in the face of constraints. Artificial intelligence applications may incorporate a huge rationalization potential because they harness the power of deep learning, big data, and algorithms when having full-sing access to big data. Rationalization is not about rightsizing and downsizing, because you cannot shrink to greatness. Moreover, it is about smart asset mobilization, coordination, and virtualization to either get an excellent payback for the spendings on sick care or to broaden the asset base. Asset exploitation and an asset exploration often go hand in hand in healthcare, because the value and number of knowledge-intensive competencies increases with its utilization. On the opposite, physical assets and core competencies are not depreciated by means of application but may increase in value in the case of activation und addressing. Rationalization corresponds with many efficiency-seeking consulting tools such as lean management, business process reengineering, objective key results, or ERP-systems. The motto: Make your resources as productive as possible!

Rationing: If the expectations increasingly exceed the asset and competency reservoir, the gap can no longer be closed through rationalization. Referring to the triage logic, it is not possible to satisfy every need and to meet any expectation because of resource constraints. For this reason, rules have to be defined according to which asset deployment should take place. Triage criteria should be fair, transparent, objective, and reasonable to be accepted among patients and physicians. Typically, the degree of emergency and the chance of benevolent outcomes score very high. Since outcomes are a function of compliance, patients will not be given the opportunity to take full advantage of therapy and treatment if they are reluctant to follow the orders of medication. Think of heart, kidney or lever transplantations addressing non-compliant patients who obviously damage their health by an obsessive lifestyle. Adopting a moral standpoint, willingness to pay or sociopolitical status are often rejected as triage criteria for ethical reasons. Should medicine discriminate between status groups reflecting different values of human capital following the logic of a discounted cashflow model? VIPs and billionaires would have much better chances to benefit from triaged capacities than underprivileged people or the working poor. Empirical studies evidence that healthcare access is a matter of income, education, and social status. There is no denying the fact that rationing is all-pervading with respect to service quantities, qualities, and right on time treatment.

Prioritization: Value on resource spendings in healthcare can be dramatically increased when focusing scarce resources on high-leverage activities and diseases that account for the vast majority of all healthcare cost. Many chronic diseases emerge as cost monsters when ignored, not diagnosed, or treated unprofessionally. Obesity, diabetes, cancer, cardiac arrest, strokes, and depressions can be prevented from the longevity perspective if health is perceived as gift and value and not as free good to be consumed by a devastating lifestyle. Nevertheless, health policies came up with the idea of disease management programs to concentrate resources on "blockbuster defects" to curb costs and improve outcomes. Prioritization in terms of therapies, medications, interventions, patients may cause moral problems because of patients without a strong political say suffering from diseases that a de-prioritized. Think of orphan diseases, displaced patients or third-world countries and their endemic healthcare problems. No money, no lobby, no prioritization! Achieving critical mass effects, scale economies, and learning curve effects in healthcare often hinges on resource condensation instead of diluting and dispersing them across a flurry of topics.

We do not want to argue against the RRP paradigm or proclaim that is has outlived its usefulness. Moreover, the problem lies in dominance of the "sick care" addressing "sick styles" that should be replaced by healthy longevity imperatives. The seminal article of Theodore Levitt diagnosing marketing myopia for many companies when defining their relevant market in the wrong way can also be applied to the hospital and therapy market encompassing acute and chronic illness or states of decompensation while not accounting for value of health, fitness, and vitality.

Longevity Economics: Beyond Sick Care. All too often management and economics are reduced to cost savings or constraint handling. Longevity economics considers the toxic cascade of sick style, sickness, and sick care that is tremendously resource consuming. Obesity, diabetes, cancer, cardiovascular diseases, and many other chronic states of decompensation are often "manmade by sick style" challenging our economic approach towards helping and healing. What are the premises, flaws, and misperceptions of sick care systems? The ten cardinal flaws can be delineated as follows:

Appetite for Med-Tech Interventions: The prevalence of advanced med-tech infrastructures may nurture an over-shooting mentality when being inclined to employ all available technologies at hand if they are reimbursed and compensated attractively. The "sex appeal of newness" attracts physicians and patients alike. But in many cases more med-tech does not equal more outcome, but only more money oscillating within the system.

Appetite for Rocket-Science Therapies: On the one hand, research, and development as well as innovations indicate the performance of healthcare systems that are one of the most knowledge-intensive areas of value creation. On the other hand, science-induced inventions and innovations may miss market and user needs if not aligned with a lead user approach. Only a very tiny fraction of diagnosed illnesses calls for rocket-science therapies while the vast bulk corresponds with states of 'bread and butter' decompensation.

Appetite for Over-Medication and Over-Servicing: Frugal innovations address the problem of over-servicing by focusing on minimum viable features that are sufficient, necessary, and beneficial to the desired outcome. To avoid legal actions and responsibility issues in face of the debate over patient safety, many doctors are inclined to do as much as possible. Others boost turnover and profits when recommending the most expensive meals of their menu card. Over-servicing is not only very expensive and resource consuming. It may also hamper the health status as sometimes you get more health with less intervention.

Appetite for Sickness and Decompensation: Capitalization on sickness and decompensation alludes to the fact that hospitals often follow rent-seeking service strategies letting the case evolve into a customer. The latter often is eager to get rid of symptoms rather than treating the cause by means of compliance, commitment, and communication. For example, obesity induced pain is targeted with painkillers such as Oxycontin instead of recommending healthy nutrition, fitness, mobility training, and mindful lifestyles. But patients must transform from pill swallowing lazy bones to energized healthcare experts. The story of the Sackler Family epitomizes the appetite for lifecycle pharmaceuticals. - Push, prescribe, persist!

Appetite for Rehabilitation: Most of the rehabs could be avoided by means of prevention and a longevity attitude towards health. A mindful health posture should make us think of rehabs as a treatment of last resort. Many citizens display a cryptic healthcare literacy with respect to their educational status on this field of life. And even if they are involved, they are not committed to take full advantage of an array of prevention steps that could be easily undertaken without disturbing daily routines to a high degree. We do not intend to stigmatize rehabilitation but want to emphasize that they will not work if the patient does not fundamentally change his mind towards self-efficacy, compliance, and commitment. Massages may make you happy, not healthy!

Appetite for Documentation, Administration, and Quality Control: Patient safety is one of the new mantras in healthcare calling for documentation and administration of patient-centered data to endorse precision medicine. But healthcare quality is not only a matter of systems and audits, it is a matter of attitude, culture, and experience. For sure, key performance indicators and performance measurement systems are important for continuous improvement. But these tools are to be seen as means to the end of quality, safety, and satisfaction. All too often they are imposed on nurses and doctors by controllers instead of offering tangible value to the users.

Appetite for Lifelong Patient Binding and High Profits: If you can make money from sick patients, there is no incentive to pay attention to prevention and non-invasive therapies. From the point of view of the pharmaceutical industry, chronic diseases are highly attractive because of the constant revenue streams from prescription policies that are easier to predict. The reward and reimbursement policies deserve critical reflection because non-invasive, light treatments in the field of prevention and early detection do not enjoy a strong political lobby.

Appetite for Rationalization, Rationing, Prioritization: Why not apply the RRP-logic to longevity and prevention instead of addressing the market for sickness more efficiently and effectively? The RRP-logic resembles the past and the present, while healthcare providers should also be preparing for the future through entrepreneurship, innovation, and digitalization. Platform-based healthcare may herald a dawning era of disruptive innovation driven by start-ups as well as digital unicorns and tycoons. The latter are eager to get a firm grip on the market for sick care, healthcare, and lifecare as they connect these three fields of value co-alignment.

Appetite for Professions, Disciplines, and Hierarchies: The progress in healthcare is a function of interdisciplinary work overcoming the interfaces of professions, disciplines, and hierarchies that are still all-pervading in the hospital sector. Service-centered, smart, and workflow-driven high-performance organizations propelled by agile projects and management processes increasingly enter the healthcare arena from outside in a pathbreaking and disruptive way. Entrenched, embedded, and established healthcare institutions will have to redesign their governance and leadership architecture to survive under VUCA-conditions.

Appetite for Information Asymmetries and Powerplay: Tacit expertise is similar to power and influence because it can be the foundation of unique negotiation positions due to information advantages. In many expert organizations, such as hospitals, knowledge sharing takes place in battles for competence that call for cooperation, coordination, and communication. While professionals in healthcare are highly competitive (up or out mentality), organizations can only thrive and grow if productive co-opetition takes place. Going for the right balance between competition and cooperation and being aware of the fact that individual performance is often highly dependent on access to complementary assets.

Harnessing the Economic and Managerial Power of Longevity. The longevity debate should enter the economic, managerial, and entrepreneurial arena for many (various) reasons. Longevity should extend and transcend the medical sphere of preventive treatments and preservative healthcare. Considering sociodemographic shifts, e.g., due to a tsunami of retiring baby boomers and aging societies, sick care is too expensive to be funded. Instead, preservative, preventive, and predictive longevity services go beyond healthcare maintenance.

Preservative Longevity: In a first step, cost savings are possible by means of healthcare preservation through teaching, coaching, and education. Target groups increase their healthcare literacy and comply with guidelines and recommendations. In the long run, they excel in self efficacy due to an array of activities contributing to health protection. Diseases can be avoided, deferred, or channeled in an acceptable way.

Preventive Longevity: High costs arise in the case of urgent and invasive treatments, or the long-term stabilization of chronic diseases as high-tech and high care outplay their usefulness in acute contexts like the shock room. The expensive motto: Treat first what kills first, irrespective of incurred cost and resource consumption. A multi-institutional objective for the macro- and micro-level should be seen in risk avoidance on the patient, the hospital, and the policy level. This could include a zero-tolerance legislation concerning unhealthy habits and products doing harm to public health. But we must concede, that restrictive longevity measures are in conflict with personal freedoms. - Even if they externalize costs to the public.

Predictive Longevity: Individualized, personalized, and localized information about healthcare target groups reflect the bedrock of precision health because patients can be traced, tracked, and tapped in a first step. In a second step, they can be profiled for the purpose of predicting health and disease scenarios. In a last step, the profit of platform-based health models increases because benefits and expectations can be targeted. Advanced digitalization such as AI, deep learning, and algorithms capitalize on data for the sake for better, faster, and smarter decision making. The aforementioned digital tycoons and unicorns are anything but path confirming and rule-taking. Moreover, they are eager to establish a new longevity norm based on the value of data.

It is safe to say that longevity represents a portfolio of options and opportunities calling for corresponding business models to be seized. The path dependent incumbents should make it a point of their honor to reflect the dominant sick care model for the purpose of triggering a process of service transformation towards longevity issues. On a macro level, policy makers are challenged to transform sick care regimes into longevity regimes of preservative, preventive, and predictive healthcare.

6 Manifesto 4 Longevity

Longevity in general is not only about the length of time that a person, organism, or other species lives or survives in an (uncomfortable) ecological niche. The potential lifespan of an individual or the average lifespan of a species is only a necessary condition to be fulfilled. The sufficient condition reflects the quality-of-life-dimension, since people and patients want to enjoy fitness, health, and independence irrespective of their calendric age. What counts is the perceived biological and mental age. The lifespan is ultimately limited, but it can be positively influenced by many sustainable lifestyle choices culminating in a beneficial healthstyle. While genetic endowments are to some extent preordaining longevity due to "excellent genes", the science also evidences the relevance of epigenetics. However, scientific advancements and improvements in healthcare have contributed substantially to an increase in average life expectancy over the past decades. Nevertheless, some critical target groups face a decrease of average life expectancy due to non-compliant and health-averse lifestyles. Obesity, diabetes, cancer, cardiovascular diseases, and severe fitness deficits are the negative hallmarks of many less educated people. Sanitation progress, access to clean water, and healthy food as well as disease prevention, precision medicine, and predictive health are often options for a privileged few, who reflect the value of health and devalue the comfort zones' laziness and lavishness. Longevity is about slowing down or reversing the process of body and soul degeneration by applying a set of self-employed choices and forming a mindset of health literacy. Longevity shares common ground with geriatric and gerontologic objectives but is somehow different with respect to the view on aging. While geriatric and gerontological studies focus on stabilizing and alleviating decompensation states, the longevity approach paints a positive picture of aging and provides a sound plan for healthy and joyful aging [1,3,12].

In brief, we define and delineate the cornerstones of longevity by concluding with ten tenets of importance and prioritization:

First, longevity is no appendix of the old normal of sick care. Moreover, it incorporates the seeds of the new normal of predictive, preventive, and precise healthcare.

Second, longevity takes full advantage of digitalization and AI solutions on behalf of involved and committed healthcare clients feeling embarrassed by paternalistic medicine.

Third, health, mankind, animals, and nature must go hand in hand because planet earth is a dynamic system of multiple and interdependent vectors that cannot be administrated as isolated and encapsulated elements. One planet = One health!

Fourth, value for healthcare implies not only rationing, rationalization, and prioritization (RRP) to employ scarce resources in an efficient and effective way. Beyond the lean and mean focus on asset exploitation we should also pay attention to new asset exploration by means of entrepreneurship, innovation, and digitalization (EID).

Fifth, the all-pervading sick care policies must be complemented by healthcare and lifecare doctrines to make patients behave as emancipated, compliant, and committed healthcare experts who do not have to worship conventional medicine anymore.

Sixth, longevity goes beyond compliance in a rule-abiding sense when prioritizing companionship with patients. Patients evolve as co-value creators of their own and self-controlled health.

Seventh, gerontologic and geriatric studies must embody the value longevity in aging societies to overcome the paralyzing pathology of sickness monitoring and disease management.

Eighth, the longevity approach does not resemble medical disciplines although resorting to their scientific and practical evidence. The purpose of this concept goes beyond individual length and quality of life on the micro-level. Political, ecological, societal, and economic ecosystems should be considered as mediating factors of sustainable health and longevity.

Ninth, healthcare systems need an institutional turnaround to pay for health instead of clinging to a sick governance structure and incentive regimes that pay for sickness and honor disease management. Sick care, healthcare, and lifecare are intertwined being the cornerstones of the longevity triangle.

Tenth, paternalistic top-down medicine has outlived its usefulness in many cases, because empowered patients postulate a paradigm shift towards a client-centered healthcare approach balancing aseptic tech-care with empathetic touch-care.

The Longevity Challenge Framework (LCF) summarizes the key essentials of longevity (Fig. 2).

7 Outlook: Market 4 Sickness or Health, Fitness, Performance and Longevity

Finally, marketing myopia means that we define the relevant market in a narrow and parochial way. All too often emphasis is placed on sick care, therapies, and interventions for the purpose repairing and healing. It goes without saying that one of the core domains of medicine implies pain relief, recoalescence, and rehabilitations by means of high-profile therapies and surgery. Adopting the standpoint of sport science, it makes sense to differentiate between health, fitness, performance, and longevity, because they foreshadow a new normal for medicine that should go beyond the market for sickness.

Market 4 Health: The market for health includes the portfolio of services that directly or indirectly contributes to the health maintenance from the viewpoint of professionals and patients often resorting to non-evidence-based problem solutions. The market for health incorporates services, products, and bundled solutions ranging from healthy nutrition to pharmaceutical and prevention offers. The lifestyle of health and sustainability epitomizes target groups displaying a high commitment to health gains and to sustaining quality of life.

Life-Care
- Self-empowerment
- Happiness and sustainability
- Quality lifetime management
- AI-assisted life companions

Health of people/ patients
- Sport, fitness, recreation
- Age-driven exercising
- Mental and physical health
- Predictive precision health

Health of animals
- Zoonosis prevention
- Animal rights and protection
- Vegan and vegetarian foodstyles
- Sustainable farming/ nutrition

Longevity challenge
- Aging as a disease or challenge?
- Regaining quality of life
- Body and soul refurbishment
- Sustaining agility and resilience

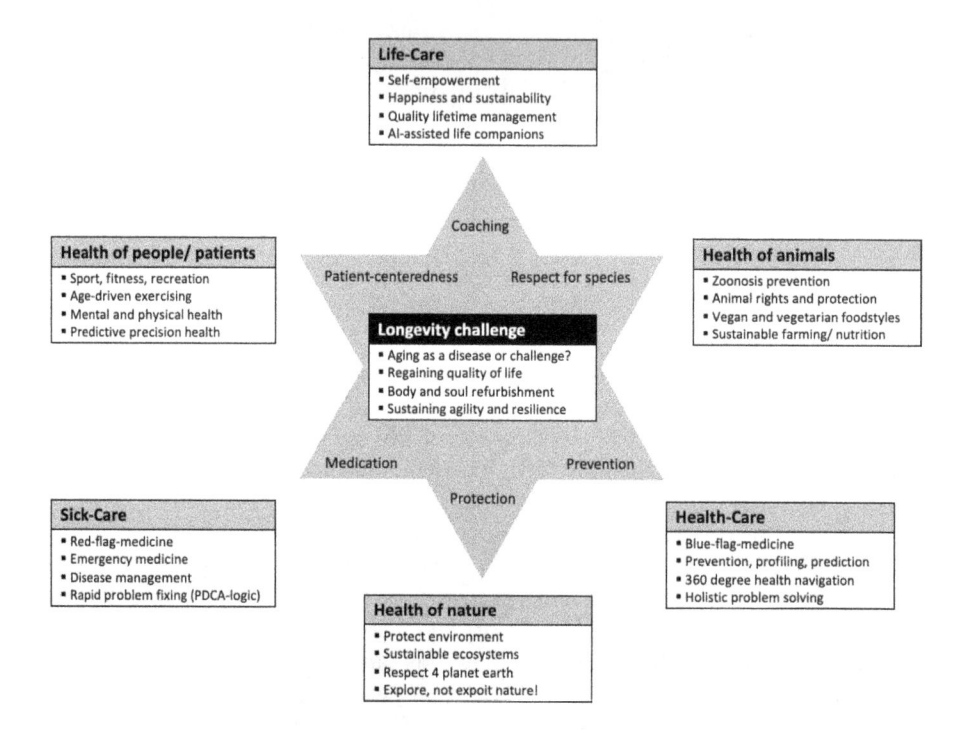

Sick-Care
- Red-flag-medicine
- Emergency medicine
- Disease management
- Rapid problem fixing (PDCA-logic)

Health-Care
- Blue-flag-medicine
- Prevention, profiling, prediction
- 360 degree health navigation
- Holistic problem solving

Health of nature
- Protect environment
- Sustainable ecosystems
- Respect 4 planet earth
- Explore, not expoit nature!

Coaching, Patient-centeredness, Respect for species, Medication, Prevention, Protection

Fig. 2. The Longevity Challenge Framework

Market 4 Fitness: You can be fit, but not healthy as drug abuse in gyms or extreme cardio and powerlifting exercises show. Social media markets the toned, shredded, and super-muscular appearance on all-pervading posts. The zest for fitness can contribute to health damage and pathologic self and body reflections with respect to Xtreme-fitness over-stretching physical and mental capabilities. Athletes have to be fit for an ironman triathlon but the ironman competition itself can be very unhealthy. Nevertheless, the market for fitness is booming with respect to nutrition, equipment, events, and supplements.

Market 4 Performance: The market for performance is exercise-driven because reaching unattained levels of performance often inspires achiever personalities to outperform themselves and competitors. Akin to fitness junkies, performance aficionados are willing to endure physical and mental stress as well as extreme training constellations to boost their performance even if they are amateurs. The performance may have many positive effects on health and well-being but resembles a curve-linear phenomenon. While couch potatoes resist slightest body challenges, high performers run the permanent risk of physical over-shooting. Economically, the market for performance is booming because success breeds success. Success driven entrepreneurs, managers or professionals of the knowledge economy want to perform outside their regular professions.

Market 4 Longevity: The market for longevity is the most inclusive one embracing all facets of the abovementioned market aspects in a balanced way when acknowledging that one-sidedness distracts from the over-arching one-health logic. Happiness research makes the point that long and healthy lives are often a function of blue zone environments representing ecosystems of social bonding, protected nature, and healthy working conditions. Physical assets, infrastructure, financial resources, or wealth are only means to the end of sustainable lives. The healthy longevity market is estimated to be an expanding business sector, interdisciplinary research makes it a point of its honor not only to find life extending therapies and promising lifestyle solutions, but to enhance quality, and not only quantity of lifespan.

Figure 3 calls the attention to the definition of the relevant market which is anything but a trivial job. While sometimes a narrow definition of the market may be appropriate when it comes to emergency cases (Treat first, what kills first! Time is heart and time is brain!), we argue that very promising business models and healthcare innovations may arise when adopting a different point of view. The four discussed markets 4 health, fitness, performance, and longevity should be related to market 4 sickness by means of a process of design thinking. It is safe to say that the conventional market 4 sickness faces states of disorder and disruption with respect to path-breaking outside investors and innovators challenging entrenched wisdoms and standard operations of incumbent players. The latter are challenged to employ complementary blue ocean strategies for the purpose of maintaining their competitiveness and service position. Interestingly, public health institutions are increasingly incentivized to promote a paradigm shift from "sickness repair" to health maintenance for economic and ethical reasons.

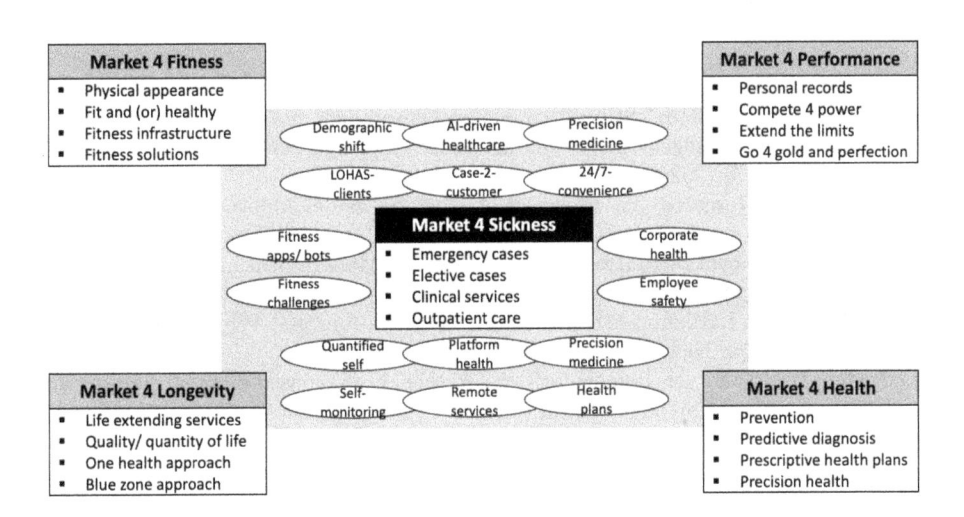

Fig. 3. Challenging Market Perspectives

Conflicts of interest. The author(s) has no competing interests to declare that are relevant to the content of this manuscript.

References

1. Attia, P., Gifford, B.: Outlive: The Science and Art of Longevity - Rethinking Medicine to Live Better Longer. Vermilion, London (2023)
2. Braun v. Reinersdorff, A.: Strategische Krankenhausführung - Vom Lean Management zum Balanced Hospital Management, 2nd edn. Bern, Göttingen, Toronto, Seattle (2007)
3. Friebe, M.: Novel Innovation Design for the Future of Health: Entrepreneurial Concepts for Patient Empowerment and Health Democratization. Springer, Cham (2022)
4. Kim, W.C., Mauborgne, R.: Blue Ocean Strategy. Harvard Business School Press, Cambridge (2005)
5. Porter, M.E., Teisberg, E.O.: Redefining Healthcare: Creating Value-Based Competition on Results. Harvard Business School Press, Boston (2006)
6. Porter, M.E.: What Is Value in Healthcare, this article (10.1056/NEJMp1011024) was published on December 8, 2010, at NEJM.org
7. Rasche C, Braun von Reinersdorff, A, Margaria, T, From Proposal 2 Profit"- Erfolgskaskade technologieorientierter Healthcare-Start-ups. Erscheint in Pfannstiehl M: Technologien und Technologiemanagement im Gesundheitswesen, Potenziale nutzen, Lösungen entwickeln, Ziele erreichen, Springer-Verlag, Wiesbaden
8. Rasche, C., Margaria, T.: Value on Data (VoD): Big Data als Chance zur Entscheidungsoptimierung in Kliniken, in: WISU 45. Jg., Heft 2, S. 182-190
9. Rasche, C., Margaria, T., von Reinersdorff, A.B.: Value delivery through IT-based healthcare architectures. In: Stephan, M., Kerber, W., Kessler, T., Lingenfelder, M. (eds.) 25 Jahre ressourcen- und kompetenzorientierte Forschung. SK, pp. 417–443. Gabler Verlag, Wiesbaden (2010). https://doi.org/10.1007/978-3-8349-8856-0_16
10. Rasche, C., Reinecke, A.A., Margaria, T.: Künstliche Intelligenz im Gesundheitswesen als Kernkompetenz? Status quo, Entwicklungslinien und disruptives Potenzial. In Künstliche Intelligenz im Gesundheitswesen, Springer: Berlin/Heidelberg, Germany, pp. 49–79 (2022)
11. Rasche, C., Margaria, T., Floyd, B.D.: Service model innovation in hospitals: beyond expert organizations. In: Pfannstiel, M.A., Rasche, C. (eds.) Service Business Model Innovation in Healthcare and Hospital Management, pp. 1–20. Springer, Cham (2017). https://doi.org/10.1007/978-3-319-46412-1_1
12. Sinclair, D.A., LaPlante, MD.: Lifespan: Why We Age?and Why We Don't Have To, Atria Books: New York, London, Toronto (2019)
13. Steffen, B., Braun von Reinersdorff, A., Rasche, C.: IT-based decision support for holistic healthcare management in times of VUCA, disorder, and disruption. Appl. Sci. **13**, 6008 (2023). https://doi.org/10.3390/app13106008

Death and Burial Data: Ireland 1864–1922 – an Interdisciplinary Collaboration

Ciara Breathnach and Rachel Murphy

Department of History, University of Limerick, Limerick, Ireland
`ciara.breathnach@ul.ie`

Abstract. Historical Big Data has posed a problem for successive national administrations, and while digitization has played an important role in ensuring the survival of invaluable social history artefacts, it has created a multitude of new problems. Digitization became the panacea for archival access over the past 50 years and it served the immediate purpose of taking fragile cultural artefacts out of the 'handling environment'. With rapid advances in technology over the past 20 years concerns have now shifted to the conservation and preservation of these digital archives. The life cycle of digitization has moved from the simple concept of preservation standard digital duplicate to more complex workflow processes enabling migration and access. In this paper we discuss some of the legacy issues that digitization has created and how meaningful collaborations between historical and computer scientists can yield exciting solutions to complicated research problems.

Keywords: Historical Big Data · XMDD · Pedagogy

1 Introduction

In this paper we discuss two bodies of historical records, civil registration of deaths, which mark the end of a life course, and cross-sectional census data taken at intervals during a lifetime. Both are widely accepted as critical indicators of national health and wealth status. With the expansion of statecraft in the late nineteenth and early twentieth centuries governments sought to implement new ways of counting the people. In the United Kingdom, for example, civil registration of births, deaths and marriage replaced ecclesiastical parish-based systems and gave rise to huge amounts of what is now recognized as historical Big Data. Over the past 60 years scholars across Europe and the United States have been engaged in efforts to render these handwritten data banks machine readable through crowd-sourced citizen science and other novel methods. The same timeframe saw the growth of for-profit commercial companies conducting large-scale digitization projects to varying standards. Because most of these companies were targeting the highly profitable genealogy market, most adopted a partial indexing system that extracted the valuable names and dates and linked them to a conservation standard TIFF of the originals. Creating an abbreviated dataset made the digitization process quicker and therefore less expensive, while providing genealogists with the information they sought. The problems associated with indiscriminate and for-profit digitization have been well described by Milligan [1], and Ahnert et al. [2]. For historians and demographers these original documents contain a lot more information about cause of death, which can reveal much more about population health, the impact of pandemics and many other things besides. Partial indexes became the gold standard in data retrieval, and the creation of digital copies fulfilled conservation and preservation purposes, but historians and other academic researchers were rarely involved in the design of such largescale digitization projects.

Unfortunately, there have been several barriers to research on individual level data, and some digitized data remains inaccessible to researchers. Historians must comply with data protection limitations and the classification of some of records as working government records has meant that research progress is uneven internationally. For example, the Statistics Act 1993 [3] placed a 100-year embargo on historical censuses meaning that scholars of Ireland could not participate in the burgeoning fields of demographic history and population studies. Aggregated reports of the Registrar General and census returns are very informative but the individual level returns have greater research potential. In countries with less stringent access rules significant scholarly advances were made in linking individual level data over the past 30 years, but with advances in machine learning processes there are now great opportunities for countries like Ireland to catch up.

This chapter charts our work together over 5 years and it is organized in line with the theme of the volume into three main sections: research, education and dissemination. It offers some insights into Tiziana Margaria's fierce intellect, commitment to knowledge and to advancing computer science research in interdisciplinary ways. In the first section we describe the research problems and the data, and the computer science solutions. One of our innovations was the development of a low code no code solution, namely an application in DIME, an eXtreme Model Driven Development (XMDD) environment, to transcribe Irish historical civil registrations of death records. In turn this work has offered several opportunities for the development of new research areas particularly in data segmentation and the potential use of neural networks in handwritten text and numeral recognition software [4]. Our work was very much rooted in research-led teaching in history and computer science, it trained 4 PhD students and offered many challenges to four cohorts of Masters' students who helped to hack at the problems unwieldy data presents. Our chapter concludes with a discussion of *Death in the Lanes*, a 15-min thematic exhibition of the history of pulmonary tuberculosis in Limerick City at the beginning of the twentieth century. The exhibition aimed to take our research beyond the academy, and used archival research, historical photographs and literary representations of the stigmatization surrounding the disease. What is less clear in this final dissemination package and the dulcet tones of our colleague Professor Joseph O'Connor reciting passages from the Pulitzer Prize-winning *Angela's Ashes* is the 5 years of interdisciplinary research and collaboration, the trial and error and the good cheer that sustained it. Underpinning the maps of the changing contours of deaths from tuberculosis is the extraordinary effort of historians and computer scientists, faculty, and students, who took the time to develop a meaningful collaboration built on mutual respect for one another's discipline.

2 Research

The Death and Burial Data: Ireland 1864–1922 project (DBDIrl) was funded by an Irish Research Council Laureate Award. As principal investigator, Breathnach sought to apply novel computer science applications to historical civil registration of death data to create new knowledge. Cause of death data is very complex and can often contain underlying illnesses as well as direct causation. The classification of disease index in 1900 was rudimentary and a fraction of the current ICD11 edition. Lack of precision coupled with limited medical knowledge permitted doctors plenty of discretion. [5]. Our work aimed to examine the dynamics of the civil registration exchange especially regarding stigmatized diseases. Tuberculosis (sometimes referred to as TB, phthisis or consumption), was associated with poverty and was rife in Ireland until the 1950s. In aetiological terms it was misunderstood until Robert Koch discovered its microbial origins in 1881. His discovery marked the beginning of bacteriology with 'germ theory' dispelling the unscientific 'miasma theory' that had held sway for centuries. After that, much scientific progress was made in testing for the disease and in the development of vaccinations, but there was no cure until the discovery of the efficacy of penicillin as drug therapy in the 1940s. Approximately 10 per cent of deaths were attributed to pulmonary tuberculosis every year, and the further 10 per cent attributed to other pulmonary diseases such as pneumonia and bronchitis should be regarded with suspicion. Contagious diseases that pose significant threats to public health are listed as 'notifiable' under national legislation, and unfortunately tuberculosis was not added to the schedule in Ireland until 1948.

In contrast with the rich and famous who leave behind a paper trail of records and personal papers, ordinary people leave a very light trail, particularly those from lower socio-economic backgrounds and those who had lower literacy levels. From 1864, everyone was required to register births, marriages (non-Catholic marriages had been registered from 1845 onwards), and deaths. For confessional reasons, it took time before the system embedded mainly because of adherence to religious requirements (e.g. baptism) more than civil requirements. Death registration yields a more comprehensive impression of some life courses especially those born prior to 1864. These civil registration records provide a rich seam of information about, if not all of Ireland's population, a high proportion of it. Death records which must include at least one cause of death (and can include two or more co-morbidities) can help historians to understand mortality more generally and the dispersion of disease. They include name and address of the deceased person which gives a spatial location, age which helps us to understand the demographic breakdown of those succumbing to the disease, and occupation which provides us with an understanding of the socio-economic status of the individual. In aggregate, all this information allows us to gain a good understanding of disease environments over space (through mapping) and time (through a timeline).

In contrast with life events like birth and death that mark the parameters of an individual life course, census returns are cross-sectional data that offer an impression of households in a moment in time. Again, the majority of the population would have been documented. This historical dataset includes the address, names and ages of each individual that was in the household on the night of the census, and other useful information such as their occupation, literacy levels, place of birth and religion.

3 Research Data and Problems

3.1 Civil Registration Data

The General Register Office of Ireland (GRO) generously allowed the project team to use its data which had been partially digitized for data retrieval purposes. The GRO is a statutory agency whose purpose is to manage the live population register. Civil birth, marriage and death registrations and marriages are official state records and must be preserved under Irish law. Since the late 1990s they have been digitized and indexed and from 2016 they have been available to view free of charge online at Irishgenealogy.ie. The years covered at the time of writing are 1871 to 1972. An example of historical Big Data they include a wealth of information that when analyzed can help historians to answer questions relating to historical demography, medical humanities, cause of death, impact of socio-economic class, the role of biopower, and the spatial aspects of disease. We can also learn more about how death is treated from civil, secular and religious perspectives. Like the death records, other Irish Big Data, such as the 1901 and 1911 censuses, are also in the public domain. All this information currently exists in separate silos. Data linkage offers enormous potential for new knowledge about past population health and life expectancy.

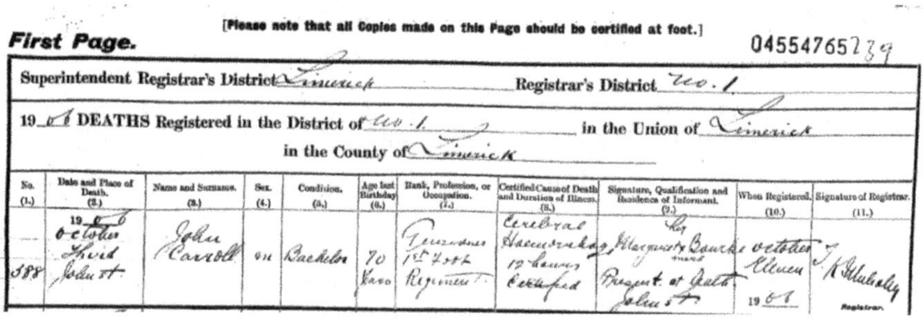
[Please note that all Copies made on this Page should be certified at foot.]

First Page. 0455476573

Superintendent Registrar's District Limerick Registrar's District No. 1

19 01 DEATHS Registered in the District of No. 1 in the Union of Limerick in the County of Limerick

No. (1.)	Date and Place of Death. (2.)	Name and Surname. (3.)	Sex. (4.)	Condition. (5.)	Age last Birthday (6.)	Rank, Profession, or Occupation. (7.)	Certified Cause of Death and Duration of Illness. (8.)	Signature, Qualification and Residence of Informant. (9.)	When Registered. (10.)	Signature of Registrar. (11.)
388	1901 October Third John St	John Carroll	M	Bachelor	70 Years	Pensioner 1st Foot Regiment	Cerebral Haemorrhage 12 hours Certified	Margaret Bourke Present at death John St	October Eleven 1901	Registrar

Fig. 1. Civil Death Record

Figure 1 shows a civil death record. Some 4.3 million individual civil registration of death records were shared with the team by the General Register Office of Ireland (GRO). The death registers have been digitized into PDFs, each image being a page of ten records which were grouped under a specific ID number. These TIFF files were linked to an index of information which is used to create the search functionality of the site. When an index file was transcribed for data retrieval purposes, nine key pieces of information were captured: Superintendent Registrar's District (SRD), Registrar's District (RD), Poor Law Union, county, date and place of death, name and surname etc. Civil registration of death data is the most complete dataset we have for Irish history. Other aspects of the life course such as births are deficient because there was no mandate for births pre-1864 to be registered. We worked together to break the information into 63 components, and this is discussed in [4].

3.2 Census Data

Only two full decennial Irish censuses survive from the period of British Administration (1801-1922). They are currently available for individual search on the National Archives of Ireland website. Again the digitisation process adopted the index/TIFF method but unlike the GRO data both datasets have been fully transcribed. DBDIrl has benefitted from a partnership that gave access to the raw data. We discuss the data further in O'Doherty et al. [6].

Census data is a cross-sectional data gathering exercise, where authorities use pre-dispersed forms to capture population levels on one particular night. In Ireland the police acted as enumerators. The forms were organized around the relationship to head of household, and they offer an extraordinary window into social life. For example, the fertility question, added in 1911 gives unprecedented information about infant mortality and maternal vulnerabilities. The public site, while more searchable than the GRO interface, does not allow for large scale research and both the 1901 and the 1911 returns exist as separate datasets (Fig. 2).

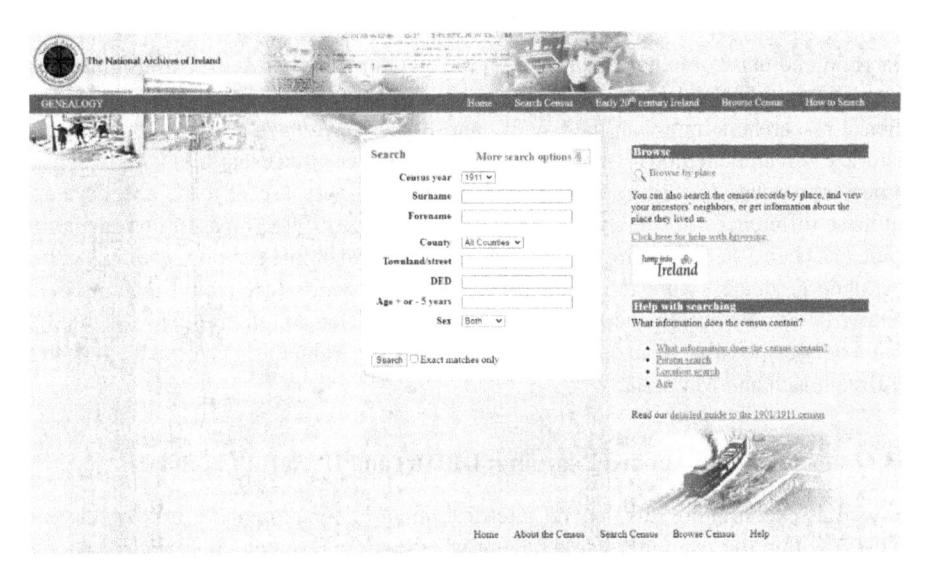

Fig. 2. National Archives of Ireland Census Website

3.3 Research Problems

In many respects DBDIrl was dealing with bodies of legacy data that were never designed to facilitate historical research or data analytics. As already alluded to, they have posed several research problems for the project team. Chief among them were how to:

1. Render bodies of 'legacy' handwritten data machine readable.
2. Create linkages within the discrete datasets.

3. Interoperate the various siloed data.
4. Design separate workflows to resolve non-standardized text.
5. Find ways of scaling up efforts

4 Education

4.1 Teaching Philosophy

Despite coming from different disciplinary backgrounds, our approaches to teaching and learning are closely aligned: our underlying philosophy is a constructivist approach, scaffolding students' learning until they are comfortable to apply new skills themselves and using practice-based learning approaches to enhance learning. We believe that there is always more to learn and as well as teaching students, we ensured that there were opportunities for doctoral candidates to use the project as a test case for new and innovative aspects of their research, and for us to learn from each other.

4.2 Interdisciplinary Knowledge-Sharing

Margaria and her Computer Science team have collaborated closely with us and other historians on the DBDIrl team. We have learned much from them about how computer science researchers approach their work, and likewise we have shared with them our historical research methods. There are differences between the disciplines – for instance, in our approaches to writing articles and it has been very useful to be able to tease out these differences in weekly meetings, as well as identifying areas of commonality. There has been a steep learning curve: our team tested an online training module for first year undergraduates, while the computer scientists were introduced to the techniques of handwriting transcription and historical demography. This adoption of new knowledge would only be possible in an open and collaborative environment such as that advocated by Breathnach and Margaria.

4.3 Innovation and Applied Learning: DBDIrl and Doctoral Candidates

As well as encouraging this general interdisciplinary education and cross-fertilisation of ideas within the team and while having very specific research aims, undergraduate and postgraduate teaching was a core part of the DBDIrl project design. So too was postgraduate research, and four PhDs students, two from history and two in CS were part of the project team. The PhD in CS was responsible for designing and developing the software application, and identifying ways in which the digital platform might be enriched. This was again an interdisciplinary effort, with the computer science PhD being co-supervised by Margaria and Breathnach.

Most importantly, additional PhD students have been able to incorporate the project into their doctoral research. Margaria identified opportunities within the project that allowed additional doctoral students to develop their expertise in very specific aspects of computer science. For example, Alexander Schieweck's focus was on developing and enriching the Historian Data App (HDA) within DIME [4], while Enda O'Shea designed a classifier to automate accuracy checks of the transcriptions [7]. More recently

Schieweck has focused on matching data from different sources e.g. civil registration of death data and census data while O'Shea has been exploring ways in which machine learning and neural networks might be used in alpha numerical character recognition of written text [8]. The project has provided a useful means for them, and other researchers, to learn more about their own field using real population data.

4.4 Practice-Based Learning: Undergraduates, Postgraduates and Beyond

Transcription is a key skill for the historian, and because we needed our data to be transcribed, it made sense to get our students to transcribe small subsets of the data in the app. PBL such as this has been demonstrated to be very effective in helping students to gain key skills; learning by doing is a more memorable experience. Since 2019, we have developed and incorporated HDA into several taught modules aimed at undergraduate and postgraduate historians. Most recently this has been in the form of a Transcribathon, a form of cultural heritage crowdsourcing event, where manuscript entries are transcribed in a fully supported group setting [9, 10].

DBDIrl incorporated the use of Transcribathons that was then used by computer scientists to refine the applications they had developed. Schieweck and others have observed how the students used the app, and along with historians have analyzed student feedback to refine the application into a user interface that worked more intuitively for students and for the researchers. At the beginning of the semester, members of the computer science team along with their colleagues from history met the students of the MA History of Family and discussed their roles on the project. This helped students to understand the nature of an interdisciplinary academic project, and their role in it. From weeks 3–10 of the semester students conducted research relating to the death records, developing their skills as a historian. Then, in Week 11 of the semester the full team met the students again and members of the computer science team walked through the app with them, while history colleagues answer any questions about how to transcribe the information. Finally, in Week 12 the Transcribathon took place. Due to the pandemic and because students were located both in Ireland and overseas this was run online. Students worked in pairs to transcribe death records and enter them into the HDA interface, while the computer scientists and historians were on call to help with any queries. Following the Transcribathon students were surveyed, and we identified any issues and how these might be addressed through further refinement of the HDA. Usually, historians grade the transcriptions, but this was aided by O'Shea's classifier which flagged any problematic entries; this helped us know which entries to focus on in the data-cleaning phase, ensuring a greater level of data accuracy. Over time the classifier was refined to create increasingly accurate results, making data checking quicker for the historians, who used this data to answer their research questions through demographic analysis, and maps. The outputs from the Transcribathons have not only been used in the exhibition, they also provided O'Shea with training data for his work on handwritten text recognition [9].

Having beta-tested the HDA with several cohorts of students, our next aim was to trial it externally with a view to it eventually forming the basis of a citizen science project. In Spring 2023, we piloted this with Clare Roots Society, a voluntary group which studies family history, genealogy and heritage of County Clare, Ireland [11]. This received positive feedback and it is hoped that in the future we will be able to collaborate on additional citizen science projects like this.

Students enjoy PBL: "Overall, it was an excellent exercise, making us think about the information in a different way" (Student B, January 2022) while we have been praised by the external examiner of this course for our teaching innovations: '[The module] should be commended for explicitly linking the study and use of big data with an important, ongoing research project, the IRC funded Death and Burial Data, 1864–1922.'(Dr Andrew Sneddon, Ulster University). In recognition of the collaborative work in education between Prof. Tiziana Margaria, Dr Ciara Breathnach and Dr Rachel Murphy, they were awarded the University of Limerick Team Teaching Award in 2023.

5 Dissemination

5.1 Introduction

Dissemination and research impact are key requirements of any funded project. Once again, this has been a highly collaborative aspect of DBDIrl. In the sections below we discuss some of the main aspects of dissemination.

5.2 Academic Conferences and Collaborative Research Papers

As an interdisciplinary team we have jointly presented at a range of academic conferences in both history and computer science, including conferences organized by the European Society of Historical Demography, the Society for the Social History of Medicine, the IEEE International Conference on Computers, Software, and Applications, and AISoLA. As well as disseminating our own research, this has proved a useful way of initiating new relationships with potential project partners and encouraging the cross-fertilisation of ideas. Similarly we have produced 9 co-authored papers across Computer Science and History. Working in this way has provided us all with a better understanding of some of the differences between the disciplines, and the problem of siloed thinking.

5.3 Public Dissemination

Government-funded research projects invariably come with public dissemination requirements, and the exhibition format is a more creative and accessible way to inform the public. While the work towards this was carried out by the historians, it is underpinned by information derived from the computer science team, through the HDA, the classifier and the data-matching of civil registration data and census data. One of our final research outputs was an online exhibition: *Death in the Lanes: Tuberculosis in Limerick City* [12] see Fig. 3. This was accompanied by the publication of an RTÉ Brainstorm piece [13].

The centerpiece of this online exhibition is three heatmaps that were created to show all deaths from tuberculosis in Limerick across three years: 1901, 1906 and 1911. These years were selected so that the data could be linked to the 1901 and 1911 census which provides us with socio-economic information about individuals and data on the

Fig. 3. Homepage of online exhibition: *Death in the Lanes: Tuberculosis in Limerick City*

quality and standard of their housing. The maps are shown in Figs. 4, 5 and 6. Data was downloaded from the HDA, checked and manually cleaned by two of the historians who added spatial information in the form of geographic coordinates. They then uploaded the data to a Geographic Information System and heatmaps were generated. These show the hotspots for TB in Limerick at these specific points in time. Such spatial analysis allows us to understand where precisely deaths from TB were occurring and showed that, aside from the public buildings such as the Limerick Workhouse, hospital and asylum, they predominantly occurred in the overcrowded tenement buildings and on the lanes, which were the location of substandard housing and insanitary conditions, and home to those of lower socio-economic status. The spatial dispersion of tubercular mortality was a source of major concern and Linda Bryder notes how the Registrar General of England was highly suspicious of historical cause of death data from other pulmonary causes occurring in close proximity [14]. Through this collaboration we can make inferences about the dispersion of disease, particularly when they are mapped.

5.4 Longevity and Preservation

A final consideration relates to the longevity of the information provided. The exhibition was built in Adobe After Effects and output as a video as it was the most stable way to meet the demands of the institutional repository requirements. The maps were created using ESRI's ArcGIS Pro software and the open source QGIS. They have been saved in several formats including TIFF for images shown in Figs. 4, 5 and 6, and as shapefiles regarding the point data in the maps. The attribute data (transcribed and cleaned information from death records and geographic co-ordinates) is saved in. csv format. The 5 versions of the HDA were preserved in DIME and most of the project interventions are available on github. The papers we have published have all been saved in the University of Limerick research repository.

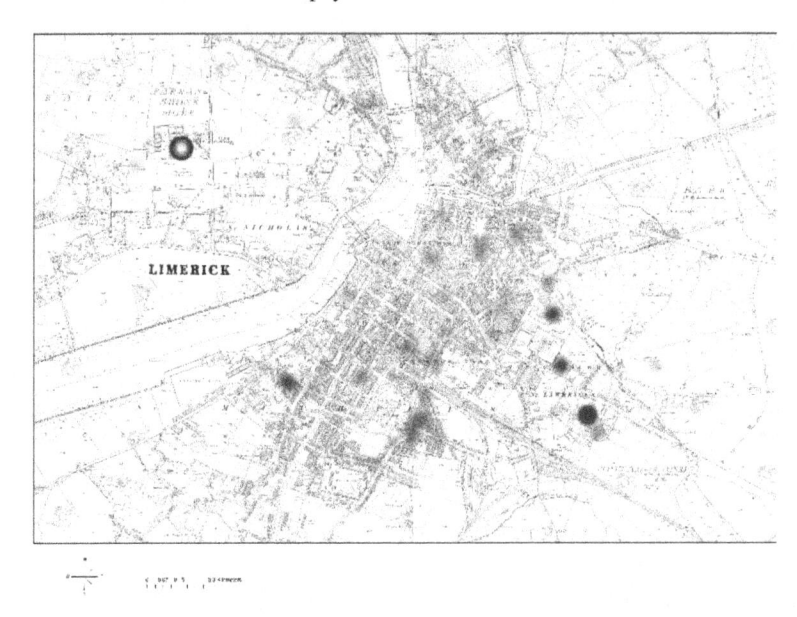

Fig. 4. Heat Map of Limerick Deaths from Tuberculosis, 1901 (Source: DBD Ireland analysis. Basemap © Tailte Éireann/Government of Ireland Copyright Permit No. MP 002223)

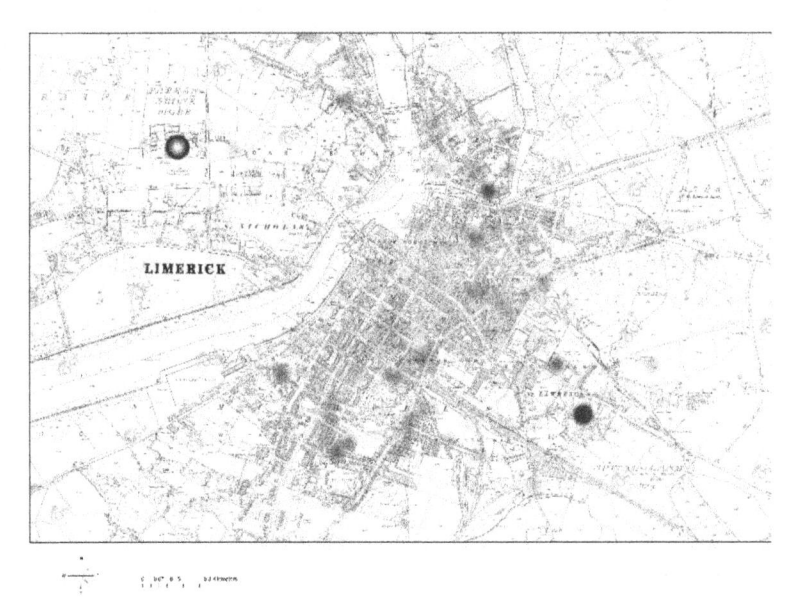

Fig. 5. Heat Map of Limerick Deaths from Tuberculosis, 1906 (Source: DBD Ireland analysis. Basemap © Tailte Éireann/Government of Ireland Copyright Permit No. MP 002223)

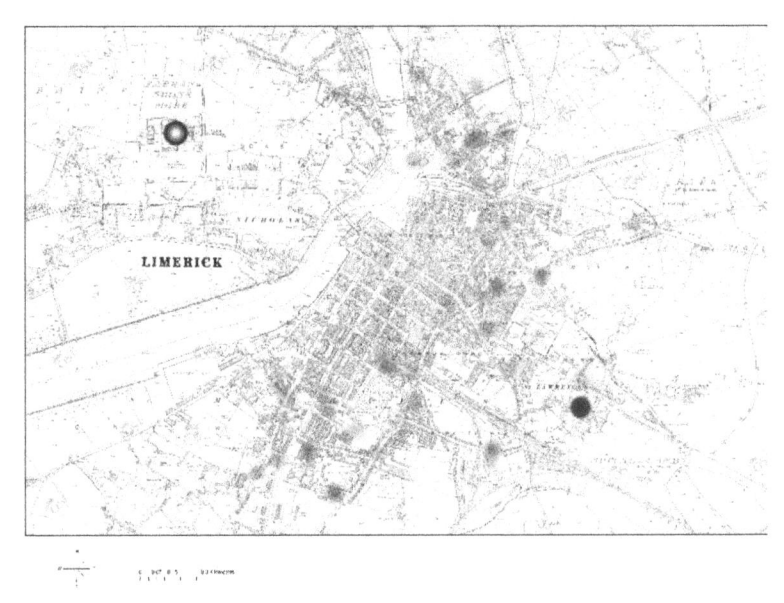

Fig. 6. Heat Map of Limerick Deaths from Tuberculosis, 1911 (Source: DBD Ireland analysis. Basemap © Tailte Éireann/Government of Ireland Copyright Permit No. MP 002223)

6 Conclusion

This chapter has shown some of the very positive outcomes that can emerge when computer science scholars such as Margaria collaborate with academics in humanities disciplines, such as Breathnach. While this phase of the project has concluded further work will be done. For example, the citizen science component of the project has been shown to work with small groups of volunteers. Over time this can be extended to larger groups and new datasets. Another opportunity is to further refine the process of matching civil registration data and census data; this has met with some initial success but with further work greater accuracy can be achieved. The GRO is supportive of this work and is keen to conduct further partnerships with the research team to make the data more accessible for the public. Once the Irish data are in a more machine-readable state there are several opportunities to make interoperabilities within GRO data, for example linking births to deaths. From robust life course data there are opportunities to link to other datasets like migration, to map mobility, or marriage to examine family formation. DBDIrl has made great progress in developing deep understandings of the data from both historical and computer science perspectives. There are many other challenges that remain unresolved but with collaborators like Professor Tiziana Margaria, there are endless possibilities.

References

1. Milligan, I.: The Transformation of Historical Research in the Digital Age Elements in Historical Theory and Practice Cambridge (2022)

2. Ahnert, R., Griffin, E., Ridge, M., Tolfo, G.: Collaborative historical research in the age of Big Data: lessons from an interdisciplinary project Cambridge (2023)
3. The Statistics Act, 1993. https://www.irishstatutebook.ie/eli/1993/act/21/enacted/en/html
4. Schieweck, A., et al.: Evolution of the Historian Data Entry Application: Supporting Transcribathons in the Digital Humanities through MDD, pp. 177–186 (2022). https://doi.org/10.1109/COMPSAC54236.2022.00033
5. Breathnach, C.: Respiratory disease and death registration, Dublin 1900–1902. 143, 1, 39–72 (2022). https://doi.org/10.3917/adh.143.0039
6. Doherty, A.J., et al.: CensusIRL: Historical census data preparation with MDD support. 2507–2514 (2022). https://doi.org/10.1109/BigData55660.2022.10021106
7. O'Shea, E., et al.: Towards Automatic Data Cleansing and Classification of Valid Historical Data: An Incremental Approach Based on MDD. 1914–1923 (2020). https://doi.org/10.1109/BigData50022.2020.9378148
8. O'Shea, E.: Tabular Corner Detection in Historical Irish Records. 25, 1–4 (2023). https://doi.org/10.1145/3573128.3609349
9. Breathnach, C., et al.: From No- to Low-Code: Transcribathons as Practice-Based Learning for Historians and Computer Scientists. 1131–1136 (2021). https://doi.org/10.1109/COMPSAC51774.2021.00155
10. Breathnach, C., et al.: Curating history datasets and training materials as OER: an experience, 1570–1575 (2023). https://doi.org/10.1109/COMPSAC57700.2023.00242
11. Clare Roots Society. https://www.clareroots.org/. Accessed 22 Dec 2023
12. Death in the Lanes: Tuberculosis in Limerick City. https://youtu.be/WFGBVjmH-g8
13. The huge human cost of tuberculosis on one Irish city. https://www.rte.ie/brainstorm/2023/0621/1390362-tuberculosis-limerick-lanes-ireland-health-history-stigma-exhibition/. Accessed 22 Dec 2022
14. Bryder, L.: Not always one and the same thing. The registration of tuberculosis deaths in Britain 1900–1950. 9, 2, 252–265 (1996). https://doi.org/10.1093/shm/9.2.253

Author Index

A
Al Machot, Fadi 215
Apt, Krzysztof R. 280

B
Belt, Jason 93
Bertram, Andreas 345
Boßelmann, Steve 118
Breathnach, Ciara 365
Busch, Daniel 118

D
de Boer, Frank S. 280
De Palma, Giuseppe 167
Demrozi, Florenc 215
Dennis, Louise A. 302

F
Fantechi, Alessandro 327
Ferraro, Gaspare 19
Floyd, Barry D. 55
Foster, Simon 302

G
Giallorenzo, Saverio 167
Gnesi, Stefania 327
Graf, Susanne 259

H
Hatcliff, John 93
Hinchey, Mike 1
Huang, Chengzi 259
Huber, Nikolaus 259

J
Johnsen, Einar Broch 129
Jonsson, Bengt 259

K
Kamburjan, Eduard 129
Khodabandeloo, Behnam 259

L
Lamprecht, Anna-Lena 81
Legay, Axel 146
Leucker, Martin 202
Lucca, Serena 146

M
Maunero, Nicolò 19
Mauro, Jacopo 167
Mendler, Michael 235
Montegiove, Sonia 19
Murphy, Rachel 365
Murtovi, Alnis 183

O
Olderog, Ernst-Rüdiger 280

P
Pferscher, Andrea 129
Prinetto, Paolo 19

R
Rasche, Christoph 345
Rümmer, Philipp 259

S
Schieferdecker, Ina K. 67
Schlatte, Rudolf 129
Schlüter, Maximilian 183
Seceleanu, Cristina 50
Sieve, Riccardo 129
Smyth, Steven 118
Steffen, Bernhard 1, 183

T
Tarifa, Silvia Lizeth Tapia 129
Tegeler, Tim 118
ter Beek, Maurice H. 327
Trentin, Matteo 167

U
Ullah, Habib 215

V
Van Ouytsel, Charles-Henry Bertrand 146
Vjerdha, Gejsi 167
von Reinersdorff, Andrea Braun 345

W
Wauters, Dimitri 146
Wirsing, Martin 44
Woodcock, Jim 302
Wright, Thomas 302

Y
Yi, Wang 259
Yu, Gino 35

Printed in the USA
CPSIA information can be obtained
at www.ICGtesting.com
CBHW051553211024
16149CB00005BA/160